THE LANGUAGE OF
TRUTH

THE LANGUAGE OF
TRUTH

The Torah Commentary of the
Sefat Emet

Rabbi Yehudah Leib Alter of Ger

Translated and Interpreted by

ARTHUR GREEN

Hebrew Texts Prepared by

SHAI GLUSKIN

The Jewish Publication Society
Philadelphia
5759/1998

Library of Congress Cataloging-in-Publication Data

Alter, Judah Aryeh Leib, 1847–1905.
   [Sefat emet (Torah). English. Selections.]
   The language of truth: the Torah commentary of the Sefat Emet: Rabbi Yehudah Leib Alter of Ger/translated and interpreted by Arthur Green.
      p.   cm.
   Includes bibliographical references and index.
   ISBN 0-8276-0650-8
   1. Bible O.T. Pentateuch—Commentaries. 2. Fasts and feasts—Judaism—Meditations. 3. Hasidism. I. Green, Arthur, 1941–
II. Title.
   BS1225.3.A46   1998
   222'.107—dc21   98-42405
                                              CIP

10 9 8 7 6 5 4

CONTENTS

PREFACE AND DEDICATION

The year was 1966. The cultural revolution of the late sixties and early seventies was just beginning to break open. Questioning of authority, including religious authority, was in the air. The Catholic Church had been transformed by the influence of Pope John XXIII and the Second Vatican Council. "Radical theology" was all the rage among avant-garde Protestant thinkers, who dared even to discuss the "death of God." In the Jewish community there was an impending sense that an age of complacency was at an end, that old ways had to be challenged and new ways tried.

I was in my final year of rabbinic training at the Jewish Theological Seminary, a Conservative Jewish institution in New York. There I had the great privilege of studying privately with Abraham Joshua Heschel, one of the outstanding Jewish religious figures of this century. Heschel, the great prophetic voice of postwar America, heir to the hasidic masters, holocaust survivor, and friend of Martin Luther King, Jr., was now becoming deeply embroiled in the anti–Vietnam War movement, a position quite unpopular among his faculty colleagues. He understood sympathetically the great student unrest that was leading to riots and violent confrontations with police at nearby Columbia University. His own antigovernment feelings grew from day to day, as he felt himself called upon to speak out ever more forcefully against policies he considered tantamount to murder and even genocide.

Heschel burned with prophetic zeal for the just causes to which he was becoming increasingly dedicated. His theology, which culminated in a demand for sacred deeds, seemed to call upon us to engage in radical action for the sake of God and divine justice. The emphasis on the prophets and their uncompromising religious and moral demands, previously the preserve of Reform "social gospel" rabbis, was now given new credence, as Heschel put the weight of his own deep learning and traditional roots behind it.

But in other ways, Heschel's theological foundations seemed far from what was being called "radical" in that era. He was more an affirmer than a questioner of religious tradition. A man of deep faith in a personal God and in the creation of humans in God's image, he spoke with disdain of the "death of God" theologians, claiming that the very phrase was a blasphemy he could scarcely bear to hear. His own prayer life and commitment to hasidic learning evoked a piety and devotionalism that seemed to belong to another era.

So it was that I entered his office one day in that spring and asked him quite directly:

"Professor Heschel, what do you think of radical theology?"

He replied immediately:

"Radical theology is very important. And it must begin with the *Sfas Emes* and R. Tsadok ha-Kohen of Lublin.*"

---

*R. Tsadok ha-Kohen (1823–1900) was an original and creative hasidic thinker and a prolific author. A disciple of the rabbis of Izbica and of R. Leibele Eiger of Lublin, his works, in contrast to most hasidic teachings, were written mainly for learned Talmud students within the walls of the yeshivah. They have enjoyed a recent upsurge of popularity, especially in Israel, where they are currently being reprinted in various augmented and well-indexed editions. In English, the unpublished doctoral dissertation of Alan Brill, *The Intellectual Mysticism of R. Zadok ha-Kohen* (Fordham University, 1994) is the most important treatment.

I have tried to take my teacher's words seriously. I had already begun several years earlier to study the works of the hasidic masters, and they had become the chief source of my own spiritual sustenance, as they are to this day, some thirty years later. I already understood some of the radical implications of hasidic thought and the ways in which it transformed Jewish theology, broadening the bounds of conventional thinking about God, the nature of Torah, and the meaning of religious life. But Heschel's challenge encouraged me to look further.

Beginning in the early 1990s, after a quarter century of teaching, quoting, and occasionally translating from the *Sefat Emet,* I began to read through the five volumes of homilies in systematic fashion. It was apparent from the outset that I would offer a selection, rather than a complete translation, of this lengthy and often repetitive work. Of the teachings on each weekly Torah reading, then each holiday, I selected those that I felt would most readily "speak" to the contemporary seeker. My hope was that these would serve as a bridge between the classical rabbinic-hasidic spirituality of the nineteenth century and the very different "mystical" or "spiritual" Judaism that I believe is just beginning to emerge in our own day. I translated the teachings into English, trying to remain faithful to the original while supplying to the reader the additional information needed to understand the text. Loving the Hebrew original of these texts as I do, it was my hope from the beginning that this selection might appear in a bilingual format, as it has. I am tremendously grateful to my student Rabbi Shai Gluskin for having prepared a Hebrew version (beginning at the opposite end of this volume) that avoids the abbreviations, ellipses, and other special features that usually make hasidic sources difficult for the uninitiated Hebrew reader.

Early in the process, I realized that the texts alone would not quite provide the intended bridge between the old Jewish spirituality and the new. I would have to do this by adding to each text my own response as a contemporary Jewish seeker. This would come in the form of commentary, but in a loose sense of that term. Only occasionally do I seek to explain the teaching in its own historical context. More frequently I ask the kind of question that the hasidic masters themselves asked of earlier sacred writings, especially biblical texts: "How can *we* use this text?" "If Torah is eternal, this text has to speak to every generation. What does it have to say to ours?" I address that question over and over again to the wealth of hasidic piety found in this volume. How might a seeker of today be addressed by this text? What would it mean for us to open ourselves to it, to fashion our lives in response to its call? What objections might we have to it? How might it be reformulated so that it speaks to our hearts as it did to those of its original hearers? Sometimes, in the course of these comments, I found myself addressing the author of the *Sefat Emet* directly. Occasionally I was moved to write a comment in the form of a prayer.

The fact that I ask such questions is a statement of my own faith that these texts can indeed address us, and very powerfully. I firmly believe that this link between the Jewish spirituality of former ages and that of tomorrow can and must be built. Hasidism, as a condensation of the Jewish mystical tradition intended to be accessible to ordinary Jews, naturally should be a key part of such an effort. This Hasidism will of course be quite different from that taught and practiced by today's surviving hasidic community. It will be hasidic thought at its broadest, challenged by our own very different life experience to open itself even more to an extended and somewhat universalized rereading, which will play an important part in the great renewal of Jewish faith just beginning in our age.

In claiming this, I hope that I am keeping faith with the call of my teacher, to whose beloved and revered memory I dedicate this volume.

TO THE READER: HOW TO USE THIS BOOK

Sefat Emet is a collection of hasidic teachings following the order of the two great liturgical cycles of Judaism: the weekly reading of the Torah in the synagogue and the annual procession of the festivals. The sections of the work follow that order, each containing several teachings based on the Torah and other classical texts associated with those occasions. The teachings in this volume were meant for study, contemplation, and discussion. It will be best used as an accompaniment to your own liturgical year, as the Hebrew *Sefat Emet* has been used for generations.

The work is preceded by a historical introduction, one that will hopefully enhance your appreciation of the teachings. You may choose to skip over the introduction at first, getting directly to the *Sefat Emet*, as you would if you had the Hebrew original in front of you. Later, after getting to know the work firsthand, you might come back to learn about its historical background. The important thing here is the texts themselves, and you are therefore urged to set sail forthwith on this sea of learning, turning first to the Torah or holiday portion approaching as you acquire and open this volume.

A. Y. G.

INTRODUCTION

I

You have before you a contemporary selection from the *Sefat Emet*, one of the most popular books of hasidic teaching and one of the most recent books to obtain "classic" status within the hasidic corpus. Originally published in Piotrkow, near Lodz, Poland, in 1905–1908, the five volumes of *Sefat Emet* have been avidly read and studied both within and beyond the hasidic community for nearly a century. This crowning literary achievement of Polish Hasidism survived the near-total destruction of the communities where it was written and first studied, following the remnants of Polish Jewry and Ger Hasidism to Israel, America, and many other lands of their dispersion.

The author of *Sefat Emet* is Rabbi Yehudah Leib Alter, the rebbe of Gora Kalwaria (called Ger in Yiddish and Gur in Hebrew),[1]* near Warsaw. He was the grandson and heir of

---

*Footnotes to the Introduction begin on page xlix.

Rabbi Isaac Meir Rothenberg (1799–1866),[2] founder of the hasidic dynasty associated with that town. In order to appreciate the *Sefat Emet* and its place in the literary corpus of Hasidism, it is necessary to understand the origins and special character of Ger Hasidism. Once we have placed the *Sefat Emet* in historical context, we will turn to an examination of its mystical teachings and the important contribution it has made to the development of hasidic thought.

R. Isaac Meir, often known by the title of his book *Ḥiddushey ha-RIM*, was an accomplished Talmudist and legal authority. He belonged to the group of hasidic masters in the movement's second period[3] who combined hasidic leadership with a significant reputation for talmudic learning, including publication in both fields. This was the period of the ascendancy of Hasidism; peace had been achieved with the movement's onetime rabbinic opponents, and hasidic influence was spreading throughout most of Jewish eastern Europe. Hasidism now sought to reintegrate itself with the values of rabbinic society, especially that of intellectual rigor.[4] More specifically, R. Isaac Meir was a key figure in the group of highly learned and intellectual leaders of the distinctively Polish school of Hasidism. This "branch" of Hasidism developed first in Przysucha[5] and Kotsk but came to dominate much of hasidic life in central Poland, including the Warsaw and Lodz areas, by the middle of the nineteenth century. The *Sefat Emet* may be seen as a key text of this "Polish school" of Hasidism—indeed, perhaps, its crowning achievement.

Hasidism had been introduced to central Poland (the former "Kingdom of Poland" or "Congress" area) around the turn of the nineteenth century by followers of the original hasidic masters who lived to the south and east in Galicia and Volhynia.[6] These traced themselves back to the original court of R. Dov Baer of Miedzyrzec (1704–1772), creator of the hasidic movement as such, and through him to R. Israel Ba'al Shem Tov (1700–1760), the central figure around whom Hasidism first began to develop. Jewish life in this part of Poland had a somewhat different character from that of the southern and eastern regions. Polish Jews tended to be more urbanized than those in Volhynia or eastern Galicia. Fewer Polish Jews lived in the relative isolation of village communities, earning their livelihood from the old "arenda" or tax-farmer contracts with Polish magnates. Jews in central Poland, a largely flat plain, lived in larger cities and in towns that were closer and more accessible to one another, compared with the more sparsely settled regions in and beyond the Carpathian Mountains. This urban tendency increased significantly over the course of the nineteenth century with the advent of the Industrial Revolution, when impoverished Jewish tradesmen and small-scale shopkeepers turned for work to the newly organized textile factories in larger cities, vastly increasing the Jewish populations of such places as Warsaw, Lodz, Radom, and Rzeszow.

Jews in this area also tended to see themselves as more sophisticated and less credulous than their Ukrainian/Galician counterparts. Ukrainian Jewish life is frequently portrayed as characterized by a rich lode of folk-belief and superstition, accompanied by relative ignorance of talmudic learning at its higher levels.[7] While Poland was not home to great yeshivot in the early nineteenth century,[8] the level of learning, or at least the self-perception of Jews as living in an area of high Jewish culture, was superior to that of those to the east.

Christian hatred of Jews was an integral part of Jewish life experience throughout the region. As the Industrial Revolution developed, economic competition and jealousy combined with ancient Christian myth to keep the Jews' situation ever difficult and precarious. Still, there seems to have been less insecurity and fear of gentiles in Congress Poland than in Volhynia and especially in Podolia (home of the Ba'al Shem Tov), an area sparsely settled by Jews and close to the trans-Dnieper section of southern Russia, where the seminomadic Cossacks still held sway and where Jewish residence was not permitted.

The dismemberment of the former Polish kingdom, beginning in 1772, meant that central Poland was under the rule of the czars. This area, the historic heartland ("kingdom") of Poland, was also the center of Polish cultural-intellectual life and the hotbed of growing Polish national consciousness. To a degree, some enlightened Poles in this region were beginning in the nineteenth century to see Jews as fellow-victims of czarist oppression, a view that somehow coexisted alongside ongoing discrimination against Jews as religious pariahs and economic rivals.

Hasidism was introduced to Congress Poland by two key figures in the third/fourth generation of hasidic leadership, R. Jacob Isaac Horowitz (1745–1815) of Lublin[9] and R. Israel (1733–1814) of Kozienice.[10] Both of them, following the general impulse within early Hasidism to spread the movement's impact ever farther, brought with them the type of hasidic religious enthusiasm and popular mystical teaching that were prevalent throughout the movement. R. Jacob Isaac, known popularly as the Seer of Lublin, was especially well known for having unusual psychic powers, a phenomenon he probably shared with the Ba'al Shem Tov himself and several other hasidic masters. He was also an unabashed miracle worker, one who did not hesitate to pray for the material as well as the spiritual welfare of his followers. The seer's writings[11] show him to have been quite at home in the teachings of the Miedzyrzec school, including the more abstract and mystical among them. In general we may say that he brought to this new region an authentic representation of Volhynian Hasidism, including both its most sophisticated and its most popular sides.

The Maggid (or "preacher") of Kozienice was a somewhat different figure. He brought the fatherly warmth of popular Ukrainian Hasidism to a court that seemed to function as an extended family surrounding a beloved elder. While not opposed to miracle working, he was less known for visionary powers than was the Seer, though the extraordinary power of his prayers and intercessions were an important factor in attracting the large following that gathered about him. He combined this folklike image with a degree of learning and a love of books for which he became especially known. The Kozienicer collected ancient Hebrew manuscripts and was responsible for the first publication of several important ancient writings of the Jewish mystical tradition.

R. Isaac Meir, the grandfather of the Sefat Emet, came from the little town of Magnuszew, which was quite near to

Kozienice.[12] When he was still a boy, his parents took him to the nearby hasidic master or rebbe, R. Israel. There he had his first exposure to hasidic learning, and he quickly came to be seen as the most promising young student in the Kozienicer's circle. Because he showed great progress in his studies (his father was the rabbi of Magnuszew and a man of considerable learning), the young Isaac Meir was wedded, immediately following his Bar Mitzvah, to the daughter of a wealthy member of the growing Warsaw Jewish banking community.[13] His father-in-law, as was the custom, took him to live in Warsaw, where he became known as "the Warsaw prodigy," a young genius of talmudic lore. After the death of Rabbi Israel of Kozienice in 1814, Isaac Meir became a follower of the rabbi's son Moses Eliakim Beriah (1777–1828). Soon,[14] however, he became attracted to the newly developing and more distinctively intellectual circle of Hasidim around R. Simḥa Bunem (1767–1827) of Przysucha.

R. Simḥa Bunem was an anomaly in the hasidic world.[15] He is the first hasidic master to have had something of a Western education; he worked as a pharmacist before he began his career as rebbe.[16] While the Ba'al Shem Tov and others had combined a knowledge of herbal medicines with amulet writing as tools of healing, their sources were strictly on the level of rural folk knowledge. R. Simḥa Bunem is of a different class. Even prior to working as a pharmacist, he had served as a business agent for the important Bergson (Berkson) merchant family,[17] maintaining commercial ties to the somewhat Germanized city of Danzig, where he is said to have traveled regularly. One has the sense (partly from repeated denials in the hasidic sources!) that the "hasidic master" phase of R. Bunem's life represented a return to greater commitment after a prior life in which at least the values of intense piety, if not the commandments themselves, might have been somewhat neglected. The sources say quite openly that he consorted with nonpious Jews and that he dressed in Western clothing during this period of his life.

The Przysucha circle[18] seems to have been more a peer group of learned young men, led by an older mentor figure, than it was a locally based center of following for a wonder-working *tsaddik*. The very exceptional group of scholars and future leaders of Hasidism, unrivaled by any save for the original disciples of Dov Baer of Miedzyrzec, came from all over the region rather than from near Przysucha itself.[19] Key figures in the circle were R. Menaḥem Mendel of Kotsk[20] (1787–1859), R. Isaac of Warka (1779–1848), R. Mordecai Joseph of Izbica[21] (1801–1853), R. Abraham of Ciechanow (1784–1875), and R. Isaac Meir. As leader of this group, R. Simḥa Bunem called for a rededication to the principles of Hasidism on the highest level. These included a prayer-life of passionate intensity, a love of learning as a religious act, and a sense of caring for one's fellow Jews. His own somewhat odd background seems to have aroused considerable opposition in more conventional rabbinic and hasidic circles,[22] creating an atmosphere of controversy that was loved and cultivated by the fiery group of young men who surrounded him.

 II

The Hasidism of Przysucha, and especially that of Kotsk which followed it, is in part to be seen as a puritanical reform movement within Hasidism, the most influential of several that have come to be during the course of the movement's history.[23] The success of Hasidism and the fact that several generations had passed since the original revival called forth by the Ba'al Shem Tov's followers had inevitably led to the emergence of a highly stylized hasidic piety. For many, self-definition as a Hasid had less to do with the heart's openness or with the simple awareness of God that the Ba'al Shem Tov had taught than with such externals as forms of prayer, special garb, dynastic loyalties, and an ever-growing welter of particular customs and practices, often in imitatation of the personal behavior of one holy man or another.[24] In Przysucha there was no room for such behavior. Personal *integrity* was seen as the key to authentic religiosity. R. Mendel of Kotsk, the successor of R. Simḥa Bunem,[25] conducted relentless war against any sort of derivative or imitative religious behavior, denouncing it all as sham piety. He offered no tolerance for a Hasidism defined by any sort of "style" or outward manifestation of religiosity. He dismissed as false display any extreme act of piety not required by Jewish Law.

From the viewpoint of other, more traditionalist, hasidic leaders, Kotsk represented a certain betrayal of the hasidic ideal. The imitation of the *tsaddik* (and his revered ancestors) played an important and positive role in hasidic life as it was usually understood. The *tsaddik*'s loving ability to accept all Jews, despite their faults and shortcomings, was also a key to the movement's growth. Kotsk had about it a strong self-critical edge that was new to Hasidism and undoubtedly frightening to those who stood outside this elite circle. There was a certain militancy evident here, a sense that the real task of Hasidism was nothing less than that of transforming the self, a battle that could be won if approached with sufficient dedication, constancy, and lack of self-deception. This was a far cry from the Hasidism—which also continued to exist in Poland—of dependence on miracle workers, amulets, and the merits of the righteous dead.[26]

Study of the law itself played an important role in this particular "Polish school" of Hasidism. While the earlier masters had also encouraged study and seen it as an essential religious duty, there was a certain ambivalence in their attitudes toward what had long been considered the essential subject of Jewish learning, especially in Poland: the legal discourses of the Talmud and its commentaries.[27] Hasidic learning had focused rather on Mishnah (the learning of which was encouraged by certain kabbalistic associations), on the aggadic or nonlegal sections of the Talmud, and on the Zohar and other mystical writings. Such learning tended toward the creation of inspired Sabbath table-talks, drawing on a wealth of these earlier sources; these in turn became the basic texts of the new hasidic literature. With only rare exceptions, the early hasidic masters did not have (or did not care to foster) the erudition to produce learned tomes of halakhic discourse in the classic rabbinic fashion.

One reason for this change in curriculum was an extreme suspiciousness, even to the point of mocking, of those who claimed to have attained understanding of mystic truths or high levels of kabbalistic knowledge. Such understanding was beyond the ken of that generation, the Kotsker taught, and claims to the contrary were to be treated with the greatest wariness, to say the least.[28] Since we cannot truly understand the mystical writings, there is little point in studying them. Thus the chief object of study among the Kotsker's disciples became *nigleh*, the "revealed" Torah, consisting of talmudic and later legal sources, especially the tractates dealing with the civil code. These most difficult legal writings, considered by non-hasidic scholars to be the very heart of Jewish law, were now the center of hasidic learning as well, though peppered with an occasional sharp flash of spiritual or moral insight into the seemingly dense and often obscure matters at hand.

Part of this change in the curriculum of studies was brought about, as we have said, by a suspicion of would-be mystics. But it also had to do with a reassertion of ethical concerns, the subject matter of those tractates. Religion needed to be re-rooted in this-worldly decency, the Kotsker insisted, rather than in lofty flights of fancy. Typical of this Polish hasidic ethical sensibility is an interesting "historiographic" comment offered on the famous Mishnah: "The world stands upon three things: Torah, worship, and deeds of kindness." This comment divides Jewish history into three periods: From the days of Moses until the time of R. Isaac Luria (1534–1572), it claims, the world was based on Torah. From the time of Luria until the advent of R. Elimelech of Lezajsk (d. 1786; seen as the "grandfather" of Polish Hasidism), the world stood upon worship. Since his day, however, the world exists because of deeds of kindness.[29] The Kotsker is often described with reference to the scriptural quotation, "Truth grows from the ground" (Ps. 85:12),[30] which is frequently quoted in sayings attributed to him, meaning either that *emet*, long known as "the seal of God," must be based on honest behavior here on earth or, even more sharply, that truth lies buried beneath the lies of a supposedly pious but corrupt society. This radical shift in emphasis did not deny the truth or value of mystical texts written in former generations, but it left virtually no room for the current cultivation of such an approach. There were mystics and even kabbalists to be found among Hasidim in the second quarter of the nineteenth century,[31] but not in Kotsk.

R. Isaac Meir was a key member of the inner circle in both Przysucha and Kotsk. While he had taken on R. Simḥa Bunem as his master, R. Mendel of Kotsk was more an older peer (he was twelve years older than R. Isaac Meir) to him, the one among the Przysucha circle who assumed leadership after their shared master's death. The years of the Kotsker's leadership saw the intimate circle of fiery young men who had gathered in Przysucha become the most important religious personalities in the Jewish community of Poland. By the time of the Kotsker's death in 1859, tens of thousands of Jews saw themselves to one degree or another as followers of those spiritual figures who had been forged in the crucible of R. Menaḥem Mendel's demanding and uncompromising school for leaders.

Paradoxically, it may have been the very elitist character of the Kotsk circle's ideology that became the source of its ultimate success. While westernization (in the form of Haskalah) had not yet made serious inroads into Polish Jewry in the second quarter of the nineteenth century, a spirit of critical thought and rationalism was able to find a home within Hasidism through Kotsk. Young men who were incredulous of the miracle tales and pious superstitions that so often accompanied Hasidism were here able to have the best of both worlds: the intense brotherhood of a community devoted to spiritual pursuits, mostly living within the approved norms of tradition, together with the legitimation of their own questioning and doubts, justified by the inevitably greater doubts and challenges to popular faith raised by the mysterious rebbe himself.

The circle of Kotsk disciples underwent a significant crisis during the later years of their leader's life. From around 1840[32] until his death in 1859, the Kotsker, always short-fused and somewhat irascible, completely lost patience with the demands of life as a public figure and became increasingly reclusive. Some who opposed Kotsk said that he had become a madman, hiding in his own room and appearing only occasionally—often to the terror of those visiting his house of study. One leading disciple, R. Mordecai Joseph Leiner, left him at the beginning of that period, founding the separate dynasty of Izbica Hasidism. Others, notably the future rebbes of Aleksander, Ger, and Warka, stood by their master, often acting in his place when the public need demanded.

By the time of the Kotsker's death, it had become accepted in Polish hasidic circles that the Hasidim would follow the deceased master's leading disciple as the new rebbe, rather than the master's son. This type of succession had already taken place in the cases of the R. Jacob Isaac of Lublin, R. Jacob Isaac of Przysucha, and R. Simḥa Bunem. In each of these cases, it should be noted, there was a son who succeeded in the direct dynastic line of his father, with a small group of locally based Hasidim connected to the family remaining loyal to him.[33] But the majority went with the disciple, there being a sense that the true charisma of leadership was passed, as in the days of the Ba'al Shem Tov, from master to disciple rather than from father to son. This too reflected the reformist character of Polish Hasidism and its desire to base itself on a search for the true presence of the spirit in the current moment rather than on tradition and memory of past glories.

R. Isaac Meir, who was then living in Warsaw, was chosen by the inner circle of R. Mendel's followers to be the next leader. Warsaw, the Polish capital that only about half a century earlier had still forbidden Jewish residence, now became the hasidic "capital" of Poland as well. A building was purchased on "Iron Street" (*Eisen-gas* in Yiddish) that was to remain the Warsaw headquarters of R. Isaac Meir's descendants and followers down to the years of Polish Jewry's final destruction. After seven years, however, the new rebbe decided that Warsaw was not a good setting for a growing hasidic court. The large numbers of young men who came to Warsaw as his followers, many of them from impoverished small towns, might be too attracted by the many commercial opportunities and even the freethinking ideas that flourished in the fast-growing capital. They would be religiously "safer" in a smaller place, one where the spiritual climate, at least of the Jewish community, could be more assuredly dominated by the hasidic spirit. For this purpose he chose Gora Kalwaria, a place where his father had once served as rabbi.[34] Moving there in about 1860, he turned that town (population in 1860: 1401 Jews, 707 Christians[35]) into one of the most important centers of Polish Hasidism and of Jewish learning. R. Isaac Meir agreed, however, to visit Warsaw at least twice a year and conduct a *tish* (a hasidic "table") there, so as not to abrogate his claim as chief hasidic influence in the capital.

III

The brief period in which R. Isaac Meir served as leader of Polish Hasidism was important in solidifying the place of Hasidism as a leading force within the "official" Jewish community. The Kotsker had disdained political influence and contacts with powerful people, even while his disciples saw to it that his court was supported by the Bergsons and other wealthy followers. Although the leading rabbis of Poland could not but have been impressed with the high level of Torah study fostered by Kotsk, the unconventional attitudes of the Kotsker kept them somewhat at a distance. R. Isaac Meir was seen as a figure of greater respectability than his master had been, particularly during the Kotsker's long period of isolation.[36] When Ger replaced Kotsk as the center of Polish Hasidism, the new leader made a great effort to link himself, through learned correspondence as well as in personal meetings, with his fellow halakhic authorities throughout eastern Europe. He had a close relationship with R. Dov Berush Meisels, Rabbi of Warsaw from 1854 to 1870, and was in touch with many of the leading rabbis of both Poland and Russia. These contacts, made possible only by R. Isaac Meir's high level of talmudic erudition,[37] effected for Polish Hasidism that which had already happened in Galicia a generation earlier: a thorough joining of the hasidic with the rabbinic leadership, so that the former lines between

Hasidim and their onetime opponents virtually disappeared. Marriages between offspring of hasidic dynasties and great rabbinic families had already become commonplace, and the same important merchant and banking families often provided the economic support for both sorts of leadership. This effort may be said to mark the final victory of Hasidism in gaining full respectability in the Polish-Jewish community.[38] That it took place in the face of a growing common enemy, Western-style "enlightenment" and the beginnings of assimilation, should come as no surprise.

R. Isaac Meir was, however, not granted a lengthy "reign" as leader of his own community. He had suffered the tragedy of seeing many of his children, including all his sons, die within his own lifetime. Of his sons, only the eldest survived to adulthood; R. Abraham Mordecai (1815–1855) was the father of the Sefat Emet. His death was a particularly great loss and disappointment to his father. In his later years, along with the burdens of communal leadership and the writing of several volumes of novellae and teachings, R. Isaac Meir devoted much time to the personal education of his grandson, who had now become his heir.[39] The future author of the *Sefat Emet* went frequently to Kotsk with his grandfather; he was twelve years old when the Kotsker died. R. Isaac Meir suffered his own final illness in 1866, leaving behind him a community once again in search of a leader, and a grandson, his successor within the family, a young man of only nineteen years. It was understood among the Hasidim that this young man was not yet ready for the large-scale following that being rebbe of Ger would entail.[40] Thus it was, again following what by now had become "tradition" within Polish Hasidism, that the disciples turned to R. Henikh of Aleksander (1798–1870),[41] the best-known surviving member of the Przysucha circle, to serve as the leader of Hasidism in Poland.

It was four years later, after the death of the Rabbi of Aleksander,[42] that the "crown" of Polish Hasidism returned to Ger. The young rebbe, married to the daughter of R. Yehudah Kaminer,[43] a member of the Warsaw circle of Hasidim and the scion of a distinguished rabbinic family,[44] had changed his name to Aryeh (another cognate of Leib) in deference to his father-in-law. Although he had begun composing written teachings from the time of his grandfather's death, he later came to dismiss those as juvenalia,[45] and his formal body of teachings, included in the *Sefat Emet,* begins in 1871, after his appointment as rebbe.

Throughout the more than three decades that he served as Gerer rebbe, from 1871 to 1905, R. Yehudah Leib maintained a distinguished reputation for great learning, for personal integrity, and for upholding the high reputation of the Gerer court in an age when Hasidism, and religious life generally, was losing its hold over a large part of the Jewish people. He and his family lived in relatively modest style, supported by the income from a tobacco shop run by his wife. While many of his Hasidim had come to possess great wealth, he refused to accept gifts from them and did not allow himself to profit personally from their successes. He maintained good relations with the rabbinic authorities of his day, continuing the trend already started by his grandfather. In his years the yeshivot in Ger, Warsaw, and other towns under his influence grew and prospered, educating thousands of young men in the spirit of talmudic acumen, strict personal piety, and a degree of openness to questioning and even skepticism, as originally cultivated in Kotsk. By far his greatest work, however, was the tremendous outpouring of discourse and personal teaching offered to his disciples on each Sabbath and festival over the course of all those years, collected in the work known to us as *Sefat Emet.*

The homilies that make up the *Sefat Emet* were not given that title by their author. Although there is little doubt that he intended the eventual publication of his carefully collected teachings, the volume was incomplete and untitled at his death in 1905. The brief introduction to the first volume, reprinted in the later offset editions, is signed by "the sons and sons-in-law of the holy rabbi, our master, teacher, and rabbi of Gur, may the righteous one's memory be a blessing unto the life of the world-to-come." There they tell us that the manuscript of this work, in the author's own hand, was lacking a title, and that they called it *Sefat Emet*, based on an interpretation of Proverbs 12:19 found in the last teaching he had entered into the collection, a comment on *parashat va-yeḥi* for 1904/05. There *emet* (truth) is associated with the speech of all Israel, "because the witness to God is not the individual person but the totality of Israel." As is often the case with later teachings in the *Sefat Emet*, this homily is a variant on one he had offered five years earlier, in the same *parashah* for 1899/1900. There Jacob represents truth, and the sons gathered around his deathbed are the lips that bring this truth to expression in language. Jacob's truth would be silent were it not for the tribes who bring it into words.

I would suggest that, in a perhaps only partly conscious way, this reading of Jacob's deathbed scene had another level of meaning to R. Yehudah Leib Alter as well. Jacob, the quality of truth, represents R. Mendel of Kotsk, who is often referred to as "the pillar of truth" and who was known, as we have said, for absolute devotion to truth and integrity in all walks of life. This utter insistence on truth had the effect of *silencing* all expressions of the spiritual life. It made the Kotsker a radical minimalist in religious language and frightened his disciples into the same position. R. Yehudah Leib realized that this necessary and well-intended cooling of hasidic exaggeration and hyperbole also had the more far-reaching effect of denying any possibility of religious speech at all. There was nothing one could say regarding the spiritual life or the inner universe of faith that did not fall victim to this ever sharp Kotsker scrutiny. The lips were silenced, and the inner Torah became truly *nistar* (hidden) once again; only *nigleh* could be spoken of in Kotsk. In fact, for the last nineteen years of the Kotsker's life there had been *total* silence when it came to religious creativity; there were no new teachings delivered by the rebbe in all those years. R. Yehudah Leib sees the task of Ger as that of restoring speech to the (silent) truth of faith, *safah* to *emet*, of recreating, on the far side of Kotsker questioning, a new and simplified religious language, one that can express higher or deeper truth without falling prey to the question of whether anyone in our time can attain such high rungs of knowledge.

He does so by insisting that the insights he offers belong to all of Israel. Expressed in simple terms, they are truths that conform to the intuition implanted within the soul of each and every Jew. No Kabbalah beyond a bare minimum of vocabulary is required here. The mystical insight offered in *Sefat Emet* is at once too direct and too profound to be the exclusive property of those who know the occult lore. This creation of a *post-kabbalistic Jewish mystical language* is a major goal of the *Sefat Emet,* which might also be translated as *Honest Talk.* The Sefat Emet, heir both to Kotsk and to the earlier hasidic tradition, was something of a mystic, though not a Kabbalist. Only very seldom in the five volumes of his collected homilies do we find him referring to the *sefirot* in anything but a psychological or moralizing way. There is no reference to the four worlds, the *partsufim,* or other key features of the language associated with later Kabbalah and present in the writings of the Lubavitch and Zydachov/Komarno schools of Hasidism, which may at least in this sense be called "kabbalistic." True, R. Yehudah Leib often quotes "the holy Zohar," and it is clear that he studied it, as he did the "Midrash Rabbah," as he prepared his weekly discourses. But the Zohar provides him essentially with homiletical material that he uses or sets aside at will, rather than with a full system of thought or symbolic expression. Most important, the Zohar provides an ancient and venerated example of a *spiritualized reading* of the *parashah,* which is precisely what the *Sefat Emet* is seeking to create for his own listeners and readers.[46]

Unlike most hasidic collections, the *Sefat Emet* is presented as a series of dated homilies on each Torah portion and festival over the period of some thirty-three years of its author's "reign" as Gerer rebbe. Like nearly all the printed collections of hasidic teachings, these are written Hebrew synopses of much longer talks given in Yiddish,[47] typically at the Friday evening *tish* (the rebbe's communal "table") and at *se'udah shelishit,* the concluding "third meal" of the Sabbath. But here we are given the opportunity to see how a theme developed in the preacher's mind over the course of several decades; the later teachings are often combinations of themes that had appeared earlier, reworked for application to a new situation that confronted his Hasidim. Although these talks, like all sermons, surely often had contemporary points of reference, these are never mentioned directly in the text. The hasidic rebbe, we should recall, is "saying Torah"; his teaching is seen as a part of the ongoing revelation of the divine Word. As such it would be unseemly for him to make mention of contemporary events that would pin down the eternal Word to a particular time and place. For us as latter-day readers, that is all to the good, as the texts retain a lasting currency they could not have if "dated" (in both senses) by reference to historical particulars.

The rebbe's *tish* is a celebratory event, a sacred meal at which he functions in a manner reminiscent of the ancient priest presiding over the holy altar. The food at this table, of which he eats but sparsely, is then considered holy, and is rapidly divided among the eager disciples. In some hasidic dynasties, song at the table takes a place of primacy, lasting nearly through the night. In Ger, however, the *tish* is to be seen primarily as an educational session, the time when the rebbe shares teachings intended to inculcate values into his assembled Hasidim. In this Torah-centered Hasidism, where both master and disciples valued learning so highly, the weekly teachings of the rebbe were the great gift of each Shabbat.

The thirty-three years of R. Yehudah Leib's reign as rebbe of Ger were a time of great transformation in the life of Polish Jewry. Urbanization was a major factor: the Jewish population of Warsaw grew from 72,800 in 1864 to 306,000 in 1910, largely due to migration from the countryside.[48] The influence of Haskalah, or Western enlightenment, and the growth of a Haskalah-oriented Hebrew press stood as an important counterpoint to hasidic domination of the spiritual life of Warsaw Jewry. Assimilation and Polonization of upper-class Jews were also widespread phenomena; the assimilationist party actually controlled the official Warsaw community throughout R. Yehudah Leib's years as rebbe of Ger and Warsaw. Secular literature in Yiddish began to appear in the mid-nineteenth century and also began to offer a contrary value system to that propounded by the hasidic community. In the later years of

R. Yehudah Leib's reign, both Zionism and socialism became major factors in the lives of a great many Warsaw Jews. While statistics are hard to come by, it is fair to say that between 1871 and 1904 an increasingly significant percentage of Warsaw Jewry was less and less faithful to the norms of Jewish practice and the old way of life that Hasidism had come to represent.

Reading through the volumes of *Sefat Emet,* the reader cannot but marvel at how clearly their author articulates his central theme of inwardness and spirituality, and how frequently he comes back to it. Especially given the battles with secularization and modernity that he and his Hasidim were fighting in the last decades of the nineteenth century, the emphasis he chooses to place on this spiritual theme is absolutely remarkable. It is by no means clear that such emphasis was to his "advantage" in this struggle. Ger was working hard to achieve and maintain dominance over Jewish religious life in central Poland; this included the building of yeshivot, educational reform from within, and efforts to overcome remaining religious resistance to Hasidism. The constant spiritualist refrain of the *Sefat Emet* is addressed primarily to his own Hasidim, as though to remind them regularly that all their efforts were for the sake of this higher goal of mystical consciousness, one that was not to be lost while at work on building the earthly trappings of a powerful religious movement. If he wanted to remind them of how their value system was essentially different from that of the non-hasidic Orthodox world, as well as from those of the increasing forces of secularism and materialism, he did so by this constant emphasis on inward spirituality as the true goal.

IV

Although the legacy of Kotsk did not permit him to be a kabbalist, I have claimed R. Yehudah Leib as a mystic. Because of this, his agenda is no longer identical to that of the Kotsker. The revolution of Kotsk has already taken place. The battle against a Hasidism centered on popular wonder workers has been won, at least within the Polish hasidic leadership circle. A group of hasidic rebbes has arisen that claims no miracles for itself other than that of fashioning disciples who combine true religious awareness with a life of learning and good deeds. This "miracle" is performed in the only way possible: by constant exemplary behavior on the part of leaders and by the hard work of self-mastery and study among the disciples.

The Sefat Emet fully believes in the principles of this revolution and remains faithful to them. Nevertheless, he represents a return to mystical consciousness, to the insights of the Ba'al Shem Tov, now to be expressed again in simple and direct language. He believes fervently that the truest existence—sometimes he insists that it is the only true existence—is that of the *innermost point*, the source and true essence of all that is. Everything else is mere garb, the infinitely varied costumes with which this point that animates all being has chosen to cloak itself. This term, offered in typically poor hasidic Hebrew, is key to his religious self-expression and comes up hundreds of times within his writings. It may be translated as "innermost point," "core of being," "inward reality." Sometimes it appears combined with the term *ḥiyyut*, "life-force"; *nekudat ha-ḥiyyut* would be the "inner life-point." Dispensing even with the degree of old mystical language that had been present in Hasidism since the Maggid of Miedzyrzec,[49] he uses his own much simpler terms to verbalize the basic mystic insight in most direct and sometimes startling ways.[50]

> All things are brought into being by Him. But the point is hidden and we have to expand it. This depends upon the point within us, for the more we expand our own souls, the more God is revealed to us in every place. This is the meaning of "When YHWH your God widens your border" (Deut. 12:20)—when the point spreads forth and expands throughout the human soul.[51]

The "jump" from speaking of YHWH as Creator to "the point" within all things takes place almost too quickly, as this book consists of briefly summarized homilies rather than clearly argued theological discourses. But the "God revealed in every place" is clearly identical to the expanded "point."

The relationship of both of these to YHWH is less than clear. Does "point" refer to the divine presence accessible to us within all things? Is YHWH identical with that point or transcendent to it? Let us try another passage. Here Torah is depicted as God's agent in creation, a well-known midrashic motif:

> Torah gives life to all of creation, measuring it out to each creature. But that life-point (*nekudah ḥiyyut* [!]) which garbs itself within a particular place to give it life—it has no measure of its own, for it is beyond both time and nature. It was of this point that the rabbis said: "It ['He?'] is the place of the world, but the world is not its ['His'?] place.". . .[52]
>
> This is true of the human soul as well; it too has no measure. Scripture refers to the One who "forms the person's spirit within" (Zech. 12:1). The more one transcends the body, the more one is capable of receiving soul. But the soul itself is without limit. The same is true of the world's soul, since the person is a microcosm.[53]

The midrashic passage quoted is the *locus classicus* in rabbinic sources for theologies of emanation and ultimately for the panentheistic position of early hasidic theology. It is universally understood as applying to God: "*He* is the place of the world. . . ." Reading it here in reference to the inner point, we come very close to an identification of God with the *nekudah*. The point is infinite, beyond measure or limit. It remains unclear how aware the Sefat Emet is of the paradox, or perhaps the mathematical ingenuity, of his claim. A point is by definition infinitesimal; indeed it is smaller than any measure. To say that this infinite smallness is in fact infinite vastness, a limitless Oneness that contains all the world within itself, would be a formulation hardly surprising to either kabbalist or contemporary physicist. Such a paradoxical formulation is precisely typical of the ḤaBaD sources that seem to stand in the background of this formulation by the Sefat Emet.[54]

There are indeed passages in *Sefat Emet* where one has the impression of reading a theistic mystic, one who believes in a transcendent and unknown God who has allowed Himself to become *manifest* in the inner point, this manifestation being knowable to those who turn away from externals, especially of the corporeal sort, and open themselves to seeing what lies within. But in other passages the *Sefat Emet* seems much closer to a panentheistic theology. Here the discovery of the inner point is a direct experience of knowing God, and thus of re-effecting the cosmic unity. In these passages no distinction appears to be made between YHWH, the innermost point of all existence, the *ḥiyyut* or life-energy that sustains the universe, and the cosmic soul. Most commonly, the *Sefat Emet* gives the impression of a work that treads carefully, seeking to maintain the theistic language of normative Jewish piety to express a theology that leans heavily toward the panentheistic side. Let us have a look at another passage, this time along with its homiletic setting, a comment on the passage immediately preceding Jacob's first meeting with Rachel at the well:

> "He looked, and there was a well in the field, and there were three flocks of sheep lying down by it, for from that well the flocks were watered. But the stone was large on the mouth of the well. When all the flocks were gathered there, they would roll the stone off the mouth of the well" (Gen. 29:2–3).
>
> This reality—the well in the field—is found within every thing and within every one of Israel. Every thing contains a life-giving point that sustains it. Even that which appears to be as neglected as a field has such a hidden point within it. The human mind is always able to know this intuitively. This [knowledge] is the three flocks of sheep, which stand for wisdom, understanding, and awareness. With wisdom and intellect a person understands this inwardness. Within all things [dwells] "the power of the Maker within the made."
>
> But "the stone was large on the mouth of the well." When corporeality spreads forth there is hiding; intellect is not always joined to deed. The answer to this lies in "were gathered there"—all one's desires and every part of the body and its limbs have to be gathered together as one places oneself in God's hands before each deed. Then "they would roll the stone."
>
> You might also read "they were gathered" to mean that you should join yourself to all of Israel. For when all of creation is united with God, the hiding will end. This will occur in the future, may it come in our days! Meanwhile, we Jews gather everything to Him. . . .[55]

Here the homilist uses allegory to an extent somewhat unusual in the hasidic sources, but let us not allow that to distract us from the essential teaching. The field stands for inwardness, the unadorned inner simplicity that lies within all things. At its center is a life-giving well. The "life-giving point *(nekudah notenet ḥayyim)*" is in everything, both in seemingly inanimate objects and in the human (or Jewish) soul.[56] The point is described by a phrase familiar to the reader of earlier hasidic sources, *ko'aḥ ha-po'el ba-nif'al,* "the power of the Maker within the made."[57] The phrase indicates a subject-object distinction between God and the creation, the *nekudah* serving as the link between the two, or the continuing presence of the Creator within the world's innermost self.

This situation as described is not the ideal or ultimate one. The hope is for the day when "all creation is united *(mitaḥedet)* with God," a day toward which Israel are actively striving. At that time one can only imagine that the separate existence of all things as well as individual souls will cease, since all will be reunited with the one.

But is that unity only a goal for the anticipated future? Here is another passage, also, as it happens, describing a field (the physicist might also be interested in these descriptions of "point" as "field"!), but one where cautious speech is set aside, and a more radically mystical and even acosmic view of reality is proclaimed:

> The Sabbath table-song of Rabbi Isaac Luria contains the phrase, "To come into the entrance-ways of the apple field (a symbolic term for Shekhinah or divine presence)."[58] Why does he refer to the "entrance-ways"? Does one not come [directly] into the apple field?
>
> The truth is that this apple field is everywhere, as Scripture says: "The whole earth is filled with His glory!" (Is. 6:3) This is also taught with regard to the verse: "See, the smell of my son is like the smell of the field" (Gen. 27:27).
>
> But the essential task of worship is the opening of this point. On the Sabbath that gate is indeed open, as is written: "The gate to the inner courtyard wll be closed on the six workdays and open on the Sabbath and the New Moon" (Ezek. 46:1). . . . Thus it is easy to experience holiness on the Sabbath.
>
> In the same way, we should understand that the glory of God's kingdom is everywhere, even though it is unseen. This is the faith that every Jew has in God's oneness. *The meaning of "One" is that there is nothing except God Himself; God is the all.* Even though we are incapable of understanding this properly, we still need to believe it. This faith will lead us to truth. . . .[59]

The point is that just as God is present throughout the week as well as on the Sabbath, but Israel are open to that presence in a special way on Shabbat, so too is God present throughout the spatial realm, even if our own "Temple gate" is to be found only in Jerusalem or the Holy Land. In this sense the Sefat Emet is a good reader of ḤaBaD thought, with its recognition (based in turn on Cordovero and Maimonides) that divinity is equally present throughout the universe. Only our capacity to attain access to that presence is varied in time and space, limited chiefly by our lack of understanding or our only partial subjugation of the lower self. Typically, the Sefat Emet simplifies and presents these ideas in his rather direct and nondialectical way.[60]

A careful reading of this passage shows no room for a distinction between "God" and the inner point; we turn in when we are open to inwardness, and there we discover that nothing but the One exists. That One is, of course God, the One whose existence makes all other "existence" pale into nothingness. This is the classic acosmic position as taught by R. Shne'ur Zalman of Liadi and R. Aaron ha-Levi Horowitz of Starroselje.[61]

All these more or less careful formulations in the public teachings of the Sefat Emet pale, however, in comparison with the words recorded in a rare private document, a letter written to a member of his family and published only recently. The letter is written shortly before Passover (the year is unknown). In the midst of a discourse on spiritual preparations for Passover, a time when one must "pass" or "leap over" all that is evil and defiled, he says the following:

> Since most people do not understand how to leap up and attach themselves to God, I shall reveal to you what I know about it in a forthright manner. The proclamation of oneness that we declare each day in saying, "Hear, O Israel," and so forth, really needs to be understood as it truly is. That which is entirely clear to me, not from hearsay but based on the holy writings of great kabbalists, I am obliged to reveal to you, in order that these matters be clear. This is it: the meaning of "YHWH is one" is not that He is the only God, negating other gods (though this too is true!), but the meaning is deeper than that: there is no being other than Him. [This is true] even though it seems other-

wise to most people who understand such things, for there are count-less feelings about these matters.[62]

The content is as follows: everything that exists in the world, spiritual and physical, is God Himself. It is only because of the contraction [tsimtsum] that was God's will, blessed be He and His name, that holiness descended rung after rung, until actual physical things were formed out of it.

These things are true without a doubt. Because of this, every person can attach himself [to God] wherever he is, through the holiness that exists within every single thing, even corporeal things. You only have to be negated in the spark of holiness. In this way you truly bring about ascents in the upper worlds, causing true pleasure to God. A person in such a state lacks for nothing, for he can attach himself to God through whatever place he is. This is the foundation of all the mystical formulations in the world. Even though it can be treated at great length, as it is in the thousands of pages of explanation written in various books, we need not go on about it now. In my opinion my few brief words suffice. If you study the matter you will see that it is as I say, and this is the essence of human worship.

Let us return to the subject. Every person can attach himself to the holiness within his own limbs, physical and spiritual, going very, very high, truly to God. . . .[63]

Here, as is the case with a now famous letter written within early ḤaBaD circles,[64] that which was said in private, in completely uncompromising language, stands as the best commentary to all that was spoken and written in public, where the formulations were somewhat more cautious. The Sefat Emet is revealed as a monist, in the tradition of monistic or acosmic mysticism that runs through Hasidism from the font of Miedzyrzec and especially through the teachings of R. Shne'ur Zalman of Liadi, clearly an important influence on R. Yehudah Leib, who now seems to be struggling to combine the this-worldliness of Kotsk with the spiritualist profundity of ḤaBaD.[65]

The interest of the Sefat Emet in mystical language is not only theoretical, nor is it merely an accident of his hasidic tradition. R. Yehudah Leib should not be depicted only as one who seeks to set out a particular position among mystical doctrines. On the contrary, the Sefat Emet is very much a living religious document, and one can feel the enthusiasm with which its author keeps renewing his emphasis on inward vision and the point within. The reading of Ezekiel 46:1 quoted above, referring to the "inner gate" that is opened on the Sabbath, must occur well over a hundred times in the *Sefat Emet*, even if alluded to only briefly. The classic themes accessible within the tradition for the spiritualization of Judaism, those used by Philo in Alexandria of late antiquity and by the Zohar in medieval Spain, are remarkably fresh and vital in this usage by a preacher in Poland at the edge of the twentieth century. The patriarchs, the liberation from Egypt, the tabernacle, the promised land: all of these are read as describing the inner "territory" of the spiritual realm, unique to each individual yet shared through this rich legacy of religious language.

There are occasional passages in the text where R. Yehudah Leib speaks out quite directly and personally as a mystic. Even through the veiling so familiar in Jewish sources, one can hear in these words an echo of someone speaking of his own religious experience:

> "All the people saw the voices" [lit.: "the thunder"] (Ex. 20:15). The meaning is like that of "I am the Lord your God" (Ex. 20:2) [in the singular]. Each one of Israel saw the root of his own life-force. With their very eyes they saw the part of the divine soul above that lives in each of them. They had no need to "believe" the commandments, because they saw the voices. That's the way it is when God speaks.[66]

The religious consciousness expressed here remains aware of divine transcendence, but in a way that brooks no contradiction to the immediate presence of God within both world and self. It is still the transcendent voice that speaks the words: "I am the Lord thy God." But as that voice is spoken, we translate it into a commandment that simultaneously demands and affirms our ability to discover divinity within our own souls. This is the transforming power of divine speech, which is able to address each of us in an intimate and unique way.

"Transcendence" in this context is surely not about the *remoteness* of God, nor can it be characterized in Rudolph Otto's phrase as the transcendence of the "wholly other." God is not "wholly other" here, for something of God's own undivided Self fills both human self and world. That transcendence remains a quality of this all- and ever-present God is a matter of wonder and mystery, expressible more by allusion than by any specific theological formulation.

> "I will sing unto the Lord for He is exalted, exalted" (Ex. 15:1). The transcendence *(romemut)* of God cannot be conceived. Each conception that we attain only shows us that God remains beyond it. Thus it is written: "You are transcendent forever, O Lord" (Ps. 92:9); Your power remains supreme. This is the meaning of "exalted, exalted"— the only exaltedness and transcendence to which we can bear witness is that He remains raised high and exalted beyond all of our conceptualizations.
>
> In the book *Qol Simhah* [by R. Simha Bunem of Przysucha],[67] in the section *Hayyey Sarah*, the author interprets a Midrash on the verse "O Lord my God, You are very great" (or "large"; Ps. 104:1). His form is larger than the tablet [on which it is drawn], referring to the parable of a sage who designs a wondrous instrument, for which everyone offers him great praise. Then along comes one person [of greater understanding] who says: "The wisdom of this sage is surely much greater than the skill displayed here." But it was by means of the instrument that they had become aware of the sage's brilliance.
>
> Thus we come to know God through all the wisdom of Creation, but He remains high and exalted beyond all that. So our understanding of God's blessed wisdom is that He is exalted beyond [our understanding]. This [is] the meaning of "exalted, exalted."[68]

This teaching, which may reflect the indirect influence of Rabbi Nahman of Bratslav,[69] understands God as an infinitely transcendent mind, but one that is nevertheless manifest in all of God's works and attainable only through our appreciation of them. In a broader sense, we may see the influence of an intellectualist mysticism here, a tradition reaching back into both the philosophical and mystical works of medieval Jewry, and in turn to their sources in neo-Platonic and Aristotelian thought. God is always transcendent because the human mind always and necessarily fails to apprehend fully that which is present within it and around it. This failure seems to be a necessary condition of our corporeal state, one that great minds and souls can push back quite considerably by their lives of self-negation, but that cannot be overcome entirely.

V

Such is the case for human consciousness in its "ordinary" or weekday state.[70] God does, however, allow us very significant glimpses into the total transcendence of our human intellectual limitations by the regular gift of Shabbat and its extra measure of soul, a "gift without limits" and "a foretaste of the world-to-come" that comes to us from the world beyond. The Jew knows two types of consciousness, that of the weekday and the special consciousness of Shabbat, the time of the extra soul.[71] "Six days shall you labor and do all your work" means that on the weekdays we are supposed to seek God out through the things of this world. Our weekday task is to discover the wisdom of the Sage by appreciating the wonders of the instrument He has fashioned, to return to the language of our parable. That weekday consciousness has something of "natural religion" about it, an appreciation of transcendent mystery within the natural order itself. In fact "miracle" and "nature" should be joined in this mind-set, reflecting together the power of the Creator:

> On the verse, "But if you should say: 'What will we eat in the seventh year, since we neither plant nor reap our harvest?' I shall command My blessing upon you . . . " (Lev. 25:20–21), the author of the book *No'am Elimelekh*[72] quotes a comment by his brother. He said that it is because of the asking that God will have to command His blessing.
>
> The meaning is as follows. What kind of question is "What will we eat?" The One who provided life itself will provide food as well! But this would make the existence of Israel dependent upon a miracle, and not every generation is deserving of miracles. It is of this [situation] that they ask: "What will we eat?" The answer is that sustenance will come about through the blessing [of abundance], and such blessing is partly natural.
>
> *Israel should really know that miracle and nature are all one. In fact there is nothing so miraculous and wonderful as nature itself, the greatest wonder we can apprehend.* When this faith is clear to us, we are no longer concerned with being sustained by miracles. Once we say: "What will we eat?" [realizing that we cannot count on miracles], the answer comes, "I shall command My blessing. . . . "

And in fact the generations when miracles occurred were firm in this faith, and to them nature and miracles were all the same. That is why God performed miracles for them.[73]

It may be said that there is nothing new about this sense of the natural world as the greatest of miracles. The 'Amidah prayer, after all, itself reflecting the biblical Psalter, thanks God for "Your miracles that are with us daily, and Your wonders at all times; evening, morning, and afternoon." The sense of wonder informs all of religious life. But there does seem to be something added in the claim that God would perform miracles (the out-of-the-ordinary sort) only for a generation that could take such miracles completely in its stride, seeing them as no different from the process of nature itself. It bespeaks a religious consciousness so elevated that it knows both the seemingly ordinary and the unique as events that equally bear witness to God's presence within them. It is that sort of religious mind that the Sefat Emet seeks to cultivate in those who hear (or read) him.

Insofar as the Sefat Emet is concerned, it is clearly Jews alone who have the power to cultivate such ways of thinking. Only Jews are able to discover divinity within the world, because this discovery itself depends upon an appreciation of God's Torah. The very structure by which the world was formed is that of Torah. He takes quite seriously the ancient teaching that God "looked into Torah" when creating the world; it is the divine Word that underlies all of creation, and it is by means of that Word, in the form of Torah, that we return to the presence of God in creation.[74] Jews alone can find this inner structure of Torah, also the structure of creation itself, within their own souls, since only the Jews have accepted God's Torah.

Hasidism is in this sense very much a product of the time and place in which it originated. Most Christians in eighteenth- and early nineteenth-century eastern Europe saw Jews as spiritual subhumans, and Jews "returned the favor." Religions other than Judaism and a Christianity laden with anti-Semitism were completely unknown. The universalist religion of the western European Enlightenment could seemingly have existed on another planet, for all the effect it had on the religious views of either Jews or Christians in Poland, geographically near but culturally light-years away from the centers of such thought. When such universalist thinking did begin to penetrate into eastern Europe (and by the time of the Sefat Emet many Jews and Christians in Warsaw were well read in Western thought), it was associated by the Hasidim with the dreaded Haskalah, a direct challenge to their own religious identity and way of life. The walls of defensiveness were raised high, and there was no way such thinking was allowed to enter the hasidic worldview.

Still, it is startling to see how Hasidism, in its own terms, is at pains to avoid this awkward subject. The very essence of hasidic theology is that divinity is everywhere; the entire world contains sparks of divine light, waiting to be redeemed. This is true of animate and inanimate matter, of the ground itself—of trees, birds, and animals. Gentiles and their culture are spiritually objectivized in the same way: there are indeed sparks of holiness to be found there, hidden in the music, dance, folktales, healing traditions, and so forth of the eastern European milieu. But only the Jew can discover and redeem those sparks; the gentile who contains them is no more aware of them than is the nonhuman bearer of divine presence. Hasidim had, to say the least, low regard for the spiritual lives of non-Jews and showed little interest in the subject. The *Sefat Emet*, like all hasidic texts, frequently makes jumps from "person" to "Jew" without any seeming self-consciousness[75] and without directly raising the question of non-Jews and their presumed lack of spiritual potential.

This Jewish exclusiveness is probably the greatest barrier between the Sefat Emet and the contemporary reader; no apology should be made for it. A Jewish spirituality appropriate to our own day will have to take a very different position with regard to the twin questions of the spiritual potential of non-Jews and the legitimacy and value of other religious traditions. We are fortunate not to live in the closed world of the shtetl, and human religious expression in its great variety is known to us in ways our ancestors could not have imagined.

But if the exclusivist views of the Sefat Emet put off the contemporary reader, his sense of universal Jewish mission seems very much in place. He has a strong sense of the Jews' vocation (literally "calling") as God's witnessing people in the world. It is the Jews who uniquely call forth the divine presence in all of Creation by discovering it within their own souls. This power exists within all Jews, no matter how far they think they may be from God or from Torah. The words of Torah cannot be entirely erased from the tablets that lie deep within every Jewish heart. The very purpose of Jewish existence is that we call forth the reality of God to all our fellow humans, making the entire world aware of the fullness of divine presence that engulfs us always.

> God has chosen the children of Israel as His own portion. One might think that this would make for a greater distance between God and the other nations. But actually, just the opposite is true. This was God's deeper plan: to bring all nations near to Him by means of Israel. Israel understand this, and it is Israel's desire to bring everyone close to God. Only the wicked interfere with this plan, as [when] "Amalek came and fought with Israel" (Ex. 17:8). But when Jethro came, they drew him near with all their strength. "The Lord is my strength"— Israel's own strength. "And my stronghold"—He gives strength to Israel. There is to be power in their hands through the Torah God has given them—"The Lord gives strength to His people (Ps. 29:11)"—for they are God's emissaries, to bring all creatures near to Him.
>
> This is the meaning of [the verse]: "The Lord spoke all these words, saying: 'I am the Lord your God'" (Ex. 20:1-2). The blessed Creator gave them the Torah. The nations were not capable of this. Even of Israel it is said that their souls fluttered out of them and they were purified like angels. That is why it says: "The day you stood before the Lord your God at Ḥoreb" (Deut. 4:10). The angels are those who "stand." The intent is that Israel speak these words, drawing them into rung after rung, until all creatures are brought close to God. The life-force of all is in the Torah, and all are to be redeemed by the power of Torah. This is the meaning of "saying" in that verse: every one of Israel has to bear witness to the Creator each day. Twice a day we say, "Hear, O Israel." These words shine forth to all the world, to all who are created.[76]

The unique place that Israel has in the human community and

sanctity of *Erets Yisra'el* in the realm of space. R. Yehudah Leib is fascinated by the claim of *Sefer Yetsirah* that the three realms of space, time, and soul *('olam, shanah, nefesh)* are parallel to one another,[77] and a great many of his teachings adumbrate this theme in one form or another. These are the three dimensions in which the holiness of the *nekudah* comes to be manifest in the world. Among souls, it is those of Israel, or sometimes specifically that of Moses or of the high priest, that reflect the inner holiness of existence; among times, it is the holy days of the Jewish calendar, but especially Shabbat (the holiness of which is not derivative from Israel's, since it was declared holy by God at Creation and its arrival is not determined by the humanly determined calendar); among places, it is the Holy Land, Jerusalem, the Temple, or the Tabernacle that is the manifestation of the *nekudah*, brimming with life-energy and bathed in holiness. It is by working through these three categories that holiness can be brought from abstraction into real and daily existence.

> The flow of the passages [in the Torah-portion Emor]: from the holiness of priests and the high priest among all souls; "You shall sanctify him . . . for he offers the food of your God" (Lev. 21:8). Because the priest draws the souls of Israel near to the blessed Holy One. The same is true of the festivals [that follow the discussion of priests], "callings of holiness"; they, too, draw the souls upward and near. That is why it says: "You shall sanctify him." The same is true in the dimension of space; the Temple and the Holy of Holies raise souls up to take greater care for their holiness.[78]

> Regarding the sabbatical year: "The land shall rest " (Lev. 25:2). The children of Israel were created in order to redeem space and time, as it is written: "I made the land and created man upon it " (Is. 45:12). "Man" here refers to Israel, as in [the verse]: "You are [called] 'man' [and the nations of the world are not called 'man.']" Just as there is redemption in the soul, so "shall you give redemption to the land" (Lev. 25:24). Just as Israel were previously mixed in among the nations in general, and were only later chosen . . . and at the Exodus they were redeemed physically and spiritually, so too was the Land of Israel formerly under the seven nations, and later it proceeded to become the Land of Israel; that is both a physical and a spiritual redemption. The same is true of time. Previously the holy times were all mixed together [with other times]. Later they were purified, Sabbaths and fes-

tivals drawn out of the category of times. This happened by means of
the redemption of Israel. That is why the festivals are "in memory of
the Exodus from Egypt," since it was through the Exodus that their
potential light was realized. . . ."[79]

Here the emphasis seems rather clearly to be placed upon
Israel. It is their soul-work to raise all things up to God or
to uncover the presence of divinity as *ḥiyyut* or *nekudah
penimit* throughout the twin domains of time and space. But
depending upon the homiletical need, sometimes one of the
other two dimensions is given priority, and Israel's holiness
follows along with it.

> On the verse: "The land upon which you [Jacob] lie" (Gen. 28:13). Our
> sages said that the blessed Holy One folded the entire Land of Israel
> beneath him. We have already written frequently that an innermost
> point exists within space, time, and soul. [This point] includes all and
> is referred to in the verse: "In every place where I mention My name"
> (Ex. 20:21). That is the Temple, which includes all places; that is why it
> is called "every place." All of space is folded up within that single
> place. On the verse "The Lord God created man from the dust of the
> earth" (Gen. 2:7), it is said that He gathered his dust from the four di-
> rections, or else from that place of which it says: "You shall make an
> altar of earth" (Ex. 20:21). See RaSHI's comment there. But the two in-
> terpretations are now one, since this dust [of the altar] contains the en-
> tire earth!
>
> Jacob was as beautiful [i.e., perfect] as Adam, and that is why it is
> said that "he reached the place" (Gen. 28:11)—he reached that place
> which belongs to him. It did not say which place, since that place con-
> tains all places. The same is true of Jacob's soul, which contained all
> souls, just as Adam's had. Only in Jacob's case the good souls had been
> separated [and they] alone [were present]. The same is true in time,
> since Shabbat contains all the six weekdays, as we have said
> elsewhere.[80]

Or we might choose an example where sacred time has the
primary role:

> "God blessed the seventh day" (Gen. 2:3). The Midrash says that
> He blessed it with lights. "The light in a person's face on a weekday
> is not the same as it is on the Sabbath." This refers to the revelation
> of inwardness, that of which it says: "A man's wisdom lights up his
> face" (Eccles. 8:1)—that is the revelation of the extra soul. For the

> inwardness of space [lit.: "the world"] as a whole is also revealed on
> the holy Sabbath. Thus it says: "And there was light," which the sages
> said was stored away for the righteous [in the world to come]. But "Let
> there be light" meant that [divine light] should be present in every par-
> ticular [of Creation]; all of Creation has a part in this light, except that
> it is hidden. But on Shabbat something of this light is revealed. The
> weekdays are compared to an opaque glass, but the Sabbath to a shin-
> ing one. That is why there is a commandment to light candles for the
> Sabbath, to show that light is revealed on the holy Sabbath. Israel look
> forward to this holy light and feel the darkness of this world. . . .[81]

There is something surprisingly modern about the use of these
three categories, even though cloaked in the timeworn meth-
ods of homiletic association. There are passages where R. Yehudah Leib seems almost as much phenomenologist of religion
as he does hasidic preacher. He understands the interplay between space and time as realms for potential spiritualization
as well as the fact that the difference between them is nulli-
fied when both turn out to be mere garb for the self-manifesta-
tion of the *nekudah* that underlies and animates them. It
would seem that the mystic, understanding that all things are
one in God (or that the same *nekudah* is the being that underlies all, to use his language), has the need to test the extent of
this insight by seeing through the most basic of distinctions
that ordinary consciousness makes among categories of being,
including such fundamental dualities as time/space, self/other,
and microcosm/macrocosm.[82]

VI

Having paid some attention to the mystical thought of the
Sefat Emet in its own terms, we should here recall again the
unique situation of R. Yehudah Leib's role as the first hasidic
rebbe to "reign" over an area that contained an ever-increasing
and visible population of Jews who denied both Jewish faith
and practice. The Gerer rebbe's strategy for dealing with this
situation is precisely the opposite of that of his older contemporary, R. Samson Raphael Hirsch (1808–1888) of Frankfurt,
and most of the rabbis of Hungary and Galicia. While Hirsch

strove to create a totally separatist *Austrittsgemeinde* and others engaged in increasingly shrill denunciations of the heretics and "evildoers," the Sefat Emet worked by a strategy of inclusion rather than condemnation. Nowhere in the five volumes of his sermons can one find sharp language used against those who opposed Hasidism and often bitterly fought its influence. Such arguments and political battles were left to the Hasidim; and Ger, even before the organization of Agudat Yisra'el (1912), was a major political force in Polish Jewry, with all that that entailed. But the rebbe, himself a pious and even humble man, tried to remain above politics. If he occasionally was forced to engage in worldly conflict,[83] he does not allow even the slightest trace of anger or hostility to sully the pages of his collected teachings.

R. Yehudah Leib insists that he is rebbe of all of Warsaw Jewry, Hasidim and self-proclaimed nonbelievers alike. He does so by addressing his hearers on the level of the "inner point" rather than by any externally defined norm. There is a place within the heart of every Jew, he insists, unaffected by one's deeds or one's beliefs, that remains a personal "holy of holies." The word of God is written in each Jewish heart and is present since birth, whether or not he or she is aware of it. With this he offered his hand to those seeking to repent of their waywardness ("Come, let me show you your truest inner self!"), or even to those many Jews, brought up in the tradition but now distanced from it, who still sought to warm themselves periodically by the light of his Torah.

It was in part for this reason that the *Sefat Emet* achieved the very wide popularity that it has always enjoyed, outside hasidic circles as well as within them. In an era when an embattled hasidic leadership began to react more and more to non-Orthodox Jewry with derision, dismissal, and even hatred, the *Sefat Emet* had an accepting and embracing glow. It welcomed Jews to open their own inner gateways, to come into the holy consciousness of Sabbath and festival joy, seemingly not requiring that they first leave behind all their outside baggage.[84]

Some time after the *Sefat Emet* began to achieve its wide popularity, a certain highly respected Jerusalem kabbalist sought to write a commentary on the book, tracing its sources to kabbalistic texts and explaining its secret meanings. For this purpose he sought the approbation of R. Avraham Mordecai, the son and successor of the author. The Imrey Emet, as R. Avraham Mordecai is called, refused to give the testament. In doing so he said: "My father, of blessed memory, wrote his book so that every Jew could read it in his own way."[85]

The selection and commentary that you have before you is one Jew's reading of the *Sefat Emet*, one who is both the great-grandson of a Gerer Hasid and a Jew who lives very far from the hasidic community and its way of life. Through it you are invited to discover and study the *Sefat Emet* in *your* own way. There are no prior requirements here, either of specific beliefs or of knowledge, beyond the barest minimum. All that is required is the faith that the teachings of a great master, interpreting the sources of a most ancient tradition, may still have the warmth to open the hearts and inner places of those who read and study them, coming from perhaps not so great a distance as they might think.[86]

Notes to Introduction

[1] The history of this town's Jewish community and the influence of the hasidic court on the town have been studied by Eleanora Bergman of Warsaw's Jewish Historical Institute. See her articles "Gora Kalwaria: The Impact of a Hasidic Cult on the Urban Landscape of a Small Polish Town" in *Polin* 5 (1990) 3–23 and *"Gora-Kalwaria (Gur): Ha-Yishuv ha-Yehudi ve-Hatsar ha-Rabbi mi-Gur . . ."* in R. Elior et al., eds., *Tsaddikim ve-Anshey Ma'aseh* (Jerusalem: Mossad Bialik, 1994), pp. 111–117.

[2] Hasidic tradition claims that the family name was changed from Rothenberg to Alter in 1831, in an attempt to hide from the Russian authorities the fact that R. Isaac Meir had been involved in financial support of the Polish rebellion of 1830. See Y. Alfasi, *Gur: Toledot Hasidut Gur* (Tel Aviv: Sinai, 1978; henceforth: *Gur*), p. 88. This work has now been expanded as *Tif'eret shebe-Tif'eret: Bet Gur le-Dorotav* (Tel Aviv: Sinai, 1993).

[3] The history of Hasidism may be divided into four periods. Though the boundaries between them are somewhat fluid, we may roughly speak of (1) the period of growth and challenge, 1750–1815; (2) the period of dominance and struggle with Haskalah, 1815–1880; (3) the period of decline and destruction, 1881–1945; and (4) the period of rebirth and transplantation, 1945–present. A new history of Hasidism, covering this entire range, is urgently needed.

[4] Ever since the first conflicts between Hasidim and their rabbinic opponents in 1772, the accusation that Hasidism was anti-intellectual, that Hasidim neglected study in favor of ecstatic prayer, storytelling, and even drink or laziness, and that Hasidim mocked and derogated talmudic scholars, had all been part of the stock-in-trade of anti-hasidic polemics. For a scholarly evaluation of early Hasidism's attitude toward study, see J. Weiss "Torah Study in Early Hasidism" in his *Studies in Eastern European Jewish Mysticism* (Oxford: Littman Library, 1985), pp. 56–68.

[5] Pronounced "Pshiskhe" in Polish Yiddish. I have tried in most cases to retain original Polish spellings of place names ("Kotsk" for "Kock" is an exception), though deleting the Polish accent markings.

[6] The classic study of Polish Hasidism is A. Z. Aescoly's *"Ha-Hasidut be-Polin"* in I. Halpern's *Bet Yisra'el be-Polin* (Jerusalem, 1954), pp. 141–186. Raphael Mahler's *Hasidism and the Jewish Enlightenment* (Philadephia: Jewish Publication Society, 1985) (Hebrew original, 1961) contains a very important chapter on "Two Schools of Hasidism in Poland," pp. 245–314. See also the important collection *Tsaddikim ve-Anshey Ma'aseh*, edited by R. Elior, Y. Bartal, and H. Shmeruk (Jerusalem: Mossad Bialik, 1994). An excellent survey of scholarship in the field is offered by D. Assaf, pp. 357–379.

[7] To some degree this intra-Jewish bias reflects Polish attitudes toward the southeast region of their country and especially toward Ukrainians, often depicted by Poles as ignorant, illiterate, and riddled with superstition.

[8] The typical setting of study in the Polish style was the local *beit midrash*, rather than the larger, regional, and more institutionalized yeshivah. Yeshivot in the late eighteenth and early nineteenth centuries existed primarily in Moravia and Hungary; they were revived in the nineteenth century in Lithuania, and only afterwards did they spread to central Poland as well. I thank Michael Silber for this information.

[9] R. Jacob Isaac's thought has recently been studied by Rachel Elior in her "Between Yesh and Ayin: The Doctrine of the Zaddik in the Works of R. Jacob Isaac, the Seer of Lublin" in *Jewish History: Essays in Honour of Chimen Abramsky* (London, 1988), pp. 393–455. Hebrew version: "*Beyn Yesh le-Ayin: 'Iyyun be-Torat ha-Tsaddik shel R. Ya'akov Yitshak, ha-Hozeh mi-Lublin*" in *Tsaddikim ve-Anshey Ma'aseh*, pp. 167–239. See also her "The Innovation of Polish Hasidism" in *Tarbiz* 57:3 (1993), pp. 381–432. The English title of that article is somewhat misleading; it deals essentially with the relationship between certain themes in the seer's writings and those of R. Mordecai Joseph of Izbica. For a bibliography of biographical (mostly hagiographic) treatments of the seer, see Elior's n. 3 on p. 168 of the former article (in Hebrew) and David Assaf's bibliography in the same volume, p. 364f.

[10] Popular biographies of R. Israel and his descendants are Ts. M. Rabinowitz's *Ha-Maggid mi-Kokhenits: Hayyav ve-Torato* (Tel Aviv, 1947); A. Y. Bromberg's *Bet Kozhenits* and H. Ts. Halberstam's *Toledot ha-Maggid mi-Kozhenits* (Tel Aviv, 1966). For further details see D. Assaf in *Tsaddikim ve-Anshey Ma'aseh*, p. 364. See also Ze'ev Gries's important study of R. Israel's writings in that same volume, pp. 127–165.

[11] For a detailed discussion of his three books (*Zot Zikkaron*, Lvov, 1851; *Zikhron Zot*, Warsaw, 1869; *Divrey Emet*, Zolkiew, 1808 [actually 1830 or 1831]), see R. Elior in *Tsaddikim ve-Anshey Ma'aseh*, p. 173f., n. 21.

[12] The biography of R. Isaac Meir has been written in several versions, mostly dependent on Abraham Issachar Benjamin Alter's *Me'ir 'Eyney ha-Golah* (Piotrkow, 1928–1932) and Y. K. K. Rakatz's *Siah Sarfey Kodesh* (Lodz, 1928–1931). For a critical review of these, see D. Assaf in *Tsaddikim ve-Anshey Ma'aseh*, p. 369ff. See also n. 14 below.

[13] R. Moshe Chalfan, owner of a well-known bank on Senatorska Street. His other daughter later married R. Mendel of Kotsk. See Alfasi, *Gur*, p. 26.

[14] Hasidic legend says that he met with R. Jacob Isaac, the "holy Jew" (1766–1813) several times during his childhood. For details see Y. Alfasi, *Gur*, chap. 2. Both R. Israel and R. Jacob Isaac of Przysucha had passed on by the time R. Isaac Meir was fifteen. Essentially, he seems to have chosen R. Simha Bunem as a teacher over R. Moses Eliakim. According to the Ger tradition, R. Moses Eliakim did not forgive him for this betrayal and caused him great suffering. For details see Abraham Issachar Alter, *Meir*

Eyney ha-Golah, p. 28. On the original attraction of R. Isaac Meir to R. Simḥa Bunem, see the account in *Siaḥ Sarfey Qodesh he-Ḥadash* (Beney Berak: Sifriyyati, 1989), p. 169. This edition is a more user-friendly re-arrangement of the original *Siaḥ Sarfey Kodesh* by Y. K. K. Rakatz, first published in Lodz, 1928–1931, the most important collection of memoirs, tales, etc. concerning mid-nineteenth-century Polish Hasidism.

[15] On R. Simḥa Bunem see the (noncritical) biography by Ts. M. Rabinowitz, *R. Simḥa Bunem mi-Peshiskhe: Ḥayyav ve-Torato* (Tel Aviv, 1945). See also A. J. Heschel, *Kotsk: In Gerangel far Emesdikeyt* (Tel Aviv: Hamenora, 1973), vol. 2, pp. 383–432.

[16] The pharmaceutical examination that he passed in Lvov would have required reading ability in Polish and Latin; it is likely that he knew German as well. Heschel claims (op. cit., p. 652, n. 6) that R. Bunem had some exposure to European literature as well as languages.

[17] This connection itself supposedly came about because of a shared devotion to R. Israel of Kozienice. See Heschel, op. cit., p. 383f., and the sources quoted there. The Bergsons, and especially Temeril, the wife of Berke Sonnenberg-Bergson, were later supporters of the Przysucha circle.

[18] Przysucha began as a hasidic center under the influence of R. Jacob Isaac, the "holy Jew" (1766–1813), a disciple of the seer who took the daring step of forming his own hasidic circle in his master's lifetime and without his approval. Some aspects of the innovations of the Polish school of Hasidism began with him, though they became much more sharply defined in the generations that followed. On R. Jacob Isaac, see the tales and other materials collected by Y. K. Kadish as *Nifle'ot ha-Yehudi* (Piotrkow, 1908) and *Tif'eret ha-Yehudi* (Piotrkow, 1912).

[19] "From all the cities of Israel," in the language of the sources (*Siaḥ Sarfey Qodesh ha-Ḥadash,* p. 174). The point seems to be that this situation was unusual. It is difficult to compare this wide circle of attraction with others, because most figures in hasidic circles are known more by the names of the towns where they later settled than by places of origin or early education. This question deserves further consideration. The Seer of Lublin also seems to have drawn disciples from a wider region.

[20] Of course these are all named for their later places of settlement, not their places of origin, as mentioned in the preceding note. R. Mendel originally came from Goray near Lublin, but he lived for a time in Tomaszow Lubelski, and was first known as R. Mendel Tomaszower. His original family name was Halperin, but he changed it to Morgenstern for reasons similar to those that motivated his friend Isaac Meir (see n. 2 above). The proper Polish spelling of Kotsk is Kock. According to hasidic tradition, R. Mendel had a key role in the selection of R. Simḥa Bunem as leader. After his predecessor, the "Yehudi ha-Kadosh" of Przysucha died in 1814, the Hasidim first began to follow R. Abba of Neyshtat (Nowe Miasto). See *Siaḥ Sarfey Qodesh ha-Ḥadash,* p. 171ff.

[21] The unique Hasidism of Izbica has been studied by a number of scholars, including Joseph Weiss, Rivka Schatz, and Rachel Elior. See the summary by D. Assaf in *Tsaddikim ve-Anshey Ma'aseh*, p. 368f. Morris Faierstein has written in English on Izbica in *All Is in the Hands of Heaven: The Teachings of Rabbi Mordecai Joseph Leiner of Izbica* (Hoboken, New Jersey: Ktav, 1990). An important contribution to this discussion is the unpublished doctoral dissertation by S. Magid, *Hasidism in Transition: The Ideology of R. Gershon Henokh of Radzin in Light of Medieval Philosophy and Kabbala* (Brandeis University, 1994).

[22] See, for example, the stories in *Siaḥ Sarfey Qodesh he-Ḥadash*, pp. 165–166 and 181.

[23] Two other very different internal reforms are Bratslav Hasidism and the circle of R. Arele Roth in interwar Hungary and later in Jerusalem. Both of these resulted in distinctive sectarian offshoots of Hasidism. On the former, see my *Tormented Master: A Life of Rabbi Naḥman of Bratslav* (University, Alabama, 1979). On R. Arele, see S. Magid, "Modernity as Heresy: The Introvertic Piety of Faith in R. Arele Roth's *Shomer Emunim*," *Jewish Studies Quarterly*, spring 1997.

[24] Lists of *hanhagot*, or personal practices, of various *tsaddikim* were a well-known phenomenon and constitute a distinct genre of hasidic literature. These have been studied by Ze'ev Gries in *Sifrut ha-Hanhagot* (Jerusalem: Mossad Bialik, 1989). An introduction to the arcane world of hasidic custom is found in A. Wertheim's *Halakhot ve-Hanahagot ba-Ḥasidut* (Jerusalem: Mossad ha-Rav Kook, 1960).

[25] A smaller portion of the Przysucha disciples remained loyal to the son of R. Simḥa Bunem, R. Avraham Moshe of Przysucha. Significantly, these included the future R. Isaac of Warka. R. Avraham Moshe died, however, only two years after his father, in 1829, and the line ended.

[26] These insights, developed in dialogue with Nehemia Polen, are an extension of R. Mahler's treatment of "Two Schools of Hasidism in Poland" mentioned in n. 7 above. Mahler tends to emphasize the economic basis for the distinction between these schools, ignoring certain aspects of the differences in religious approach.

[27] Polish Jewry had long been known for an exclusive devotion to Talmud as the single subject in the curriculum of higher Jewish learning. In contrast to such other communities as Spain, Italy, the Netherlands, or the symbolically important settlement in Safed, Polish Jews engaged more sparingly in such ancillary intellectual pursuits as philosophy, poetry, biblical exegesis, etc. Within the realm of talmudic studies, it was the civil and domestic orders *(Nezikin* and *Nashim)* of the Talmud that were the central areas of study and the objects of Polish rabbis' notorious addiction to *pilpul* (intellectual casuistry).

[28] See A. J. Heschel, *Kotsk: In Gerangel far Emesdikeyt*, vol. 1, p. 60ff. See also the response of R. Simḥa Bunem to a so-called "famous kabbalist"

quoted in *Ramatayim Tsofim*, a commentary on *Tanna de-Vey Eliyahu* (Warsaw, 1881, rep. Jerusalem, 1970), p. 227. This work contains important material on Polish Hasidism.

[29] Quoted in the name of R. Aaron (II) of Karlin in A. H. Michelson's *Ohel Elimelekh* (Przemyszl, 1915), p. 7. The mishnah is Avot 1:2.

[30] This verse is widely quoted in the later literature on Kotsk. I thus find myself in disagreement with Yoram Jacobson, *"Emet ve-emunah be-Ḥasidut Gur"* in *Studies in Mysticism, Philosophy, and Ethical Literature Presented to Isaiah Tishby* (Jerusalem: Magnes Press, 1986), p. 613ff., where he derives the Sefat Emet's interest in this verse directly from the MaHaRaL of Prague, without mention of Kotsk. The immediate historical context is impossible to ignore; the question would then be whether the MaHaRaL helped shape the Kotsker's thinking in this regard. Of course, R. Mendel's Hasidim must have rejoiced in discovering that *erets* in this verse was numerically equivalent to the Yiddish spelling of Kotsk itself, so that the verse could also be read to hint: "Truth will rise from Kotsk!" The fact that no version of this widespread association is to be found in either of Jacob Levinger's lists of original Kotsk teachings ("The Authentic Sayings of Rabbi Menaḥem Mendel of Kotzk," *Tarbiz* 55:1 [1985], pp. 109–135 and "The Teachings of the Kotzker Rebbe According to His Grandson Rabbi Samuel Bernstein of Sochatchow," *Tarbiz* 55:3 [1986], pp. 413–431) does make one wonder whether it might not be an invention of the disciples, precisely based on this wordplay! It is thus not clear whether this is an actual saying of the Kotsker or a later literary flourish, though the idea behind it certainly is appropriate to Kotsk.

[31] The hasidic line that most preserved traditional kabbalistic knowledge and praxis was the Galician dynasty of Zydaczov/Komarno. The writings of several members of that family should really be considered kabbalistic, rather than specifically hasidic works, though the interplay between the two makes for interesting questions of definition. See Louis Jacobs's "Translator's Introduction" to his translation of *Turn Aside from Evil and Do Good* by Zevi Hirsch Eichenstein of Zydaczow (London: Littman Library, 1995). Close to these circles are such other figures as R. Zevi Elimelech of Dynow and some of his descendants in the Munkacz dynasty. Mysticism of another sort, but one also based on a deep knowledge of kabbalistic sources, was cultivated in the ḤaBaD/Lubavitch school.

[32] It is not entirely without significance that this seclusion took place early in the Hebrew year 5600, the year in which the so-called TaRniks hoped for messianic redemption. For a description of the seclusion from within Kotsk circles, see P. Z. Glickman, *Der Kotsker Rebbe* (Lodz, 1938), p. 48. An Izbica version of the events is found in H. S. Leiner's *Dor Yesharim* (Lublin, 1925), p. 34f. On the TaRniks and their expectations more generally, see Aryeh Morgenstern, *Messianism and the Settlement of Erez Israel in the First Half of the Nineteenth Century* [Hebrew] (Jerusalem, 1985) , pp. 38–65; 197–215.

[33] Such was the case also with R. David Morgenstern, the son of the Kotsker, who was proclaimed rebbe with the agreement of his father's major heir, R. Isaac Meir. See Alfasi, *Gur,* p. 67f., and sources quoted there.

[34] I see no warrant for Eleanora Bergman's denial of this well-attested hasidic tradition. See her offhand dismissal in her "Gora Kalwaria" in *Tsaddikim ve-Anshey Ma'aseh,* p. 111, n. 2. The traditional report is found in Alfasi, *Gur,* p. 69f.

[35] Bergman, op. cit., p. 114.

[36] This is partly due to the fact that R. Isaac Meir tended to be more strict in his halakhic views than had been the case previously in the Przysucha-Kotsk tradition. See the discussion by Y. Mondshine in *Ha-Tsofeh le-Doro* (Jerusalem, 1987), p. 243f.

[37] The published writings of R. Isaac Meir include talmudic novellae on several tractates, novellae on *Shulḥan 'Arukh,* responsa, and hasidic teachings. The last were first published as *Sefer ha-Zekhut* (tellingly as an addendum to one of the volumes of his *Ḥiddushim*) in Warsaw in 1876. It has been reprinted several times. Further teachings were included in *Sefer Ḥiddushey ha-RYM ve-Gur Aryeh* (Bilgoray, 1913). In recent years there have been several augmentations of a collection called *Sefer Ḥiddushey ha-RIM 'al ha-Torah,* edited by Yehudah Leib Levin, first (?) published in Jerusalem (Nahaliel, 1965).

[38] On the role of R. Isaac Meir in unifying Polish Hasidism, see Raphael Mahler, *Hasidism and the Jewish Enlightenment* (Philadelphia: Jewish Publication Society, 1985), p. 311ff.

[39] R. Abraham Mordecai was married twice. He had one daughter by his first wife and, after he was widowed, he was remarried to Esther, the daughter of R. Ḥanokh Henikh Landstein. They had three daughters and one son, the Sefat Emet. R. Yehudah Leib was born on Rosh Ḥodesh Iyyar in 1847.

[40] This decision too was not so simple or clear-cut as first appears. In an exchange of letters between the young R. Yehudah Leib and an older confidant-adviser named R. Baruch Shapira, written in 1866, the future Sefat Emet denies accusations that he intrigued to be named rebbe at that point. These letters were published shortly after the death of the Sefat Emet in *Sefer Ḥiddushey ha-RYM ve-Gur Aryeh* (Bilgoray, 1913), p. 48f. and are now reprinted in *Otsar Mikhtavim u-Ma'amarim* (Jerusalem: Makhon Gahaley Esh, 1986), p. 82f. R. Baruch Shapira, a disciple of R. Bunem and the Kotsker, later became rebbe of Stochyn and Ciezew (?). See Y. Alfasi, *Sefer ha-ADMORim* (Tel Aviv: Ariel, 1961), p. 98. In 1866 R. Judah Leib did accept the position of *rav* [official rabbi] of Ger, a position he gave up four years later when he became rebbe.

[41] Correcting an error in Mahler (see note 39), p. 312. It was R. Ḥanokh Henikh, not R. Yehiel Danziger, who succeeded R. Isaac Meir by becoming rebbe in Aleksander (Aleksandrow Lodzki). The Danzigers were in fact the rebbes of the later Aleksander dynasty, but that began, according to Y. Alfasi, *Sefer ha-ADMoRim* (Tel Aviv: Ariel, 1961), only in 1878.

[42] He died on 18 Adar in 1870.

[43] The text of the wedding invitation is printed in *Otsar Mikhtavim u-Ma'amarim*, p. 119. The second part of *Me'ir 'Eyney ha-Golah* contains much correspondence between R. Isaac Meir and R. Yudel Kaminer, indicating that they were both close friends and business associates. The wedding took place in 1862, while R. Isaac Meir was still alive. R. Judah Leib's wife's name was Yocheved Rivka. Many years later, after her death, he was married again, to a granddaughter of R. Hayyim of Sandz (Nowy Sacz).

[44] That of R. Baruch Fraenkel-Teomim (1760–1828), rabbi of Lipnik in Moravia and author of *Barukh Ta'am* as well as important marginalia to the Talmud included in all the later printed editions. The Fraenkel family, originally from Vienna, was considered a part of the ancient Jewish aristocracy. See *Encyclopedia Judaica*, s. v. Fraenkel and references cited there.

[45] These early teachings, the originals of which were partially destroyed by their author, were nevertheless preserved among the Hasidim. These were edited by his grandson R. Abraham Issachar Benjamin Alter (Radomsk, 1896–Treblinka, 1943) as *Sefat Emet—Likkutim*, published in Warsaw (?) in 1934 and 1936. This grandson also edited other collections of teachings by the Sefat Emet. These include a commentary on Psalms, 1928 (an original manuscript augmented by selections from *Sefat Emet 'al ha-Torah*), and commentaries on Proverbs and Pirke Avot (mostly culled from *Sefat Emet 'al ha-Torah*). The major talmudic work by R. Judah Leib Alter, in his grandfather's tradition, is *Sefat Emet 'al Seder Mo'ed, Kodashim, ve-Likkutim 'al Seder Zera'im*, 3 vols. (Warsaw, 1925–31). R. Abraham Issachar Benjamin Alter is also author of *Meir 'Eyney ha-Golah* (discussed above in note 13), an important collection of historical-biographical materials around the life of his great-grandfather R. Isaac Meir, and the chief source for such a work as Alfasi's *Gur* and other later biographies.

[46] There does exist a "commentary" by the Sefat Emet on the *Tikkuney Zohar*. This very rare little book was published in Piotrkow (or Warsaw?) in 1938 or 1939, and nearly all the copies were destroyed in the war. The Gershom Scholem Collection at the Jewish National and University Library in Jerusalem has a photocopy of it. This is an independent work, not culled from *Sefat Emet 'al ha-Torah*, but probably collated from notes in the margins of his copy of *Tikkuney Zohar*. Examination of it confirms that these are essentially hasidic insights that use the text as a point of departure, rather than evidence of true involvement in Kabbalah.

[47] See my prior discussion of this in "On Translating Hasidic Homilies" in *Prooftexts* 3:1 (1983).

[48] This included a significant migration of Russian Jews (mostly Lithuanian/Belorussian *mitnaggedim*) after the pogroms began in Russia in 1881.

[49] As Rivka Schatz-Uffenheimer demonstrated in her book *Hasidism as Mysticism* (Princeton: Princeton University Press, 1993), an augmented translation of *Ha-Ḥasidut ke-Mistikah* (Jerusalem: Magnes Press, 1968), Hasidism had developed or adapted from Kabbalah a distinctive mystical terminology. This involved much discussion of the term *ayin* ("nothing-

ness"), the union/identification of *hokhmah* and *malkhut* as transcendent and immanent aspects of the deity, etc. This language is mostly absent in Polish Hasidism after the Seer of Lublin.

[50] Various aspects of the thought of the Sefat Emet have been studied by Yoram Jacobson in several important articles: "*Galut ve-Ge'ulah be-Hasidut Gur*" in *Da'at* 2:3 (1978/79), 175–215; "*Emet ve-Emunah be-Hasidut Gur*" in *Studies in Jewish Mysticism, Philosophy, and Ethical Literature Presented to Isaiah Tishby* (Jerusalem: Magnes Press, 1986), pp. 593–616; "*Kedushat ha-Hullin be-Hasidut Gur*" in *Tsaddikim ve-Anshey Ma'aseh*, pp. 241–277. In general I very much appreciate and learn from Jacobson's work. I agree with many of his conclusions. I do find, however, that he tends to study the *Sefat Emet* too much as an isolated literary text, ignoring its historical context and the ways in which it reflects its setting in the Polish hasidic school.

[51] *Sefat Emet* 5:54.

[52] *Bereshit Rabbah* 68:9; ed. Theodor-Albeck, p. 777f. See the discussion by E. Urbach in *The Sages* (Jerusalem: Magnes Press, 1975), p. 66ff.

[53] *Sefat Emet* 1:9.

[54] On the influence of both HaBaD and Bratslav Hasidism on the idea of the "inner point" in the *Sefat Emet* and elsewhere in later Polish Hasidism, see the remarks by M. Piekarz in the addendum to his article "'The Inner Point' of the *Admorim* Gur and Alexander as a Reflection of Their Ability to Adjust to Changing Times" in *Studies in Jewish Mysticism, Philosophy, and Ethical Literature Presented to Isaiah Tishby* (Jerusalem: Magnes Press, 1986), p. 657ff. This article has been severely criticized by Y. Jacobson in his above-mentioned (note 51) article in *Tsaddikim ve-Anshey Ma'aseh*, p. 242f., n. 5. I agree with his criticisms and will not repeat them here. Piekarz does add some of the historical context lacking in Jacobson's treatment, but his tendency, well documented in several of his writings, to dismiss the mystical nature of the text before him, offers a completely inadequate reading of the material.

[55] *Sefat Emet* 1:124.

[56] Thus I demur from the interpretation of *nekudah penimit* offered by M. Piekarz in his article mentioned in note 55. His claim is that the notion of "inwardness" and the "inward point" was created as a strategy for dealing with a particular historical situation. But this would not explain why *all* things, including natural and inanimate objects, should have such a center. While I certainly agree that the usage, a usage to which I will return at the end of this introduction, functioned as he describes, I do not believe that it was created intentionally or exclusively for that purpose, as he seems to imply.

[57] Rivka Schatz-Uffenheimer, in her edition of *Maggid Devarav le-Ya'akov*, p. 19, attributes this phrase's origin to Judah ha-Levi's *Kuzari* 5:20. Y. Jacobson, in *Da'at* 2:3 (1978/79), p. 177, n. 10, suggests *Sefer ha-Yashar* as the source. A full history of this usage would prove interesting.

[58] The Lurianic table-songs have been explicated by Y. Liebes in *Molad* 4 (1972), pp. 540–555. On the apple field image, see also Liebes's discussion in his *Studies in the Zohar* (Albany, 1993), p. 175, n. 99.

[59] *Sefat Emet* 1:247. Emphasis mine.

[60] For a full discussion of the ḤaBaD idea of the equal presence of divinity throughout all worlds and the implication of that reality for Jewish theology, see R. Elior, *The Paradoxical Ascent to God* (Albany, 1993), p. 67ff.

[61] The most accessible introduction to this aspect of hasidic thought is Louis Jacobs's *Seeker of Unity* (London: Vallentine-Mitchell, 1966). A fuller and more scholarly discussion is found in Rachel Elior's *The Paradoxical Ascent to God* (Albany: SUNY Press, 1993).

[62] The meaning of this sentence is somewhat obscure, and the text may be garbled.

[63] *Otsar Mikhtavim u-Ma'amarim*, p. 75f.

[64] I refer to the letter of R. Yizḥak Isaac Epstein of Homel to R. Hillel of Paritch (both disciples of the second Lubavitcher rebbe, R. Dov Baer), where he defines the difference between Hasidism and other Judaism as turning on the realization that "all is God." This letter has been translated by Louis Jacobs in *Seeker of Unity*, p. 159ff.

[65] I agree with Y. Jacobson ("*Emet ve-Emunah be-Hasidut Gur*," p. 595, n. 10) that the doctrine here is not properly acosmicism, as it surely is in some of the ḤaBaD sources. R. Judah Leib tends to view the mystical through the lens of the Kotsk tradition that *insists on worldliness but battles superficiality.* Seeing all in terms of the *nekudah* and working to "expand" that *nekudah* until it covers all is a properly mystical formula that reflects this background.

[66] *Sefat Emet* 2:91f.

[67] *Qol Simḥa* (Breslau, 1859) 9a.

[68] *Sefat Emet* 2:80.

[69] On R. Naḥman's view of God as One who constantly eludes comprehensibility, see the sources quoted in my *Tormented Master*, p. 292ff.

[70] The *Sefat Emet* avoids the classic hasidic distinction between *katnut* ("small" or ordinary consciousness) and *gadlut* ("large" or expanded consciousness). See note 40 above.

[71] Shabbat in the *Sefat Emet* is treated extensively by Y. Jacobson in "*Kedushat ha-Ḥullin be-Hasidut Gur*" in *Tsaddikim ve-Anshey Ma'aseh*, pp. 241–277.

[72] Cf. R. Elimelech of Lezajsk. See *No'am Elimelekh, be-Har*, ed. G. Nigal (Jerusalem: Mossad ha-Rav Kook, 1978), p. 350. His brother is R. Zusha of Hanipol'.

[73] *Sefat Emet* 3:190f. Emphasis mine.

[74] Here, too, we see the typically Torah-centered character of Polish Hasidism. The vehicle frequently used to convey this message is the parallel between God's ten utterances in Creation and the Ten Commandments. According to well-established tradition, all of Torah is contained in the Ten Commandments, and prior hasidic writings (*Tanya* 2:1, for example) make it clear that all of Creation is contained within the ten creative utterances of God. For the Sefat Emet, the commandments are then *a divine reformulation of the ten utterances in imperative form.* As such, their observance becomes the way to seek and follow the ways of divinity within creation.

[75] Hasidism in this sense is very much a part of the tradition that runs from Yehudah ha-Levi into the Zohar and such later Kabbalah-influenced thinkers as the MaHaRaL of Prague. For such thinkers, there is an ontological difference between the souls of Jews and non-Jews. Today this view would rightly be called "racist," though its historical context should not be forgotten.

[76] *Sefat Emet* 2:91.

[77] See *Sefer Yetsirah*, chap. 3, and the commentary of Pseudo-RABaD (R. Joseph ben Shalom Ashkenazi) to 3:4.

[78] *Sefat Emet* 3:186.

[79] *Sefat Emet* 3:197.

[80] *Sefat Emet* 1:138.

[81] *Sefat Emet* 1:13.

[82] I have discussed the parallels between the categories of sacred time, sacred space, and sacred person in two previous contexts. See my articles "The Zaddik as Axis Mundi in Later Judaism," *Journal of the American Academy of Religion* 45:3 (1977), pp. 327–344; and "Sabbath as Temple: Some Thoughts on Space and Time in Judaism," in *Go and Study: Essays and Studies in Honor of Alfred Jospe* (Washington: B'nai Brith Hillel, 1980), pp. 287–305.

[83] A rare example is to be found in the sharply worded condemnation of Hasidim who read the secular press, dated 25 Tishrey 5663 (1902) in *Otsar Mikhtavim u-Ma'amarim*, p. 66. It is almost hard to believe that this fierce attack came from the same pen that wrote the *Sefat Emet.*

[84] This strategy of the Sefat Emet served as the paradigm for two great leaders of traditional Jewry in the twentieth century, Rabbi Abraham Isaac ha-Kohen Kook (1865–1935) and the late Lubavitcher rebbe, R. Menahem Mendel Schneersohn.

[85] The story is told in the introduction to *Otsar Mikhtavim u-Ma'amarim.*

[86] I am grateful to my friends Dr. Nehemia Polen of Hebrew College in Boston and Dr. Shaul Magid of the Jewish Theological Seminary of America for their thoughtful reading of this introduction and for a number of suggestions that I have incorporated into the text.

בראשית

SEFER
BERE'SHIT

BERE'SHIT

≡ 1

"In the beginning" (Gen. 1:1). RaSHI opens his commentary by quoting Rabbi Isaac, who asked why the Torah did not begin with: "This month is the first of months for you" (Ex. 12:2) [since that is the first commandment to Israel]. He answered by quoting, "He declared to His people the power of His acts" (Ps. 111:6).

Now we have to understand how this answer applies to all that takes place in the Torah, from "In the beginning" all the way down to "This month." Its meaning is as follows: Indeed, Torah was revealed primarily for the commandments. That is the written Torah. But God also wanted to make it clear that all of Creation, including this world itself, had come about by the power of Torah. "In the beginning," we are told, means that "He looked into the Torah and created the world." That is called oral Torah—and it depends upon human acts.

All the sections that tell of the patriarchs are there to show how Torah was made out of their actions. This is "the power of His acts"—the power that God placed within [human] deeds. That is why we refer to "the *act* of Creation." The world was created by ten divine utterances [of "Let there be"] so that the very life of the world would also derive from Torah. The task of humans is to make this clear, to show how every deed takes place through the life-energy of God. A person who acts in accordance with this Torah-power, fulfilling the Creator's will, renews the light that lies hidden within the natural world.

Of this, Scripture says: "I have placed My words within your mouth . . . to plant the heaven and to establish the earth, saying unto Zion: 'You are My people'" (Is. 51:16). But instead of *'ami* (My people) the rabbis in the holy Zohar read *'immi* (with Me), for the human being is a partner in the act of Creation.

The word "Zion" [*ziyyon/ziyyun*="distinguished"] in this verse refers to the point that exists within each thing, an imprint or sign that reminds us of its divine origin. It is this force that gives life to all. The person who is joined to this inner point, and all of whose life is drawn to this point, indeed becomes a partner in the act of Creation. . . .

1:5

What a radical rereading of the notion of oral Torah! He completely transforms the relationship between written and oral teaching. Written Torah here refers to the commandments as found in the Torah text, which are binding on all Israel. Oral Torah is Torah in process of creation: the actions of the righteous are seen by those around them and are made into Torah, that is, norms of communal behavior. This creation of oral Torah began with the patriarchs. The seemingly nonlegal sections of the Torah in fact are a source of oral Torah; that is why God wanted to give them, to show how Torah is made. So, too, we would presume, are the tales of the rabbis who lived after Torah was given, sources of ongoing oral Torah. As a hasidic master, the author would surely believe the same of the lives of the righteous in his own day; they, too, become sources of living Torah, constantly recreated in partnership with God. The world is ever created anew out of Torah—but so, too, is Torah ever created anew out of the world.

2

"Heaven and earth were completed, they and all their hosts" (Gen. 2:1). The Midrash says that they were made into vessels *(va-yeKhuLu/KeLim)*. It also says there: "I have seen an end to every purpose" (Ps. 119:96).

We can understand this by recalling the prayer we recite on Shabbat: "God spreads out the tabernacle of peace."

Every thing has its root in heaven, as it has been said: "Not even a blade of grass grows without its star striking it and saying: 'Grow!'" Scripture also tells us that "God separated between the waters that were below the heavens and those that were above the heavens" (Gen. 1:7). In this verse we are told that the lower waters wept, saying: "We, too, want to be before the King!" But whatever was done with those "waters above the firmament" is not told in the Torah. Neither is the creation of the angels mentioned in the Torah. The reason is that they are the other halves that belong to all the lower creatures. Lower beings are themselves half-creatures. As each thing is created, something is also born in the upper world that belongs to this creature.

On the Sabbath, the power of that upper root comes down, and the two parts are joined together. This is what we mean by God's "spreading out the tabernacle of peace" [or wholeness]; the upper part comes down. That is why we say "Shalom" to the ministering angels on the holy Sabbath.

Now that upper part [of all things] really has no end, since it is beyond both time and nature. The Creation expounded in the Torah is only that of measures and limits.

That is why Jacob, of whom it is said that he kept the Sabbath, "inherited the world without limits," as the Midrash says. This came about through the wholeness that exists on the holy Sabbath. For it is a vessel that contains blessing. The power of the root comes to dwell within it, that which never ceases and has no measure.

1:9

How do we become more whole? By learning that we are only half. Each of us has another "half," the part of us that ever remains with God, never fully "descending" into this world of change and action. It is this other self whom we call an angel, the one to whom we sing "Shalom Aleikhem" as the Sabbath begins. Rooting ourselves in that higher self is also our opening to infinity, for that which is "above" (or "within") has no limits. Each of us, as we exist in this world and ordinarily know ourselves, is but a "lower" or outer manifestation of an endless and infinite whole.

"Heaven and earth were finished . . ." (Gen. 2:1). The Midrash quotes the verse: "I have seen an end to every purpose, but Your commandment is very broad" (Ps. 119:96). "Everything has a fixed measure," says the Midrash, "but Torah has no measure."

Torah gives life to all of Creation, measuring it out to each creature. But that life-point which garbs itself within a particular place to give it life—it has no measure of its own, for it is beyond both time and nature. It was of this point [that] the rabbis said: "it is the place of the world and the world is not its place."

The verse says: "Your commandment is very broad." *Very* means that it is broader than the place which contains it. This is like the teaching of our sages concerning the Land of Israel, [which is called *erets tsevi* ("beautiful land," but lit.: "land of the deer"), to which the sages added:] "It is the deer among all the lands." Just as the deer's skin seems not to contain its body properly, so does the Land of Israel expand when Israel* are upon it, and so forth. The same is true within everything: the inward point has neither measure nor limit.

This is true of the human soul as well; it, too, has no measure. Scripture refers to God as the One who "forms the person's spirit within" (Zech. 12:1). The more we transcend the body, the more we are capable of receiving soul. But the soul itself is without limit. The same is true of the world's soul, because the person is a microcosm.

The Sabbath is a revelation of this inwardness, and it is called "the day of the soul, not the body." Elsewhere we have interpreted the word *va-yekhal* ("God *completed* on the seventh day all the work that God had done") to refer to measuring, for the Sabbath measures out life to all things. . . . But Shabbat itself has no measure or bounds, for it belongs to those entities that transcend the world of nature. . . .

1:9

Here our author takes us from boundless soul to the place of boundless Torah. The other view of Torah is surely there in the tradition: that it is all about bounds and measures, that its purpose is to set limits and controls. But Torah in its root, the author reminds us, is beyond all this; it is nothing but the limitless wisdom of God. Torah is the infinite font of Creation: it is manifest in the innermost point, itself unfathomable, within each creature. As each creature knows its deepest self, it knows Torah. Only when Torah enters into this-worldly human discourse does it require tsimtsum, *the contraction that makes it take on limits. So, too, the soul; its root is boundless. Only as it lives in this world does it have to exist within limits. This is why the soul loves Torah; it recognizes within it a secret partner from the world of infinity.*

---

* Here, and throughout the text, Israel appears in the plural form to preserve the author's sense of "Israel" as a collective body, singular and plural at the same time.

4

"The Lord God sent him forth from the Garden of Eden" (Gen. 3:23). The word *sent* sounds as if Adam was on some sort of mission. Within the garden, too, he was supposed "to work it and guard it" (Gen. 2:15), meaning that he was to keep the positive and negative commandments. But he was like the king's child, one who is welcome to rummage about among the royal treasures, the innermost secrets of Torah and its commandments.

Now it says in that verse: "God took the human. . . . " This word *took* indicates intimacy and attachment. This is the other side of the rabbis' reading of [the verse:] "He expelled the human He had made" (Gen. 3:24), on which they said: He divorced him as one does a woman *(GaReSH/GeRuSHin)*. In that case *took* in this verse should be read as in: "When a man takes a wife."

But after Adam sinned, he was sent forth to work the land like a servant. Only later did Israel deserve to reenter the state of sonship, when they received the Torah by the merits of the patriarchs and Moses, who had set aright the sin of Adam. Then they moved from the status of servants to that of God's children.

Of this it is said: "An intelligent servant rules over a disgraceful son" (Prov. 17:2). Adam disgraced the entire world, bringing death into the world. Abraham our Father—of whom Scripture says: "For the sake of Abraham My servant" (Gen. 26:24)—was raised from the rank of servant to that of son. In fact he was elevated higher than Adam. Scripture refers to "the great man [adam] among giants" (Josh. 14:1), and the rabbis say: This is Abraham our Father, who was greater than the first human. . . .

1:18

Divorced wife, beloved child. No wonder it's hard to figure out who we are. Out here, that is. Out of Eden. The point is that God is never happy with that divorce/expulsion, but

longs for an Abraham who can repair the damage in our rela-
tionship. The state of exile and alienation, endemic to the
human situation since Adam and Cain, is not one that God
desires. The divine call is that we all be children of Abraham,
not "merely human" (beney Adam), but seekers striving again
to be "taken" by God.

In more abstract terms: the One that is the source of all
being longs to be known and manifest in each of us. In our
struggle for individuation and separate identity, we forget and
even violently break the ties that bind us to all others and to
our shared Root. Selfish deeds, augmented by guilt and then
defensiveness, widen the gap between us and our own deepest
Self. The One that lives forever waits in infinite patience for
each of us to feel, mourn, and begin to heal the breach. The
journey from Adam to Abraham belongs to each of us.

5

On the verse "Let the waters beneath the heavens be gathered
to a single place, that dry land might appear" (Gen. 1:9), the
Midrash tells this parable. Once there was a king who had
mute subjects living in his palace. They would make all sorts
of motions to ask about the king's welfare. He thought: "If
only I had subjects who could speak, how much more would
this be the case!" He brought in speaking subjects, and they
sought to take over the palace!

All that the blessed Holy One created was for God's glory,
to bear witness to God. Thus Scripture says: "The heavens
tell of the glory of God, the firmament proclaims His handi-
work" (Ps. 19:2). "There is no speech, there are no words;
their voice is not heard" (vs. 4). These are the creatures ges-
ticulating to bear witness to their Creator. But only the
human being, who has intellect and speech, can bring this
unspoken testimony into verbal expression. That is why God
gave humans wisdom and intellect, to enable them to bear
this witness. Intellect itself depends upon this act of testifying. The more a person directs the mind and uses intelli-

gence only to know God and bear testimony, the more intellect and wisdom are given to that person. Of this the psalm goes on to say: "The testimony of the Lord is faithful, making wise the fool" (vs. 8). For it is by bearing such witness that a person comes to comprehend even more, and to testify to that as well.

Of this the rabbis said: "The ark bore those who carried it." The same is true of all one does for the sake of God's name. The deeds themselves add to our power to understand what to do further.

The counsel of the cursed primal snake—"You shall be as God" (Gen. 3:5)—was intended to mix evil with good, so that the intelligent human would desire to rule on his own over those beneath him. But intellect was truly given only to know the Creator and to bear God's witness. This in fact is why Adam was created close to the Sabbath—because the Sabbath is itself testimony that this is the purpose of Creation, for humans to attest to their Creator.

Because of this sin of the mind, human intellect itself came to be diminished. Only when Torah was given did Israel attain undiminished intellect. Thus Scripture says: "You have been shown in the mind (la-da'at) that the Lord is God; there is none else besides Him" (Deut. 4:35), and also: "This people I created for Myself, that they tell My praise" (Is. 43:21) and: "I have placed My words in your mouth and hidden you in the shadow of My hand, to plant the heavens and lay the foundations of the earth, and to say unto Zion: 'You are My people'" ('ami) (Is. 51:16). And the holy Zohar reads that word as 'immi: "with Me in partnership."

Since the purpose of heaven and earth was to bear witness to God, Creation is renewed in response to Israel's testimony. This is even more true on the holy Sabbath, which is the designated time for bearing witness, just as Israel are so designated among the souls. Thus the one who says "Heaven and earth were finished" (Gen. 2:1) becomes the blessed Holy One's partner in that primal deed, since this is the purpose of Creation.

1:19

How right you are, and yet how not-so-simple all this is! The mind needs to stretch, to grow, to challenge. How will it do all that without real freedom? The human being is defined by intellect and will, not just speech. Do we fulfill our humanity by becoming mere automatons in the praise of God?

And yet what good is freedom if it only leads us away from who we really are, from what we really need to know and do in life? Our rebellion has become exhausted in the frightful excesses of this century. We are ready again to bear witness, but we need to choose that act of witness freely.

Help us, O Lord, to know You in our freedom! Each day take us out of Egypt, and then lead us to Your holy mountain.

NOAḤ

1

"These are the generations of Noah; Noah was a righteous man" (Gen. 5:9). The holy Zohar says that *Noaḥ* (which means "rest") refers to the Sabbath. RaSHI comments on this verse that the true "generations" of the righteous are commandments and good deeds. All creatures have to bring forth generations. This means that the blessed God placed a holy point within all of Creation. All creatures, but especially humans, are charged with broadening this point until its force spreads out over all the earth. This is the process of "generation;" it takes place only through human self-negation. Each person has to engage in self-negation before the Creator. We need to know that it is not within our power to generate anything. It is only by the power of God that there is a place for us. Only in knowing this can we bring about such generation. That is why Scripture says: "These are the generations of Noah." The word *noaḥ* means rest and self-composure, where everything returns to its source. It is the one who understands that he has no life on his own who brings forth generation. Even though rest and self-composure seem to be the very opposite of generation, they allow it to be.

The holy Zohar comments that [the verse:] "God blessed the seventh day and hallowed it" (Gen. 2:3) refers to manna. But the Zohar asks: Since no manna was to be found on the seventh day, what was its blessing? It answers that all blessings above and below depend upon this day. They depend not on the spreading forth but on the negation before God. This is the source of all generation. Thus Shabbat gives blessing to all the days of the week, since it is through Shabbat that all the days are negated into their source. . . .

1:23

Bittul (self-negation) is the hardest thing the Sefat Emet demands of us, but perhaps the only thing that really counts. It is a self-negation that is in no way negative, but merely realistic. Bittul does not come about from moaning over our human inadequacies, nor from burdening ourselves with overwhelming guilt. Instead, as our author shows us here, it comes from a place of inner rest and peace. The path to self-transcendence begins with self-acceptance. True surrender of self can be undertaken only by one who is at peace.

2

On RaSHI's comment that the true "generations" of the righteous are mitsvot and good deeds.

Note that he did not say this about all "generation," [but specifically about the righteous]. But isn't it obvious that the righteous follow the mitsvot? The point is that not every mitsvah brings about this birthing of a new "generation." Only the *tsaddik*, who joins all of his life-force to the mitsvah, fulfills [the verse:] "In my flesh I see God" (Job 19:26). This becomes like the physical act of union: because all of one's life-force is drawn into that act, it creates a new birth. In the same way, when one does a mitsvah with all [one's] life-energy and strength, it brings about birth.

Now it is also true that there is a birthing that comes about through every mitsvah. That is the way God made things to be, that actions above should depend upon those below. But for this birth to be called that person's "offspring," for the one who did the mitsvah to have an attachment and relationship to it—this depends on desire as well as upon the deed itself.

But the simple meaning of the verse is this. Because Noah was a *tsaddik*, certainly his offspring were as they should be. In their coupling, he [and his wife] considered mitsvot and good deeds above all else. The children born of such union followed the root from which they came.

1:21

How right it is that these two readings come together in a single teaching! The first could sound almost like a monastic ideal: put all your energy into the mitsvah, as though it were an act of physical union; there you will bring forth true "generation." But this devotion does not come to replace the human act of coupling. The second reading, simple and direct as it could be, shows that the same Jew who is concerned about how to make the mitsvot into true spiritual "offspring" is no less devoted to finding holiness in the act of this-worldly union and the very real children who will be born of it.

 3

Regarding the generation of dispersion [after the tower of Babel]. "And the Lord said: Behold, they are one people and have a single language" (Gen. 11:6). The Torah here teaches us how we lower creatures fell away from the root of oneness. Of an earlier generation, Scripture had said: "Behold, he has become as one of us" (Gen. 3:22), truly cleaving to oneness. The rabbis taught that he became like one of the angels, of whom it says: "They call to one another" (Is. 6:3), meaning that they all join together to become one. Thus we say: "They sound forth together aloud the words of living God [all of them as one]."

The Holy One created everything through the twenty-two letters. Each school of angels flies up to the root of its own special letter. Then the twenty-two letters are joined together through various endless permutations. Thus they are made one.

The same was true of humans before the fall. Then we were expelled from Eden "to work the land." But we still had a single language [the holy tongue], and by joining together the twenty-two letters below, we retained access to the letters above. Thus the Zohar says that we "cleave below to secret oneness, just as above." There are various rungs of letters: special large ones, special small ones, and just ordinary letters.

But the power to become one below is only preparation for the root of oneness above. Of this it says: "He builds His upper stories in the heavens, but establishes His foundation upon the earth" (Amos 9:6). Because the generation of dispersion was a gathering not for the sake of heaven, since they abandoned the root and separated between the unity above and that below, they had to lose their own unity and become divided into the seventy nations.

But the holy tongue was preserved for the children of Israel, who are called "a singular people in the earth." They are "a gathering for the sake of heaven, whose end is to be sustained."

1:39

Warsaw in 1900 was a center of Jewish socialist and communist activity. Many children of Hasidim were attracted by the message of labor organizers, and they began to follow these leaders of the Left as previous generations had followed hasidic masters. Here the rebbe shows that he was aware of such thinking, and attuned to both the good and bad within it. The desire to draw humanity into a universal bond was an attempt to recreate Eden. But doing it without a sense of true oneness and its divine root would lead instead to Babel.

But the conclusion of the teaching returns to Israel. If humanity is not united for the sake of God's oneness, surely the Jewish people are! Here we can see how a true religious viewpoint would criticize all our secular Jewish efforts at proclaiming: "We are one!" If our unity does not see itself as a way to the oneness of all things in God, it is not better than the unity of Babel.

LEKH LEKHA

1

"Get you from your land, your birthplace, and your father's house" (Gen. 12:1). The Midrash quotes the verse: "Listen, O daughter; look and give ear. Forget your people and your father's house" (Ps. 45:11). Abraham our Father was a great sage even before this, as the holy Zohar tells us: "God gives wisdom to the wise."

Now surely [each] person was created for a particular purpose. There must be something that we are to set right. A person who achieves that is called righteous (tsaddik), walking a straight path of justice. But Abraham our Father is called a lover of God (ḥasid); he went beyond the line demanded by the law. The one who serves God out of love can arouse a desire within God to let flow the source of his own soul in a way

19

that cannot be comprehended by the human mind. Thus they interpreted the verse: "Those who fulfill His word to hear the voice of His word" (Ps. 103:20). By properly mending our deeds, we can come to hear more and more. This goes on forever. The *ḥasid* serves God in order to become attached to the root of the mitsvah, ever seeking to hear new things.

This is why Scripture said: "Hear, O daughter," referring to that which we can understand, and afterward "give ear," meaning that *all* hearing and listening should be attuned only to God. This is the complete surrender referred to in [the verse:] "Get you from your land, your birthplace, and your father's house." In this way we attain a new enlightenment, one that is beyond nature, just as did Abraham our Father.

The verse continues: "which I show you." This refers to that which a person cannot see on his own. And so the children of Israel, being drawn after Him "in the wilderness, an unsown land," attained Torah, that law of fire. . . .

1:48

There is a rare union here: the religious life and the creative life turn out to be deeply intertwined. The Sefat Emet says it in a way you might expect of a poet. The ability to hear and to follow, even beyond our capacity to comprehend, opens the inner well and allows the soul to spread forth. The ḥasid as poet can ask no more than this: to have the inner ear attuned forever, to go on hearing without end. This openness beyond all limit transcends all other meaning in life, even that of the tsaddik *who has found his purpose.*

 **2**

In the Midrash: "'Listen, O daughter, look and give ear. Forget your people and your father's house' (Ps. 45:11). . . . A tale is told of one who was wandering from place to place and saw a certain castle that was on fire. He said: 'Could it be that this castle has no master?' The owner of the castle looked out at him and said: 'I am owner of the castle.'"

A person is essentially set aright when he forgets the vanities of this world—"Forget your people"—and remembers that he is sent into this world to do God's bidding. This is the meaning of "remember" and "keep" [in the two versions of the Sabbath commandment], referring to the positive and negative commandments.

This is also "remembering" and "forgetting," both of which a person needs to do. When we forget the world's vanities, we are able to remember and attach ourselves to a higher world. Of this the rabbis said: "Whoever is obligated to 'keep' is obligated also to 'remember.'"

The Sabbath, when all Israel cease from labor, is truly a time to forget this world. That is why we merit an extra soul; we remember and are attached to the world to come, for Sabbath is "something like the world to come." This is the meaning of "remember" and "keep" the Sabbath.

But Sabbath is really there to teach us about all the rest [of time] as well. A person always has to guard these two aspects of "Hear, O daughter" [remember] and "Forget." Abraham was the first one to cast all worldly vanities aside and thus to draw light into the world. Of him Scripture speaks when it asks: "Who caused the sun to shine from the East?" (Is. 41:2).

This is the meaning of the burning castle. This whole world was created only so that its vanities be forgotten and negated; this is the world's true fulfillment, since it is the corridor that leads into the great hall. It is the will of the castle's owner that it be burned and consumed. Thus it is with a candle: the white fire hovers over a black, consuming fire. The more the black fire consumes, the more the white light burns. "Remember" and "keep." This is why we light candles for the Sabbath.

1:58

"The Lord your God is a consuming fire." The burning Shabbat candles are here given an almost apocalyptic message: the very purpose of existence is that it be consumed, or restored to its oneness with God. Our task is to "forget" the outer world, to turn only to the Source of the fire that consumes it.

But this reading of Abraham's burning castle does not suffice for us. We have seen our author's entire world burned up and consumed in the fires of evil and hatred. For us the master who calls out from the burning castle is also the God we meet when we act to fight that fire, when we do what little we can to save the world from being consumed by evil flames. Here the balance of "remember" and "forget" has to be established in a new way. That is key to our religious task.

3

[Concerning the same verse and parable:] The human being is called a walker, always having to go from one rung to another. For habit makes things seem natural, and this sense of "nature" hides the inner light. This is true even of Torah and the commandments: when we do them out of habit, they become our nature, and we forget their inward meaning. Therefore we need always to seek out some new counsel.

That is why God "renews, in His goodness, each day, the work of Creation," so that we not be overpowered by the sense of nature. This is the burning castle, this world of nature and all that passes through it. Even though all of nature came to be only through the transcendent single point of life, it becomes stamped with the imprint of nature [the ordinary] and all things are thus consumed, as Scripture says [of the cows in Pharaoh's dream]: "And you couldn't tell that they had come inside them" (Gen. 36:21). Therefore, the blessed Holy One renews each day the work of Creation. The person has to search and seek out this renewal, "to watch My doorways each day" (Prov. 8:34).

That is why Scripture first said "Hear, O daughter" and afterwards "and give ear." Be ready to hear always. And therefore also: "Get you out of your land"—a person should always keep walking. "To [that which] I will show you"—always some new attainment. This is why the person is called a walker. Whoever stands still is not renewed, for nature holds him fast. The angels above are beyond nature; they can be said to "stand" (Is. 6:2). But the person has to keep walking.

1:60

Thank you, Lord, for all that nervous energy. Life as an angel might have been easier—standing still to do Your bidding. But it is our walking, our ever climbing (and sometimes falling!) from rung to rung that makes us human. Despite all the struggle and pain that go along with growing, we wouldn't have it any other way.

 4

Human beings were sent into this world in order that all places be restored, that holy sparks be drawn forth from everywhere. This is the meaning of all Abraham's wanderings from one place to another, and then to Egypt. Our sages said that this [descent into Egypt] was preparation for the children of Israel.

Scripture says [of Abraham after his return from Egypt] that he was "very rich in cattle, in silver, and in gold" (Gen. 13:1). These are the many holy sparks he brought out of there. "Silver" and "gold" stand for the love and fear of God, for he came out of there in love and fear. He did it all for the sake of heaven, and so everything was restored.

Silver and gold are not mentioned in the case of Lot; there it just says that "Lot too, who went with Abram, had flocks, herds, and tents" (vs. 5). This is why Lot came to sin after the journey to Egypt; he did not have the proper fear and love. The same applies to Lot as to the "mixed multitude" that came up out of Egypt with Israel. And of Israel it says: "He brought them forth with silver and gold" (Ps. 105:37). That is why "none of [Israel's] tribes stumble" (ibid.). These holy sparks that have come from the places of evil require careful guarding, lest they afterwards become the cause of stumbling.

1:54

Our love and our fear are indeed very precious, and we are very fragile as we bring them to You. They are the true shining sparks of "gold" and "silver" that we can offer up on the altar within our hearts. Ours is a God who wants us whole, with all of our emotions. Holding on to these in order to uplift them does not make the walking easier. The path is a more dangerous one than it would have been if we had left them all behind, but it is a path to greater wholeness.

5

On the verse, "Walk before Me and be perfect" (Gen. 17:1), the Midrash Tanḥuma has Abraham ask: "Until now was I lacking something? And when I circumcise myself will I be more whole?"

An interpretation: this is the true wholeness, when a person diminishes himself in order to be negated unto God, to show that we creatures have no wholeness except that which flows into us from the Creator. This in itself bestows wholeness; here the negation of the thing is its very fulfillment.

That is why the mitsvah of circumcision was assigned to this particular limb, for it is the source of flow and generation. This [sexual and progenerative] function is the most essential human power. It is here that there needs to be a sign of recognition that humans on their own are lacking, and that they need the Creator in order to be whole. . . .

Therefore this mitsvah is called *berit,* or covenant, for it connects the receiver to the Giver, and that is true wholeness. That is why it was given to man [as a task]. The uncircumcised asked: "If circumcision is really so beloved, why was man not created that way?" The answer is that circumcision really does diminish the body, but it has to be undertaken by the person for the sake of [connection with] the Creator. In this way it makes for wholeness. That would not be the case if the person were created that way.

1:45

This explanation of circumcision, unlike so many, is offered without a shred of apology or defense. Yes, he recognizes that circumcision is a diminishing of the body. But it is one that we undertake for the sake of God. The organ of sexual union, that which will allow for the making of future generations, is the place where we are told to demonstrate symbolically our awareness that generation comes from God and is carried on for the sake of heaven. Life is a divine gift; circumcision is our way of saying that the new life comes from God, not only from our own act of union.

VA-YERA'

It is said that Abraham cleared the way for all the exile. "Israel were exiled only so that converts would be added to them." This means drawing all creatures near to Torah. Therefore, Abraham chose to take himself to all these places, in order to set them right and raise them up. Thus it is taught that while Noah still needed [God's] help to walk [in the proper path], Abraham found his own strength in his righteousness. "As a person goes, so is he led." He chose this path, that of seeking out truth, on his own.

This is why the righteous who lived previous to Abraham's time were born circumcised, while he, by his own service, attained circumcision as a commandment. He was mending the mundane world, so that humans by their own work should be able to remove the foreskin.

Because of this, those who serve God should not be too concerned by those times of "hiding" that happen to every religious person. "According to the suffering is the reward." This way was chosen by our father Abraham, who so loved God that he took himself into dangerous places, in order to rejoin all of Creation to Him. That is why Creation itself is called by his name *(Be-HiBaR'aM/Be-'aBRaHaM)*.

Thus it is for all generations. "In the beginning" means "for Israel, who are called 'beginning,'" for they bring all of Creation near to God and thus arouse the power of new beginnings in the world.

This is also why it says that Abraham established the dawn prayer service, as Scripture tells us: "He arose early to that place where he had stood in God's presence" (Gen. 19:27). On the simplest level, this tells us that as soon as he arose, he was able to get back to that [spiritual] place where he had been when he lay down the previous night.

This is the way of those who serve God. They are called "walkers," as Scripture says: "Speak of them when you sit in your house and when you walk by the way, when you lie down and when you rise up" (Deut. 6:7). All of a person's days are a single journey; of this Scripture speaks when it says that someone "was come in his days." Thus we say in our prayers: "May we arise and find our heart's hope." For this is a sign that we truly love God: if as soon as we awaken we can recall our Creator, before we do anything else. . . . Thus Scripture testifies that Abraham, the Pillar of Love, "Abraham My Lover" (Is. 41:8) "arose early to that place where he had stood." This is what they mean when they say that he established the dawn service: he gave the power to each Jew to arouse the dawn every day.

1:67

The way of Abraham as defined here is that of 'avodah. It is no accident that this term can be translated as both "work" and "service." Abraham understands that the arousal has to

*come from below; it is in our prayers and deeds that we
awaken the love of God. The power to begin each day with
this sense of 'avodah is one of the great strengths of Jewish
spiritual practice. No wonder our tradition attributes it to
none other than Abraham, the first seeker.*

2

"God appeared to him" (Gen. 18:1). RaSHI follows the
Midrash and the Gemara in saying that He was there to visit
the sick.

Of this it is written: "For I am sick with love" (Cant. 2:5).
The community of Israel is filled with love and longing to be
united with the blessed Holy One. On the verse, "The righteous blossom like a palm tree" (Ps. 92:13), the Midrash says
that just as a palm has desire [the "male" tree and "female"
trees for one another], so do the righteous have desire for God.

Soul and spirit long for their root, but they are bound to the
body. By means of circumcision, the removal of the sheath,
this desire of soul and spirit wins the day. The body really has
the same form as the soul. On the verse, "There is no rock
(tsur) like our God" (1 Sam. 2:2), the sages said: "There is no
artist *(tsayyar)* like our God." Just as in the body desire and
longing are concentrated in this limb, so too within.

That is why "the righteous blossom like a palm tree"; the
entire soul truly desires to ascend, just as any derivative being
longs for its source. As long as the foreskin covers that limb,
the body wins over the soul's desire. The wicked have no idea
that they are imprisoned by the body. But after circumcision, a
person is as though reborn. He feels himself to be a prisoner
and becomes sick with love.

The same is true on the holy Sabbath, when the power of
the other side is removed, and the full light of soul, the "extra
soul," is seen. This is revealed in the desires and longings of
the soul that come out on the Sabbath. The word *va-yekhulu*
("Heaven and earth *were finished*" [Gen. 2:1]) can also refer to
passionate longing. *Va-yinafash* ("and on the seventh day He

rested and *was refreshed*" [Ex. 31:17]) can mean: "Woe, the soul is lost!" For on weekdays that longing and desire are missing. Shabbat is to time what circumcision is to the soul.

1:81

Religion, he seems to say, is a matter of recognizing and rechanneling desires. The religious soul knows the power of human passions; it may also be aware that its own longing for God is related to other passions that fill the human heart. The task is one of directing the energy of longing to its finest and most precious goal—the love of God.

The relationship of body and soul taught here is the legacy of kabbalistic tradition. The soul is not just a formless entity within the body. The bodily form itself is in the divine image, and the soul is structured in the same pattern as its bodily sheath. The removing of the foreskin in circumcision is thus a symbolic removal of the coarse power of the outer self from the holy form in which we are created.

 3

The Midrash quotes the verse: "From my flesh I see God" (Job 19:26). "Had I not done this," Abraham asks, "from where would God have been revealed to me?" This is because [the verse] "God appeared to him" comes after the circumcision.

This is the meaning of the commandments. They set aright the 248 limbs [of the human body] so that the grace of God might dwell upon them. This reflects great love, that the image of God be revealed in the human soul, by the power of the commandments.

Circumcision is the first of those 613 commandments that are distinctively Israel's. It is the root of Father Abraham, the positive commandment "that he command his children" (Gen. 18:19). Thus we say in our prayers: "With Your shining face You gave us the teaching of life, gracious love." "Gracious love" refers to the commandments; this is the "great love," to cleave to the Creator with every limb of our bodies. This is the power of the mitsvot.

Abraham our Father represents the 248 positive commandments; Isaac stands for the 365 prohibitions. Jacob [who embodies them both] is "the teaching of life." It was because of Abraham's own great love that he was able to draw forth the commandments, this "gracious love."

This is the meaning of "God appeared to him" and "From my flesh I see God." This is Abraham's covenant, that by fulfilling the commandment down here he could be joined to the root above. The grace of God was upon him by the power of this covenant God had made with him. Through circumcision we come into this covenant. Therefore, at a circumcision we recite the blessing: "to bring him into the covenant of Abraham our Father."

1:78f.

Here we see the side of Hasidism that sought to end the Jew's ancient war of the soul against the body. The commandments involve the physical world, and this is their special strength. When we follow them, the body—and with it the physical universe as a whole—is bound to its root in the realm of spirit. The understanding that this regimen of transforming the bodily self begins with the mitsvah of circumcision shows profound psychological insight.

"Now I know that you fear God" (Gen. 22:12). But was not Abraham's service out of love? And is that not higher than serving from fear? Then why should Scripture here attribute to Abraham the fear of God?

This was Abraham's trial. He who had left his land and his birthplace, who had thrown himself into the fiery furnace for the sake of his Creator, would not have considered it a trial to slaughter his son. Of course a person like Abraham, one who serves out of love, would be drawn to follow God's will with all his heart and innards. Each of his limbs is drawn by its very nature to fulfill the will of God; their very life is the divine command.

But in this case it really *wasn't* God's will that he slaughter Isaac! Abraham's heart [discerning this] felt no love or attachment to God in this act, since it was not God's true will. That was the trial. And that is why it says: "He saw the place *(hamakom)* from afar" (vs. 4), meaning that he saw God *(hamakom)* was far from him [since this commandment was not really God's will]. Now all he had was the fear of God, not to question Him at all.

That is why Abraham insisted that God try him no more, that God never be far from him again. For Abraham's path was that of love.

1:67

This is a startling interpretation of the binding of Isaac, one that restores the equanimity in the God/person relationship that seems so greatly thrown off balance in this tale. As one who stands in an ongoing love relationship with God, Abraham senses that this command to offer up his son could not bespeak the true will of his Lover. The command is real, and Abraham has to follow it, but he does so in the faith that the God whom he has known in love cannot will this thing; his God is far from him as he goes toward that mountain. Having survived that trial, one in which he felt abandoned by the God of love, Abraham is given the strength to say: "No more!" Never again should I or my children have to choose between love and the divine command.

In this 'akedah, both man and God are tried, tested, and refined, never to be the same again.

חיי שרה

ḤAYYEY SARAH

1

"Sarah's life was a hundred and twenty and seven years" (Gen. 23:1). RaSHI comments that [they are written out this way to show that] all of them were equal in goodness.

It is the way of ordinary people that as you get older your awareness increases and you settle out your ways. The older you get, the more you are able to put aside certain bad qualities and stop doing some of the bad things you used to do. But in that case, the real "days of your life" are only the last minute, the time when you are really whole. And only some merit that chance.

But righteous Sarah, all her days were good and unspoiled. Surely she rose higher in her old age, but not by having to push away anything she had done in her youth. She just grew higher according to the natural course of her being. Every day of our lives we are given [the opportunity of] some special thing to set aright. Thus we can ascend, rung after rung. In Sarah's case there had been no damage done along the way, no spoiling for which she had to repent in order to behave properly. This is the meaning of "all equal in goodness." Think about this.

1:82

For some of us teshuvah, *the return to God, needs to consti-tute a drastic or even violent change in the way we have been living. But there are those for whom* teshuvah *is constant throughout life, who are always turned to God, returning en-ergy to the One. For them* teshuvah *is as natural as breathing and as indispensable a part of life.*

≡ 2 ≡

"Sarah's life was a hundred and twenty and seven years, the days of Sarah's life" (Gen. 23:1). The Midrash says: "'The Lord knows the days of the perfect *(temimim)*; their inheritance shall be forever' (Ps. 37:18). Just as they are perfect, so are their years perfect."

. . . The first meaning of *tamim* (perfect) is "without blem-ish"; this refers to perfection or wholeness. It may be applied to time as well. The human being was created in order to re-alize self-perfection. And since we were created in this world, each of us given but a limited time, perfection applies to time as well.

This is most obviously understood if referred to the aware-ness we gain every day. My grandfather and teacher (of blessed memory) said that the day itself is called after the light it con-tains, for Scripture says: "God called the light day" (Gen. 1:4). This means that the blessed Holy One in goodness renews Creation each day. Each and every day God places a point of awakening in each one of Israel, to which they may attach themselves. That is the meaning of "which I command you this day" (Deut. 6:6). "Each day they are to be new to you."

Of the one who accepts all these daily enlightenments, Scripture says: "The Lord knows the days of the perfect," since it is through the days that this person's perfection is fulfilled. Thus the Zohar says that a person's days make up a "garment." For in the upper worlds there are various hidings [of the divine light] by the "other side"; not everyone can approach the Holy. But triumph over this world and the transformation of nature bring about a "garment." This allows nature, which is called "time," to be joined and subjected to holiness. This is the meaning of "their years are perfect"—the *tsaddik* joins each day to its root. By attaining awareness and spirituality within time, a person shows that time itself has value, so that time, too, is uplifted.

"God knows the days of the perfect"—their days are filled only with knowing God, new knowledge coming along each day.

1:84

We have seen that the holiness of time—particularly as exemplified by Shabbat—is a major theme in the Sefat Emet. *But here we see clearly that this holiness is only a potential. Time is made holy by the way we use it, by the way we search ever anew for holiness in the days and years that are given to us. Each day, according to the kabbalists, we weave part of that garment that will clothe and protect our soul throughout eternity.*

 3

[On the same Midrash and RaSHI comment:] This the quality of equanimity, written about in *The Duties of Hearts*. It is a very great quality for a person to remain perfect [whole, innocent] despite all that happens. Both rich and poor are tried in this matter.

Sarah had lived through some very hard times early in her life. There had been hunger, and then she had been taken both to Pharaoh and to Abimelech. Now, at the end of her days, she and Abraham lived in great comfort. But nothing changed in her, despite all these differences.

This is what the Mishnah means when it says that Abraham our Father went through ten trials, all to show his great love. Abraham loved God so much that all the changing winds in the world couldn't move him from his place. He remained whole, not feeling at all those things that passed over him.

Most people are not like this; they go through several changes each day. But Sarah and Abraham were unchanged throughout all their years. Of them was it said: "She did him good and not ill, all the days of her life" (Prov. 31:12). This includes all those changes and trials, both in poverty and in wealth. "Just as they were perfect, so were their years. . . ."

The essence of this "perfection" is to be attached to the upper root, as Scripture says: "Be perfect with the Lord your God" (Deut. 18:13). Everything below has a root above; when the lower portion is attached to its root, the thing is perfect and whole. This is the purpose of the religious life: to attach ourselves to our upper root. . . .

1:99

Sarah and Abraham have left their children the greatest of gifts: models of wholeness toward which each generation in its own way can aspire. The task of being ourselves, remaining faithful to our truest values in the face of both temptations and trials (those of plenty as well as those of deprivation), is one that confronts each of us. Being able to face these challenges knowing that we are the children of such parents gives us a much-needed extra measure of moral strength.

This teaching reflects the fact that Ger Hasidim were well represented among the rising middle class of Warsaw Jewry in the late nineteenth century. The figures of Abraham and Sarah are taken here to provide such listeners with a model of Jews who remain faithful to the values of Judaism as it was in the impoverished shtetl, despite the temptations of expanding economic opportunity. The model is even more needed in our own day, when we live in a society of luxury far beyond previous centuries' wildest dreams.

TOLEDOT

1

. . . My grandfather and teacher used to say this about the wells the patriarchs dug. Everywhere there is a hidden point of God. We only have to remove the external covering in order to reveal that innermost point, which is called "a well of living waters" (Gen. 26:19; Cant. 4:15). On weekdays this well is called *'esek* or *sitnah* (lit.: "preoccupation" or "accusation"; cf. Gen. 26:20ff.). But on the Sabbath it is called *rehovot* (expanse). The words of the wise are gracious.

But Scripture says: "Wisdom cries out in public; in the streets *(rehovot)* she sounds her voice" (Prov. 1:20). The sound of Torah is always there to arouse the hearts of Israel. We have only to turn our ears, as the holy Zohar says: "There is no one who turns his ear." Scripture also says: "If you hear, hear My

37

voice" (Ex. 19:5), as well as "Because Abraham heard My voice" (Gen. 26:5). The divine voice is always present. It comes from the ten utterances by which the world was created and the Ten Commandments by which God gave the power of His words to all of Creation.

On Shabbat Israel testify that the world and all its fullness belong to God. Then the divine voice is awakened; it is easy to hear that voice on the holy Sabbath. "In *rehovot* [in the expanse of Sabbath] she sounds her voice."

1:105

A great number of the teachings on each Torah-portion deal with the Sabbath; we should recall that these teachings were all Sabbath table-talks in their original form, so it was natural that Shabbat itself be a frequent theme. Often his message was the one expressed here with special clarity: Sabbaths and festivals are given us as a special gift, a time when the divine presence is clear and obvious, when God's voice can readily be heard. Time is dotted with these moments of special grace so that the rest of time, the weekday on which we struggle so hard to find God's voice, will not completely overwhelm us. But for those whose ears are truly open, the divine voice can be heard through the din of the weekday world as well.

 2

Regarding the wells the patriarchs dug: the word *be'er* (well) is to be read as in: "Moses agreed to explain *(be'er)* this teaching" (Deut. 1:5). In the same way, even before the Torah was received, the patriarchs explained/"welled" the wisdom of Creation, since everything was created through Torah and for God's glory.

We have to contemplate all of Creation in order to understand the Creator's purpose. Abraham our Father explained/"welled" how to derive the love of God from all of Creation. He showed us how to look upon the kindnesses and goodness of the Creator, whose goodness and glory fill the world. In the same way, Isaac explained/"welled" how to attain the fear of God from all of Creation. All this was before the Torah was given. This is "the well dug by princes" (Num. 21:18), which is followed by "a gift from the wilderness." Then the Torah, which explains the true meaning of all Creation, was given. But this can be acquired only as a gift.

As for Jacob, it says of him: "You give truth unto Jacob" (Mic. 7:20). The well/meaning came upon him of its own accord, as it says: "He looked, and there was a well" (Gen. 29:2).

1:122

Torah comes to us from above, brought down from the mountaintop, given from the highest heavens. But what of the Torah that our patriarchs knew before that Torah was given? Their Torah flowed from a well, water deep within the earth. We have here a key metaphor for understanding the Torah that comes from within, rather than from above or beyond. Religion today would do best to seek out and cultivate this internal metaphor, knowing full well, of course, that both "above" and "within" are meant in nonliteral ways. Here the Sefat Emet reminds us—as he does so frequently in other ways—that the first Torah to be discovered is that which lies within. The need to contemplate all of Creation in order to learn God's purpose is one that we could well affirm today.

3

"Isaac loved Esau, for he relished his venison, but Rebecca loved Jacob" (Gen. 25:28). Scripture gives a reason for Isaac's love; it was not a true love, for it depended upon a particular thing. If that thing were to disappear, so would the love. Therefore when Jacob approached him with venison, his love for Esau disappeared.

But Rebecca loved Jacob without any reason, and her love lasted forever. This is what the Midrash means when it says that "whenever she heard his voice, she came to love him more." This means that it did not depend upon any particular thing.

God's love for Israel is of the same sort. It does not depend on anything, not even . . . deeds. God has simply chosen Israel; "God's people is His portion (Deut. 32:9)." Of *Him* it is said: "Who is wealthy? The one who takes delight in his portion."

Therefore Scripture [records the following dialogue]: "'I love you,' says the Lord. But you say 'In what do You love us?' 'Was not Esau Jacob's brother,' says the Lord, 'but I loved Jacob'" (Mal. 1:2). This love does not depend on any reason. Israel are just attached to God in their root.

1:107

Can we accept God's choosing of Israel, presented here with the fullest measure of its arbitrariness? There is something very attractive about the total lack of apology in this passage: God simply fell in love with Israel, for no particular reason. This love can no more be explained than any other. Can we imagine a God so moved by the particularity of passion? Or is God as Rebecca, the mother possessed by a "special" love for one of her children, too much for us egalitarians and democrats to bear? Can we create a Judaism for our age that does not stand or fall over this indeed "scandalous" and morally difficult claim?

4

"May God give you of the dew of heaven and the fat of the land" (Gen. 27:28). The Midrash says: May God give you godliness. The verse [is read this way even though it] concludes with "the dew of heaven and the fat of the land."

The real intent is that the Jew receive godliness from everything that exists in the world. That is why it is written: "Love the Lord your God with all your heart, with all your soul, and with all your might" (Deut. 6:5)—to receive divinity from everything. For all of life comes from the blessed Holy One—there is nothing without Him. This is the blessing—that He give you God "from the dew of heaven and the fat of the land"; that you find godliness in all of it.

Now afterwards the Midrash interprets "the dew of heaven and the fat of the earth" to refer to offerings, libations, and sacrifices. But this is all the same, for it shows that in the Temple, by means of sacrifices *(QoRBanot)*, all things were brought near *(nitQaReBu)* to the root. This is witness that everywhere "the whole earth is filled with His glory" (Is. 6:3).

"The fat of the land" indicates that desirable things in this world, even earthliness itself, have a potential [godliness] to be realized. All was made in wisdom. That is why the earth needs to be worked in various ways: plowing, planting, reaping, and so forth, until food is prepared. This shows that by the power of human effort, the true "food," or the hidden sparks of holiness, can be brought forth in this world. . . .

1:120

This charge to find godliness in everything was given to a community of Jews diverse in their economic means, including some wealthy Hasidim, to be sure, but one that also included the poor and struggling. What of us, who have so much of "the fat of the land," who daily consume far more than our share of earth's resources? Does too much "fat of the land" keep us from seeing the simple "dew of heaven"? Or can our very richness of experience, the ability to encounter more diversity, greater wonders both geographically and culturally than our ancestors ever dreamed possible, enrich also our chances for seeing godliness everywhere we turn?

VA-YETSE'

1

"The land upon which you are lying will I give unto you and your descendants" (Gen. 28:13). The rabbis taught that the blessed Holy One folded up the entire Land of Israel and placed it beneath him. Just as our Father Jacob included all the souls of Israel, so did he now have the entire land. Jacob is the [ideal] person whom God created in His world, and his image is engraved beneath the Throne of Glory. Thus this place belonged to him, since it includes all places.

The Talmud says that one who gives joy to the Sabbath is given an inheritance without limits. There it quotes the verse: "Then you will rejoice *on* the Lord; I will cause you to ride upon the high places of the earth, and I will feed you from the inheritance of your Father Jacob" (Is. 58:14). This inheritance is not attributed to Abraham, of whom Scripture says: "Walk about in the land, its length and its breadth" (Gen. 13:17), but rather to Jacob, of whom our chapter says: "You will spread forth to the sea and to the east, to the north and to the south" (vs. 14). On the Sabbath everything ascends to its root. That is the meaning of [the verse:] "Let no man go forth from his place on the Sabbath day "(Ex. 16:29).

This was the purpose of man's creation: that each find the place belonging to him. Then surely the blessing "You will spread forth" will apply. That is the meaning of "the land upon which you are lying will I give unto you." It is the place that belonged to him. Jacob our Father contained all six directions: "the ladder set in the ground, but with its top reaching heaven" (Gen. 28:12) represented the two vertical directions, and then he was told: "You shall spread forth," and so on, representing the four others. . . .

1:131

Jacob is the perfect human being, the parallel within humanity to the Sabbath in time and the Holy Land in space. According to the rabbis, he was "as beautiful as Adam"; and his image, inscribed on God's throne, was an object of godly devotion. This image of a perfected human has ancient roots in all of our religious traditions, both East and West. We lesser humans live out our religious lives by imitating those great souls or by discovering, sometimes to our great surprise, that we, too, partake of their wholeness.

This rabbinic and later mystical image of Jacob as the ideal of human perfection stands in strong contrast to the Bible's own account of him as trickster, a tradition reflected even in his name. Perhaps there is a message of hope in this irony: Jacob, even Jacob, was capable of becoming Israel, the one who prevailed over God and man. You too, O ordinary mortal. . . .

2

"He looked, and there was a well in the field, and there were three flocks of sheep lying down by it, for from that well the flocks were watered. But the stone was large on the mouth of the well. When all the flocks were gathered there, they would roll the stone off the mouth of the well" (Gen. 29:2–3).

This reality—the well in the field—is found in every thing and in every one of Israel. Every thing contains a life-giving point that sustains it. Even that which appears to be as neglected as a field has such a hidden point within it. The human mind is always able to know this intuitively. This knowledge is the three flocks of sheep, which stand for wisdom, understanding, and awareness. With wisdom and intellect a person understands this inwardness: within all things dwells "the power of the Maker, within the made."

But "the stone was large on the mouth of the well." When corporeality spreads forth, there is hiding; intellect is not always joined to deed. The answer to this lies in "were gathered there"—all one's desires and every part of the body and its limbs have to be gathered together as one places oneself in God's hands before each deed. Then "they would roll the stone."

You might also say that "they were gathered" means that you should join yourself with all of Israel. For when all of Creation is united with God, the hiding will end. This will occur in the future, may it come in our days! Meanwhile, we Jews gather everything to Him. And even when a single person negates himself and joins into all of Israel, acting for the sake of all, we call this action "in the name of all Israel." This too can roll away the stone and remove the hiding.

The fact that in Jacob's case Scripture says *va-yegal* (vs. 10) [which looks like "he revealed" rather than "he rolled"] means that he found it from within himself, for he was the whole of Israel. He was also *tsaddik*, foundation of the world, by whose merit the world exists. Therefore, "he revealed it" from within himself.

1:124

There can be something frighteningly simplistic about hasidic teaching: "the sparks of light are everywhere," "the inward point lies within all things," and all the rest of such formulations. The teaching is saved from this danger only by our awareness of how large the stone really is on the mouth of that well, of how far we seem to be from the realization of that inward truth. The rest is all a matter of counsel: what can we do to "reveal" or unmask the stone?

3

My grandfather taught in the name of Rabbi Isaac Luria that the Sabbath is called a field. Scripture refers to this when it says: "Come my beloved, let us go out into the field" (Cant. 7:13). This world is a wilderness, one where there is no sign of God's providence. On the Sabbath it is called "field," ready to be seeded. Then the power of inwardness, the divine life-point within it, is aroused, and it receives its seed.

On this basis we can understand the verse: "He looked, and there was a well in the field, and there were three flocks of sheep lying down by it, for from that well the flocks were watered. But the stone was large on the mouth of the well." This means that on the Sabbath a source of living water is opened; this is "a well in the field." The three flocks of sheep are Israel, negating themselves unto God with all their heart, soul, and might. These are called [the three levels of] self, spirit, and soul; all are to be negated unto God.

1:124

Shabbat is a magical time, a moment when the world that often seems a barren "wilderness" is transformed into "field," waiting to be planted. The well is open. But that magic is still only potential, waiting for us to plant the seed and nurture it to grow. Only we can do that; the true miracle is that of our ability to open in response.

4

"But the stone was large on the mouth of the well." It should have said: "There was a large stone on the mouth of the well." This may hint that although the stumbling-stone, our evil urge, is to be found everywhere, "on the mouth of the well" it is at its largest. It does not allow us to open our mouths in prayer, the service of the heart. Prayer is this well, the teaching that is in the mouth. That is why we say [before each *'Amidah* prayer]: "Lord, open my lips, that my mouth may declare Your praise" (Ps. 51:17). The main goal of the evil urge is to postpone prayer, as every religious person knows. That is why it is taught that "the one who defeats this snake gets to marry the daughter of the King."

Really, there is no advice regarding prayer. The more you serve God in all you do, the better you will be able to open your mouth in prayer. That is why it is called the "service of the heart"; it depends upon the longing of the heart—all day long, in all one's deeds. These are "all the flocks" that were gathered there—this is the final result of all one's service.

But of Jacob it says *va-yegal*, which was read to mean "like taking a cork out of a barrel." The *tsaddik* fully understands that this stone is there for special guarding, just as the cork is in the barrel to keep its contents from defilement. To one who stands on the outside it can surely feel as if heavenly forces are holding him back, placing a stone on his heart. But this is all for his own good.

It is also written: "Jacob drew near" (Gen. 29:10). This may be hinting at a parallel to "Abraham drew near" (Gen. 18:23) [when he prayed for Sodom]. There the Midrash taught that "drew near" could mean three things: appeasement, war, and prayer . . . "Come and draw near to pray." These might also be the three prayers we recite each day, the three flocks that enable us to roll away the stone.

1:130

This teaching shows a deep wisdom of religious life, of the sort that is born only of long experience. The difficulty of true prayer, the sense that one is being held back, and the need for divine help in breaking through—these are attested by great seekers the world over. The reminder that prayer or meditation is not an isolated event in human life, but one that needs to be nurtured by one's thoughts and deeds throughout the day, is also a bit of counsel offered by teachers of many traditions. We see here a spiritual master who speaks fully within the particularist language of his own tradition, commenting on a verse of Scripture, using Hebrew wordplays, and all the rest. But the advice he gives has breadth as well as depth and can be understood by anyone who has truly struggled to pray.

וישלח

VA-YISHLAḤ

1

"A man wrestled *(va-ye'aVeK)* with him until the break of day" (Gen. 32:25). Our sages say that they raised up dust *('aVaK)* that rose as high as the Throne of Glory.

This hints at the tradition telling us that Jacob's form is engraved on the Throne of Glory. But in that case, the power of the struggle with the "other side" also reaches that high. Thus it is written: "There is a hand raised over the Throne of God" (Ex. 17:16), meaning that God swears that the Throne will not be whole until Amalek's name is wiped out.

But can it really be that there is some imperfection in God's glorious Throne? This rather means that God's glory cannot be revealed in this world as long as Amalek exists. So, too, the spreading forth of Jacob's power and the revealing of his form—that, too, cannot yet happen in a full way.

That is why "the children of Israel do not eat of the vein sinew on the thigh to this day, because he [the angel of the "other side"] touched the vein sinew in Jacob's thigh" (Gen. 32:33). Of him it says: "The sun shone for him" (vs. 32).

That is why the Midrash teaches that the verse "Jacob was left alone" (vs. 25) is parallel to [the verse] "The Lord will be exalted alone on that day" (Is. 2:11). Neither of them may be revealed until [that day in] the future.

1:156

As long as Amalek continues to exist in this world, Israel, like God, will remain a mystery. Our true nature cannot be revealed, perhaps not even to ourselves, as long as we are distorted by having to defend ourselves against the attack of our ancient and ever-present foe, the one who is manifest in the Hamans and Hitlers of each generation.

The claim makes a good deal of psychological sense. The need to be ever on guard against enemies, whether imagined or real, surely does distort the individual's personality, and even self-perception. This is true of the people as a whole, as has been witnessed so clearly in our generation. The struggle to stand tall enough to say "Never again!" has extracted a great price from the Jew. The need to examine the heart of every non-Jew we meet to ask: "What would he or she have done if . . . ?" has made it infinitely harder to ask what the hasidic master would have us do as we meet the other: "How do I find a way to this person's heart, so that I may share something of God's greatness and our love of God's Torah?"

2

"Your name will no longer be called Jacob, but Israel, for you have struggled with God and with men and have prevailed" (Gen. 32:29). The children of Israel merited both of these names, and they refer to the body and the soul. Every person has to set aright the body, so that the power of soul will dwell upon it. Then one is called "Israel."

Jacob's struggle with the angel took place because the human soul is on a higher rung than the angels are. But this applies to the soul alone. With regard to body, the angel is higher, for the human body is of the world of action [the lowest of the "four worlds"].

But Jacob made his body so right that it merited becoming a throne for God; his body was like soul. Thus he was able to struggle with that angel, even with his physical self. That is why it says: "Your name will no longer be called Jacob," even though the body is called Jacob; in his case it was no longer body, but had been turned into spirit like the soul. That is what Scripture means by [the verse:] "Jacob came to Shalem" (lit.: wholeness; Gen. 33:18). This equalizing of body to soul is called *shalom*.

The struggle of body and soul goes on in every one of Israel. The better you deal with the body, the more wholeness you will attain. That is why the Sabbath is also called *shalom*: it is the time for righting the body, "a foretaste of the world to come." In the future, bodies will be set right, truly just like souls. We have a taste of this on the Sabbath. . . .

1:143

The tradition seems to offer two ways to understanding a teaching such as this. One is the ascetic path. Read this way, the text would be claiming that Jacob so transcended any attachment to base lusts or desires that his body itself became of the category of soul. Even his bodily self was perfected, that is, went beyond its corporeal nature while yet in this world, just as will be the case in the world to come.

The other reading is an older one, yet it may also strike a chord with the biases of today's reader. Jacob worked to perfect himself in body as well as in soul. The Midrash says that Jacob's beauty was as great as that of Adam; this hardly seems to refer to his skills in ascetic self-mastery. It may be that the Sefat Emet understands and appreciates something of this latter reading, one that was so much a part of the program to create a "new Jew" that Zionists would preach in the next generation.

3

"God has been gracious to me, and I have all" (Gen. 33:11). The *Or ha-Hayyim* wrote on this that it was because of God's gift that Jacob lacked nothing. . . .

The meaning of "all" seems to indicate more than Esau meant when he previously said: "I have much" (vs. 9). But how can any person say "all"? Surely there were some things that he didn't have!

But for one who is attached to the upper root, whatever he has is "all." For everything contains a point of divine life. In that point all is included. Thus the Midrash says: "All are considered blind," with regard to Hagar who found the well.

This means that all is really found everywhere, because everything contains that godly life. That is why God is called *shalom*, because every point of divine energy contains all. In this way, the one who draws everything to its source has all. It makes no difference whether it is more or less.

This is the Sabbath, the time when "all [our] desires are fulfilled" and we lack for nothing. That is true wholeness. But Esau referred to "much"; he wanted that "muchness" that comes about from human hands. That which comes by God's power is in oneness; it is only there that the "all" is found.

This also is the meaning of [the aphorism,] "Better one hour of return and good deeds in this world than the entire life of the world to come," and certainly better than this world itself as well. That "one hour" means that all is in oneness, attached to its root above. That is why Jacob can say: "I have all." Understand this.

1:140f.

Here the religious spirit gives the lie to the life of acquisition in which most of us spend our days. The one who has insight—including the insight that the whole dwells fully within each one of its parts—has acquired all that a person needs in this world.

4

"He camped *(HaN)* in front of the city" (Gen. 33:18). It has been taught on this that the place was gracious *(HaN)* to those who dwelt there. For the Land of Israel is set aside for the children of Israel and our holy ancestors. There like found like, as Scripture says: "God has chosen Zion" (Ps. 132:13) and "God chose Jacob as His own" (Ps. 135:4). Therefore it is also written: "God will not abandon His people, nor will He leave His inheritance [the land]" (Ps. 94:14), for each depends upon the other.

It was by the power of our ancestors that the Holy Land was made into a holy place, a dwelling for God's glory. Of this Scripture says: "Happy are they who dwell in Your house" (Ps. 84:5). The sages taught with regard to "Seir the Hurrite, dwellers in the land" (Gen. 36:20), that "they tasted the land like snakes," meaning that they understood the land physically, how to turn it into a dwelling-place. But Israel made it an inner dwelling; that is why [only] they are called "they who dwell in Your house." They understood that the place was waiting for holiness. "God desired it as His dwelling" (Ps. 132:13). This was brought about by the patriarchs and by King David, who said [in that same psalm]: "Surely I will not come into my own dwelling-tent, nor go up to my bed; neither will I allow my eyes to sleep nor my eyelids to slumber, until I find a place for God, a dwelling for the mighty One of Jacob" (vv. 3–5).

1:154f.

The holy land and the holy people are drawn to one another; this theme is repeated numerous times in the Sefat Emet. *For all his strongly mythic sense of the land's holiness, our author is very much in the biblical tradition when noting that the land becomes holy only through Israel's dwelling there. Unlike sacred time, which is proclaimed from the moment of Creation itself, sacred space is such only because of the presence and the efforts of the holy people.*

But the land is holy, and is home, to others besides Jews. Spoken in Poland, before Jewish propriety over the land was conceivable, these claims of unique spiritual rootedness existed in the safety of a historical vacuum. When read in our own day, they also contain a dark and dangerous side that their author, never having encountered either the physical land or its non-Jewish inhabitants, could not have predicted.

VA-YESHEV

1

"His brothers saw that Jacob loved him more than all his brothers; they hated him and were not able to speak well of him" (Gen. 37:4). The verse does not mention that Joseph's brothers hated him because of his talebearing. In fact, it seems likely that Jacob did not tell them of the bad reports Joseph brought about them. Rather, it seems that the reason the Torah tells us that "Joseph brought ill reports about them to their father" (vs. 2) is to establish a reason why Joseph had to be sold to Egypt. Had he remained with their father and continued to bring those ill reports, the tribes would have been pushed aside altogether.

The meaning is thus: The task of the *tsaddik* is to raise up before God the good deeds of Israel. But Joseph was not yet

55

sufficiently whole until after his trial; only then is he called Joseph the *tsaddik*, bringing up only the good deeds. Then they could all be together with their father. But prior to this, when he would still bring in those bad reports, it was necessary for him to go down into Egypt.

Why, then, should any sin be ascribed to the brothers in selling [Joseph] to Egypt? Because if all their deeds had been proper in the first place, there would have been no danger in his telling their father of all they did. Then he never would have had to go down to Egypt. Thus they are, after all, the cause of his descent.

1:165

The tale of Joseph appears to the modern reader as a surprisingly "secular" narrative within the Torah. God seems to recede as an active participant in the events of the story, one that is about human destiny and the complexities of family relationships. But for the hasidic reader, the tale of Joseph is about the education and forming of a tsaddik; *Joseph is the figure most commonly called* tsaddik, *or "righteous one," in the rabbinic tradition. A prime task of the* tsaddik *is to defend mortals before their heavenly Father. The righteous one should be able to judge every person generously, bringing only "good reports" about each one to the Father. Joseph has to go through the trials of being sold into Egypt in order to become such a person. Hasidic teaching, especially in Poland, became very sensitive to the question of inherited spiritual leadership as it was practiced within the movement. Our Father Jacob was a true* tsaddik, *but that alone did not qualify Joseph to follow him. The son needed his own formative suffering in order to become the one who would speak up for his people before their Father.*

2

. . . There are two sorts of trials. One sort can be overcome by a person's own efforts. The other trial is a greater one, in which sheer strength cannot be victorious at all. In a case like this, the pure desire and the honest and just heart of the righteous person allow choice to be removed altogether, thus avoiding the trial. This is considered divine intervention.

[Hear this in Joseph's words regarding his trial with Potiphar's wife, where] Scripture says: "He refused, saying to his master's wife: 'My lord knows nothing of that [which I do] in the house; all that is his he has placed in my hands . . .'" (Gen. 39:8). Now I have elsewhere said that God gives us choices in all we desire to do, asking only one thing of us: that we remember the yoke of God's blessed kingdom, recalling that all comes to us from God. This much we surely have to keep.

Now understand this meaning within the ongoing words of Joseph: "And he [He] has kept nothing from me, except for you insofar as you are his wife" (vs. 9). That should suffice for the wise.

In this way Joseph was able to avoid having to choose; he remembered that choice itself is given by God. Therefore, it is not fair that we transgress the divine will. Even though he couldn't overcome temptation by his own strength, the pain he felt over this caused God to deliver him from his trial.

This was our first preparation for exile, since Egypt contained within it all of our exiles. The essence of exile is that it makes for additional choice. If there were no need to choose, humanity would be truly free. When we are able to avoid choosing we [will] come to complete redemption. Understand this.

1:164

In this teaching we see reflected an approach most closely associated with Mordecai Joseph of Izbica, a fellow disciple of the Kotsker with the Sefat Emet's grandfather Yizḥak Meir. The Izbicer believed in the abandonment of freedom of the will. He sought to have his disciples see freedom as illusory, recognizing that all comes from God, and that the only seeming "freedom" humans have is that of doing evil and abandoning the path of truth. One who wants to lead the good life should pray that such freedom be taken from him; only in this way can our willfullness be fully subjugated to the good.

3

"He left his garment in her hand and fled outside" (Gen. 39:12). He fled right out of his bodily garb. This is as in [what was said of Abraham]: "He took him *outside*" (Gen. 15:5), as I have explained elsewhere.

It is written: "You have joined a person to our head; we have come through fire and water, but You have brought us out to satiety" (Ps. 66:12). Because of the first sin, we were given "garments of skin" that came from the primal snake. We were garbed in "personhood" and corporeality. Now we first have to set the body aright. We do this through love and fear, which are bodily feelings. Only afterwards can we attain inwardness.

In principle the patriarchs set right the sin of Adam. "Fire and water" refers to Abraham and Isaac; "You have brought us out to satiety" refers to Jacob, of whom it is said: "You give truth to Jacob" (Mic. 7:20). "Truth" is that which was before the sin, for it was the snake who brought falsehood into the world.

Joseph was drawn after the way of Jacob, as it says: "These are the generations of Jacob: Joseph" (Gen. 37:2). "And he made him a colorful garment" (vs. 3)—these were the "garments of light" that existed in Eden. That is how "he fled outside"—he stripped off his corporeal self.

1:180

This teaching may be considered one of the more "kabbalistic" passages in the Sefat Emet, *which does not often use those mythic symbols in an ordered way. Abraham and Isaac respectively represent water and fire, the grace of God and the judgment of God, the right and left hands. Jacob, called "truth," is the mediating force between them, containing the satiety of proper balance. Joseph, in the chart of divine potencies or* sefirot, *is positioned directly below Jacob, following in his path. Jacob is seen already by the rabbis as the most perfect of humans, the one who repairs that which Adam had destroyed. Here Joseph follows in that path by returning to the way of Eden, the time before the garments of light had turned into those of skin. This is taken by the kabbalists to mean that Adam had a light-body, a more pure or less corporeal self, when he still lived within the Garden of Eden. Joseph, who represents sexual purity in this world, was able to replicate that self.*

MI-KETS

1

The Torah here tells of dreams, referring to the seven years of plenty and the seven years of famine. They are a hint to us that the power of the "other side" [or the evil forces] exists only because divine bounty is hidden in times of exile. They have no power, God forbid, outside the divine life-energy. This is the meaning of the "swallowing up" in the dreams and the fact that the cows or sheaves of plenty "could not be detected." It appears as though these forces had some power of their own, but that is not the case.

This had to be shown to Pharaoh before the exile. Even though Israel were going to be subject to him, there is no power that stands opposed to God. This is why the Torah speaks of a Pharaoh "who had not known Joseph" (Ex. 1:8), meaning that he had forgotten this lesson as well.

What can we learn from this passage? To prepare ourselves well in days of plenty, in those times when holiness is apparent to us. We should fix that radiance firmly in our hearts, so it may be there for the bad times when holiness is hidden . . .

1:182

Though heir to the kabbalistic tradition, which taught of an ongoing battle between forces of good and very real evil powers, Hasidism rejects this dualistic view of the mystical tradition. Divinity is everywhere; there is no other source of being. All that exists is of God, whether revealed or in hiding. But the power of hiding, the exile of the mind from any awareness of divine presence, can sometimes be very great. And the evil that human beings can perpetrate in the course of hiding from God's light can indeed be without end.

Scripture says: "He placed testimony in Jehoseph [adding the letter *heh* to Joseph] when he went forth over the land of Egypt; I heard a language I did not know" (Ps. 81:6). The rabbis say that Gabriel came and taught Joseph the seventy languages of humanity, but he could not fully learn them. Then the angel added a *heh* to his name and he learned them. This is a surprising comment. First of all, what kind of Torah is it to learn seventy languages? If Pharaoh knew them all, could Joseph [in his wisdom] not learn them? And of what help was the letter *heh* in all this?

But we have to understand this together with another Midrash, one that comments on [the verse:] "Moses agreed to explain this entire Torah" (Deut. 1:5). This means, says the Midrash, that he explained it to them in seventy languages. For all seventy languages flow forth from the holy tongue; it is the Torah that gives life to all those languages. They are something like varied garments, but their intent is all one. The languages indeed differ in their movements [lit.: "vowels"], but the things said in the Torah can be garbed in all languages.

Now Joseph the *tsaddik*, who came to rule over Egypt by the power of Torah, had to know all the languages and join them to the holy tongue. As preparation for the exile in Egypt, Israel's first exile, Joseph had to attain mastery over all the languages. That is why the *heh* was added to his name, for "this world was created by a *heh*, as it is written: *be-hibar'am/be-he bera'am*" (Gen. 2:4); "He created them with a *heh*." It is therefore within the power of this letter to draw all languages after the life of inwardness, which is the holy tongue.

1:185

The faith that Hebrew is the original language of Creation, or the core of all human speech, is deeply embedded in Jewish tradition. This has particular meaning for the mystics, who describe God's Creation by means of the word as closely related to the inner workings of the sacred tongue. Joseph not only learned all the languages of humanity, he learned them through the heh, *the sacred letter by which this world was formed. In this way he learned to redeem them from their status as merely profane speech, and to tie them to true, that is, sacred, language, the brimming cup of inner divine and human meaning. It is this act of Joseph's that allows for the translation of sacred speech, and the bearing of Torah's truth into all the endless varieties of human language.*

A contemporary and more universalist mystical Judaism will balk at this claim for Hebrew, even though it was once widely believed by Christians as well as Jews. We would have to say that our version of God's universal Torah is in Hebrew, while we trust that the God of all has versions of the Primal Teaching in each of the "seventy" (and many more!) languages and cultures. The original Torah, that which existed before the world, was not yet divided into words or letters. Only as it was "given" to each people did the universal Word of God have to be translated into specific words and letters.

3

[Another comment on the same passage:]

. . . For Joseph's descent into Egypt was preparation for the exile in Egypt. The purpose of that exile was to prepare for receiving the Torah, to purify speech. That is why the Psalm goes on to say: "I am the Lord your God who brought you up from the Land of Egypt; open wide your mouth and I will fill it" (vs. 11).

Thus, when Joseph came forth from prison he had acquired knowledge of all the seventy languages, as preparation for all of Israel, who were created to bear witness to the Creator. They have to make this witness clear in every language, as Scripture says: "Hear, O Israel!" (Deut. 6:4), meaning "in every language in which you can hear."

But the covenant of the mouth [the revelation at Sinai] depends upon the covenant of the flesh [circumcision]. These two covenants are represented by Judah and Joseph. It is true that testimony is mainly through the mouth; this is Judah's strength, and that is why the other tribes followed him. But the root that underlies the possibility of opening the mouth for this testimony belongs to Joseph, [the symbol of circumcision and sexual purity]. This is, "He placed testimony in Jehoseph," for testimony depends on him.

The Talmud says that Joseph, who sanctified the divine name in secret [by not submitting to temptation with Potiphar's wife], merited having a letter of God's name added to his own. But Judah, who did so in public [at the splitting of the sea], is called entirely by God's name [YeHUdaH contains the full divine name within it]. This is as we have said: speech belongs mainly to the public realm, that of Judah, but the secret root of speech belongs to Joseph.

1:196

The two covenants represent two purities, the verbal and the sexual, which the tradition sees as deeply tied to one another. They represent the two ways in which the individual reaches out to the human other in order to form ties. In both of these parallel realms, we are capable of beauty and degradation, of holiness and betrayal. Speech is the more public of these realms; thus Judah receives the greater reward for sanctifying God's name in public. But the authenticity of his testimony depends also on the holiness with which he lives his private life. There it is Joseph, resister of temptation, who remains the ideal of the tsaddik.

VA-YIGGASH

1

The Sabbath table-song of Rabbi Isaac Luria contains the phrase: "To come into the entrance-ways of the apple field" (a symbol-term for Shekhinah). Why does he refer to "the entrance-ways"? Does one not come directly "into the apple field"?

The truth is that this apple field is everywhere, as Scripture says: "The whole earth is filled with His glory!" (Is. 6:3). This is also taught with regard to the verse: "See, the smell of my son is like the smell of the field" (Gen. 27:27).

But the essential task of worship is the opening of this point. On the Sabbath that gate is indeed open, as it is written: "The gate to the inner courtyard . . . will be closed on the six workdays and open on the Sabbath" (Ezek. 46:1). We see that the

Sabbath is holy among days, for it is a foretaste of the world to come, even though it is within time. The difference between Sabbath and weekday is the opening of inwardness. "The light of a person's face on the Sabbath is unlike that on weekdays." Thus it is easy to experience holiness on the Sabbath.

In the same way, we should understand that the glory of God's kingdom is everywhere, even though it is not apparent. This is the faith that every Jew has in God's oneness. The meaning of "One" is that there is nothing except God Himself; God is the all. Even though we are incapable of understanding this properly, we still need to have faith in it. This faith will lead us to truth.

I have taught elsewhere that truth and faith represent two rungs. These are represented by Joseph and Judah, as the Midrash on [the verse] "One approaches the other [lit.: the one]" (Job 41:8) says. This is also the meaning of [the verse:] "On that day shall the Lord be one and His name one" (Zech. 14:9). This oneness within all of Creation will become clear in the future; it is called "the secret of oneness" because it is now a hidden mystery. God's oneness is beyond our creaturely power to conceive. It is referred to in [the verse:] "All that is called by My name I have created, formed, and made for My glory" (Is. 43:7), for this world was created by His blessed name.

This is the meaning of "*Bi* [lit.: 'please' but read here as 'within me'], my lord" (Gen. 44:18). Rabbi Isaac Luria noted that the letters of Judah's name contain "YHWH within me." By means of faith that God oversees all, a person can set himself right even in times of hiding. Then you should have faith that you have within yourself the soul of the living God, as every Jew says [in the daily prayers]: "The soul You placed within me is pure."

When you negate yourself before this divine life-point, wanting to know the truth, it will be revealed to you. We find this with Judah [for right after he said, "my Lord is within me"] we read that "Joseph was no longer able to hold back" (Gen. 45:1).

1:247

Here we have one of the most unabashedly mystical teachings in the Sefat Emet, *a brief but classical statement of the unique faith of Hasidism. Nothing but God exists; this world lies entirely within His glory or His holy apple field, which is not separable from the divine self. It is only to us that divinity seems distant or closed off; we have to seek the entranceway, our own path into consciousness of the all-enveloping divine reality. You will do this best, the reader is here told, by recognizing the same ultimately simple truth that Judah did.* Bi adoni *("my Lord is within me"). When you have learned this lesson and can live it, with regard to both yourself and others, all the rest is indeed just commentary.*

2

[A composite of three teachings:]

"Joseph was no longer able to hold back." For it is written: "Judah approached him" (Gen. 44:18). The "him" here refers to Joseph, to Judah's own self, and also to God. The meaning is as follows: Judah offered nothing new in his words, nor did he have a good claim with which to approach Joseph. But as he clarified the truth of the matter, salvation came to him. "Truth grows from the earth" (Ps. 85:12).

The fact is that this entire account of Joseph and his brothers is an allegory for Israel's worship of the blessed Holy One . . . and this is its meaning. The whole world is filled with God's glory; even in the place of darkness, God's glorious rule is hidden. "Even darkness is not dark for You" (Ps. 139:12). For this reason, any person in trouble who negates himself before truth and hands over his soul, as did Judah, can have truth revealed to him. Judah said: "How will I go up to my father?" (Gen. 44:34) and was willing to be a servant in Egypt, so as not to sin before his father. Because of this, he came to see that all was for the good, and he had nothing to fear at all, for [Joseph said] "I am Joseph. . . . " (1:249)

"Judah approached him . . . [for your servant took responsibility for the lad]." Each person is responsible for his soul, the

King's daughter, to bring her back to her Father in heaven. Even if that soul is very sullied by sin, an act of repentance from the depth of the heart, as expressed in [the question,] "How will I go up to my Father?" can transform sins into merits. Thus Scripture says, "I am Joseph." Even though we have no clear understanding of how this process of transformation of sins into merits takes place, it is the power of the Maker in that which He has made. Just as a person can transform the heart by an act of true repentance, so can all the deeds of sin be transformed as well.

Israel are in fact God's own portion and lot. "Even a Jew who sins remains a Jew." Because of this, we can be strong enough to approach that divine power hidden within us. . . . "Judah approached him" mean[s] that he approached himself. He said: "My Lord is within me," as we have already written. . . . (1:248)

. . . Then surely "Joseph was no longer able to hold back." It is the inner point within each thing that is called Joseph [meaning "more"; that "extra something"]. This is hidden only because of our defilement. There is a "shell" that hides and darkens as though, God forbid, the thing were separate from God. But through humility and true self-negation, the inward becomes revealed, and it is clear that it is "your brother."

This is the meaning of "my Lord is in me." He still maintained the faith that the divine life was contained within him, even though it was hidden and he did not know how. All this had brought about the sin. But truly, "my Lord is within me." This is true of every hiding. . . . (1:246)

1:246, 1:248, 1:249

Mystical religion as described here begins not in experience but in faith. Judah knows, perhaps intuits, that his Lord is within [him] even while sin still blinds him from the realization that this is the truth of experience. The tenacity of this faith built up within him is so powerful that it finally tears the blinders off his eyes, allowing him to see the inner point. Even after that initial experience of seeing, faith and trust in the truth of such a moment are key to the mystic's ongoing

religious life. As every God-seeker knows, insight we had yes-
terday is worth little to us, except as a reminder when we
struggle for it again tomorrow.

3

The Midrash quotes the verse: "Counsel is like deep water in
the human heart; the wise one draws it forth" (Prov. 20:5).

It was the task of Judah and the tribes to draw water from
deep wells, as it is said: "Drink water from your own cistern
[and water from your well]" (Prov. 5:15). In every individual
Jew in this world, and within the world as a whole, there are
hidden lights, because "God has founded the world with wisdom" (Prov. 3:19). This is the religious work of the weekday:
to separate the "food" from the waste.

But the aspect of Joseph draws new light from the heavenly
root. This is [the meaning of] "and water from *Your* well," the
well that flows forever, the one of which it says: "I will pour
pure water over you" (Ezek. 36:25). This is the written Torah.
"Deep water in the human heart" is the oral Torah, the "eternal life implanted within us."

These treasures are hidden in the human heart. Of these
Scripture says: "Seek it like silver; search for it as for a treasure" (Prov. 2:4). On this verse the Rabbi [R. Simḥa Bunem] of
Przysucha taught the following: The verse says that you
should seek it like silver and search for it like a treasure.
"Seeking" is like a person who wants to acquire something,
while "searching" is usually a matter of getting back something you've had and lost. The difference is that the latter, the
one who has lost something, is the more upset while in the
process of searching. But when he finds it, his joy is not so
great, because that which he finds was, after all, already his.
The "seeker" [who does not think he has lost anything] is just
the opposite. His sorrow is not so great, but his joy is even
greater. That is why Scripture says that the religious life requires both: you should feel sorry and struggle hard to find
that which you lost. But when you find it, you should have

great joy, like one who just happened upon a tremendous treasure. How gracious were that wise man's words!

I think both are true, that both sorts of worship are to be found in every person. You need to realize the potential within you, to seek out the lost treasure within your own soul. This search after your own loss is the religious work of the weekday. But you also have to seek "help from the Holy" (Ps. 20:3), the newness that comes from heaven. That is the Sabbath, which is called "a goodly gift." That is why there is so much happiness and joy on the Sabbath, while the week requires so much of struggle and hard labor.

1:257f.

The first part of this teaching returns to the theme of written and oral Torah that we have seen earlier. The oral Torah is that which comes from within the self; it is the basis for our commentary on, hence our understanding of, the written Torah that comes from God. The one who has no sense of Torah from within the self cannot live the life of Torah, since the written Torah without commentary stands beyond our grasp. Religious life demands inner search.

Of this search for Torah within the self, R. Simha Bunem asks a nice question: Are we recovering something that we had and lost, or gaining something new? The answer, like the answers to many of these seeming "either/or" questions, is of course yes!

VA-YEHI

1

"Jacob lived in the Land of Egypt" (Gen. 47:28). My grandfather and teacher said on this verse: "With the quality of truth you can live even in the Land of Egypt! And it says: 'Give truth unto Jacob'" (Mic. 7:20). Scripture could have just said: "Jacob *was* in the Land of Egypt." It wanted to teach that he was truly alive, even in Egypt. "Life" here means being attached to the root and source from which the life-force ever flows. The holy Zohar in fact says something similar in *Parashat Va-Yiggash* on "the spirit of their father Jacob came alive" (Gen. 45:27).

It seems to me that this "life" is the same as that in the phrase "living waters." The soul's joy arouses the source of life, and more of the life-force flows forth. (That may also be

why it says: "And Adam became a living soul" [Gen. 2:7].
"Soul" refers to desire; it is the innermost soul that constantly
draws forth life.)

Even though he was in the Land of Egypt, he knew that all
of "Egypt" was just a hiding "shell," inside which there was
nothing but that divine life-force. That is why the sages say
that "the wicked are called dead in their lifetimes," because
they are separated from the source of life.

The Midrash says on the verse "For we are strangers before
You" (1 Chron. 29:15) that human beings were not created in
this world in order that [they] attach [themselves], God forbid,
to worldly things. The purpose was just the opposite: when
humans attach themselves to the root of life, this-worldly
things are drawn near to God along with them. The word *ger*
(stranger) means "drawing forth," or "bringing up," just as the
cud-chewing animal brings up its *gerah*. But *ger* also refers to
one who is converted, for such a person brings forth a holy
point that was lost among the heathen. The same thing is true
of the exile in Egypt, where [it is said:] "Your seed will be
strangers" *(ger)* (Gen. 15:13), in order to draw forth holy sparks
that were lost there. That is why it says: "And afterwards they
will go forth with great property" (Gen. 15:14, referring to the
sparks).

This is why RaSHI says that "Jacob sought to reveal the end,
but it was hidden from him." He wanted to make it clear that
exile is just a matter of hiding, and that the power within
comes only from God. But had this been revealed, there would
have been no exile at all, so "it was hidden." Still, the holy
Zohar tells us, he revealed what he wanted, but in a hidden
way. This means that by faith you can find the truth, and it
can become clear that it's all a matter of hiding.

That is why "Jacob lived" is a closed section [that is, it begins in mid-paragraph in the Torah scroll]. The fact that this
source of life is to be found even in the Land of Egypt is hidden
(and this was the beginning of enslavement). I believe my
grandfather quoted the Rabbi of Przysucha as wondering why
Jacob wanted to reveal the end. His answer was that when the
end is known, exile is made easier. That's all I remember, but

it seems to mean the same: revealing the end means knowing there is an end to exile, and that shows it to be but a matter of hiding, not a force of its own. Inwardness is truth, and that is endless; only the hiding has an end. Jacob wanted to reveal this, but then there would have been no exile at all, so it remained hidden. Nevertheless, by the faith Jews have that there is no power other than God, even if it is all hidden, even if you can't see it with your eyes, you can still come to see truth within faith. Jacob our Father just wanted there to be no mistake about this, that it all be obvious, but that goal eluded him. You need to struggle to find truth. This is the quality of King David, who has nothing of his own. He achieves truth only by self-negation. And that is the difference between truth and faith.

Thus my grandfather and teacher wrote about the passage in the Talmud where Rabbi Yohanan says: "Jacob our Father did not die." When the sages objected: "But was he mourned, embalmed, and buried for naught?" Rabbi Yohanon answered: "I am just interpreting Scripture." When a person seeks to interpret Scripture and struggles at it, oral Torah is created. Such a person can find some of the light that comes from Jacob our Father's *living* even within the hiding. . . .

1:264

Jacob represents the quality of truth, a power so great that it can live, *in the emphatic sense of having true vitality, even in the darkness of exile. Jacob was truly alive even in Egypt. This means that none of the tribulations of this world is a sufficient excuse to keep us from being fully alive, from appreciating God's world to the highest of our abilities.*

The only danger was that the light of Jacob's truth might have been so bright that it would have given the lie to exile altogether, showing Egyptian bondage to be no more than an illusion. But the time was not right for this: Jacob's truth has to remain hidden up to a certain point, so that exile can seem real and we see our need to struggle against it with all our might. Only in that way will we do our work of redeeming sparks, of bringing ever more points of light out of hiding.

That is the task we are given. But how do we sustain ourselves when truth has to be hidden? That is the role of faith. Faith gives us the courage to struggle against the darkness until finally we reveal its secret and come to the place of truth, which will finally tell us that really there was only light all along. Our model in this struggle is King David the psalmist, who cries out to God in faith even from the midst of the darkest night, trusting that God's light still shines.

2

The Midrash asks why this is a closed *parashah*. Scripture would seem to praise the actions of Jacob, who lived in Egypt for seventeen years and remained attached to life. All the defilement of Egypt couldn't stand up against his holiness. Those seventeen years were preparation for the entire exile.

Yet this *parashah* remains closed to us. We still don't understand how he drew that holy life into Egypt. If we really got that, there would be no exile at all. But surely it is within the Jew's power to arouse life anywhere! Of this it is said: "He has placed our souls in life" (Ps. 66:9), and it is written: "He blew the breath of life into his nostrils, and the person became a living soul" (Gen. 2:7). "Soul" refers to desire, and a person can arouse the life-force through desire. The children of Israel are attached to life.

But the sages taught that Jacob sought to reveal the end and it was hidden from him. They compare this to the king's friend who was about to reveal the confidences of the king, until he saw the king standing over him; then he changed the subject to something else. This is surprising: surely Jacob could not have wanted to hide his deeds from God! The meaning is rather that he sought to show them the depths of evil. He wanted God's kingdom to be revealed to them everywhere, even down to the lowest rung. That is why he referred to "the end of days" (Gen. 49:1), the time when God's face is hidden.

But the blessed Holy One did not want this [revealed], in order that there be an exile, for such was God's will. That is why the Shekhinah was revealed to Jacob; because there was a revelation taking place, he could not "reveal the end." "The end" is only there in hiding.

This was Jacob's way: he was always putting himself into places where there was danger. He wanted to open them up for his descendants. He hinted at this when he said: "The angel who redeemed me from all evil, may he bless the lads" (Gen. 48:16). This shows that he had gone down into all the evil places and bcen saved from them. He wanted to teach this way to his children, but it was closed to him.

1:267f.

Jacob our Father is here depicted as a good hasidic rebbe, willing even to defy God out of love for God's children. He had hoped to show his sons that God is present even in the lowest and darkest corners of existence. This would take the fear out of those places and reveal them not to be intrinsically evil after all. But perhaps no loving ancestor can do this work for descendants yet to come. Each generation has to struggle on its own with the relationship between God and evil.

 3

"Jacob called his sons and said: 'Gather and I will tell you what will happen to you at the end of days'" (Gen. 49:1). The Midrash asks whence Israel earned the right to recite "Hear, O Israel" and answers that it came from Jacob. Thus it says: "This is what their father said to them" (49:28)—he gave them the power of speech.

It is by this power that Israel bear witness to the Creator, as it is written: "the lips of truth *(sefat emet)* will stand forever" (Prov. 12:19). Jacob stands for truth, as it says: "Give truth unto Jacob" (Mic. 7:20). The tribes, his sons, are "the lips of truth," for speech is made whole by the lips. Previously there had been a single language *(safah)*, but in the generation of Babel, because they did not cleave to truth, the power of speech was taken from them and left only for Israel. Scripture

says: "You *['atem]* are My witnesses, says the Lord" (Is. 43:10).
This means that the power of the twenty-two letters [from
'aleph to *tav*] and the holy tongue [represented by the letter
mem], the language used by the ministering angels, has been
given to Israel. This is one of the ways we are similar to angels, in speaking the holy tongue.

This is the difference between *safah* and *sefat* (both mean
either "lip" or "language"): the lips both complete the word
and hide or seal up that which should not be spoken. *Safah,*
ending in the *heh,* is open; *sefat,* ending in *tav,* is closed until
that future when "I will convert the nations to a pure language *(safah),* that they all call upon the name of the Lord"
(Zeph. 3:9).

But truly it is through the *sefat emet* ("true speech" or
"honest talk") of Israel that all the restoration of the future
will come about. This is [the meaning of] "will stand forever,"
in an active sense: by means of this true speech, all languages
will be restored. Jacob left to his children this power of the
holy tongue. Therefore, Scripture says: "Remember the days
of yore; consider the years of generations. Ask your father and
he will tell you; your elders and they will say it to you" (Deut.
32:7). [This continues] "I will tell you" [of Gen. 49:1]. Every
day the children of Israel have to seek out the truth and it will
be revealed to them. Thus Scripture says: "Give truth unto
Jacob"—in the present. Every day, by the power of calling out
the *Shema'.*

1:281

*The relationship of truth and language is a key theme in this
book entitled* The Language of Truth. *Israel know the truth
of God deep in their hearts. But they also need the power to
express that truth; this gift of language and expression, the
power to cry out "shema' yisra'el," begins with the tribes' response to their dying father, in the moment when they
wanted to assure him that his ways had not been forgotten
in the exile of Egypt. "Listen, Father Israel!" they called out,
"as we still proclaim that God is One!"*

שמות

SEFER SHEMOT

SHEMOT

1

"It came to pass in the course of those many days that the king of Egypt died. The children of Israel sighed because of their bondage, and they cried out, and their cry rose up to God because of the bondage" (Ex. 2:23).

My grandfather and teacher commented that until the king died they were so deeply sunk in exile that they did not even feel it. But now the process of redemption began, and they became aware of their exile and started to sigh. This is also the meaning of [the verse:] "I will bring you forth from beneath the sufferings of Egypt" (Ex. 6:6), meaning that [Israel] will no longer be able to put up with the ways of Egypt.

Surely there are several rungs in each exile. "He brings forth the prisoners"; "He delivers the humble"; "He helps the poor"—these are three different aspects [of redemption from exile].

The middle rung [comprises] those who are prisoners in exile; they are unable to broaden out that point of divine life that is within them. They need to be brought forth from that prison. "The humble" are the righteous; they themselves are not really in exile, but they remain there only for the common good. Such was the case with Moses, who had already been a shepherd. He was prepared for redemption. In essence he was no longer in exile at all, but was there just to redeem Israel. The same was true of the light in those seventy souls who came into Egypt; they were there just to make for redemption. This is "He delivers the humble." But "He helps the poor" refers to those lowly ones who do not yet even feel their exile; they are in need of the greatest salvation. This is the beginning of redemption: "I will bring you forth from beneath the sufferings of Egypt."

This is why there are four terms for redemption [mentioned in the Torah. Those are three, and the fourth is] "I will take you as My people" (Ex. 6:7). This is the purpose of redemption, the uplifting that was the reason for the entire exile.

Something like this is true of every exile. But more than that, all these rungs seem to exist in every person as well. Every Jew has some inner place in which he is a free person. This is especially true since we have already come out of Egypt: now there is surely something free in every Jew. This helps the person to prepare for redemption. That which is true of the people as a whole is true of each individual person as well.

2:18

Each of us slaves has a free inner tsaddik, *a part of us that has never submitted to our bondage, or that has already been made free. Finding that self within us and allowing it to help us become free—that's how we are going to find the rest of our way out of Egypt. We will only be truly motivated to seek out that redeemer within ourselves when even our inner "poor," even the lowliest part of us, is no longer willing to put up with the suffering and degradation of our enslavement.*

The hasidic master sees himself as rebbe both to the Jewish people and to each individual. That which is true of the nation is true of each person; Hasidism sees much of liberation as an inner individual struggle. But the collective desire to liberate Jewry as a whole from bondage is also never far from the surface in these teachings.

2

The Midrash quotes the verse: "He announces His ways to Moses, His acts to the children of Israel" (Ps. 103:7).

We are told that "whoever participates in the pain of the community will get to see the community's consolation." Thus it is written about mourning for the destruction: "Rejoice in gladness with her, all you who did mourn for her" (Is. 66:10). Now we have to understand what this claim means: if this means that the one of whom we speak will see the building of Jerusalem in his own lifetime, will this merit not be shared by the whole generation [even the undeserving]? But if it means that this person who participated in the community's pain will keep on living until Jerusalem is rebuilt, we have to note how many righteous persons have already died before that has taken place!

The real meaning is that one comes to see the community's consolation right there in the midst of its suffering. Exile is only a hiding. If you can manage to remove that hiding from yourself by making your heart pure and clear, you will be able to see "the community's consolation." This is the meaning of "Rejoice . . . with her"—with the community of Israel; even while she is in exile, joy is hidden up within her, for she knows that she is one day going to be the crown upon the king's head. So whoever truly takes part in her suffering is able to see her joy as well.

This is what happened with Moses. Because "he saw into their suffering" (Ex. 2:11), the blessed Holy One showed him the redemption and the giving of Torah, for this was the entire purpose of the exile. The Midrash says that the exile of Egypt was the suffering that preceded [and led up to] Torah. Every exile since then and until now is preparation in suffering for the world that is still to come. And just as in Egypt, "the more they tortured them, the more they flourished" (Ex. 1:12), so it is in all our exiles. And since the reward of messianic days and the world still to come is without measure, so is the suffering that leads up to it without a fixed limit of time.

Now let us go back to our verse. God showed Moses the special hidden light that was to be born out of this suffering. "He announces His ways to Moses." Israel were able to see it only after it had come to pass; thus "His acts." Moses saw the "ways" before they came to be, "in a flame of fire, in the midst of the bush" (Ex. 3:2). So it is with the righteous who take part always in the pain of exile: that of Shekhinah and that of Israel. They deserve to feel the light of redemption while it is still on its way.

2:11

But now something of redemption surely has come about. Israel are in the Land of Israel, the exiles are gathered together, and peace is hopefully, if ever so slowly, on its way. Surely all of us should be able to see something of it by now. But do those who for so long took part in Israel's suffering get to see the glimmer of hope for redemption? Here I think of the generation of holocaust survivors who built new lives and gave so much toward the building of Israel. Surely the faith they had to go forward bears within it something of what the Sefat Emet is describing here.

 3

The Midrash on "Moses was" (Ex. 3:1) says that he was prepared for redemption. Thus it says: "a refuge in times of trouble" (Ps. 9:10); the word *misgav* (refuge) is numerically the same as "Moses." He is the prince of Torah, which is called "strength." Freedom depends entirely on Torah, as our sages have said: "There is no one free except the one who studies

Torah." Now if the one who studies Torah is considered free, surely Moses, who brought the Torah down from heaven, is the master of freedom.

The real freedom that comes about by means of Torah is the freedom of the soul from its bodily prison. This takes place through the Torah. "In the beginning God created"—for the sake of Torah, which is called "beginning"; God consulted the Torah and created the world. This was the way of Torah: to create the world and to hide within it the power of His deeds. By means of Torah, Israel would be able to realize this hidden light throughout Creation.

That is why the Book of Exodus begins: "And these are the names." The *and* indicates that this is adding on to what came before. Just as the world was created by Torah, so did the whole of both exile and redemption in Egypt come about by the power of Torah. This completed Creation. "The mouth that bound is the mouth that loosened." It was the power of Torah that hid everything within nature; this same power now loosens the bonds, "saying to the prisoners: Go forth!" (Is. 49:9).

2:17f.

The real exile is a universal one, beginning with Creation, not Egypt. It is the hiding of divine light, the slipping of supernatural, wondrous truth into the sheath of the natural and the ordinary that has us in bondage. Israel's exile in Egypt— and later—is a dramatic representation of this universal human situation. The mystics understand the redemption from Egypt as the first phase of the needed redemption of the human mind from this "exile" or "slavery" of inner blindness. In this sense all humanity may be said to participate in the symbolic Exodus. Exile of the mind surely does not belong to us Jews alone!

"In a flame of fire from the midst of the bush" (Ex. 3:2). The Midrash says that this is to show [that] "there is no place devoid of the divine presence—not even a thornbush." This is the purpose of exile: that Israel make visible His kingdom, which is indeed everywhere. The true meaning of the word *galut* (exile) is *hitgalut* (revelation), that the glory of God's kingdom be revealed in every place. This task is completed by the souls of Israel in this world, as the Midrash says on the verse: "I am asleep but my heart wakes. The sound of my beloved knocking: 'Open for me!'" (Cant. 5:2).

The blessed Holy One has chosen us and given us the Torah. Torah is beyond time; just as for the Holy One, past and future are all one. In that case, the choosing of Israel and their attachment to God that happened when Torah was given were already revealed to God "beforehand" as well. This powerful attachment to Torah—even though it was still hidden and unrealized by Israel—was still "the sound of my beloved knocking: 'Open for me,'" calling them to make this attachment real by opening "as wide as the eye of a needle."

Holiness can be revealed in this world only through the opening that Israel make. When we said: "We shall do and we shall listen" (Ex. 24:7), we were making real the light of Torah, to which we were already attached somewhere deep within ourselves. Now that we have accepted the Torah, this is even clearer. The sound of Torah pounds in Israel's hearts. Even though exile hides it, we need only long that it be revealed. Thus it was in the *galut* (exile) of Egypt that "the Holy One *nigleh* [was revealed] upon them and redeemed them" (Haggadah).

It is of this that Scripture says: "As in the days when you came out of Egypt, I will show you wonders" (Mic. 7:15).

2:19

The pounding of my own heart,
the sound of Torah,
the voice of my Beloved—
Help me to learn again that they are all one voice!

VA-'ERA'

1

"I appeared to Abraham, to Isaac, and to Jacob as El Shaddai, but by My name YHWH I did not become known to them" (Ex. 6:3).

All of the patriarchs' efforts were for the sake of the children of Israel; that is why they are called our "forefathers." They went into all the hidden places within nature, struggling until there, too, they found the light of holiness. This is the conduct of the name El Shaddai, which our sages explained to mean that "there is enough *(she-dai)* of godliness for each creature." This means that God placed in each thing a point of divine life, powerful enough to draw to itself all that which surrounds it.

This world is called "the world of lies"; there is much falsehood for every point of truth. Of this it is written: "The wicked walk all about" (Ps. 12:9) and also: "Save my soul from lips of falsehood" (Ps. 120:2). Every bit of truth is surrounded by falsehood on all sides. Nevertheless, by means of struggle, that point of truth can be found in every place.

This was the holy work of our forefathers. That is why Scripture refers to "the land of their sojourning, where they sojourned *(garu)*" (Ex. 6:4). The same word *ger* (sojourner) refers also to the proselyte. We are told that "Abraham would convert the men [and Sarah the women]." This act of "converting" is one of drawing everything back to its root. The exile of Egypt, and indeed all exiles, are of this order. And in this work, the merit of our ancestors stands by us.

We are taught that "Moses prophesied through a lucid glass, and all the other prophets through an unlucid glass." But why is their vision called a "glass" at all, if it is not translucent? This refers to the point that is in hiding; it is revealed in the very midst of its hiding. Moses merited seeing things as they will be in the future: One God and His name One. Then there will be nothing but the divine life-force. But in this world everything is garbed in nature. It is by sanctifying yourself in this-worldly matters that you attain some bit of understanding. This is called the "unlucid glass"; it is through the hiding that you come to merit revelation. But this is hard work, the task we do through the week. The holy Sabbath is the lucid glass, when there is an abundance of revelation for every Jewish soul. . . .

2:25

Torah has been given, and Moses is our teacher. Nevertheless, for six out of seven days each week we still have to do things the hard way: seeking out bits of truth, though they are surrounded by mountains of falsehood; finding the divinity that is there within the ordinary, the miracle within nature. In this the patriarchs are our best guides.

 2

"I appeared to Abraham, to Isaac, and to Jacob as El Shaddai, but by My name YHWH I did not become known to them."

And after the four terms for redemption, the Torah says: "And you shall know that I am YHWH" (Ex. 6:3,7), for this is the true purpose of redemption. They had to be in Egypt for four hundred years to merit this "knowing" *(da'at)*, which is Torah.

Scripture says: "YHWH will grant wisdom, from His mouth knowing and understanding" (Prov. 2:6). The Midrash says: "Wisdom is great, but knowing is still greater. To the one He loves He gives a morsel from His own mouth." "Appearance" is a matter of wisdom. You can see from a great distance as well, as it says: "From afar the Lord appears to me" (Jer. 31:3). But knowing is an intimate attachment; it is knowing in your very soul.

The children of Israel are witnesses to God, as it says: "You are My witnesses, says the Lord" (Is. 43:10). Of the witness it says: "if he either saw or knew" (Lev. 5:1); there is testimony based on either seeing or knowledge. Truly "the Lord has made all for His sake" (Prov. 16:4), which means "that He be witnessed." See the Midrash there. So the world and all within it are witness to the blessed Holy One. Even the sages among the gentiles have to bear witness to the Creator; the natural scientist surely sees the Creator's wonders.

But of Israel it is written: "You have been shown knowledge *(da'at)*" (Deut. 4:35)—we are witnesses both by seeing and by knowing. We attained this when we came out of Egypt and received the Torah, of which Scripture says: "Let him kiss me with the kisses of his mouth" (Cant. 1:2). . . .

2:40

This is what it means to know God: a closeness that can only be described in the language of the Song of Songs. Such knowing is the very antithesis of what we usually call "knowledge" in our modern world. Scientific knowledge is supposedly guaranteed by detachment and "objectivity." The knowledge spoken of here is unabashedly that of total subjectivity. It can come about only through full engagement of the self as subject, through being wholly present to the One who seeks to be revealed to us and through us, if we are only there to witness.

3

"Indeed, the children of Israel have not listened to me, so how will Pharaoh listen, since I am a man of uncircumcised lips?" (Ex. 6:12). We have already explained that it is because Israel refused to listen that he has these "uncircumcised lips." The prophet prophesies by the power of those who listen. This is the meaning of "a prophet from your midst . . . [to him you shall listen]" (Deut. 18:15); it also says: "Hear, my people, and I will speak" (Ps. 50:7). The rabbis teach that a witness must be one who can hear.

This is what delayed the giving of the Ten Commandments. Speech was in exile as long as those who were to receive Torah had not yet readied themselves to hear the word of God. When it says [of the people in Egypt] that "they did not listen to Moses" (Ex. 6:9), the Midrash says that it was hard for them to abandon their "foreign worship." Thus it is said: "No man would cast away the abomination of his eyes" (Ezek. 20:8). This does not necessarily refer to idols, but to worship that was foreign to them.

Hearing requires being empty of every thing. "Hear, O daughter, and see, give ear; forget your people and your father's house" (Ps. 45:11). This is the essence of exile today as well: our inability to empty ourselves, to forget this world's vanities so that we empty the heart to hear God's word without any distracting thought. This is the meaning of the verse: "Do not turn after your hearts [or after your eyes]" (Num. 15:39). And it was because "no man would cast away the abominations of his eyes" that they walked about amid "the idols of Egypt." Had they been ready to hear God's word, they would have been redeemed immediately.

Now Torah has already been given to Israel by "a great voice that did not cease" (Deut. 5:19). It has never stopped. Each day we say: "Hear, O Israel, YHWH our God, YHWH is One" (Deut. 6:4); this is the voice saying: "I am YHWH your God"; it has never stopped. But we have to prepare ourselves to truly hear the *Shema'* without any distracting thought.

That is why we mention the Exodus [in the Song at the Sea] before the *Shema'*. By being redeemed from Egypt we are emptied of all distraction and become ready to hear God's word. . . .

2:40

Rabbi Ishmael taught that the basis of the entire Torah is our opposition to idolatry. Here, idolatry is taken in an expanded sense that makes it still applicable to us. Anything that keeps us from hearing the divine voice, our over involvement in the vanity that occupies most of our attention in this world and keeps us from being empty enough to receive the word of God—all that is our idolatry.

Since Torah has already been given to us, the voice of God we are to hear comes from within ourselves. The power to hear the voice of God's "I am" in our own recital of the Shema'—that requires concentration to the point of emptiness. Sound and silence come together in this profoundly contemplative teaching. It calls for a faith in ourselves and in the power of our own prayer that would transform our lives.

BO'

"[For I have hardened Pharaoh's heart and the heart of his servants] so that I might show these, My signs, in his midst" (Ex. 10:1). RaSHI notes that "might show" seems to indicate the future, though it could refer to the past as well.

All these deeds that were done in Egypt took place because God had already placed in Egypt hidden treasures that Israel still had to take out. "My signs" (otot) refers to the letters (otiyyot) through which heaven and earth had been created. The children of Israel, who were ready to receive the Torah, first had to bring forth words and letters that already existed in the world.

Thus the Midrashim say that originally there were just seven mitsvot. Only when Israel came along did they merit receiving the entire Torah. But first they had to clarify the light of Torah that already existed within the natural order. This is "the way of the world" that preceded Torah; it is something impressed within nature itself. Always one must first set right the physical and the natural, and only afterwards can we come to new insights.

Now Scripture explains why God did it this way, placing "My signs in his [Pharaoh's] midst." When they clarified the lights that came out of such a place, they would go on to live [and shine] throughout the generations. Therefore the verse goes on to say: "so that you will tell it in the ears of your children and your children's children." This made it into something that would last.

2:48

Yes, the memory of a struggle for freedom makes freedom more real. Indeed it is the Jewish experience that such memory can live and inspire for a very long time. But here the struggle is also one for words and language, as though the people all shared in the experience of their stammering prophet who struggled for words. This memory, too, we are told, can last forever and make the words of Torah ever precious and new. God indeed gave Torah to Israel. But it could only be received in those verbal vessels that they had formed by redeeming language itself from its own Egyptian bondage.

2

[On the same verse] the Midrash quotes "A stone is heavy and sand is weighty, but a fool's wrath is heavier than both" (Prov. 27:3).

Israel are witnesses to the Creator, as Scripture says: "You are My witnesses, says the Lord" (Is. 43:12). Just as we have to testify and make it clear that God created the world, so do we have to bear witness that all choice, all human actions and undertakings, come about in accord with God's will. Thus we can counter the "fool's wrath" that says: "I did it by the power of my own hand."

All this was revealed to Israel in Egypt. On the verse: "You have been shown to know" (Deut. 4:35), RaSHI says that the seven heavens were opened up before them, and just as He opened everything above, so did He open everything below, [to show them that He is only One].

In fact this has to do with the conflict between divine foreknowledge and free will, a subject spoken of by teachers early and late. This is how the Jew serves: we seek to make clear in this world that which the Creator already knows, and thus to negate choice, both for ourselves and in the world as a whole. This is just like what we saw in Egypt, where the blessed Holy One performed signs and wonders for us, "so that Egypt know" and their choice was taken away. He both strengthened Pharaoh's heart against his will and had him send us out against his will.

Now Scripture says: "According to two witnesses will the matter stand" (Deut. 19:15). The Creator's conduct of the world in fact stands by the witness of the Jews. "You are My witnesses, and I am God." And King David said: "I too will praise You with the harp, speaking Your truth, O my God" (Ps. 71:22). This is an amazing thing: truth depends upon human effort in this world of lies. This is why the opening letters of the words "Truth shall spring up from the ground" (Ps. 85:12) stand for truth itself.

So truth is hidden in this world. "Darkness covers the earth" (Is. 60:2). Up above, truth is clear and revealed; the Lord is a God of truth. But His deed is also true; this is the power of the Maker in that which He has made. This refers to the divine point within the person; that is "Your truth, O my God." The wicked turn things upside down and are called "dead" within their lifetimes. The divine power vanishes from them; for them truth turns into lies. The righteous clarify that truth. This is apparent to every religious person who works at the service of God. "The ways of the Lord are straight; the righteous shall walk in them, but the wicked shall stumble in them" (Hos. 14:10). All of this comes about through the power of Torah, the Torah of truth. . . .

2:63

Truth is already implanted within us, in our deepest selves and within the earth. It is this truth from below, the one that has to "spring up from the ground," that is the object of our real religious work. Even Pharaoh testified to God's truth, but he did so unwillingly; he stands as a memorial to the fact that no person can long defy the will of God. Our job is to attest to this truth willingly and in joy. Our discovery of the divine point within is also an acceptance of our own limitations. All our individual dreams will fade; that which is eternal in us is our witness to Eternity.

3

"You shall take a bundle of hyssop, dip it in the blood that is in the basin, and touch your lintel and two doorposts . . ." (Ex. 12:22). The Midrash says that even though they are lowly . . . , if they join into a "bundle," their very lowliness will bring them help from the Holy.

The Exodus from Egypt was only the beginning, the time when they came out from under Pharaoh's hand. Afterwards they had to enter the category of God's servants in order to receive the Torah. This is hinted at in the smearing of blood on the lintel and the doorposts: so that they know this is only the beginning.

Of this, Scripture says: "Open for me, my sister, my love" (Cant. 5:2). The rabbis said: "You make an opening as wide as a needle's eye, and I'll open it up for you like the entrance-way to a palace." This took place at the Exodus from Egypt, just like the opening of a doorway. God defended that little point, as it says: "God will protect the opening" (Ex. 12:23).

Even though they went out from Egypt with great victory, God wanted Israel to be in their own eyes like that bundle of hyssop, to know that they were just at the open doorway, hoping to truly come inside. Then it is written: "The king has brought me into his chambers" (Cant. 1:4), referring to the giving of Torah.

2:49

Our hope is to enter the chamber, to live inside Torah, and not just to stand "before the Law." But we also hope never to forget the anticipation and the promise of that first moment, the time when we just began to open up the door. The rabbis insist that the Exodus itself was a time of revelation, an encounter at which Israel "saw" God. But this was just a first opening of the door, the beginning of a relationship that bore with it the promise of much more love and intimacy to come.

BE-SHALAH

1

In the Midrash: "One who recites the *Shema'* is obligated to mention the splitting of the sea . . . in the prayer 'true and firm.' If one does not mention it, however, the prayer does not have to be repeated. But if the person has not mentioned the Exodus from Egypt, the prayer does need to be said again. . . . "

Why does the splitting of the sea have to be mentioned? Because that is when they came to [have] faith in God, as the verse says: "They believed in God and in His servant Moses" (Ex. 14:31). By the power of this faith they were able to sing, with the Shekhinah dwelling upon them. . . . And just as they purified their hearts [by faith] and then sang . . . so too does any person coming to pray first have to purify the heart, and then begin to pray.

The verse says: "then sang Moses and the children of Israel" (Ex. 15:1). "Then" means that at this moment the chief purpose of redemption had been accomplished. The point is that Israel was created to bear witness to the blessed Creator: "This folk I have formed [that] they tell My praise" (Is. 43:21). The Egyptian bondage was an iron furnace in which they were made pure, to serve as proper instruments for song and hymn before God. When redemption was complete, their mouths opened and they began to sing. *Therefore*, they had faith.

When Israel came forth from Egypt, they did not understand what value there had been in exile. But then, as they became God's instruments, they came to understand. The Midrash here also quotes: "My dove in the cleft of the rock, in the secret of the cliff; show me your appearance, let me hear your voice" (Cant. 2:14). They were in those clefts, hidden among the rocks, so that their voices might come forth and be heard.

Some of this is true each day as well. A person has to set this right on a daily basis. Our urges threaten to overpower us, making us like the dove in the cleft of the rock. We then have to purify our hearts in order to recite the *Shema'* and say our prayer.

2:78

The theme of exile and redemption is a central drama of the Jewish soul. Our people's historical sufferings—and their triumphs, with God's help—are there as paradigms by which we live. Each of us has been to (and often revisits!) our own Egypt. We have to learn to see this Egypt—even in the form of our daily struggles with our own desires—as a purifying furnace, making our voices into instruments that will sing God's praise more clearly as the sea splits once again for us. Remembering that Egypt and transforming its meaning is a process vital to our religious lives; hence, any prayer service that fails to mention it "needs to be repeated."

2

"Then sang Moses and the children of Israel." After the Exodus they became instruments to witness to the Creator. . . . The Midrash quotes the verse: "He brought me up out of the gruesome pit . . . and He placed in my mouth a new song of praise to our God" (Ps. 40:3–4).

The meaning of "new" is that it forever carries this power of renewal. It can never be forgotten by the souls of Israel. It was hardly for naught that they insisted this song be sung each day. Israel's faith [at the sea] was that this saving act would last for all generations. Thus Scripture says: "He is become my salvation" (Ex. 15:2), which the rabbis read as, "He was and He will be."

This song and the attachment to God have been implanted in the Jewish soul forever. But until the Exodus from Egypt, we were not able to call it forth. Only after this was the longing [for God] revealed. Of this, Scripture says: "Our soul has escaped like a bird out of the hunters' trap" (Ps. 124:7). In Egypt our very desire was imprisoned. "Release my soul from prison, so that I may give thanks to Your name" (Ps. 142:8).

So it is on every Sabbath that soul and desire are set free. That is why Shabbat is "in memory of the Exodus from Egypt." And we say: "It is good to give thanks to the Lord" (Ps. 92:2) in the song for the Sabbath day.

2:83

Shabbat Shirah, the day this song is read, is also traditionally called "the Sabbath of the Birds." It is customary on this winter day to put crumbs or other food out for the birds to eat, to sustain them through the coldest part of winter. Our author reminds his hearers that we and those birds have more in common than we might have thought. We, too, have escaped from the trap only so that we can sing our song to God for just a bit longer. Shabbat is here to give us the freedom we need to do that.

3

The manna is called "food from heaven" (Ex. 16:4). The Midrash quotes: "Go eat My food and drink of the wine I have poured" (Prov. 9:5), [referring to Torah]. For the generation of the wilderness were sustained truly by Torah itself, by "food from heaven."

But humans had previously been prepared for this. "He placed him in the Garden of Eden . . . " but then "lest he stretch forth his hand and eat of the Tree of Life . . . He expelled . . . the turning flaming sword to guard the way to the Tree of Life" (Gen. 2:15; 3:22,24).

It is taught that "whoever slays this snake will marry the King's daughter." So after the Exodus from Egypt, Israel were ready for the Tree of Life. "I thought you were divine beings, children of the most high" (Ps. 82:6), and so they were given this "food that the angels eat."

The rabbis say that had Israel kept the first Sabbath, no nation would have had rule over them, for it says: "And it happened on the seventh day that some of the people went out to gather it" (Ex. 16:27) and then "Amalek came and fought with Israel" (Ex. 17:8). But we interpret this "first Sabbath" to mean really the first, the Sabbath of Creation, when "He placed him in the garden." This is the true rest that God desires.

Some of that light is present on every holy Sabbath. That is why an extra soul comes down from the Garden of Eden, and that is called "rest. . . . "

2:75

Now that we have come out of Egypt, the historic exile, we are ready to "return" from the cosmic exile as well, to that rest first promised in Eden. The universal human exile and the national exile of the Jewish people are taken to be one and the same. This time the snake—in the person of Pharaoh— has been defeated, and Israel can eat the manna, the fruit of the Tree of Life, the food of angels.

Each Sabbath contains within it a return to the original Sabbath of Eden, waiting for us to reclaim it. It is only our entanglement with the mundane world that keeps us from it. How can we prepare ourselves to reenter Eden each Sabbath?

 4

On the manna: the Midrash claims that Israel merited the manna because of the food that Abraham our Father had given to the ministering angels. The manna first came to them in Alush (cf. Num. 33:14), because Abraham had said to Sarah "knead *(lushi)* and make cakes" (Gen. 18:6). The Torah hints that Israel's souls were so purified that they could eat the food that sustains the angels. This came about because of Abraham, who himself had become pure enough to feed the angels. "He stood over them beneath the tree and they ate" (vs. 8). The deeds of the patriarchs were so holy, and the Shekhinah so dwelt in their midst, that the angels ate of their food. Of this, Scripture says: "Go eat of My food" (Prov. 9:5) [for the manna is called "bread from heaven"].

There is [also] "bread from the earth"—this refers to the redemptive work the righteous have to do each day. That bread rises upward. And then there is the bread that comes down to them from heaven. On the Sabbath we have two loaves joined together, to point to these two kinds of bread. Thus the holy Zohar comments on "between Me and the children of Israel" (Ex. 31:17), that on the Sabbath those above and below rejoice together.

2:84

The two Sabbath loaves represent the meeting of two sorts of bread: that which we uplift from earth in the course of our transforming work, and that which comes from heaven as a blessing to our rest. It is the combination of these two that makes for Shabbat. Our preparation is vital, and the rabbis say that "the one who has worked hard on the Sabbath eve will eat on the Sabbath." But Shabbat is also a divine gift that comes upon us from a mysterious place both beyond and within; a gift from God's own treasure-house, as it is taught, that is given to Israel each week.

YITRO

1

"All the people saw the voices" [lit.: "the thunder"] (Ex. 20:18). The voice was that which said, "I am the Lord your God" (vs. 2; in the singular). Each one of Israel saw the root of his or her own life-force. With their very eyes each one saw the part of the divine soul above that lives within. They had no need to "believe" the commandments, because they saw the voices. That's the way it is when God speaks.

2:91

The dramatic setting of the Sinai revelation is so powerful that we sometimes forget to ask the internal question about what this event of God's self-revealing meant to those who were present (and we too are among them, of course). Here

105

we are told that the supernatural "seeing the voice" means that each one uniquely experienced the divine voice speaking within his or her own soul. To this all the rest of religion—indeed, perhaps all the rest of life—is merely commentary.

2

Of Sinai it says: "The day you stood before the Lord your God at Ḥoreb" (Deut. 4:10). At Sinai Israel reached a state of perfect wholeness, like that of the angels. The human being is a walker, always having to go from one rung to the next; we are ever on the way to wholeness. Only when we reach it can we "stand [like the angels]." And some of the light of that wholeness reaches us every Sabbath. That is why we cease from work. Scripture points to this in [the verses]: "If you restrain your foot because of the Sabbath" (Is. 58:13) and "May no person go forth from his place on the Sabbath day" (Ex. 16:29).

Of this we say: "Spread over us the tabernacle of Your peace."

2:102

The spiritual life has its own rhythms: weekdays for walking, Sabbaths for rest. But sometimes the period between two of those Sabbaths can stretch out to years.

3

The Midrash quotes: "The Lord is my strength and my stronghold, my refuge on the day of trouble; unto You nations will come from the far corners of the earth" (Jer. 16:19).

God has chosen the children of Israel as His own portion. One might think that this would make for a greater distance between God and the other nations. But actually, just the opposite is true. This was God's deeper plan: to bring all nations near to Him by means of Israel. Israel understand this, and it is their desire to bring everyone close to God. Only the wicked interfere with this plan, as [when] "Amalek came and fought with Israel" (Ex. 17:8). But when Jethro came, they drew him near with all their strength. "The Lord is my strength"—Israel's own strength. "And my stronghold"—He gives strength to Israel. There is to be power in their hands through the Torah God has given them—"The Lord gives strength to His people" (Ps. 29:11)—for they are God's emissaries, to bring all creatures near to Him.

This is the meaning of [the verse]: "The Lord spoke all these words, saying: 'I am the Lord your God'" (Ex. 20:1–2). The blessed Creator gave them the Torah. The nations were not capable of this. Even of Israel it is said that their souls fluttered out of them and they were purified like angels. That is why it says: "The day you *stood* before the Lord your God at Ḥoreb" (Deut. 4:10). The angels are those who "stand." The intent is that [every one of] Israel speak these words, drawing them into rung after rung, until all creatures are brought close to God. The life-force of all is in the Torah, and all are to be redeemed by the power of Torah. This is the meaning of "saying" in that verse: every one of Israel has to bear witness to the Creator each day. Twice a day we say, "Hear, O Israel." These words shine forth to all the world, to all who are created.

RaSHI comments on "saying" that Israel called out "Yes!" at each positive commandment and "No!" at each negative commandment. This means that God's words are not like those of flesh and blood. These utterances were engraved in their hearts; Israel "saw the voices." In their hearts they saw the words fulfilled in that very instant; their souls were redeemed as they were drawn after God's words. This becomes the oral Torah, of which we say: "Eternal life has He implanted within us." The words of Torah were absorbed into their souls. This is "my stronghold"—their very selves became Torah.

2:91

But the nations and the creatures cannot hear our shema' *yisrael. And even if they do, they have no idea that it is addressed to them, a universal call to come near to God. How do we translate our* Shema' *so that the world can hear? How do we learn to share God's word with all, while still keeping*

*it enough our own to give us strength? It is in these challenges
that the voice of Sinai calls out to us today. We still do not
have a Judaism that lives up to the high universal standards
demanded here.*

*The task has gotten both easier and harder in our day. No
one will kill or persecute us for bearing God's witness to the
world; we are free to deliver our testimony. But the job has
gotten so much more complex. Recognizing, as we should,
that there are other testimonies to God in the world, sometimes we forget the special value of our own unique witness
and the need the world still has to hear the call of Israel.*

We are commanded to remember each day the giving of the
Torah, "The day you stood before YHWH" (Deut. 4:10) or
"these words that I command you today" (Deut. 6:6). This is
[the] "I am" of the Ten Commandments. It is spoken of also in
[the verse:] "If you will truly listen unto My commandments
that I command you this day" (Deut. 11:13), in the second passage of the *Shema'*. [One is singular, one is plural, command-
ing] the individual and the group.

Thus is the commandment of Torah aroused each day. The
Ten Commandments contain within them the entire Torah.
They stand parallel to the ten utterances of God in creating
the world. Just as all of Creation and all that has happened
since, in general and in particular, were included in those ten
"Let there be"s, so is all of Torah—all the commandments as
performed by every one of Israel, general and particular—included within these Ten Commandments.

The difference between these two sets of ten is that the divine utterances of Creation are fixed within nature, while the
commandments are constantly renewed. They are the inner
side of the ten utterances. That is why the Mishnah (Avot 5:1)
can teach that the world was created with ten utterances "to
give goodly reward to those who preserve" it. This "goodly reward" is Torah.

Scripture says: "The Lord founded earth with wisdom; He establishes the heavens with understanding" (Prov. 3:19); "founded" [in the past tense] refers to Creation, but "establishes" [in the present] is constant, as the holy Zohar says. This refers to Torah, which is renewed constantly. And by the power of Torah, the utterances of Creation are renewed as well. Of this we say: "By His goodness [=Torah] He renews each day the work of Creation." By means of the commandments we can find that renewal of Torah each day. . . .

2:103

The relationship between these two sets of ten can be seen in both directions. The Sefat Emet wants to find the Ten Commandments within the ten utterances, seeing Torah as the essence of Creation itself. The commandments are God's "translation" of the fixed utterances into a language of humanity that is ever on the move, growing and evolving in new directions, taking the commandments along with it. It is only in the language of imperatives for behavior that the words of Creation become truly dynamic rather than static.

But we also need to seek God's ten repetitions of "Let there be" within the Ten Commandments. That, too, would give us a renewed Torah, one that becomes a way to affirm all that is, since everything that has come to be is derived from the ten utterances. Within the written Torah we learn to discover God's secret Torah, the one manifest in Creation itself. This Torah is the true law of nature, the loving affirmation of all life; we find it within and behind each commandment of our Torah, "both general and particular."

MISHPATIM

1

"And these are the statutes that you shall place before them" (Ex. 21:1). The Midrash comments that "and" means that these were in addition to what had been said previously (cf. Ex. 15:25 and 18:22). It brings a parable of "a lady who went out walking with armed soldiers on either side of her, while she walked in the middle. Thus is the [giving of the] Torah preceded by laws and followed by laws, while she walks between them."

RaSHI notes that "just as those preceding are Torah [so too are those that follow]." In fact everything comes from Torah, and she is the one who blesses both that which comes before her and that which follows her, since all the world was created for the sake of Torah. It was the generation that received the

111

Torah who brought this potential into realization, but the work of the preceding generations served as preparation for Torah.

The same is true for every individual of Israel. First we have to straighten our ways, as we are taught: "Prepare yourself to study Torah." This refers to the judgments that precede Torah. Thus it says [before the giving of the Torah]: "They shall judge the people at all times" (Ex. 18:22). These were not judgments specific to Moses, but such as had existed before Torah. Afterwards it says: "And *these* are the statutes"—specifically these, after the giving of Torah.

These rungs are always present in everyone who serves God. It is as we straighten our paths that we come to attain Torah. Afterwards, by the power of Torah we are able to straighten our ways even more properly. And thus it is forever. When Israel said "we shall do" before "we shall listen," they did not do so just for that moment, but forever. First we set right our actions; then we listen. After we hear, there comes the time to correct our deeds even more, by the power of that Torah. Then we deserve to hear yet more of the inward Torah.

The main thing is that this process has to be directed for the sake of heaven. Work to straighten your heart as a way of preparing to receive Torah and to serve God; then Torah will help you to complete the task. Of this Scripture says: "You shall be people of holiness *unto Me*" (Ex. 22:30)—a person has to seek out holiness in order to serve God, not just in order to be a holy person. For holiness is above nature. How can it be found within this world? Only by the power of Torah and the blessed Holy One, who has made us holy by means of His commandments. Thus: "people of holiness *unto Me*. . . ."

2:116f.

This eternal cycle of doing and hearing is deeply characteristic of the Jewish spiritual life. Here the Sefat Emet joins such diverse Jewish teachers as Naḥman of Bratslav and Franz Rosenzweig: each of the three has his own version of this cyclical process. This reading is one that insists on constant growth as the model for true religious living and a dialectical relationship between "life" and Torah. Only the angels stand still; we humans are constantly on the ladder, the rungs of which include our life in the world as well as our encounter with divinity.

The cycle begins not with Torah itself but with that which we bring with us when we come to study Torah. "Prepare yourself to study Torah" here means that everything that precedes Torah in your life is a part of your path; bring it with you as you turn to Torah. The "judgments" that preceded Sinai are in the category of derekh erets—*those universal norms that make a person into a* mensch. *You have to bring these with you when you come to Torah.*

But another point is being made here as well. Sometimes, especially in religious societies, the quest for sanctity becomes an end in itself. The rebbe here warns his Hasidim—including ourselves—that the saintly and the sanctimonious are only a hairbreadth apart. Remember that it is for God, the Life of all worlds and all creatures, that you are to be holy, not for yourself.

"You shall be people of holiness unto Me"—*Tiheyun* ("You shall be") means a new being. It is within the power of every Jew to bring about constant renewal, to cause a garment of holiness to dwell upon him, by means of the Torah and commandments. Now it says: "Come up to Me upon the mountain and *be* there" (Ex. 24:12)—this means that Moses was transformed into a new being, like one of the ministering angels. Our sages taught that he entered the cloud and was garbed in cloud, to make him like one of the angels. That is why he was there for forty days, the amount of time it takes for a fetus to be formed. He received that form in fullness. The Zohar says that "be there" *(sham)* can be read as "be a name" *(shem)*, meaning that Moses became the Holy Name.

All of Israel have a part in that form. Before the sin [of the Golden Calf] it says : "I said, 'You are God'" (Ps. 82:6). And it is taught that on the holy Sabbath Moses restores that light to every Jew. This is the "extra soul," and that is why "the light of a person's face on the Sabbath is not the same as it is during the week." We come to merit this form through the 613 commandments, which are our own limbs and sinews. In this world it seems that the body is primary and that the 613 commandments are known only by a hint. But really it is the other way around. The true essence of the human form is the 613 spiritual limbs, the root of the commandments. The bodily limbs are pointers to that which is within.

In Moses our Teacher this inner garment was revealed. The farther we distance ourselves from the corporeal, the more we merit inwardness. On weekdays our struggle is to distance ourselves from the physical. On the holy Sabbath we have to work at receiving the inner light and spirit.

2:117

The Judaism of the mystics has long asserted that all of Israel were there in Moses' soul as he stood atop the mountain—or even as he entered the cloud. We are participants in Moses' journey, not mere followers who stood at the mountain's base and waited for him to return. And yet those same mystics also knew full well that we were indeed back there at the base of the mountain—impatient, childish, frightened—prepared to block our own transformation into divinity by worshipping the Golden Calf. Both of those selves are still present within us.

 3

In the name of the holy rabbi of Kotsk, on the verse: "You shall be *people* of holiness unto Me" (Ex. 22:30). The guarding of holiness has to be within the realm of human deeds and activities. God has no lack of sublime angels, seraphim, or holy beings. But God longs for the holiness of people; it was for that reason that He caused sparks of holiness to enter this world, in measured and reduced form. Therefore, "meat that is torn by beasts of the field you shall not eat" (ibid.); from this the rabbis derived the principle that anything taken out of its proper place is forbidden. This means that the flow of holiness is in all things, but in a measured way. We have to guard the corporeal, that it not transgress the border of holiness.

But "you shall be" can also be read as a promise [rather than as a commandment]. In the end Israel are to be "holy unto the Lord." That is why we have to guard ourselves now, so that we are ready to be placed upon the King's head. The Midrash says in a parable, [referring to one making a crown], "as many precious stones and pearls as you can put unto it, do so, for it is going to be placed upon the King's own head."

2:111

Here we see how Ger has taken the legacy of Kotsk and transformed it. The Kotsker's reading of the verse was ultimately an earthy one: "God wants this-worldly holiness; that is why He made us human!" "Make your humanity holy" was his message. The Gerer has taken this reading and turned it right back to heaven: "Be holy because you are the crown of God!" We live somewhere between these two.

 4

"And these are the statutes"—adding to what had come before. The Ten Commandments refer to matters between person and God, but these statutes are between person and person. They are placed here to remind us that we merit Torah in accordance with the peace that exists among Israel when we are united. Of this the rabbis said: "'Love your neighbor as yourself' (Lev. 19:29)—that is the basic rule of Torah." The psalmist (29:11) says: "The Lord will give strength to His people," referring to Torah, right next to "the Lord will bless His people with peace," referring to the well of oral Torah, about which we say: "He has implanted eternal life in our midst." This well is opened by the peace wrought by these statutes. For this reason the Midrash quotes here: "You have established uprightness" (Ps. 99:4), because these statutes lead people to love one another.

A person has to set aright his conduct in matters concerning the relationship with God in order to merit the written Torah.

But to merit oral Torah, we have to concern ourselves with the relationship with others. And this latter is the higher rung, for it says: "He declares His words unto Jacob, His laws and statutes unto Israel" (Ps. 147:19), and we know that the name Israel is higher than the name Jacob. It is of greater merit to repair one's ways with regard to fellow humans. That is the "straightness" of the name Israel, which can be derived from *YaSHaR EL* (godly straightness). "For God made man straight" (Eccles. 7:29), and so forth. But after the sin we became involved with "multiple accounts" (ibid.); now we have crookedness, jealousy, and hatred, all of which need to be straightened out. It is the statutes that can help us to do this.

That is why it says: "These are the statutes which you shall place before them." This is reminiscent of [the verse:] "They shall place My name upon the children of Israel" (Num. 6:27)—putting it in order before them. This well of oral Torah that is within the children of Israel needs to be brought out into reality; truth has to be drawn forth from the midst of falsehood. Of this it is written: "The paths of the Lord are straight; the righteous walk in them" (Hos. 14:10). This is the meaning of "before them."

2:117

From the very minute written Torah is given, it is in need of oral interpretation to make it work. The wellspring of this oral Torah is found within Israel; it is we who are given the power to read, understand, and apply the teaching. But this power can be exercised only when Israel are at peace with one another. That is why Mishpatim, containing the rule of law, has to follow Sinai immediately; only this rule of law will bring about peace in the human community, allowing us to receive Torah.

The statutes can only be placed "before" us; it is we who have to choose to walk in their ways. In our day it seems harder than ever to find out how to walk in a way that will lead us all to peace with one another. But the message here is one we need to take to heart: there is no path to God's teachings, no way to open the divine wellsprings that lie within us, except that of peace.

תרומה

TERUMAH

1

The Midrash quotes the verse: "You went up to the heights and took a captive, you took gifts for humans [lit.:'in man']; even for sinners, so that God might dwell" (Ps. 68:19). This teaches that it was because of Torah that Israel merited having the Shekhinah dwell in their midst. The Zohar says that at Sinai Israel were prepared to have God bring down the Temple from above for them, just as will happen in the future. Only because their sin caused them to fall from this rung did the indwelling of the Shekhinah have to be in reduced form, in the earthly *mishkan* and Temple.

"You took gifts *in man*" means that they were ready to have the Shekhinah dwell *in the person*, without any intermediary. This is also the meaning of [the verse:] "A foundation for Your

117

dwelling did You establish, O Lord" (Ex. 15:17). Israel at the sea felt themselves to be vessels ready to have the Shekhinah poured into them. Thus they said: "This is my God and I will enshrine Him" (vs. 2), meaning that I will make [myself into] a shrine for Him. The children of Israel themselves were a foundation for "Your dwelling"! But after the sin: "Let them make Me a sanctuary" (Ex. 25:8), and [only] through it "I will dwell in their midst."

In fact this refers to the distinction between weekdays, when the revelation of holiness comes about through physical deeds, and the holy Sabbath, when the light is revealed spiritually. The Midrash says that the Torah was like a king's daughter who was about to be wedded to a faraway prince. Her father said that neither could he keep her from marrying, nor could he live without her. So he asked her to make a small room for him in her new home, so that wherever she might be, he could come and dwell with her. Previously, Israel had been intensely attached to God [in a direct way]. Afterwards, as they descended from this rung, Scripture says: "Let them make Me a sanctuary," a little chamber that I might dwell in their midst.

This might also refer to the mitsvah of tefillin, which contain special little "houses" in which holiness dwells. The divine names in those tefillin parchments draw holiness to the person. The Zohar quotes "Let them make Me a sanctuary" as referring to the mystery of tefillin. These inscriptions are really written in the innermost souls of Israel, as Scripture says: "Set me as a seal upon your heart" (Cant. 8:6). But it is by means of tefillin that "like finds like." That is why the rabbis say that on the holy Sabbath Israel themselves are a sign, and they need no tefillin.

On the holy Sabbath the light of revelation is restored, something of what it was like before the sin. We are told that on Shabbat Moses returns to Israel the crowns they had received when they said: "We shall do and we shall listen" (Ex. 24:27) [which had been taken away after they sinned]. And that is why the work of building the *mishkan* was interrupted on Shabbat, as RaSHI says (in Ki Tissa'): "Moreover, you shall keep My Sabbaths" (Ex. 31:13)—this excludes the building of the *mishkan* on Shabbat. For on the holy Sabbath there is a revelation of holiness like that before the sin, and there is no need for the "reduction" of a sanctuary.

2:144

Every soul is a chamber for God, a vessel that contains the divine light. This is the message the hasidic masters repeatedly associate with the tabernacle and all the details of its making; in all these ways are we to fashion our inner chambers, to make them a proper dwelling place for God. In our souls we light a lamp for God, set a table, raise up an altar. Truly, God needs no intermediary. The divine light seeks out only the soul and would be pleased to dwell directly within us. It is only our sin, that which makes us feel separate from God, that causes us to need ritual forms, chambers in which we can allow God's presence to dwell. These outward signs, whether in the grand form of the tabernacle or the little boxes of tefillin, help to attract the light, to bring it to its true home within the soul.

2

In the Midrash: "I am asleep but my heart is awake" (Cant. 5:2)—"I am asleep in exile, but my heart wakes that I be redeemed; I am asleep because of the Golden Calf, but my Beloved knocks to awaken me."

"Let them bring Me gifts *(terumah)*." "How long shall I wander without a home?" asks the Midrash. The point is that the children of Israel have a portion in the Torah that is higher than the sun. Their connection to this root is never severed. Ever since God said at Sinai: "I am the Lord your God," every person of Israel contains a divine force. How much more is this true of the Jewish people as a whole! Even when sin causes the bodily self to become distanced from this inwardness, from the soul, our root in heaven still defends us, seeking that we return to our place.

The fact is, however, that this too depends on our desire to cleave to our source; the source longs for us in the same measure that we long for it. This is the meaning of "I am dark but comely" (Cant. 1:5)—the body and the garbing may be dark, but the inner self, the soul or the root, is glorious. Thus "my heart wakes"—this is the godliness that longs to dwell within Israel below. "How long shall I wander without a home?" But this [indwelling] will come about through the longing within Israel's hearts.

Thus it was surely not for naught that God said: "Let them bring Me gifts." They were filled with longing to return to their prior rung, that which they had attained as they received the Torah. But because of the sin, they just weren't able to reach it. Then God was compassionate with them and gave them the idea of the *mishkan* and its vessels.

All this is written in the Torah to tell us that this desire is constantly present in the hearts of Israel. If we seek intensely enough, we will merit the indwelling of the Shekhinah. Now it should in fact be easier to draw this forth, since we have already had a *mishkan* and the Temples. This is the secret of "and so shall you make it" (Ex. 25:9)—it is forever according to Israel's desire and generous spirit that the people are able to "make Me a holy place" (Ex. 25:8). But it has to be with true longing of the soul, as was the case for David: "I will not give sleep to my eyes, or slumber to my eyelids until I find a place for the Lord, an abode for the Mighty one of Jacob" (Ps. 132:4–5).

Thus he earned the right to do it.

2:141

The message is that of the wakeful heart—and of our endless struggle to heed its longings and to build a home for God in this world. Here it is stated with great clarity that God's presence in this world depends upon the depth and sincerity of human desire. That desire has resided in the heart of every Jew ever since we all heard God speak and had His words inscribed within us at Mount Sinai. As the Sefat Emet never tires of saying, that inscription can be covered over or forgotten, but never erased. Each of us stands ready to be redeemer

of the wandering Shekhinah, to repeat King David's act of
making a home in this world for God's presence.

3

The Midrash Tanḥuma quotes: "I have given you good teaching" (Prov. 4:2). [The term *lekaḥ* (teaching) can also refer to
something acquired by purchase.] It offers a parable of two
merchants, one who has silk and the other peppers. Once they
exchange their goods, each is again deprived of that which the
other has. But if there are two scholars, one who has mastered
the Order of Seeds and the other who knows the Order of Festivals, once they teach each other, each has both orders.

The point is that each one of Israel has a particular portion
within Torah, yet it is also Torah that joins all our souls together. That is why Torah is called "perfect, restoring the
soul" (Ps. 19:8). We become one through the power of Torah; it
is "an inheritance of the assembly of Jacob" (Deut. 33:4). We
receive from one another the distinctive viewpoint that belongs to each of us.

Of this, Scripture says: "God gives strength [=Torah] to His
people; God bless His people with peace" (Ps. 29:11). The
blessed Holy One's name is "peace"; God is called the King of
Peace, who makes peace in the heights. Torah, too, is composed of names of God, and that is why Torah leads us to
peace. So, too, it says: "He calls them all by name" (Is. 40:26),
for the name of God includes all the hosts of heaven, joined
together by that name. So, too, are the souls of Israel joined
together by Torah.

The same was true in the building of the tabernacle. Each
one gave his own offering, but they were all joined together by
the tabernacle, until they became one. Only then did they
merit Shekhinah's presence.

This oneness has to exist on the three planes of thought,
word, and deed. The tabernacle and Temple represent oneness
in deed, Torah stands for unity of word, and God is the One of
thought or contemplation.

The word *nefesh,* used for the "seventy souls" [who went into Egypt], appears to be singular. They all worshipped the same God, had the same longing and desire in their hearts. All of them were turned to Him, and thus they became a single nation.

2:150

Calls for Jewish unity, so it appears, were as common in the Sefat Emet's time as they are in our own. Remembering a Warsaw divided among Hasidim and socialists, Zionists and assimilationists, this teaching was as needed in early 1900, when it was spoken, as it is today. But his message is more defined than that: the way to achieve unity is through everyone holding on to his or her own distinctive viewpoint while sharing with all others in a context that fully accepts the infinite variety of minds and opinions, all of them making up a single divine whole. Here no view is to be dismissed or rejected, for such would only diminish the whole, defacing the name of God. Such a truly pluralistic model of Jewish life has yet to be tried.

TETSAVVEH

1

In the Midrash: "A candle of God is the soul of man" (Prov. 20:27). "The blessed Holy One said: 'Let My candle be in your hand and yours in Mine.' And what is the candle of God? That is Torah, as Scripture says: 'For a commandment is a candle and Torah is light'" (Prov. 6:23). "What is 'a commandment is a candle'? Whoever does a mitsvah is like one who lights a candle before the blessed Holy One and gives life to his soul which is called a candle—'a candle of God is the soul of man.'"

The meaning of "a candle of God" is that God's providence in the lower world is through the souls of Israel. By means of their service Israel draw divine providence and the light of God's countenance into the world.

123

There are two sorts of darkness. One comes about through the evil inclination and the "other side"—that is true darkness, but it can be negated by means of the mitsvot. That is why doing a mitsvah is like lighting a candle before God—it is preparing a place where His glorious Presence can dwell. By means of this you enliven your soul, the candle. But the supreme light is also considered darkness to us, since it is beyond our reach. The holy books thus refer to it as darkness. The more light a person brings about in the physical darkness, through doing the mitsvot, the more that one will enlighten his soul from the ["dark"] light above.

"Now you shall command" *(tetsavveh)* (Ex. 27:20)—bring the mitsvah into the souls of Israel so that they themselves become mitsvot! All our limbs are really there for the sake of doing mitsvot. The Talmud offers two meanings for "you shall do them" (Num. 15:39). One is that whoever fulfills a mitsvah is considered by God as one who had made [invented] it. The other is "as though he had made himself." The two interpretations are really one: it is the remaking *(tikkun)* of the person that takes place through mitsvot, forming him into one dedicated to God, bless His name. That person is then sent into this world only to do the will of His Creator. He himself has become a mitsvah. This is the meaning of *asher kideshanu be-mitsvotav*—"Who has made us holy through His mitsvot"—*ve-tsivvanu*—"and made us into mitsvot"!

2:154

To become a mitsvah, and thus to make God's dark light visible in the world through your own very being—that is the purpose and meaning of your life as a Jew.

2

In the Midrash: "You command" . . . "The Lord named you verdant olive tree, fair, with choice fruit" (Jer. 11:16).

There is a hidden point within the souls of Israel, of which Scripture says: "If you seek it as you do silver and search for it as for treasures . . . " (Prov. 2:4). This inwardness reveals itself as a result of great effort, a struggle of the soul and the body, to purify the physical. Thus we are like the verdant olive tree: what an effort it is to bring forth that oil!

Now Scripture also says: "For a commandment is a candle and Torah is light, and the way to life is the rebuke that disciplines" (Prov. 6:23). The souls of Israel are the wicks that draw the oil after the light. Moses our Teacher, peace be upon him, the root of Torah, is the light. Thus we read: "Let them take olive oil unto you" (Ex. 27:20)—drawn toward the wick. The mitsvot are the lamps, vessels in which oil and wick are joined to the light.

All these elements exist within every person, just as they exist within Israel as a whole. The Midrash here also quotes: "From them shall come cornerstones, from them tent-pegs" (Zech. 10:4). God made humans upright, bearing within themselves the perfect totality (*shelemut*) of all creatures, from the deepest depths to the greatest heights. Aaron the priest was chosen to serve God; this was for the sake of Israel, for after the sin they contained a mixture of good and evil. The blessed Holy One's counsel was to choose one person in each generation to represent purity, through whom purity would flow to all of Israel.

You too can do the same. Set aside one quality, or one special mitsvah, about which you take fabulous care. Through this you will be able to draw light and redemption to all your qualities. "From them shall come tent-pegs"—the choosing of Aaron set a firm grounding for Israel's tent. The blessed Holy One raised him up, removed him from all evil. It was through this [uplifted one] that Israel were always able to return, to cleave again to their blessed Creator.

2:155

The metaphor of the olive tree also contains an unspoken understanding that it is only through the pain of divine rebuke—the pressing of the olive—that its fine oil is drawn forth. Israel is made pure by its suffering, drawn after the wick that makes its fire burn.

As God appoints a leader for the people, so may you also appoint a "leader" within your own religious life. The mitsvah or quality that you choose to make your own in this special way will become a mirror to your soul. Choose it wisely—or let it choose you.

≡ 3 ≡

In the Midrash: "'Were not Your Torah my delight, I would have perished in my affliction' (Ps. 119:92). When God said to Moses: 'Bring near to you your brother Aaron [to serve Me as a priest]'" (Ex. 28:1), "Moses felt bad. God said to him: 'I had a Torah and I gave it to you. Without that I would have lost My world!'"

Even though Moses was greater than Aaron, the priesthood was given to Aaron, who was separated from the people, as Scripture says: "Aaron was separated" (1 Chron. 23:13). Moses, as prince of Torah, had to be attached to all of Israel. That is why Moses did not pass the crown on to his sons, but rather left "an inheritance for the community of Jacob" (Deut. 33:4). Had Moses also been separated, we would not have been able to stand.

Such is the power of Torah, which is called "more precious than pearls" *[peninim]* (Prov. 3:15)—more precious than the priest who enters to the innermost place *[li-fenai veli-fenim]*. Torah causes the world to stand firm. This is the way the blessed Holy One consoled Moses for his not being able to separate from all Israel. Because Moses gave his life for Israel, God repaid him by having his power remain within them forever. Nearly every Jew has the light and spark of Moses our Teacher.

That is why Moses wasn't given the priesthood; the priest has to be separated. So our sages said: "Aaron merited and received the crown of the priesthood; David won the crown of royalty." But the crown of Torah remains for every Jew.

2:163

Something of Moses' soul is there in every Jew. When we study Torah, we stand there with him on the mountain, bound together in a single universal soul that transcends all barriers between the generations. Moses thus remains rabbenu—*our teacher—forever. This is the true sacred "democracy" of Israel.*

Aaron the priest needs to be separate from the people in order to maintain his priestly bearing, to preserve the magic of his holy role. Here the Sefat Emet may be subtly attacking the high style of some other hasidic masters, those who remained aloof from the people, living like "high priests," supposedly in order to maintain their own holiness. The rabbi, he reminds us, is supposed to be the disciple of Moses, living fully within the community of Israel.

כי תשא

KI TISSA'

1

"You shall only keep My Sabbaths" (Ex. 31:13). Note "Sabbaths" in the plural. Everything contains the life-force of the holy Sabbath; this point makes everything whole. Thus RaSHI reads: "On the seventh day God ended His work" (Gen. 2:2), meaning that only on the Sabbath was the work finished.

The Sabbath completes each thing; it is the finishing or fulfillment of all, since it is the root of life. On the holy Sabbath this root is aroused in each thing. That is why Sabbath is called "rest," because it returns each thing to its root.

RaSHI interprets the phrase *shabbat shabbaton* (Ex. 31:15) to mean "a tranquil rest, not a casual rest." Of course every Jew puts his work aside and doesn't do it on the Sabbath. But this leaving of one's work behind must not itself become a

129

burden. All week long we should look forward to this turning to our root and the place of our rest, since this is where we truly live. That is what it means to "keep" the Sabbath—to be in a state of anticipation all week long, saying: "When will the holy Sabbath come so that I can go back to my place!"

This is the meaning of [the verse:] "You shall *only* keep . . .": Have no desire or longing for anything else in the world. Only for God, who is the root of human life—hold fast to Him on the holy Sabbath.

It also says: "to do the Sabbath" (vs. 16). But isn't the commandment one of *not* doing? And what "keeping" does the Sabbath need? Isn't it in fact the Sabbath that "keeps" and preserves us? This verse means that you have to take the Sabbath and draw it into all your deeds throughout the week. There, indeed, it needs to be "kept" or guarded. . . .

2:198

The real Shabbat is not that of restriction or confinement. These outer bounds serve to create for us a temporal "territory" in which we are free to be our truest selves. That inner Shabbat, the place where the burden of worldly concerns is lifted off us and the crushed spirit is given the "extra soul" that it needs to breathe, remains a rare gift, even among those who are perceived to "keep" the Sabbath.

2

"You shall only keep My sabbaths, a sign between Me and you throughout the ages, that you may know that I the Lord make you holy" (Ex. 31:13). The sages note that Shabbat was given to Israel in secret.

This can be understood in connection with the verse [concerning the future Temple]: "The gate of the inner court which faces east shall be closed on the six working days; it shall be open on the Sabbath . . . " (Ezek. 46:1). For on the Sabbath the innermost secret is revealed. Just as this is true for our blessed God, so is it the case for the souls of Israel: their innermost hearts are opened on the holy Sabbath. And wherever there is inwardness, there needs to be protection. That is why the verse says *"keep My sabbaths."*

Our sages commented on [the verse:] "Remember the Sabbath day to keep it holy" (Ex. 20:8)—"remember it with wine." This is to show that the secret within is to be revealed, for that is the function of wine. "Wine causes young women to speak" (Zech. 9:17). Hence the saying: "Wine in—secrets out!"

In the book *Torat Hayyim* it is said that we recite *kiddush* over wine on Shabbat because the Sabbath is a foretaste of the world to come, where [the righteous will drink of] "the wine that has been kept with its grapes" [fermenting since Creation]. But in an inward sense, this "wine kept with its grapes" is the power of the soul, hidden away within the body. No one else can touch it, for it is sealed within. This is the sense of [the verse:] "No eye but Yours, O God, has seen it" (Is. 64:3), referring to this kept wine. And the future, when "the righteous sit with crowns on their heads"—that is when the soul will be revealed in fullness.

Since the Sabbath is a foretaste of the world to come, on this day the soul is revealed just a bit. This is what the sages meant when they spoke of an "extra soul" on the holy Sabbath. And that is why we recite *kiddush* over wine—to show that the soul is now open. And wine, like the soul, must be guarded from the stranger's touch. . . .

2:208f.

This and the preceding Torah should be read together. When does the Sabbath need "keeping"? Once his answer is "during the week," as we work to bring Shabbat and its spirit into all our weekday doings. There it brushes up against the harshness of the weekday world, and it needs special guarding. Our Sabbath has to be strong enough to go with us out into our daily lives, but there we need to take special care to preserve it. But his second answer is of a different sort. It is we who need guarding or keeping on the Sabbath. On this day our souls are open and vulnerable in a special way. The casks of wine that are slowly fermenting within us over the course of

*our whole lives are exposed to the air each Sabbath, if we
allow that "inner gate" to open. Doing so requires great care;
the exposed inner self needs our guarding.*

3

In the Midrash: "He hurled the tablets from his hands and
shattered them" (Ex. 32:19). "Once Moses saw that Israel
would not be able to withstand God's wrath at the Golden
Calf, he bound his soul to them and smashed the tablets. Then
he said to God: 'They have sinned and I have sinned, for I
smashed the tablets. If You forgive them, forgive me also,' as
Scripture tells us: 'Now if You will forgive their sin . . . then
forgive mine as well. But if You do not forgive them, do not
forgive me either, but rather 'wipe me out of Your book that
You have written'" (Ex. 32:32).

The meaning of this midrash is not clear. It is also difficult
to understand the midrash that tells us it was the sight of the
letters flying off the tablets that caused Moses to smash them.

The meaning of the matter seems to be this: Torah depends
on the preparation of Israel, on the readiness of those who are
supposed to receive the Torah. Scripture says that the words
were "incised [harut] on the tablets" (Ex. 32:16). The rabbis
comment: "Freedom [herut] from the evil urge, from the
Angel of Death, from death itself" and so forth. But what does
"incised on the tablets" really mean? Only as the light of
Torah is engraved and incised on the hearts of Israel are the
letters incised on the tablets as well. The real writing is on
the heart, of which Scripture says: "Write them upon the
tablet of your heart" (Prov. 3:3). That is why the letters flew
off when Israel sinned.

But Moses our Teacher had not really sinned; he had it in
his power to hold on to Torah, as the blessed Holy One said
to him: "I will make of you a great nation" (Ex. 32:10). Because he risked his life for the children of Israel and refused to
separate himself from them, he and they were truly joined together, not to be divided.

Moses loved the whole community of Israel even more than he loved the tablets. He also knew the will of God, and he knew that Israel were more beloved to God than anything. It was for this very reason that the letters flew off the tablets, and that is why he smashed them [for they no longer contained God's word].

By this act of joining himself to Israel, Moses in fact redeemed them. Once he and they were united in this way, they did not sin. In the hour when they did sin, he was not with them.

I heard something similar from my saintly grandfather, of blessed memory. Our rabbis taught that "I am the Lord thy God" was said in the singular so that Moses might claim [in defense of Israel]: "You said it to me and not to them." My grandfather interpreted this as follows: Surely the commandment was to all of Israel! But since they are all a single one, attached to Moses who draws them all together, the commandment was to him and to them at once.

This offers a way of dealing with the sin of the Golden Calf. Israel clearly had fallen into disunity before the calf was made. On the rung where they then stood [that of separation], they indeed had received no command. Their only real sin was that of falling out of oneness, the sin of disunity. But this is surely not so severe as the sin [of idolatry] itself.

2:200

Moses is the true rebbe, joining his soul to that of his people in the moment after their sin, forcing God, as it were, to save them from destruction, and accepting no forgiveness for himself unless they are forgiven as well.

But the joining has to go both ways. Moses, who was with God on the mountain, has to come down and join his soul to ours. His task is to unite himself with God's people, the ones he loves so much, and whom God loves as well. But that love makes a demand on those of us who were down here, dancing before the Golden Calf. We have to leave all our idols behind us and join our souls to that of Moses, up there on the mountain, worshipping God alone. And the price is quite clear: as long as we hold fast to those things that divide us—from one another or from the soul of Moses that still dwells in our midst—there can be no going up that mountain.

4

According to RaSHI, the commandments of the tabernacle were given only after the sin [of the Golden Calf]. This means that the first tablets were prepared to be right there in Israel's midst, without any ark or tabernacle. Israel were supposed to exist in a noncorporeal way.

Our sages pointed to this with their parable [of the king's daughter who married a prince. The king, who could not keep them at home, but who could not live without his daughter, said to them]: "Wherever you go, make a little chamber for me, and I will dwell with you." This seems to mean that had it not been for the sin, they would not have been separated from the Creator at all. But now there was a bit of distance, so the counsel was [to fashion] the tabernacle and its vessels.

2:204

We only need "religion" because of our distance from God. The One who cannot bear to see us so far off gives us a way to come closer—this is the Temple, tabernacle, synagogue, and the whole world of sacred forms. While we need these and use them as a way to come closer, all of us also bear in our hearts the memory of a moment when the word was right there, inscribed clearly within us, readable in our own hearts. Then we had no need for such "means" of access to the holy at all.

VA-YAKHEL

1

"'The people are bringing more than is needed. . . .' Moses thereupon had this proclamation made throughout the camp: 'Let no man or woman make further effort toward gifts for the sanctuary!' So the people stopped bringing. Their efforts had been enough for all the tasks to be done, and more" (Ex. 36:5–7).

This is the comment by Midrash Tanḥuma on [the verse:] "Moses saw all the work" *(mel'akhah)* (Ex. 39:43). It does not say: "All the work of the sanctuary," the Midrash notes, but rather [that] Moses looked at *"all* the work"—all of [God's work in] Creation. The point is that the whole purpose of making the sanctuary was to affirm Creation. This is the Creation, of which it is said: "And God saw all that He had made,

135

and behold it was very good . . . heaven and earth were completed . . . and God blessed [them] . . ." (Gen. 1:31–2:3). So, too, the sanctuary, which confirms that Creation: "Moses saw . . . and it was good in his sight . . . Moses blessed them."

Thus the Zohar explains in several places that God created the world by the power of Torah, and the righteous affirm that Creation by the power of Torah. Therefore "Moses saw": he saw that they had set right "all the work"; all of Creation—all of doing, in fact—had been put straight. . . .

We find in the story of Creation that heaven and earth kept on expanding when they were created, so that God had to stop them and say, "Enough!" So it was that the children of Israel kept giving until he said to them, "Enough!" This is the meaning of [the verse:] "Their efforts had been enough. . . ." But what is the meaning of "and more"? Don't "enough" and "more" contradict one another? But now we understand that this was how it had to be: they had to contribute more than was needed, until they had to be told, "Enough!" This too was part of the "work" that was needed for the sanctuary.

2:222

Overflowing generosity was what was needed for the making of the mishkan, *an act of human giving that did not put limits on itself. This act is comparable only to God's first gift of overflowing generosity in the creation of heaven and earth. Every* mishkan, *or dwelling-place for God, that we make in our lives requires such generosity of spirit.*

The account of Creation referred to here is also a somewhat frightening one. Once God's creative energies were released, the process might have gone forward, with almost instantaneous effect, until all of Creation—including each soul or spark that is to exist down to the end of time—would have come forth immediately. Such a Creation would have contained its own destruction, exhausting at once all the resources of existence. In order for the world to exist over a course of time, God had to hold back Creation by calling out, "Enough!" In the parallel suggested here, human activity needs the same self-

limitation; knowing when to stop is part of the task of our human doing. We need to leave some room, after all, for the countless future generations coming after us, who will also want to take a hand in building God's dwelling-place on earth.

2

"Take from among you gifts for the Lord; everyone whose heart so moves him shall bring them" (Ex. 35:5). The Midrash quotes: "Vast floods cannot quench love, nor rivers drown it" (Cant. 8:7), commenting: "My children made Me a sanctuary of [mere] skins, and I came down and dwelt among them."

The point is that the love and attachment to God that Israel received at Mount Sinai remain alive in them forever, even when sin prevents them from bringing this hidden love out into the open. So after the sin [of the Golden Calf], they needed to give this offering. By the act of giving they brought forth their own inner generosity, their longing and attachment, so that they were able to draw the Shekhinah [into their midst]. That is why the sanctuary is called "the tabernacle of witness"—it bears witness that the Shekhinah dwells in Israel.

When the sanctuary and Temple were standing, however, this presence was so palpable that there was no need for such "witnessing." The witness is rather for all later generations, saying that even when it cannot come forth, the imprint of holiness is still there in the innermost hearts of Israel.

In fact this is true of all the mitsvot, which are counsels on how to bring that inner sense of giving and desire into reality, as in [the verse:] ". . . everyone whose heart so moves him." This act of offering and uplifting brought forth all the giving and desire that lay hidden within their hearts. Thus are all the mitsvot called a "lamp": "For the commandment is a lamp and Torah is light" (Prov. 6:23), and also: "The soul of man is the lamp of the Lord, revealing all his inmost parts" (Prov. 20:27). You can raise up all your desires to God by means of the commandments.

The work of the sanctuary bears witness for all generations, calling out to us that even when sin separates us from God, the love in our hearts is never extinguished.

2:227

The sanctuary or Temple has never really been destroyed; it has only taken on another form. The life of the mitsvot is now the holy "place" we enter in order to witness God's presence in our midst. Our task is to make that presence as apparent through our life of holiness as it was in ancient times when the Shekhinah almost visibly filled the Holy Temple. This remains the task of the Jew forever. And if old forms seem to fail, our witness requires both that we renew them and place new ones by their side, through which God's light will also come to shine.

 3

"Six days shall work be done" (Ex. 35:2). This refers also to the six directions, the four "winds" and above and below. All the powers and qualities gather together to build a palace for that innermost place, the Sabbath. This is the true building of the *mishkan*, of which it says: "Where is the house you will build Me?" (Is. 66:1).

2:221

Here the kabbalistic structure underlying hasidic teaching is more apparent than usual. The six days and six directions are both extensions of the sefirot, *the primary number-structures of existence, embodying them in time and space. The heart of the* sefirot, *in this hasidic reading, is Shabbat, equated throughout this book with the deepest human heart and the innermost core of being, revealed to us on the Sabbath.*

PEKUDEY

1

"All the labor of the tabernacle was completed; the children of Israel did just as God had commanded Moses; such did they do" (Ex. 39:32).

The tabernacle redeemed doing itself; that is why, according to the sages, everything in it is referred to as *mel'akhah* or "work," [the same word used for God's "work" in Creation]. The labor of the tabernacle redeemed every deed that exists in the world. It is called "the tabernacle of witness," for by it Israel make it clear that all of Creation belongs to God. Just as in Creation it was said of each thing: "And God saw that it was good" and then over the Creation as a whole: "God saw all that He had made, and behold, it was very good. . . . And

139

He completed . . . and He blessed . . . " (Gen. 1:31–2:3), so too
in the tabernacle each detail was "as He commanded," and in
the end "the labor was completed" (Ex. 39:32). . . . "And
Moses saw all the work, that they had done it just as God
commanded . . . and Moses blessed them" (Ex. 39:43).

Now Creation was redeemed in a way that was distinctive
for Israel. That is why it was all done through Moses. . . .

By means of the *mishkan* Israel separated out the goodness
within doing; of it the tabernacle was made. Thus "doing" as a
whole was redeemed. That is why the verse says "the tabernacle was completed" and afterward "the children of Israel did
as God had commanded. . . . " Now all doing could follow the
command of God.

2:232

*The tabernacle was Israel's own distinctive way of repeating
and thus fulfilling God's work in creating the world. Like
every religious society, we celebrate the most universal of
truths in the most particular of ways. Because their celebration is so distinctive, setting Israel off from the other nations,
the blessing of the tabernacle comes about through Moses. It
is Moses who "saw all the work . . . and blessed them." Why
Moses and not God? Because God's own blessing was already
given to all that exists, at the very moment of Creation. God
did not have to repeat that blessing here, not to a form that
separated the creatures from one another. But Israel needed to
feel its work was blessed, and indeed the tabernacle was a
place of holiness. Such a blessing, one that appreciated the
human need for difference as well as the human need to value
our work, had to come about through a human vessel, and
was pronounced by Moses.*

 2

"The tabernacle of witness" (Ex. 38:21). It witnessed to Israel
that God had truly forgiven them for making the Golden Calf,
for now He was causing His presence to dwell among them.

Why did they need this witness? Israel had been deeply disgraced by that sin. Now God gave the [people] the tabernacle as witness, in order to strengthen their hearts, to show that they had indeed repaired the damage wrought by their sin. The fact is that Israel are God's witnesses, as it says: "You are My witnesses" (Is. 43:12). But how is it possible that Israel, who were created to bear witness to God's oneness, could themselves worship idols? This thought caused Israel to neglect their witnessing, until God had to demonstrate that the sin was incidental to who they were, brought on by the "mixed multitude." Thus they really were worthy to witness God, just as they had been previously. The rabbis in fact teach that "Israel were not deserving of such a sin; it came upon them only to teach the way of *teshuvah.*" It came to teach every person who returns not to let himself fall too low in his own eyes, for by *teshuvah* we really are restored to what we were before.

That is why Yom Kippur, the day of forgiveness and atonement, is followed by the *sukkah,* another indwelling of Shekhinah in the Temple. This gives strength to all who return, telling them they are worthy to have Shekhinah dwell upon them.

2:239

The insight that guilt is the great impediment to true religious life is one that was well known to hasidic masters, beginning with the Ba'al Shem Tov himself. Among the most essential innovations of Hasidism is the insistence expressed here that teshuvah, *return to God, really does work, and that the one who returns is fully renewed in God's presence. The real task is to be sure that our witness goes forward, not interrupted by our own sense of inadequacy to the task. If we wait until we are perfect to attest to God, we will never do our job.*

 3

The Midrash quotes the verse: "A man of trust has many blessings, but he who runs after wealth will not be cleansed"

(Prov. 28:20). The man of trust, says the Midrash, is Moses, and "whoever is trustworthy, God brings about blessing by his hand." But the one who runs after wealth is Korah.

We have learned that *"shalom* is a vessel that contains blessing." This is the "man of trust": all his deeds are attached to his root, "planted firmly into a trustworthy place" (Is. 22:23). Then he is called *shalom,* for the lower portion is not whole *(shalem)* unless it is joined to that portion [the root of the person] above. This was the character of Moses our Teacher, of whom it says, "Moses, Moses" (Ex. 3:4), without any indication of a break between them. And he is called "a man of God" (Ps. 90:1), meaning that he is "half man and half God." Thus too the tabernacle, for it says: "These are rules of the tabernacle, tabernacle of witness" *(mishkan)*(Ex. 38:21). Of this, Scripture says: "like a city joined together" (Ps. 122:3).

This was the whole purpose of the tabernacle: to be a vessel containing *shalom* for the entire world. The same is true of Shabbat with regard to time. That is why all its deeds are doubled: two loaves of bread, "A psalm, a song for the Sabbath day" (Ps. 92:1), "Remember . . ." and "Keep . . . ," and it gives blessing to all of time. . . . So, too, "the man of trust" with regard to souls. Moses our Teacher gives blessing to all souls, as it says: "This is the blessing with which Moses the man of God blessed the children of Israel" (Deut. 33:1), because he was a man of trust. But of Korah it says: "And Korah took" (Num. 16:1), meaning that he caused division. The quarrelsome person is the very opposite of *shalom.* . . .

Here Scripture speaks of "tabernacle of witness," for this is the essence of Israel's witness: to bring divine blessing into the world. "You are My witnesses, says the Lord, and I am God" (Is. 43:12). This refers [to those times] when they are answered from heaven. Thus there is witness in space and in time. Israel deserved by their deeds to build the tabernacle and to have the Shekhinah dwell in their midst. Shekhinah comes forth also on Shabbat and at holy seasons because of Israel's merit. And the same is true in the realm of souls, when we bring forth holiness from above into our soul.

Scripture says that Bezalel, in building the tabernacle, "did all that God had commanded Moses" (Ex. 38:22). For the building of the tabernacle points to all 613 commandments. There are 248 positive commandments [paralleling the human limbs] and 365 prohibitions [parallel to the sinews of the body], to set right the entire human form so that holiness may dwell within it. This is the purpose of the commandments: to attach the very limbs and sinews of the person to their source. The same structure is present in the tabernacle. That is why it is called "the labor of the Levites," for the word *levi* can mean joining or attachment to the root.

This is all one matter.

2:239

Here is one of the clearest expressions of a key theme in the Sefat Emet, *the presence of holiness in the three realms of space, time, and person, and the parallels between them. Shabbat is the tabernacle or Temple transferred from the realm of space to that of time. The Sefat Emet speaks only rather rarely of the* tsaddik, *their parallel in the realm of person. Such avoidance of this topic is typical of Polish Hasidism of the later period, which had reacted against the excesses of other groups and their claims. But the figure of Moses here, the half-divine man, stands in that role. He, too, can be like the tabernacle or the Sabbath, a source of blessing for all who draw near.*

וייקרא

SEFER VA-YIKRA'

VA-YIKRA'

1

The Midrash opens by quoting: "Bless the Lord, O His mighty angels, who do His word to hear the sound of His word" (Ps. 103:20). The plain meaning here follows the sages' teaching on the question of why the *Shema'* precedes the passage: "It shall be if you truly listen" (Deut. 11:13ff.). First, a person has to accept the yoke of divine rule and afterwards the yoke of the commandments. "All that the Lord has spoken we shall do" (Ex. 19:8) is the general acceptance of divine rule. Only afterwards were they entitled to "hear the sound of His word." This refers to the commandments, and thus the second section of the *Shema'* opens: "It shall be if you truly listen unto My commandments."

This means that the sound of God's speech is present in each commandment. Our sages taught that each limb calls out to the person: "Fulfill the commandment that depends on me!" Each fulfillment is an acceptance of divine rule, and afterwards one comes to hear more. Thus we should "do His word" in order "to hear" more. We should never see ourselves as having dismissed our duty, but should ever do more in order to hear more so that we will do still more—constantly. . . .

3:5

This very modern insight is well known throughout Hasidism. It is indeed possible to hear the word of God, still calling out each day. But we come to such hearing only by means of doing. Enter into the commandments, live your life through them, and thus you will come to hear. The one who stands outside, waiting first to hear the word of God addressed to him or her alone—such a one will neither hear nor enter.

2

My grandfather and teacher said in the name of the Rabbi of Przysucha: Our sages taught that "It is all one, whether you do more or less, as long as you direct your heart to heaven." The famous commentator Turey Zahav opened his work with a question regarding this statement. "But suppose," he said, "that the one who does more also directs his heart to heaven? Is his conduct not still preferable?"

The Rabbi of Przysucha answered this with a parable, a tale of two merchants who went on the same journey. One arrived quickly, while the other was prevented from doing so and got there only some time later. When asked what his delay was all about, he replied: "The point is that I'm here. Whatever happened, happened." He did not comment further.

The meaning seems to be as follows: "As long as you direct your heart" says that the final goal of your deeds should be that your heart be directed to God, whether this comes to you rather easily or takes a great deal of effort. Deeds are to help one to direct the heart. This is very true.

Here this is said of the gift offering. Since one's offering is a coming near (*korban* = sacrifice/drawing near) to God, and that is the desired goal and the end of the matter, it makes no difference whether you give more or less. The end is one: coming near to God. This is the very meaning, in fact, of "direct your heart"—like the offering, you are drawn after your own root. This is the life-force of divinity, which has been placed in every thing.

3:3

The point that R. Simḥa Bunem of Przysucha seems to be making is that God is the undepletable wholesaler; He has "merchandise" for everyone who comes along on the journey, no matter when you arrive. The Sefat Emet is making the same point, though in his typically more mystical language: since the divine life is in every thing, even the smallest offering to God is enough to set your soul into connection with its root and to bring it back to the One. That is what religious doing is all about.

3

With regard to the small *aleph* of *Va-Yikra'*:

There are three sorts of letters in the Torah: those of enlarged size, those of reduced size, and the ordinary letters. These reduced letters seem connected to matters that depend upon action, the light of Torah flowing in a reduced and concentrated way into the actual doing of the mitsvah, as in "the commandment is a candle" (Prov. 6:23). This entire book, called *Teaching of the Priests*, is about deeds. For there are [three] categories: thought, word, and deed.

Torah itself is the category of word. This belongs particularly to Moses our Teacher, as it was when Torah was given. There it says: "And Moses went up" (Ex. 19:3), on his own, since he was specially designated for this rung. But the enlarged letters are still higher, in the very root of the written Torah, the category of thought. That is why they are written large, because thought can transcend reality and nature. Word is the intermediate category, between thought and action.

That is why *Va-Yikra'* is written with a small *aleph*, because action was "a small matter with regard to Moses." Here the Midrash quotes: ". . . who do His word, to hear the sound of His word" (Ps. 103:20)—for deed has to be joined to the word, and word to thought. That is why the *Teaching of the Priests* was given through Moses, so that he would join deed to word. The Midrash tells us that Moses was like a king's servant who built a palace, and on every single thing he fashioned he would write the name of the king. Thus Moses writes repeatedly: ". . . as the Lord commanded Moses."

The matter is thus: "Forever, O Lord, Your word stands in the heavens" (Ps. 119:89). "His words are alive and standing." Every word of God stands [forever] in the heavens. Therefore, one who fulfills even a single commandment "for its own sake" (lit.: "for its name") like Moses our Teacher truly joins this deed to the word of God that is in the mitsvah. This is the signature of the king. Therefore, we ask [before performing a commandment]: "May the pleasantness of the Lord our God be upon us" (Ps. 90:17). This is the meaning of "for its own sake—for its name's sake," since the entire Torah is composed of the names of God. There is thus a particular name that belongs to each commandment in the Torah. This again is [the meaning of] "who do His word to hear the sound of His word."

On weekdays we attain Torah by the deed. The holy Zohar says that donning tefillin before prayer is a way of fulfilling [the commandment:] ". . . they will make Me a sanctuary and I will dwell in their midst" (Ex. 25:8). But on Shabbat Israel need no tefillin, since they themselves are a sign; the light of Torah shines forth in the day itself. That, too, is why the work of the tabernacle, "who do His word," was not done on the Sabbath.

3:10

The inner linkage of thought, word, and deed goes to the heart of the mystical meaning of the commandments. Each mitsvah, we are told here, is linked to a particular name of God. So, too, we understand, is each name linked to a particular contemplative configuration in the mind of God, the realm of thought. For mortals of lesser rank than Moses, however, even the path of names is too profound for us to follow. We perform the commandments in the realm of action, filling them with the inner direction of our hearts, and that causes them to be joined to their counterparts in the realms of word and thought. But since the link is there and the flow goes in both directions, some glimmer of those great lights can be given to us as we light our little candle of the mitsvah, here in the world of action.

TSAV

≡ **1** ≡

"This is the Torah of the burnt-offering . . . a fire must always burn on the altar; it may not go out" (Lev. 6:1,6).

This is the purpose of human worship. Each day a new light comes down upon those who serve God, as the Scripture says: "And the priest shall burn wood upon it each morning, each morning" (vs. 5). So, too, is it written: ". . . in His goodness He renews each day . . . " (Prayerbook). This love comes to us as a gift of divine grace. Something of this light should remain imprinted on the heart throughout day and night; "it may not go out."

When this is the case, whatever thoughts and doubts that arise upon the heart will be burned up by the inner flame of

153

this imprint. "It is the burnt-offering upon its altar" (vs. 2); as the holy Zohar says, evil thoughts are consumed in this fire. "The burnt-offering upon its altar" means that no evil thought arises until the fire-power to consume it is already present. So says the RaMBaN: God does not bring any trial upon a person unless he has the power to withstand it.

In fact the fire that "must always burn" is the fear of God, but the wood that "he shall burn upon it each morning" is love, the "thread of grace" that we are taught is drawn forth each day. "God commands His grace by day, and at night His song is with me" (Ps. 42:9)—that is the fire that "burns upon its altar all the night."

This order is present with us each day, as the light of Torah works in the person, burning and consuming improper thoughts. All this takes place through Torah, which is called fire. There is fire that gives light—this refers to the 248 positive commandments of Torah, [performed] out of love. And there is a fire that burns—[these are] the 365 prohibitions, [observed] from fear of heaven.

The commandment here to remove the ashes hints that as we burn up the waste in our lives we are uplifted each day, and then we are given new light. This redemptive process is with us every single day. For the one who serves God in a simple way, daily accepting divine rule in reciting the *Shema'* and saying, "you shall love" then reads: "These words which I command you today shall be upon your heart"—that is the light made new each day. "And you shall speak of them when you dwell in your house and when you walk by the way, when you lie down and when you rise up"—we receive this light until we lie down and arise again. That is [the fire that burns] "all night, until the morning" (Lev. 6:2).

3:24f.

These opening verses of Parashat Tsav *are recited in the Sephardic and hasidic prayer-rite each morning, as part of the introduction to worship. They have long been interpreted as referring to spiritual or inner fire, the undying fire of prayer that is rekindled each morning. Here the two most basic prop-*

erties of fire, its power to warm and to burn, are joined to the two "wings" of prayer, the love and fear of heaven.

In a move typical of the much older rabbinic sources, the fire of the altar is here identified with Torah, rather than with prayer alone. This shows Ger as belonging to that Polish school within Hasidism that valued study and tried to combine the ancient intellectualist traditions of Judaism with the hasidic fire and enthusiasm for the religious life.

For us too, the study of texts such as these may itself be a religious act, no less filled with **kavvanah** *or directed intensity than is prayer or meditation. Sacred study as an act of devotion is an aspect of Judaism that continues to live on, right here in our own reading of the hasidic sources.*

2

"A fire must always burn, it may not go out" (Lev. 6:6). The Midrash begins by quoting: " . . . love covers over all sins" (Prov. 10:12). Scripture elsewhere says: "Great waters cannot douse love" (Cant. 8:7).

In the soul of every Jew there lies a hidden point that is aflame with [love of] God, a fire that cannot be put out. Even though "it may not go out" here (Lev. 6:6) refers to a prohibition, it is also a promise. Thus our sages said: "Even though fire descends from the heavens, it is a commandment to bring it from a common [i.e., human] source." The same is true of the human soul: there needs to burn in it a fiery longing to worship the Creator, and this longing has to be renewed each day, as we read: "The priest shall burn wood upon it each morning, each morning." Everyone who worships God may be called a priest, and this arousal of love in Israel's hearts is the Service of the Heart, that which takes the place of sacrificial offerings.

When this fiery love is present, any distracting thought that enters the heart is consumed. Thus the holy Zohar says that the evil thought is "the burnt-offering upon its altar." That in fact is the true purpose of all those thoughts that rise up within the heart: they are there to be overpowered in the fire of worship. In this way those distracting thoughts are purified and uplifted.

That is the reason it says "all night until the morning." The phrase appears redundant: why "until the morning" if we already said "all night"? But this is to show that the very admixture of distractions and their "darkness" in the worshipper's heart will itself bring about the "morning." For that is the order: "There was evening and there was morning": the mixture of good and evil is purified. Weekday prepares for the Sabbath, this world prepares for the next. So, too, the struggle in the heart of the one who serves goes on "all night until the morning." Our exile is also called night, but it too will bring about a morning. . . .

3:23

We long for a perfect act of worship, one in which there is no distraction, no doubt, no holding back, no wandering of the mind, nothing but the pure gift of love. But we miss the point! Our worship is all about struggle, an ongoing inner process of transformation. Indeed there is pure fire of love in our hearts, but it is there in order to meet and consume our lower passions, our distractions, all those thoughts that seem such unwelcome guests in our hearts when we try to pray. But their presence is the very point of prayer. They—or the "we," the self who is represented by them—come to us in that moment in order to be consumed, to be taken up into that secret fire that burns within us.

☰ 3

"This is the Torah of the burnt-offering" (Lev. 6:2). The Midrash quotes: " . . . love covers over all sins" (Prov. 10:12).

It has been said that "sin douses [the flame of] a mitsvah, but not [that of] Torah." "A fire will always burn" refers to Torah, of which it is written: "Are not My words like fire?" (Jer. 23:29). "It may not go out." Thus says the Faithful Shepherd in the holy Zohar.

This is why Torah teaches how to atone for all sins by means of sacrifice *(QoRBan)*. Note that in each of them the word "Torah" is used, showing that by means of Torah Israel can always return and draw near *(hitQaReB)*. It says twice: "Fire will burn upon the altar; it may not go out," pointing to the two Torahs, the written and the oral. Of these it says: "Sustain me with raisin cakes" *(ashishot* = "two fires") (Cant. 2:5), the fire above and the fire below, written Torah and oral Torah. So, too, they said that "even though fire comes down from heaven, the commandment is to bring it from a common source."

Israel eternally have a place in those two fires. "Are not My words like fire?" is the written Torah, and "The House of Jacob [is] fire" (Ob. 1:18), the "eternal life implanted within us [is the oral Torah]." This was the "stamp of fire" that the Holy One showed Moses, indicating that Israel would always have a place in this form of fire. Half the form is above and half of it below.

In the Temple, which was capable of receiving fire from heaven, it was commanded to arrange [wood upon the altar and] fire from below. So, too, in time: on the Sabbath there descends an extra soul, particular to Israel. The two Sabbath loaves represent bread from heaven and from earth. They are the same two fires: the written and the oral Torah.

The essence of love, of which it says: "'I love you,' says the Lord" (Mal. 1:2) is because at Mount Sinai Israel received [the commandment] "I am the Lord your God," the essence of Torah, carved into their souls. Through this inscription they can continually return and draw near to Him. This is "the continual rising upward that was made at Mount Sinai" (Num. 28:6).

3:29

We have learned several times that the human soul is half above and half below, united on the Sabbath. Now we learn that Torah too is half above and half below. Written Torah was spoken and given by God; oral Torah is that which lies deeply implanted within our souls. But even God in heaven, Master of the eternal Word, prefers the fire that comes from below. It is the working out of this internal Torah, and the fashioning of a life in response to it, that we have to bring as our "fire from below," our uniquely human offering to God.

SHEMINI

1

"On the eighth day Moses called Aaron and the elders of Israel" (Lev. 9:1). The Midrash teaches: "Beloved are the elders, and if they are young, their youth is secondary to them." The Tanḥuma adds: "God ages them quickly." This needs an explanation. Rabbi Akiba had said [just above in the Midrash]: "Israel are compared to birds. Just as birds cannot fly without wings, so too Israel cannot exist without their elders." Moses' *calling* the elders was a sign of affection and intimacy; "call" is the term used by the ministering angels [when "they *call* to one another"]. This is uniting and being one with the Root.

Just as there are seventy elders in the lower Sanhedrin, so too are there [seventy] above. That is why the Midrash mentions here that they sat in a semicircle. The same is hinted to

159

in the verse: "Her husband is known in the gates, as he sits with the elders of the land" (Prov. 31:23). What is "the land" doing here? The verse refers to the angels above; among them are those in charge of the lower world, and they are called "elders of the land." Those above eternally give light to those below.

On the verse, "Gather seventy men unto Me" (Num. 11:16), the Midrash notes that "unto Me" always refers to things that will last forever. Through the seventy elders below, the yeshivah [parallel to the Sanhedrin] was established above. They forever shine their light below. When the generation merits and there is a Sanhedrin of wise elders, they certainly are beloved. But even if those below are youthful [and inexperienced], the help from above that shines into them makes their youth secondary to the flow of upper light. The help from above is greater than any human power. Essential knowledge occurs in the world when the gates above are open. . . .

3:119

The shape of the Sanhedrin's chamber is read as a symbol of their being but half a Sanhedrin; their counterpart, filling the other half of the circular cosmic "chamber," is the yeshivah or court above. Just as we have seen the Sefat Emet claim that the human being in this world is but a half, joined to the "upper root" that eternally remains with God, here we see the same structure of thought applied to the legislative body of Israel, the rabbis, who are ever seated together with their counterparts in the upper realm. The wisdom that is expressed in their teachings and in the halakhic process continually flows into this world from "above."

The original hasidic masters, young men when the movement was created, were often accused of straying from the ways of their elders. Perhaps the Sefat Emet, who was forty-four years old and quite well established when this teaching was spoken, was defending a young colleague within the hasidic world, which by his time also tended to be dominated by the respect offered to elders.

2

"On the eighth day." The Sifra teaches that on this day there was joy before God in heaven like that of the day when heaven and earth were created. Of Creation, Scripture says: "There was evening and there was morning, one *day.*" And of this day [the dedication of the tabernacle] Scripture says: "Go forth and gaze, O daughters of Jerusalem, upon King Solomon, upon the crown with which his mother crowned him on the *day* of his marriage, the *day* of his heart's delight" (Cant. 3:11).

The children of Israel now brought forth a new path in the world, by means of their repentance. This prepared the way for future generations to come. Thus the rabbis taught that "Israel did not deserve to do such a deed" [the worship of the Golden Calf], but did so only to teach repentance.

God made humans straight, a part of the Creation that was all for God's glory. But this way was only for the righteous, as Scripture says: "The ways of the Lord are straight: the righteous shall walk in them [and sinners shall stumble in them]" (Hos. 14:10). But now Israel set forth a way by which even the weak who had turned crooked would be able to return to the straight path, by means of repentance. Only the lower creatures could bring this possibility to fruition, since "the ways of the Lord are [only] straight." That is why there was joy before God like on the day of Creation—for this would set the world aright.

This is "the crown with which his mother crowned him." ["Solomon" here refers to God; Scripture calls Israel] His "mother" because they brought forth this new path. And this took place "on the eighth day," the one that reaches beyond nature, past the seven-day cycle of Creation.

See how great repentance is! The rabbis teach that sin is powerful, since before Israel had sinned, they were able to look upon "the appearance of God's glory. . ." (Ex. 24:17), while after the sin they were afraid to gaze even at the intermediary [Moses]. Once they had repented, however, it says: "The glory of God appeared to all the people" (Lev. 9:23).

3:124

Here the teaching that humans are "in the image of God" takes on new meaning. God creates heaven and earth but needs us also to be creators. Our creation is in the moral realm, one in which a perfect God cannot create alone. Only flawed humans like ourselves could have given birth to the reality of teshuvah, to the sense that other flawed humans will always be able to change their ways. To do this, Israel themselves had to go through the experience of sin and repentance. The tabernacle dedicated on this eighth day stands as a symbol of God's forgiveness of their sin and of the possibility of forgiveness for all future generations.

3

"Moses said to Aaron: 'Approach the altar'" (Lev. 9:7). Aaron was ashamed [to draw near], but Moses said to him: "Why are you ashamed? For this you were chosen!" (RaSHI). The commentators say that it was because of this shame he had that he was chosen. But it could also be read otherwise: that the goal of being chosen was to reach this state of shame. Thus Scripture itself says about the giving of the Torah: "so that His fear be upon your faces in order that you not sin" (Ex. 20:20). The rabbis said that this refers to shame and that "if one has no shame, it is known that his ancestors never stood at Mount Sinai." So the purpose of Israel's coming near to Mount Sinai was to merit shame.

All that God metes out is as deserved. Just as Aaron was one who "loved people and brought them near to Torah," which the sages took to mean that he even brought sinners close so that they would be ashamed of themselves and repent, so did God mete out to him that He would draw him near to be high priest over all Israel. Aaron was deeply ashamed of himself; this is the token of true perfection.

But by means of shame you can really come close to each of the commandments. Take true shame to heart, [thinking:] "How can a clod of earth do the will of the Creator?" In this way you will be able to fulfill the mitsvah. And if it is done in a whole way, then a further measure of shame will come upon you. This testifies to the wholeness of the deed.

So [with regard to Aaron,] both interpretations are correct: it was because of his sense of shame that he deserved to be chosen as high priest, and this choosing caused the quality of shame to be established in him.

3:123

The Hebrew word bushah *has a wide range of meanings, reflecting the original link between "shame" and "shy" in English as well. We have lost too much of the sense that blushing or shame at a disgraceful act—evil talk or gossip, for example—is a sign of good breeding. That sense is forcefully contained in this text: the memory of Sinai continues to make us ashamed to transgress. The distinction between "shame" and "guilt" might be a good one for us to recover from our renewed contact with the tradition.*

 4

In the first chapter of Mishnah Avot: "Do not be like servants who serve the master in order to receive reward; be rather like servants who serve the master not in order to receive reward, and let the fear of heaven be upon you."

It could have been said more simply: "Do not serve in order to receive reward." But the meaning here is that all of a person's efforts should be directed toward doing the Creator's will. "Let the fear of heaven be upon you" means that fear of heaven is truly present in every Jew. But we need to work or to serve in order to draw our hearts near to that truth, rather than to walk in darkness. When the heart is aroused *constantly* to do the will of God, fear of heaven falls upon the person on its own.

So too we can understand the verse: "This is the thing the Lord has commanded you to do that the glory of God may appear to you" (Lev. 9:6). Let your will be only to do God's will, as He has commanded, and through this "the glory of God may appear to you"—the presence of Shekhinah within your heart will be revealed.

3:112

Serving God "for its own sake" rather than for reward is a matter of being, not just of doing. The Mishnah uses the expression "do not be" to indicate this: such service of God involves the entire way a person lives, not just specific actions. A life wholly dedicated to selfless service has its own built-in reward: true fear of God, implanted deep within the human heart, will come to the surface and be revealed. By serving without thought of reward, you "let the fear of heaven be upon you."

Only one who stands outside the life of faith will ask: "But what kind of reward is the fear of heaven?" As though to answer this question, however (for indeed the scoffer, too, lives in every human heart), our author ties his interpretation to the verse in this parashah. Here it is the "glory of God" that is revealed, surely a more attractive-sounding goal. But this glory too turns out to be just that which has been dwelling in the human heart all along—now brought into view by a life of selfless service. The final connection is not made here, but is perhaps implied: God's glory is our "fear of heaven."

5

"These are the living creatures of which you may eat" (Lev. 11:2). "Because Israel are attached to life," as RaSHI says.

On the verse (11:44–45) "[You shall not defile yourselves with any creeping thing that crawls upon the earth,] for I am the Lord your God who brought you forth from the Land of Egypt . . . ," the Talmud comments: "Had I brought Israel forth only so that they not defile themselves with creeping things, it would have been sufficient." The One "who brought you forth" has to be greater than the Exodus itself. Thus we say: "who brought us forth from the Land of Egypt and redeemed us from the house of slaves." There is a redemption from the narrow straits *(Mitsrayim/metsar)*, but there is a still higher rung, one above all places of constriction, an "inheritance without constraints." Since God has brought us into [this] true freedom, we are not permitted to eat any of those things that enslave the soul to the body. The essence of the soul's liberation is that it not be tied down to bodily things. . . .

3:121

. . . indeed the life of Torah is to be found everywhere, as it says: "You made them all in wisdom" (Ps. 104:24). But the life-force cannot be drawn forth from some things because [they contain] an admixture of good and evil. These are the signs: chewing the cud and having the split hoof. Each thing contains two keys, an inner and an outer. First the lock of nature has to be opened, so that the physical itself not be too entirely corporeal. This is the split hoof, one not completely closed, showing that there is a crack in the outer shell, in that which hides. Afterwards, the holy point within has to be opened. The animal that chews its cud hints at one who can bring forth that which lies within.

In these [the life-force] is drawn after the Jew who eats of them in holiness. The forbidden species are those from which we cannot bring forth that holiness. That is why the blessed Holy One has separated us from them.

3:120

The rules of kashrut, like all the commandments, are given to enable Israel to live in greater holiness. This was the purpose of our liberation from bondage and remains the essence of our higher freedom. We are to be freed from the universal human enslavement of soul to body, of deepest and purest self to the whims of physical desire. This liberation is attested by a system of restraint in the realm of eating. By consuming only the flesh of animals that symbolically offer openings to inwardness, Israel are reminded that even in the mundane and corporeal aspects of their lives, they are to seek always to discover and uplift the holy that everywhere lies within.

תזריע

TAZRIA'

1

The Midrash opens by quoting: "'You formed me backward and forward' (Ps. 139:5). Said R. Yoḥanan: A deserving person thus inherits two worlds, this one and the world to come . . . and one who is not deserving has to give an accounting, as the verse goes on to say: 'And You placed Your hand upon me.'"

All of Creation is in need of redemption [*tikkun*], as Scripture says: " . . . which God created to do" (Gen. 2:3). The human was created last in deed, but first in the order of redemption. It is through humanity that Creation and redemption are joined together. This is what the sages meant by noting that humans were created last, so that they could [immediately] enter the Sabbath, since the Sabbath belongs to redemption.

"Backward" in the Midrash refers to the weekdays, the days when we labor to purify those things of this world that are not yet redeemed. Through this we come to merit the Sabbath, the "forward" time, that of contemplation and redemption.

The human being is the one who links and joins all of Creation together. That is why we contain the most base corporeality and the most lofty spirit; "He created the person in the image of God" (Gen. 9:6). If that is the case, then just as God contains all beings—"You give life to them all" (Neh. 9:6)—so, too, do we humans contain all those creatures that are under us. And when we redeem all those who depend upon us, we then merit the place that awaits us, above them all. Thus we are taught [in the Midrash] that a deserving person is told: "You preceded all of Creation!" But one who does not merit, that is, who has not come to this place of redemption, is told: "This flea preceded you! This worm preceded you!"

"Backward" comes before "forward" in the verse, in accordance with RaSHI's explanation (Lev. 12:1) [that just as the creation of humans followed that of all the beasts, so too does the teaching concerning purification of the human body appear in Leviticus after the teaching about various matters relating to animals.] This is to indicate that we cannot achieve true understanding of Torah, the way we are to walk forward, until we first redeem the animal soul and our corporeal selves. Only then can we come to "teaching concerning humans."

3:128

The human being as a denizen of two worlds is a frequent theme in hasidic teachings. Often the hasidic masters were more positive in attitude toward the body or the physical world than were their predecessors or non-hasidic contemporaries. But they still retained a sense of separation between the two realms of spirit and flesh, the one charged always with the uplifting and transformation of the other.

From a contemporary point of view, this notion of the human community's relationship to nature can be called one of enlightened stewardship. We are certainly "higher" than

*the animals, as our human nature is internally "higher" than
our animal self. But the corporeal can by no means be disre-
garded, and in fact our first task in tikkun is that of redeeming the "lower" creatures that so depend on us. This teaching
has special meaning in our own day, when the dependence of
many species—and perhaps of the natural order as a whole—
upon human behavior has become so clear. To this contemporary reader, the Sefat Emet calls out clearly to say that all
our redemptive efforts within the human—and surely within
our more narrow Jewish—community will not be grounded
unless we turn first to the redemptive task of enabling Creation itself to survive.*

2

[On the same Midrash] . . . the human being contains the form
of this entire world. We are called microcosm or "small
world," since all the world is contained within each of us.
Everything exists because it is needed for human sustenance.
Therefore, the human has to contain something of the root [of
each thing that exists]. Humanity may thus be called the soul
of all created beings; they are the body or matter, and the
human is the soul or the form. That was why all of Creation
took place before the creation of humans, since the body
comes first. Creation first took on bodily form, and only then
did it receive its human soul. That is why it is taught [that humans were created on the sixth day] "so that they enter the
Sabbath immediately," since Shabbat is called by the Zohar
"the day for souls."

Just as these rungs exist in Creation, so are they present
later in Torah. God "says and does, speaks and fulfills." The
world was created by ten acts of speech and continues to exist
through Torah and its ten utterances (or "commandments").
That is why there is a place in Torah for each detail of Creation; thus "the teaching concerning the animal," "the teaching concerning the bird" (Lev. 11:46), and afterwards comes
the teaching concerning man.

So that is the meaning of [the verse:] "You formed me backward and forward." The human contains all, both upper and lower. Just as the human body contains the form of all the lower creatures, so does our soul contain the upper; that is the "forward." And that is why the sages took note that *va-yiytser* ("He created," referring to Adam—Gen. 2:7) is written with two *yods*: we are created twice, for this world and for the world to come. The Midrash refers to this as "inheriting two worlds."

3:131

At first reading this is a difficult text from the point of view of contemporary ecological awareness. Its radical anthropocentrism goes so far as to see all the rest of Creation existing only to serve human need, a viewpoint that these days is considered deeply suspect encouragement of a violation of earth's resources.

But I believe the text can be reread in a very different spirit, one that may provide a key to other retranslations as well. Yes, the human being is a very late product of the evolutionary process. We were created, as it were, on "Friday afternoon" of the earth's "week." And we do contain within us, in the form of DNA, genetic memory of all that came before us and led up to our evolution; in that we may indeed be called a "microcosm," though we have not yet learned to gain conscious access to the great wealth of "memory" stored within each of us. To call us the "soul" of Creation may seem like hubris, but to say we are existence made articulate and self-conscious, the first being in the evolutionary process that has developed the power to see its interrelationship with all other beings and to understand the process itself, does not seem out of line.

To this view of humanity we would also want to add a note of transcendence: memory and understanding of the evolutionary process do not exhaust the depths of the human spirit, whose greatness is in going beyond biological origins and limits, not merely in reaching back to them. Translated this way, the message of the Sefat Emet *suddenly does not seem very far from us at all.*

≡≡ **3** ≡≡≡≡≡≡≡≡≡≡≡≡≡≡≡≡≡≡

["The Lord spoke to Moses and Aaron, saying: If a person has in the flesh of his skin a sore . . . " (Lev. 13:1–2)].

. . . The verse makes these afflictions depend upon the skin (*'or*). This is based on the verse that says: ". . . the Lord God fashioned garments of skin for the man and his wife and He dressed them" (Gen. 3:21). The Midrash refers to a distinction between these "garments of skin" and "garments of light" (*'or*). It was because of sin that they came to be garbed in this coarse clothing, the skin of the snake. All of corporeality derives from there. Previously, they were in a spiritual state, as is said of the future. At the giving of the Torah, too, Israel were ready for this state. That is why it says of Moses that the skin of his face shone. He so redeemed "skin" that he was lit up through the shining speculum.

But we did not remain at that rung. Therefore, the afflictions reappeared; the Midrash teaches that it was sin that made us again impaired.

It is also known, however, that the skin is porous, containing many tiny holes. These allow the light to shine through its "shells." Only sin clogs up those pores, so that "darkness covers the earth" (Is. 60:2). That is why "the leprous affliction" is translated [into Aramaic] as *segiru* or "closing."

Now we also understand why the purification rites are assigned to Aaron and his sons the priests: it was they who set right the sin of the Golden Calf.

3:130

Here the wordplay between the Hebrew 'or and 'or ("skin" and "light") becomes the vehicle for a profound assertion of ancient Hebrew myth: that behind and within the person of flesh there lies another self, one dressed only in pure light. That this is our true self is attested by the fact that it was our identity at the beginning of human history, and will be so once more at the end.

Again, we have matter and spirit opposed to one another. But the hasidic master, wanting to lessen this dichotomy, notes that our inner light can shine through the very pores of our human skin! Even though we are again "blemished" and our skin has "closed up" again after Sinai, the light still shines within us.

METSORA'

1

"When you come into the land of Canaan, which I give you as a possession, I will cause a plague of leprosy to be upon a house in the land you possess" (Lev. 14:34).

What sort of strange announcement is this? RaSHI explains that the Canaanites [had been hiding gold treasures inside the walls of their houses, which the Israelites would find upon destroying the houses]. Now really! Did the Creator of the universe need to resort to such contortions? Why would He have given the Canaanites the idea of hiding [things in the walls] so that Israel would have to knock down the houses!

The real meaning of these afflictions of houses is in fact quite wondrous, a demonstration that Israel's holiness is so great that they can also draw sanctity and purity into their dwelling-places. Scripture tells us: "A stone shall cry out from the wall and a wooden beam shall answer it" (Hab. 2:11), regarding a person's sin, to which the walls of his house bear witness. How much more fully does the *tsaddik* have to bring a feeling of holiness into all that belongs to him, including both plants and ordinary physical objects!

That is just what Israel did when they brought the Land of Canaan forth from defilement and into the realm of holiness. Then it became the Land of Israel, and the blessed Creator caused His presence to dwell in the holy Temple. This is part of loving God "with all your might" (Deut. 6:5); we have to bring the light of holiness into all of our possessions. In this sense the "plague of leprosy" can fall upon houses too; the announcement is the good news that Israel can redeem all those places.

This is the real "hidden treasure"—that in the most corporeal of objects there are hidden sparks of the greatest holiness. . . .

3:139f.

What more is there to say? The only "hidden treasures" we need seek out are those hidden by God Himself, and these are hidden throughout reality. The only houses we need to destroy in order to find them are those walls we ourselves construct, the blinders we keep setting up to keep us from seeing the light within. We are our own Canaanites; we are our only Israel.

The Sefat Emet chooses to read the passage in this intrapsychic way, thus saving it from the obvious moral problems of a more literal reading. But a Jew living after 1945 cannot hear this RaSHI comment quoted without recalling the tales of Jews in Poland and elsewhere being asked by their gentile neighbors, as they were being led out to slaughter: "Where did you hide the gold?" In the face of this horrible memory, the aggadic tradition underlying RaSHI here serves to protect us from any moral superiority that our status as victims might give us. Under different circumstances, we are reminded, we might have been the ones to go searching for other people's treasures.

2

"This is the teaching concerning the leper" (Lev. 14:2). The Midrash quotes the verse: "To the wicked one God says, 'Why should you speak of My laws and bear My covenant upon your mouth?'" (Ps. 50:16) and declares that "the blessed Holy One does not desire the praise of the wicked."

The Torah offers to Israel counsel appropriate to all times, as it is written: "Peace, peace, to the far and to the near" (Is. 57:19). The far one, the Midrash tells us, is the leper, who was distanced and has now drawn near.

There are some who attain wholeness by drawing near and others who do so by distance. These are the two sorts of *shalom* to which the verse refers. Such a verse as "Why should you speak My laws?" is a part of the Torah's way, telling the wicked one to distance himself. His healing will come about through his being sent out of the camp. The same is true of a person who simply did some misdeed and became distanced from holiness. He has to accept this distancing with love and learn that within it is to be found his redemption. The Midrash says that the ways of the blessed Holy One are not like those of man. Man cuts with a knife but heals the wound with a bandage, while God heals with the very same thing by which He wounds. The wound itself is the healing!

That is why the portion opens with [the verse:] "This is the teaching *(torah)* concerning the leper," for his *torah* is in his being sent far off. The [lowly] hyssop also points to this; by humbling himself he will earn the right to draw near. Everything the Torah has one do is for the good, as it says: ". . . all her paths are peace" (Prov. 3:17). Even those paths that distance a person lead to wholeness; this is "peace to the far." Scripture says: "'Am I a God nearby?' says the Lord, 'and not a God far off?'" (Jer. 23:23), to which the Midrash adds: "Do I bring near and not make distant?" God's divinity is not to be found only in closeness, but even the distancing God does ultimately brings us near. . . .

3:141

Modernity has been defined by our sense of distance from God. This distance then becomes alienation, a sense of being cut off also from our own true selves, from our natural roots, and from the world around us. The hard-won freedom of modernity is also the root of our modern pain and sense of emptiness.

Dare we allow ourselves to see this entire process from the viewpoint of a higher rung of consciousness? To say that our modern selves are God's way of sending us far off so that we might draw near again? Modernity has surely brought us new sorts of wholeness, just as it has broken us. Can this breaking, too, be a tool of the Spirit, intended ultimately to heal?

3

"Then shall the priest command to take for the one to be cleansed two living birds . . . " (Lev. 14:4). RaSHI comments that "leprosy" is a punishment for evil speech and birds are chatterers. The holy Zohar says that such afflictions come about both through evil words and through good words that we pass up an opportunity to speak. "I was silent of good and my pain was frozen" (Ps. 39:3).

It is written that "death and life are in the hands of the tongue" (Prov. 18:21). Because the power of language is so great, we have to take special care concerning idle talk, which prevents the mouth and tongue from bringing forth words of holiness. Scripture says: ". . . you shall speak of them" (Deut. 6:7), which the sages interpret to mean: "Whoever engages in idle talk transgresses a positive commandment, since it says 'of them'—and not of other things." This is a condition: to the degree to which you guard your tongue from meaningless talk, you are able "to speak of them. . . . "

The birds are there to atone for two sins. The one that is slaughtered is there so that one will cut himself off from idle chatter, and how much more from evil talk itself. The bird that is set free is to prepare the mouth and tongue to speak words of Torah. That is why the slaughtered bird is forbidden [to be eaten], while the one set free is [later] permitted. On the verse "every pure bird you may eat" (Deut. 14:20) the sages noted: "This includes the bird set free [in the leper purification ceremony]." This bird points to pure speech, which is the very essence of the human being. The verse ". . . man became a living soul" (Gen. 2:7) is translated: "a speaking spirit. . . . "

3:143

Gossip and evil talk are great dangers in any circumstance. Their power is especially great in the sorts of small and overly familiar communities that typified the shtetl and Hasidim as a group; it is no wonder that we find much concern with the evil power of the tongue in the teachings of traditional Jewish sages, both hasidic and not.

But this passage goes further than warning against evil speech. It suggests a true abstinence of talk, one that would keep us close to silence except for words of prayer and Torah. This counsel, also found very widely in the devotional classics of Judaism, suggests a gate that we would do well to re-open in our day, at least for limited periods. The notion of ta'anit dibbur, *a "speech-fast" in which one chooses to remain silent—except for prayer and study—for a day or some other period of time, is a Jewish tradition worth reclaiming.*

AḤAREY MOT

1

"You shall not do like the deeds of the Land of Egypt in which you dwelt, nor shall you do like the deeds of the Land of Canaan into which I am bringing you; you shall not follow their statutes. You shall do My judgments and keep My statutes to go by them. . . . These are the things a person shall do and live by them" (Lev. 18:3–4).

The passage is difficult. If it refers to the forbidden sexual liaisons that are about to be explicitly listed, why does it make them dependent upon "the deeds of Egypt and Canaan"? Rather, the intent is that in *all* our deeds we not do things as they are done in Egypt and Canaan. Every deed has an inner and an outer side; the [inner] root of all things is surely in holiness, since all was created for God's glory. This innermost

179

point has been given to Israel. That is the meaning of [the verse:] "Let all your deeds be for the sake of heaven." That is why the deeds of the other nations are referred to as "statutes," as in "you shall not follow their statutes." They have no relationship to the inner meaning of all things, and cleave to mere externals.

In fact it is by means of the commandments that Israel can do all their deeds in holiness. That is the meaning of "You shall do My judgments. . . ." In this way you will be able to do all your deeds not in the way of Egypt or Canaan. This is "to go by them . . . things a person shall do and live by them." We have also explained that through the commandments one draws life into all things. On a simple level, this refers to the rabbis' teaching that every mitsvah is parallel to a particular limb. By devoting all of the life-force in that limb to the commandment alone, you can bring new life from the commandment into that limb. In this way you can do all your deeds in holiness. This is the meaning of "who made us holy through His commandments. . . ."

3:144f.

The teaching contains an interesting reversal of a common Christian complaint about Judaism, whose halakhic structure has often been depicted by Christians as devotion to "mere externals." Here it is the nations of the world, that do not understand the inner workings of things, whose laws are only ḥukkot, statutes "carved in stone." The laws of Israel, as our author has frequently reminded us, are carved rather on the tablets of the heart. Each side in this long debate has thus painted the other as lacking in real faith, real heart.

Of course this sort of interreligious sparring only makes sense in a world where each tradition holds fast to its exclusivist truth-claim. When each learns to see the other as also having a hold on the inner meaning of life, however different the symbol-system through which it gains that access may be, the denigration of the other's faith no longer has any meaning. Parts of humanity have taken some important steps in that direction in the years since the Sefat Emet was written, but only as a result of the most horrible dehumanization of all time that included among its victims the Hasidim of Ger and the Jews of Poland. It behooves us to remember, as victims of that unique event, that any denigration of the other's faith is a step toward seeing that other as less than human.

2

I heard my grandfather interpret the verse "These are the things a person shall do and live by them" (Lev. 18:5) to mean: "You should put most of your life-force into Torah and commandments."

One could add that in this way you truly "live by them," since Torah also gives life to those who fulfill her, life in this world and the world to come. Just like the wicked, whose desire to live is so that they can enjoy this world, and therefore all their life comes through eating and drinking, so the righteous, who seek to live for the sake of God's commandments and His Torah, are sustained by the Torah and mitsvot themselves. "For they are our life and the length of our days." Our life is given to us by Torah.

The sages said of "to walk in them" (Lev. 18:4)—"put them first and not second." This really depends upon a person's devotion: insofar as you put Torah and commandments first, Torah gives you life in this world as well. This is the meaning of "a person shall do" and then "live by them." The true root of Torah is above, and it contains all the worlds. But when Israel act in accordance with Torah, it gives them life in this world as well. That is, after all, why the blessed Holy One gave us the Torah, so that through us its light [would] spread forth in this world as well.

3:147

We place our life-energy in Torah, and Torah gives us new life. The mutuality of this exchange allows for its eternal renewal. Good teachers will understand this easily. We devote our energies unstintingly to the texts and traditions that we teach, and these sources themselves become a font of constant renewal for us.

But the Sefat Emet wants more here than just devotion to Torah. It is the Torah that contains all the worlds to which we are to give ourselves, the Torah that was God's plan for Creation. An openness to that Torah will necessarily give us a love of this world as well, but one that is rooted in the divine perspective.

3

Another reading of "the things a person shall do and live by them": The sages referred this to the world to come, because in this world one does ultimately die. The commandments set aright the inner image of the human being, the 248 [positive commandments, parallel to the limbs] and the 365 [prohibitions, parallel to the sinews]. When a person attains this garment, death has no power over him, as was the case with Adam before the sin. After sinning he was garbed in a body that is subject to death. The commandments give us access again to our original garment.

This teaching is also to be found in "the things a person shall do and live by them," for by doing them you fulfill your true image as a person. Even in a more direct sense, by doing the commandments you become a vessel to receive the life-force that is beyond death, of which Scripture says: "He blew into his nostrils the breath of life" (Gen. 2:7). There is no place for death here. Only due to sin did we lose this original vessel; in the next world we will regain it, prepared by the commandments.

Here Scripture says "shall do," and elsewhere we also read: "No eye but Yours has seen, O Lord, what You *shall do* for the one who waits for You" (Is. 64:3). The "eye" refers to the form or image; in the future Israel will be garbed in a spiritual image comprehended by no creature, but only by [God]. Thus the sages taught that in the future [the angels] will recite "Holy!"

when Israel stand before them. All this will come about because of the commandments in this world.

But the sages say of the Sabbath that it is "something like the world to come." So something like that form or image is revealed on it. That is why "the light of a person's face on a weekday is not like the the light of his face on the Sabbath."

3:149

The path of Torah is a path back to Eden, a return to "the way of the Tree of Life." It is no accident that the phrase gan eden *in Hebrew refers both to biblical Eden and to life after death. We seek to return to the Eden whence we came, to the primal holiness, even divinity, that humans once had, but lost at the very beginning of time.*

But once again an other-worldly teaching is referred back to this world as well. If we want to see something of what that Eden is like, the Sefat Emet tells us, we should just look into the face of a Jew who truly keeps the Sabbath.

KEDOSHIM

1

"You shall be holy, for I the Lord your God am holy" (Lev. 19:2). This section was spoken in public assembly. No one can attain holiness except by negating his own self before the whole of Israel. Thus Scripture says: "The whole community, all of them, are holy" (Num. 16:3). This means that when they are all one, they are holy. That is why most of the laws in this section deal with interpersonal matters. When Israel are one, the hand of the nations also has no power over them. Insofar as they are separate from the nations, holiness dwells in their midst. Thus RaSHI teaches: "Wherever guard is kept regarding interpersonal borders [avoiding sexual misdeed], there you will find holiness." So it is on the Sabbath, when "all of them

185

are united in secret oneness" that "the 'other side' passes away from them," and there is holiness.

But it says: ". . . for I the Lord your God am holy." Holiness, too, has to be so that we merit being attached to God, blessed be He. This is what the Midrash means when it asks here: "Might you think 'You shall be holy' means 'just like I am'?" It learns from the case of Pharaoh, who declared [when appointing Joseph to office]: "I am Pharaoh" (Gen. 41:44), meaning that Pharaoh elevated Joseph only for his own sake. He saw that Joseph was clever, and he raised him up to protect Pharaoh's kingdom. Our holiness should not be separated off in this way [of self-glorification], but should be only for the sake of attaching ourselves to God. "For I am holy," and you can be attached to God only by attaining holiness.

This "assembly" applies to each individual as well. We have to gather together all of our 248 limbs and all our desires into one. Thus our sages taught on the verse: "The Lord your God walks about in the midst of your camp . . . so your camp must be holy" (Deut. 23:15)—in the midst of your own 248 limbs. So it is by means of the commandments [sanctifying the limbs] that one attains holiness; "He has made us holy through His commandments." And we ask: "Sanctify us by Your commandments." It is by means of the commandments that the limbs are joined together and come to oneness. Then there is holiness.

But the holiness of all Israel remains higher. This is the "assemblage for the sake of heaven" whose "end is to persist," since the name of heaven is called upon it and holiness dwells in it. Thus it was in actual history: because Israel were united, they had both the tabernacle and the Temple, God's presence dwelling in their midst. Now destruction has come upon that assemblage, because of baseless hatred, for holiness can be present only where there is oneness. . . .

3:158f.

Even holiness has to be for the sake of heaven. The perfection of the self as an end can be idolatry, a kind of spiritual self-aggrandizement comparable to that of Pharaoh, who took

himself for a god. Here the Sefat Emet seems to foresee some-
thing of the danger in the recent "New Age" joining of the
search for self-realization and the quest for God. These two
are indeed deeply related, as the mystic is the first to under-
stand. But the essential value of self-transcendence makes all
the difference. Mystics in all the great traditions have under-
stood this. Only humility and the negation of self that allows
one to join with all of Israel—and we would add, all of hu-
manity, all of Creation—can make room for God's presence.

2

"You shall be holy." RaSHI comments: "Be careful about sexual misdeed and transgression." RaMBaN reads it: "Sanctify
yourself within the domain of the permitted."

In my humble opinion RaSHI has the correct intent here.
Surely, "You shall be holy" is one of those commandments
that has no fixed limit. The more you abstain, the greater the
holiness you attain, and there is no end to this. That is why it
says: "You shall be" [pointing to the future], for a person
should always add holiness to holiness. A hint of this may be
seen in the verse: ". . . sanctify them today and tomorrow"
(Ex. 19:10), showing that there is no end point at which you
can say: "I am already holy!" The proof of this is to be found
in that generation [when Torah was given]. They really were
"the whole community, all of them holy," and yet God said
to them: "You *shall be* holy."

This is the meaning of "Might you think: 'Just like I am
holy . . . ,'" since the verse indicates that there is no limit to
holiness. Now a limit is added: "My holiness is above your holiness." But this in fact shows how limitless holiness is, that
right here in this world, a person can become more holy than
the Seraphim.

But surely holiness has to begin with abstaining from sexual
misdeed and transgression. That is where you enter into the
boundary of holiness; this much is required of every Jew. From

there you can add on, just as you can with learning Torah and those other things for which "there is no fixed measure."

3:157

Here the Sefat Emet affirms the classic Jewish moral position. Holiness comes about only through the training of discipline. There is no holiness without a degree of withholding and self-control. The beginning-place of these is where human beings are most likely to be controlled by their passions rather than by the dictates of the inner heart and soul. Sexual control and self-limitation are the training-grounds where we prepare for the rest of holiness.

Hasidism began as a rejection of the kabbalists' excessive concern with sin and repair of the specific "damage" it could cause. The Ba'al Shem Tov taught a love and embrace of the corporeal world as the dwelling-place of divine light. Excessive worry about sin, he taught, kept one from doing the real work of seeking out sparks of light everywhere, even in the most unlikely places. But those rather risqué formulations were never meant as permission for licentiousness. Hasidism maintained, even beyond its formal commitment to halakhah, a strong belief that curbing the passions was essential to the religious life. Here the Sefat Emet is being entirely faithful to hasidic tradition.

This is not a popular position in our world, one in which many have tried for holiness without abstention. The most serious seekers ultimately learn that such is not possible, though the learning of that lesson alone may sometimes exhaust a lifetime, one that might have been better spent in a more advanced form of seeking.

 3

"Do not hate your brother in your heart; reprove, reprove your neighbor, do not bear sin on his account" (Lev. 19:17). The commentators have written that *reprove* is doubled to indicate that the one who reproves should be included in the rebuke he offers. He should know that he, too, has a part in this sin. That is, "do not bear sin on his account." Do not cast the entire burden of sin onto the transgressor. Involve your own self in this matter and repent for the sin. Then surely your neighbor will feel aroused to repent as well.

"Love your neighbor as yourself" (vs. 18) we interpret as a [causative] form, referring to the love of God. Where have we found [it written] that a person is supposed to love himself? Then what does "as yourself" mean? The meaning rather is: "Make God as beloved to your neighbor as He is to you." In fact our sages interpreted "You shall love the Lord your God" (Deut. 6:5) to mean: "May the name of heaven become beloved through you." Just as you struggle to bring the love of God into your own heart, so should you do for your neighbor as well.

This is why the sages taught that "Love your neighbor as yourself" is an underlying principle of Torah.

3:159

Here we have a reading of the "underlying principle" quite different from the well-known teaching of Hillel. He said the most basic rule was: "That which is hateful to you, do not to your neighbor." That seems to be a direct interpretation of "Love your neighbor as yourself." But the hasidic master reads the verse in a more devotionalist context: the greatest gift you can give your neighbor is not just to treat him or her decently, but to share with them your love of God.

The ground that lies between these two readings of the same verse provides the context for an essential question of religious ethics. What is my obligation to my neighbor? To treat him decently, out of respect for our shared humanity? Could the Torah's message be that humanistic and seemingly "secular"? Or is it to treat him not just with decency, but with the sacred respect due him as the image of God? And does that not mean helping him to realize that he is created in God's image? But how do I do that while respecting his right to believe and live differently? The Torah contains a strong imperative that we teach and "witness" our faith to others, both Jews and non-Jews. We need to find a way to do this work, but one that will save us from the pitfalls of "missionaries" who have too much exclusiveness and self-assurance and too little respect and love for human variety and the many garbs in which God's presence can be found.

4

"When you come into the land and you plant every food-bearing tree . . . " (Lev. 19:23). The Midrash quotes: "It is a tree of life to those that hold fast to it" (Prov. 3:18).

This means that the power of planting has been given to the children of Israel. They are able to plant every thing, to join it to its root, by the power of Torah. This is the meaning of "He has implanted eternal life in our midst." "You shall plant every food-bearing tree" shows us that we are to negate each thing unto its root. This is the essence of [coming into] the Land of Israel; for this reason we pray: ". . . implant us within our border." First we have to implant our own souls within their root, because "man is the tree of the field" (Deut. 20:19).

3:156

"The power of planting" is a wonderful description for the religious task. Here it is used as a metaphor for connecting each thing to its root. Elsewhere we have seen it in connection with the oral Torah, the power of interpretation implanted within Israel that allows us to "plant" meaning within the Torah text.

This brief discussion of "spiritual husbandry" was offered in 1878, four years before the first Jews went to establish the BILU colonies in the Land of Israel and began real planting. Some among the early agricultural pioneers, especially the founders of the kibbutz movement, had a quasi-religious sense of their work: they were "planting" a new Jewish people, rerooting an alienated folk both literally and figuratively in the soil of their own national life. A few among them— both A. D. Gordon and R. Abraham Isaac Kook immediately come to mind—had a truly transcendent understanding of this planting. Rav Kook knew well that Israel's rerooting in its soil was part of the return of all things to their root in God, a view that may be a concretization, against the background of Zionism, of ideas already found in the Sefat Emet.

אמור

'EMOR

1

"You shall sanctify him" (Lev. 21:8).

[Moses is to sanctify Aaron as priest, showing that] the holiness of the priests depends upon that of the people Israel. They, too, have to sanctify themselves. Even those who cannot become truly holy, when they take on a bit of holiness, add strength to the one who has been designated as holy, [enabling him] to be properly sanctified. Thus Scripture refers to "the priest who is greater than [lit.: "great from"] his brothers" (Lev. 21:10). The rabbis read this to mean: "Make him great by that which is of his brothers," as we have said.

3:172

Hasidic teachings on the Book of Leviticus very often make an unspoken jump from the priest, holy man of the Torah, to the rebbe, holy man of the hasidic community. This interpretive leap is so natural to the hasidic preachers that they frequently seem to assume it, without need for special mention or justification.

In the tradition of Kotsk and Ger, however, the powers of the tsaddik *or* rebbe *are very much downplayed, and his humanity and vulnerability are emphasized. This teaching is built around a typically Kotsker* vort, *or brief flash of insight. The Kotsker would have to do no more than quote the verse "the priest who is great from his brothers" for his disciples to understand that the holiness of the* tsaddik *depended upon his community and that it was the gifts of "his brothers," including the sort of material riches that the Kotsker utterly disdained, that made the* tsaddik *great. The passage here is simply an embellishment of that sharp insight.*

Today's seekers will do well to remember the Kotsker's critique of hasidic leadership. In our search for an old/new Jewish spirituality, there is no need to repeat all the mistakes of the past.

2

The Midrash opens with the verse: "The utterances of the Lord are pure utterances" (Ps. 12:7).

Torah was given to the children of Israel so that through it they could redeem all deeds. Therefore, words of Torah cannot become defiled. That is the special value of their purity; wherever you take them, they do not come into contact with anything alien to them.

It is only in accord with one's personal purity that one can deserve to attain Torah. That is why the days of Omer counting were given, as a period of purification to make us ready to receive Torah. While it is true that anyone may study Torah, attachment to the innermost Torah, the "utterances of the Lord," of which we say: "Cause our hearts to cling to your

Torah," indeed requires purity. This [inward attachment] in itself bears witness to the purity of the person's words, for this
Torah is attained only through purity. Thus the verse (Ps. 12:7)
goes on to say: ". . . as silver tried in a crucible on the earth."
The Torah is truth and bears its own witness. A person can
enter into Torah only insofar as that person is pure. Otherwise, no tricks will help.

But this too is true: Words of Torah themselves serve to purify the one who studies them. Thus our sages said: "Just as
water purifies, so do words of Torah." In fact the verse the
Midrash quotes is preceded by [the verses:] "May the Lord cut
off all the slippery lips, the tongue that speaks of great things.
They say: 'Our tongue is powerful; we have our lips. Who is
Lord over us?'" (vv. 4–5). This is the point of the Midrash: just
as evil speech is terribly destructive, so does holy speech bring
one to purity. Parallel to his cry: "May the Lord cut off," here
the psalmist says: "But the utterances of the Lord are pure utterances." This refers to those who occupy themselves with
the words of the Lord. Therefore, the Psalm concludes: "May
You guard them, O Lord," which according to the Midrash
refers to children who study Torah.

3:173f.

*This teaching is rich with psychological insight and nuance.
Purity of heart bears witness to itself. An experienced hearer
of spiritual teachers can learn to see that purity as it expresses
itself in the person's words. Such teachers are rare among the
great many who espouse religious teachings.*

*But if true Torah requires purity of heart, how are we im-
pure ones ever to attain it? Must self-purification always precede receiving Torah, as the Omer days precede the revelation
on Shavu'ot? What about those of us who never feel pure
enough to receive the Torah?*

*The Sefat Emet responds to this plea with another side to
what is revealed as a dialectic of learning and purity. The
study of Torah in itself, he claims, helps one to become pure.
But of course it has to. Without this there would be no hope,
and learning would be of no value.*

3

The Midrash quotes the verse: "The fear of the Lord is pure; it stands forever" (Ps. 19:10). Aaron's fear of God caused this chapter [concerning priestly purity and avoidance of contact with the dead] to remain with his descendants for all generations. . . .

The fear of God that is "for life" is awe before God's sublimity. The priest who served God in the Temple was subject to this sort of fear of heaven, just as the ministering angels were. It is said that one way God differs from flesh and blood is that fear of God is greater upon those who are closest; "about Him is a mighty storm" (Ps. 50:3).

This most essential fear of heavenly rule was present in the Temple. The people of Israel received [an infusion of] this fear three times a year, as it says: "All your males shall fear [lit.: 'be seen,' at the pilgrimage festivals]" (Deut. 16:16). We also pray for this when we say: ". . . and there we will serve You in fear." Of Aaron it is said: "My covenant was with him of life and peace, and I gave them to him, and of fear, and he feared Me, was afraid of My name" (Mal. 2:5).

The holy Zohar teaches that wholeness comes to those who fear the Lord, as Scripture says: "There is no lack for those who fear Him" (Ps. 34:10). Since they lack for nothing, they may be called whole or "at peace" *(shalom/shalem)*. This is how Aaron attained the quality of peace and became a lover and pursuer of peace. *Shalom* is God's own name. Since he had that pure fear of God, he was able to attain peace.

That is why the holy city is named *Yerushalayim,* for she contains both *yir'ah* (fear) and *shalom.*

On the Sabbath the fear of God comes upon the Jewish people. It is said that even an ignorant Jew feels the awe of the Sabbath. That is why the Sabbath too is called *"shalom."*

3:181

"Fear" and "peace" are not two attributes that we generally expect to see together. Our fears rather disturb our peace and

keep us from its wholeness. Here we see the great difference between "awe before God's sublimity" and any ordinary human fear. This awe is a fear that takes us beyond our ordinary selves, allowing us to leave behind all other fears, all attachments to the vanities of this world, even our attachment to our own individual selves. It is the fear of the angels, those who stand eternally in the chorus of God's praise, knowing without interruption that it is for this alone that they were created.

4

"I will be sanctified in the midst of the children of Israel; I am the Lord who sanctifies you, who brings you from the Land of Egypt to be a God unto you; I am the Lord your God" (Lev. 22:32–33).

RaSHI, based on the Midrash, says: "For this purpose [of being your God did I bring you forth]."

Whenever a Jew sacrifices himself for the sake of God's holy name, the Exodus from Egypt is aroused, since the purpose of that Exodus was "to be a God unto you." Self-sacrifice means accepting upon oneself God's divinity, and hence the power of the Exodus is awakened. It is by that power that one is able to perform the sacrificial act.

It says "in the midst of the children of Israel" to indicate that holiness is hidden in the collective body of Israel, since "His people is a part [lit.: 'the portion'] of God" (Deut. 32:9). The sages said: "Wherever there are [lit.: 'In every house of'] ten Jews, the divine presence rests." The use of "house" here means "when they are truly one, with a single heart." "In the midst of the children of Israel" refers to the heart, since the souls are close and only the bodies prevent their becoming one. But an act of self-sacrifice denies the physical self. Then the person is truly joined to that collective body of Israel, and "I am sanctified."

That is why the sages established that the Exodus from Egypt should be mentioned in connection with the *Shema'*. In reciting the *Shema'* we accept God's rule and [acknowledge our willingness for] self-sacrifice. Thus we become united and are reminded of the Exodus from Egypt.

3:186

The glorification of martyrdom, or willingness to give one's life for God's sake, has a long and unfortunately real history in the life of the Jewish people. How was the Sefat Emet to know that just forty years after he spoke these words the reality of forced martyrdom—one that left few, if any, choices— was to be the lot of all of his beloved Polish Jewry?

But mesirut nefesh (self-sacrifice) also has another, more mystical meaning. A person who cares not at all about bodily existence but only about the presence of God becomes part of a "house" in which that presence may dwell. Because that person's ego-self has been set aside, room is made for others; such a one is joined into the community that together bears God's presence in this world.

5

On the verse: "Bring an 'omer-measure of your first harvesting unto the priest" (Lev. 23:10), the Midrash quotes the verse: "What value is there for man in all his work that he does under the sun?" (Eccles. 1:3). The Midrash then mentions that there was an attempt to "hide" the Book of Ecclesiastes [i.e., to exclude it from the canon due to its "heretical" views]. The potential heresy of this particular verse was resolved by Rabbi Samuel bar Naḥmani, who noted that *"his* work" does not include "the labors of Torah."

But it is hard to understand the view that was of concern here. The whole meaning of Ecclesiastes is to show the vanity of all this world's doings, so that one be concerned solely with Torah and mitsvot. But in truth all that God created was for His glory; "the Lord with wisdom established the earth" (Prov. 3:19). There is value to all of Creation. This opposes the heretical view that claims: "the Lord has abandoned the earth" (Ezek. 8:12).

The wisdom hidden within Creation since its beginning can be discovered only by the power of Torah, as it is written: "In the beginning" (Gen. 1:1), which is interpreted to mean "for the sake of Torah, which is elsewhere called "beginning." By the labors of Torah one can raise up this "beginning" that is found within nature. This is the "labor"—working to find words of Torah everywhere. A Jew must have faith that everything is Torah, that the power of God's ten utterances is hidden within nature. Of these, Scripture says: "The utterances of the Lord are pure speech, beaten silver" (Ps. 12:7). Just as silver is found within the soil and has to be beaten and purified until pure silver emerges, so too the words of Torah are to be found throughout Creation. "Seek it out like silver; look for it like hidden treasure" (Prov. 2:4).

This is what is truly meant by "redemption" or "freedom"—bringing the precious forth from the ordinary. The Jewish people are instruments for this. When they came out of Egypt, this purification was performed by them for the entire world, so that the transformed ten utterances became the Ten Commandments.

Not only did that take place once, but each year on the day after [the beginning of] Passover, that "beginning" is again raised up by the power of the Exodus from Egypt. Therefore, it says: "Bring an 'omer-measure of your *first* harvesting. . . ." That "first" or "beginning" is purified in the ensuing forty-nine days until it becomes actual Torah, just as happened at the Exodus itself.

This is the meaning of [the verse:] "I am the Lord your God who brought you out of the Land of Egypt" (Ex. 20:2). Note this carefully. Each year has its own particular matter [in which Torah can be found], until in the future "earth will be filled with knowing the Lord" (Is. 11:9). Everything will truly be Torah, and all of this because of Israel. That is why Israel are called "makers of His word" (Ps. 103:20), and it is taught that the righteous cause the world, created by ten utterances, to exist.

3:184f.

This is a very important teaching for understanding the position of the Sefat Emet regarding God, world, Torah, and Israel. The interpretation of Ecclesiastes 1:3 gives him a chance to state quite clearly the place of Hasidism, as he sees it, among three opposing camps. Some say "the Lord has abandoned the earth," meaning that God cares not at all for what humans do in this world, whether in Torah or in secular pursuits. This would be a deist view, essentially the world-view of the maskilim, *or "enlighteners," whom Hasidism fought. There may indeed be a God, but not the God of revelation or the election of Israel. The Jewish people is thus bereft of its divine mission. The second view is that God cares only about Torah, defined in a narrow way. This would be the view of the* mitnaggedim, *who care only for the "four ells of the law" and see nothing broader as the proper domain of Jews. Our task is only to study and live the life of Torah. But Hasidism has a third view, one that sees Torah everywhere; Torah is the key by which the Jew unlocks the hidden secrets of Creation. True engagement with Torah as the Sefat Emet, an enlightened hasidic sage, wants to see it studied means an embrace of all of God's wondrous Creation. This was the very purpose of our liberation from Egypt, the beginning of our national existence: to seek Torah everywhere. In the ongoing process of seeking and finding Torah throughout Creation, we transform God's ten creative utterances into commandments, through which all humans will be able to enter a deeper and more harmonious relationship with the created world in which we live.*

בהר

BE-HAR

1

"The Lord spoke to Moses at Mount Sinai, saying" (Lev. 25:1).
On the relationship of [this chapter concerning] sabbatical and
jubilee years to Mount Sinai:

The Midrash says that the verse "Bless the Lord, O His angels, powerful heroes who do His word" (Ps. 103:20) refers to
those who observe the sabbatical year. The rabbis also taught
that when Israel said "we shall do" before "we shall listen,"
the blessed Holy One said: "Who revealed to My children that
secret used by the ministering angels?"

When the children of Israel received the Torah, they were
prepared to become like the angels above. After all, lower creatures are also God's emissaries; all of us were created for God's
glory. The difference is that the angel has nothing else, only

the bearing of that message. His whole being is called *mal'akh* [which means both "angel and "messenger"] because of that message. His existence is in fact negated before God, since he is sustained by the light of divine presence, just as the righteous will be in the future.

When the children of Israel received the Torah, they were ready for this as well. That is why they were sustained by manna, "the food that the angels eat." In fact, "By the sweat of your brow shall you eat food" (Gen. 3:19) is a curse that followed sin; before that all Adam ate was from the Garden of Eden. This is what Israel were ready for at Mount Sinai. Of this, Scripture says: "I said: 'You are gods'" (Ps. 82:6).

But even after they sinned [by worshipping the Golden Calf], there remain for Israel times when this former power is awakened. This is true of the Sabbath, when they set aside all other tasks and are prepared only to serve their blessed God. That is why the Sabbath food is considered holy. In the times when there were sabbaticals and jubilees, the whole year was Sabbath-time, as they took no part in planting or harvesting. . . .

During sabbaticals and jubilees, as on Sabbaths, Israel enjoy some of their former enlightenment, from before the sin. That is why they rest at these times, to return to their former rung that they had attained at Mount Sinai. This is the true freedom of the jubilee, of which it says: ". . . you shall return each man unto his possession" (Lev. 25:10), meaning that they should be attached to their root.

That is why those who observe the sabbatical year are called God's "ministering angels who do His word"—they have only this task to perform, and they abstain from worldly matters, just like the angels. That, too, is why their food comes to them in miraculous ways, as is taught in the verse: "But if you say, 'What will we eat in the seventh year? . . .'" (Lev. 25:20). It was God's intent that they not raise this question at all, and then they would have been fed miraculously. But because of the question, the food had to come about by blessing [of abundance, rather than by pure miracle]. . . .

3:195f.

The difference between humans and angels lies in the human ability to be distracted. We, too, are God's messengers in this world, but we have forgotten our message. The rebbe—or his book—is here to remind us.

2

On the verse: "But if you say, 'What will we eat in the seventh year? . . .'" (Lev. 25:20), see the comment in the *No'am Elimelech* [by R. Elimelech of Lezajsk] in the name of his brother. He said that because of this question the Everpresent was forced "to command the blessing."

But what kind of question was it? "What will we eat?" The One who gave life will give food! [Should not the Torah assume Israel would be more trusting?] But then the existence of Israel would have depended upon a miracle, and not all generations are deserving of miracles. That is what they meant by [the verse:] "What will we eat?" The answer was that their sustenance would come about by means of "blessing," and blessing is somewhat closer to nature.

Really, Jews should understand that miracles and nature are all one. In fact there is no miracle so great and wondrous as nature itself, the greatest wonder we can know. When this faith becomes clear to Jews, it is no longer any problem to be fed by miracles. Only "if you ask: 'What will we eat?' then will I 'command the [partly natural] blessing.'"

The word *nes* (miracle) refers to uplifting; this is a way of conducting the world that is lifted out of the natural state, especially for the children of Israel. The MaHaRaL claimed that just as there is a natural order, there is also a miraculous order, one set aside for Israel.

In fact, the generations for whom miracles were performed were those when faith was firmly established; nature and miracle were all the same to them. That is why God performed miracles for them.

3:190

This passage offers a glimpse into a very interesting theology of the relationship between the natural and the supernatural. The only ones for whom God provides miracles are those who don't notice them as such, those whose faith is so great that for them nature and miracle are all one. For the rest of us, God does not perform miracles, presumably because we do not deserve them, lacking the faith to take them in our stride. But the upshot is that there are no miracles encountered by their recipients as such. "Miracles" stand out only afterward; the miracle is named as such by a lesser generation. Those of greater faith know such happenings simply as part of the natural/divine whole, a way of being that cannot be divided into "natural" and "supernatural" realms.

3

"When you come into the land which I give to you, the land shall have a Sabbath-rest for the Lord" (Lev. 25:2). God gave us the Land of Israel to show that the entire earth belongs to Him. Thus the Midrash teaches that God gave ownership of the earth to Abraham, who turned and gave it back to Him. This is the meaning of the sabbatical year: The land is being given to Israel anew; each sabbatical renews that gift. Thus it has been taught regarding the verse: "And may God give you . . ." (Gen. 27:28)—may He give and give again! Indeed "which I give" is in the present tense.

Israel are prepared to receive that gift. "You are strangers [*gerim* also comes to mean 'converts'] and sojourners with Me" (Lev. 25:23). This is in Israel's praise, for they are such *gerim* as to make clear that the earth is the Lord's; they forever hold fast to the power of that giving. This may explain the verse: "You made a covenant with him [Abraham] to give the land of the Canaanite, the Hittite, the Amorite, the Perrizite, the Jebusite, and the Girgashite, to give to his seed . . . " (Neh. 9:8). Why does it say "to give" twice? So that they be attached always to that act of giving. "May He give and give again." For in every sabbatical "the land rests [*ve-shavetah*/and 'returns'] to the Lord."

This is similar to what the *Or ha-Hayyim* [R. Hayyim ibn Attar] has taught on "Heaven and Earth were completed"— that on each Sabbath new life is given to the Creation. Have a look there. That which is true of the [weekly] Creation-Sabbath applies also to the sabbatical year.

3:196

This teaching is a play on the similarity of two Hebrew roots: shin-bet-tav, meaning "rest" and shin-vav-bet, meaning "return." Because of the conjugation patterns of Hebrew verbs, the forms of the two take on similar appearance. Thus our author interprets the ve-shavetah of Lev. 25:2 to mean that in resting, the land also returns to its primal divine ownership.

The similarity of verbs may or may not be coincidental. Some would claim that there is no coincidence in the Torah's language. But in any case the idea is basic to our vision of the Sabbath and is parallel to the understanding of meditation or other forms of inner rest in many traditions. Stillness, or inner rest, returns us to our source.

 4

The Midrash quotes the verse: "Death and life are in the hands of the tongue" (Prov. 18:21). It goes on to quote Ben Sira, who told of one who found a glowing ember and blew on it, lighting up a flame. Then he spat on it and it was extinguished.

This ember is to be found everywhere; it is the spark of Torah, which is called fire. The word *gahelet* (ember) is numerically equivalent to *emet* (truth). "Truth" refers only to Torah, by which everything was created. Thus the ember is to be found everywhere, in every thing.

The Jew is capable of fulfilling the potential of this spark. Of this it is written: "He blew the breath of life into his nostrils, and man became a living soul" (Gen. 2:7). "Living soul" is rendered by the Targum as "a speaking spirit." We have the power in our mouths to awaken the life that lies everywhere. That is why "If you walk in My ways" (Lev. 26:3) is read as "working at Torah." This means [making] a real effort to find words of Torah everywhere, [to seek out] the stamp and imprint of Torah that is to be found in every place. The Midrash refers to "the imprint in which I formed [sun and] moon." Time itself has been given to Israel, who declare times to be sacred. The same is true of sabbaticals and jubilees, for it says: "Count for yourself" (Lev. 25:8). It is the court that declares a year to be a sabbatical or a jubilee.

This power was given to Israel when they received the Torah; that is why [the account of the sabbatical] says: "at Mount Sinai." "The power of the tongue" refers to Israel, who were given the holy tongue. Originally all humans had a single language, but at the generation of division [the Tower of Babel] tongues became confused. The holy tongue was later given specifically to Israel when they received the Torah.

3:200

This teaching combines interpretation of Be-har and Be-Ḥukkotay, which are often read together. It contains a very radical expression of the notion that Torah is to be found and sought everywhere. This view should certainly encourage religiously seeking Jews to engage in the sciences and in all other branches of knowledge, ever hoping to expand the realm in which sparks of divinity are to be found and uplifted. It seems hard to understand how contemporary Hasidism's disdain for and fear of "secular" learning could be derived from the teachings of one of such broad vision as the Sefat Emet. Warsaw of 1900 may have been a more open place for the Hasid than Brooklyn or Jerusalem a century later.

But this teaching is also a hard one for the contemporary reader. For Adam's "breath of life" to refer to a power of sacred speech that belongs to Jews alone shows the narrow and overly exclusivist side of the older hasidic tradition. In the author's own spirit, the postmodern reader here has to liberate the spark and expand the "everywhere" in which the presence of God can be found. This surely includes all tongues, each of them derived from the original holy speech of Adam, and each capable of being spoken in purity and holiness. Per-

haps Hebrew had to become a "secular" as well as a sacred vehicle in our day in order for us to understand that "holy tongue" means something more than a specific language. Hebrew surely retains that place of holiness for us as Jews, but we can also recognize holiness in speech elsewhere when we encounter it.

בחקותי

BE-ḤUKKOTAY

1

"If you follow My laws" (Lev. 26:3). RaSHI follows the Midrash in understanding this as making an effort at Torah study. To put effort into Torah means to follow His laws. This [includes] even one who does not understand, but still expends effort on study because he takes pleasure in contemplating God's word even without getting at the meaning of it. In fact, the Torah is "hidden from the eyes of all the living" (Job 28:21), and one should study it even while recognizing that less than one part in a thousand of it can be grasped. A person who "learns" this way partakes in the root of Torah.

Thus the MaHaRaL noted that the blessing says "to occupy ourselves with words of Torah." Even one who doesn't understand may still be occupied with matters of Torah. The holy

209

Zohar, too, always refers to "making an effort at Torah." The Talmud in Tractate Nedarim reads "they did not follow it" (Jer. 9:12) to mean: "they did not recite the blessing before study of Torah." The meaning is simple: once people have tasted the meanings of Torah, who would be fool enough to deny blessing God for that great joy and pleasure? But the point is that one blesses beforehand, *before* understanding, when one only *desires* to contemplate holy words, the words of the living God.

The next verse continues: "[If you follow My laws and observe My commandments,] I will give you your rains in their seasons." Even though the sages taught that there is no reward in this world for fulfilling the commandments, that is true only rationally and from our human point of view. But in fact, God has made the law of the entire universe depend upon Torah. Since it is taught that the world was created through Torah, the connection between world and Torah is higher than the rational mind [can reach]. But a person who transcends his own self, truly "following His laws," is given sustenance by Torah in this world as well.

3:210

The problems raised in this teaching show the very rich and complex texture of a Jewish religious consciousness that holds fast to many elements at once. The Torah text obviously talks of concrete, this-worldly reward for fulfilling the commandments: the rain will fall, crops will be abundant. But the rabbis, writing in a much later era, one when the sufferings of the righteous in this world were all too apparent, taught that reward belongs only to the world to come and is not to be found in present reality. But this claim of theirs seems to conflict with another rabbinic belief: that all the world was created in accordance with Torah. How then can there not be reward in this world?

The hasidic preacher resolves the conflict by positing a multilayered understanding of reality. For the one who rationalizes his religion, counting up the good deeds performed and seeking appropriate payment, there is indeed no reward to be had in this world. The reward is more subtle and cannot be seen by such a mind. Who is the one who perceives this reward? The person who lives by faith, seeking always, even without understanding, to do nothing other than to "follow His laws." Such a person partakes of Torah at its root, where the deep connection between divine teaching and divine Creation lies whole and unchallenged.

2

The Midrash quotes the verse: "I considered my ways; I returned my steps [lit.: 'feet'] to Your testimonies" (Ps. 119:59). It comments: "David said, 'Master of the Universe! Every day I consider going to such-and-such place, to such-and-such dwelling, and yet my feet bring me to synagogues and houses of study.'" "A man's steps are from God and He desires his way" (Ps. 37:23).

Each Jew has certain particular paths to walk. One who serves God, longing always to find those paths that are unique to him, will be led by God in a true way. The Midrash says that "my feet bring me"—because he would "consider" and long each day to find the way of God.

This is the meaning of "If you follow My laws": it is within a person's power to see the ways and patterns that God has inscribed into the human soul. The Midrash says that laws are called ḥukkim (lit.: "inscriptions, engravings") because they are carved within us to stand out against the evil urge. Just as a person may feel his soul drawn to the temptations of that urge, that soul even more clearly contains ways and paths that distinctly lead to God. These are imprinted or engraved upon the human soul. But to bring these to fulfillment requires divine help, [aroused by] human desire and struggle at Torah. Thus it says: "If one says to you, 'I have struggled and found,' believe it."

"I considered my ways"—in the plural. David was always considering those paths that were uniquely his. And because he thought so much about it, he was helped from heaven.

"I returned my steps"—this refers to the restoration of one's [human] nature and habits [*regel* can also mean "habit"], to bring the light of wisdom and awareness into them. Just as the sages have taught that "thoughts of sin can be worse than sin," we need to learn that thoughts of mitsvah can be more pleasing than the mitsvah itself. The soul is redeemed through much longing and desire to serve the blessed Creator.

3:208f.

Typically hasidic is the concern here for intent and desire. David the psalmist, transformed once by the Midrash into one who always found himself, even unwittingly, walking into synagogues and houses of study (neither of which existed in the historical David's day, of course!), is here transformed yet again, into one who thinks of nothing other than how to find his own unique ways to God. It is by knowing our own heart, by learning to read God's word as it is inscribed upon our soul, that we find our way to Him.

≡ 3 ≡

[Another comment on the same Midrash:]

Scripture says: "The Lord made all for His own sake" (Prov. 16:4). The sages read this to mean: "as testimony to Him, to bear His witness." This witnessing is the duty of every Jew, as it says: "You are My witnesses" (Is. 43:10). Therefore, we have to find this testimony everywhere and in each thing.

This is what David meant: he was proud that in every thought he considered all day long he would find some witness to God. In the Talmud at the end of Tractate Berakhot, it says: "What is a short passage upon which depend all the weighty teachings of Torah? 'Know Him in all your ways'" (Prov. 3:6). That means finding this testimony in all things.

But what is the matter of [David's feet bringing him to] synagogues and houses of study? It is said that "His greatness and goodness fill the world." "His greatness" refers to Creation, which took place through His ten utterances. "His "goodness" refers to Torah or the Ten Commandments. These "fill the world"—there is no place and no thing where the power of the ten utterances and Ten Commandments is not found. A Jew has to make this clear, to find the Torah-light in every place.

All the events and thoughts that occur to a person are for this purpose, to make his witnessing more clear. They are like the questioning, investigation, and cross-examination that a witness has to undergo in order that the testimony be clarified.

Just as the Sabbath is called a witness, in which the good of all the six weekdays is purified and uplifted, so are Israel called witnesses, purifying and raising up all the good from this mixture [in which we live]. That is why it says: "You are my witnesses."

3:213

The most dramatic part of this interpretation of the Midrash is left unspoken. What does it mean that David's feet always took him to synagogues and houses of study? Everywhere his feet took him was a house of prayer or study! Nature itself, filled with God's greatness and goodness, is the universal synagogue, the place where God's glory is spoken. Anywhere he went was a house of study, a place where he could learn of and bear witness yet again to the goodness of God! Such "synagogues and houses of study" did indeed exist in the time of King David, as they have in all ages, and it is precisely these places of prayer and learning of God that the psalmist knew like none other.

The hasidic master has worked his way through the mediating tradition of the rabbis and has come out with a call for an essentially unmediated encounter with the divine in each moment and in every place, a call not unlike those of a voice often heard in the ancient Psalter.

"Your threshing shall overtake the vintage, and your vintage shall overtake the sowing" (Lev. 26:5). It is written: "Light is sown for the righteous" (Ps. 97:11). This is the light of Torah that a person takes into his heart and it bears fruit. Then he has to purify his deeds, so that they be without anything rotten. If he purifies sufficiently, he will receive another dose of light, and onward forever. This is the meaning of [the verse:] "Your threshing shall overtake the vintage." This is the [ongoing process of] purification.

3:205

Insight inspires you to deed; deed becomes the locus of new insight. Midrash and ma'aseh. *Halakhah and* aggadah. *The yin and yang of Judaism.*

 5

"[I am the Lord your God . . .] who made you walk erect" (Lev. 26:13). RaSHI follows the Midrash in interpreting the word *komemiyyut* this way. But did the sages not teach that it is forbidden to walk erect, [a sign of excessive pride]? When redemption comes about, as it will in the future, people will be able to have devotion to God even with an erect posture. That is the way humans were created, after all. Only in this world, because of its vanities, do we have to bend and be quite bowed over in order to have the proper awe.

This too is spoken of in the Midrash. Where it says: "I will walk in your midst" (vs. 12), the Midrash adds "and you will not be shaken." Might this mean that you will have no fear of God? No, because Scripture says: "I am the Lord your God." This means that they will be able to accept the yoke of God's rule just as they are, without having to transform or humble themselves excessively. This is the promise—that they will be able to walk erect.

3:205f.

A surprisingly "Nietzschean" insight for the hasidic master: the problem with this world is that we have to bend our backs to receive God's yoke. Redemption will be a time when we can continue serving God, but do so tall and proud.

No wonder that the Sefat Emet *has been read and studied far beyond the bounds of the ultra-Orthodox community. The religious kibbutz movement (or even the so-called "secular") could derive much nourishment from a passage such as this. In a society that truly overcomes materialism and competitiveness, the mix of pride and devotion may look different than it does in this materialistic and self-aggrandizing world where most of us still live.*

במדבר

SEFER
BE-MIDBAR

BE-MIDBAR

1

Rabbi Meir says: "Whoever studies Torah for its own sake merits many things." The obvious meaning of "for its own sake" is "in order to do it." This is the meaning of the word "Torah" or "teaching"—it teaches a person what to do. The real effort in Torah is that of negating your own mind and opinion in order to understand the will of God and the opinion of Torah.

The Midrash likens Torah to a wilderness: it has to be as ownerless as wilderness. Scripture says: "From the wilderness to Mattanah" (Num. 21:18), which can be read as: "From wilderness, a gift." The Midrash tells of a prince who entered one city after another only to see the populace flee before him, until he came to [a] ruined city, where he was greeted with praise. Said the prince: "This is the best of all the cities. Here I will set my throne."

The word *midbar* (wilderness) comes from a root meaning "to lead" or "rule." The *midbar* is one who submits to that rule, the person who negates his own self, realizing that he has no power to act without the life-flow of God. This is the difference between the populace of the various cities. Those who fled also feared the prince, but they retained power to act on their own. The nations of the world also revere the Lord as "God of gods." But Israel are like a *midbar;* they have no power or leadership at all on their own.

Thus we are told that fear of heaven applies "in the open and in secret." "In the open" means to know that God oversees all things; this brings you to a state of awe. But "in secret" means that the fear of God attaches itself to a person's very life-force so that he can do nothing, not even make a simple movement, without remembering that it takes place through the power of God and that he himself is as but an axe in the hand of the one who chops with it.

Such is the study of Torah: to negate yourself before the way that Torah leads you, so that every deed be only to fulfill God's will and desire. Since it was by Torah that God created the world, you can cleave to God in every deed you do through the power of Torah. You do that by self-negation, by submitting in every act to the inner life-force, which is the life of God, by means of the letters of Torah that lie within the deed.

This the meaning of "for its own sake." All creatures were made for His glory . . . the glory of God's blessed name.

4:2

The discovery of God comes about through self-negation and submission. When we accept that we ourselves are utterly without power, even to make the smallest movement, we open ourselves to feeling and receiving the power of God. The nations call upon God as well, to be sure, but they are not able utterly to negate themselves before God's glory.

The hasidic master sees a sign of this self-negation in the utter powerlessness of the Jewish people in this world; Jewish powerlessness is an indication of our closeness to God. We wonder what he would say today, when we Jews, having had quite enough of powerlessness, have become significant players in the game of power. Are we, too, now like the "nations" in his teaching? Can we again make ourselves like a midbar, *ready to respond to God alone? Or do we have too much to lose this time?*

═══ **2** ═══════════════════════

[On the same Mishnah]: What is the meaning of "for its own sake?" For we realize that no one knows the worth of Torah.

The Torah that lies before us is the garb of Torah. It is by means of study that we arouse the force that lies within it. That is the real power of Israel: to awaken the root of Torah. For the same is true of the human soul; the *nefesh* is but the garb of the *neshamah* that lies within it. And that *neshamah*, or deeper soul, is a part of God above.

The Midrash refers to this counting of the children of Israel as being "like the scribe's count." Just as the Torah has words and letters that are subject to counting but its root is high above, beyond all count, so, too, are the souls of Israel countable in this world, while in their root they are beyond all number. Thus the holy books say that the 600,000 Jews [who came out of Egypt] are parallel to 600,000 letters in the Torah.

One who studies Torah for its own sake merits all the good qualities listed in the Mishnah, since all of these are found in the root of Israel's soul. Study of Torah brings them out into the open. "She sounds her voice forth in the open places" (Prov. 1:20). Through our struggle, the inner Torah spreads through the Torah-garb; outer and inner become one. This is the meaning of "for its own sake. . . . "

4:6

Torah is an outer vehicle through which to express the quali-ties of goodness that lie within our own souls.

How right you are, Master, in seeing Torah as "garb" and as outer instrument. That is the hasidic spirit within you, ever reminding you that the "real thing" is something deeper, that which lies within each soul. The soul is holy and Torah is holy teaching, a mirror held up to allow the soul to uncover the great depths that lie within.

How close you seem, and yet how far, from realizing the next step: the acceptance that these qualities are the root of every soul, not just that of the Jew. Each tradition will have its own instruments, parallel to Torah, that will allow those powers of the soul to be discovered, expressed, and shared. The limitless God cannot have but one covenant with one people. It is only we, living wholly within that one, who can see no other.

3

On the matter of counting "by heads" (Num. 1:2). Scripture says: "There is no counting [or 'telling'] His understanding" (Ps. 147:5). The holy Zohar says on the verse "Her husband is known in the gates" (Prov. 31:23) that the word "gates" (she'arim) refers to imaginings of the heart. Each and every Jew has a particular knowledge of God's greatness, according to that person's own rung. It can be shared with no other. This is what the Mishnah teaches: ". . . showing the greatness of God, for each person was stamped out in the stamp of Adam, yet no two faces are alike." Rabbi Pinhas of Korzec adds that because "the difference is in minds, not only in faces," each of us becomes excited by a different quality or aspect [of religious life]. This is the meaning of [the verse:] "There is no counting His understanding" [referring to the many ways of understanding God].

In this count each of us was given that mind and those capacities appropriate to us. That is the meaning of "by their heads" as well as "according to their fathers' houses." The patriarchs contained all their children's minds, but in a general way. Afterwards each mind was formed individually. Of this the Midrash quotes: "I raise my mind from afar" (Job 36:3).

4:14

Here is a lesson we still have to learn, and one we teachers especially need to recite again every day. Each person has been given a unique understanding of God, one that can be fathomed by no other. Our job as teachers is to awaken that individual to his or her own inner understanding, not to convince the person of the truth of our own. How hard it is to learn this lesson—but how rich the reward when we do!

Once again, the contemporary reader wants to push the Sefat Emet. To whom does this beautifully open teaching apply? Only to Jews? Surely not—it goes right back to Adam! Here there is no escape from the universalist inner logic of the Mishnah itself! Every person, man or woman, Jew or gentile from any of the many tribes of humanity, has a unique capacity to know God, before which all others can only stand in awe.

נשא

NASSO'

1

My grandfather taught that the mitsvah of *teshuvah* is based on the verse: "They will confess their sin" (Num. 5:7). But this verse is written in connection with theft. Every transgression, he taught, is a sort of theft. One who restores everything to God, the source of life, recognizes God's mastery over all Creation. Such a person surely will be free from sin.

4:54

What is sin, after all, but a separating of persons or things from their source in God? Here R. Yitzḥak Meir was being faithful to kabbalistic tradition: the root of all sin is separation; the core of all good is union with the Source.

2

"May the Lord lift His face up to you" (Num. 6:26).

The Midrash quotes [a seemingly contradictory verse]: "He will not lift up His face" (Deut. 10:17), and reconciles them by saying that one applies when Israel do God's will and the other when they do not. But . . . when one is doing God's will, what need is there for God to "lift His face" [to show favor, since the blessing is earned by the deed]? The point is that the blessed Holy One accepts our little bit of service as though it were much. This is what the Midrash means when it says: "As they lift their faces toward Me, so will I lift My face toward them." Just as the person rejoices in a good deed and is glad to have done God's will, whether great or small, so does the Creator accept this offering with a smile. [God knows that] this is a sign of the person's inwardness, from where the joy comes forth.

This is the meaning of "and may He give you peace." *Shalom* or *shelemut*, wholeness, is the inner point of truth. Within even the smallest bit of light, all is there. That's why God is called Shalom, for God is the wholeness of all. And when Israel have this wholeness, even a tiny point is considered a lot.

4:55

The spirit of this truly hasidic teaching is diametrically opposed to the notion of God as cosmic accountant, maintaining a balance sheet of our good deeds and transgressions. A single mitsvah done in joy contains God—all of God, for God cannot be divided!—within it, and may give us all the wholeness we need. The seeming smallness of the deed or the moment is no obstacle to its containing the infinite fullness of God's presence.

3

"To the sons of Kehath he did not give any, because the divine service was upon them; they raised it up upon their shoulders"

(Num. 7:9). The Midrash here speaks of song, linking this verse to "raise up a song and offer a drum; a sweet harp and a lyre" (Ps. 81:3). But what has song to do with raising things up on one's shoulder?

This can only be understood by recalling the verse: "The cows went straight *(va-yiSHARnah)* along the way" (1 Sam. 6:12), which is interpreted to mean that the cows sang *(SHARu)* [as they carried the Ark to Jerusalem]. Because they were carrying the Ark, they were given the awareness to sing. Thus the Zohar says: "It was the Ark on their backs that enabled them to sing."

The same is true of the Levites! It is the fact that they carry the Ark on their shoulders that gives them the power to lift their voices in song. This is true also of every person who serves God. True service fills a person with light and joy.

Of this Scripture says: "This people I created; they will tell My praise" (Is. 43:21). True worship consists of Torah and mitsvot; these of their own accord fill a person's mouth with song and exultation. And this in itself serves as testimony; truth is its own witness. The worshipper comes to understand that his soul is in fact joined to the true root, and his soul rejoices. This in itself bears witness to the Creator.

The same is true of all our prayers and songs. First, mitsvot need to be done as deeds, and then the mouth can speak.

4:57

The religious life is not meant to be a weighty burden, but one that helps us to feel the lightness and joy of knowing God's presence. The Levite who carries the ark on his shoulder is also—or is therefore—the one who sings! What a great message, and a typically hasidic one: life in God's service is a life of happiness and fulfillment. Like those privileged cows who merited carrying the Ark of the Lord on their backs, the service of God should so fill us with joy that we cannot keep from breaking into song.

BE-HA'ALOTEKHA

1

"Facing the front of the lampstand shall the seven lamps cast their light. Aaron did so; he mounted the lamps to face the front of the lampstand" (Num. 8:2–3). What does Scripture mean by "facing" the front of the lampstand? And what praise is it for Aaron that he did not change what he was told to do? And why does it say that the *seven* lamps faced the lampstand? Was it not in fact *six* that faced the central lamp?

We can understand this according to a parable taught in the Midrash. A king asked his loving subject to prepare a meal for him. [The subject] did so gladly, but all in his own ordinary vessels. When the king arrived, accompanied by all his retinue and finery, the subject became embarrassed, and put all his own things away. When the king asked where the meal was

229

that he had prepared, the loving subject had to admit that he had been ashamed. But the king immediately insisted that all the royal finery be set aside and that they use only that which this devoted subject had prepared for him.

We see from this story that it was proper for the subject to prepare the meal as he did, even though he saw all the king's fancy vessels. Despite everything the king already had, the subject had to do his bit. For the sake of his shame alone, the king insisted that all the finery be hidden away.

But why, indeed, should the king's glory be lessened? This is what Scripture refers to when it speaks of the "seven lamps facing the front of the lampstand." The blessed Holy One should not have to hide His own upper light. The only reason God's glory and holiness are hidden in this world is for the sake of humans' service. Were the glory to be revealed, all our attempts at worship would be seen as mere efforts of flesh and blood, and they would be cast aside.

The *tsaddik* is one who can go ahead with his own service even though he sees God's glory. Everything in the upper worlds may be shown to such a one who is prepared for it, since the only reason for its hiding is so as not to "shame" our worship.

This is the meaning of "facing the front of the lampstand"—even if you see all those lights from above, you should not be ashamed, but go right on and do that which is yours. This is what Aaron did; he did not change anything. There was thus no need for change or hiding. This indeed is worthy of great praise.

This is the way it will be in the times to come. On the verse "I will walk in your midst" (Lev. 26:12) the sages say that "you will not be shaken [by My presence]." A person will no longer have to stand at a distance, out of awe. Then we will be like the angels, of whom it is said: "I will cause you to walk among those standing ones" (Zech. 3:7). The angels can stand right there and minister to God, even though God is highly exalted over the angels, just as God is far above earthly creatures. The Creator is so very exalted that from God's perspective there is no difference in rung between humans and angels.

But the angel is whole enough to stand still and do what is commanded, even while seeing and grasping the exaltedness of God. . . .

4:71

Hasidism follows in old rabbinic tradition by insisting that God loves the simple worship of ordinary human beings. While we are supposed to be in awe of God, we should not be so overawed that we become incapable of bringing our simple gifts, the offerings of our heart, since it is these that God most desires.

But there is more here as well. We could be like angels, if only we weren't so insecure about the adequacy of our gifts. The angel and the tsaddik *are just like the rest of us—except that they have learned to stand still, to be at peace in the knowledge that God accepts their offerings in love.*

2

"Take the Levites from among the Israelites" (Num. 8:6). The Midrash asks: "How many strings were in the lyres that the Levites played?" It answers that there were seven strings, but that when Messiah comes there will be eight and, in the final future, ten, as Scripture says: "I will sing to You on a ten-stringed harp" (Ps. 144:9).

Music requires time. That is why each day has its own unique song. The renewal of each day brings forth a new song. The sun sings a song as it shines forth, as our sages said on the verse: "O sun, be still in Gibeon" (Josh. 10:12). Each day has its own unique light. Thus the ARI taught: no day is exactly like another, since the creation of the world.

Now the Levites seem to belong especially to the realm of time. There are three dimensions: space, time, and person. Every person—and the whole of Israel even more—has to redeem space and time in a way particular to the transformation of that particular soul. The people of Israel transform space by the power of the Land of Israel; that is why the land was divided among them. But the tribe of Levi was given no portion, for it is their task to redeem time [rather than territory]. That is why Levites become disqualified for their service by years [i.e., when they reach fifty years of age] and not by blemishes. Thus the Mishnah says: "One who might be fit among the priests [an unblemished man over fifty] is disqualified among the Levites."

The priest belongs to the realm of person, and that is why he must be without blemish. But years do not disqualify the priest.

Thus song belongs to the realm of time. In messianic days and in the future to come, time will be changed, and music will be changed as well. The same is already true on the Sabbath, which is a foretaste of the world to come. That is why we say: "A song to the Sabbath day . . . on the ten-stringed lyre and the harp" (Ps. 92:1–4). The Sabbath is the Song of Songs, for it is made up of all the songs of the workday week.

4:81f.

This is one of the many Sefat Emet teachings on the three realms of holiness: time, space, and person. Each Jew, he would say, contains all three classes represented by our ancient people: kohen, levi, *and* yisra'el. *The* kohen *(priest) represents sacred person; he, like the sacrifice he offers, must be without blemish, for holiness resides in his own person. The Levite embodies sacred time, the sound of his song in measured beats marking the passage of minutes and hours. As such he represents Shabbat, or the cycle of time that brings weekday to Sabbath. Shabbat is also the Song of Songs, representing the way time will be transformed in the world to come. The tribes of Israel are those who inherit the land: they are to invest it with holiness by the love with which they sow and reap, finding the divine presence in the very soil on which they live.*

All three of these live in the heart of every Jew (we would say "of every person"), and we need to seek out the holy in each of these three dimensions.

3

In the Midrash: "The Lord desires to justify [Israel]; therefore He has magnified and glorified Torah" (Is. 42:21), and also: "For the commandment is a lamp and Torah is light" (Prov. 6:23). For the light of Torah is beyond human grasp. We cannot cleave to that light except by means of the commandments. These are vessels that prepare our own limbs and sinews to become vessels themselves in which Torah-light can be contained.

Moses our Teacher belongs to the category of "Torah is light." But Aaron is [in the category] "the commandment is a lamp," referring to the deed. Therefore, at the end of the preceding *parashah* it says that Moses "heard the voice bespeak itself to him, and it spoke to him" (Num. 7:89). This leaves out Aaron; Moses [alone] cleaves to the very essence of Torah. That is immediately followed by this section on [Aaron and] the lamps, which teaches how to cleave to Torah by means of transforming the externals, through the mitsvot.

That is why this portion will end with the distinction between Moses [and all other prophets, including Aaron and Miriam]. "If there be a prophet among you, I make Myself known to that one in a vision" (Num. 12:6). *Be-mar'eh*, "in a vision," numerically equals 248, [the number of positive commandments in the Torah and limbs in the body]. It is through the 248 commandments that [I am revealed]. But of Moses it says: "Mouth to mouth I speak with him" (vs. 8).

We learn that on the holy Sabbath Moses restores to Israel the crowns they were given when they said "we shall do" before "we shall listen." For upon receiving the Torah, all of Israel cleaved to that very essence of Torah itself, just like Moses. That is why all 613 commandments are included in the Ten Commandments, which are the very essence of Torah's light: "I am the Lord your God" is the entire Torah.

Only after we fell from this rung, Torah light came to us by means of the 613 commandments. This is [the meaning of] "The Lord desires to justify [Israel]; therefore He has magnified and glorified Torah." But on the Sabbath we have an "extra" soul; this is a light that comes from that essence of Torah, higher than its garbing in the 613 commandments. That is why it is called "extra," because it cannot be contained within the body. The weekday soul is indeed garbed in [the category] "the commandments are a lamp." But on the holy Sabbath we have something higher, a light that comes from the giving of Torah. That is why Torah was given on Shabbat: so that it be always clearly known to God that on Shabbat Israel remain forever on this rung.

4:82f.

Here we see that the most radical of ancient mystical ideas survives in the teachings of one who sometimes appears to be a cautious or conservative teacher. The higher Torah, that originally given to Moses on Sinai, was one of pure light. It was nothing other than God's own self that God gave. This intimate gift was given "mouth to mouth," a revelation that was nothing other than the divine kiss, all of Torah contained in the moment when Israel understands "I am the Lord your God."

The Torah as we have it is that of commandments, specific "lamps" that can contain the infinite divine light. This is the way of service, the gift of Aaron, who understands that we need specific forms or vessels. Our weekday service is that of seeking out the holy in the ordinary, and it is these lamps, or sacred forms, that light our way. But on Shabbat the original "crowns," the higher mental powers of that first moment of insight, are restored to us, and we should be able to catch a glimpse of that light which remains undiminished, just as it was in that first moment of revealed glory.

SHELAḤ

1

In the Midrash: "Nothing is beloved before God like an emissary sent to do a mitsvah who risks his life for the misson to succeed." You know that my grandfather and teacher said that we are all emissaries to do mitsvot; we were sent into this world by God in order to fulfill His commandments. Surely it would have been impossible for God's holiness to be drawn into this world, if not for Israel's service. For that reason Israel are enabled to remain holy in this world by means of the commandments. "Send Your light and Your truth and they shall lead me" (Ps. 43:3).

Holiness is present in everything, as it says: "Your kingdom is a kingdom of all the worlds" (Ps. 145:13). Thus everything that happens is the supreme will, but that is hidden in this

world. The commandments are called "candles," shining
light, by the power of Torah, onto every deed. There is no deed
that does not contain some mitsvah. But before doing anything, you have to offer up your soul as an emissary, gathering together all of your own desires in order to negate them, so
that you can fulfill only the will of God. This is how to succeed in your mission, to do the mitsvah properly. Even in
doing corporeal things, if you concentrate on keeping it clear
that your only desire is to do God's will, you can be saved
[from the power of desire.] . . .

4:87f.

*Here we see the broadened hasidic view of the command-
ments stripped down to its essential meaning. The commandments are not only the 613 enumerated by the rabbis.
These extend forth into all of life, until there is nothing one
does that does not contain some mitsvah. But everything we
do should be only to fulfill the will of God—which is itself
the basis of all the commandments. So the religious life de-
volves down to a single principle: negate your will before that
of God, and do all you do only for the sake of heaven.*

2

"If the Lord desires us, He will bring us into this land and give
it to us" (Num. 14:8).

The spies surely felt that they were not ready to enter the
Land of Israel. "There is a time for everything, a season for
every desire beneath the heavens" (Eccles. 3:1). They would
not be ready until forty years had passed.

But this refers only to desires "beneath the heavens." Surely
the generation of the wilderness, that of Moses, were "above
the heavens" in all their paths. This is what the sages pointed
to in [Joshua and Caleb's words] "Let us surely go up" (Num.
13:30), which they took to mean: "Even if [Moses] said to us:
'Make ladders to go up to heaven!' would we not listen to
him?" This is as we have said, that only in a natural way were

they incapable of going up [to the land]. That is why Scripture seems to say: "Send yourself!" (Num. 13:1). Had they succeeded in their mission, entering the land in a way that is above both time and nature, Moses himself could have entered with them.

The same is true of the final redemption. Scripture says: "At its time I will hurry it" (Is. 60:22), which we understand to mean: "If they merit, 'I will hurry it,' and if not, the redemption will come 'at its time.'" Everything depends upon Israel's desire. If they are truly impassioned in their love of God, they arouse His desire as well. Then there is no impediment on the part of time or nature. That is, "If the Lord desires us He will bring us. . . . "

From this chapter we should learn that even though the time had not come, if Israel properly longed for God in their hearts, they would have come [to the land]. The same is true in our own exile: if we have enough desire to return to God, He will hurry and speed up our redemption.

4:94f.

This teaching was offered in the spring of 1883, the same year the first BILU pioneers began the rebuilding of Erets Israel.

 3

In the chapter on the fringes it says: "on the corners of their garments" (Num. 15:38).

We wrap ourselves in a *tallit* in order to unite with the root of oneness. The holy Zohar, discussing this verse, quotes: "From the corner of the land we have heard singing" (Is. 24:16). The Tosafot mention the six wings (or "corners"—two meanings of *kanaf*) on each of the holy creatures and note that they sing one day out of each of these wings. On the Sabbath they say: "We have no other wing [with which to sing]." God replies: "I have a certain corner of the earth. . . . "

This is the "Song of the Sabbath day. It is good to give thanks to the Lord" (Ps. 92:1–2). This song comes about because of the unity, one that is not present in our World of Separation. It is given to Israel only in the soul.

The same is true of the days themselves; unity belongs only to the holy Sabbath, of which the Zohar says that it unites "in secret oneness." The parallel in the realm of "world" is the Land of Israel and the holy Temple. Indeed Jonathan ben Uziel translates "the corner of the land" as "the Land of Israel." That place which contains all places is called "the corner of the land." By this power song was present in the holy Temple. And on the Sabbath, when all of Creation unites, "it is good to give thanks to the Lord."

Israel are given the power to wrap themselves up and gather all the corners together. That is why we pray: "And gather us together from the four corners of the earth." RaSHI notes that the four corners are also parallel to the four terms used for redemption [in the Exodus account]. Thus Scripture says: "I have swept you there like the four winds of heaven" (Zech. 2:10). Israel were sent to every place so that all the sparks would be gathered into their hands to be restored to their source. And by the commandment of fringes a Jew can bring himself into the realm of unity. That is why "unto their generations" is said with regard to the fringe. Wherever they are outcast, this commandment helps them not to be separated from their root. A person who is wrapped up in a fringed *tallit* is like one separated and distinguished from this world; this is the spreading forth of God's tent of peace that He gave us to separate us from those who have gone astray, that we might dwell in the holy shade. The more Israel are separated from this world, the more they can enter into His shade. It is written: "I longed to dwell in his shadow. . . " (Cant. 2:3).

4:97f.

Here the author turns again to his much-loved pattern of person-space-time parallels. Israel among humans, Sabbath among days, and the Temple or Holy Land among places are all chosen for special holiness and therefore given to one another. The symbol here of Israel's cosmos-sustaining role is the four corners of the tallit, *drawn together into one as we prepare to recite the* Shema' *and proclaim God's oneness. Israel are also drawing together the four "corners" of the earth and the wings of God's holy angels, the source of songs that fill the earth each day. Israel are unifiers of the upper and lower worlds, dwellers in God's universal tent of peace.*

≡ **4** ≡

"You shall see it [the fringe on your garment]" (Num. 15:39) is read by the sages to mean that you shall see God's presence, for "whoever fulfills the commandment of the fringes merits greeting the Shekhinah."

Thus we may look at the glory of God's kingdom, which exists in every thing, as it says: "The whole earth is full of His glory" (Is. 6:3). But it is hidden, and a truly wholehearted act of self-negation allows one to see His shining glory. Such is the meaning of wrapping oneself in fringes to "look at Him," meant in the simplest sense, to desire only to see and come to know the glory of God's name. So, too, we find [in the table-hymns of R. Isaac Luria]:

> We will gaze at His glory
> He will show us His secret
> That had been said in a whisper.

This means that there is light locked away in each thing, hidden from us. But by negating ourselves, which is the "whisper," turning our sensations all toward God and becoming deaf to all else, the secret light is revealed to us. This is that "said in a whisper."

This too is the meaning of "you shall see it"—"you shall see His sign" *(oto)*. This refers to the sign that is within each thing, bearing witness to our blessed God. The sages taught this about the word *tseva'ot* (hosts), that "He is a sign *(ot)* amid His host *(tsava')*." All the creatures of heaven and earth are His hosts, each one a sign of His kingdom, which in this world remains hidden.

"And you shall remember the commandments of your Lord and do them, turning not aside after your hearts or your eyes . . . so that you remember to fulfill all My commandments and be holy unto your God" (Num. 15:39–40). Observing the commandments also has to be for this purpose, in order to cleave to God and remember that we were created only to fulfill His will. "Remembering" means cleaving to God. "Turning not aside" is also in order to remember the attachment to God.

Any intelligent person could reject this world on his own. But our sages said that "a person should not say: 'I cannot eat the meat of pigs,' but rather: 'My Father in heaven commanded me . . .'" This is why we should "turn not aside . . . so that you remember . . . and be holy." Our turning aside from the material world should be for God's sake, to cleave to Him. The true power we Jews have to reject materialism comes about because God brought us out of Egypt. That is why this passage ends: "I am the Lord your God who brought you out of the Land of Egypt to be your God; I am the Lord your God."

4:88

Here the teachings of Hasidism are emphasized in contrast to both non-hasidic Orthodoxy and the early growth of secular antimaterialism. On the one hand, R. Judah Leib emphasizes that the goal and reward of observance are true religious experience, the seeing of God within all things. It is for this purpose that we are to fulfill the commandments, which remain instruments toward this higher goal. Here Hasidism is clearly distinguished from non-hasidic Judaism, which does not know about finding and seeing God within all of existence. There the commandments often become ends rather than means, expressions of the arbitrary will of God rather than gateways to the divine presence.

On the other hand, the rejection of the material world also has to be for God's sake alone, directed toward the same religious vision. An intelligent secular person might also see through materialism, recognizing the need for some higher purpose. This is a step in the right direction, but by itself it does not suffice. Simply rejecting the vanities of the material world is not the same as seeing through those vanities to discover the face of God looking back at one from within each of God's creations.

≡ 5 ≡

In the chapter on fringes, the Midrash quotes: "Light is sown for the righteous" (Ps. 97:11). The word *tsitsit* (fringe) is interpreted by RaSHI as coming from [the verse:] "He peers between the cracks" (Cant. 2:9). [The purpose of] this mitsvah is to open a Jew's eyes. That is why the Talmud says that "one who is careful [or 'bright'] about the commandment of the fringes merits greeting the Shekhinah," since it says, "and you will see Him."

Tsitsit are mentioned three times in this passage, parallel to the three times in the year when Israel were to "be seen." These both came about by means of the three patriarchs to whom prophecy was granted. Thus Scripture says: "I was seen by Abraham, by Isaac, and by Jacob" (Ex. 6:3). Because of Abraham our Father's great love for God, God was revealed to him. To Isaac it was because of his great fear, which can also be read as "insight" *(YiReʾaH/ReʾiaH)*, and to Jacob because of his truth. God gave Israel this commandment so that we could all come to the patriarchs' level. And it is also true that God watches over Israel, "peers *(metsits)* between the cracks" (Cant. 2:9) because of this commandment.

The same is true of the "seeing" God and "being seen" by God in connection with the pilgrimage festivals, where it says both "see" and "be seen." And Scripture also says: "You have been shown to know" (Deut. 4:35), meaning that Israel have both "seeing" and "knowing." We are God's witnesses, and of the witness it is said: "If he sees or knows" (Lev. 5:1). The holy Zohar in *Parashat Va-ʾeraʾ* says that knowing is higher than seeing; knowing is the rung of Moses himself. Perhaps that is why they were here given the commandment of fringes. When they fell from their rung by no longer fully accepting Moses' leadership, they would have need of this "seeing," a step lower than knowing.

4:106

It is typical of the intellectualist tendency of Jewish mysticism to say that knowing is higher than seeing. An awareness of God that fills the mind is greater than one of the single sense of sight alone. This way of understanding also says something about "religious experience" and its place within the mystical consciousness. Many a Jewish teacher has been less than fully impressed with the sort of experiences that consist of graphic visions or the hearing of holy voices. The deeper experience is one that wells up from within, transforming consciousness itself from the inside rather than confronting it with sound or sight of that which still manifests itself as "other." Only when Israel are slipping from their highest rung are they given, as a way of reassurance, the "lesser" power of seeing God.

KORAḤ

1

"Koraḥ took . . . " (Num. 16:1). [The Targum translates:] "He divided."

The Mishnah teaches: "Controversy for the sake of heaven will come to fruition, while that which is not for the sake of heaven will not. Controversy for the sake of heaven: that of Hillel and Shamai. Controversy not for the sake of heaven: that of Koraḥ."

This world is in fact called the "world of separation," one where each creature looks out for itself. That is why it is "all strife." But Israel attain peace and wholeness by means of Torah. Whoever truly serves God properly, in order that God's will be fulfilled in the world, and acts only for the sake of heaven, can be jealous of no person. What is any single human being that his deeds should be accepted above? It is only through the entire community of Israel that God's will is fulfilled in the world. So everyone has to give his portion thoroughly over to the community. Once you do that, you see that there is no difference between you and your fellow.

This was the quality of Aaron, who "loved peace and pursued peace." That is why God chose him to be priest. Thus Scripture says: "Aaron, what is he that you complain against him" (Num. 16:11)—he does not divide himself off at all; all his deeds are given to the community. But of Koraḥ it says: "He took"—for himself. And even the very greatest person, when he is just for himself, what is he?

Scripture teaches: "Love your neighbor as yourself, I am the Lord" (Lev. 19:18), and the sages said: "This is the basic rule of Torah." RaSHI interprets "your neighbor" to refer to God. This means that when you serve God for God's own sake, you naturally love your neighbor, one who serves God just as you do. This is the basic rule of Torah: "your neighbor" as God and your real neighbor—it is all one. . . .

4:127

He reads the verse to mean: "Love" God. In doing so you will come to see "your neighbor as yourself."

The vision of human community and its necessary relationship to the religious life as presented here is both inspiring and frustrating to the contemporary reader. The Sefat Emet is clearly expansive and generous in his reading of religion and community as deeply tied together—when it comes to Jews. How can we envy others when we see that we are all one in God's service? How can we help loving our neighbors when we see them as fellow-worshippers of the same God? Our task as readers of this teaching is to let ourselves be inspired by his vision, but also to think of how we can expand it to include all of humanity, or even all of our fellow creatures, without losing the uniqueness and special power of our own language, in which these things are said so well.

≡ **2** ≡

"In the morning God will show who is His and who is holy . . . the one He will choose" (Num. 16:5). On this the sages commented: "Just as I separated morning from evening, [light from darkness, so did I separate Aaron to make him holy]."

Koraḥ was an important person. The sages note that he was one of those who carried the Ark. But there are words and deeds, as the Zohar tells us. "Whoever seeks [to study] Torah may do so, but when it comes to deeds one needs the help of heaven." This category of deeds is that of the priest who serves God; the whole world is renewed each day through his service in the holy Temple. That is why the verse says "will choose" in the future, as it says: "Who is the man who fears God; He will show him the way He will choose" (Ps. 25:12).

There is a new way each day. The Midrash teaches that each day God gives some new law, "an utterance *will come* from His mouth" (Job 37:2). The person who truly fears God is shown these ways that are made new each day. But even for those who are on a lesser rung, as we are in exile, our fear of heaven directs us in accordance with this renewal.

In the time of the Temple this process took place in a revealed way. This was surely true of Moses and Aaron, upon whom the whole world depended. The verse "Your grace and truth have forever formed me" (Ps. 40:12) refers to them. Through the high priest a thread of grace was drawn forth into the world each day. This was the testimony to Aaron: each day he brought new light into the world.

That is why Moses said: "In the morning God will show. . . ." How can you rise up against the high priest when every day itself bears witness to him . . . ?

4:117

The hasidic masters had a deep appreciation for the powers of priesthood, including an intuitive understanding of the cosmic significance of ancient priestly religion. The notion that the priest is responsible for the daily renewal of Creation is one that is entirely absent from the Hebrew Bible and one that would be hard to find explicitly stated in the teachings of the early rabbis. But the kabbalists and hasidic masters saw priesthood in its fullest and most powerful senses, sometimes exceeding the sources that lay before them in articulating the true implications of the Temple service.

3

It is said that "the blue [of the fringe-thread] is like the sea, the sea is like the sky, and the sky is like the Throne of Glory." These three levels of sea, sky, and throne remind us of three events. The sea is the Exodus from Egypt, for it says: "I am the Lord your God who brought you forth" (Num. 15:41), a redemption that ended at the sea, of which it says: "On that day the Lord saved Israel" (Ex. 14:30). "Sky" points to the receiving of Torah from Heaven. "Throne of Glory" refers to the dwelling of God's presence in the tabernacle and the Clouds of Glory.

These three also connect to the three gifts that Israel were given. The well is like the sea [and was received through the merit of Miriam]. The sky refers to the manna or "bread from heaven" that came down because of Moses. The Clouds of Glory were by the merit of Aaron. These are also the three pilgrim festivals, and at root this matter is related to *nefesh, ruaḥ,* and *neshamah,* [the three levels of soul]. When we left Egypt the redemption was that of *nefesh,* we received Torah on the level of *ruaḥ,* and only afterward comes *neshamah.*

[This order might seem surprising, placing Aaron higher than Moses.] It is true that Moses' rung is a high one. But Aaron, because he caused Israel to return in penitence, reached a still higher level. Therefore, he was given the innermost service on the Day of Atonement, equivalent to both *teshuvah* and *neshamah.* Of this they said: "Penitents stand in a place where the wholly righteous cannot stand." And also, "great is *teshuvah* for it reaches the Throne of Glory." That is why the Clouds of Glory were by Aaron's merit.

Now we understand the controversy of Korah. He made a *tallit* that was entirely blue, when Moses had explicitly said only a thread of blue should be placed among the fringes. From the upper blue [Moses believed], it is only possible to draw forth a bit of light, and even that is not certain. Korah did not reach that understanding.

We can add to this in accordance with the midrashic remark that God called Israel by three names: daughter, sister, and mother. Korah said: "The entire assembly is holy" (Num. 16:3) and heard "I am the Lord your God" (Ex. 20:2). He thought there was no rung higher for Israel than that of receiving the Torah. And since the Levites had not participated in the sin of the Golden Calf, he held himself superior to Aaron. But in fact it was Aaron who merited and gave merit to the people, who after the sin rose to a rung higher than that of receiving the Torah. The Midrash hints at this by reading the verse: "A brother led to sin by the bastion of strength" (Prov. 18:19) [to mean that "the brother who had sinned—Aaron—is greater than the bastion of Torah—Moses"].

These three categories of daughter, sister, and mother are themselves the three festivals. Just as it was in the generation of the wilderness, so it is forever. A Jew has to mend these three categories: to be redeemed from the evil urge and the "other side" is the Exodus from Egypt or liberation. After this, one reaches Torah, the category of *ruah*, spirit. But then you have to go on and do some new redemptive act in the world, for that is why human beings were sent here. Every Jew has a part in this. By means of prayer and the return to God, even a simple person can arouse some act of redemption, something specific to that person, each in accordance with his own measure.

Now of Korah it says that he "took," and that is translated "divided." Moses was the choicest of God's prophets. He negated himself before the Jewish people; he referred to Torah as "the inheritance of the community of Israel" (Deut. 33:4). He brought himself into the situation of Israel; when they had fallen from their rung because of sin, he joined himself to them. Korah, being quite a brilliant fellow, tried to hold himself off and did not want to be joined to the fate of the masses. That is why God did not choose him.

4:130

This very rich teaching is filled with associations that we might want to carry further as we develop these ideas. For that purpose a chart of parallels suggested here will be useful.

Nefesh	Ruaḥ	Neshamah
Sea	*Sky*	*Throne of Glory*
Well	*Torah*	*Clouds of Glory*
Miriam	*Moses*	*Aaron*
Passover	*Shavu'ot*	*Sukkot*
Daughter	*Sister*	*Mother*
Liberation	*Spirit*	*Redemptive Deed*

A further word is needed in connection with "daughter, sister, mother." The Midrash, quoting a series of biblical verses, suggests that at various times God had occasion to call Israel by each of these female terms of endearment. The hardest, of course, is "mother," as it is hard to imagine Israel depicted as the mother of God. Indeed, the Midrash must creatively distort a verse (Is. 51:4) in order to get it. But the usage here means that Korah could not imagine a state of being higher than that of receiving the Torah, when Israel are raised to being God's "sister" as opposed to His "daughter." The term "sister" in the Canticle is often associated also with "bride"; the point is that here God and Israel are equals, of the same generational standing. But Aaron understands that there is a still higher rung for Israel, that of "mother," by which God calls them when they do the redemptive work in God's world that they alone can do, giving "birth" to holy deeds.

Would we be too far off the mark in naming such a teaching "a Jewish mystical humanism"?

חקת

ḤUKKAT

1

"This is the law of the Torah" (Num. 19:2). Scripture here makes purification depend upon Torah, the Tree of Life. Purity derives from this tree, the opposite of the Tree of Knowledge, from which came death, the most basic category of impurity. By means of Torah, Israel can purify themselves of this defilement. We say in our prayers: "My God! The soul you placed in me is pure." "Pure" means that it is not capable of becoming defiled, for it says: "He blew into him the breath [= soul] of life" (Gen. 2:7).

The soul of every one of Israel belongs to Torah, the Word of God. Every soul has a portion in that Torah, in some letter or vowel point. This is the living soul within the person, and it cannot be defiled. Thus our sages taught on the verse "Are not

My words like fire?" (Jer. 23:29) that "Just as fire cannot be defiled, so words of Torah cannot be defiled."

Scripture says: "Who can bring forth the pure out of the impure?" (Job 14:4). Our sages read this as referring to the drop of semen, which is impure, and the person formed from it, who is pure. When the soul is joined to that drop, it takes on life and goes from defilement to purity. Thus it is forever: the one who studies Torah attains both soul and purity. This must be what the sages meant when they said: "There is not a single letter of Torah that does not contain the resurrection of the dead, except that we do not know how to interpret."

4:149

"Soul" and "Torah" are understood here as aspects of the same metaphysical entity; both represent the flow of divine ḥiyyut (life-energy) into the person. The miracle of birth, the greatest sublime wonder known to us humans, is repeated in the miracle of Torah study. In both of them the divine soul or an extra measure of life is added to mere flesh and blood. In this spirit the author offers a brilliant reinterpretation of a phrase in the talmudic discussion about whether the resurrection of the dead, seemingly not a biblical idea, is to be found in the Torah. Indeed, he says, study of Torah itself is that very resurrection.

The notion that "words of Torah cannot become defiled" serves as an ongoing assurance to us teachers of Torah who feel ourselves to be impure vessels, inadequate to the lofty and pure teachings we bear from one generation to the next. There is great consolation in being reminded of that level of truth where the teachings of Torah remain forever pure, no matter through what channel they may be transmitted.

 2

Regarding "the mouth of the well, [one of the ten things]" created on the eve of the first Sabbath:

Scripture says: "Drink water from your cistern *(bor)* and flowing water from your well *(be'er)*" (Prov. 5:15). The sages tell us that one who says [in the Grace after Meals] "From His goodness we live" is a boor, but one who says "In His goodness we live" is a disciple of the sages. *"From* His goodness," as we have interpreted it, would mean that we are sustained by a distinct part of His goodness, something separate from God's own self. "In His goodness" means that we cleave to the whole of goodness itself.

Everything derives from Torah, which is called "good," since God created the world "in the beginning" for the sake of Torah, which is called "beginning" (Ps. 111:10). The root of all is in Torah. The Zohar adds that Torah [as the Tree of Life] includes roots and fruit, leaves and bark. Israel and the sages cleave to the body of the tree itself. This is the difference between *bor* (cistern) and *be'er* (well): the cistern just contains gathered water; its contents are limited by the size of the vessel that contains them. The well, on the other hand, is joined directly to the source of an ever-flowing spring.

The same thing is true on the inside. Every soul contains enlightenment and wisdom; "You made them all in wisdom" (Ps. 104:24). This [outer soul] is the cistern.

Such, too, is the distinction between weekday and Sabbath. On the weekdays "it will be closed" (Ezek. 46:1); the inner gates are not open. But on the Sabbath the inner wellsprings are opened. That is why Shabbat is called "a gift without restraints." This is it: the mouth of the well, the inner gate.

But there are two openings, because Scripture says it is open "on the Sabbath" and "on the new moon" (ibid.). Those two openings are the two letters *yod*, placed around the letter *vav* [to form an *'aleph*], and transforming the "cistern" into a "well." The letter *yod* is a gateway. Thus we learn in the verse "You open Your hands" (Ps. 145:16) that the word *yadekha* (Your hands) can also be read as *yudekha* (Your *yods*). The preceding verse in the Psalm refers to "giving them their food in their season." That is the specific and measured time that belongs to each individual. But "You open Your hands" refers to the source itself, "satisfying all life with favor," directly connecting to the root of all. . . .

4:144f.

This is a rich and complex teaching, clearly reported in an only fragmentary way. He means to say that the innermost human soul, the one accessible to us Jews through our Shabbat-consciousness, is a wellspring ever joined in a direct way to God, the endlessly flowing source of life. Thus it is that we live "in His goodness" and not merely "from" it. Adding the 'aleph, which also stands for our awareness of the ever-present One, transforms life as cistern, receiving that which God gives in limit and measure, to life as living well. This transformation is miraculously recreated for us on the eve of each Shabbat.

3

Regarding the song at the well (Num. 21:17ff.) and the fact that Moses is not mentioned there. In the prior song it says: "Then Moses and the children of Israel sang" (Ex. 15:1).

The well refers to the oral Torah. The sages said: "There is no water but Torah" [and this refers to the oral teaching]. There is written Torah, the "food from heaven" (Ex. 16:4), belonging to Moses, who brought it down from heaven. That is why we are told that the manna was given by the merit of Moses, since it is that food. But this well belongs to the realm of water, the oral Torah.

I heard from my grandfather and teacher that the reading of Torah, preceded and followed by a blessing, is like a meal, when we thank God beforehand for having given us this food and afterwards for having sated us and nourished us for life by the food. That is why the blessing after meals must be recited before the food has been digested. The blessing after the Torah reading is about the way we draw life from words of Torah, which are absorbed into our soul. This is the oral Torah, in which a person becomes a "child of Torah," attached to Torah, as in [the verse:] "He implanted eternal life within us." This is the well of water to which our sages refer when they say: "You shall eat, be sated, and bless the Lord your God" (Deut. 8:10). "You shall eat" refers to eating, but "you shall be sated" refers to drinking, since drinking allows the food to be digested, so that the person may be nourished by it.

A hint of this may be found in the Midrash on the Song of Songs, where it mentions that the word "well" is found forty-eight times in the Torah, parallel to the forty-eight means by which Torah is acquired. Written Torah, in other words, is a gift from heaven, available to anyone who wants it. But for a person really to acquire a portion in the Torah, to be a "child of Torah," where Torah is truly absorbed into one's bloodstream—this comes about only through those forty-eight things.

The first song was sung before the giving of the Torah. "Then Moses and the children of Israel sang," since they felt in their souls that they had become God's servants, ready to hear the word of God. But this latter song took place forty years later, when they felt that Torah was truly absorbed into their blood. The sages tell us that after Moses had learned Torah for forty days [on the mountain] he forgot it all, and God gave it to him as a gift. So, too, the service of Israel for those forty years in the wilderness: they struggled to attain Torah until it was finally given to them as a gift. That is why Moses is not mentioned in this song, which refers to a higher rung than that of the one who brought Torah down from heaven.

4:145

Moses brought to Israel Torah from heaven. But Israel, having struggled to learn, apply, and absorb Torah into their own lives, are now higher than they (or even he?) had been earlier and are thus no longer dependent upon Moses. Forty years later Torah has become truly their own, present in their very blood, and they can speak and teach it freely, without turning first to their master. This reading is true to the spirit of Polish Hasidism, which sought to show how the Hasidim of each generation, while nourished by their masters' teachings, eventually need to become independent and seek out their own path.

Unstated in this teaching, but obvious from the symbolic connections behind it, is the attribution of oral Torah to Miriam, by whose merit we were given the well. In this generation, which is blessed by so many female Torah teachers, we are no longer surprised to learn who stands as the source of our wellspring of oral Torah.

4

On the verse "Israel sent emissaries to Siḥon" (Num. 21:21), the Midrash quotes "Trust the Lord and do good" (Ps. 37:3) and "Turn from evil and do good; seek peace and pursue it" (Ps. 34:15). In the case of any other commandment, the Midrash explains, you must do it only if the opportunity comes before you. Peace alone has to be pursued; "Seek it" in your place "and pursue it" beyond your place.

Actually we find "pursuit" prescribed for two things: truth and peace. "Justice, justice shall you pursue" (Deut. 16:20) and "Seek peace and pursue it." These two qualities are the opposite of this world. In fact they both opposed the creation of the human being, "since he is all lies, all quarrels." These qualities are not to be found in this world of lies. That is why they have to be pursued, why divine help needs to be sought. Such was the case of Israel, who received Torah from heaven. "God gives strength [=Torah=truth] to His people; God blesses His people with peace" (Ps. 29:11).

Moses our Teacher represents that quality of truth—"In all My house he is the trusted one" (Num. 12:7)—and he brought Torah down from heaven. Aaron represents peace. Israel attained peace by the merit of being in the wilderness, the place outside human settlement. That is "'Pursue it'—beyond your place." Because they trusted in God and were drawn to follow Him out into the wilderness, they attained the quality of peace, *shalom.* That is why Israel are referred to [in the Song of Songs] as the Shulamite.

But Scripture also has God saying, "I am peace" (Ps. 120:7). Once Israel attained this quality of peace, it was within their power to draw all the nations close to God. . . .

4:147

The teaching continues with a troubling passage about the nations' refusal to accept Torah, all of them being like the Amorites and Canaanites, who sought only war when Israel approached them in peace.

This teaching makes it clear how urgent peace is, in order for Israel to do the work for which we exist. The message we have to offer the world is one of shalom. *We cannot deliver it as a nation of warriors, occupiers, or arms merchants.*

Why were Israel chosen (however we understand that term) to bear God's message to the world? Because they, like their father Abraham, were willing to leave the settled world behind and follow the fire of an unknown God into the wilderness. Only there, in that place where all the conventions and arrangements of ordinary human society do not exist, could God's word be spoken in a whole and undisturbed way. It was that place, cut off from the world of lies, from the deceitfulness of all human-made idolatries, that gave them access to true inner peace. And only there, where existence itself depended on the love and trust Israel had for their loving God, could they become God's Shulamite, faithful bearer of the Teaching.

BALAK

1

The Mishnah says that whoever possesses the three characteristics of a good eye, a lowly spirit, and a humble soul is a disciple of our father Abraham, while one who has the three opposite characteristics is a disciple of wicked Balaam (Avot 5:19). Our sages here reveal to us that Balaam was the precise opposite of righteous Abraham.

This fits with their comment on the verse, "What may I curse that God has not cursed?" (Num. 23:8). This wicked man sought out the precise moment of divine wrath, of which it is said: "The Lord is wrathful each day" (Ps. 7:12). But this wrath lasts only for a moment, since it also says: "The compassion of God is all the day long. . ." (Ps. 52:3). The entire goal of the wicked is to find that [moment of] wrath.

The righteous, by contrast, seek out the good will of Heaven. "As for me, my prayer is for a time of good will" (Ps. 69:14). Even beyond that, they seek out the thread of grace that exists in this world. This world is indeed founded on judgment, but still a thread of grace is found each day. The righteous seek to find that point of grace or time of good will.

Now in fact the momentary anger that exists above comes about through the wicked. It is taught that they worship the sun and God becomes angry. And the thread of grace exists in this world only because of the righteous. It was father Abraham who brought this thread into real existence in this world, as is taught around the verse, "Will I take even a thread or a sandal-lace?" (Gen. 14:23).

So the teacher said that one who has these three good characteristics is a disciple of Abraham, deserving of finding grace each day in this world "for those who await His grace" (Ps. 33:18). And the wicked by their evil qualities bring about divine wrath above. But we still find that goodness is more plentiful. When the righteous succeed in finding grace in this world, all that the wicked do is not able to take that grace from them. Of this Scripture says: "Many waters cannot douse love, nor can floods drown it. If a man were to put up all the goods in his house against love, people would despise him" (Cant. 8:7). Wicked Balaam offers the same testimony when he says: "If Balak were to offer me his house filled with silver and gold, I could not transgress the word of the Lord my God" (Num. 22:18).

But when the wicked seek to gain strength from that moment of anger that exists in heaven, God holds back the anger. Thus it is taught that for all those days [when Balaam was in Balak's hire] God was not wrathful, "so that the righteousness of God be known" (Mic. 6:5).

This war goes on every day. It also takes place within the individual Jew, and we have to arouse the quality of grace every day. The wicked and the will to do evil also strengthen themselves each day, arousing the forces of judgment. It was for this reason that the rabbis wanted to place the account of Balak as part of the *Shema'*.

4:156

This is an important teaching, offering a hasidic version of the kabbalistic idea that evil as well as good has its root in God. There is a moment of divine wrath, one against which God Himself, as it were, is in struggle. The wicked glorify that moment, seeking in it justification for their own evil behavior. But this is not God's desire. The Lord whose grace is "all the day long" wants us to seek out that grace and bring it into this world, becoming channels for this divine gift as we give it to others.

What does it mean that God struggles with an inner moment of divine anger, wrath, or impatience? Among other things, it means that we in our very imperfection, amid our own messy and imperfect lives, are images of God. Only a God who knows an inner wrath with which He is not content can be with us as we struggle each day for the little victories of love and grace over impatience and anger.

2

The Midrash quotes the verse, "O Rock, whose work is perfect, all of whose ways are just" (Deut. 34:2), applying it to the fact that "the blessed Holy One did not leave the nations of the world a chance to say: ['it was You who distanced us from You'] . . . He established prophets for them. . . . "

The point is that prophecy brings speech forth from potential to real. The prophet is the collective "mouth" of Israel. Just as in the individual it is through the mouth that we bring forth our innermost selves . . . , so it is with the prophet who is the mouth of Israel. That is why the prophet's power is dependent upon the efforts of all Israel, since it says: "A prophet from within your midst . . . will arise for you" (Deut. 18:15). More than Israel needs the prophet, the prophet is in need of them. This is "the general that requires the particular and the particular that requires the general." That is why the prophets bear witness to the general community, to whom they prophesy.

The nations are not prepared for prophecy. That is why God gave them Balaam. He was a vessel for prophecy, but since they were not prepared, it did not go well for him.

We can say the same thing about the reason prophecy was taken away from us. Even though it was "because of our sins," it is also a way of testifying for Israel. Let the nations not say that we followed Him, because He drew us near and set up prophets for us. We no longer have prophets, and yet we still hold fast to our faith in God and busy ourselves with His commandments! This shows the inwardness of Israel, even though we have no prophets who can draw forth existence from potential to real. "We have seen no signs; there is no longer a prophet, and none among us knows until when" . . . (Ps. 74:9).

4:158

The claim that Balaam was prophet to the nations as Moses was to Israel is an ancient one. Usually, however, it is made in the context of the vilification or even demonization of both the heathens and their prophet. They are pictured in the Midrash, and even more so in Kabbalah, as the negative or wicked counterpart of Moses and Israel. Here we see just a glimmer of another view, one that will be essential to any contemporary reappropriation of Jewish spirituality. Each nation (read "religious community") has its own prophet, whose powers all derive from the one God. The quality and clarity of each prophet's message depend upon the community he or she represents and the degree to which that community is willing to say, "Let us do and listen," as Moses' people was. The claim of Judaism would thus be not that Moses is superior to all other prophets but that the Jewish people, ever standing at Sinai, constitute a community prepared to follow the word of God. This claim should seek to serve as a paradigm for others, recognizing that other such faithful communities do potentially exist everywhere, rather than as a means of claiming superiority over other nations and their paths to God.

3

On the verse: "How goodly are your tents, O Jacob, your dwelling places, O Israel!" (Num. 24:5). Holiness follows Israel wherever they may be, as Scripture says: "In every place where I cause My name to be mentioned, I shall come unto you and bless you" (Ex. 20:21). Now the Land of Israel and the Temple have a permanent and unique relationship with the Jewish people. This is referred to in "your dwelling-places, O Israel." But wherever else Israel happen to be, even in a temporary way, there, too, holiness is revealed to them. [The following verse reads:] "Like streams that flow," for the wellsprings of Torah indeed flow with them wherever they dwell. This is why Scripture refers here to Jacob, who wandered outside the Land. The same was true in the wilderness, when they had not yet entered the Land. . . .

4:163f.

Offered in 1896, the very year when Theodor Herzl's The Jewish State *was published, the Sefat Emet here as elsewhere in these teachings is seeking to confirm a hasidic point of view on the Holy Land and the Jews' relationship to it. Ger was in fact less opposed to Zionism than were many other hasidic groups, and a number of its followers were to settle in the Land of Israel between the two world wars. But this sermon makes it clear that while Israel and the land are indeed spiritually bound together, holiness is found in the temporary "tents" of Jacob in Poland and elsewhere as well as in the permanent "dwelling-places" of Israel in Jerusalem or on the Temple Mount.*

4

. . . It is taught that "the broken tablets lie in the Ark." Surely the gift God gave us was not for naught. If we were not yet ready to receive that gift, it was hidden away in the Ark.

The breaking of the tablets took place on the seventeenth of Tammuz, [the date when the wall of Jerusalem was breached by the Romans]. All these breaks have to be healed. That is why Israel are dispersed and exiled throughout the lands, in order to gather those fragments. When all is restored, we will be able to receive those "first tablets."

Thus it is taught in the name of Rabbi Isaac Luria that [Aaron's words when erecting the Golden Calf], "A holiday unto the Lord tomorrow!" (Ex. 32:5), mean that one day the seventeenth of Tammuz will indeed be a festival. As the day when the tablets were given, it is properly a time for great celebration. It was only because we were unable to receive them that our dance was turned into mourning. When everything is restored, this date will be transformed into a time of gladness and joy. So, too, the prophet says: "The fast of the fourth month . . . will be a time of gladness and joy" (Zech. 8:19).

4:157f.

This homily assumes the identity of the "broken tablets" of Sinai and the "broken vessels" of Lurianic Kabbalah, which are scattered through the universe and which Israel are dispersed in order to retrieve and uplift to God. Both of these are then identified also with the broken walls of Jerusalem. The healing of all these breaches is the same task, and its completion will be heralded by the transformation of all our mourning—on the three levels mentioned here and perhaps some others—into joy and thanksgiving.

PINḤAS

═══ **1** ═══

The letter *yod* is added to the name of Pinḥas. This is a sign of peace; the *yod*, like the *vav*, contains no empty space and does not take up space like the other letters. These [two letters] represent two kinds of peace, as in "Peace, peace, to the far and the near" (Is. 57:19). The holy Zohar says that the "far" is Jacob and the "near" is Joseph. These are the two sorts of peace: Jacob makes peace between Abraham and Isaac. This is [the meaning of] "I shall return in peace to my father's house" (Gen. 28:21), "sweetening" the harshness of Isaac [who represents the force of judgment]. Joseph makes peace among the tribes.

It is taught that Pinḥas [with the *yod* added] numerically represents 208, the same as Isaac, who stands for the quality of judgment [or the "left" side]. The priesthood, however, is of

lovingkindness [or the "right" side]. Priesthood was given to
Pinhas as a gift, as though to say that when Israel are deserving, even the "left" becomes "right." Something like this is
found in the Zohar, to the effect that priesthood had to be
given to him, since one who has killed a person is [ordinarily]
disqualified from priesthood. The point is that he belongs to
the side of judgment.

So, too, it says: "He makes peace in His heights" (Job 25:2),
meaning that God makes peace between angels of love and
justice. But there may also be a single angel who contains both
of these. Such a one was Pinhas in this world; the "covenant of
peace" was given to him, to be a priest, even though he came
from the side of judgment.

4:182

*Abraham and Isaac represent the qualities of lovingkindness
(the "right" side) and harsh judgment (the "left" side) with
God, according to the kabbalists.*

*Much of the material around Pinhas, in this as well as
many other traditional sources, is difficult for the modern
reader. The texts do not seem to share our instinctive horror
at Pinhas's act. Here we come somewhat close: the shedding
of blood indeed renders one unfit for priesthood. A special divine exemption had to be made for Pinhas. This was done in
order to show that the left side, as seemingly vicious as it
may become in the terrible act of judgment, is not beyond redemption. God may restore it to balance with lovingkindness. Here Pinhas emerges like King David: warrior and
psalmist at once.*

*For us latter-day readers, however, it remains important to
remember that David and Pinhas were both murderers. In
David's case God accepts his remorse, though only his son's
hands, and not his, are clean enough to build the Temple. We
need to see the remorse of Pinhas as well. We need a hasidic
master to do for us what even the Sefat Emet has not quite
done—to tell us that the yod is added to Pinhas's name only
when he realizes and repents of his terrible deed.*

2

"Among these shall the land be divided" (Num. 26:53). It is taught that the division took place by the casting of lots, but guided by the holy spirit.

Scripture says: "Portions have come to me pleasantly; my inheritance is pleasing to me" (Ps. 16:6). The main gift of the Land of Israel is in the upper root. Every Jew has a portion in the root of the Land of Israel, both above and below. That is why they were counted again before entering the land, so that each be aware of his root, just as was the case with the prior countings. These refer also to the written and oral Torah, for Israel all have a part in both of these. Thus we say: "May it be Your will that the Temple be rebuilt, and grant our portion in Your Torah."

It is taught that "all Israel have a place in the world to come." This teaching is based on the verse: "Your people are all righteous; they will forever inherit the Land" (Is. 60:21). Even though the plain meaning of this verse refers to the [earthly] Land of Israel, it still serves as a sign that we all have a place in the world to come. This comes about through our earning the right in this world to attach ourselves to the Land of Israel, the root of Israel's souls.

Scripture says [referring to Jerusalem]: "There the tribes of God went up, a witness for Israel, to acknowledge the name of the Lord" (Ps. 122:4). Pilgrimage to the Temple was a way of witnessing the [people's] attachment to their root. The fact of this pilgrimage testified to them and their lineage.

These were the songs, [the fifteen "psalms of ascent"] that the Levites would sing while the pilgrims ascended the fifteen steps of the Temple. These are also the fifteen "rungs" Israel went through from the Exodus from Egypt until "He built for us the Chosen Dwelling [as described in the Passover song "Dayyenu"]. These are fifteen categories or paths by which to get to the root.

4:174

The openness expressed here to the need for spiritual attachment to the this-worldly Land of Israel is typical of Gerer Hasidism. It provided the background against which the son of the Sefat Emet, R. Avraham Mordecai, in 1921 bought land in Jaffa and encouraged his Hasidim to do likewise, so that every one of them would be rooted in the Land of Israel. Certain other hasidic groups were critical of Ger for this and much more uncompromising in their opposition to anything that smacked of compromise with the newly emerging Zionist forces. While the founder of Agudat Yisra'el was still far from what might be called Zionism, he felt the same instinct as did more secular Jews that the time had come to renew our roots within the land. The origins of this desire are already reflected in passages like this one in the Sefat Emet, whose writings were also read by Rabbi Abraham Isaac Kook and other leaders of religious Zionism.

3

"Command the children of Israel and tell them to bring the food offerings for My fires . . . " (Num. 28:2). . . . RaSHI here quotes a midrash [that offers the parable of a king and his dying wife. On her deathbed she asks that the king take care of her children. He replies to her:] "While you are leaving me a testament concerning your children, command your children also [that they not rebel against me]."

There is food that comes from heaven and food that comes from earth; these correspond to the written Torah and the oral Torah. Moses our Teacher brought Torah down from heaven to earth. The manna also [was food from heaven], as Scripture says: "Behold I will rain down upon you food from heaven" (Ex. 16:4). Moses hoped that [this flow from heaven] would continue after his lifetime as well. But this was in fact the beginning of "food from the earth": it was time for the lower creatures to bring offerings for the sake of heaven. This is [the meaning of] "command your children also." This refers to sacrifices and then to prayer, which came in their place, the "worship within the heart," the longing of the heart to be attached to its root above.

Even if we have fallen from that height, we can get back to where we were. That is why it says of the daily sacrifice: "A regular offering that was offered on Mount Sinai" (Num. 28:6). We have already been on a very high rung at Mount Sinai, where it says: "The Lord descended upon Mount Sinai" (Ex. 19:20). Because of that we can raise ourselves back up to heaven.

Moses in fact prayed for this. When he said, "I supplicated the Lord at that time" (Deut. 3:23), the rabbis derived rules of prayer from his prayer. Here Moses was preparing the way of prayer. Until then there had been only Torah, the shining speculum, all revealed. But from now on there began to be a way to find everything by means of struggle, as it is said: "*Your deeds* will draw you near."

This is the meaning of sacrifice and prayer. Understand it.

4:170

To follow the interesting image created by the Midrash, we may say that it is only in the childhood or immature years of the life of faith that we primarily expect God to provide for us. As we grow "older" in our faith, we understand that our primary act is one of giving; it is within our giving that we glimpse some reward as well. The easy and direct path of revelation is replaced by the life of spiritual struggle, of climbing back up the mountain where we know we have been already. It is only that assurance, the memory that once God did "descend upon Mount Sinai," that allows us to go on with a life of endless giving, endless struggle.

MATTOT

1

The Midrash quotes the verse: "You shall swear by the living God in truth, judgment, and righteousness" (Jer. 4:2). I have already noted that these three are parallel to "with all your heart, with all your soul, and with all your might" (Deut. 6:5). "Truth" refers to the soul, which is the life within. "Judgment" applies to the heart, for it has two directions and needs proper balance. "Righteousness" applies to might [interpreted to mean material wealth; *tsedakah* means both "righteousness" and "charity"]. Only then can it say: "These words which I command you this day shall be upon your heart" (Deut. 6:6). Only after both body and soul have been set aright can we receive words of Torah.

In fact the entire Torah is the names of God; the words of the holy Torah cause our hearts to be attached to God. That is why it says: "You shall contemplate it ['Him?'] day and night" (Josh. 1:8). The same is true of the commandments to recite the *Shema'* and the *'Amidah*: "You shall speak of them" (Deut. 6:7) means adding to the life-force of God. By accepting God's kingdom each day, verbally, the words help our deeds to fall in line with our acceptance. "I have sworn and I shall fulfill it" (Ps. 119:106); one may take an oath to fulfill the commandments, and that oath may be of help. ". . . as all that comes out of his mouth, he will do" (Num. 30:2).

This is also a promise that we will be able actually to fulfill that which we have accepted verbally. That is why it says: "as all" and not just "all." Deed is really greatly distanced from desire and acceptance. It is only the acceptance itself that allows the deed to become like it. . . .

4:186

Our deeds are often very far from our intentions. This gap can be bridged, the hasidic master teaches, only within the framework of a true commitment to accept God's kingdom. Such an oath of acceptance can have tremendous power over us, if we let it.

2

[On the same verse:]

Swearing by God's name is meant to help the one who serves God . . . "A tower of strength is the name of God; in it run the righteous and the uplifted" (Prov. 18:10). The involvement with study of Torah and prayer gives holiness to ordinary Jews and allows them to purify their hearts. How much more does it do for the truly great among Israel. They are like [the angels] above, of whom it says that when they cannot rise so high as to crown God, they administer an oath to the crown, which then proceeds on its own and seats itself on the king's head. Of such help is the oath to the truly righteous, when they need it!

But "not anyone who wants to take the name may do so." It is rather, as the Midrash goes on to say: we need to "fear the Lord your God, serve Him, and be attached to Him" (Deut. 10:20). Only afterwards does it say "and swear by His name."

So the power of oaths is here given to the heads of the tribes. But the acceptance of God's kingdom, recited by ordinary Jews every single day, is also an oath. Thus it says: "Seven times [*sheva'* means both 'seven' and 'oath'] a day I praise You" (Ps. 119:164), referring to the *Shema'* and its [seven] blessings each day. This acceptance is a help to them, just as they have been given help from above, for we are taught that "before a person comes into this world, he is given an oath that says: 'Be righteous, not wicked.'" Just as God renews Creation each day, so is this oath renewed on a daily basis, as it says: "which I command you this day" (Deut. 6:6). But this depends upon our awareness, as Scripture says: "You have affirmed the Lord your God . . . and the Lord your God has affirmed you . . . " (Deut. 26:17–18).

5:187

While very little of the magical element in Hasidism remains in the Sefat Emet, *here we see some trace of it. The righteous have recourse to oaths (or "adjurations") as do the angels, in seeking to reach into those places where they as mortals have no other authorization to go. This might be used as justification for recourse to amulets in healing and other practices that, while by no means the chief focus of religious life in the Hasidism of Ger, were never explicitly rejected. But how like the Sefat Emet, as soon as he has made the slightest mention of such a view, to hurry back to the daily oaths of ordinary Jews and provide another reminder, in the spirit of Kotsk, that everything depends upon us, and that God is present "only where you let Him in."*

 3

. . . There are three sins for which you are supposed to sacrifice your life rather than transgress. These are murder, forbidden sexual liaisons, and worshipping idols. But evil talk is considered as wicked as all three of these together, as the Midrash teaches. Parallel to them are three positive rungs: "fear Him"; "serve Him"; and "be attached to Him" (Deut. 10:20). After these comes [the commandment:] "and swear by His name," referring to the power of the mouth and the tongue of the righteous, making an impression both in heaven and on earth. These three plus one refer also to the three patriarchs and King David.

But something of this is found in each person as well. First you must struggle to fulfill the Torah and commandments as they are set out for us; only then do you deserve to add something of your own. Of this they said: "If someone says to you, 'I have struggled and found,' believe him." This is the "eternal life You have implanted in our midst"; God has hidden secrets of Torah within the mouths of Israel, as it says: "I have placed My words in your mouth" (Is. 51:16). When we struggle with Torah, this oral Torah within our hearts and mouths is reawakened. . . .

4:189

Israel are the vehicles of oral Torah; there is no such teaching until we give articulation and bring into language that which has been eternally hidden within our hearts. God's secrets are waiting within us to be discovered and spoken. Only study of Torah, that same Torah by which we and all creatures were made, can so stimulate our hearts as to call forth the Torah hidden within each and every one of us.

This is perhaps the most essential and valuable teaching in all of Hasidism: true Torah lies within you; the collective Torah and commandments are but a vehicle—albeit an essential vehicle—to help you release that endless flow of divine life and teaching that lies within your soul.

Our sages noted that all the other prophets opened their words with: "Thus says the Lord!" but Moses went beyond them and said: "This is the word that the Lord has commanded" (Num. 30:2). The difference between these two formulations is like that between the ten utterances *(ma'amarot)* of Creation and the Ten Commandments *(dibrot;* "words"). The utterances were only directed outward, announcing the divine will, as in "Let there be a firmament!" or "Let there be luminaries!" But *word* refers to the inner essence of speech itself, just as the noun "speaker" *(medabber)* defines the human being [and distinguishes us from the animal kingdom]. The word is an essential speech-act, not an incidental one, as is the utterance.

Such is also the distinction between "this is" and "thus." There are various rungs of prophecy. The essential word is "garbed" and then flows forth to the rungs of utterance. That is why utterance is initiated with "thus" and speech with "this is." That is why [at Sinai] Scripture says: "The Lord spoke all these words, saying . . ." (Ex. 20:1). First came speech; utterance [or "saying"] came only later. And such was the rung of Israel, as they received the Torah, that the inner divine word was revealed to them in speech, going beyond the ten utterances.

Something like this distinction applies also to weekdays and the Sabbath. During the week, which exists by the power of the ten utterances, there is a particular creation on each day, as in "Let there be light!" or "Let there be a firmament!" But on the Sabbath there is no creation, and it says: "God blessed the seventh day" (Gen. 2:3). That was the essence of speech. On other days, when there is divine blessing, the word "bless" alternates with "said" or "saying," as in "He blessed them and said: 'Be fruitful and multiply'" (Gen. 1:28). But on the Sabbath it just says "bless," for this is speech itself.

That is why the Torah, meaning the Ten Commandments [or "speech-acts"], was given on Shabbat, as we said above. Thus the Zohar says of the Sabbath that even though it has no food [i.e., manna] given on it, it is the source of all blessing. . . .

4:190

Though this text is somewhat obscure, both because of the inadequate terminology available to the Sefat Emet and due to its inadequate reflection in translation, careful attention should be paid to it. The Sefat Emet is hinting here at a profound theology of language. He suggests that there are two types of speech-acts, which he designates by the terms ma'amar ("saying" or "utterance") and dibbur ("word" or "speech"). Ma'amar is an act of speaking that is outer-directed; it has a goal beyond speech itself that it seeks to accomplish. Such are God's ten ma'amarot in Creation; their purpose is not that they be spoken, but that the world come to be. Such verbal activity is instrumental, rather than being an end in itself. Dibbur, on the other hand, exists for its own sake. It is an act of deepest self-revelation; its only intent is to bespeak the speaker. Such, our author hints (and this is indeed a radical theological idea), is the divine speech of Sinai. God gives of Himself, turns Himself into language, as the Sefat Emet suggests elsewhere (Shavu'ot 4:41; Ki Tavo' 5:105). It is our ability to do the same, to offer of ourselves in verbal form—both to God in prayer and to others in the verbal sharing of intimacy—that makes us human. We are distinguished from the beasts not because of what we can do by means of verbal communication, but by the pure rung of shared rest and blessing to which that same verbal vessel can be raised.

MASSE'EY

1

"These are the journeys of the children of Israel who came out of Egypt. . . . Moses wrote down their comings forth and their goings forward according to the word of the Lord; these are their goings forward and their comings forth" (Num. 33:1–2).

Notice that the order is reversed from the beginning to the end of the verse. Scripture is telling us that all this "going forward" depends upon "coming forth" from Egypt. Only after all those journeys is the Exodus from Egypt complete; with each "going forward" they got farther from Egypt, until they reached the Land of Israel.

A person who turns away from material things has to do so in order to cleave to God, to be a person of heart. We should not turn away from the corporeal because we find it repulsive.

275

In fact, that is why God gave such great beauty to physical things, so that our deed [in turning away from them] should be only for the sake of heaven. This is "their coming forth and their going forward." But later, the farther one travels and the closer one comes to God, the more complete is the "coming forth," the separation from the corporeal world. Each of these two helps the other.

4:193f.

There is a nice bit of spiritual insight here, a counsel that one could imagine exists in parallel forms in all the great traditions of monasticism and abstinence. We should not turn from the corporeal world out of disdain for matter, but rather to seek God. On the other hand, the very process of seeking is surely aided by the degree to which we train ourselves to turn from the corporeal world. "Coming forth" from the Egypt of enslavement to wealth and material things and "going forward" in the journey to God and the Promised Land are two processes deeply intertwined with each other.

 2

"This is the land that will fall to you by inheritance" (Num. 34:2). The Midrash says that here God showed to Moses each generation and its teachers.

Surely the Canaanites had never experienced the category of the "Land of Israel." It was only due to Israel's preparation as they entered the land that the heavenly "Land of Israel" descended upon that earthly land. Thus we have been taught that the earthly Temple is parallel to one above. The same is true of the Land of Israel and of Jerusalem. It was this inward land that God showed to Moses.

The children of Israel are themselves "borders" into which the holiness can flow; it was as they entered into their physical borders that the [upper] Land "fell" into their inheritance. That is why God commanded that they leave none of the Canaanites, for the upper land could not bear them.

The same is true of the individual as well: as we prepare our hearts and souls with Torah, so does God cause holiness to flow into us. Our sages spoke of this when they said [that a person should conduct himself] "as though a holy being were present in his loins."

4:194

This text is translated here despite the disturbing nature of its message if translated into contemporary politics. The Canaanites, who had never known the true "Land of Israel," were to be utterly exterminated, for the Holy Land could not bear their impure presence.

When the Sefat Emet said these things, it was still inconceivable that Israel in premessianic times would have political power, along with the responsibility that comes with it. The "Canaanites" to him were a purely symbolic entity, a category of defilement symbolized by that ancient and now wholly nonexistent nation. But today, only a bit more than a century later, there are forces within the Jewish people that want to resurrect the "Canaanites," identified with today's non-Jewish inhabitants of the Holy Land, and demonize them as well. This reading of Judaism must be forcefully countered and rejected. We may claim that Jews have a unique relationship with the Land of Israel, one indeed not quite shared even by Christians or Muslims. But we must do this entirely without transforming others into demonic or less than fully human beings.

We also have the alternative of reading such texts on the individual moralistic level, as the Sefat Emet does. But when we do, we should recall that Islam too has a way of internalizing its aggressive side in the form of the "spiritual jihad." We would do well to see this parallel. It was perhaps only our many centuries of alienation from power that allowed us to carry out this spiritual sublimation of violent imperatives to such a high degree. Our return to power politics threatens to undo this process much more quickly.

3

Our sages said: "Whoever gives joy to the Sabbath is given an inheritance without limits." They based this on . . . "the inheritance of your father Jacob" (Is. 58:14).

From God's point of view, the flow is without interruption or limit. It is only because all that flows forth to a person has to come into this world (since we, while in the body, are attached to this world) that on the receiver's end there are limits. On the Holy Sabbath, however, all creatures ascend to their true place. Thus it says of the Sabbath: "No person may go forth from his place" (Ex. 16:29). The Zohar says that "place" here refers to God. On the Holy Sabbath all is negated before Him, so surely the inheritance is "without limits." This refers to the extra soul that Israel have on the Sabbath. A person's capability to grasp things is limited on all other days, but on the Sabbath it is expanded beyond all quantification or measure.

This comes about through our ancestors, the patriarchs. A person who truly negates himself to return to his root is helped by the merits of our forefathers.

The extra soul of the Holy Sabbath leaves an imprint on the body as well. Holy books teach us that after a person dies there is some "breath" [of that soul] left amid the bones. The same is true of the extra soul; it, too, leaves an imprint through all the days of the week. This of course depends upon how attached we are to that extra soul, how much we long not to be separated from it, and how hard that separation is for us.

4:194

Shabbat in the mystical tradition is a time for an entirely different rung of existence to enter our lives. On Shabbat we live as spiritual superhumans, stepping beyond the ordinary limits of human consciousness, able to receive God's blessing in the absolutely limitless way in which it is given.

The experience described here is a real one, though one known by most who speak of it as a rare and spontaneous event. The power of Jewish spiritual insight, linked always to the normative and halakhic tradition, is the ability to make such experiences regular and attainable, at least in some moments of prayer, on each Sabbath day.

דברים

SEFER DEVARIM

DEVARIM

1

"These are the words Moses spoke" (Deut. 1:1). The Midrash comments that the language of Torah heals the tongue, as Scripture says: "The tree of life is a healing for the tongue" (Prov. 15:4). The Zohar compares Torah to a tree; it has branches, fruit, leaves, and bark in addition to the trunk of the tree itself, to which all these are joined. So, too, the Torah: it gives sustenance and life to all of Creation; each being is attached to it according to its own rung of holiness. For by Torah the Holy One created the world; all things are as a garment to the innermost point.

The languages in which Torah is explained are also but a garb. The divine utterance is Torah itself, which is then garbed in other tongues. From this derives the "healing to the

283

tongue." That is why the sages permitted bibles to be written in every language. Our text goes on to say: "Moses agreed to explain this teaching" (Deut. 1:5), and RaSHI says that he explained it to them in seventy languages. This is why it says "explain" (be'er can also mean "well"): the more broadly Torah's light expands through its outer garments, the closer everything gets to the innermost. In this way the inner wellspring becomes most open.

Scripture says: "Drink water from your cistern (bor), flowing from your well (be'er)" (Prov. 5:15). God placed a holy point into the very nature of each creature. The Jew in particular has a holy soul. It is called "your cistern" for it is attached to the body. The more you take this soul-light upon yourself, drawing your deeds to follow this light, the more of spirit and higher soul is added to you. This opens the wellspring that flows without end; this is "flowing from your well."

So it is that after all this journeying about in the desert, during which Israel drew holy light into all those places, now Moses "explains" Torah like a flowing well.

5:2

The teaching that Torah preceded the world is well known to the ancient rabbis and is widely quoted. But the mystical view of that primordial Torah, represented here, is quite transformative. Torah as God speaks it is beyond any language; that includes the Hebrew of our own Torah-text. The written Torah itself is thus already commentary, the interpretation that Moses or ancient Israel gives to the transverbal utterance of God.

Torah can exist in all the seventy (or, we would say, the many thousand) languages of humanity. For us as Jews, Hebrew is first among those languages, and our Torah (our own cistern) is the first place we turn to discover the hidden speech of God. But even prior to Torah-text, as the Sefat Emet understands so well, is the silent turning inward, toward that silent wellspring out of which all words and interpretations ever flow.

2

In the Midrash: "The tree of life is a healing for the tongue" (Prov. 15:4). The language of Torah releases the tongue. The Midrash Tanḥuma here quotes: "Then shall the lame leap like a deer, and the tongue of the mute shall shout aloud" (Is. 35:6). Because Moses said: "I am not a man of words" (Ex. 4:10), he earned the right to say: "These are the words" (Deut. 1:1). Thus we are told: "As a person measures himself, so is he measured." Moses longed to be entirely Torah; that is why he said: "I am not a man of words." [He sought to be] "a man of [only the Torah's] words," to be entirely Torah. We are defined as human by the power of speech, and that is what our speech should be. We should negate all our powers and our own form before the Word, the power of soul and divinity, that lies within us.

This is how the rabbis understood Moses' statement: "Who am *I* that I should go before Pharaoh" (Ex. 3:11). "Did You not say," Moses demands of God, '*I* will surely raise you out?'" (Gen. 46:4) [i.e., it is God's "I," not Moses', that should go before Pharaoh]. But this word was actually fulfilled *through* Moses, who was entirely Torah; "Shekhinah spoke from within his throat."

Thus Scripture says: "'Are not My words like fire?' says the Lord" (Jer. 23:29). It is the way of fire that all who draw near to it are turned into fire. So it was with Moses: he became entirely Torah. Something like this happens to everyone who studies Torah; such a person is transformed into a "master of Torah," all in accordance with the amount of study.

But in fact all of Creation came about through Torah; "In the beginning God created" (Gen. 1:1) is interpreted to mean: "God looked into the Torah and created." Thus too it is written: "All is called by My name, and for My glory I created it" (Is. 43:7), to which the rabbis said: "All God created in the world was created only for God's glory," and "glory" refers only to Torah. Every creature teaches us something; there is a way to learn from each of them the glory and the will of God. This is the song that lies within each creature.

In the future, when all is redeemed "and the tongue of the mute shall shout aloud," God's glory shall be raised up from within all tongues. But for now "the tongue is mute," so covered by corporeality that the inwardness hidden within it cannot be seen. The redemption of all tongues shall come about through the power of the holy tongue given to Israel. Thus Scripture says: "he explained (be'er) the Torah," in seventy languages.

This is also the meaning of "These are the words that Moses spoke . . . in the desert, in the plain, facing Suf, between Paran and Tofel . . . " (Deut. 1:1). All those places were far from the holiness, and Moses created openings, gates of Torah, in each one of them, something like what will be in the future. This is also the meaning of "Moses agreed to explain." He began; Messiah ben David will complete it.

5:16–17

There is an openness in this teaching to an authentic universalism that is rare in Jewish sources. All the tongues of humanity praise God, each in their own distinctive way but as part of the universal chorus. The Moses who "created openings, gates of Torah" in all the places and tongues of the world is not like the religiously imperialistic missionary who translates his own Bible into all the languages and thus rejoices at the spread of God's word. Here the "openings" have to come from within those languages and the cultures that are an inseparable part of them. If we understand that there is really but one God and listen to the prophet who says: "Everywhere incense and sacrifice are offered to My name" (Mal. 1:11), we will begin to understand our task as participants in and listeners to the truly universal human chorus.

 3

[In the *haftarah*] "An ox knows its owner; an ass its master's crib: Israel does not know, My people takes no thought" (Is. 1:3). Does this mean, God forbid, that Israel know God even less than an ox? Do they not recite blessings and prayers to God?

But it is God's will that Israel discover and raise up God's rule in all creatures. Thus it was in the time of wholeness, when the Temple stood. When we offered regular sacrifices each day, we were drawing all creatures near and joining them to God. Then were the nations also submissive to God's blessed name. Thus Jerusalem is called "the faithful city" (vs. 21). This really refers to the entire world, because in those days all creatures were drawn to their root. This is the meaning of "Israel does not know"—to bring forth this "knowing" and attachment to all creatures. . . .

5:1

Here we are appropriately reminded that the chorus is not only human. It is all of God's creatures that we are to perceive in harmonious praise of the Creator. The Temple-nostalgic Judaism of the past was able to see this "uplifting" of all creatures to the praise of God through the sacrificial system: by offering the animal on the altar and consuming its flesh in holiness we brought it to participation in the praise of God. A new Judaism will have to be more humble about our role in relation to the animal kingdom, finding ways other than slaughter and consumption by which to seek out the spirit of the One that lies within the animal world as well as all that lives.

VA-'ETHANNAN

1

"You shall love YHWH your God" (Deut. 6:5). The Midrash quotes: "Whom do I have in heaven; I desire none alongside You in earth" (Ps. 73:25). This means one should want nothing but God.

"With all your soul"—"with every single soul-breath that God has created in you." And the meaning of *"be-khol levavekha"* is not "with all your heart," as most people interpret it. But rather, we need to become aware that each feeling we have is only the life-force that comes from God. "A person does not bang his finger below unless it is decreed from above"; we are but "the axe in the woodchopper's hand."

This is the meaning of "YHWH is one." It goes beyond the fact that there is just one God; there is YHWH and *nothing* else.

Every thing that exists is only His blessed life, but it is hidden. The same is true of His blessed will. Therefore, the love of God has to be in every feeling a person has. This is "all your heart."

5:18

Here we have the mystical claim of Hasidism in its most undiluted form. Since nothing but God is real, we should both seek and find nothing but God in all of our lives. Every feeling and emotion, every want and desire, come from nowhere other than the being and will of God. To worship God with "all your heart" requires recognizing this truth and living in response to it.

How would we begin to make this teaching real in our religious and emotional lives? It would require two steps: a great opening and a great directing. The first step is one of radical self-acceptance and inclusion. "I will stop fighting off my thoughts, stop picking and choosing among my desires. All of them, even those I like least, have their root in God, for there is no other root." The second step is that of directing and uplifting each of these thoughts and desires. Try addressing each of your desires this way: "The game is up, O desire. You can't fool me any more. I know that you too come from God, even if in fallen form. Now I will take you back to your root, using the energy you arouse in me to give to God in yet a more whole way."

This teaching does not answer for us the critical question of which desires or emotions we may act upon, celebrating God's presence in the fulfillment of desire, and which we must hold back, worshipping God with transformed desire alone. The spiritual life requires a proper balancing between these two; it is the critical role of halakhah—whether the old or a new form—to offer us guidance as to where those lines are drawn.

2

The commentators raise an objection in Maimonides' name to the commandment of "You shall love" and similar passages, asking how it is possible to command regarding matters that have to do with human nature. But the truth is that this objection is its own answer, for from it we learn that it is in the nature of every Jew to love God with full heart and soul. But this natural inclination is buried deep within the heart; of the willful longing to seek out this love it is said: "I have struggled, I have found."

In *Sifre* it says: "'These words . . . shall be upon your heart' (Deut. 6:6). Why is this said? But because it says 'You shall love' and I do not know how [to fulfill that commandment, Scripture teaches that] when you place the words upon your heart, you will come to know the One who spoke and caused the world to be." By placing the words on your heart always and longing to come to the love of God, the spirit of holiness that dwells within you will be revealed to you. Of this we say (in the Torah blessings): "He implanted eternal life with us."

The point is that all the commandments of Torah are general rules. But the details—how to achieve fulfillment of the commandment—are oral teaching. That is why "the words of the scribes [i.e., the oral law] are more beloved than words of Torah." The words of the sages are introductions on how to fulfill those commandments laid out in Scripture. The words of Scripture are addressed to the perfected person, the one who has such wholeness as to grasp it all on his own [from within]. This is why it is literally called "the Torah that is in your mouth."

Even if it is hard for us to imagine fulfilling "with all your heart," we should still have that willful longing to reach it at all times. For it is through this longing that gates open in the human heart.

5:20

Why are we to place the words "upon our heart"? To ask the question more broadly, what is the function of "organized religion"? Why do we need all these symbols, sacred times, holy words, and all the rest of religion's endowment to us? Here we are given a clear hasidic answer: "So that the spirit of holiness that dwells within you will be revealed to you."

The Spirit is already there in you, as it is in every person. God endows each of us with a soul fully capable of the deep-

est spiritual understanding. What we need to do is to become aware of this, to open ourselves to a presence that awaits us from within. Religion is there to help us do that, to give us the language and tools with which to bring our own divine souls to life.

3

"This day we have seen that God may speak with a person, and that person may live. Now why should we die, for this great fire will consume us if we continue to hear. . . . You approach and hear all that the Lord God will speak, and you speak to us . . ." (Deut. 5:21–24).

New life was added to the children of Israel as they heard each one of the Ten Commandments. We can learn this by inference from lesser to greater. When Scripture says, "He blew into his nostrils the breath of life and Adam became a living soul" (Gen. 2:7), we learn that the divine breath gave him vitality. How much more must this have been true as God spoke these Ten Commandments to the children of Israel. Surely Israel were created again, made into new beings, with each and every one. That is why the sages said that at each commandment the souls of Israel passed away from them. As they were created anew, their former rung passed away, just as we have to die prior to the coming resurrection of the dead.

This is the real meaning of "God may speak . . . and that person live"—more and more life was added to them with each word God spoke. They rose upward, level after level, until they were prepared to become just like the angels. Now the rung of Moses, the man of God, was one that obliterated all corporeality. But Israel were not able to receive that much. That is why they said to him: "You approach. . . . " He was standing right there with them! But as they kept going up, rung after rung, they found that they could reach no higher.

This is also why Israel were warned: "Take great care for your souls, for you saw no form" (Deut. 4:15), while of Moses Scripture says: "He sees the form of the Lord" (Num. 12:8).

Only because he was totally separated from corporeality was he entitled to see. For surely it is impossible to grasp the form of God as long as you have any relation to corporeal form. Only as the corporeal is completely negated [can one "see" God]. That, too, is why God reproved Aaron and Miriam, saying: "Why were you not afraid to speak against My servant Moses?" (ibid.).

That is why Moses said this to them. Because they did not go up to that rung, and they asked him to approach God, they were told "You saw no form." Your souls were not fully separated from the corporeal, and thus you need to take great care. If only they had been on the rung of Moses! For he, as we know, is entirely good—and needed no such care.

5:25

At Sinai all of Israel were "born again." Letting go as much as we could of the corporeal world and our corporeal selves, we were allowed to ascend to higher consciousness, or to descend into ever deeper levels of understanding God, the world, and ourselves. We could not get to the point, however, where all the lines between these are obliterated and where there exists but one form, the shi'ur komah, *or "form" of God. This is a state of perception that requires total separation from the corporeal, and we are allowed to know it only through our participation in Moses' vision, but not through our own.*

The unwillingness of Israel to let go entirely of attachment to the corporeal world should not be viewed as failure. What we have here is a conscious self-portrayal of Judaism as the religion of a people that does not seek complete detachment. We have too many commitments to this world—seeking justice and equity in it, raising up the downtrodden, bringing it to wholeness and peace—to let it simply evaporate into nothingness and illusion. By holding onto our this-worldly commitments, we sacrifice some levels of mystical depth, to be sure. But a glimpse of these, too, is allowed us through the prophet, who is permitted to let go more and thus travel higher.

עקב

'EKEV

1

"If you surely listen to My commandments . . . " (Deut. 11:13). RaSHI, quoting the *Sifre,* notes that this passage constitutes a warning both to the individual and the community. Every day the Torah's warning is renewed in the souls of Israel, in general and in particular. But a person gets to hear this voice "which I command you this day" only insofar as he worships God. Everything depends upon the person.

That is why it says "If you surely hear" (lit.: "If you hear, hear"). The first "hear" refers to the raising of that voice and the second to our "hearing" and accepting the command. The same is true of the verse that says: "They do His word" and then goes back to say again "to hear the sound of His word" (Ps. 103:20–21).

" . . . which I command you *(etkhem)* this day." All was created by the twenty-two letters of the Torah [from *aleph* to *tav*, the first two letters of *etkhem*] and every Jew contains an imprint of those letters that belong to him. All Israel contain the twenty-two letters. These letters are renewed each day in their various permutations. So "which I command you" can also be read as "which I command the twenty-two letters within you."

If Israel merit this renewal, all of Creation is blessed for them. Thus: "I will put grass in your field" (Deut. 13:15) and so forth. And this is [the conclusion of the passage] "like the days of heaven upon the earth" (Deut. 13:21). "Days" refers to spiritual lights. As long as heavenly "days" shine upon the earth and can be revealed in the world, Israel will continue to inherit the land.

5:49

How is it that we are capable of hearing God's word? What is it about the human being that gives us the consciousness with which to respond to the divine command? The hasidic tradition answers that it is the Torah within us, the divine letters implanted within the human soul, that respond to those same letters when they rearrange themselves as divine commandment. The voice of Torah beyond calls forth to the Torah within. Our response brings about a renewal of life that affects not only us but all the world around us.

2

"If you surely listen to My commandments . . . to serve Him with all your heart" (Deut. 11:13). RaSHI comments that one should not study in order to become wealthy or to be called "rabbi" [or for any other extraneous reason], but only out of love.

The verse then means that the purpose of the commandments is to come to the love of God. How is it possible for a person to love his Creator [given the vast difference between God and humans]? The philosophers also ask how a commandment can apply in the case of love, if the soul doesn't love of its own accord. They asked this not out of wisdom, however, but because they were lacking in commands. In Israel love is aroused through the commandments.

In the *Sefer ha-Yashar* of Rabbenu Tam it says that the root of love is the lover becoming like unto the beloved. Thus when God sanctified us through His commandments and ways, and when we make our ways and deeds like His, we become attached to Him. "Become attached to His ways"; the mitsvah is thus called because it indicates joining and attachment, as in the verse: "They are a joining of grace . . . " (Prov. 1:9).

God's giving us the mitsvot was an act of unearned love. It was to offer Israel merit that we were given so much of teachings and commandments, in order that we purify our deeds to become like our Creator. The 613 commandments purify the 248 limbs and 365 sinews in the person. In this way we attain the love of God. . . .

5:50f.

"Do all for the sake of love!" is a cry heard from the lips of mystics throughout the world. Each tradition clothes this longing in its own garb; here in the heart of a Judaism very much centered on laws and commandments, we find a passage that could be read and appreciated by anyone who has experienced the love of God and the attraction that ever draws the beloved to the One. In Judaism it is the commandments themselves that play this role. There is no tension here between "love" and "law." How can there be, when the mitsvot in all their finest detail serve as pathways to the love of God?

 3

When commanding the blessing after meals, the Torah says: " . . . you will eat and be sated. Take care lest . . . " (Deut. 11:15–16). For "a person rebels only when sated." So it appears that [the verse] "you will eat and be sated and bless the Lord your God" (Deut. 8:10) comes to set this aright, to keep one from rebellion. On the contrary, the verse shows that one can derive blessing [and not only rebellion] from food.

Scripture says: "A person does not live by food alone; one lives by all that comes forth from the mouth of God" (Deut. 8:3). The ARI of blessed memory explained that the life-energy of God's word within the food is that which sustains the soul, just as the corporeal food sustains the body. It is by means of the blessings we recite that we find the inner food to nourish the soul. Surely, since God made the food that nourishes humans, there is sustenance in it for the inner self as well. By means of Torah we find that inward food.

All the commandments contain the two basic aspects of "remember" and "keep." "Remember" is the positive side, to awaken the inner self and the sparks of holiness that dwell within everything. "Keep" is the negative side, that which guards against outwardness and the "shells," so that one does not go too far in this drawing out. These two aspects exist in everything in the world. That is why the Torah says: "be sated and bless"; this refers to "remember," mentioning aloud. This is immediately followed by "Take care lest . . . " which refers to guarding in the heart.

That is why the rabbis taught: Whoever speaks words of Torah at the table, it is as though they had eaten from the table of the Everpresent, as Scripture says: "He said to me: This is the table that is before the Lord" (Ezek. 41:22). Once words of Torah are spoken there, it becomes God's table. This is as we have said above, that words of Torah enable one to find the holy inward aspect of food.

The sages pointed at this when they said: "If there is no flour [sustenance], there is no Torah." That refers to the inner part of "flour" that sustains the soul. But also: "If there is no Torah, there is no flour"; without the power of Torah, the inward quality of the food would not reveal itself. That is why the Talmud teaches that both "covenant" and "Torah" are to be mentioned in the blessing after eating. By means of both the covenant sealed in our flesh and Torah, we can set about finding that inward sustenance which comes from the place of holiness to nourish our souls.

5:46

The view of eating as a sacred act has an important place in Judaism, reaching back to most ancient sources. The communal meals of the early Pharisaic brotherhoods, at which the blessing after meals was probably first formulated, saw the table as God's altar and the meal eaten in holiness as a copy of that which took place in the Holy Temple. Much later, the table (tish) of the hasidic master, the setting where teachings like these were usually offered, was regarded in the same way. When the hasidic masters spoke of serving God through ordinary everyday human activities, eating and drinking are frequently mentioned as examples.

Satedness can indeed lead us away from God, down the path of "rebellion"; we in our oversated generation certainly know that truth. But Judaism does not call upon us to reject plenitude or to take on voluntary poverty. The fact that we are blessed with plenty can also be turned around, by mindfulness combined with generosity, keeping us aware that both soul and body are sustained by the unending gifts of God.

RE'EH

1

"See, I place before you this day a blessing and a curse. The blessing, that you listen to the commandments of the Lord your God . . . " (Deut. 11:26–27).

The Midrash says here that both soul and Torah are compared to candles. "The soul in the verse: 'A candle of the Lord is the soul of man' (Prov. 20:27) and Torah in [the verse:] 'The commandment is a candle and Torah is light' (ibid. 6:23). God says to the person: 'My candle is in your hand and yours is in mine. . . .'"

In everything there is a living point from the Life of Life. But that inwardness lies hidden in this world. The Jew has to arouse and reveal this inwardness that lies within all things by means of the commandments. Every deed involves some divine command, either a "Do" or a "Do not." Through the

301

mitsvot we bring all our deeds near to Him. This is [the meaning of] "My candle is in your hand." Each person has to give light to the hidden point, which is as though in prison until we have the strength to light up its darkness.

This point is itself "the blessing, that you listen. . . . " When you attach yourself to the point within each thing, you will come to see that it is the blessing. Then, indeed, "See"—by negating yourself before the point.

This is the meaning of the Sabbath, of which it says: "And He blessed . . . " (Gen. 2:3). Shabbat is a self-negation and inclusion within the point; that is where the blessing dwells. The sages also spoke of peace as a "vessel that holds blessing." This, too, is the point from God. It brings all things to be and is called "peace," because it is the fullness *(shalom/shelemut)* of all things, the blessing.

5:54

This strongly mystical teaching features a rather concrete image of divine blessing; it is something like a substance that dwells or inheres in all that is, forming the innermost substratum of being. As we turn inward, something that can be done in every human deed, we discover the fullness of God's blessing, waiting for us to release it from the prison of hiddenness and bring it to light.

"See, I place before you this day a blessing and a curse. The blessing, that you listen to the commandments of the Lord your God that I command you this day, and the curse, if you do not listen . . ." (Deut. 11:26–28).

Note that in the blessing it says "that you listen," but in the curse it says "if." Goodness exists within the Jewish people by their very nature; sin is only incidental. That is why a Jew's good intentions are joined to his deed [even if inadequate, according to the law], but such is not done with ill intentions. Israel as a whole certainly heard and accepted the

Torah. Even if they have fallen away since then, each day they are given the choice anew; "I place before you *this day.*" The "I" of receiving the Torah [of "I am the Lord your God"] allows the two choices to stand before us every day. Thus we are taught to accept the yoke of God's rule each day as we recite the *Shema'.* This is [the meaning of] "that you listen."

Even if there is some sin—and indeed "there is no one so righteous as to do good and never sin" (Eccles. 7:20)—it is only passing.

5:61

The generosity with which the Sefat Emet was willing to judge Jews, including the large number in the Warsaw of his day who were flagrantly violating the commandments, shows Hasidism at its finest. Only a truly expansive soul would have been able to love Torah as he did and at the same time see through to the essential goodness of Jews, even those who stood outside the domain of Torah.

Our day calls for a universalization of this ethic. Since every person is born with the essential divine point within, each child of the human race must contain that essential goodness. If not all have been to Sinai, all are descended from Eden and thus contain a memory of the hidden light, to which they long to return. As Jews we find the way to seek out that light in the commandments of Torah; that is our special gift. Others may find other wise and inspired teachings that lead them back to the light. But the essential inner goodness of humanity knows no boundaries of nation. Neither does the ease with which both persons and societies can shut out that light, keep their own inwardness hidden, and commit the most unspeakable violations against their own humanity and that of others.

 3

"The place where the Lord your God shall choose from amid all your tribes to place His name; you shall seek out His dwelling and come there" (Deut. 12:5).

The sages said: "Seek by means of a prophet . . . seek and you shall find, and then let the prophet confirm it, as is told of David who swore: 'I shall not come home to my own tent or lie upon my bed, giving sleep to my eyes or rest to my eyelids, until I find a place for the Lord, a dwelling for the Mighty One of Jacob," (Ps. 132:3–5). See the discussion in *Sifre*.

Scripture says "which the Lord . . . shall choose," but this choice was not revealed to them at once; they had to seek it out. The Land of Israel and the Temple depend upon human service, and that is why the sages taught that they require seeking.

The same was true in the case of Abraham our Father. When God said to him: "Go forth . . . to the land that I will show you" (Gen. 12:1), He did not at once tell him where it was to be. The same was true of the specific site of the Temple; Israel had to seek it out.

First Scripture tells us to "destroy utterly all the places where the nations worshipped" (Deut. 12:2), cleansing the land of all defilement, and only afterwards [to] "seek out His dwelling." The Temple is called "rest and inheritance." Just as the Sabbath contains rest, which is holiness revealed in time, and all the darkness of time passes away before it, so, too, is there a place of rest, that of the Temple, the place where the "other" force has no power. The same is true in the realm of souls; the holy spirit is called rest, as in the case of Baruch [ben Neriah, Jeremiah's scribe], who said: "I have not found rest" (Jer. 45:3). A person should seek out those places, times, and souls in which holiness is revealed. This is the meaning of "seek out His dwelling."

This commandment really applies to each individual: first we have to remove the "other" from our souls, then "seek His dwelling." But how much more is it true of all Israel: we seek, plead, supplicate God to restore prophecy, so that the holy spirit [may] dwell in our midst as it did of old.

5:62

The Sefat Emet's fascination with the parallel between these three dimensions of existence—space, time, and person—is a frequent theme in his teachings. Each of them contains a sa-cred element, one that can be discovered and realized only as a result of our ongoing search.

4

"When the Lord your God widens your border as He has promised, and you say 'Let me eat meat,' for your soul desires to eat meat, according to the whole desire of your soul shall you eat meat" (Deut. 12:20).

The Midrash quotes: "A person's giving broadens him and places him before the great" (Prov. 18:16) and also: "He deals justly with the oppressed and gives bread to the hungry; the Lord releases the captive" (Ps. 146:7).

Obviously, one who gives to God a gift from the heart is broadened by this very act. All of constriction comes about only through the hiding caused by externality; it is only a trial. When a person overcomes his own willfullness and sets it aside for the sake of God's will, this in itself opens up the inward and negates the hiding. This is the meaning of "broadens him."

Now the verse says: "According to the whole desire of your soul you shall eat meat," responding to . . . "Let me eat meat." But the commentators have noted that Scripture does not say "the whole desire of your body" but rather "your soul." See the words of Rabbi Moses Alsheikh: "The whole desire of your soul" is that of which the Torah has already said: "You shall love the Lord your God with all your heart and all your soul" (Deut. 6:5). Then "the whole desire of your soul" must mean "for the sake of heaven."

The meaning is as follows: if you will not be removed from your innermost attachment to God even by this will, then the eating is permitted, as long as it does not remove you from your main love, "the whole desire of your soul." Once you are attached to God by that main love, this permits the forbidden [*mattir issur*] and [diminishes] the power of the "other side" found in all material things. This is the meaning of "the Lord releases the captive" [*mattir asurim*].

All things come to exist through YHWH. But the point is hidden, and we have to broaden it. This depends upon the point within us: the more we expand our souls, the more God is revealed to us in every place. This is the meaning of "when the Lord your God widens your border"—the point spreads forth and "broadens" or expands throughout the human soul.

5:54

The very radical implications of this teaching sound more like Hasidism in its first generations than in the late nineteenth century. It may be no surprise to the experienced reader that it comes from the Sefat Emet's first year as rebbe. If attachment to God is so intense that it can permit the otherwise forbidden with regard to eating meat, why could it not do so with regard to eating only certain (i.e., nonkosher) meat? Or even more strongly, could not such an argument be used to justify immoral behavior, removing all restraints before the self-proclaimed lover of God?

For the hasidic rebbe, one may argue, the issues are settled. The law of Torah is in force, and this explanation is brought only in a case where the Torah itself seems to have changed the prior law (cf. Lev. 17). But for those of us who stand in a less clear position regarding the law, this view is indeed a challenging and dangerous one. Yes, we must ever work to broaden the bounds of the holy. But we also need forms within which the holy can be contained, as well as a commitment to restraint and self-control that will not allow us to say: "For those who love God, everything is permitted!" Nothing could be further from the intent of the Sefat Emet.

For a later teaching on the same theme, see the following text.

5

In the Midrash: "Listen and give ear; do not be haughty, for the Lord has spoken" (Jer. 13:15). Said Rabbi Tanḥuma: The blessed Holy One said: "Listen to words of Torah and do not speak haughtily, for the Lord has spoken." Therefore, Scripture says [in the present tense]: "Behold, I place before you today blessing and curse" (Deut. 11:26).

Indeed, these two paths stand before a person at all times. The *Sifre* offers a parable of an elder standing at the crossroads and warning those who pass, saying: "This path that begins in brambles ends up being straight [whereas the path that looks straight will end up in brambles]."

The *tsaddik* also stands always between two paths that branch off right and left. That is why they said: "Whoever is greater than his companion, his [evil] urge is also greater." The sages further said: "In the future, the blessed Holy One will bring forth the evil urge and slaughter it. To the righteous it will appear as a great mountain, and they will weep, saying: 'How were we ever able to battle it!' But to the wicked it will appear as a hairbreadth, and they will weep: 'How were we never able to conquer it!'"

The fact is that there is always only a hairbreadth. But the righteous, as they overcome each hairbreadth, go on to encounter another. They keep doing so forever, until they accumulate so many as to seem like a mountain. But the wicked is one who stands still, always facing that same hairbreadth. This is why "the righteous have no rest in this world."

This is also the reason no one should become too proud for having ascended some rung. For in that place, too, there will be two paths. But this is how the righteous earn their blessing, by ever leaving the wicked path and choosing the good. This is their reward for the future. . . .

5:57

Here is a passage of which the Sefat Emet's contemporaries, the mussarists, *or moral teachers, would have been proud. Every moment in life is one of choice. This is the very essence of our human situation. "Righteousness" is here defined as moral courage—the ability to meet each of these situations, make the decision, and move forward to the next. This vision of life is at once endlessly challenging and endlessly exciting.*

שפטים

SHOFTIM

1

"Appoint for yourselves judges and officers throughout your land" (Deut. 16:18). This can be read in connection with the hint that my grandfather, of blessed memory, found to the month of Elul in the verse: "He has made us and not we our-selves" (Ps. 100:3). There is a variance between the written text and the oral reading in this verse. One says *ve-lo' anaḥnu* ("and not we ourselves") while the other reads *ve-lo anaḥnu* ("and we are His"). These two words *lo'* and *lo* make up the spelling of the name Elul.

These two aspects depend upon one another. The more a person can negate his own self ("and not we ourselves"), the closer that person can draw to God ("we are His"). These are the two parts of the service of God. First we have to negate the body and the corporeal world. For this we need "officers," who can force the body to change its ways, to "turn from evil" (Ps. 34:15). Then one can draw near to the Creator "and do good." For this we need to be judges, to take hold [of God] with our minds. . . .

5:72

At first sight the contemporary reader may rebel against this text. "Negating the body" is not what we had hoped to find in Hasidism! Is not the body, too, divine Creation? Surely that seems to be the thrust of many other teachings in this volume.

Today we might choose our words differently; we might say "train" or "discipline" rather than "negate." But the twin aspects of religious life as presented here remain constants. The regularity of discipline requires an overcoming of willfulness, a training of the self, including the body, to accept a pattern of regular religious forms even when it seems unwilling. It also includes liberating the self from compulsive behaviors that do the body harm. This life of religious discipline alternates with moments of grace and insight when the mind reaches to heights or depths of awareness that are the fruit of its daily training.

 2

Certain times, we are told, are "times of favor" before God. These include the month of Elul, the time of the third Sabbath meal, and others. We are told this even though we know that time itself does not apply to God! The truth is that these are times of favor for humans, moments in which we are more able to draw near and attach ourselves to God with the inward desire of our hearts. God is filled with favor, but we must deserve to come close to Him. "As the face in the water is to the face" (Prov. 27:19)—as a person has compassion on himself, seeing that he contains a holy point of godliness, while yet formed of matter, so too is great compassion for him aroused in heaven.

5:68

Here the hasidic master offers a partly "naturalistic" reading of divine favor. Nothing in God is changed by the coming of certain moments in the calendar or special times. The divine well overflows with grace at every moment. It is only we who need those sacred times to inspire and refresh us, so that we will have mercy on ourselves and go drink of those ever-flowing waters. When we treat ourselves with compassion and forgiveness, those same forces will reveal themselves from beyond us as well.

3

"Appoint for yourselves judges and officers." This is [not only a commandment, but] also a promise to the Jew, saying: "You will be able to make yourself into your own judge and officer." Thus it says that "a person is led in whatever direction he seeks to go." Some want to seek the truth. Others find their minds not whole enough and long to be forced along the way. In this, too, a person can find help; these are the [inner] "judges and officers."

The main thing is to seek truth. Scripture says: "Justice, justice shall you pursue" (Deut. 16:20), and of lies it says: "Stay far from false words" (Ex. 23:7). I heard from my grandfather in the name of the Rabbi of Przysucha that of no other prohibition does the Torah say to "stay far" from it. Only the sages added their warnings to that effect. But of lying, the Torah itself says: "stay far," to show you how serious this prohibition really is.

We find the converse with regard to truth. "Justice, justice shall you pursue" is a formula said in no other case, because this is the foundation of everything. That is why it says "pursue." We can never really come to truth in the fullest sense within this lying world. We have to keep pursuing justice, knowing that we have not yet attained it.

When we pursue justice in this world, we attain it fully in the world to come. The verse goes on to say "so that you will live and inherit. . . . " This is a hint at the next world, one that is all life.

5:72

The call for honesty in this teaching is an important one to keep in focus, especially when dealing with religious thought and the life of the spirit. The line between being subtle and being slipshod, or between transcending intellectual objections and simply avoiding them, is itself very hard to draw. The traditions of Przysucha and Kotsk, in which this book was written, stood firmly against any sort of dishonesty or self-deception in the religious life. So should we.

"Justice, justice shall you pursue." There is no final depth or end to justice and truth; we always have to go deeper, seeking out the truth within truth. It is not "true" until the person is entirely unified and prepared for God's service. Thus 'emet (truth) contains the first, middle, and last of the Hebrew letters.

The Yehudi of Przysucha taught that the word "justice" is repeated here to say that even in the pursuit of justice, you have to engage justly, without lies.

5:68

In a biblically based vision of social justice, it always remains clear that the ends never justify the means.

"For these nations . . . listen to sorcerers and magicians. You should not do thus, but [to] a prophet from within your midst . . ." (Deut. 18:14).

. . . Sorcery and magic are [a way of tuning in] to the forces of nature. These come about through the ten utterances by which God created the world. But Israel were chosen in a way that elevates them above nature, [where the ten utterances become manifest as] the Ten Commandments. Of them it is written: "They do His word to hear the sound of His word" (Ps. 103:20). By committing all their actions to the Creator and saying: "All that the Lord says, we shall do" (Ex. 19:8), they merited hearing the spoken word.

This was to prepare them for future generations, when all the people of God were supposed to become prophets. They were forever to hear the word of God. But then their souls passed out of them as the first words were uttered, and they said to Moses: "I can listen no more to the voice of God . . . " (Deut. 18:16). Then the power to hear God's word remained only with the prophets, and their power depended upon Israel's resisting the magicians. . . . This was all part of the divine intent: these powers were to exist in the world, and Israel were to negate them, [giving the power back] to God. Thus Scripture says here: "Be perfect [for the sake of] the Lord your God." It is this that makes us worthy to hear God's word.

That is why it says "a prophet from within your midst," for the whole thing depends upon Israel. But something of this is to be found within each person as well: the more you negate everything else for God's sake, the more you are able to hear and attain God's word.

5:73

Hasidism never denied the reality of the spirit-world, both holy and demonic, that was so much a part of the folk culture of eastern European Jews. Nor did it deny the possibility of magic, which was practiced by Jews as "practical Kabbalah" as well as by the non-Jews among whom they lived. But from the days of the Ba'al Shem Tov, Hasidism also taught that the spiritual place of Israel was higher than the world of magic: it was always better to turn to God, without need of reward, than to trust the "lower" forces that could be thus manipulated.

The teaching becomes interesting in a different way if we follow those anthropologists who see science, beginning with the Greeks, as an extension of magic's attempt to control and predict the forces of nature. Then the confrontation becomes one of science and religion, not magic and religion. In this case the Sefat Emet, read for our times, would say that the sciences are correct in their perception of the universe, basing themselves on laws that are part of Creation. But the religious reading of Creation is one that transforms those fixed laws ("the ten utterances") into forms of address ("the Ten Commandments") in which the universe speaks to us humans in a special way, and demands of us that we devote our lives to bringing the energy of Creation back to its divine Source.

KI TETSE'

1

"When you go forth to war against your enemy and the Lord your God places him in your hand and you take him captive . . . " (Deut. 21:10).

In every thing there is a point of divine life, but it is secret and hidden. Throughout the days of the week we are engaged in a battle and struggle to find that point. Then comes the Sabbath, on which it is revealed that God gives life to all. The Sabbath is Israel's way of bearing witness to Creation, since even now heaven and earth exist only by virtue of God's ten utterances.

During the week we need to do battle over this. The Sabbath comes only in response to our weekday struggles: "One who has struggled on the eve of the Sabbath shall eat on the

Sabbath." The "eve" *('erev)* of the Sabbath here refers to the mixing *(ta'aruvot)* of Sabbath and weekday, as we say in our evening prayer "who by His word makes mixtures" [*ma'ariv 'aravim*, lit.: "brings on evening"].

We must realize that the strength we have to fight the evil urge also comes only from God, as in [the verse:] "And the Lord your God places him in your hand." Even though this battle takes place by human power, "in your hand," it is the limitless power of God that helps us. . . .

"You, Lord, are gracious, and you pay each one according to his deeds" (Ps. 62:13). The question asked on this verse is: "What is the grace [if you pay a person only in accord with his deeds]?" But the answer is that everything [including our own deeds] is from God, but you reward us as though it were ours.

"And you take him captive" (lit.: "when you capture his [His!] captivity") means, "when you know that it comes from God." The point is that in every good deed or commandment, there is an act itself, followed by the giving of the thing back to God. For as hard as a person struggles, even if he performs wonders, if he hasn't returned the mitsvah to God, he has done nothing. He has not properly attributed the mission on which he was sent to the One who sent him. This is the "return"; it takes place only when you become aware that everything comes from God. This is "when you capture His captivity," restoring the point to God, knowing that all comes from Him.

5:83

The statement, "he has done nothing" in this final paragraph is an unusually definitive declaration of the hasidic position. Mitsvot without **kavvanah** *are worthless exercises. The whole purpose of them is to provide forms through which we can do the work of uplifting and transforming the ordinary and of celebrating God's presence throughout the world and in our own selves. Without these, the forms are indeed nothing at all. The mitsvah is a holy deed, one we are enabled to do solely because of the divine presence at work within us. To do the deed without becoming aware of that presence is to miss the point.*

2

"If a bird's nest comes before you" (Deut. 22:6). The Midrash says: "Just as He shows compassion for humans, so does He for beasts and birds." But an objection is raised from the Mishnah, which teaches that if [a prayer-leader should] say, "Your mercies reach [even] the bird's nest," he should be silenced. The Talmud explains that "he is making God's qualities into mercies, when they are really only decrees."

The meaning of the midrash is that He has placed His mercies in all of His creatures, as it says: "His mercies are upon all His works" (Ps. 145:9). Humans have mercy upon humans, but not upon animals, for man does not grasp or comprehend the animal mind at all. We humans do not understand either animal consciousness or animal compassion. In the same way, angels do not understand the human mind; we are like animals to them. Only God, who knows all, comprehends at once the minds of angels, humans, beasts, and all the rest of Creation. That is why it says: "His mercies are over all his works." God understands the feelings of the mother bird sitting over her chicks, if she should be taken together with them. God similarly understands [the animal's feeling if] "both he and his son are slaughtered on the same day" (Lev. 22:28).

In truth God placed this measure of compassion into the nature of each species; it is due to these commandments found with regard to animals and birds that compassion is to be found in them. The whole existence of Creation is through mercy; "He conducts His world with grace and His creatures through mercy." Thus compassion is to be found throughout Creation. And Israel, who are the essence of Creation, are the most compassionate.

But this compassion exists only by His decree [= Torah, through which He created the world]. This is what the Midrash means when it says: "Just as He showed compassion," and so forth. But the Talmud is commenting on one who thinks that His mercy upon the bird is the reason for the commandment. Just the opposite is the case: it was through this mitsvah that God placed compassion in the bird itself. This is the meaning of "they are nothing but decrees"—it was God who decreed that compassion should be found in each creature in a particular manner.

5:92

As editor, I am tempted to omit "And Israel, who are the essence of Creation, are the most compassionate" from this otherwise beautifully universal teaching about compassion. Though my own instincts urge me to do so, however, for the sake of honesty to the source, I cannot. The Sefat Emet remains a faithful follower of the strand in Jewish thought that runs from R. Yehudah ha-Levi through the Zohar, R. Judah Loew of Prague, and R. Shneur Zalman of Liadi, emphasizing the uniqueness and essential moral superiority of Jews in relation to other humans. Today we thank God that the climate of hatred and mutual dehumanization among religious groups that wrought such views has begun to pass away from at least part of the human community.

But the essential point here is an important one. We humans deceive ourselves in thinking that we know the mind or hearts of other species. True empathy with them eludes us insofar as we are bounded by our own human experience. Our compassion for them rather goes back to our source in God, Creator of all species and source also of whatever spirit is in them. It is the Creator's living word (manifest to us in the form of Torah) that binds all creatures to one another and transcends all boundaries, allowing compassion to flow from human to animal, and surely also sometimes from animal to human, even beyond the limits of understanding.

 3

"Guard what comes out of your lips" (Deut. 23:24). This refers to keeping one's tongue. The mouth is the most inward of our limbs; all the breath and the inward self come out as we open our mouths. That is why the mouth needs special guarding. It seems that the mitsvah of Torah study is there to guard the mouth, just as each commandment stands in relation to one or another of our limbs. That is why this mitsvah requires full-time duty—day and night—because the opening of the mouth needs to be so guarded.

The very root of a person's life is in that inner breath. Guarding this stands at the root of all one's deeds, and it says: "Guard . . . and do." The rest of our deeds all depend upon guarding the mouth.

Human beings are distinguished from animals by the fact of speech. That is why "a living soul" (Gen. 2:7) is rendered by the Targum as "a speaking spirit." This main quality [of our humanity] is what we have to give to God. The creation of the human faculty of speech is more wondrous than anything else in Creation, as anyone who contemplates this phenomenon will understand. All that God created was created for His glory, "so that they tell My praise" (Is. 43:21).

While it is no easy matter to bring forth words before God, we can at least guard ourselves from idle talk.

5:84

This seems to be an incomplete record of a teaching, as happens not infrequently in hasidic writings. The point is that since all is created to tell God's praise, telling, or the gift of speech, is the apex of Creation. It is only human speech that raises the silent praises of all God's creatures to the level of articulation, and as such we humans are the channel through which the life-force of all Creation is given back to God. All this can be done, of course, only if speech remains pure.

"Be careful of the scaly affliction . . . remember what the Lord your God did to Miriam on your way out of Egypt" (Deut. 24:8).

. . . The purpose of all the commandments, both positive and negative, that were given to Israel, is so that every person of Israel be free. That is why the liberation from Egypt comes first [before the giving of the Torah]. Torah then teaches the soul how to maintain its freedom, by not becoming attached to material things. These are its 613 "counsels." Every mitsvah in which the liberation from Egypt is mentioned is to tell us yet again that by means of this mitsvah one may cling to freedom. In the commandment regarding the [gifts to the poor of] leftover gleanings, the corners of the field, and forgotten sheaves, Torah says: "Remember that you were a slave" (Deut. 24:22). In this way your food will have no waste, and you will not become overly attached to wealth. That is why Torah commanded such things as tithes and gifts to the poor; these guard one from [overattachment to] wealth.

A Jew has to be free in soul, in body, and in all he or she has. That's why with regard to dwellings we have the *mezuzah*; for clothes, the fringe; all of this is to help us be free, "in memory of the Exodus from Egypt." That is why the commandment of the fringed garment is next to that which forbids mixed [wool and linen garment] mixtures (Deut. 22:11–12). The mixing would bring waste into the garment, and the fringes make for freedom with regard to clothes.

This is the purpose of the entire Torah. That is why they read "engraved on the tablets" (Ex. 32:16), as though it said "freedom on the tablets" (*harut/herut*). "The only free person," they added, "is the one who is engaged in Torah," for Torah teaches a person the way of freedom.

Guarding the tongue [from evil speech] is freedom of the soul, since "a living soul" is rendered as "a speaking spirit."

5:98

Freedom here seems to be defined as nonattachment. By limiting our devotion to things of this world, Torah tries to teach us how to be free of them, how not to be controlled by material possessions, by the worldly "image" we try to create by the way we dress, or by worldly and especially malicious talk that keeps us from the pure speech we need to express our deepest selves. That power of expressing what is within us is the deepest freedom, one so easily lost that we often even forget to feel that it is missing from our lives.

An attachment to Torah that would help to awaken all these freedoms within us would indeed be a great gift. It becomes harder to find when many of those we meet who are engaged in Torah study do not seem to be free at all. A master like the Sefat Emet knew something that he was not able to pass on to most of the community of Torah learners. To find what he meant, we will have to start anew, reading and learning Torah in a different and more liberating way.

KI TAVO'

1

"This day the Lord your God commands you to observe all these statutes and laws" (Deut. 26:16). Midrash Tanḥuma quotes: "Come let us raise a joyful shout before the Lord" (Ps. 95:1). Moses saw that the first fruits (Deut. 26:1–11) would one day no longer be brought, so he instituted prayer in their place. My grandfather of blessed memory said that prayer, too, was a way of giving the first [of each day] to God, another sort of "first fruits."

But the meaning of "this day" in the verse still needs to be clarified. The Midrash and RaSHI both say: "Each day these should be like new in your eyes." [Why "like new"?] Is someone out there trying to fool the person, giving him something that isn't really new, but is "like new"? God forbid! It is really within human power to renew each thing. The renewal is there within everything, since God "renews each day, constantly, the work of Creation." "Constantly" means in each moment. Nothing exists without the divine life-force, and the point in each thing that comes from Him never grows old, since His words are constantly alive and flowing.

However, "darkness covers the earth" (Is. 60:2). The outward "shell" hides that flowing point. Thus Scripture says: "Nothing is new under the sun" (Eccles. 1:9). That is the natural world that hides the renewal. But it is within the power of man to light up that point within the darkness; "This day the Lord your God commands you. . . . " God commands you to find [or "to make"!] "this day," the revelation of light, the shining speculum, within the very deed that hides the point.

You do this by means of the commandments, since "the commandment is a candle." The mitsvah exists within the corporeal world of deeds, but it also contains the divine life-force in the command to do it. Thus it gives the person power to become attached, by means of it, to the hidden light. This is the meaning of "This day . . . these statutes . . . ." By means of the commandments, God gives you the power to find "this day" also in the deed. . . .

5:99

This is a marvelously optimistic passage. Its emphasis on human power, even though a God-given power, to be sure, is especially refreshing in a work that speaks so much about self-negation.

But just what is it that the person is able to do by the power of the mitsvot? Is the mystic's claim here a metaphysical or an epistemological one? Does he bring about some change in the nature of reality, actually causing a renewal of life, or does he allow himself to see (our eyes being those from which the "shells" have kept the light hidden) a renewal that God is ever affecting, with or without our awareness? As we might expect of a semimodern mystic, he stays very close to the line between these two. If we do change something other than perception, it is because the deed *itself overflows from the mystical into the "real" world, and that creates its own dynamic effect.*

2

"If you listen, listen to the voice of the Lord your God . . . " (Deut. 28:1). The Midrash comments: "Happy is the one whose listenings are to Me, hovering always at My doorways, door within door. . . . "

"Listenings" means that one should always be prepared to receive and listen closely to the words of God. The voice of that word is in every thing, since each was created by God's utterance and has the power of divine speech hidden within it. This is the hidden light that we are told to find.

Inwardness goes on, deeper and deeper, truly beyond measure. This is the meaning of "My doorways." Never think that you have come to the truth; understand that you are always standing at the entrance. The word "doorway" *(delet)* is related to "poverty" [or "humility"] *(dalut)*. This is the way you find door after door opening for you, [by always knowing how little you have achieved thus far].

This is especially true of the Jew, whose living soul constantly hears the voice of Torah. But this too is hidden from us. This is why the verse says "listen, listen"—listen to that which you already are hearing.

The Midrash goes on to say: "to guard the doorpost of My entrance." Just as the *mezuzah* is fixed, so you too should not depart from synagogues or houses of study. This means that a person has to be ready always only to hear the word of God. Then, when a moment of grace occurs, something opens for him. But he has to be standing always at that doorway. That is "whose listenings are to Me." All the senses have to be prepared to receive and listen closely to the word of God and nothing else.

5:99f.

The concept of infinite inwardness, here and elsewhere in the Sefat Emet, is an important one. We usually think of "transcendence" in religion as belonging to a realm of the beyond, something outside and "higher" than the universe in which we live. But the hasidic sources point to a transcendence within being, a truth so deep that it cannot ultimately be fathomed. This, too, is a transcendent reality, one that lies eternally beyond our grasp. But when transcendence is seen as the deepest "within" rather than as the highest "beyond," it does not lend itself to being understood as a force of reality "other" than this world.

3

"The Lord has not given you the heart to know, eyes to see, or ears to hear until this day" (Deut. 29:3). My grandfather of blessed memory quoted the Rabbi of Przysucha, who said that all the miracles and wonders God had performed for them, since they were outside the realm of nature, were only one-time events. But now that the whole Torah was completed and all their own behavior had been made into Torah, there was something fixed for all generations.

This is the meaning here of "this day." All the lights were now cloaked in good deeds; Torah had been formed out of all their own actions. This was the great merit of Israel in accepting Torah. Torah itself is completely beyond measure, "hidden from the eyes of all who live" (Job 28:21). But Israel deserved to "garb" that Torah; from all their deeds a cloak was made for the light of Torah, in the teachings and commandments of that Torah which is before us. Understand this.

This could also be the meaning of "You have affirmed [*he'emarta*; lit.: 'given speech'] to the Lord this day" (Deut. 26:17). Out of the ten utterances there came an entire Torah.

5:101

This passage, read together with the following passage, provides a key opening for a radical rethinking of revelation and

*the relationship between revelation and commandment. The
Torah God reveals at Sinai is one of pure divine light, a vision
of infinite love and giving that as yet has no particular form.
Israel, because their hearts are open to receive God's light,
come to stamp the revelation with the particular forms—
ethics, rituals, beliefs, taboos, and all the rest—of their own
culture. For later generations these come to be associated with
the revelation and are accepted as God's commandments.*

 4

"You have affirmed *(he'emarta)* the Lord this day to be your
God . . . And the Lord has affirmed *(he'emir)* you" (Deut.
26:17–18).

See the commentary of ibn Ezra. [Ibn Ezra quotes Yehudah
ha-Levi, who says that *he'emir* is the causative form of the
verb *'amar,* "speak."]

This interpretation can be read more deeply in connection
with the well-known teaching that "Torah, God, and Israel are
one." The Midrash interprets the word *"anokhi"* ("I am"—Ex.
19:2) as an abbreviation for the words ["I Myself wrote it and
gave it.] This could also be read as "I wrote and gave Myself."
Torah is truly divinity [i.e., is God Himself]. The children of Israel, as it were, made God into Torah and they too were made
into Torah. Understand this carefully.

5:105

*Torah, classically the intermediary that Judaism poses be-
tween God and Israel, is here made up of the two of them,
the product of their meeting. Torah in its deepest essence is
nothing but God; what God gives at Sinai is God's own self,
but now transposed into the medium of words and language,
in order that humans can receive it. The specific details of
Torah, as we have seen above, are derived from the actions
and life-experiences of Israel. Through these Israel are "made
into Torah." Torah is then at once a thoroughly divine and
thoroughly human product.*

This way of thinking about Torah and revelation should provide the way for going beyond the challenge to Jewish faith posed by biblical criticism and historical study. To the seemingly crucial and vexing question: "Is the Torah of divine or human origin?" the Sefat Emet encourages us to answer: "Yes!" All the rest proceeds from there.

NITSAVIM/VA-YELEKH

1

"You stand this day before the Lord your God . . ." (Deut 29:9).

The Midrash here notes that the evening prayer has no fixed time. [This is the prayer that comes at the time of darkness,] the darkness in the human heart that causes us to call to God out of our pain. This outcry opens the gate of prayer more than any fixed time, since Israel ever stand before the Lord, in a way that is beyond time.

5:121

Judaism seems to be terribly concerned with specific times, holy hours, particular measures, holy and profane places, and all manner of other such careful distinctions and separations. But at its deepest core, it knows that we are ever with God,

329

and that time and space themselves cannot touch this constant truth. When it really counts, in the moments of deepest human pain, it is to this truth that we need have recourse, and not only to that of fixed words, places, or hours.

Gerer Hasidim were notorious for ignoring the fixed times of prayer; here the principle behind that seemingly unorthodox behavior is laid bare.

2

". . . To cause you to pass through the covenant of the Lord your God" (Deut. 29:11). This covenant is Torah, and it is taught that "God, Torah, and Israel are all one."

The numerical equivalent of the word "Torah" is 611. Add two for love and fear, which are the root of all positive and negative commandments [and the count will reach 613, the number of commandments in the Torah]. These also stand for "I am the Lord your God" and "You shall have no other gods besides Me" (Ex. 20:2–3) [the first two commandments], of which Scripture says: "The Lord spoke one; I have heard two" (Ps. 62:12).

Love is really the gift of God. This is the meaning of [the verse:] "I am the Lord your God" [God Himself is the source of your ability to love God]. This is what King David meant when he said: "One thing I have sought of the Lord" (Ps. 27:4). Fear is the essential power of each person on his own, as in: "What does the Lord your God ask of you but that you fear Him?" (Deut. 10:12).

Add one [for "fear of God"] to the 611 and you get the value of "covenant" *(berit)*. This covenant goes from God to Torah and from Torah to Israel. The covenant is made with all of Israel, "not with you alone am I making this covenant" (Deut. 29:13). The covenant can only be with all of Israel, those of past and future generations all together. Just as God is, was, and will be, all in a single unity, so must His covenant include all the generations at once. But every individual Jew also has a part in this. Each person who brings himself in to receive this covenant arouses all the generations of past and future to be present with him as well.

5:128

The Sefat Emet is very little given to gematria, *or number associations, especially when compared to others among the later hasidic masters. Here his real point is the linking of Torah, covenant, and the commandments, which are numerically in a series (611, 612, 613). It is love and fear that link Torah to commandments; these elements represent the first two (those Israel heard "directly" from God) of the Ten Commandments as well.*

The reading of the first two commandments as representing an originally undivided root of love and fear is especially striking here. God speaks a single word, the psalmist says, but I, in my bifurcated human mind, can only hear it as two. It is we who have to divide between affirmation and negation, between love and fear, between giving and holding back. No such division is present in the divine word until it reaches human ears.

3

"I bring heaven and earth to witness to you this day . . . " (Deut. 30:19). RaSHI comments: "Just as heaven and earth have not betrayed their nature . . . you . . . how much more so!

What kind of proof do heaven and earth seem to offer? They have no freedom of choice! Nevertheless, the point is that even in nature all things seem to be drawn to follow God and His command. Surely humans should do no less than this! The only difference is that we have been given the choice to follow our good or evil urge. If evil does not overwhelm us, we will naturally follow the good, just as all other creatures do.

Thus we may understand the verse: "Yours, O Lord, is lovingkindness, repaying each person in accord with his deeds" (Ps. 62:13). The Talmud asks what sort of lovingkindness this is, if the person is given only what he has earned. But our doing good also comes from God; if we keep ourselves free from domination by the evil urge, the inner self God has implanted within us is aroused to do good. So all of this is itself due to God's lovingkindness.

This is the real answer to the question raised by Maimonides as to how there can be a commandment to love, and for other matters that depend upon the heart. The love of God is impressed upon the heart of every Jew. All we have to do is keep ourselves from those desires that pull this love toward evil, for then the true inner point gets hidden. A person who is guarded in this way will be wholly drawn after God, in heart and soul.

5:120

Here the Sefat Emet offers a psychology that combines two essentially different traditions found within Judaism. The old rabbinic sources see the human soul as a moral tabula rasa, *the battlefield of equally strong warring forces called the "good urge" and "evil urge." Free will is the core of the system; the individual's task is to seek out and cultivate the good while fighting off his or her own temptations toward evil. A different psychology stands at the core of the Jewish mystical tradition. Every person is essentially good, even essentially divine, in innermost core. This divine spark or soul has been covered over by layers of* kelipot, *or "shells," hard crusts formed as defenses in the course of living, abetted by external demonic forces that encourage the development of* kelipot *by leading us into sin. These* kelipot *serve their own purposes, nourishing the forces of evil from our own vital energies.*

Here the hasidic author chooses the kabbalistic model, that which sees humans as essentially good. This fits most clearly with his own notion of the "inner point" within all reality. But that which keeps us from our own innermost and truest selves is no demonic power other than our own bad decisions. Anyone who takes care to turn away from evil—and the choice is entirely ours—will come to know the godly presence that dwells within.

HA'AZINU

1

"Listen, O heavens, and I shall speak; let earth hear the words of my mouth" (Deut. 32:1).

Torah has its roots in heaven; its power is to draw everything in earth up to heaven. These two factors are dependent on each other: the more a person binds each mitsvah or teaching to its root, the greater its chances of spreading forth below as well. The greatest heights and the greatest depths depend upon each other.

The purpose of this section is to explain that Israel have to uplift all corporeal and lowly things. Thus you should never be depressed about having to concern yourself with humble or worldly matters. "The Rock, His work is perfect and all His ways are just" (Deut. 32:4). So, too, does the person contain all of Creation: "He set the borders of the nations according to the numbers of Israel" (Deut. 32:8). This is true of each individual: every Jew contains all the hidings [of divine light] brought about by the powers of all the nations; the Jew has to redeem them.

> He found him in a desert land,
> in a desolate howling void.
> He surrounds him, He gives him understanding;
> He guards him as the apple of His eye   (Deut. 32:10).

Even though it is written here that God chose Israel from most ancient times—"For the Lord's portion is His people" (32:9)—the statement that He "found him" refers especially to times of trouble and hiding; it is in the darkness that you "find" something. The Jew is ever anticipating that God's holiness will be revealed here in this lowly world. This is the "desert land," a place where all we have is desire.

That is the way we worship on weekdays. But when Shabbat comes, "He surrounds him," spreading forth the tent of peace. "He gives him understanding" with the extra Sabbath soul; a person has an added measure of awareness on Shabbat. But of weekdays too we could say: "He surrounds him" with the *tallit* and "gives him understanding" in tefillin. These commandments give a person light each day in this world.

After Rosh Hashanah and Yom Kippur [when this *parashah* is read] a person has been made pure, but he does not yet know how to find divine light in this desertlike world. That is why "He surrounds him" with the *sukkah* and "gives him understanding" with the *lulav*, which stands for the drawing forth of awareness. "He gives him understanding" may also point to Simḥat Torah, as RaSHI already commented on "gives him understanding," referring to Torah.

5:176

The essential religious task, as Judaism understands it, is that of sanctifying the ordinary, of uplifting the most common or worldly objects, deeds, and moments to reveal themselves as repositories of divine light. In order to do this, the religious person—and the Jewish people as a whole—must experience inner darkness, living in the "desert land." It is from there that the uplifting is greatest, that the miracle of revealing God is most profound.

2

"Listen, O heavens, and I shall speak" (Deut. 32:1). This refers to the Ten Commandments. "Let earth hear the words of My mouth" refers to the ten utterances of Creation. That is the oral Torah. God gave the Torah so that Israel would repair, by means of Torah, all that had been created by the ten utterances. Torah is thus a commentary or interpretation of Creation itself. That is why we are taught that "the righteous give existence to the world that was created by the ten utterances."

That is why this Ha'azinu song was sung by Moses and Joshua together, joining the written Torah to the oral Torah. It says: "May my teaching drop as rain" (32:2), for the purpose of Torah is to bring forth into reality all that which God has hidden in the world, just as rain brings the fruits of the soil forth from the earth.

5:180

"Torah is a commentary on Creation" is a beautifully Jewish way of saying that the purpose of religion is the self-fulfillment of the natural order, through human agency. God is revealed constantly from within all of Creation; nature is but the garbing of divine presence. Torah is our people's guide to finding God throughout the created world, then to do the work of uplifting and fulfilling the intent of Creation. It also gives us a language for articulating and sharing that discovery, both within our community and beyond it.

3

"May my teaching drop as rain" (Deut. 32:2). Within every Jew there is a living point. That life-force has to be awakened by means of Torah. Just as earth has the power to bring forth fruits and produce, but needs the rain to arouse its powers, so too with us humans, who are called *adam* (earthling) since we come from *adamah* (earth). That is the oral Torah, the "eternal life He has implanted within us" in order to bear fruit. So too are we taught that "the offspring of the righteous are their mitsvot and good deeds."

This is the symbolic meaning here of "heaven" and "earth"; they [and the relationship between them] are the basis of all Creation. It is from heaven that rain comes down upon the earth. Israel, too, contain a "heaven" and an "earth": the written Torah and the oral Torah. Thus it is written: "You shall become a land of desire" (Mal. 3:12).

Israel enable the world to exist. This can be seen in the lower world as they bring about His kingdom. But they also add strength above, in a way that is less apparent. Heaven and earth are in fact one; it is because Israel make clear this truth below that the two of them are able to unite.

Scripture says: "The rock whose work is perfect," even though Israel are still given the task of perfecting Creation. "Who came before Me, that I be perfect?" (Job 41:3). All that is demanded of us is that we stand truthfully, straight in deed and thought. When a person stands firm, the life-force in him is necessarily aroused. God has placed within each person sufficient measures of holiness, purity, and the fear of heaven. All we need to do is actualize them. This is [the meaning of: "If a person says to you] 'I have struggled and found,' believe him." "I have found" means, within the human body I have found that "the soul You placed within me is pure."

Thus it is taught that God's actions lack for naught; we only have to put ourselves in the proper place. The same is true of the way all species are propagated. God gave them the power to procreate; they only have to put themselves in their proper places. "Not for naught did He create it; He formed it that it be dwelt upon" (Is. 45:18).

The same is true with regard to the religious life: when a person attaches himself to the right place, he "dwells" there, returning to the place of his root. This takes place on the holy

Sabbath, when blessing dwells and arouses the inner life-force within the person. It turns out that the person has done nothing but put himself in his proper place. But when we receive words of Torah into our heart, we join heaven and earth, bringing forth the true fruits [of that union]. This is "light is sown for the righteous" (Ps. 97:11), the light of Torah. . . .

5:175

Here we have a most interesting union of the active and passive readings of the mystical tradition. On the one hand humans play a vitally active, even dominant, role in the union of heaven and earth. Humanity adds strength to the heavenly forces that in turn water and fructify the ground, bringing about the union and the bearing of fruit. On the other hand, all that human action consists of is the pure passivity of being in the right [mental!] place, so that the ever-flowing energy that proceeds from "heaven" or from the "inner point" will have a place to alight; we are only the channel through which the divine forces flow.

ימים טובים

FESTIVALS

ימים טובים

YAMIM TOVIM

1

"These are the appointed seasons of the Lord, holy assemblies that you shall call forth in their appointed times" (Lev. 23:4). The inner life-force of God that exists within all creatures is revealed on these festivals. That is why they are called *mikra'ey kodesh*, "holy assemblies" (lit.: "callings of the holy"). I heard from my grandfather, of blessed memory, that you can call forth the holiness on these days, and also that the holiness itself calls forth to us.

"Holy" refers to the innermost point. Even though this point gives life to all, it remains separated from physical being; God is holy and separate. Even though it is written: "The whole earth is filled with His glory" (Is. 6:3)—for God gives life to all—in this world God remains hidden. But on the festivals God is revealed.

341

Thus says the holy Zohar on the verse: "How great is the good that You have hidden away for those who revere You" (Ps. 31:20). On the festival the innermost life-force, which is the light hidden away for the righteous, can be felt even in the ordinary world. My grandfather also said in the Zohar's name that the festival is called *yom tov* (lit.: "good day" or "day of the good") because . . . "God saw that the light was good" (Gen. 1:4). The festival has within it some of that hidden light. This is also why we call them "seasons for joy." When the root of all life—in people and in all creatures—is revealed, surely there is great joy. So on the festival we can see into the inward light that exists within every thing.

Scripture also says, when speaking of the festival: ". . . all your males will be seen with the face of the Lord your God" (at the pilgrimage; Deut. 16:16). To see and to be seen; "just as you come to see, so you come to be seen." The Talmud there means to say that a person can see that inner life-force. Such a one is called "your male" or "the one who notices You" *(ZeKHuR/ZaKHaR).* "The face of the Lord your God" also refers to the innermost point *(PaNIM/PeNIMi),* which is called "the face of God."

On the festival we pray *ve-hasi'enu:* "Raise up for us, O Lord our God, the blessing of Your appointed seasons." We are asking that human deeds be tied to their root by the light of the festival. But the word *hasi'enu* is also related to *masu'ot,* the fire signals of ancient times. It is the flame of love that ties us to the root of life. "The blessing of Your appointed seasons"—the life of the entire year comes about through this connection to the root of life, revealed to us on the festival.

3:42

The festival is a time of inner light, a moment of special opportunity for us to become open to the light that exists within us always. While we know that such forms are only instrumental, and that the real purpose is the light and the inner seeing it allows, such special moments are rare gifts in the spiritual quest, special opportunities that the seeker dare not allow to pass by.

ROSH HASHANAH

1

"Inscribe us for life." There is a holy point in each Jewish person's heart. This is the living soul, of which it says: "God has implanted eternal life within us." But over the course of each year, as we become accustomed to sinning, the material self overpowers and hides that holy point. We then have to seek compassion from the blessed Holy One, asking that this imprint in our heart be renewed on Rosh Hashanah. This is what we mean when we say: "Inscribe us for life."

This is the same as "engraved on the tablets" (Ex. 32:16), which our sages read as "freedom on the tablets" (*ḥarut/ḥerut*), referring to freedom from the angel of death and the evil will. At the moment of receiving the Torah, Israel were prepared to have that writing never erased. But along came sin and spoiled that. Now we need to renew that "for life" every year.

The "sealing" for life, to which we refer in the *Ne'ilah* prayer on Yom Kippur, means that this inward point has to remain sealed up, so that the life-flow does not go just anywhere. Thus Scripture refers to the [inner self as] a "locked garden . . . the fountain sealed" (Cant. 4:12).

5:139

Here we have an important spiritual reading of an ancient theme, that of inscription in the Book of Life. The Book of Life is within you, the Sefat Emet teaches. God needs to write "Life!" on the tablets of your heart each year. Your task is to keep those inner tablets free enough from the accumulated grime caused by sin, guilt, the insanely fast pace at which we live, and all the rest, so that you have time to read (and follow!) that holy word.

2

"The Head of the Year" means before the flow of divine bounty is differentiated. When God sends life into this world, it enters under the rule of time and nature, becoming transformed from spirit to matter. But Rosh Hashanah is at the head, the source of that renewal, for within the source it as yet has no material form.

The Midrash quotes the verse: "Forever, O Lord, Your word stands in the heavens" (Ps. 119:89). It is said in the name of the Ba'al Shem Tov that God's utterance "Let there be a firmament" (Gen. 1:6) gives life to that firmament in each moment; so, too, are all the other divine utterances fully alive. So the root of all things and their very existence are the point that ever flows from divine speech.

The shofar blasts are sounds without speech. Speech represents the division of sound into varied and separate movements of the mouth. But sound itself is one, united, cleaving to its source. On Rosh Hashanah the life-force, too, cleaves to its source, as it was before differentiation or division. And we, too, seek to attach ourselves to that inner flow of life.

5:138

The consciousness of this holiday should take us to a place of absolute inner simplicity and purity, to that inner rosh, *that place of new beginnings, before the* shanah, *meaning both "year" and "change," begins on its inevitable complicated course. So, too, the sound of the* shofar *takes us to that moment of outcry from deep within, to a place prior to the division of our heart's cry into the many words of prayer.*

We find in the Talmud that the angels asked the blessed Holy One: "Why do Israel not recite *Hallel* before You on Rosh Hashanah and Yom Kippur?" The Holy One answered: "Could you imagine the King sitting on the throne of judgment with the books of the living and the dead open before Him—and Israel singing praises?"

We have to understand the nature of the angels' question. We have learned elsewhere that from each mitsvah a Jew performs, an angel is created. Now Rosh Hashanah and Yom Kippur are indeed holidays; they are "appointed times." The hearts of Israel are filled with joy at these times, but they just cannot articulate that joy in the form of *Hallel*. But because they have such longing—even though it cannot be realized—the angels are created anyway. And perhaps these angels are even higher than those created from the actual saying of *Hallel*—since thought is higher than speech.

(And maybe this is the true meaning of the shofar. The holy Zohar says that there is an outcry within the heart that the lips cannot speak. So, too, the shofar sound is hidden, as in [the verse:] "I will answer you in the secret of the thunderclap" (Ps. 81:8). And this is also the meaning of [the verse:] "Sound the shofar on the new-moon, in the hiding of our festive day" (vs. 4). This is also why there is a supplication in our prayerbook that refers to the angels who emerge from the shofar sounds.)

5:146

The mute Hallel-*angels of the Days of Awe serve as a powerful metaphor. They are created by the fullness of our hearts and our desire to sing, but kept silent by the awe before these days and the inevitable confrontation with our own mortality and questions of life and death.*

The wordless shofar blast (in a comment possibly added by the next generation's editors of these texts) also partakes of this deep dialogue between sound and silence. When we have gone beyond anything that words could possibly express, we come before the One with only the bleating, wailing, wordless cry that comes through the shofar. These sounds, we are told, come forth from the deepest places and rise higher than any words our mouths could utter.

"Now lest he stretch out his hand and take from the Tree of Life as well" (Gen. 3:22).

The root of humanity is in the Garden of Eden, for it says: "He placed there the person He had made" (Gen. 2:8). But because of sin we were expelled from there. By the power of *teshuvah* however, we are enabled to hold onto the Tree of Life. "Now" in the verse refers to *teshuvah*. "Stretch out his hand" refers to power and place, referring also to the ten days of penitence, since *yado* (his hand) has the same letters as *yod* (ten).

Abraham our Father also "stretched out his hand" (Gen. 22:10). He was willing to risk life itself in this trial, by which he was lifted out of the natural state and held fast to the Tree of Life. When Scripture says: "God tried Abraham" (Gen. 22:1), the rabbis read the word *NiSSaH* to mean "uplifted"; he was raised up and went forth from the natural state. The same is said of Joseph when "he fled *(va-yaNaS)* and went outside" (Gen. 39:12). This is the meaning of "The Lord *NiSSaH* Abraham."

While it is true that even earlier it says: "He took him out-side" (Gen. 15:5), meaning "above the covering of the sky," now Abraham was uplifted by his own power. This is the meaning of the "trial," as the Midrash says, quoting the verse: "You give those who revere You trials by which they uplift themselves as banners" (Ps. 60:6). They do it on their own.

That is why it says afterward: "Abraham, Abraham!" (Gen. 22:11). He has now become whole, cleaving to that root of "Abraham" above. This is why they said: "The patriarchs are the Chariot" [i.e., their lower selves were a "seat" for the upper hidden self]. . . .

4:157

This teaching should be read along with the second teaching here on Parashat Bere'shit. *There it is taught that each of us, as we exist in this world, is only half a self. Our infinite "other half" remains within the realm of God, and true self-fulfillment means transcending the limits of this natural world and being thus joined to our own personal root in infinity. This is what happens to Abraham in the* 'akedah, *as he abandons any hope of self-fulfillment other than in God. This is his moment of attachment to the true Tree of Life.*

This is a powerful and deeply religious reading of the 'akedah *story. But is it enough to mitigate the horror we still feel, and must feel, as humans and as parents, at Abraham's willingness to put the knife to his child? Do we want the Tree of Life if it has to be acquired by the near-death of all we love?*

SHABBAT SHUVAH

The verse says: "Return us to you, Lord, and we shall return" (Lam. 5:21).

This refers to the two kinds of *teshuvah:* that of fear and that of love. When a person is defiled by sin, it is impossible to return from love. Only the return due to fear is possible, and this requires the help of heaven. Thus the ancients have told us that God helps the one who returns. This is the meaning of "return us."

But those who return from love do so on their own, because of the love of God that burns within. This requires no help. Thus the Midrash recounts that Noah needed help to "walk with God," while Abraham needed no help to "walk before Me." One acted from fear, the other from love.

Now the two sorts of *teshuvah* also divide according to the verse "Turn from evil and do good" (Ps. 34:15). Returning from fear is turning from evil; the penitent seeks to be cleansed of

349

the defilement of sins. But *teshuvah* from love is "doing good"; this penitent realizes that sins keep one from attachment to God. Therefore, this one seeks *teshuvah*, in order to return to doing good.

The verse continues: ". . . renew our days as of old." This refers to the root attachment that all Israel have to God; "For God's people are a part of YHWH" (Deut. 32:9).

That is why it is easier to return on the holy Sabbath. Then the root of Israel is aroused, as Scripture says ["the inner gate] shall be open on the Sabbath day" (Ezek. 46:1). This refers to the extra soul that Jews have on the Sabbath; it is the force of that root, something that does not depend upon human deeds. That is why it is called "extra," for it is beyond that which we would merit. This force is not destroyed by sin, and that is why we are able to return on the holy Sabbath. . . .

5:161

Hasidism has always been identified with the "return from love." Since the days of the Ba'al Shem Tov, it has believed that a life of doing good with a loving heart is far greater than one of dreading sin or fear of punishment. But a careful reading of the sources shows that hasidic masters were not ready to let go entirely of the "return from fear." For those immersed deeply in the blinding or deadening routines of daily life, shock therapy is sometimes needed to awaken us to the glory both within us and around us. There is nothing like a confrontation with mortality, a reminder of how brief the time is that we have to exist as separate conscious beings, to bring us to our senses. That can serve as an important first step.

YOM KIPPUR

1

The Mishnah says that "for transgressions between one person and another, Yom Kippur does not atone until you appease your fellow-person." For on Yom Kippur all Israel are made into a single one. This is described as "If only they were one" (Ps. 139:16), referring to Yom Kippur. Just as this day unites all days, so, too, on it are all souls united.

In fact our souls really are close [to one another and to God]; only sin creates distance and separation. Thus it says: "It was only your sins that separated between you and your God" (Is. 59:2). Some sins bring about separation between the person and the Everpresent; others bring about separation between one person and another. We might read this verse to refer to separation "between *you*" on its own! Then too it brings about separation between you and your God.

Both of these sorts of separation need repair. Transgressions between people include not only such obvious damages as stealing, but also those things that bring about division between people, as in "You shall not hate your brother in your heart" (Lev. 19:17) and the like. "Until you appease your fellow-person" really means "until you again favor *(yeRaZeH/RoZeH)* and love that person." Thus "'Love your neighbor as yourself' (vs. 18)— that is the most basic rule of Torah."

On Yom Kippur, when all transgressions find atonement, Israel are made one. That is how they merited the second tablets on this day. Before that, sin had made them "wild" (Ex. 32:25), and their unity had been broken. Now that Moses came down from the mountain, he "assembled the whole community of the children of Israel" (Ex. 35:1), and they were returned to oneness. Torah depends upon this oneness, as Scripture says: "An inheritance of the *community* of Jacob" (Deut. 33:4). This is the meaning of "the most basic rule of Torah."

5:171f.

Torah could not have been given without unity among Jews; it cannot exist in the absence of its most basic principle: "Love your neighbor as yourself." How, then, does Torah exist in our day? Perhaps it does not exist at all. New and convincing readings of the texts elude us because we do not love enough. Until we can all open our hearts to one another, crossing all the lines defined by "Orthodox," "Secular," "Reform," "Zionist," and all the rest, there will be no revelation for us; we are not yet singularly "encamped" at the mountain.

Responsibility for this division falls heavily on the heads of "leaders," each of them so committed to an intractable position that nothing is allowed to change, no new Torah can be received. But for how long can Jewish souls be nourished by mere repetitions of teachings or translations (even one such as this) of old sources? God will bring about the real renewal of Judaism only when we put down our loudspeakers of division and hatred long enough to listen.

2

[The Talmud, discussing the Yom Kippur fast, rhetorically asks whether] one should fast on the ninth of Tishre as well. "On the contrary!" is the reply. "Whoever eats and drinks on the ninth day [in joy] is considered as deserving as one who had fasted on both the ninth and the tenth!" We further learn from these two days that one is supposed to take from the profane and add on to the holy [the Yom Kippur ritual beginning before sundown].

Yom Kippur is considered a foretaste of the world to come, where there is no eating or drinking. Thus it is a day of true joy for Israel, even though we are not quite able to grasp that joy, still being creatures of this world. That is why we have to take hold of the Yom Kippur joy both before and after the day itself, adding on from the profane to the holy. The rejoicing on the ninth day allows us afterward to attach ourselves to the light of Yom Kippur.

Rabbenu Jonah says something similar to this: Since we are unable to rejoice on Yom Kippur itself, we celebrate a bit earlier. Yom Kippur is in fact a day of complete self-negation before God. The rabbis say on the verse "God is the hope *(mikveh)* of Israel" (Jer. 17:13) that just as a *mikveh* purifies the ritually defiled, so does the blessed Holy One purify Israel. He specifies that just as a person has to enter into the *mikveh*'s waters with the whole body, so does the entire self have to be negated before God.

After death, those who merit are purified in a *mikveh* by the blessed Holy One. Something of that takes place on Yom Kippur as well.

5:170

The place of purification, the ritual bath, or mikveh, *has now been transferred to the temporal realm: the day is itself a cleansing experience. The association of Yom Kippur with death and with life in the world to come is an ancient part of this day's power and a reason why Jews who have given up much else in our ritual life continue to observe Yom Kippur.*

The annual contact with mortality—a moment to see death, life, and rebirth all cojoined and to emerge alive—is not something that many would want to miss.

≡ 3 ≡

In Tanna de-Be Eliyahu it is taught that for the period of Moses' second forty days on the mountain, Israel fasted. On the final day they called for a fast that would last through night and day. God was appeased, and He thus established that day as one of forgiveness and atonement for all generations. This must have come about through the power of Aaron: just as he participated with them in the sin of the Golden Calf, so did he lead them to repentance. This is why the Day of Atonement ritual is led by the high priest, the descendant of Aaron.

In this way they atoned for their violation of [the commitment:] "We shall do and we shall listen" (Ex. 24:7), which they had promised [to fulfill]. They lost the "we shall do" when they sinned, but now they regained it, as they declared a fast day before God commanded it.

The second tablets were given on Yom Kippur. It is of these we speak when we say in our Shabbat prayers: "He brought two tablets down in his hands, in which it is written to keep the Sabbath." The [first] tablets said: "Remember the Sabbath day," and [the second] said: "Keep the Sabbath day." Remembering is an oral act, that of mentioning the Sabbath; but "keeping" means to guard it in one's heart. The true writing of the tablets was an engraving directly into the hearts of Israel, as it says: "Write them upon the tablets of your heart" (Prov. 3:3). Sin made them incapable of receiving these tablets, but once their hearts were forgiven and purified on Yom Kippur, the inscription in them reappeared.

The sin of the Golden Calf is carried down through all the generations. Each year a bit more of it is forgiven; we enter into the Gates of Holiness and receive the imprint in our hearts once again.

5:173

The association of Yom Kippur with the giving of the second tablets, while of ancient midrashic origin, is especially emphasized by the Sefat Emet. So is the sin of the Golden Calf, which for the kabbalistic tradition is Israel's version of "original sin." The dangers of idolatry, especially in the midst of highly ritualized religious behavior, are ever with us. *Perhaps Moses, when he looked ahead and saw "each generation and its interpreters," shuddered when he saw Israel turning God's living word into an idolatry, and that was why he smashed the first tablets. The second tablets were given on Yom Kippur, which has become the most highly ritualized day in the Jewish calendar. Here we are, supposedly confronting our innermost selves, and instead we are busy chanting triple acrostic hymns written in the Middle Ages! How important it is to recall on Yom Kippur, in the midst of all this elaborate ritual (recalling yet another more ancient ritual that lies behind it), that the real goal of all these rites is cleansing our heart, so that God's word will once again shine forth from within it.*

 4

Yom Kippur exists by the merit of Moses our Teacher, of blessed memory; it is the day when he brought down the second tablets. Israel joined with him by fasting on the final day of those forty, and his merit was attached to them all. Moses is called "the Man of God" (Ps. 90:1). All of Israel were supposed to attain that state, as it says: "I said you were gods, all of you children of the most high" (Ps. 82:6). We were all supposed to become like angels. Moses remained on that rung, but no one else. On Yom Kippur we again become like angels, through the power of Moses our Teacher, since he joined himself to the whole community of Israel. That is why we have to be one on Yom Kippur, for it is only then that Moses dwells in our midst. . . .

5:175

The moment of revelation on Shavu'ot was supposed to be a breakthrough for humanity; Israel were to lead in the trans-

formation of us humans into angels, beings who would learn to transcend entirely our corporeal selves. Our existence as denizens of two worlds, the spiritual and the physical—with all the conflicts that seem to exist between them—was to come to an end. But we were not ready, and we rushed to find a physical representation of divinity in the Golden Calf. Ever since then we have but a taste of divinity, moments like Shabbat and Yom Kippur, when we know what transcendence is. In each of us, however, there lives a bit of Moses, the one who went up the mountain and did not falter. Each Jew contains something of Moses, the Man of God.

SUKKOT

The *sukkah* is like a *ḥuppah*, concluding the marriage of man and wife. "For I caused Israel to dwell in *sukkot* when I took them out of the Land of Egypt" (Lev. 23:43). At the Exodus from Egypt Israel were sanctified (="wedded") to God, as it says: "I am the Lord who sanctifies [or 'weds'] you, who brought you forth from the Land of Egypt to be your God" (Lev. 22:32–33).

There is a claim to be made against this: why should Israel be selected from among all creatures to be God's own possession? [Scripture says of our father Jacob:] "For his possessions he made *sukkot*" (Gen. 33:17). It is also written [in the prayerbook] "who spreads out *(pores)* a *sukkah* of peace." But the word *pores* also means "to divide" or "to choose a portion," for "God's portion is His people" [Israel] (Deut. 32:9), which He has chosen from among all creatures.

God is wholeness itself. Why then did He choose a fragment of something? Scripture answers: "I dwell with the lowly and those of humble spirit" (Is. 57:15). The Zohar adds that a person with a broken heart is indeed whole. This in fact is to be said in God's praise: wherever He dwells there is wholeness; He makes a whole out of the half.

This is the real meaning of "who spreads a *sukkah* of peace." The inner point that is everywhere is wholeness; Israel represents this among God's creatures. On Sukkot seventy bullocks are offered for the seventy nations. The water libation [of Sukkot] is also interpreted by the Talmud to mean that Israel should pray for God's kingdom to spread over all Creation. This is the meaning of [the verse:] "Do not be like servants who serve the king only to receive [your own] reward."

5:181

The teaching is based upon the triple meaning of the root peh-resh-samekh. In the prayerbook passage it means "to spread forth." Elsewhere it means "to divide" or "set off." Related to this meaning is "prize" or "reward," that of the final quotation, a well-known adage from Pirke Avot.

The point is that Israel are chosen to serve God for the sake of all humanity and all Creation. If they think only of their own good and their own needs, they are like the faithless servant, the one concerned only with reward.

This highly universalist message, forgotten in our years of struggle for survival, is one we need to learn again. Jewish life will ultimately be meaningful only if its content is ultimate: a contribution to the survival and maintenance of all existence, not just of the Jewish people.

 2

"Take unto yourselves the fruit of the goodly tree" (Lev. 23:40). On Sukkot God draws Israel near to Him, as it says: "He spreads forth a *sukkah* of peace." He protects us as His own children. Israel, too, want to be attached to God; they seek to do good deeds so that it not be God's grace alone that helps them. This is the meaning of "Take unto yourselves"—of your own accord.

Scripture also says: "Tell me the way to live, to be sated with joy in Your presence" (Ps. 16:11). *Lulav* is numerically equal to *ḥayyim* (life); Israel desire the true life of their inner selves. This is what it means to be "sated with joy"—the more deeply you take life into your heart, the more you are sated. This happens through the *lulav* and the species that accompany it. Israel actually point to God, taking in the light of the *sukkah*, which is given to them as a gift. When the king invites guests, he gives them what their heart desires. "Whoever invites someone does so with the intent that they eat and drink."

That is why He says to us: "Take unto yourselves," meaning that we should choose life for ourselves. On Sukkot all Israel are granted awareness, as it says: "So that all your generations be aware . . . " (Lev. 23:43). Awareness for the whole year comes about on Sukkot, the last of the three "legs" on which the year stands. The mitsvah of *sukkah* stands on its own, but the *lulav*-species represent the awareness that Israel receive and take into the depths of their hearts. . . .

5:181

The teaching interprets the wavings of the lulav, *the way we point in each direction and then move inward. The Sefat Emet suggests that in each direction we are pointing to God, and then taking deep into our hearts the awareness that God is to be found there. Wherever we point—north, east, south, or west, up or down—we are pointing at God. The instrument we use for that pointing, the* lulav, *also means "life"; we use our entire lives as ways of seeking out ever new sacred awareness and bringing it home, to deepen and expand the knowing in our hearts.*

3

The joy of the water-drawing place is one of the ceremonies of Sukkot. For it is from there, from joy, that we draw the holy spirit. Joy is the vessel with which we draw the living waters, the holy spirit, of which it says: "He blew into his nostrils the breath of life" (Gen. 2:7). As a person holds fast to the life-force that each of us has from God, life spreads forth through all his limbs.

It says [of these festive days]: "We saw no sleep." The Midrash says the same of Moses, that for forty days and nights he was unable to sleep, knowing there was no measure to that which he was receiving in every hour. Of Sukkot it says: "seven days in the year" (Lev. 23:41), something it says of no other festival. The light of the entire year depends upon these seven days. And the vessel through which we receive that light is joy.

5:182

Sukkot is called zeman simḥatenu, *"the season of our joy."*
Hasidim celebrate the entire week in song and dance, staying
up late into the night in celebrations that seek to recreate the
joy of Sukkot in ancient Israel, including the water-drawing
festival. The ecstasy of this celebration, we are told here, has
the purpose of enlightenment and the renewal of life itself.

4

Sukkot is said to be in memory of the Clouds of Glory that went with Israel in the wilderness. But how did they merit being accompanied by Clouds of Glory? The Zohar attributes it to [the verse:] "I remember the lovingkindness of your youth, the love of your betrothal, when you followed Me in the wilderness, the unsown land" (Jer. 2:2).

The main point is that they placed themselves under God's blessed rule. After coming out of Egypt they feared for their souls, lest they fall again under the domain of the "other side."

Even though choice is given to a person, there is a choice about that as well. One can choose with all his soul not to have choice, but rather to follow God's lead and be guided in an upright path.

After the days of judgment, Rosh Hashanah and Yom Kippur, have passed, Israel are cleansed of sin. Now they have to choose God as their leader; this too is a form of *teshuvah*. Previously we returned out of fear, but this *teshuvah* is from love. We see that in God's grace we have been forgiven and purified of all our sins. But we still [need to] return to Him, realizing that we have no place of our own, but only dwell in His shade.

5:183

Can we "choose not to choose"? This seemingly strange question is an important one in our age, a time when many are plagued by an excess of choice. So many things that once seemed to be given and unchangeable circumstances of life are now matters of chosen "lifestyle" that some are tempted to reject choice itself as a "demon" of the age. Yet all our commitments, even those seemingly most choice-rejecting, are themselves chosen. Somewhere within our hearts there always lurks the possibility that we might have chosen otherwise, or that we still may.

The Sefat Emet was a perceptive reader of modernity. He wished he could hold back the new vistas of choice and temptation by urging a collective decision not to choose. But he was wrong about choice: once we know that we are the choosers, no firmness of decision or mythic denial of choice ("Israel stand under oath since Mount Sinai"—therefore, they have no choice) will make a difference. We may indeed still choose the upright paths of tradition, but this choice is one that has to be struggled with and reaffirmed each day.

 5

Sukkot is called the Festival of Ingathering, when everyone harvests and gathers his property into his home. This is a good time to remember that we and all we possess belong to God; He, too, gathers us into His home, the *sukkah*.

5:184

 6

The days of Sukkot are called "season of our joy," because God has privileged us to dwell in His shade. The *sukkah* is something like the Garden of Eden, where it says: "He placed there the person whom He had made" (Gen. 2:8). The true intent of Creation was that humans dwell there, in that place of joy, of which we say [in the wedding blessings]: ". . . as You gave joy to Your creature in Eden of old." Even though we are also told that "He expelled the human" (Gen. 3:24), there are times when some bit of Eden still glows. God has brought us into this dwelling that belongs to the realm of heaven, as the Talmud says [prescribing the grace after a wedding-banquet]: "There is joy in His dwelling-place." That is why being in this place brings us joy.

God above is surely happy because Israel have purified themselves before Him on Yom Kippur. We now partake of His joy. Of this, Scripture says: "Before the Lord [or 'for the Lord's sake'] you will be purified" (Lev. 16:30). We rejoice not only at our own purification but also in the joy God takes in us.

5:199

The memory of Eden has not disappeared; we humans manage to stay alive in this world because the spark of that memory is not quite extinguished, and can be rekindled in us at special moments. The moments of bride and groom under the ḥuppah often have that quality, as two evocations of the wedding blessings here indicate. So, too, does the simple act of dwelling in the sukkah, *another protective bower touched by divine grace, open us to the possibility of a renewed Eden.*

7

The Talmud recalls a difference of opinion regarding the verse: ". . . for I caused the children of Israel to dwell in booths when I brought them out of the Land of Egypt" (Lev. 23:43). One says this refers to real booths, while the other says it refers to the Clouds of Glory.

Both must somehow be true. But we have to understand the one who said "real booths." What did he have in mind? He must have been thinking of [another rabbinic interpretation of the *sukkah*], where "Torah says: 'Go out of your fixed dwelling and dwell in this temporary shelter!'" That indeed is the true meaning of the freedom given to every Jew when we left Egypt: not to be stuck in the ways of nature. "I caused the children of Israel to dwell in booths when I brought them forth" means that [God] implanted in the hearts of Israel the power to escape the prison of the body and nature, to dwell in this world as temporary visitors. On the verse "They traveled from Raamases to Sukkot" (lit.: "to booths"—Ex. 12:37) the sages quoted: "I have raised you up on eagles' wings and brought you unto Me" (Ex. 19:4). He gave them the power to be high above nature, complete with wings with which to fly to their Father in Heaven.

As much as a person fulfills this sense of "dwelling," not being stuck in this-worldly things, in that very measure do the name of heaven and the *sukkah* of the Clouds of Glory go with him. . . .

5:202

This is a beautiful, almost ecstatic description of freedom as understood in a religious context. Liberation from Egypt means that we are truly free, free from all attachments to worldly things, if only we are willing to live our lives that way. Each of us has the power to release ourselves from nature and to make use of those wings God gave us to fly to His place in the Clouds of Glory.

But alas we are human, all too human, and our way is to be householders rather than renunciates. Once a year, therefore, we are both reminded (and challenged) by dwelling in the sukkah *of the freedom each of us has within us since the day we were brought forth from Egypt. The "eagles' wings" are still there awaiting us.*

☰ 8 ☰

The holiday of Sukkot draws Israel to repent in love and joy. Of this it is said: "Love covers over all sins" (Prov. 10:12). That is the *sukkah*, which shields Israel. Of this, Scripture says: "Many waters cannot douse love" (Cant. 8:7). Israel's love for God remains forever in their hearts. It is only sin that hides the love, so on these days [when sin has been forgiven] it is revealed. . . .

My grandfather always used to say that there is a point within each Jew's heart that God protects. In this way He is [the] "shield of Abraham." This is the point of love, the love that many waters cannot douse.

This holiday of Sukkot is like the tabernacle; it, too, was a dwelling given to the children of Israel after they had repented of their sin [the Golden Calf]. RaSHI interprets "Moses assembled the people" (Ex. 35:1) to have taken place on the day after Yom Kippur, when he came down from the mountain and God had joyously been appeased by the children of Israel. It was then that they began to contribute to the tabernacle, on those days between Yom Kippur and Sukkot. Since it says "each morning" (Ex. 36:3), one gets the impression that it was only a few days. In the joyous giving for the tabernacle, preparation was made for this "season of our joy" each year. The Midrash quotes "He loves them freewillingly" (Hos. 14:5) to show that the freely willed and joyous giving for the building of the tabernacle awakened love between Israel and their Father in Heaven. . . .

5:203f.

The love of God is ever present in the hearts of all Israel. We would have to expand this to say "all humanity." There is no human being who is not capable of gratitude to the Source of Life for the gifts that he or she has been given. But that which "covers" love, which makes it difficult for us to reach or express that deeply natural feeling, seems more complicated. "Sin," and especially the guilt we feel in response to sin, is certainly an important factor. But in our time anger is a factor as well. We Jews are still struggling and learning to "forgive" God for the holocaust (as though it were God who needed forgiveness!). Doubt also keeps us from expressing our love of God. But perhaps more than all else it is our fear of vulnerability that makes us hide our love of God. "Do I want to get involved?" "Do I want to take the risks of love?" Loving God in that sense is like any love: dangerous, demanding, leaving us open to hurt.

The difference is our faith that God is always there, present even to heal the heart that breaks for love of God.

 9

The commandment of *sukkah* comes after the Day of Atonement. It is said that "only your sins separate you from your God" (Is. 59:2). So now that they have been purified of sin, the separation has been taken away. Some sins cause separation of the unity of the person and his fellow-man; this is "separate you" in the limited sense. Others bring about separation between man and God.

On Sukkot all becomes one and all the souls of Israel unite. This is pointed to by the four species [representing various types of souls,] all joined in one grouping. And the *sukkah* joins the souls of Israel to be one with their Father in Heaven. That is why it is called "the holiday of ingathering."

5:236

The essential claim of all mystics here receives clear and deeply Jewish expression. Separation is caused by sin, by attention to externals, by turning to the material world. When these are removed, all the barriers to oneness, the true natural state of being, fall away, and we are all joined into a single One.

HOSHA'NA RABBAH

The *'aravah* (willow) has neither aroma nor taste [referring, according to the Midrash, to Jews who have neither learning nor good deeds]. What, then, is its importance? The willow-leaf is shaped like the mouth, which is the locus of all of Israel's power; "the voice is the voice of Jacob" (Gen. 27:22).

The willow thus refers to King David [symbolizing *malkhut*, the fourth and passive member of the kabbalistic quaternity]. The three other species refer to the three patriarchs; David is the one who says: "I am prayer" (Ps. 109:4). Now it is true that the sound of prayers of the righteous, those who come with "aroma" and "taste," reach to much higher rungs. But their attainment is due in part to the [learning and] good deeds that accompany them. The one who comes with neither aroma nor taste indeed has only prayer itself.

This is the meaning of "the prayer of a poor man who is enwrapped" (Ps. 102:1). He wraps himself entirely in his prayer, as in [the verse:] "I am prayer." This is pleasing (*'arev*) to God and is thus called *'aravah*. That is why this day is called Hosha'na Rabbah, the Great Salvation, because on this day even the lowly, those without taste or aroma, are saved. This salvation reaches out to lowly generations like ours, a time when [all of us] have only prayer. On this day the gates of prayer are open in Israel's mouths. . . .

5:194

The last line is especially worthy of note. Where are the gates of prayer, those that seem to be sometimes open, sometimes closed? They are in the mouths of human beings who seek to pray. God has no gates. God is everywhere, hears every sound as a part of the great eternal chorus. It is only we who sometimes close the gates, losing for a while our ability to open our mouths in prayer. On this day of days, the day called Yom 'Aravah, *the Day of the Willow or the day of the mouth itself, all our mouths are open once more to the possibility of prayer.*

≡ 2 ≡

Our sages composed many supplications to be recited on this Day of the Willow. The power of Israel lies in its mouth, and the willow is shaped like the mouth or the lips, as our sages have taught.

The two lips seem to represent two forms of praise: one that can be uttered by the mouth in speech and the other in silence. Of these the rabbis taught: "A word for a penny, but silence for two" [i.e., silence is worth more than speech]. The two willows or the two lips thus also stand for Moses and Aaron, Moses being the verbal power of Torah, while of Aaron it says: "And Aaron was silent" (Lev. 10:3); his was the power of silence.

Since we find that the sin of evil talk is worse than any other, the power of the one who can keep his mouth closed at times of conflict is very great. The sages read "He hangs the earth upon *belimah*" (Job 26:7) to refer to the one who closes his mouth. This refers to Aaron, who loved peace and pursued it.

These two [speech and silence] in fact depend upon one another. The more you guard your mouth, the better you can open it when it comes to Torah. . . .

This may be the difference between the willow when attached to the *lulav*, where it refers to speaking words of Torah, combining with the other three species, each of which stands for some great principle, and the willow alone, representing the power of silence and the value of guarding one's tongue. That is why we are taught that there is no blessing to be recited for beating the willow, since it in itself stands for silence.

5:226

These words in praise of silence are most noteworthy. They follow an old Jewish tradition of carefully measuring speech and not allowing oneself to engage in anything that might be termed vain or wasteful talk. How much we wish that the value of guarding speech was more widely appreciated by Jews in our time. Silence as a value has almost disappeared from Judaism, even where Torah study and sacred language are still very much alive. We may have to relearn the discipline of silence, if only to provide counterpoint for our sacred language, which will then speak all the more clearly.

SHEMINI 'ATSERET/
SIMHAT TORAH

1

Why do Shemini 'Atseret and Simhat Torah follow the holiday [of Sukkot]? The Faithful Shepherd [of the Zohar] suggests that there are two types of *teshuvah*. One sort intends only to mend the sin itself, while the other, more complete *teshuvah* includes a return to Torah study with all one's strength. The goal of this "return" is not only to atone for one's soul, but to be purified in order to serve God. You repent in order to remove the barrier [between yourself and God] that sin has erected in your soul.

That is why we accept the yoke of Torah immediately after the days of repentance. Scripture says: "On the eighth day there shall be an assembly for you" (Num. 29:35). It is *for you* because the gates of *teshuvah* are open to all. But Israel take greater joy in accepting God's service anew than they did in having their sins forgiven. . . .

5:186

This is a hasidic teaching very much in the spirit of the Ba'al Shem Tov. The problem with sin is that it is a hindrance; it keeps us from doing the work we are here to do. Israel knows that humans are placed on earth in order to serve God; fulfilling that task is our greatest joy. Sin creates a barrier of guilt that keeps us from serving. When that barrier is removed, either through the penitential season or through any human act of contrition and teshuvah, *we can get back to being who we really are, faithful and joyous servants of God and God's creatures.*

The Midrash says that Shemini 'Atseret really should occur fifty days after Sukkot, just as Shavu'ot takes place fifty days after Passover. The reason it is held immediately is so as not to trouble people during the winter season.

When Israel came out of Egypt, they counted forty-nine days of purification, which the Zohar compares to a woman counting the days after her period until she is ritually pure. The same is true of these days. On Rosh Hashanah and Yom Kippur Israel are liberated from the evil urge. They, too, need days of purity before they are ready to receive the Torah [on Simḥat Torah]. But here the purification takes place on the seven festive days of Sukkot, parallel to the seven weeks of counting before Shavu'ot. Here we have the help of the mitsvot of *sukkah* and *lulav*, God's grace hovering over us closely. It may also be, as the Zohar says, that those who have just repented bear great strength, and they can repair a great deal all at once. In this season we are all *ba'aley teshuvah*; we can restore what we need so that we get right to Shemini 'Atseret and Simḥat Torah.

The point is that in the preceding holy days, our souls were set right and made into vessels that can receive the holy pouring forth of God's blessing. Shemini Atseret is the time for that blessing. "An assembly *for you*" (Num. 29:35) means that this is the time when we receive. We have become whole enough to be vessels that will contain God's blessing, which comes forth on these days. That is why we read the portion "This is the blessing" (Deut. 33:1).

5:186

The parallel between the spring and fall festivals is an interesting one, made in a number of hasidic sources. The Jewish calendar may essentially be said to contain two holy periods of approximately the same length, one in spring and one in fall. The spring period celebrates the nation, beginning with its liberation from Egypt, continuing for a period that recalls "your going after Me in the wilderness" (Jer. 2:2), and climaxing fifty days later with the receiving of the Torah.

The fall season is that of the individual. It begins on Rosh Ḥodesh Elul. Because the liberation here is from our inner demons, representing a more constant struggle, the great events take place in the middle of the period, rather than at its beginning. The cleansing or liberation of the self is followed by a lyrical period of following God out into the wilderness, represented by the sukkah *and branches, culminating in our joy at the renewed acceptance of Torah on Simḥat Torah.*

The message of both seasons is the same: first you must become free, no longer dominated by idolatrous or materialistic concerns. This liberation will give you a sense of joyous worship, a closeness to God born of your love set free. But this period of intimacy and spontaneous faithfulness will not last. Out of it you must find Torah, norms of behavior, and ways of remembering that will sustain your religious life, even when the sacred season is no more and you have to survive in the profane workaday world in which we are destined to live.

≡ **3** ≡

"This is the blessing" (Deut. 33:1). The Midrash says that Torah came in order to bless Israel.

Before Moses died he handed over his power, the Torah given him at Sinai, to the entire Jewish people. Therefore he called it "an inheritance for the communiy of Israel" (Deut. 33:4). Whenever the children of Israel gather together we fulfill [the commandment]: "There is a king in Jeshurun when the heads of the people gather" (Deut. 33:5).

We recite blessings before and after we read from the Torah. I heard from my grandfather and teacher that these two blessings are parallel to the blessings over food. The blessing we recite before we eat is for the food itself, which God created. The blessing after eating is for the power the food contains to satisfy us as we digest it, and for the strength that food gives to our bodies. That is why the blessing after meals may be said until the food is digested. The same is true of Torah. In addition to giving the Torah, God also gave "a blessing after it," that the words light up a person's heart.

It may be that the two holidays are parallel to these: Shavu'ot celebrates the giving of the Torah itself, while Simhat Torah is "an assembly for *you.*" That is for the power left by Torah, that which shines and gives forth blessing within the hearts of Jews. . . .

This is Torah's blessing: it gives life to those who study it. That is why the blessing says: "He implanted eternal life within us." This is the oral Torah, that which gives forth blessing in the heart and bears fruit. This, too, is a gift of God, as it says: "From Me does your fruit come forth" (Hos. 14:9). Even what is added, the new interpretations offered by the sages, is a gift of God. This is the power that Moses left to the entirety of Israel through all generations, to the end of time. . . .

5:202

The mystic understands well that no sharp lines can be drawn between divine gift and human creativity. The power of humans to create, and here especially to create through constant reinterpretation, is itself a divine gift. So Torah, the same Torah in its entirety, is thus God's Torah, the one we receive and accept anew each Shavu'ot, and our Torah, the one recreated each year by the collective reinterpretations of all Israel, which we celebrate on Simhat Torah.

4

"Moses commanded us Torah" (Deut 33:4). Elsewhere, Scripture says: "For the commandment is a candle and Torah is light" (Prov. 6:23) and "A candle of God is the human soul" (Prov. 20:27). The souls of Israel are vessels into which the light of Torah is able to flow. Thus it is that the light of Torah is interpreted and illuminated in accordance with the worthiness of each generation. In a lowly generation, God forbid, Torah's light becomes hidden. Of this, Scripture says: "I am with him in sorrow" (Ps. 91:15), "I" *[anokhi]* referring to Torah, which is dependent upon the repair of Israel's souls. This is the meaning of [the verse:] "Moses commanded us Torah." "We" and "Torah" are thoroughly bound together. Therefore, Torah rejoices in Israel, and Israel rejoices in Torah. Moses is the go-between, the one who kindles the light of Torah in the candle-souls of Israel.

[The verse continues: "An inheritance for the community of Jacob."] The sages said: Do not read it as "inheritance" *[morashah]* but rather as "betrothed" *[me'orasah]*, like a bride to her bridegroom. Both readings are correct. Torah really is a gift within the souls of Israel, but it is only as the person prepares himself that the light of Torah is renewed for him. Of this we say [in the Simhat Torah hymns]: "It is strength and light for us." "Strength" refers to Torah in its essence, while "light" is the shining forth of Torah, renewed for us constantly, but according to our efforts. [Thus it is said of Torah:] "Her breasts will slake your thirst at all times" (Prov. 5:19).

That is why Scripture first says: "The Lord will give strength to His people" (Ps. 29:11) and then "God will bless

His people with peace." The blessing is that which is added through the constant renewal of Torah. Thus it is taught that "when a person sits and studies Torah, the blessed Holy One sits and studies facing him."

5:229

The teaching seems to be a defense of ongoing creative reinterpretation of Torah. Perhaps an ultraconservative voice was raised against the urge within Hasidism, very much present in this work, to keep teachings fresh and ever "new." By the late nineteenth century, the Sefat Emet was exceptional in this regard. Here he warns against those who view Torah only as an "inheritance," something to be passed on unchanged to the next generation. Such a Torah will indeed have "strength," the power to protect Jewish existence, but it will be without "light," the true purpose for which Torah was given. This message is an urgent one in our day as well. "Preserving the tradition" is not an end in itself, but only a means to making God's light shine forth through it.

ḤANUKKAH

1

It is written: "A lamp [candle] of the Lord is the soul of man, searching out all the belly's chambers" (Prov. 20:27). The Gemara notes that searching requires a candle. One candle from another. "I will seek out Jerusalem with candles" (Zeph. 1:12).

Sanctuary and Temple are found in every one of Israel, as Scripture says: "I will dwell within them" (Ex. 25:6). These are present insofar as a person makes it clear to himself that all of life-energy comes from the soul. Thus we say each day: "The soul You have placed within me is pure. . . . " This means that there is a certain pure place within each Jew, but it is indeed deeply hidden.

When the Temple was standing, it was clear that all life-energy came from God. This is the meaning of [the verse:] "the

377

indwelling of Shekhinah [in the Temple] was witness that God dwells in Israel." But even now, after that dwelling-place has been hidden, it can be found by searching with candles. The candles are the mitsvot; we need to seek within our hearts and souls in order to fulfill a mitsvah with all our strength. The word *NeR* (candle) stands for *Nefesh Ruah* ("soul" and "spirit"). To fulfill a mitsvah in this way we also make use of all our 248 limbs. These, combined with love and fear, together add up to the equivalent of the word *NeR* (248 + 2 = 250/*Ner*). Then we are ready to find the sanctuary, to come to that hidden point within.

Especially at this season, when lights were miraculously lit for Israel even though they did not have enough oil, there remains light even now to help us, with the aid of these Ḥanukkah candles, to find that hidden light within. Hiding takes place mainly in the dark; we need the candles' light to seek and to find. . . .

But Scripture also says: "At that time I will seek out Jerusalem with candles." This means that even now Jerusalem and the Temple can be found by searching. Even when it says: "She is Zion; none seeks her" (Jer. 30:17), this means that she requires seeking! This happens by the power of the mitsvot that you do with all your strength. They arouse the inner life-energy, which is the pure point. Of this, Scripture says: "Seeking out all the belly's chambers." By the power of inwardness we can find the hidden light within all our own inner chambers.

[This is the meaning of the verse: "A person must always measure himself as though a holy being dwelt within his innards." Of a person who conducts himself in this way it is written: "Let them make Me a sanctuary and I will dwell within them." Truly within them!]

1:198

The Ḥanukkah candles are here reinterpreted as a spiritual symbol. They are the light of the mitsvot by which we search out our inner selves. We are looking for the hidden divine light within ourselves; the mitsvot are light-seeking candles, instruments given to us to aid us in that search.

Ḥanukkah is the time of rededication, making the Temple once again pure enough to be a dwelling-place for God. Our inner Temple, too, needs to be dedicated anew, to become again the place where God can dwell "within them."

═══ **2** ═══

My grandfather and teacher quoted the Gemara that says: "Wicks and oils that the sages said not to use to light Sabbath lamps may be used for the lights of Ḥanukkah." This, he explained, refers to the impure souls within Israel. The word *NeFeSh* (soul) stands for *Ner/Petilah/SHemen* (lamp/wick/oil). Those that cannot rise up on the Sabbath—because "the light skips in them and [the wicks] are not drawn up"—can be brought up on Ḥanukkah. Thus far my grandfather's teaching.

These holidays of Ḥanukkah and Purim belong to the oral Torah. The three festivals God gave us are commanded expressly in the written Torah. God gave us those holy times, sanctified since Creation, for all was created through the Torah. They bear witness that the blessed Holy One has chosen Israel and is close to them, giving them his holy testimony. The word *mo'ed*, used for these festivals, is related to *'edut* (testimony).

But Ḥanukkah and Purim are special times that Israel merited by their own deeds. These are called oral Torah; they are witness that Israel chose the blessed Holy One. Israel are joined to God and their deeds arouse God, for here they are capable of creating new sacred times by their deeds. And because these holidays were brought about by Israel's own deeds, every Jewish soul can be restored through them. Every single Jew can find a way of belonging and attachment to them.

1:207

Every Jewish soul is kosher enough to be a candle in God's menorah! This is our holiday, one that became sanctified only because of our actions, not by original divine intent. For this sort of holiday no one needs to feel inadequate or insufficiently holy to participate.

It is interesting to note that such "Ḥanukkah and Purim" Jews existed already in Warsaw of the 1870s, when this teaching was given. Jews who were not "holy" when it came to observing the Sabbath every week still showed up at the rebbe's for the lighting of Ḥanukkah candles and were given a chance to warm their souls by the light of his teachings.

≡ **3** ≡

Ḥanukkah is the last miracle that was performed for us. Therefore, we have to find special strength in it.

Why did all the miracles take place for Israel? Surely God could have guarded Israel in such a way that their enemies never would have ruled over them. Then there would have been no need for miracles! But the miracles were to demonstrate that Israel exists only by virtue of lights that come from above, from beyond nature. The miracles are particular to the way Israel is led, and this itself is the reason for the four kingdoms [who have subjugated them], that Israel constantly be in need of miracles.

So it was that when God performed a miracle for our ancestors, they would be sustained by it [for some period of time]. When the light of that miracle vanished, He would have to perform another for them. That's the way it always was.

This means that the light of the Ḥanukkah miracle still shines for us, since God has not yet performed another outright miracle. It must be that we are still sustained by that light.

But in saying that when the light of one miracle passes, God performs another for us, we don't mean to say that the light completely disappears, God forbid. Each miracle is in fact beyond time and shines forth forever. Thus Scripture says: "He did so that His miracles be remembered" (Ps. 111:4). We mean rather that the renewal-force of the miracle grew old, due to the heavy burden of exile. Then God performed another miracle for us.

But Ḥanukkah contains within it the power to keep renewing until the redeemer comes (speedily, in our day!). That is why it is called Ḥanukkah, meaning rededication or renewal. This miracle will keep renewing itself until the messiah comes (speedily, in our day. Amen!).

1:208f.

The real miracle of Ḥanukkah is that the miracle remains with us forever. Perhaps that is because its true meaning lies in our power to rededicate and purify ourselves. That sort of miracle, though it takes hard work and discipline, will remain alive as a possibility as long as human life exists, indeed "until the messiah comes."

The word Ḥanukkah can be divided and read *ashanu koh,* meaning: "Thus did they camp."

The essential miracle of Ḥanukkah was the victory in battle over the wicked Hellenistic kingdom. The sages, wanting to show that the true joy of liberation from human bondage is that we are enabled to become servants of God . . . gave it this name.

We are taught that although there was sufficient oil to burn for only one day, it lasted eight days. This does not have to be seen only in temporal terms. "Eight" represents wholeness [completing the Sabbath cycle and beginning again]. Under the yoke of Hellenistic decrees, the power of holiness in the Jews was weakened, until only a tiny bit of it remained within them. After the terrible struggles and battles against the Greek kingdom, they had no strength left to attain wholeness. Here God helped them, and the tiny point of holiness within them miraculously led them in an instant back to wholeness. They called this Ḥanukkah, "thus did they camp," because here they attained true rest. Wholeness is the peace and rest of coming back to one's root, as I have explained elsewhere.

All this shows that were it not for the evil forces and the wicked who cover over the power of holiness, Israel would be ready to ascend to the highest rung, to cleave to the Root above. But "darkness covers the earth" (Is. 60:2). As soon as they overpowered the Hellenists, they were blessed in a single moment and enabled to cleave to that Root above.

This should console our generations as well. Even though we see how lowly we are, how we sink lower and lower in each generation, we retain our hope that in a single moment, when the time of redemption comes, we may, with God's help, be carried all the way back to wholeness.

1:211

Here the miracle of the Ḥanukkah lights is interpreted symbolically, as it properly should be. The bit of oil that remained, miraculously lasting eight days, stands for the bit of strength that was present in the Jews, allowing them to last out the struggle with a much stronger enemy. In this hasidic version it is the bit of holiness still within them, despite the violations of Judaism imposed by the Greeks, that blossomed forth into true wholeness as soon as the oppression was removed.

But this reading, like many interpretations of the Passover, Ḥanukkah, and Purim stories, bears within it the dark side of our tradition as well. We survived many centuries of oppression because we were sure that God was with us and our enemies were all incarnations of evil. That "black and white" vision lends great strength but also has its dangers. In our own era, now that we are not an oppressed group, we have an obligation to expand it and become conscious of the many gradations of gray. Can we do that and still maintain the strength we had when we knew so clearly that we were God's only candle in this world, shining forth against all incarnations of evil?

PURIM

1

[On Purim we sing:] "You have been their salvation forever; their hope from one generation to the next."

The salvation on Purim was eternal, for all generations. Just as the decree was "to destroy all the Jews" (Esth. 3:13), so does the miracle apply to all generations. The Jewish people exists only by virtue of this miracle. It has been taught that in this case there was a heavenly decree against the Jews, but that God acted miraculously without regard to their merit. Only because we are His people, trusting in Him always, did He have to save us at this time. That is why this holiday gives us such strength and hope, throughout our exile, to trust in God simply because we are joined to Him.

This seems to be why one is obligated to become so drunk on Purim that one cannot tell the difference between "Blessed be Mordecai!" and "Cursed be Haman!" We thereby show that this day has nothing at all to do with our merit. It is called Purim because of the casting of lots; the fate [of destruction] was entirely natural and appropriate, the forces of evil having been strengthened by our own sins. God saved us out of love alone. . . .

It is taught that Purim is like the Day of Atonement, called *Yom Ki-Purim*. On Yom Kippur we reach beyond the natural state by negating our bodies, by abstaining from food and drink. This brings us to a certain freedom, one where transgressions are forgiven. On Purim we get to the same place by means of drinking and merrymaking, all with the help of God, not because of our own deeds.

2:179

Some parts of the teaching seem not to be recorded, but can be inferred from the connections made. The parallel between Purim and Yom Kippur is widespread, especially in hasidic sources. Some express the hope that on Yom Kippur God will become so intoxicated by "drinking" the prayers of Israel that He will no longer be able to distinguish between the righteous and the wicked, and thus have to save us all. Here the hopeful claim seems to be that on Yom Kippur God will perform a miracle similar to that of Purim, a time when He ignored the question of merit and saved all Israel out of love alone.

2

The Talmud says we should be so intoxicated on Purim that we cannot distinguish "Blessed be Mordecai!" from "Cursed be Haman!" I heard my grandfather and teacher say that one has to rise to a place higher than the Tree of Knowledge of Good and Evil. I don't recall it all in its proper order [!]. But the point was that the tree Haman prepared for Mordecai's hanging was fifty cubits high, one higher than the forty-nine measures of defilement and purification. The power of

Amalek is found on all those levels, [where one can be either pure or impure]. But the fiftieth gate is that of holiness; there are no two ways there, but only that of goodness, for that is the root of oneness. That is why it says [in the battle against Amalek]: "When Moses lifted his hand, Israel was victorious" (Ex. 17:11), for he raised it toward the fiftieth gate, the Tree of Life, which is the Torah.

When the power of Moses, Prince of Torah, is awakened, Amalek is defeated. That is why we are told that on Purim there was another receiving of Torah, the revelation of that Tree of Life. That is a place that does not know about "Blessed be Mordecai" and "Cursed be Haman," since evil does not reach there at all, to the root of unity.

The intoxication of Purim also reminds us of the sweet fragrances with which the world was filled as the Ten Commandments were spoken. The fragrance of myrrh and *deror* is referred to in Aramaic as *marey dakhia,* as my grandfather used to say. That is Mordecai, the bearer of Moses' light, the root of Torah.

2:181

Purim here becomes a third festival of revelation. On Shavu'ot the original written Torah was revealed; because its light was too great for mortals to bear, the tablets had to be broken. Yom Kippur is the day of the second tablets, the Torah as restored by human participation in the revelatory event; it is thus the source of oral Torah. Purim hints at a third level, the revelation of a Torah beyond rules and statutes, Torah as the Tree of Life itself. This Torah is purely mystical; it is the name of God, that which was before the beginning and will finally be revealed only at the end. That is why we are taught that Purim, unlike the other holidays, will continue to exist even in messianic times.

3

It is taught that all the holidays will be canceled in the [messianic] future, except for Purim, of which Scripture explicitly says: "These Purim days will not pass away from among the Jews, and their memory will not cease amid their descendants" (Esth. 9:28). The holidays depend upon Israel, as it says: "These are the holy assemblies that you shall call . . . " (Lev. 23:4). It is Israel who sanctify these days, unlike the Sabbath, which is established as a holy day [since God's rest in Creation]. Israel draw holiness into the course of time; "holy assemblies" are "calling forth the holy" *(mikra'ey kodesh)*.

In the future there will be a "day that is all Sabbath," transcending time itself. Then, as a matter of course, the holidays will be negated. "Who needs a candle at noontime?" The same is true of the rabbis' teaching that the commandments will be abolished in the future. This does not mean, God forbid, that anything in the Torah will be negated. They will be abolished [because of the greater light,] like the light of a candle next to a great torch. "Torah is light and the commandment is a candle" (Prov. 6:23): when the light of Torah, the root of all commandments, will be revealed, the lesser light of the commandments will be obliterated.

But in this world the deeds of Israel are beloved of God, for this is a world of darkness. The holidays are still of great importance, those "three times a year when you appear" (Deut. 16:16), since it is because of them that holiness exists in this world. But on "the day that is all Sabbath," when holiness is revealed from above, the holiness that we arouse by our deeds will be set aside.

But on Purim holiness was revealed without human deeds; therefore, it will exist forever. Like the Sabbath, it does not depend upon the actions of those below.

2:191f.

This aligning of Purim with Shabbat is somewhat strange. The Sabbath is holy in itself because it dates from before *history; Purim is instituted by Esther and through the authority of the sages who lived* after *the sacred times of the Torah. On the face of things, Purim seems to be the most secular of Jewish holidays, a time when salvation takes place through human cunning and without benefit of divine interference at all.*

Of course the hasidic tradition cannot see it this way. Because providence here is hidden, it must be of a higher order, entirely transcending the realm of human action. Here too, as in the preceding teaching, Purim points to a higher realm, the nature of which will be revealed only in the mysterious future.

PESAḤ

1

The holiday of Pesaḥ is called Shabbat in the Torah, as in "from the day after the Sabbath" (Lev. 23:15). Pesaḥ is like Shabbat, of which Scripture says "remember" and "keep." Of Pesaḥ too it says: "this day will be a remembrance for you" (Ex. 12:14) or "so that you remember the day you came out of Egypt" (Deut. 16:3) and "Keep the month of Aviv" (Deut. 16:1); "Keep the matzot" (Ex. 12:17). For memory is a point within, one where there is no forgetfulness. Since this point is revealed within the souls of Israel on Shabbat, it has to be "kept" or guarded from flowing into that place where forgetting occurs. That is why "keep" and "remember" were said [in the Ten Commandments] in a single utterance.

The same is true of the redemption from Egypt. On every Pesaḥ a Jew becomes like a new person, like the newborn child each of us was as we came forth from Egypt. The point implanted by God within our hearts is renewed. That point is called *leḥem 'oni* (poor people's bread), because it is totally without expansion. Matzah is just the dough itself, not having changed through fermentation. Every Jew has this inner place, the gift of God. Our task is really to expand that point, to draw all our deeds to follow it. This is our job throughout the year, for better or worse. But this holiday of matzot is the time when the point itself is renewed, purified from any defilement. Therefore, it has to be guarded from any "ferment" or change on this holiday.

"Keep the matzot, for on this very day I brought the children of Israel forth from the land of Egypt" (Ex. 12:17)—*be-'etsem* ("this *very* day") refers to that inward point, just as it is in itself *(be-'atsmo)*, without any change. This is why it needs "keeping." "This day is a remembrance"—for the renewal of that point within, the point of memory. One could also read it "a remembrance" indeed, a day that reminds us of the real reason we were created in this world: to do His will. . . .

3:99

The liberation from Egypt happened to Israel be-'etsem, *"in their very selves." Here, no place is given to the old debate between those who first want to transform the inner life or renew the human spirit and those who believe first in alleviating the social and economic woes of humanity. In this paradigmatic event of liberation, both take place at once: both the souls and the bodies of Israel become free. Of course the biblical tale is somewhat different. They may be free* be-'etsem *from this moment, but the realization and acceptance of that freedom will take forty hard years and the passing of a strife-torn generation.*

2

"Even if we were all wise, all understanding, and all knowing the Torah, we would still be commanded to tell of the Exodus from Egypt. And one who goes to great lengths in telling this tale is considered all the more praiseworthy." Scripture tells us: "When you bring the people forth from Egypt you shall serve God . . . " (Ex. 3:12), and also: "I am the Lord your God who brought you forth from the land of Egypt to become your God" (Num. 15:41).

This process is renewed each year: Pesaḥ is the season of our freedom. This is the meaning of [the verse:] "You are My servant Israel, in whom I take pride" (Is. 49:3). Afterwards, on Shavu'ot, is the time when our Torah is given. Torah is renewed on Shavu'ot in accordance with the freedom that has been awakened on Pesaḥ. Something like this happens every single day as well, as we recall both coming forth from Egypt and receiving the Torah. Even though we have already received the Torah, there is still a renewed revelation of Torah in each generation, each year, and each day—a revelation peculiar to that time. That is why freedom, too, needs to be renewed each year; through this we are able to renew our acceptance of divinity.

"To become your God"—this is something that takes place in the present and is forever happening anew.

3:103

The relationship of liberation from Egypt to the revelation at Sinai is here taken to a point of abstraction from the concrete historical circumstances. Every person, at all times, must first become free; only then can he or she hear the word of God and enter into the sacred covenant.

The constancy of this ordering, repeated for every nation and for each individual, has great significance for a Jewish social ethic. We cannot expect a person or a group to come to responsible commitment or to true community until they are first liberated from the Egypt that binds them, however com-

plex or subtle their enslavement might be. Our Jewish role should encourage others to follow this ordering: to support people's need for liberation and to help them move from Egypt to Sinai, from the exultation of being free to hearing the commanding voice that calls for community based on mutual caring and shared symbols that evoke the divine presence.

As individuals as well, each of us needs to renew this process each year, each day: to declare first our freedom from bondage and then our free choice for love and commitment.

3

"The more one tells about the Exodus from Egypt, the more praiseworthy." For the Exodus from Egypt never ends, as Scripture says: "[So that you will remember the day when you went out of Egypt] all the days of your life" (Deut. 16:3). In the act of telling about the Exodus, the miracle itself is continually fulfilled and enhanced. Since this tale of the Exodus is a section of Torah, it has to go on forever. That is why the rabbis added to the tale, saying that there were really fifty plagues rather than ten, and even more. Now, they felt, the fifty could be revealed, while previously they had been hidden within the ten. That's what telling the tale does: it keeps drawing out further potential. The real point of the story is that we are liberated from the force of evil. The root of that force was back there in Egypt, but the specifics of our liberation are worked out each year.

3:69

The root of evil is the enslavement and the degradation of the human spirit, the denial, inherent in slavery, that each human being is the image of God. That principle is constant and unchanging; we are as committed to it now as we were on the day we left Egypt. But the many ways in which that evil force manifests itself, the human communities still crying out for liberation from bondage, the subtleties of enslavement even among those who think they are free, the new categories of evil and degradation we had failed to notice for so long—all these need to be discovered and worked out each year. In this sense our liberation from bondage is truly an eternal process, one that continues to grow through the telling and through our deeds.

 4

"The wise son says: 'What are these testimonies and statutes. . . ?' And you answer him: 'One does not conclude the Pesaḥ feast with *afikoman.*'"

It is written: "I remember the devotion of your youth, your love as a bride—how you followed Me in the wilderness, in a land not sown" (Jer. 2:2). When we came out of Egypt, we as yet had no comprehension of the ways of Torah or the commandments, not until God gave us the Torah and bestowed upon us other fine qualities. When we left Egypt, the main thing was to go forth into freedom. Thus we entered the category of those who serve God.

So it is every year in this season of our freedom: every Jew is made a free person and is redeemed from all bondage, from all that binds us to worldly vanities. Later, on Shavu'ot, the giving of the Torah is reawakened. That is why the wise son, who is ever ready to enter the gates of wisdom and awareness, understands that this night is the gate of freedom and nothing more. So he asks what all the joy is for, since we have already attained much more than that [i.e., we already have received the Torah, the stage beyond liberation]. The answer, "One does not conclude the Pesaḥ feast with *afikoman*," means that right now this joy of freedom goes beyond everything else. This is [the meaning of the verse:] "You followed Me in the wilderness, in a land not sown." Don't ask for anything more than to be drawn after His blessed divine rule.

That is why the haggadah refers to [the verse:] "How many great gifts God has given us," [the first of which is,] "Had God only brought us out of Egypt . . . it would be enough." It was through this act of coming forth into freedom that we got to all the rest. Therefore, the haggadah goes on to speak of "How much greater is the redoubled good that God has done for us, taking us out of Egypt," and so forth. Coming out of Egypt was a double gift, for through it we came to all the rest.

How much more true is this in our own exile! All we long for is redemption! Of this we say: "Draw me after you, let us run!" (Cant. 1:4), just as we were drawn after God in that unsown land, knowing nothing of Torah or mitsvot. But now that "the king has [already] brought me into his chambers" (ibid.), certainly "we will delight and rejoice in you" (ibid.). Surely we will now follow You into the unsown land; "as in the days when you came forth from Egypt will I show him wonders" (Mic. 7:15). So the redemption of the future will also be followed by a sojourn into an unsown land, for a new path will be created. Of this, Scripture says: "A new teaching will come forth from Me" (cf. Is. 51:4).

3:86f.

In this passage and some others like it, the Sefat Emet appears as a precursor of Rabbi Abraham Isaac Kook (1865–1935), one who well understood that the new liberation of Israel taking place in modern times would require "a new teaching," as already predicted in our ancient sources. Like the successors of the Sefat Emet, however, Kook remained very much a conservative in practice; their "new teaching" was indeed theologically radical, but that barely touched their views on halakhah.

For those of us who live on the far side of that great divide, the stakes are infinitely higher. We indeed are waiting to discover, or for God to reveal, the new teaching. Until that teaching is revealed, however, faithfulness to divine guidance "in the unsown land" is all we have.

 5

"In every generation a person should see himself as one who had come forth from Egypt." Shortly afterward the haggadah says: "He brought *us* out from there."

By means of faith that the Exodus takes place in each generation, such an event is truly revealed. The MaHaRaL of Prague wrote that in a collective sense each Jew was indeed there at the Exodus from Egypt, but he "should see himself as though he had come forth" as an individual ["in each generation"].

The fact is that faith draws us into the collective; surely the redemption from Egypt happened to that collective body, to the "point of Jewishness" from which each Jew draws life. We come to awareness of this, however, only through faith.

But once you see yourself as though having come forth from Egypt, knowing that the awareness you have could not have come to you without your leaving Egypt, you begin to understand how that "leaving" really happens.

That is why the haggadah says: "Even if we are all wise, all understanding, all knowing the Torah, it is incumbent upon us to tell of the Exodus from Egypt." Even a wise person, one attached to the living God, has to realize that this has come about because he has left Egypt. This is the truth, but we need to make it clear to ourselves by means of faith.

"Telling" *(sippur)* of the Exodus can also mean "making pure" or "shining." We reveal with absolute clarity that there is an Exodus in every generation, according to the need of that generation. All this was there at the moment of the [first] Exodus from Egypt. The more you have faith that you are as one redeemed from Egypt, the more this redemption is actually revealed. Then you will feel the present redemption, each one coming forth from his own straits.

3:45

The various commentaries on the haggadah often seem to wrestle with the question of whether Passover is a commemoration of a historical event that once was or an actual reliving of the Exodus in the present. The hasidic commentators prefer the latter explanation: each of us must come forth from our own straits, and that is the true and ever-recurring Exodus from Egypt. Here the Sefat Emet tries to reconcile the two views, seeing faith as the bridge that transforms the historic event of the past, one in which we all took part in a general and collective sense, into the spiritual event of the present, one that can happen to each person only in his or her own way.

 6

"Then Moses and the children of Israel sang" (Ex. 15:1). After the exile, after the redemption: now they understood that the whole process had taken place so that the rule of heaven be manifest. When it says "They had faith in the Lord and in His servant Moses" (Ex. 14:31), it means that they looked back at the whole of their exile and accepted it in love. Their song was about the whole thing; they even sang to God for hardening Pharaoh's heart [thus prolonging their suffering]! They sang: "The enemy said: 'I shall pursue, catch up, divide the spoils, consume them, put them to the sword, destroy them by my hand'" (Ex.15:9). For this too they offered praise, for they saw that it had all led to greater glorification of the name of God. This is how Moses gave them strength, saying: "Stand firm and see the salvation of the Lord" (Ex. 14:13). Once they heard that all would be for God's glory, they accepted it all in love.

We need to know the same thing in this present exile, as Scripture says: "As in the days when you came out of Egypt, I will show you wonders" (Mic. 7:15).

3:68

This was said on Pesaḥ in 1882, the year after the pogroms began in Russia. Some day, he says, after the redemption, we will understand that it was all for God's glory, and in retrospect we will accept it all in love.

Could he have said this after 1945? What would we say of one who did? Would we call it faith, folly, or blasphemy?

7

In the Midrash on the Song of Songs: "Let us sing to the One who made us like princes in the world!" "This people I formed to tell of My glory" (Is. 43:21).

When they came out of Egypt, Israel were re-formed, like new creatures set aside to manifest the kingdom of God in the world. This is why we tell the tale of liberation from Egypt, bearing witness each day to our Creator. This act of manifesting God's kingdom depends upon the inner work we do in our hearts, as we make clear in our hearts how our deeds are joined to God.

We do this [especially] in the days of counting, as it says: "Count for yourselves" [or "Tell yourselves"—*u-SeFaRtem/ ve-SiPpaRtem*].

The entire Song of Songs is based on this: Israel creating light by their deeds, drawing all things in the world to their Root, raising them up as with pleasing scent to the Lord. We see this especially on this holiday and in the telling of the tale, "so that you remember the days when you came out of Egypt all the days of your life" (Deut. 16:3). "Remembering" means "mentioning" orally; the telling of this night gives us the power to continue "telling the tale" all year long. . . .

3:65

Here the telling of the Exodus tale is uplifted from the realm of ritual to become, as in the Bible itself, a description of the sacred task of Israel throughout our lives. Each day, by our deeds as inspired by our words, *we are to tell the world that God brought us slaves out of Egypt and that we have not forgotten!*

The religious life that stems from this imperative is one that most of us have hardly begun to live, but one that calls upon us from the pages of Scripture as it does from the Sefat Emet.

SHAVU'OT

1

"On the day of the first-fruits, as you offer a new gift to the Lord . . ." (Num. 28:26).

God created the world through Torah. Therefore, the inner life of all creatures is the power of beginning that derives from Torah. Thus the sages taught: "[God created the world] for the sake of Torah, which is called 'beginning'." Or, as Scripture says: "He declared to His people the power of His acts" (Ps. 111:6), for Torah is the original power of creation. Creation was in such a fashion, however, that this inwardness was hidden. Now, with the giving of Torah, it was revealed, and everything became joined to its root.

This is the meaning of "Face to face [or 'Facing inward'] God spoke to you" (Deut. 5:4). So, too, their statement: "With every word the whole world filled up with spices." This also explains [the verse:] "Torah was divided into seventy languages." It is all as we have said, for then the life-force of Torah was drawn forth and revealed to all creatures.

The Ten Commandments (lit.: "words") are parallel to the ten utterances [of Creation], as the holy Zohar says. But the "utterance" is silent and secret, while the "word" is revealed. "The king's word" is his rule. Then it was revealed that the power of Torah gives life to all and rules over all that is. The most essential "receiving of the Torah" was this revelation. That is why the Targum translates "The Lord *descended* upon Mount Sinai" (Ex. 19:20) as "was revealed." God fills the entire world, but until then it was hidden.

That is why this day is called "the day of the first-fruits." Everything now becomes attached to its beginning and is in this way renewed. Thus, too, it says: "He renews in His goodness each day the work of Creation." "His goodness," the rabbis explain, is Torah, since the inner life-force of Creation comes from Torah. Each day, to be sure, Creation is renewed, but in a hidden way. On Shavu'ot it is more revealed. The evil urge is negated on this day, since it is revealed that even the life-force that animates the demonic side comes from that inner point. . . .

4:22

The real revelation of Torah is the uncovering of the great secret of existence: that everything is animated by the single life-force that derives from the word of God. We are not given a Torah that is in any way separate from that which we are given in Creation itself. Torah is the key that unlocks the hidden meaning of all existence. As such, Torah has to be manifest in seventy languages and accessible to all God's creatures. While this interpretation of revelation is offered in a deeply Jewish context, its understanding of revelation's true meaning gives it an inevitably universalist tone. The Sefat Emet shows us once again that these two values do not have to stand in conflict with each other.

2

"Face to face the Lord spoke to you" (Deut. 5:4).

It is taught: "May the good one [Moses] come and receive the good [Torah] from the Good [God] for the good [Israel]."

The inwardness of all things is good. It has only been admixed with evil because of sin. But the hour when the Torah was given was one of complete freedom. The hidden goodness was then distinguished, just as in [the verse:] "God saw that the light was good and He distinguished between light and darkness" (Gen. 1:4). He hid the light away for the righteous.

It is also written: "God is good to all" (Ps. 145:9). This means that God is good to the whole. When it says: "Assemble the people for Me" (Deut. 4:10), referred to as the day of assembly, we are told that "Israel encamped there facing the mountain" (Ex. 19:2). The verb *encamped* is singular, for they were "like a single person." That is why inwardness, which is called the good, was revealed to them.

Torah is called "good," but the inwardness of Israel's own souls is also goodness. That is the oral Torah, of which it is written: "He implanted eternal life within us." This is the meaning of "I am the Lord *your* God" (Ex. 20:2)—the portion of the transcendent God hidden within every Jewish person.

It is written: "The Lord is my strength and the source of my strength" (Jer. 16:19). Torah is called strength. This refers to the power [to create] oral Torah, placed by God into the very essence of Israel's souls. Not only that—He continually keeps adding power and strength to Israel. That is why He is both "my strength" and "source of my strength"—the strength that is within me also comes from Him! These are the two loaves that get waved about on this day, to show that Israel's portion, the oral Torah, also comes from God.

Scripture says: "All the people saw the thunder and lightning, the shofar sound and the smoking mountain; the people saw, trembled, and stood far off" (Ex. 20:18). Why does the word "saw" have to be repeated? Because through these light-visions their own selves were revealed to them. The sages read "face to face" as a mirror: each one saw his own form. This is the meaning of "face to face is as in water" (Prov. 27:19). As the inner person is revealed to Torah, so is each Jew's inward portion in Torah revealed to us. Every Jew has a particular portion within Torah; that is why Torah appears to us as water, [reflecting our own souls].

That is why we are told that Israel's souls passed out of them [at Sinai]: each saw through the holy spirit the root of his or her own soul above. That is why they trembled, so excited [were they] at the realization that while they were yet in this lowly world, their form was engraved above. Israel at Sinai were like the souls that first come into this world, as they are adjured: "Be righteous, not wicked!" We, too, are adjured since Sinai to keep the Torah. Just as those souls come into this world against their will, so did Torah restore the souls of Israel against their will, for they had attached themselves [above], because of so much love. "My soul leapt forth as he spoke" (Cant. 5:6).

4:30

This teaching could serve as a fine introduction to the religious philosophy of the Sefat Emet. There is a single inward goodness, or Godliness, of which God, Torah, and the souls of Israel all partake. Torah and the moment of its revelation are the means through which Israel discover that their own souls are of the essence of that same goodness, on the innermost level not separated from God and Torah. This includes the oral teachings they create throughout all generations: these, too, are part of that same goodness. This realization brings Israel to ecstatic "death" in the passionate love aroused by this ultimate self-discovery; they have to be forcibly revived at Sinai so that they go on living in this world, even while knowing the true nature of their own souls.

 3

We have a prayer that says: "May He open our hearts in His Torah, placing His love and awe in our hearts, so that we not sin." The Talmud, [referring to one who has learning but no awe,] says: "Woe to the one who has no dwelling-place but makes himself a gateway for a dwelling." All of wisdom and Torah is but an entrance-way into "Awe before the Lord; that is his treasure" (Is. 33:6). Once Israel's hearts are opened by the power of Torah, they are able to receive awe and love. . . .

In this way I heard my grandfather explain why they established that the Scroll of Ruth be read on Shavu'ot. People say that the main thing is "study and prayer." Prayer is derived from King David, of blessed memory. David *[malkhut]* also represents awe, showing that "if there is no awe, there is no wisdom."

4:30

Here is a very powerful statement that undercuts the Torah-centeredness that we are likely to feel on Shavu'ot. It reminds us, even at this moment, that Torah-learning is instrumental, not an end in itself. This awareness is maintained throughout Hasidism, even in the very learned and study-centered circles represented by the Sefat Emet. The Book of Ruth, culminating in the birth of David, is a counterpoint to the Torah reading of this day, showing us that all of Torah is only a gateway, one that leads to the real work of opening our hearts in joyous love and awe.

The teaching implies a reversal of the usual kabbalistic symbols. Here, based on a Talmudic passage, Torah-learning [hokhmah] *is shown to be a gateway to awe* [malkhut], *showing once again the circular quality of God's sefirot.*

 4

With regard to the reading of Ruth on Shavu'ot:

This is a matter of oral Torah. The blessed Holy One asks of Israel that by their deeds they add on to the written Torah, since the deeds of the righteous are Torah. Out of the deeds of Boaz and Ruth, this scroll was composed in the holy spirit.

The Torah says: "God spoke all these words, saying" (Ex. 20:1). The "saying" [or "to say"] means that Israel should say words like these of their own accord. That is why we bless the One "who gave us the true Torah and implanted eternal life within us." This is the oral Torah, and it is in this sense that Torah particularly belongs to Israel. They have a special awareness for comprehending secrets of Torah, things that are not explicit in the text.

This itself is the matter of Boaz. His name means *bo 'oz* [lit.: "strength (= Torah) is within him"]. He believed the sages when they said that an Ammonite, but not an Ammonitess, and a Moabite, but not a Moabitess, to be kept outside the community of Israel. He had no doubts about it, unlike the other fellow who said: "Lest I destroy my own inheritance" (Ruth 4:6). Boaz, by contrast, was happy to show that the interpretation of the sages *is* the Torah that was given from Sinai. Faith in the sages is the basis of oral Torah. . . .

4:23

This idea that the deeds of the righteous themselves make Torah, and that the oral Torah is composed of those deeds, is one that appears several times in the Sefat Emet. *This is an original notion, derived from the hasidic view that the* tsaddik *is an embodiment of Torah and that one can learn from all his deeds. The "sages" who created Torah in rabbinic times are seen already by earlier hasidic authors as the* tsaddikim *of their generations. But our author takes the notion further in saying that oral Torah is an actual recording of the deeds of the patriarchs, prophets, and other holy Jews of ancient times, going beyond their interpretation of the written Torah. Boaz represents this oral Torah as one who understands that he has Torah within his own self, waiting to be recorded and preserved as he leads his holy life.*

This is also a halakhically courageous Boaz, one willing to stake his life on his faith that the sages in each generation have the power to interpret and even restrict the meaning of Torah. Would that more teachers of Torah in our day had such courage!

5

"Face to face the Lord spoke to you" (Deut. 5:4). The Midrash likens them to a teacher, the one who gives, and the pupil, who receives.

The blessed Holy One both gives the Torah and gives Israel the power to receive Torah. Everything comes from Him! Israel's readiness for Torah is itself a unique form of God's grace: there they were, face to face with God, prepared to receive the commandments.

This came about by means of Moses our Teacher, as Scripture says: "I stand between the Lord and you" (Deut. 5:5). This, too, is aroused each year, and that is why "stand" is in the present tense, not the past.

The waving of the two loaves of bread on Shavu'ot has the same meaning: they represent "bread from heaven" and "bread from the earth," the written Torah and the oral Torah. Both giving and receiving are awakened on this day.

4:25f.

Here only fragments of a much longer homily are preserved. The point is that everything comes from God, who both gives us the Torah and gives us the power to receive it. We think of revelation as a dialogue, one side giving and the other receiving. But in fact there is only one: God gives and God (operating within us) receives.

This teaching is attested by the comments on the two loaves: we might think that bread from heaven (manna) is the gift of God and bread from the earth our own product. But we thank God as the One "who brings forth bread from the earth," showing that both forms of food are equally divine gifts. So too the written Torah, given directly from heaven, and the oral Torah, that which seems to well up from within our own minds. They, as he has already frequently reminded us, are gifts too, one being "implanted within us" by the hand of God.

6

All [the Talmudic authorities] agree that the Torah was given on the Sabbath, since Scripture says: *"Remember the Sabbath day"* (Ex. 20:8), referring to that very day.

The essence of receiving the Torah is that Israel's souls were drawn near to their own "place" and source, as in [the verses:] "Face to face the Lord spoke to you" (Deut. 5:4) and "I am the Lord your God" (Ex. 20:2), when each one saw and understood the divine power that God had placed within each soul of Israel.

This is the true meaning of the holy Sabbath, the rest and cessation *(SHeBiTah)* when each thing returns to its place and root; that is why it is called *SHaBBaT.* Scripture calls upon us to "remember" the Sabbath day. But "remember" applies only to something that you have already experienced once. Because the revelation, this true "Sabbath," had happened once as Israel received the Torah, God calls upon us to remember it always.

Now it is true that the principle of Sabbath was given before Sinai, at Marah. But now [at the revelation] [the people] felt the holiness of Sabbath right in their souls. This is the true "added soul" that every Jew gains on the holy Sabbath; it comes about through . . . being "bound together in secret oneness" on the Sabbath. It is an "inheritance of the *assembly* of Jacob" (Deut. 33:4).

4:28f.

Here the key themes discussed above are attached to teachings around the Sabbath. The weekly day of rest is a time of returning to our own deepest selves and to the primal experience we have all had of standing before God at Sinai.

Said in broader terms, religion begins with the primal experience of closeness or identification with the One. Since we are fated, for better and worse, to live our lives in this world of multiplicity and fragmentation, however, we are given the gift of moments of cessation, regular times to return to the oneness of all being. In that sense Shabbat truly is what the rabbis said: a gift from God's own store of treasures.

=== **7** =================

On Shavu'ot there are two sorts of drawing near. The hearts of Israel draw near to God, and the Everpresent draws close to Israel. These two forms of closeness are the two loaves that are waved on this day.

We Jews glory in this day by calling it "the day of the giving of our Torah," [referring to God's closeness to us]. But God, in the Torah, delights in the closeness of Israel's hearts to heaven, so there this day is called "the day of offering the first fruits."

4:27

Each lover calls the day after receiving gifts from the beloved.

GLOSSARY

aggadah narrative; the portions of rabbinic corpus that deal with narrative and interpretive, rather than legal, matters.

'akedah the binding of Isaac.

'Amidah lit. "standing"; the central prayer of rabbinic Judaism, recited while standing each morning, dusk, and evening. Seen as a verbal "offering" to replace the ancient Temple sacrifices.

'avodah lit. "service"; worship, especially regular prayer and daily devotion.

Ba'al Shem Tov R. Israel ben Eliezer (1700–1760), mystic and healer, the first central figure of Hasidism in its later eastern European form.

berit covenant, especially the covenant of circumcision.

bittul self-negation; the overcoming of ego required for mystical insight.

bushah shame; embarrassment.

derekh erets lit. "the way of the world"; respect, proper behavior, the unspoken rules of conduct that should be known even to those who have no knowledge of Torah.

emet "truth"; said by the rabbis to be the seal of God.

Erets Yisra'el the Land of Israel; the Holy Land.

galut exile, designating the geographical, political, and metaphysical condition of Israel.

gan 'eden "the Garden of Eden," referring either to the biblical paradise or to the dwelling-place of righteous souls after death.

ger (-im) proselyte, one who converts to Judaism.

HaBaD lit. H*okhmah* ("wisdom"), B*inah* ("understanding"), D*a'at* ("awareness"); a type of intellectual Hasidism associated primarily with the Belorussian Lubavitch dynasty, beginning with R. Shne'ur Zalman of Liadi (1745–1813).

haftarah portion from the writings of Israel's ancient prophets, read each Sabbath and festival following the reading from the Torah.

halakhah lit. "the way"; Jewish religious law.

Hallel a collection of Psalms of thanksgiving, recited with joy on festivals and new moon days.

Hasid (-im) lit. "devotee"; in the context of Hasidism, a follower of one of the hasidic rebbes.

Haskalah lit. "enlightenment"; the movement of Westernization and modernization among Jews in Europe, beginning in the late eighteenth century.

ḥiyyut the life-force; the presence of divine life-energy within all things.

ḥuppah the canopy under which bride and groom stand during the wedding ceremony.

Kabbalah lit. "that which is received; tradition"; the speculative and theosophical aspects of Jewish mysticism, based on texts dating from the twelfth century.

kashrut lit. "fitness"; the Jewish dietary code.

kavvanah lit. "direction" or "intent"; the direction of the heart toward God in prayer; more generally, inwardness or religious intensity.

kelipot lit. "shells"; outer husks or demonic forces that separate humans from God. In Hasidism they are seen mostly in psychological terms.

lulav the palm branch carried and waved as part of the Sukkot festival celebration.

MaHaRaL R. Judah Loew of Prague (1525–1609), influential preacher and exegete.

makom lit. "place"; also used as a name of God in early rabbinic sources.

mal'akh lit. "messenger"; an angel.

malkhut lit. "kingdom"; the last of the ten *sefirot*; symbolically identical with Shekhinah and various other female-associated terms, seen by kabbalists as the female consort of the blessed Holy One.

maskil (**-im**) an "enlightened" one, meaning a Westernized or modernized Jew, opposed to Hasidism.

mezuzah a parchment inscription, containing two portions of the *Shema'*, placed on the doorposts and gates of Jewish homes.

midrash the process of rabbinic interpretation of biblical texts, including significant elaboration, expansion, cross-matching of verses, etc., as well as the literary works containing such interpretations.

mikveh ritual bath, used for immersion by proselytes, by women following completion of their menstrual cycle, and (mostly by hasidic men) in preparation for prayer or for entry into a more holy time or place.

Mishnah the early rabbinic code of Jewish praxis, around which the Talmud was formed.

mishkan lit. "dwelling-place"; the portable tabernacle erected by the Israelites during their wandering in the wilderness.

mitnaggedim lit. "opponents"; the rabbinic opponents to Hasidism, chiefly in the late eighteenth century; by extension, pious eastern European non-hasidic Jews.

mitsvah commandment, one of the 613 obligations of the Torah; by extension, a good deed.

mussar chastisement regarding proper behavior, emphasizing ethics. The Mussar Movement was a revival of ethical pietism among mitnaggedic Jews in the late nineteenth century.

nefesh soul, from a word originally meaning "self"; considered by the rabbis to be the lowest portion of the tripartite soul, the life-force itself.

Ne'ilah the concluding service of Yom Kippur, recited just at sunset, the time of the "locking" of the Temple gates.

nekudah point; used to designate the inward point of godliness within each Jew and within all things.

nes miracle. A well-known play on words also associates it with the word for "banner."

neshamah soul, from a term meaning "breath"; the highest or divine portion of the human soul.

nigleh the "revealed" Torah; nonesoteric aspects of the Jewish tradition, especially talmudic law.

nistar the "hidden" Torah, referring primarily to Kabbalah.

'omer originally an ancient grain-measure; refers to the period of fifty days between Passover and Shavu'ot, a time when each day is counted, in anticipation of the renewal of the revelation at Sinai.

parashah lit. "section"; the Torah reading assigned to a particular week in the yearly cycle.

partsufim the reconfiguration of the ten kabbalistic *sefirot* into five "faces" or aspects of divinity, rooted in parts of the Zohar corpus but central to kabbalistic thought after Isaac Luria (1534–1572).

RaSHI Rabbi *SH*elomo *I*tshaki (1040–1105); French rabbi, the leading rabbinic commentator to both Bible and Talmud.

rebbe hasidic leader or master.

ruah spirit; the intermediary level of the tripartite human soul.

Sanhedrin the court of seventy-one elders, which served in antiquity as the high court of rabbinic law.

Sefer Yetsirah an early (third–eighth century) short speculative treatise on cosmology and language, later used by both philosophers and mystics in the development of their thought and terminology.

sefirot the ten emanations of divinity that form the basis of symbolic thought within Kabbalah.

se'udah shelishit lit. "third meal"; the concluding meal of the Sabbath, generally held communally among hasidim, a time of special communal intensity.

Shekhinah lit. "indwelling"; the Divine presence in this world; in Kabbalah, the feminine aspect of divinity that unites with the blessed Holy One.

Shema' a collation of three Torah passages, beginning with the line, "Hear, O Israel, YHWH our God, YHWH is One," recited twice daily at the center of traditional Jewish worship.

shi'ur komah a series of ancient Hebrew writings, now preserved only in fragments, concerning the supposedly gargantuan measurements of a divine ethereal body.

shofar ram's horn, blown as part of the Rosh Hashanah service.

shtetl town (Yiddush); the typically Jewish-dominated small town of eastern Europe, in which most Jews of the region lived before 1880.

Sifre an ancient rabbinic midrash on the books of Numbers and Deuteronomy.

sukkah the frail outdoor booth in which Jews are to dwell during the fall harvest festival of Sukkot.

ta'anit dibbur a "speech fast"; a period of time for which a person takes on silence as a religious obligation.

tallit a fringed shawl worn during prayer.

tefillin phylacteries, leather boxes containing passages from the Torah, tied to the head and arms by straps, worn during weekday morning prayers.

teshuvah lit. "return"; repentance, the return to God of those who have strayed; hence also, for the mystics, the longing of all things to return to their single Source.

tikkun lit. "fixing"; the redemptive process, the restoration of cosmic wholeness.

tish lit. "table" (Yiddush); the public Sabbath or holiday table conducted by hasidic rabbis, at which discourses were offered.

tsaddik (-im) lit. "righteous one"; hasidic master or holy man.

tsimtsum lit. "contraction"; the withdrawal of divine light that preceded creation, allowing for an empty "space" in which the non-God might exist.

vort, gut vort lit. "word," "good word" (Yiddush); an aphorism or brief but witty hasidic teaching.

yeshivah academy for higher-level Torah study.

YHWH the tetragrammaton or the mysterious, unpronounceable four-letter name of God.

Zohar the chief work of medieval Kabbalah, composed in Spain in the late thirteenth century; revered as a canonical holy book by later Jewish mystics.

INDEX

Note: The Sefat Emet (person) is not italicized in the index; the *Sefat Emet* (text) is.

A

Aaron, 126, 127, 159, 162, 163, 171, 193, 196, 229, 233, 244, 245, 246, 254, 293, 368–69
Abba (rabbi) of Neyshtat (Nowe Miasto), xxiii n.21
Abraham: circumcision of, 24, 27–28, 30; dawn prayers by, 28–29; fear of God, 31–32; "garment of skin" of, 58; and love of God, 38–39, 241; and manna, 103; ownership of Earth by, 204; trial of, 36, 346–47; veneration of, 8, 21; wanderings in Egypt, 23, 27, 28, 304; and water and fire symbolism, 58; wisdom of, 19, 20
Abraham of Ciechanow (rabbi, 1784–1875), xxii
acosmic mysticism, xliv, xlvi
acquisition ("muchness"), 52
Adam: creation of, 10, 170, 292, 336; expulsion from Eden, 8–9, 16; as living soul, 74
afflictions, 171, 176

afikoman, 393
aggadah, 214, 409
Agudat Yisra'el, lvi, 266
Aharey Mot, 179–83
'akedah (binding of Isaac), 32, 347, 409
Akiba (rabbi), 159
alienation, 176
Alsheikh, R. Moses, 305
Alter, R. Abraham Issachar Benjamin, xxxiii n.46
Alter, R. Avraham Mordecai ("Imrey Emet"), lvii–lviii, 266
Alter, R. Judah Leib (of Gora Kalwaria). *See* Sefat Emet (R. Judah Leib Alter)
Amalek, 49, 50, 102, 106, 385
'ami (My people), 4, 10
'Amidah ("standing") prayer, 1, 47, 270, 409
anthropocentrism, 170
anti-Semitism, Polish, xviii, li
atonement, 351, 352, 354
Attar, R. Hayyim ibn, 205
'avodah ("service"), 28–29, 409
ayin ("nothingness"), xxxix n.50

415

B

C

D

ע"ו ע"ב)" "לא יבוא בקהל ה' (דברים כ"ג:ד)." ולא היה לו ספק בדבר כפלוני שאמר "פן אשחית (רות ד:ו)." והוא אדרבה היה שמח בדבר, להראות שדרשת חכמים היא התורה שניתנה מסיני, ואמונת חכמים היא יסוד תורה שבעל פה... (4:23)

ה

"פנים בפנים דיבר ה' עמכם (דברים ה:ד)." במדרש: "הרב נותן והתלמיד מקבל."

פירושו כי הקדוש ברוך הוא נותן התורה ונותן גם כח בישראל לקבל התורה, כי הכל ממנו הוא. והכנת בני ישראל אל התורה היא חסד בפני עצמה, שזכו בני ישראל להיות מכוונים פנים בפנים לקבל הדברות.

זה היה על ידי משה רבינו עליו השלום כמו שכתוב "אנכי עומד בין ה' וביניכם (דברים ה:ה)." וזה מתעורר בכל שנה כן כמו שכתוב "עומד" ולא כתיב "עמדתי."

וזהו גם כן תנופת שתי הלחם, לחם מן השמים ומן הארץ, בחינת תורה שבכתב ושבעל פה. פירושו: הנתינה והקבלה שתיהן מתעוררות בחג הזה. (4:25-6)

ו

הכל מודים שבשבת ניתנה תורה דכתיב "זכור (שמות כ:ח)' בעצומו של יום (שבת פ"ו ע"ב)."

פירושו דעיקר קבלת התורה הוא שנתקרבו נפשות בני ישראל למקומם ושורשם, כמו שכתוב "פנים בפנים דיבר ה' עמכם (דברים ה:ד)." וכן כתוב "אנכי ה' אלהיך (שמות כ:ב)," שראו והשיגו כל אחד כח אלהות שנתן הבורא יתברך בכל נפש שבישראל.

והוא באמת בחינת השבת קודש שהיא המנוחה והשביתה, שכל דבר חוזר למקומו ושורשו—אז נקרא שבת. וכתיב "זכור את יום השבת" ולא שייך "זכירה" רק בדבר שכבר השיגו פעם אחת. ולכן כיון שבעת קבלת התורה היתה בהתגלות בחינת השבת, צוה אותם לזכור זאת תמיד.

ובאמת עיקר השבת ניתן מקודם במרה. אבל עתה השיגו בנפשותם קבלת קדושת שבת, והוא באמת ענין נשמה יתירה שניתוספת לכל איש ישראל בשבת קודש. והוא על ידי דמתאחדין ברזא דאחד בשבת דכתיב "מורשה קהלת יעקב (דברים ל"ג:ד)." (4:28-9)

ז

בשבועות יש שני מיני התקרבות: לבות בני ישראל להשם יתברך והתקרבות המקום ברוך הוא לבני ישראל. וזה שתי הלחם.

ובני ישראל מתפארין [וקוראים אותו] "יום מתן תורתנו." והשם יתברך בתורה מחשב עיקר החג על התקרבות לבות בני ישראל דכתיב "וביום הביכורים בהקריבכם (במדבר כ"ח:כ"ו)." (4:27)

"עוזי ומעוזי" כלומר שעוז שעוז בי גם כן ממנו. וזה רמז שתי הלחם שמניפין אותן, להראות שגם חלק בני ישראל בבחינת תורה שבעל פה מאתו יתברך.

כתיב "וכל העם רואים את הקולות ואת הלפידים ואת קול השופר ואת ההר עשן וירא העם וינעו ויעמדו מרחוק (שמות כ:י״ח)" וקשה: "וירא" השני מיותר. אכן יש לומר שראו במאורות הללו שנתגלו להם את עצמותם כמו שדרשו חז"ל "פנים בפנים—כאספקלריא שכל אחד רואה שם צורה שלו (על פי מדרש הגדול דברים עמוד צ״ח)." והוא פירוש "כמים הפנים לפנים (משלי כ״ז:י״ט)." כמו שמתגלה פנימיות האדם אל התורה כן מתגלה אליו פנימיות חלקו בתורה, דיש לכל נפש ישראל חלק בתורה. לכן נדמה התורה למים.

ולכן "יצתה נשמתן (שבת פ״ח ע״ב)" על ידי שראו כל אחד ברוח הקודש את עצם נפשו למעלה. לכן "וינעו" שנתפעלו מאוד איך הם בעולם השפל וצורתם חקוקה למעלה. ובני ישראל בקבלת התורה היו כמו נשמה היורדת בעולם הזה דמשביעין אותה "תהי צדיק!" כן [ישראל] "מושבעין ועומדין מהר סיני." וכמו שבעל כרחה הנשמה יורדת לעולם הזה כן התורה החזירה נשמתן בעל כרחן, כי הם נתדבקו מרוב אהבה כמו שכתוב "נפשי יצאה בדברו (שיר השירים ה:ו)." (4:30)

ג

בנוסח הבקשה "הוא יפתח לבנו בתורתו וישם בלבנו אהבתו ויראתו (תפלת ובא לציון)." על פי הגמרא (שבת ל״א ע״ב) "וי מאן דלית ליה דרתא ותרעא לדרתא עביד [אוי לאדם שאין לו דירה ועושה פתח לדירה]." כי כל החכמה והתורה רק פתח לכנוס ל"יראת ה' היא אוצרו (ישעיה ל״ג:ו)." ועל ידי שנפתחין לבות בני ישראל מכח התורה יכולין אחר כך לקבל היראה והאהבה...

כעין זה שמעתי מפי מורי זקני ז"ל שתקנו מגילת רות בשבועות כמאמר העולם כי העיקר תורה ותפלה. ותפלה היא בחינת דוד המלך עליו השלום. והוא גם כן בחינת יראה, ולהודיע כי "אם אין יראה אין חכמה (אבות ג:י״ז)." (4:30)

ד

ענין קריאת רות בשבועות, שהוא ענין תורה שבעל פה, שהקדוש ברוך הוא מבקש שבני ישראל במעשיהן יוסיפו על התורה שבכתב, כי הרי מעשי צדיקים הם תורה. ונעשתה ממעשי בועז ורות מגילה שהיא ברוח הקודש.

כתיב "וידבר אלהים את כל הדברים האלה לאמר (שמות כ:א)." פירוש שבני ישראל יאמרו מעצמם כדברים האלה. וכן כתוב "אשר נתן לנו תורת אמת וחיי עולם נטע בתוכנו," והוא תורה שבעל פה שמצד זה מיוחדת התורה לבני ישראל, שדעתם מיוחדת להשיג סתרי תורה שנסתרים ואינם מפורשים בתורה.

וזה עצמו ענין בועז דאיתא הפירוש "בו עז." והיינו שהיה מאמין בדברי חכמים שדרשו "עמוני—ולא עמונית, מואבי—ולא מואבית (יבמות

שבועות

א

"וביום הביכורים בהקריבכם מנחה חדשה לה' (במדבר כ״ח:כ״ו)."

כי באורייתא ברא קודשא בריך הוא עלמא. נמצא חיות פנימית של כל הנבראים הוא כח הראשית שמהתורה, כמו שדרשו "בשביל התורה שנקראת ראשית (רש״י בראשית א:א, פסיקתא זוטרתי)." וכמו שכתוב "כח מעשיו הגיד לעמו (תהלים קי״א:ו)," שהתורה היא כח מעשה בראשית, אך כי נברא להיות נעלם הפנימיות, אבל ביום מתן תורה נתגלה זה ונדבק הכל בשורש.

וזה שכתוב "פנים בפנים דיבר ה' עמכם (דברים ה:ד)." וכן מה שאמרו "מכל דיבור נתמלא העולם בשמים (על פי שבת פ״ח ע״ב)" וכן מה שאמרו "שנחלק לשבעים לשונות (שם)." שאז נתגלתה ונמשכה חיות התורה לכל הנבראים.

ועשרת הדיברות נגד עשרה מאמרות [שבהם נברא העולם] כמו שאמרו בזוהר הקדוש שפירוש "מאמר" בחשאי ובהסתר ו"דיבור" הוא התגלות, דבר מלך שלטון, שאז נתגלה שכח התורה מחיה הכל ומושל על הכל. ועיקר קבלת תורה הוא התגלות. וזה שכתבו בתרגום על פסוק "וירד ה' על הר סיני (שמות י״ט:כ)" "ואתגלי." כי הקדוש ברוך הוא מלא כל הארץ כבודו, רק שמקודם היה נסתר.

ולכך נקרא "יום הביכורים" שנדבק עתה הכל בבחינת הראשית ונתחדש על ידי זה. וכן כתוב "מחדש בטובו בכל יום תמיד מעשה בראשית (סידור התפלה)." ופירשו "בטובו" בתורה שפנימיות חיות מעשה בראשית מהתורה. ובכל יום מתחדש גם כן מעשה בראשית בדרך נסתר, ובשבועות נתגלה יותר שיש ביטול יצר הרע גם כן על ידי שנתגלה שגם חיות סטרא אחרא מנקודת פנימיות... (4:22)

ב

כתיב "פנים בפנים דיבר ה' עמכם (דברים ה:ד)."

דאיתא "יבוא טוב ויקבל טוב מטוב לטובים (מנחות נ״ג ע״ב)." כי הפנימיות שבכל דבר טוב הוא, רק שנתערבו טוב ורע על ידי החטא. ובשעת קבלת התורה שהיא חירות לגמרי נתברר הטוב הגנוז דכתיב "וירא אלהים את האור כי טוב ויבדל אלהים בין האור ובין החשך (בראשית א:ד)" שגנזו לצדיקים.

וגם כתיב "טוב ה' לכל (תהלים קמ״ה:ט)" אל הכלל, כמו שכתוב "הקהל לי את העם (דברים ד:י)" ונקרא יום הקהל "ויחן שם ישראל נגד ההר (שמות י״ט:ב)," כאיש אחד. לכן נתגלתה הפנימיות שנקראת טוב.

ותורה שנקראת טוב—כמו כן פנימיות בני ישראל הוא טוב והוא תורה שבעל פה שכתוב "חיי עולם נטע בתוכנו." וזה בעצמו פירוש "אנכי ה' אלהיך (שמות כ:ב)" הוא חלק אלוה ממעל שנגנז בכל איש ישראל.

וכתוב "יהי עוזי ומעוזי (ירמיה ט״ז:י״ט)," שהשם יתברך נתן עוז בעצם נפשות בני ישראל. ולבד זה מוסיף תוקף ועוז לבני ישראל תמיד. וזה פירוש

נראה כי על ידי אמונה שיש יציאת מצרים לכל דור ודור נתגלה זה. ומהר"ל [רבי יהודה ליווא מפראג] כתב כי בכלל היה כל אחד ביציאת מצרים, רק חייב לראות "כאילו" יצא בפרט.

ויש לומר גם כן שעל ידי אמונה נכנס לתוך הכלל. ובוודאי בכלל היתה יציאת מצרים לנקודה הישראלית, שמשם נמשכים חיים לכל איש ישראל. רק על ידי אמונה באין לזה.

ואחר שרואה עצמו כאילו יצא, ויודע ומאמין כי גם ההארה שיש לו לא היה לולי יציאת מצרים, על ידי זה נתגלה לו שרואה איך יוצא באמת.

וכן הפירוש בסיפור יציאת מצרים: "אפילו כולנו חכמים, כולנו נבונים כולנו יודעים את התורה מצוה עלינו לספר ביציאת מצרים" כי אף שהוא חכם דבוק בהשם חיים, יש לו לידע כי כל זה על ידי יציאת מצרים. שהאמת כן, רק שצריך לברר זה על ידי אמונה. והוא הסיפור [מלשון ספיר] לשון בירור וגילוי מפורש כי בכל דור יש יציאת מצרים לפי ענין הדור, וכל זה היה בשעת יציאת מצרים. וכפי אמונת האדם כאילו יצא, נתגלה בחינה זו ומרגיש מיציאת מצרים של עתה ויוכל לצאת כל אחד ממיצר שלו. (3:41)

ו

"אז ישיר משה ובני ישראל (שמות ט"ו:א)." פירוש אחר הגלות ואחר הגאולה, כי הבינו עתה שנתבררה מלכות שמים על ידי כל תהלוכות הגלות. לכן "ויאמינו (שם י"ד:ל"א)" פירוש שהאמינו למפרע על כל הגלות וקבלו באהבה. ועל הכל אמרו שירה, גם על מה שחיזק ה' לב פרעה. וזה שכתוב "אמר אויב ארדוף אשיג אחלק שלל תמלאמו נפשי אריק חרבי תורישמו ידי (שם ט"ו:ט)." על כל זה נתנו שבח על ידי שראו שנתגדל על ידי זה שם שמים. ובזה חיזק משה רבינו ע"ה לבם: "התיצבו וראו את ישועת ה' (י"ד:י"ג)." וכיון ששמעו שעל ידי זה יתפרסם כבודו יתברך, קיבלו באהבה.

וכן יש לנו לידע בגלות הזאת כמו שכתוב "כימי צאתך מארץ מצרים אראנו נפלאות (ז:ט"ו)." (3:68)

ז

במדרש שיר השירים "נשיר למי שעשאנו שרים בעולם דכתיב עם זו יצרתי לי תהלתי יספרו (ישעיה מ"ג:כ"א)." ביציאת מצרים נעשו בני ישראל כבריה חדשה ונתיחדו לברר מלכות שמים בעולם. וזהו סיפור יציאת מצרים, וכן בכל יום שמעמידין על הבורא יתברך. ובירור זה תלוי בעבודה שבלב, כפי מה שמברירין בלב יחוד המעשה אליו יתברך.

וזה ימי הספירה דכתיב "וספרתם לכם (ויקרא כ"ג:ט"ו)." וכל שיר השירים נתיסד על זה, שהאירו בני ישראל במעשיהם והמשיכו כל הדברים שבעולם לשרשן להעלות מהם ריח ניחוח אליו יתברך. וזה הבירור עיקרו מזה החג, ומצות סיפור יציאת מצרים דכתיב "למען תזכור את יום צאתך ממצרים כל ימי חייך (דברים ט"ז:ג)," וזכירה היא בפה. ולילה זה נותן כח על הבירור והסיפור של כל ימות השנה... (3:65)

מצרים אין לו הפסק כמו שכתוב "כל ימי חייך (דברים ט"ז:ג)." וכפי מה שמספרין ביציאת מצרים, נגמר ומתרבה הנס דיציאת מצרים. כיון שענין יציאת מצרים היא פרשה בתורה היא נצחית. וזה שהוסיפו כל התנאים "אמור מעתה במצרים לקו חמישים מכות כו' (הגדה)," הרי שהוסיפו שמעתה מתגלות חמישים המכות שהיו מקודם גנוזים בשם עשר בלבד. וזה ענין סיפור יציאת מצרים: להוציא מכח אל הפועל. כי עיקר יציאת מצרים הוא חירות משיעבוד סטרא אחרא. רק במצרים היה שורש סטרא אחרא. ובפרטות נגמר בכל שנה יותר. (3:69)

ד

"חכם, מה הוא אומר? 'מה העדות והחוקים והמשפטים אשר צוה ה' אלהינו אתכם?' אף אתה אמר לו... 'אין מפטירין אחר הפסח אפיקומן' (הגדה)."

הנה כתיב "זכרתי לך חסד נעוריך אהבת כלולותיך לכתך אחרי במדבר בארץ לא זרועה (ירמיה ב:ב)." כי כשיצאנו ממצרים עדיין לא היתה לנו שום השגה בידיעת דרכי התורה והמצוות, עד שנתן לנו הקדוש ברוך הוא התורה ושאר מעלות טובות. ביציאת מצרים היה העיקר היציאה לחירות, להיות נכנסין בכלל עבדי ה'.

כמו כן בכל שנה הוא זמן חירותינו עתה, שנעשה כל איש ישראל בן חורין ונפדה מכל מאסר והתקשרות שנקשר בהבלי עולם. ואחר כך בחג השבועות מתעורר זמן מתן תורה. לכן החכם שמוכן תמיד לכנוס בשערי חכמה ודעת, והלילה הזה הוא שער החיות ולא יותר, חכם זה שואל "מה שמחה זו עושה?" אחר שכבר זכינו למעלות רבות מזאת. והתירוץ הוא "אין מפטירין אחר הפסח אפיקומן," ששמחת החירות עתה היא עולה על כל המדריגות שהיא בחינת "לכתך אחרי במדבר בארץ לא זרועה." ואין לבקש השגות, רק להיות נמשך אחר מלכותו יתברך.

וכן הנוסח "כמה מעלות טובות למקום עלינו אלו הוציאנו ממצרים... דיינו (הגדה)." שמתוך מעלת היציאה לחירות זכינו אחר כך לכל המעלות. וזה שכתבו "על אחת כמה וכמה טובה כפולה ומכופלת," פירושו שיציאת מצרים היא מעלה אחת כפולה, שמזה באנו לכל המעלות האחרות.

מה כל שכן עתה בגלות בודאי אנו מצפין רק לגאולה. על זה מבקשין "משכני אחריך נרוצה (שיר השירים א:ד)," כמו שנמשכנו אחריו יתברך בארץ לא זרועה, הגם שלא ידענו מדרך תורה ומצוות. ומה כל שכן עתה שכבר "הביאני המלך חדריו (שם)," בודאי "נגילה ונשמחה בך (שם)," להיות נמשך אחריו בארץ לא זרועה דכתיב "כימי צאתך מארץ מצרים אראנו נפלאות (מיכה ז:טו)." אם כן אחר הגאולה העתידה תהיה גם כן המשכה בארץ לא זרועה, כי יתחדש דרך חדש כדכתיב "תורה חדשה מאתי תצא (על פי ישעיה נ"א)..." (3:86-7)

ה

"בכל דור ודור חייב אדם לראות את עצמו כאילו הוא יצא ממצרים (הגדה)," ואחר כך כתוב "ואותנו הוציא משם (הגדה)."

פסח

א

יום טוב של פסח נקרא בתורה שבת כדכתיב "ממחרת השבת (ויקרא כ"ג:ט"ו)." כי פסח דומה לשבת. כמו שכתוב בשבת "זכור" ו"שמור" כן בפסח "והיה היום הזה לכם לזכרון (שמות י"ב:י"ד)" "למען תזכור את יום צאתך ממצרים (דברים ט"ז:ג)" וכן "שמור את חודש האביב (דברים ט"ז:א)" "ושמרתם את המצות (שמות י"ב:י"ז)." כי זכירה היא נקודה פנימית שאין בה שכחה. ולפי שבשבת מתגלה נקודה זו בנפשות בני ישראל, לכן צריכה שמירה שלא תתפשט נקודת הפנימיות למקום שיש בו שכחה. ולכן זכור ושמור בדיבור אחד נאמרו.

והוא עצמו העניין בגאולת מצרים, שבכל חג המצות נעשה איש ישראל כבריאה חדשה כמו שהיה ביציאת מצרים, כקטן שנולד. ומתחדשת בו אותה הנקודה שנטע הקדוש ברוך הוא בנפשות בני ישראל. נקודה זו נקראת "לחם עוני," שהיא בלי התרחבות, כי מצה היא עצם העיסה ואחר כך נשתנית ומתחמצת. כמו כן כל איש ישראל יש בו נקודה, מתנה מאת אלהים. ובאמת צריך אדם להרחיב זאת הנקודה ולהמשיך כל המעשים אחריה. זה התיקון של כל ימי השנה, לפי מה שזוכה האדם לטוב ולמוטב. אבל כשבא חג המצות מתחדשת הנקודה ונטהרת מכל הלכלוכים. לכן צריכין לשמרה מחימוץ ומכל השתנות בזה החג.

"ושמרתם את המצות כי בעצם היום הזה הוצאתי בני ישראל מארץ מצרים (שמות י"ב:י"ז)." פירושו פנימיות הנקודה כמו שהיא בעצם ואינה מקבלת שינוי. לכן צריכה שמירה. "והיה היום הזה לזכרון (שמות י"ב:י"ד)" שמתחדשת בו הנקודה שנקראת "זכרון." גם יתפרש "והיה לכם לזכרון" ממש, שיזכור האדם עיקר בריאתו בעולם, לעשות רצונו... (3:99)

ב

"אפילו כולנו חכמים כולנו נבונים כולנו יודעים את התורה, מצוה עלינו לספר ביציאת מצרים. וכל המרבה לספר ביציאת מצרים הרי זה משובח (הגדה של פסח)." דכתיב "בהוציאך את העם ממצרים תעבדון את האלהים (שמות ג:י"ב)." וכן כתוב "והוצאתי אתכם מארץ מצרים להיות לכם לאלהים (במדבר ט"ו:מ"א)."

וכן זה הסדר מתחדש בכל שנה: פסח זמן חירותנו והוא בחינת "עבדי אתה אשר בך אתפאר (ישעיה מ"ט:ג)," ואחר כך בשבועות זמן מתן תורתנו. וכפי החירות שמתעורר בפסח, כך מתחדשת התורה בשבועות. ומעין זה גם בכל יום ויום יש זכר ליציאת מצרים ולקבלת התורה. ולכן אפילו שקבלנו כבר התורה, מכל מקום יש התגלות התורה בכל דור ושנה ויום, מיוחד לזה הזמן. ולכן צריכין לחדש החירות בכל שנה ובזה זוכין להתחדשות קבלת אלהותו יתברך שמו.

"להיות לכם לאלהים"—הוא דבר ההווה ומתחדש תמיד. (3:103)

ג

"כל המרבה לספר ביציאת מצרים הרי זה משובח (הגדה)." כי יציאת

ב

איתא בגמרא "מיחייב איניש לבסומי בפוריא עד דלא ידע בין ברוך מרדכי
וארור המן (מגילה ז ע"ב)." שמעתי בזה מילין מפה קדוש מורי זקני ז"ל
לעלות עד למעלה מעץ הדעת טוב ורע. ואיני זוכר הדברים על בורין. אבל
נראה תורף הדברים דכתיב "עץ גבוה חמשים אמה (אסתר ה:י"ד)." והם כל
מדריגות שערי טומאה, שיש מ"ט פנים טמא ומ"ט פנים טהור. כי כח של
עמלק נמצא בכל המדריגות, אבל באמת שער החמשים הוא של הקדושה.
שם אין שני שני הדרכים, רק כולו טוב, כי שם שורש האחדות. ועל זה כתיב
[במלחמת עמלק] "כאשר ירים משה ידיו (שמות י"ז:י"א)," לשער החמשים
ועץ החיים שהוא התורה.

ולכן כשנתעורר כח משה רבינו עליו השלום שהוא שר התורה, יש
מפלה לעמלק. לכן איתא שבפורים קבלו התורה, והיינו התגלות עץ החיים.
ושם נקרא "דלא ידע" שאין שם שום אחיזה לסטרא אחרא כלל, כי הוא
שורש האחדות. "בסומי" הם ריחות הבשמים שנתמלא העולם בהם בעשרת
הדברות. ומורי זקני ז"ל אמר רמז בשמים "מר דרור (שמות ל:כ"ג)" שמתרגמין
מרי דכי. ומרדכי הוא הארת משה רבינו שורש התורה. (181:2)

ג

איתא "כל המועדים בטלים לעתיד חוץ מפורים דכתיב יומי הפורים האלה
לא יעברו מתוך היהודים וזכרם לא יסוף מזרעם (אסתר ט:כ"ח)'." כי
המועדים תלוין בבני ישראל כמו שכתוב "אלה מועדי ה' מקראי קודש אשר
תקראו... (ויקרא כ"ג:ד)"— ישראל דקדשינהו לזמנים, ושבת קביעא וקיימא.
כי בני ישראל מושכין קדושה בתוך הזמן כמו שכתוב "מקראי קודש."

ולכן לעתיד שיהיה יום שכולו שבת למעלה מהזמן, ממילא קדושת
המועדים תתבטל "דשרגא בטיהרא מה מהני [מה ערך יש לנו באור היום]?"
ובעניין זה גם כן מובנים מילין דרבנן: מצוות בטלות לעתיד לבוא. וחלילה
לומר שיהיה דבר מן התורה בטל. רק כדמיון ביטול הנר לגבי אבוקה
דכתיב "תורה אור ונר מצוה (משלי ו:כ"ג)." וכשיתגלה אור התורה ושורש
המצוות יתבטלו המצוות שלמטה לגבי אור תורה.

ובעולם הזה חביב מעשה בני ישראל לפניו כיון דהוא עלמא דחשוכא.
ולכן חשובין המועדות דכתיב "שלוש פעמים בשנה יראה (דברים ט"ז:ט"ז)"
כיון שעל ידיהם חלה הקדושה בעולם. אבל ביום שכולו שבת, ותתגלה
הקדושה למעלה, בטלה הקדושה שהתחתונים מעוררים במעשיהם.

ולפי שבפורים היתה התגלות הקדושה שלא על פי מעשה התחתונים,
לכן לא יתבטל לעולם כמו בחינת השבת שאינו תלוי במעשה התחתונים.
(2:191-2)

ד

חנוכה: "חנו כה." כי עיקר הנס היה במלחמה שגברו על מלכות יון הרשעה. אכן חכמים רצו להראות כי עיקר השמחה מגאולת מלכות בשר ודם כדי שנוכל אחר כך להיכנס בכלל עבדי ה'... לכן קבעו שם חנוכה.

ואיתא שלא היה להדליק רק יום אחד והדליקו בו שמונה ימים. ואין הפירוש בזמן דוקא, רק שמונה הוא כל השלימות. ובני ישראל על ידי גזירת יון הרשעה נחלש אצלם כח הקדושה ורק נקודה אחת נשארה בהם. ולכן אחר יגיעות מלחמות גדולות עם מלכות יון, לא היה כח לבני ישראל לעמוד על השלימות. ועזר להם הבורא יתברך בדרך נס, שנתברכה זאת הנקודה ובאו ברגע אחד לכל השלימות. ועל זה קראו בשם חנוכה, שזכו לבוא מיד אל המנוחה. כי השלימות נקראת מנוחה שזוכין לבוא אל השורש.

ובאמת כל זה להראות כי לולא כח ההסתר מסטרא אחרא ורשעים שמסתירין כח הקדושה, היו בני ישראל מוכנים לעלות במעלה עליונה להתדבק בשורש עליון. אך "החושך יכסה ארץ (ישעיה ס:ב)." ולכן מיד כשגברו ואיבדו מלכות יון, ברגע אחד נתברכו ונדבקו בשורש העליון.

והוא נחמה גם לדורותינו עתה, בראותינו שפלותינו בכל דור יורדין מטה מטה, עם כל זאת תקוותינו רבה בהשם יתברך אשר בבוא עת הגאולה במהרה בימינו אמן, ברגע אחד נוכל לבוא אל השלימות בעזרת השם יתברך. (211:1)

פורים
א

"תשועתם היית לנצח ותקוותם בכל דור ודור (שושנת יעקב,' פזמון לפורים).''

כי התשועה בפורים היתה לדורות עולם. כמו שהגזירה היתה "להשמיד כל היהודים (אסתר ג:י"ג)," ממילא גם הנס היה לכל הדורות. והרי קיום כל זרע ישראל הכל על ידי הנס הזה. ואיתא כי הגזירה היתה גם בשמים, כן על בני ישראל. והקדוש ברוך הוא עשה זה הנס בלי זכות ישראל, רק מצד שאנחנו עמו וחוסים בו תמיד, לכן עליו להושיע לנו בעת צרה. ולכן יום טוב זה נותן כח ועוז ותקוה לבני ישראל בגלות לבטוח בו, מצד שמיוחדים אנחנו אליו.

ונראה שלכך תקנו (מגילה ז:ע"ב) לבסום עד לא ידע [בין ברוך מרדכי וארור המן] להראות שאין היום טוב מצד זכות ישראל. ולכן נקרא פורים על שם הפור, כי הגורל הוא סימן שכך היה ראוי מכל צדדי הטבע, ותגבורת כח הסטרא אחרא על ידי עוונותינו. ורק בחסדו השם יתברך הצילנו...

ואיתא כי פורים כמו יום הכפורים. וביום הכפורים באין למעלה מהטבע על ידי ביטול הגוף מאכילה ושתיה "ועניתם את נפשותיכם (ויקרא כ"ג:כ"ז)" על ידי זה באים לעלמא דחירות, ויש בו סליחת עוונות. כמו כן בפורים על ידי משתה ושמחה יכולין לבוא גם לזה בעזר עליון שלא מצד מעשינו. (179:2)

מקדש ושכנתי בתוכם." בתוכם ממש. (198:1)

ב

אדוני מורי זקני ז"ל הגיד בשם רבותינו פירוש הגמרא "פתילות ושמנים שאמרו חכמים אין מדליקין בהן בשבת, מדליקין בהן בחנוכה (שבת כ"א ע"ב)." דהיינו נפשות מבני ישראל אשר לא טהורים הם כי "נפש" ראשי תיבות נר פתילה שמן. ואלו שאין להם עליה בשבת, היינו שאור מסכסך בהם ואין נמשכין למעלה, מכל מקום יש עליה להם בחנוכה. עד כאן דבריו.

כי ימים טובים אלה חנוכה ופורים הם בחינת תורה שבעל פה. כי שלושת המועדים שנתן לנו הקדוש ברוך הוא הם תורה שבכתב שמפורשין בתורה, והקדוש ברוך הוא נתן לנו זמני קדש אשר נתקדשו בעת הבריאה, שהכל בתורה נברא. והם עדות שהקדוש ברוך הוא בחר בישראל ויש לו התקרבות אליהם, שהרי מסר לנו מועדות שלו. וזהו שם "מועד" מלשון עדות.

וחנוכה ופורים הם מועדות שזכו להם בני ישראל במעשיהן, וזה נקרא תורה שבעל פה. והם עדות שהם בוחרים בקדוש ברוך הוא ומיחדים אליו ושמעשיהן מעוררין אותו יתברך, שהרי חידשו במעשיהם זמנים מקודשים. ועל ידי שאלה המועדות זכו בני ישראל להם במעשיהם, לכן יוכל למצוא בהם כל נפש ישראל תקונו, כי יש לכל בני ישראל דביקות ושייכות להם. (207:1)

ג

חנוכה הוא נס האחרון שנעשה לנו. על כן יש להתחזק בזה הנס יותר.

כי הנה כל הנסים הנעשין לבני ישראל, הגם כי היה ביד הקדוש ברוך הוא לשמור את בני ישראל שלא ישלטו עליהם השונאים ושלא יצטרכו לנס, אך אדרבא הוא להראות כי אין לבני ישראל קיום רק בהארות הבאים מעולם העליון למעלה מהטבע. והנסים הם מיוחדים להנהגת בני ישראל. וזה עצמו טעם כל הארבע מלכויות, כדי שיצטרכו בני ישראל תמיד לעשות להם נסים.

ולכן כשנעשה הקדוש ברוך הוא נס לאבותינו היתה להם מזה חיות, וכשנסתלקה הארת הנס, הוצרך לעשות להם נס אחר. וכן היה תמיד.

נמצא כי נס דחנוכה עדיין מאיר לנו, כיון שהקדוש ברוך הוא לא עשה לנו עדיין נס נגלה אחר. זה מוכיח שעדיין יש הארת הנס דחנוכה. ואשר אמרנו כשנסתלקה הארת הנס עושה נס אחר, אין הפירוש שנסתלק לגמרי חס ושלום, שהרי כל נס הוא למעלה מהזמן ומאיר לעולם, כמו שכתוב "זכר עשה לנפלאותיו (תהלים קי"א:ד)." רק הפירוש שהתחדשות של נס נתיישנה על ידי כובד הגלות, ואז הקדוש ברוך הוא עושה נס אחר.

ולכן כיון שנס דחנוכה יש בו התחדשות עד ביאת הגואל במהרה בימינו, שיעשה עמנו הקדוש ברוך הוא נסים חדשים, לכן נקראת חנוכה מלשון חינוך והתחדשות, כי נס זה יש בו התחדשות עד ביאת הגואל במהרה בימינו אמן. (9-208:1)

וישראל בתורה. ומשה רבינו הוא הסרסור והמדליק אור התורה בנשמת בני ישראל שהם הנרות. ואמרו חז״ל אל תקרי ״מורשה״ אלא ״מאורשה״ ככלה לחתן. ושניהם אמת, כי באמת התורה מתנה בנפשות בני ישראל, אבל כפי תיקון האדם כך מתחדש לו אור התורה. ועל זה אומרים ״כי היא לנו עוז ואורה (מפזמוני שמחת תורה).״ עוז בעצם, ואורה בהתפשטות התורה, כפי מה שזוכים בה כך מתחדשת להם בכל עת כמו שכתוב ״דדיה ירוך בכל עת (משלי ה:י״ט).״

לכן כתיב ״ה׳ עוז לעמו יתן״ ואחר כך כתיב ״ה׳ יברך את עמו בשלום (תהלים כ״ט:י״א).״ והברכה היא תוספת בהתחדשות התורה בכל עת כדאיתא ״היושב והוגה בתורה הקדוש ברוך הוא יושב ושונה כנגדו.״ (229:5)

חנוכה
א

כתיב ״נר ה׳ נשמת אדם חופש כל חדרי בטן (משלי כ:כ״ז).״ ובגמרא ״חיפוש מנרות, ונרות מנר (פסחים ז ע״ב).״ ״אחפש את ירושלים בנרות (צפניה א:י״ב).״

כי ענין המשכן ובית המקדש נמצא בכל איש ישראל גם כן, כענין ״ושכנתי בתוכם (שמות כ״ה:ו).״ וכפי מה שמברר האדם אצלו כי כל החיות מהנשמה, כמו שאומרים כל יום ״נשמה שנתת בי טהורה היא,״ והיינו שיש נקודה אחת טהורה בכל איש ישראל רק שהיא נסתרת וגנוזה באמת.

ובזמן שהיה בית המקדש קיים היה זה נגלה כי כל החיות מהשם יתברך. וזה ענין ״השראת השכינה עדות היא שהשם יתברך שורה בישראל (שבת כ״ב ע״ב).״ ועתה שהמשכן נגנז, מכל מקום יכול להיות נמצא על ידי חיפוש בנרות. ופירוש נרות, המצוות, והיינו שמחפשין בכל לב ונפש לעשות המצוה בכל החיות. ״נר״ הוא נפש רוח, וגם כן רמ״ח [248] איברים שבהם עושים המצוות [בתוספת] דחילו ורחימו [יראה ואהבה] הם בגמטריה נר. ואז הוא הכנה וכח למצוא על ידו בחינת המשכן, שהוא לבוא לנקודה הגנוזה.

בימים הללו שנעשו נסים [ונדלקו הנרות] על פי נס שגם בחינת הנרות היה חסר לבני ישראל אז, ממילא ההארה גם למצוא סיוע על ידי מצות נר חנוכה למצוא על ידי הנרות בחינת הנגנז. ועיקר גניזה הוא בחושך שצריכין נרות לחפש ולמצוא...

ועל כל פנים מאחר דכתיב ״אחפש את ירושלים בנרות,״ מבואר כי יש למצוא גם עתה בחינת בית המקדש וירושלים על ידי החיפוש. וכן כתוב ״ציון היא דורש אין לה (ירמיה ל:י״ז)״ אמרו בגמרא ״מכלל דבעי דרישה [שצריך לדרוש אותה] (ראש השנה ל ע״א).״ והוא על ידי כח המצוות שאדם עושה בכל החיות, נתעוררת החיות הפנימית שהיא הנקודה הטהורה. עליה נאמר ״חופש כל חדרי בטן״ שיוכל למצוא בכח הפנימיות הארה הגנוזה בכל חדרי בטן.

[הוסיפו תלמידיו] וזה ענין ״לעולם ימוד אדם עצמו כאילו קדוש שרוי בתוך מעיו (תענית י״א ע״א-ב).״ וכשאדם מתקן עצמו כן נאמר ״ועשו לי

שהוא בעזר מצוות סוכה ולולב, בחסד ה׳ החופף עלינו. גם נראה כי הטעם
כמו שאמרו בזהר הקדוש שבעלי תשובה באים בכח גדול, וברגע אחד
מתקנין הרבה. לכן עתה שהוא בבחינת בעלי תשובה, נעשה התיקון במהרה
ווכין מיד לשמחת תורה בשמיני עצרת.

הכלל כי בימים טובים שמקודם נתקנו נפשותינו ונעשו בני ישראל
כלים לקבל שפע ברכה וקדושה. ולכן בעצרת שהיא גוף הקבלה כתוב
״עצרת תהיה לכם (במדבר כ״ט:ל״ה),״ שעתה יש לכם לקבל, שבאתם אל
השלימות שהיא כלי המחזיק ברכה. והברכה היא בשמיני עצרת ושמחת
תורה. לכן קורין ״וזאת הברכה.״ (5:186)

ג

״וזאת הברכה (דברים ל״ג:א).״ במדרש (דברים רבה י״א:ד) כתוב שבאה
התורה לברך את ישראל.

כי הנה משה רבינו עליו השלום קודם פטירתו הוריש כחו שהיא
התורה שניתנה לו מסיני לכללות בני ישראל, כמו שכתוב ״מורשה קהלת
יעקב (דברים ל״ג:ד)״ שבכל עת שמתאספין בני ישראל מתקיים ״בישורון
מלך בהתאסף (שם ה).״

ואיתא שיש בתורה ברכה לפניה ולאחריה. ושמעתי מפי מורי זקני ז״ל
שהענין כמו במזון, שיש ברכה לפניו והוא על גוף המזון שברא השם יתברך,
וברכת המזון לאחריו הוא על כח המזון שיש במזון, שהוא השביעה והעיכול
שמתברך המזון במעיו ומחזק כחו של האדם. לכן שיעור [זמן אמירת]
ברכת המזון קודם זמן העיכול. כן בתורה: מלבד שנתן השם יתברך גוף
התורה, נתן גם כן שתהיה בה ברכה לאחריה, שיאירו הדברים באדם, עד
כאן דבריו.

ויתכן שכנגד שני אלו העניינים יש חג השבועות, שהוא זמן מתן תורה
ממש, ושמחת תורה בשמיני עצרת, בחינת ״עצרת תהיה לכם״ שהוא הכח
הנשאר מהתורה, שהדברים מאירים ומתברכים בלבות בני ישראל...

וזאת הברכה של התורה שנותנת חיים לעוסקים בה. ועל זה נאמר
״וחיי עולם נטע בתוכנו.״ והיא בחינת תורה שבעל פה, מה שמתברכין
הדברים בלב האדם ועושים פירות. וגם זה מתנה מהשם יתברך כמו
שכתוב ״ממני פריך נמצא (הושע י״ד:ט).״ דהיינו גם מה שמתוספ, וחדושי
תורה שהוסיפו חכמינו ז״ל הכל מתנה מהשם יתברך. וזה הכח שהוריש
משה רבינו עליו השלום לכללות ישראל עד סוף כל הדורות... (5:202)

ד

בפסוק ״תורה צוה לנו משה (דברים ל״ג:ד).״ דכתיב ״נר מצוה ותורה אור
(משלי ו:כ״ג)״ וכן כתוב ״נר ה׳ נשמת אדם (משלי כ״כ:ז).״ נשמות בני
ישראל הן הכלים שאור התורה יכולה להתפשט בהם. לכן כפי זכות הדור
כך מתפרש ומתגלה להם אור התורה. וכמו כן חס ושלום בשפלות הדור
נסתר אור התורה, כמו שכתוב ״עמו אנכי בצרה (תהלים צ״א:ט״ו).״ ״אנכי״
הוא התורה, והיא תלויה בתיקון נפשות בני ישראל. זהו שכתוב ״תורה צוה
לנו,״ שהתורה וישראל מקושרים ומחוברין. לכן שמחת התורה בישראל

ב

קבעו חכמים הרבה בקשות ליום הערבה. כי כחן של ישראל בפה, וערבה
דומה לשפתים ופה כמו שאמרו חז"ל.

והנה יש שתי שפתים, ונראה הרמז כי שבח הפה הוא בדיבור ובשתיקה,
כמו שאמרו "מלה בסלע משתוקא בתרין [שתיקה בשתים] (מגילה י"ח
ע"א)." והרמז שתי הערבות ושתי שפתים הן בחינות אהרן ומשה. כי משה
רבינו הוא כח הפה בתורה, ובאהרן כתיב "וידום אהרן (ויקרא י:ג)" והוא
כח השתיקה.

ומאחר שמצינו כי גדול לשון הרע מכל העבירות, נמצא הבולם פיו
בשעת מריבה גדול כחו. וכמו שאמרו ז"ל "יתולה ארץ על בלימה (איוב
כ"ו:ז)' על הבולם פיו (על פי חולין פ"ט ע"א)." והוא אהרן אוהב שלום
ורודף שלום.

ובאמת שני אלו תלוין זה בזה. כי כפי שמירת הפה כך יכולין לפתוח
הפה בתורה...

ואולי זה החילוק בין ערבה שבלולב, שהוא בחינת הדיבור בתורה
ומתחבר בארבע מינים שהם עמודים גדולים, וערבה בפני עצמה שהיא כח
השתיקה ושמירת הפה. לכן אמרו "חבט ולא בירך" [שאין ברכה לחביטת
ערבה] כי היא בחינת השתיקה. (226:5)

שמיני עצרת

א

ענין שמיני עצרת ושמחת תורה אחר החג. דאיתא ברעיא מהימנא [בספר
הזוהר] פרשת נשא שיש שני מיני בעלי תשובה: יש מי ששב כדי לתקן
החטא בלבד, אבל תשובה שלימה היא אחרי ששב משתדל בתורה בכל
כחו; עיין שם. פירוש הדבר שאין התשובה בעבור כפרת נפשו, אלא רק כדי
שיהיה טהור לעבודת הבורא. לכן שב: להסיר המחיצה שנעשה בנפשו על
ידי העוונות.

ולכן זה סימן שמיד אחר ימי התשובה מקבלין עול תורה כראוי. ולכן
"ביום השמיני עצרת תהיה לכם (במדבר כ"ט:ל"ה)." לכם דווקא, כי שערי
תשובה לכל פתוחין. אבל בני ישראל שמחין יותר בקבלת עבודה מחדש
ממה שמחל הקדוש ברוך להם עונש החטאים... (186:5)

ב

איתא במדרש תנחומא כי שמיני עצרת היה צריך להיות חמישים יום אחר
החג כמו עצרת [שבועות] אחר הפסח, רק שאינו מטריח אותם בימות
החורף.

הענין הוא כמו כמו ביציאת מצרים שאחר שנגאלו מנו ארבעים ותשעה ימי
הטוהר, כמו שכתוב בזוהר הקדוש פרשת אמור "כההיא איתתא [כאישה
הזאת," אחר נדתה," כמו כן בימים אלו ראש השנה ויום הכפורים שנגאלו
בני ישראל מיצר הרע צריכין גם כן ימי טהרה לזכות לתורה. רק שהטהרה
נעשתה עתה בשבעת ימי החג, שהן כנגד שבעה שבועות של ימי הספירה.

הסוכה שמגינה על בני ישראל. ועל זה נאמר "מים רבים לא יוכלו לכבות את האהבה (שיר השירים ח:ז)" ולעולם נשארת אהבה לה' בלבות בני ישראל. אך החטאים מכסים, ובימים אלו נגלית האהבה...

אבי זקני ז"ל היה אומר תמיד שיש נקודה בכל איש ישראל שהקדוש ברוך הוא מגין עליה ועל זה נאמר "מגן אברהם." והיא נקודת אהבה שעליה נאמר "מים רבים לא יוכלו לכבות."

חג הסוכות הוא מעין המשכן שניתן לבני ישראל אחר החטא כשנתקנו בתשובה. כתיב "ויקהל משה (שמות ל"ה:א)" פירש רש"י ז"ל למחרת יום הכפורים כשירד מן ההר, שנתרצה הקדוש ברוך הוא לבני ישראל בשמחה. ואז התחילה נדבת המשכן בימים שבין יום הכפורים לסוכות, שכן כתיב "בבוקר בבוקר (שמות ל"ו:ג)" והיה רק איזה ימים. ובנדבת המשכן שהיתה בשמחה נעשתה הכנה להיות זמן שמחתינו בכל שנה ושנה. ואיתא במדרש "אוהבם נדבה (הושע י"ד:ה)," שעל ידי נדבת המשכן בשמחה נתעוררה אהבה בין ישראל לאביהם שבשמים... (203-4 :5)

ט

מצות סוכה אחר יום הכפורים, דכתיב "כי אם עוונותיכם היו מבדילין ביניכם לבין אלהיכם (ישעיה נ"ט:ב)." לכן אחר שנטהרו מעוונות ניטל ההבדל. ויש עוונות שמבדילין האחדות בין אחד לחבירו: זה הוא שכתוב "ביניכם" ממש. ויש שמבדילין בין אדם למקום.

ובסוכות נעשה הכל אחדות אחת ונפשות בני ישראל מתאחדין. ולזה רומזים ארבעת המינים שבלולב שנעשין אגודה אחת, וכן הסוכה שבה מתאחדין נפשות בני ישראל לאביהם שבשמים. ולכן נקרא חג האסיף. (236 :5)

הושענא רבה
א

ערבה נגד אלו שאין להם טעם וריח. אם כן מה חשיבותם? אך [הערבה היא בצורת] הפה שהוא עיקר כחן של ישראל "הקול קול יעקב (בראשית כ"ז:כ"ב)."

והיא בחינת דוד המלך עליו השלום [ספירת המלכות, שאין לה טעם וריח לעצמה]. כי שלושה מינים הם שלושה אבות ודוד המלך אמר "ואני תפילה (תהלים ק"ט:ד)." אם כי בוודאי קול הצדיקים שיש להם טעם וריח עולה למדריגות רבות ביותר, עף על פי כן יש להם תערובות מעשים טובים. ומי שאין לו טעם וריח הוא רק תפילה בלבד.

וזה שכתוב "תפילה לעני כי יעטוף (תהלים ק"ב:א)," היינו שמתעטף כולו בתפילה כמו שכתוב "ואני תפילה." וזה ערב לפניו יתברך ונקראת ערבה. ולכן נקרא הושענא רבה כי ביום זה נושעים בו גם השפלים שאין להם טעם וריח. והיא ישועה גם לדורות השפלים שלנו, שאין לנו רק תפילה. וביום זה נפתחו שערי תפילה בפיהם של ישראל... (194 :5)

שרואין חסד ה׳ שמחל לנו וטהרנו מן החטא. עם כל זאת שבין אליו ומבינים שאין לנו מקום מעצמינו, רק לחסות בצלו יתברך. (5:183)

ה

סוכות נקרא חג האסיף שכל אחד מאסף כל רכושו לביתו. ולכן צריכין לזכור כי אנחנו וכל אשר לנו להשם יתברך. וכמו שכאן הוא זמן אסיפה, כמו כן לעילא, שהקדוש ברוך הוא מאסף אותנו לביתו והוא הסוכה. (5:184)

ו

ימי הסוכות שנקראו זמן שמחתנו כי השם יתברך זיכה אותנו לישב בצלו. והיא מעין בחינת גן עדן דכתיב ״וישם שם את האדם (בראשית ב:ח).״ ועיקר הבריאה היה להיות דירת האדם שם. ושם היתה השמחה כמו שאנו אומרים ״כשָׂמֵחַ יצירך בגן עדן מקדם.״ והגם שכתוב ״ויגרש את האדם (בראשית ג:כ״ד),״ אף על פי כן יש זמנים שמתנוצצת קצת הארה מבחינת גן עדן. והשם יתברך הכניסנו לדירה זו שחל עליה שם שמים כדאיתא בגמרא ״והשמחה במעונו (כתובות ח ע״א).״ לכן דירה זו מביאה שמחה.

ובוודאי על ידי טהרתן של ישראל ביום הכפורים יש שמחה לפניו במרום. לכן יש לנו לשמוח בשמחת הבורא יתברך. וזהו שכתוב ״לפני ה׳ תטהרו (ויקרא ט״ז:ל).״ ומלבד שזכינו לטהרה יש לנו להתענג בשמחת השם יתברך בנו. (5:199)

ז

איתא (ספרא אמור י״ז) ״כי בסוכות הושבתי את בני ישראל בהוציאי אותם מארץ מצרים (ויקרא כ״ג:מ״ג).״ יש מי שאומר סוכות ממש ויש מי שאומר ענני הכבוד.

ומסתמא הכל אמת, דצריכין להבין למי שאמר סוכות ממש מה ענין זה? ויש לומר על פי אמרם ז״ל ״אמרה תורה... צא מדירת קבע ושב בדירת עראי (סוכה ב ע״א).״ וזה באמת עיקר החירות שניתנה ביציאת מצרים לכל איש ישראל, שלא יהיה מוטבע בעניני הטבע. וזהו שכתוב ״בסוכות הושבתי את בני ישראל בהוציאי אותם מארץ מצרים״ שהיתה נטיעה בלבות בני ישראל לצאת ממאסר הגוף והטבע להיות בעולם הזה בארעי. כמו שכתוב ״ויסעו מרעמסס סוכתה (שמות י״ב:ל״ז)״ שדרשו חז״ל זה על פסוק ״ואשא אתכם על כנפי נשרים ואביא אתכם אלי (שמות י״ט:ד).״ והוא שניתן להם כח להיות למעלה מהטבע, להיות להם כנפים שלמים לפרוח בהם לאביהן שבשמים.

וכפי מה שמתקיימת בכל איש ישראל דירה זו שלא להיות מוטבע בעולם הזה, כך חל עליו שם שמים וסוכת ענני הכבוד... (5:202)

ח

חג הסוכות הוא שמקרב הקדוש ברוך הוא את בני ישראל בתשובה מאהבה ושמחה. ועל זה נאמר ״על כל פשעים תכסה אהבה (משלי י:י״ב).״ והיא

ב

"ולקחתם לכם ביום הראשון פרי עץ הדר (ויקרא כ"ג:מ)." כי בסוכות השם
יתברך מקרב את בני ישראל כמו שכתוב "הפורס סוכת שלום" והוא מגן
עלינו מצד שאנחנו נקראים בנים למקום. ובני ישראל מצד עצמם חפצים
להתדבק בו ושיעשו מעשים טובים לפניו שלא תהיה קרבתן מצד החסד
בלבד. וזהו "ולקחתם לכם—מצדכם.

כתיב גם "תודיענו אורח חיים שובע שמחות את פניך (תהלים ט"ז:י"א)."
ואיתא לולב גמטריא חיים ובני ישראל חפצים לקבל חיים אמיתים בפנימיות
שלהם. וזה נקרא "שובע שמחות," כפי עומק הקבלה בלב עד שנקרא
שביעה. וזהו על ידי מיני הלולב שבני ישראל מרמזים במעשה להשם
יתברך לקבל אור הסוכה שניתן להם במתנה. וכשהמלך מזמן אורחים נותן
להם משאלות לבם כדאיתא "מאן דמזמן, למיכלא ולמשתיה זמין [מי
שמזמן אורחים, לאכול ולשתות הוא מזמינם] (זוהר ח"ג צ"ג ע"ב)."

לכן אומר לנו "ולקחתם לכם," שנבחר לנו החיים ובסוכות ניתנה דעת
לכל איש ישראל כדכתיב "למען ידעו דורותיכם (ויקרא כ"ג:מ"ג)." וכן
נראה כי הדעת של כל השנה באה בחג הסוכות שהוא רגל אחרון משלוש
הרגלים שכל השנה עומדת עליהם. מצות סוכה היא מעצמה, ומיני הלולב
הן הקבלה שבני ישראל מקבלין ומביאין הדעת לעומק לבבם... (181:5)

ג

שמחת בית השואבה, שמשם שואבין רוח הקודש. כי השמחה היא כלי
לשאוב מים חיים והוא רוח הקודש דכתיב "ויפח באפיו נשמת חיים
(בראשית ב:ז)." וכפי שאדם מתדבק בעיקר החיות שיש לו מהשם יתברך,
כן מתפשטין החיים בכל איבריו.

ואיתא [בימי שמחת בית השואבה] "לא ראינו שינה (סוכה נ"ג ע"א)"
כדאיתא במדרש על משה רבינו עליו השלום שכל ארבעים יום שהיה
בשמים לא היה יכול לישון, שידע שאין שיעור במה שיכול לקבל בכל שעה
ושעה. וכן כתיב "שבעת ימים בשנה (ויקרא כ"ג:מ"א)" על ימי הסוכות, מה
שלא נאמר כן בכל הרגלים. שעיקר הארת השנה תלויה בשבעה ימים אלו,
והכלי לקבל הוא השמחה. (182:5)

ד

סוכות זכר לעננני הכבוד. ומהיכן זכו בני ישראל לעננני כבוד? הזוהר הקדוש
מביא "זכרתי לך חסד נעוריך אהבת כלולותיך לכתך אחרי במדבר (ירמיה
ב:ב)."

וכלל הענין שהכניסו עצמם תחת מלכותו יתברך. כי אחר יציאת
מצרים יראו לנפשותם שלא יפלו שנית תחת ממשלת הסטרא אחרא. ולכן
אף כי הבחירה ניתנה לאדם, עם כל זאת יש גם לזה בחירה, שבוחר בכל
נפשו שלא להיות בבחירתו, רק בוחר בהנהגתו יתברך שינחנו באורח מישור.

וכדברים אלו גם כן אחר ימי הדין ראש השנה ויום הכפורים, שבני
ישראל נקיים מחטא צריכין גם כן לבחור בהנהגתו יתברך. והיא גם כן
בחינת תשובה. מקודם היתה תשובה מיראה, ועתה היא מאהבה על ידי

לצוות להם.

ביום הכפורים ניתנו לוחות האחרונות. על זה אומרים בתפלת שבת "ושני לוחות אבנים הוריד בידו וכתוב בהם שמירת שבת." דיש "זכור" ו"שמור": זכור בפה ושמור בלב. וכתיבת הלוחות היא החקיקה בלבות בני ישראל כמו שכתוב "כתבם על לוח לבך (משלי ג:ג)." על ידי החטא לא יכלו לקבל הלוחות, ואחר שנמחל להם ונטהרו הלבבות ביום הכפורים נחזרה להם זו החקיקה בלב.

ובאמת חטא העגל שמור לדורות, ולעומת זה בכל יום הכפורים בכל שנה ושנה נמחל קצת מזה החטא ונכנסין בשערי הקדושה לקבל הרשימה בלב. (173:5)

ד

יום הכפורים הוא בזכות משה רבינו עליו השלום שהוריד לוחות האחרונות. והנה בני ישראל נשתתפו בתענית יום האחרון של ארבעים יום עם משה רבינו עליו השלום. וזיכה משה רבינו את כל בני ישראל. הוא נקרא "איש האלהים (תהלים צ:א)" וכתיב "אמרתי אלהים אתם ובני עליון כולכם (תהלים פ"ב:ו)," שהיו עתידין להיות כמלאכי השרת. ומשה רבינו נשאר בזאת המדריגה ולא "כולכם." רק ביום הכפורים נדמו כל בני ישראל למלאכי השרת בכח הארת משה רבינו עליו השלום שהכניס עצמו בכלל ישראל. לכן צריכין להיות אגודה אחת ביום הכפורים, ואז שורה זכות משה רבינו... (175:5)

סוכות

א

ענין סוכה כמו חופה שגומרת הקנין אשה לבעלה "כי בסוכות הושבתי את בני ישראל בהוציאי אותם מארץ מצרים (ויקרא כ"ג:מ"ג)." כי ביציאת מצרים נתקדשו בני ישראל לשם יתברך, כמו שכתוב "אני ה' מקדשכם המוציא אתכם מארץ מצרים (ויקרא כ"ב:ל"ב-ל"ג)." ועל זה יש קטרוג שיהיו בני ישראל מבוררין, להיות קנין להשם יתברך יותר מכל הברואים. ועל זה כתיב "ולמקנהו עשה סוכות (בראשית ל"ג:י"ז)," וכתיב "הפורס סוכת שלום" פריסה לשון פרס וחלק כמו שכתוב "כי חלק ה' עמו (דברים ל"ב:ט)," שבחר לו השם יתברך חלק מהנבראים.

השם יתברך בחר לו השלימות ולמה לו חצי דבר? אך כתיב "אשכון את דכא ושפל רוח (ישעיה נ"ז:ט"ו)," וכתוב בזוהר הקדוש כי זאת היא השלימות, אדם שנשבר לבו. עיין שם פרשת אמור. ואדרבא זה שבחו יתברך, כי בכל מקום שהוא שורה הוא שלימות, והוא עשה מחצי דבר דבר שלם.

וזה פירוש "הפורס סוכת שלום." כי באמת הנקודה הפנימית שבכל מקום היא השלימות. והנה בסוכות מקריבים שבעים פרים כנגד שבעים אומות. וניסוך המים פירשו בגמרא כי בני ישראל צריכין לבקש שתתפשט מלכותו יתברך על כל הבריאה. וכן אמרו "אל תהיו כעבדים המשמשים... על מנת לקבל פרס (אבות א:ג)." (181:5)

לחבירו. ויתכן לפרש "מבדילים ביניכם" ממש, וגם "בין אלהיכם."

וצריכין לתקן שני מיני פירוד אלו. וזה שאמרו "עבירות שבין אדם לחבירו" אינו דוקא גזילה וכדומה, רק עבירות שגרמו פירוד בין אדם לחבירו כמו "לא תשנא את אחיך בלבבך (ויקרא י"ט:י"ז)" וכדומה. ו"עד שירצה את חבירו" פירושו שיחזור להיות רוצה ואוהב את חבירו, כמו שאמרו חז"ל "ואהבת לרעך כמוך' זה הוא כלל גדול בתורה (ירושלמי נדרים ט:ד)."

וביום הכפורים שמתכפרין העבירות נעשין בני ישראל אחד. ולכן זכו ללוחות אחרונות ביום הכפורים, שמקודם על ידי החטא כתוב "כי פרוע הוא (שמות ל"ב:כ"ה)" ונתפרדה האחדות. אבל אחר כך כשירד משה מן ההר כתוב "ויקהל משה (שמות ל"ה:א)," שנחזרו לאחדות. והתורה תלויה בזאת האחדות כמו שכתוב "מורשה קהלת יעקב (דברים ל"ג:ד)." וזהו שאמרו "כלל גדול בתורה." (2-171:5)

ב

איתא "וכי בתשעה מתענין! אלא כל האוכל ושותה בתשיעי מעלה עליו הכתוב כאילו התענה (ברכות ח ע"ב)." וכן למדו מכאן תוספת מחול על הקודש.

העניין הוא כי יום הכפורים הוא מעין עולם הבא שאין בו אכילה ושתיה. והוא באמת יום שמחה מאוד לבני ישראל. אך שאין יכולין להתדבק בשמחה זו כראוי בעודנו בעולם הזה, וצריכין להתדבק בהארת יום הכפורים לפניו ולאחריו, בתוספות מחול על הקודש. ובשמחת התשיעי יכולין להתדבק בהארת יום כפור אחר כך.

כן אמר רבינו יונה ז"ל בטעם הסעודה: שאין יכולין לשמוח ביום הכפורים, ומקדימין השמחה. כי יום הכפורים הוא הביטול אליו יתברך לגמרי כמו שאמרו חז"ל "מקוה ישראל ה' (ירמיה י"ז:י"ג)'—מה מקוה מטהר את הטמאים, אף הקדוש ברוך הוא מטהר את ישראל (יומא פ"ה ע"ב)." ומינה מה טהרת המקוה כשנכנס כל קומה של האדם במים, כן צריך כל האדם להתבטל אליו יתברך. וכשזוכה האדם אחר פטירתו לזה, מתטהר על ידי הקדוש ברוך הוא במקוה. ומעין זה יש ביום הכפורים. (170:5)

ג

איתא בתנא דבי אליהו (סדר אליהו זוטא סוף פרק י') כי בארבעים יום האחרונים שעלה משה רבינו עליו השלום להר, התענו בני ישראל. וביום האחרון קבעו תענית לילה ויום ונתרצה להם הקדוש ברוך הוא וקבע אותו ליום סליחה ומחילה לדורות. ובודאי היה זה בכח אהרן: כאשר נשתתף עמהם בחטא החזיר אותם בתשובה. ולכן נמסרה כפרת היום ביד אהרן כהן גדול.

ותקנו בזה מה שבראשונה הקדימו "נעשה" ל"נשמע" (שמות כ"ד:ז) ועל ידי החטא איבדו בחינת "נעשה," ועתה על ידי התשובה הקדימו נעשה לנשמע, שקבעו לעצמם יום תענית מה שעתיד הקדוש ברוך הוא אחר כך

ואף על פי שמקודם גם כן כתוב "ויוצא אותו החוצה (שם ט״ו:ה)"
—למעלה מכיפת הרקיע, אבל עכשיו נתעלה אבינו אברהם בכח עצמותו.
וזהו פירוש הנסיון כמו שכתוב במדרש (בראשית רבה נ״ה:א) "נתת ליראיך
נס להתנוסס (תהלים ס:ו)." פירוש בעצמו.

ולכן כתיב אחר כך "אברהם אברהם (בראשית כ״ב:י״א)," שנעשה
שלם ונתדבק בשורש אברהם שלמעלה. שאמרו "האבות הן הן המרכבה
(בראשית רבה פ״ב:ו)."... (5:157)

שבת שובה

א

"השיבנו ה' אליך ונשובה (איכה ה:כ״א)." והם שני מיני תשובה: מיראה
ואהבה. ובהיות האדם מלוכלך בחטא, אי אפשר לשוב מתוך אהבה, רק
מיראה. ואז צריכין סיוע משמים כמו שאמרו הקדמונים כי השם יתברך
מסייע לבעל תשובה. וזה "השיבנו."

אבל השב מאהבה מתקרב בעצמו מתוך אהבת הבורא יתברך שבוער
בו, ואינו צריך עזר. והרמז "נח היה צריך סעד לתומכו ואברהם אבינו לא
היה צריך סעד (רש״י בראשית ו:ט על פי בראשית רבה ל:י)," כי זה מיראה
וזה מאהבה.

וענין שתי התשובות כמו שמתחילה יש "סור מרע ועשה טוב (תהלים
ל״ד:ט״ו)." כן תשובה מיראה היא בחינת "סור מרע" שמבקש להתנקות
מלכלוך העוונות. אבל מאהבה היא בחינת "עשה טוב." ועל ידי שהעוונות
מעכבים האדם מלהתדבק בו יתברך, לכן מבקש התשובה כדי שיוכל לחזור
לבחינת "עשה טוב."

וזהו שכתוב "חדש ימינו כקדם (איכה ה:כ״א)" הוא דביקות השורש
שיש לבני ישראל בו יתברך, כדכתיב "כי חלק ה' עמו (דברים ל״ב:ט)."

ולכן בשבת קודש בנקל לשוב יותר, כי מתעורר השורש של בני ישראל
כמו שכתוב "וביום השבת יפתח (יחזקאל מ״ו:א)." וזה ענין נשמה יתירה
שיש לבני ישראל בשבת, שהוא כח השורש שאינו תלוי בעבודת האדם. לכן
נקראת "יתירה," שהיא יותר מכפי זכות ועבודת האדם. וזה הכח אינו
נאבד על ידי החטא. לכן יכולין לשוב בשבת קודש... (5:161)

יום כפור

א

איתא במשנה "עבירות שבין אדם לחבירו אין יום הכפורים מכפר עד
שירצה את חבירו (יומא ח:ט)." דהנה ביום הכפורים נעשין בני ישראל
אחדות אחת כדאיתא "ולא אחד בהם (תהלים קל״ט:ט״ז)"—זה יום הכפורים.
וכמו שיום זה מאחד כל הימים, כן מתאחדין בו כל הנפשות.

כי באמת הנפשות קרובין, רק על ידי החטאים בא הריחוק ופירוד, כמו
שכתוב "עוונותיכם היו מבדילים ביניכם לבין אלהיכם (ישעיה נ״ט:ב)." יש
עבירות שגורמות פירוד בין אדם למקום, ויש שגורמות פירוד בין אדם

ב

"ראש השנה." פירוש: קודם התחלקות השפע להיות נשתנה. כי כשבאה חיות השם יתברך לעולם הזה תחת הזמן והטבע, משתנה מרוחניות לגשמיות. וראש השנה הוא המקור וההתחלה קודם ההשתנות, כי במקורו הוא בלי ציור גשמי.

במדרש "לעולם ה' דברך נצב בשמים (תהלים קי״ט:פ״ט)" כמו שכתוב בשם הבעל שם טוב כי מאמרי השם יתברך חיים וקיימים. ונמצא שורש כל דבר וקיומו הוא המקור והנקודה שנמשכת מן מאמר השם יתברך.

וזהו התקיעות שהוא קול בלי דיבור, שדיבור הוא התחלקות הקול לתנועות נפרדים ושונים. אבל הקול אחד מיוחד דבוק במקורו. והיום בראש השנה החיות דבוקה בשורשה קודם התחלקות והשתנות. ורוצין לדבוק עצמן בפנימיות החיות. (5:138)

ג

איתא בגמרא (על פי ראש השנה ל״ב ע״ב) אמרו מלאכי השרת לפני הקדוש ברוך הוא "מפני מה אין בני ישראל אומרים לפניך הלל בראש השנה ויום הכפורים?" אמר הקדוש ברוך הוא "אפשר מלך יושב על כסא דין וספרי חיים ומתים פתוחים ובני ישראל יאמרו הלל!"

וצריכין להבין עניין שאלת מלאכי השרת. והעניין הוא כמו שכתוב שמכל מצוה שבני ישראל עושין נברא מלאך. ובאמת ראש השנה ויום הכפורים המה מועדות, ונמצא אז השמחה גם כן בלבות בני ישראל, רק שאינם יכולין להוציא מכח אל הפועל לומר הלל. אבל מרוב התשוקה נבראו מלאכים גם כן, ואפשר מלאכים אלו המה למעלה מבחינת המלאכים שנבראו מאמירת ההלל—כידוע שמדריגת המחשבה למעלה מהדיבור.

[הוסיפו תלמידיו] ואפשר זה עצמו בחינת השופר כדאיתא בזוהר הקדוש (שמות כ ע״א) שיש צעקה בלב שאין יכול לפרש בפה. וכמו כן קול שופר הוא סתום והוא בחינת "אענך בסתר רעם (תהלים פי״א:ח)." וזהו "תקעו בחדש שופר, בכסה ליום חגינו (שם שם ד)." ועל זה סידרו הבקשה "מלאכים היוצאים מן התקיעה והתרועה." (5:146)

ד

כתיב "ועתה פן ישלח ידו ולקח גם מעץ החיים (בראשית ג:כ״ב)."

כי שורש של האדם היה בגן עדן כמו שכתוב "וישם שם את האדם אשר יצר (שם ב:ח)." אך על ידי החטא נגרש משם. ובכח התשובה יכולין לאחוז בעץ החיים. "ועתה" הוא בחינת תשובה. "ישלח ידו" הוא הכח ומקומו, והוא עשרת ימי התשובה. "ידו"—יוד—[10].

ובאברהם אבינו עליו השלום כתיב "וישלח אברהם את ידו (שם כ״ב:י)" שמסר נפשו בזה הנסיון ונתעלה למעלה מן הטבע ונתאחז בעץ החיים. וכתוב "והאלהים נסה את אברהם (בראשית כ״ב:א)" דרשו חז״ל הרים אותו (על פי בראשית רבה נ״ה:א). והוא שנתעלה לצאת מן הטבע כעניין שכתוב ביוסף "וינס ויצא החוצה (בראשית ל״ט:י״ב)" לזה הרמז נסה את אברהם.

ימים טובים

"אלה מועדי ה' מקראי קודש אשר תקראו אותם במועדם (ויקרא כ"ג:ד)."
פירוש שביום טוב מתגלה חיות פנימיות מהשם יתברך שיש בכל הנבראים.
"אשר תקראו וכו'"—מקראי קודש. שמעתי מאבי אדוני זקני ז"ל כי יכולין
לקרוא הקדושה ביום טוב, וגם הקדושה קוראת לאדם, עד כאן [דברין].

ופירוש "קודש" הוא נקודת הפנימיות, שאף שמחיה הכל היא נבדלת
מהגשמיות—שהשם יתברך קדוש ונבדל. וכתיב "מלא כל הארץ כבודו
(ישעיה ו:ג)" שמחיה הכל—רק שנסתר בעולם הזה, וביום טוב מתגלה.

וזה שכתוב בזוהר הקדוש (פרשת אמור) "מה רב טובך אשר צפנת
ליראיך, פעלת לחוסים בך נגד בני אדם (תהלים ל"א:כ)," כי ביום טוב
נתגלה חיות הפנימיות שהוא אור הגנוז לצדיקים שהם מרגישין אור זה גם
בעשיה. וכן אמר אדוני אבי זקני בשם הזוהר הקדוש שנקרא "יום טוב" על
שם "וירא אלהים את האור כי טוב (בראשית א:ד)," שיש בו מאור הגנוז.
וזה שכתוב "מועדים לשמחה" כי כשמתגלה שורש החיות של האדם ושל
כל הבריאה ממילא יש שמחה. ולכך ביום טוב יכולין למצוא הארת הפנימיות
שיש בכל דבר.

"יראה כל זכורך את פני ה' אלהיך (דברים ט"ז:ט"ז). יֵרָאֶה יִרְאֶה.
"כמו שבא לראות, בא להֵרָאות" עיין שם בגמרא (חגיגה ב ע"א). שהאדם
יכול לראות חיות הפנימיות והוא נקרא "זכורך." "פני ה' אלהיך" היא גם
כן נקודת הפנימיות שיש בכל דבר שנקראת פני ה'. ומבקשים "והשיאנו ה'
אלהינו את ברכת מועדיך (תפילת העמידה)" להיות נדבק מעשה האדם
בשורש על ידי אור היום טוב. ויש לומר "השיאנו" כמו משיאים משואות,
להיות מקושר בשלהבת אהבה לשורש החיים. "ברכת מועדיך" כי כל חיות
השנה על ידי התקשרות בשורש החיות שזה מתגלה ביום טוב. (3:42)

ראש השנה

א

"כתבנו לחיים." כי בכל איש ישראל יש נקודה קדושה בלבו והיא נשמת
חיים שנאמר "וחיי עולם נטע בתוכנו." אך בכל השנה שמסוגלין עוונות, כל
שהחומר גובר ומכסה הנקודה, צריך האדם לבקש רחמים מהקדוש ברוך
הוא לחדש זאת הרשימה בלבו בראש השנה. ועל זה מבקשין "כתבנו
לחיים."

והוא שנאמר "חרות על הלוחות (שמות ל"ב:ט"ז)" שדרשו חז"ל "חירות,"
ממלאך המוות ויצר הרע. כי בקבלת התורה היו בני ישראל מוכנים שלא
תהיה נמחקת הכתיבה לעולם. רק על ידי חטא נתקלקל אחר כך, וצריכין
לחדש החיים בכל שנה.

וה"חתימה" היא להיות זאת הקדושה חתומה, שלא להתפשט החיות
בכל מקום, כמו שכתוב "גן נעול... מעין חתום (שיר השירים ד:י"ב)."
(5:139)

מכח אל הפועל כל אשר הטמין הקדוש ברוך הוא בעולם, כדמיון המטר
שעל ידו מוציאין מן האדמה מכח אל הפועל כל הפירות. (180:5)

ג

"יערוף כמטר לקחי (שם ל"ב:ב)." כי בכל איש ישראל יש נקודת חיות, רק
שצריכין לעורר הפנימיות על ידי התורה. וכמו האדמה שיש בה כח להוציא
תבואה ופירות והמטר מעורר כחה, כן נקרא אדם על שם האדמה. וזה ענין
תורה שבעל פה שכתוב "וחיי עולם נטע בתוכינו"—הוא הכח להוציא פירות
וכן איתא "תולדותיהם של צדיקים מצוות ומעשים טובים (על פי רש"י
בראשית ו:ט)." וזהו כל ענין המשל משמים וארץ שהם מנהיגים כל הבריאה,
שמשמים יורד מטר לארץ. וכן בני ישראל יש בהם ענין שמים וארץ, תורה
שבכתב ותורה שבעל פה. וכן כתוב "תהיו אתם ארץ חפץ (מלאכי י"ג:י"ב)."

בני ישראל מקיימים הבריאה. ובארץ ניכר שעושים רושם ומבררין
מלכותו יתברך בעולם. אך גם בשמים מוסיפין כח, אף שאינו ניכר, מכל
מקום מאחר ששמים וארץ הם אחד ועל ידי בני ישראל מתברר בארץ
האמת, על ידי זה מתיחדין שמים וארץ.

וכתיב "הצור תמים פעלו (דברים ל"ב:ד)." אף כי נודע שבני ישראל
צריכין להשלים הבריאה כמו שאמרו "לצדיקים שמקיימין העולם (אבות
ה:א)" "אך מי הקדמני ואשלם (איוב מ"א:ג)" כתיב. כי כל המבוקש מהאדם
שיהיה במעמד האמיתי לישר מעשיו ומחשבותיו, וכשעומד על מכונו ממילא
מתעורר כח החיות שבו. כי השם יתברך נתן בכל איש ישראל קדושה
וטהרה ויראת שמים ככל הצריך לו, ורק שצריך האדם להוציאו מכח אל
הפועל. וזה "יגעתי ומצאתי, תאמין (מגילה ו ע"ב)," פירוש "מצאתי" בתוך
גוף האדם כמו שאנו אומרים "נשמה שנתת בי טהורה היא."

וזה שאמרו שפעולת השם יתברך בלי חסרון רק שהאדם צריך להתישב
במקום הראוי. ודוגמא לדבר כל הנבראים על ידי פריה ורביה מתרבים
בעולם, ומכל מקום זה כח השם יתברך שברא כן להיות פרים ורבים על
ידי שמתישבים במקום הראוי כמו שכתוב "לא תהו בראה לשֶׁבת יצרה
(ישעיה מ"ה:י"ח)."

וכן בענין עבודת הבורא: כשהאדם מדבק עצמו במקום הראוי לו
ונקרא "לשבת" ששב למקומו לשורשו. וזה ענין שבת קודש, על ידי זה
שורה ברכה ומעוררת חיות פנימית שבו. נמצא שאין האדם מוסיף דבר, רק
שמעמיד עצמו במקומו. וכשמקבל דברי תורה בלבו מחבר שמים וארץ
ומוציא פירות ממש כמו שכתוב "אור זרוע לצדיק (תהלים צ"ז:י"א)" והוא
אור תורה... (175:5)

וזה התירוץ האמיתי על קושיית הרמב"ם איך שייכת מצות עשה "ואהבת"
וכדומה, דברים התלוין בלב. אך כי נטבעה האהבה להשם יתברך בלב כל
איש ישראל. אך ורק צריך האדם שלא להתדבק בתאוות למשוך אהבה
לרע, שעל ידי זה נסתרת הנקודה האמיתית. ובשמרו את עצמו יתמשך
ממילא אחר השם יתברך בכל לבו ונפשו. (120:5)

האזינו

א

"האזינו השמים ואדברה ותשמע הארץ אמרי פי (דברים ל"ב:א)."
כי התורה שורשה בשמים וכחה להמשיך כל מה שבארץ עד לשמים.
שתי בחינות אלו תלויות זו בזו: כפי מה שאדם מקשר כל מצוה ותורה בכח
השורש, כמו כן מתפשטת עד למטה יותר. כי רום מעלה ורום מטה תלוין
זה בזה.

וכל ענין הפרשה הוא לבאר כי בני ישראל צריכין להעלות כל הדברים
הגשמיים והתחתונים. ולכן אל יפול לב האדם עליו במה שצריך לעסוק
בדברים גשמיים ושפלים, כי הלא "הצור תמים פעלו (דברים ל"ב:ד)." וכמו
כן האדם כולל כל הבריאה, וכן כתוב "יצב גבולות עמים למספר בני
ישראל (דברים ל"ב:ח)." וכן הוא בפרט: שיש בכל איש ישראל אלו ההסתרות
שהם מכוחות כל האומות ואיש הישראלי צריך לתקנם.

"ימצאהו בארץ מדבר... יסובבנהו יבוננהו (דברים ל"ב:י)." אף שכתוב
שבחר בבני ישראל מימי קדם, "חלק ה' עמו (שם שם ט),", אבל עיקר
המציאה הוא בעת צר והסתר, מקום חושך אשר איש הישראלי מצפה
להתגלות הקדושה בעולם הזה השפל. זה נקרא "ארץ מדבר" שאין לו רק
הרצון.

כן היא עבודת האדם בחול. אבל כשבאה שבת קודש "יסובבנהו"
בפריסת סוכת שלום, "יבוננהו" בנשמה יתירה, שנתוספת דעת לאדם
בשבת קודש. גם בכל יום "יסובבנהו" בטלית וציצית, "יבוננהו" בתפילין,
שמצוות הללו מאירין לאדם בכל יום בעולם הזה. גם אחר ראש השנה
ויום הכפורים שאדם נעשה טהור אבל אינו יודע איך למצוא הארת
הקדושה בעולם הזה שהוא כמדבר, לכן "יסובבנהו" בסוכה ו"יבוננהו"
בלולב שהוא המשכת הדעת. גם "יבוננהו" רמז לשמחת תורה כמו שפירש
רש"י "יבוננהו" בתורה. (176:5)

ב

"האזינו השמים ואדברה (דברים ל"ב:א)." זה בחינת עשרת הדברות. "ותשמע
הארץ אמרי פי (שם)" הוא בחינת עשרה מאמרות, והוא בחינת תורה שבעל
פה שהקדוש ברוך הוא נתן בתורה, שבני ישראל יתקנו כל הנעשה בעשרה
מאמרות על ידי התורה. שהתורה היא ביאור ופירוש הבריאה. ועל זה
איתא שהצדיקים מקיימים העולם שנברא בעשרה מאמרות. ולכן נאמרה
שירת האזינו על ידי משה ויהושע, שהוא חיבור תורה שבכתב ושבעל פה.
ואמר "יערוף כמטר לקחי (שם ל"ב:ב)" שתכלית התורה להוציא על ידה

נצבים—וילך

א

["אתם נצבים היום כלכם לפני ה' אלהיכם (דברים כ"ט:ט)."]

במדרש "תפלת הערב אין לה קבע [אין לה זמן קבוע] (דברים רבה ח:א
על פי משנה ברכות ד:ה)." פירוש: על ידי החשכות בלב האדם שצועק
מכאב לבו, נפתח שער לתפלה יותר מכל הזמנים שמיוחדים לתפלה, כיון
שבני ישראל נצבים לפני השם יתברך והם למעלה מן הזמן. (121:5)

ב

בפסוק "לעברך בברית ה' אלהיך (דברים כ"ט:יא)." זאת הברית היא
התורה, כדאיתא "קודשא בריך הוא ואורייתא וישראל כולהון חד."

תורה גימטריא תרי"א [611] ועם דחילו ורחימו [יראה ואהבה], שהן
שורש כל מצוות עשה ולא תעשה, [תרי"ג]. והם בחינת "אנכי (שמות כ:ב)"
ו"לא יהיה לך (שם ג)" וכתיב "אחת דיבר אלהים שתים זו שמעתי (תהילים
ס"ב:י"ב)."

ובאמת אהבה היא מתת אלהים וזה "אנכי." ועל זה ביקש דוד המלך
ע"ה "אחת שאלתי מאת ה' (תהלים כ"ז:ד)." ויראה היא עיקר הכח של איש
ישראל בעצמו ועל זה כתיב "מה השם אלהיך שואל כי אם ליראה (דברים
י:י"ב)."

נמצא א' עם תורה הוא גימטריה ברית, וזה הברית מהקדוש ברוך הוא
לתורה ומהתורה לישראל, וזה הברית הוא לכלל ישראל, כמו שכתוב "לא
אתכם לבדכם אנכי כורת את הברית הזאת (שם כ"ט:יי"ג)." פירוש שזאת
הברית אי אפשר להיות רק לכלל ישראל, הדורות שהיו ושיהיו. כמו הקדוש
ברוך הוא היה הוה ויהיה, והכל אחדות אחת, כן בריתו אי אפשר להיות
רק בכלל כל הדורות. ומכל מקום יש לכל איש ישראל חלק בו, שכל אחד
מישראל כשמכניס עצמו לקבל עליו זה הברית מעורר כל הדורות עמו,
שהיו ושיהיו. (128:5)

ג

"העדותי בכם היום את השמים ואת הארץ (דברים ל:יי"ט)."

פירש רש"י ז"ל "כלום שינו שמים וארץ מידתם...אתם...על אחת כמה
וכמה." ולכאורה מאי ראיה מהם, שאין להם בחירה? אך על כל פנים מובן
כי מדרך הטבע להיות נמשך כל דבר אחר השם יתברך וציוויו. אם כן וודאי
לא נגרע הטבע האדם מזה, רק שניתנה לו בחירה [בין] יצר הטוב ויצר הרע. ואם
לא יגבור הרע על הטוב, ממילא מצד עצמו יימשך אחר הטוב ככל הנבראים.

ומזה מובן "ילך ה' החסד כי אתה תשלם לאיש כמעשהו (תהלים
ס"ב:י"ג)." וקשה: מה החסד? כדכתבו בגמרא. אך גם מי שעושה טוב הוא
מהשם יתברך, ורק שהוא נקי ולא נמשך אחר יצר הרע, ממילא נתעוררת
הפנימיות שנתן השם יתברך באדם לטוב. ואם כן הכל רק חסד השם
יתברך.

במדרש ״אשרי ששמעותיו לי... ישקוד על דלתותי (משלי ח:ל״ד)׳...
דלת לפנים מדלת (דברים רבה ז:ב)."

פירוש ״שמועותיי״ להיות מוכן תמיד לקבל ולהאזין דברי השם יתברך,
שיש בכל דבר קול דבר ה׳, שכל דבר במאמר נברא ונגנז בו כח דבר ה׳. זה
שצריכין למצוא הארה הגנוזה.

ויש פנימיות יותר ויותר עד אין שיעור, וזה שאמרו ״דלתותי,״ שלא
יסבור שכבר בא לאמת, רק ידע תמיד שעומד אצל הפתח. וי״דלת״ מלשון
דלות, שעל ידי זה נפתח לו דלת לפנים מדלת.

ובפרט באיש ישראל יש נשמת חיים ששומעת תמיד קול התורה, רק
שגם זה נסתר להאדם. וזה שכתוב ״שמוע תשמע,״ שישמע הנשמע לו.

ועוד במדרש ״לשמור מזוזת פתחי (שם)״ כמו שהמזוזה קבועה ״כך
לא תהא זז מבתי כנסיות ומבתי מדרשות (שם)." פירוש שצריך האדם
להיות מוכן תמיד בלי הפסק רק לשמוע דבר השם יתברך, וממילא נפתח
לו כשיש עת רצון. רק שיהיה האדם עומד תמיד אצל הפתח. וזהו ״ששמעותיו
לי,״ שכל החושים יהיו מוכנים לקבל ולהאזין דבר השם יתברך לא דבר
אחר. (5:99-100)

ג

״ולא נתן ה׳ לכם לב לדעת ועינים לראות ואזנים לשמוע עד היום הזה
(דברים כ״ט:ג)."

אדוני אבי זקני מורי ורבי ז״ל הגיד בשם הרב הקדוש מפרשיסחא ז״ל
על פסוק זה כי כל הניסים והנפלאות שעשה עמהם השם יתברך, הואיל
והיו שלא על פי הטבע היו רק לשעה. אבל אחר שגמר להם כל התורה
ונעשה מכל ההתנהגות תורה, נעשה מזה בנין קבוע לדורות. עד כאן דבריו
ז״ל.

והוא ענין ״היום הזה,״ היינו התלבשות כל ההארות במעשים טובים,
שמכל מעשיהם נעשה תורה. והוא באמת עיקר הזכות הגדולה לבני ישראל
בקבלת התורה. כי התורה אין לה שיעור כמאמר ״ונעלמה מעיני כל חי
(איוב כ״ח:כ״א)." רק שבני ישראל זכו להלביש התורה, שמכל מעשיהם
נעשה לבוש לאור התורה בתורה ומצוות שבתורה זו שלפנינו. והבן.

וזה יש לפרש גם כן ״את ה׳ האמרת היום (דברים כ״ו:י״ז)״ פירוש
שנעשה מעשרה מאמרות תורה שלימה. (5:101)

ד

[״את ה׳ האמרת... וה׳ האמירך (דברים כ״ו:י״ז,י״ח)."]

עיין באבן עזרא [המביא דברי ר׳ יהודה הלוי המפרש ״האמיר״ מלשון
״אמירה.״]

ויש להעמיק יותר זה הפירוש על פי הידוע כי אורייתא וקודשא בריך
הוא וישראל חד. וזה שאמרו ״אנכי—אנא נפשאי כתבית יהבית [אני עצמי
כתבתי נתתי] (שבת ק״ה ע״א)." כי התורה אלהות ממש ובני ישראל עשו
כביכול מקודשא בריך הוא אורייתא. וכן בני ישראל נעשו בחינת תורה.
(5:105)

כי עבד היית (דברים כ"ד:כ"ב)" לומר שעל ידי מצוה זו יהיה הלחם בלי
פסולת, ולא ידבק בעושרו יותר מדאי. לכן נתנה תורה מצוות מעשרות
וצדקות שהן שמירה ל[ענין] עושר.

איש ישראל צריך להיות בן חורין בנפש וגוף וכל אשר לו. לכן גם
בדירה ניתנה מצות מזוזה, ובטלית מצות ציצית, שהכל מסייע אל החירות
והוא "זכר ליציאת מצרים." לכן מצות ציצית סמוכה לכלאים, שעל ידי
הכלאים מתערבת בו פסולת, וציצית הוא חירות אל המלבוש.

וזה כלל כל התורה לכן אמרו "חרות על הלוחות (שמות ל"ב:ט"ז)' אל
תקרא חרות אלא חירות—אין לך בן חורין אלא העוסק בתורה (אבות ו:ב)"
שמלמדת לאדם דרך החירות. ושמירת הלשון היא חירות בנפש "נפש חיה
(בראשית ב:ז)" בתרגום "רוח ממללא." (5:98)

כי תבוא

א

"היום הזה ה' אלהיך מצוך לעשות את החוקים האלה ואת המשפטים
ושמרת ועשית אותם בכל לבבך ובכל נפשך (דברים כ"ו:ט"ז)."

במדרש תנחומא מביא "לכו נרננה ה'... נשתחווה ונכרעה (תהלים
צ"ה:א-ג)." "צפה משה רבינו ע"ה שביכורים עתידין ליפסק, תיקן תפלה."
אדוני אבי זקני מורי ורבי ז"ל פירש שגם תפלה הוא ליתן הראשית בכל
יום להשם יתברך, כמו ביכורים.

אך השייכות ל"היום הזה" צריכה ביאור. במדרש וברש"י הביאו "היום
הזה"—"בכל יום יהיו בעיניך כחדשים." וכי הרצון להטעות להאדם אף
שבאמת אין התחדשות חס ושלום? אך בכח האדם לחדש כל דבר. כי ודאי
יש בחינת התחדשות בכל דבר, שהרי הקדוש ברוך הוא מחדש בכל יום
תמיד מעשה בראשית, ופירוש "תמיד" בכל רגע. וגם כי הלא אין דבר בלי
חיות השם יתברך. והנקודה שממנו יתברך לעולם לא תתישן, כי דבריו
חיים ונובעין תמיד.

אך כי "החושך יכסה ארץ (ישעיה ס:ב)." הקליפה החיצונית היא
מסתרת הנקודה הנובעת דכתיב "אין כל חדש תחת השמש (קהלת א:ט)"
והיא הטבע והעולם הזה שמסתיר ההתחדשות. אך בכח האדם להאיר
הנקודה מהחשיכה, וזה שכתוב "היום הזה ה' אלהיך מצוך לעשות" פירושו
למצוא בחינת "היום הזה" שהיא התגלות האור בחינת אספקלריא דנהרא
[המאירה] גם בתוך המעשה ממש שהוא מסתיר הנקודה.

והיא על ידי מצוות דכתיב "כי נר מצוה (משלי ו:כ"ג)" שכיון שמצוה
היא במעשה גשמי אבל יש בה חיות השם יתברך בציווי לעשותה, בכח
האדם הוא להתדבק על ידה באור הגנוז. וזה שכתוב בפסוק "את החוקים"
כלומר על ידי המצוות השם יתברך נותן לך כח למצוא בחינת "היום הזה"
גם במעשה... (5:99)

ב

"והיה אם שמע תשמע בקול ה' אלהיך... (כ"ח:א)."

"רחמיו על כל מעשיו." והשם יתברך יודע כי רחמנות של האם על האפרוחים
בענין זה, אם תלקח אם על הבנים. וכמו כן אם "ישחט אותו ואת בנו ביום
אחד (יקרא כ"ב:כ"ח)."

ובאמת זה עצמו שהטביע הקדוש ברוך הוא ענין רחמים בכל בריה
במדה ידועה. ואדרבא מחמת אלה המצוות שנתן השם יתברך בבהמה
ובעוף, מחמת זה נמצא בהם ענין זה הרחמים. ובאמת כל קיום הבריאה
הוא ברחמים, כמו שאנו אומרים "המנהג עולמו בחסד ובריותיו ברחמים."
לכן נמצאו הרחמים בכל הבריאה. ובני ישראל, שהם עיקר הבריאה הם
רחמנים ביותר.

אך בכל בריאה יש מן הרחמים כפי גזירתו יתברך, וזה שאמר המדרש
שנתן רחמיו עליהם. [אבל] בגמרא הפירוש מי שאומר שטעם המצוה [הוא]
על ידי שהשם יתברך מרחם על קן הצפור, זה אינו. אדרבא, במצוה זו נתן
השם יתברך הרחמים בציפור עצמה. וזהו שאמרו "שאינן אלא גזירות,"
שגזר שיהיו רחמים בכל בריה במדה ידועה. (92:5)

ג

"מוצא שפתיך תשמור ועשית כאשר נדרת (דברים כ"ג:כ:ד)." הוא שמירת
הלשון. הפה הוא אבר פנימי ביותר, שכל ההבל ופנימיות האדם הוא יוצא
על ידי מוצאות הפה. על כן צריך שמירה יותר. ונראה שמצוות תלמוד תורה
הוא שמירת הפה, שכל מצוות עשה כנגד אבר מיוחד. לכן מצוה זו תמיד,
יום ולילה, כי מוצאות הפה צריכין יותר שמירה.

כל שורש החיות באדם הוא בהבל הפנימי. כשאדם שומר הבל פיו זה
שורש לכל המעשים, כדכתיב "תשמור ועשית" שכל המעשים תלויים בשמירת
הפה.

יתרון בריאת האדם על בעלי החיים הוא כי האדם מדבר, וכן כתוב
"ויהי האדם לנפש חיה (בראשית ב:ז)" ותרגומו "לרוח ממללא [רוח מדברת]."
לזאת צריך לתת עיקר המעלה שלו להשם יתברך. כי בריאת הפה ודיבור
האדם הוא דבר נפלא יותר מכל הבריאה, כמו שמבין מי שמתבונן בפלא
זה. וכל מה שברא הקדוש ברוך הוא הכל לכבודו ברא כמו שכתוב "תהלתי
יספרו (ישעיה מ"ג:כ"א)."

ואם כי להוציא דברים לפני השם יתברך אינו בנקל, אבל על כל פנים
נשמור הפה מדברים בטלים. (84:5)

ד

בפסוק "השמר בנגע הצרעת לשמור מאד ולעשות ככל אשר יורו אתכם
הכהנים הלוים כאשר צויתים תשמרו לעשות. זכור את אשר עשה ה'
אלהיך למרים בדרך בצאתכם ממצרים (דברים כ"ד:ח-ט)."

... זה כלל מצוות עשה ולא תעשה: כולן ניתנו כדי שיהיה איש ישראל
בן חורין. לכן הקדים לנו יציאת מצרים ואחר כך התורה שמלמדת איך
להיות נשאר הנפש בחירות, שלא להתקשר בגשמיות, על ידי תרי"ג עיטין
[עצות] שבתורה. וכל מצוה שכתוב בה יציאת מצרים הוא לומר שעל ידי
המצוה יתדבק בחירות. כמו כן בפרשת לקט, שכחה, ופיאה כתוב "וזכרת

נמצא בכל איש ישראל כפי הביטול אליו יתברך זוכה לשמוע ולהשיג דבר השם. (73:5)

כי תצא

א

כי תצא למלחמה על אויביך, ונתנו ה׳ אלהיך בידך ושבית שביו (דברים כ״א:י).״

כי בכל דבר יש נקודת חיות מהשם יתברך, רק שנסתר ונעלם. וצריך מלחמה ועבודה כל ימות החול למצוא זאת הנקודה. אחר כך נעשה שבת, שמתגלה כי השם יתברך מחיה הכל שזה ענין שבת קודש, שבני ישראל מעידין על בריאת שמים וארץ, שגם עתה קיומם רק בעשרה מאמרות.

ובחול צריכין מלחמה על זה. ומכל מקום גם השבת באה כפי הטירחה והעבודה בחול, כמו שאמרו ״מי שטרח בערב שבת יאכל בשבת (עבודה זרה ג ע״א).״ וערב שבת הוא התערובות, שיש מבחינת שבת גם בחול, כמו שאנו אומרים ״בדברו מעריב ערבים.״

וצריך האדם לידע כי גם הגבורה נגד יצר הרע רק בכח השם יתברך, כדכתיב ״ונתנו השם אלהיך בידך,״ פירוש אף שהיה על ידי כח התגברות האדם כדכתיב ״בידך״ שהוא על שמו הכח, עם כל זאת השם יתברך כל יכול והוא מסייע לאדם שיהיה בדרך כחו, אף שהוא מהשם יתברך, כמו שכתוב ״ילך אדני חסד כי אתה תשלם לאיש כמעשהו (תהלים נ״ב:י״ג).״ ומקשין ״מה החסד?״ אך אדרבא, אף שהכל מהשם יתברך, נותן לאדם באופן שיהיה מן האדם עצמו.

״ושבית שביו״ כשיודעין זה, שהוא מהשם יתברך. והכלל כי בכל מעשה טוב ומצוה יש ענין הנעשה והחזרת הדבר להשם יתברך. כי אף שיטריח האדם ויעשה נפלאות, אם לא יחזיר המצוה להשם יתברך לא עשה כלום, כי לא החזיר את השליחות לבעליו. והחזרה לא יוכל להיות רק על ידי זה שיודע שהכל מהשם יתברך. וזה ״ושבית שביו״ שיחזיר הנקודה אליו יתברך על ידי שיודע שהוא רק ממנו יתברך. (83:5)

ב

[״כי יקרא קן צפור לפניך (דברים כ״ב:ו).״] במדרש: ״כשם שנתן רחמיו על האדם, כך על הבהמה ועל העוף (תנחומא נח ו).״ ומקשים מדאיתא במשנה ״האומר על קן צפור יגיעו רחמיך... משתקין אותו (ברכות ה:ג).״ ופרשו בגמרא ״שעושה מדותיו של הקדוש ברוך הוא רחמים, ואינן אלא גזירות (ברכות ל״ג ע״ב).״ עיין שם.

אכן נראה דכוונת המדרש שנתן רחמיו בכל הברואים, כדכתיב ״ורחמיו על כל מעשיו (תהלים קמ״ה:ט).״ פירוש הענין כי האדם מרחם על הבהמה ולא על הבהמה, כי אין האדם יודע ומשיג דעת הבהמה כלל. לכן אין בו רחמנות עליה, כי אין ענין דעת ורחמנות של בהמה מושגת לאדם. וכמו כן מלאכים אינם מבינים דעת האדם, וכבהמה המה להם. אכן השם יתברך, היודע הכל, הוא יודע דעת המלאכים והאדם והבהמה וכל בריאה. לכן

ג

"שופטים ושוטרים תתן לך בכל שעריך (דברים ט"ז:י"ח)." הוא הבטחה גם
כן שביד איש הישראלי למנות על עצמו שופט ושוטר. כמו שכתוב "בדרך
שאדם רוצה לילך מוליכין אותו (מכות י ע"ב)." ויש מי שרוצה להשיג
האמת וגם מי שאין בו דעת שלימה ורוצה להיות נכפף בעל כרחו. גם בדרך
זה מסייעין לאדם וזה פירוש "שופטים ושוטרים."

והעיקר לבקש את האמת, כמו שכתוב "צדק צדק תרדוף (דברים
ט"ז:כ)." וגם בשקר כתיב "מדבר שקר תרחק (שמות כ"ג:ז)." ושמעתי
ממורי זקני ז"ל שהגיד בשם הרב מפרשיסחא ז"ל שלא מצינו הרחקה
בשום איסור בתורה, רק חכמים תיקנו סייג, זולת בשקר שהתורה עצמה
אמרה "תרחק," להראות חומר האיסור. עד כאן דבריו.

וכמו כן מצינו כאן באמת "צדק צדק תרדוף" מה שלא מצינו במקום
אחר—כי הוא יסוד הכל, וכתיב "תרדוף." והיינו כי אי אפשר לבוא לגמרי
לאמיתות האמת בעלמא דשיקרא, לכן לעולם יש לרדוף אחר הצדק, לידע
כי עדיין אינו מוצדק כראוי. וכשרודפין הצדק בעולם הזה משיגין אותו
בשלימות בעולם הבא. וזה שכתוב "למען תחיה וירשת (דברים ט"ז:כ)"
שהוא רמז לעולם הבא, עולם שכולו חיים. (5:72)

ד

"צדק צדק תרדוף (דברים ט"ז:כ)." שאין חקר וסוף לבחינת צדק ואמת, כי
ה' אלהים אמת. ולכך לעולם יש להוסיף ולהעמיק שיהיה אמת לאמיתו, כי
אינו אמת עד שנעשה כל האדם אחד, מיוחד לעבודתו יתברך." וי"אמתי"
מראש עד סוף אותיות התורה.

בשם הרב הקדוש מפרשיסחא היהודי ז"ל להיות רדיפת הצדק בצדק,
לא בשקר. דברי פי חכם חן. (5:68)

ה

בפסוק "כי הגוים האלה... אל מעוננים ואל קוסמים ישמעו. ואתה לא כן...
נביא מקרבך... (דברים י"ח:י"ד-ט"ו)."

...מעוננים וקוסמין הם על ידי כוחות הטבע מעשרה מאמרות. ובני
ישראל נבחרו באופן נעלה מהטבע והוא עשרת הדברות. וכמו דכתוב "עושי
דברו לשמוע בקול דברו (תהלים ק"ג:כ)." שעל ידי ביטול המעשה להנהגות
הבורא יתברך שאמרו "כל אשר דבר ה' נעשה (שמות י"ט:ח)" זכו לשמוע
בקול דברו.

והיה זה ההכנה לדורות שהיה ראוי להיות כל עם ה' נביאים לשמוע
לעולם דבר ה'. אך כי יצאה נשמתן ואמרו "לא אוסף לשמוע את קול ה'
(דברים י"ח:ט"ז)," ונשאר זה הכח לנביאים. וכפי זכות בני ישראל, על ידי
זה עצמו—שאין נמשכים אחר הקוסמין, וזה שכתוב "כי הגוים האלה"
עשה כן להיות הכוחות הטבעיות האלה בעולם, ובני ישראל מבטלים הכל
אליו יתברך כמו שכתוב "תמים תהיה לפני ה' (שם י"ח:י"ג)," על ידי זה
זוכין לשמוע בקול דברו.

וזה שכתוב "נביא מקרבך" ממש שתלוי בכלל בני ישראל. ומעין זה

וקללה (דברים י"א:כ"ו)."

פירוש: שבכל עת וזמן יש שני הדרכים לפני האדם. כמו שכתוב בספרי (פרשת ראה א) משל לזקן שעומד על פרשת דרכים ומזהיר: זה הדרך תחתיו קוצים וסופו מישור [והדרך תחתיו מישור סופו קוצים].

נמצא הצדיק גם כן עומד תמיד באמצעיות שני הדרכים, ימין ושמאל. וזה שאמרו "כל הגדול מחבירו יצרו גדול (סוכה נ"ב ע"א)." ואמרו חכמים לעתיד לבא הקדוש ברוך הוא מביא יצר הרע ושוחטו. צדיקים נדמה להם כהר ובוכין "איך יכלנו להלחם בו!" ורשעים נדמה להם כחוט השערה ובוכין "איך לא יכלנו לכבוש חוט שערה כזה!"

והענין כי לעולם יש רק חוט השערה. והצדיקים שגוברים עליו פוגעין אחר כך בחוט שערה אחרת וכן לעולם, עד שמתרבה ונעשה כהר. אבל זה הרשע הנשאר עומד, הרי הוא עומד בחוט השערה האחת. וזה ענין הצדיקים "אין להם מנוחה (ברכות ס"ד ע"א)."

וזה שכתוב שלא יתגאה האדם בהיותו נתעלה באיזה מדרגה. כי גם שם יש לפניו שני הדרכים. אמנם על ידי זה מרוויחין הצדיקים הברכה בהיותם מניחין דרך הרע ובוחרים בדרך הטוב. והוא השכר שלעתיד... (5:57)

שופטים

א

"שופטים ושוטרים תתן לך בכל שעריך (דברים ט"ז:י"ח)." יש להבין על פי מה שכתב אדוני אבי זקני מורי ורבי ז"ל רמז על שם חודש אלול על פי הפסוק "הוא עשנו ולא אנחנו (תהלים ק"ג)." דיש קרי וכתיב "לו אנחנו." ועל שתי בחינות אלו נקרא אלול.

כי זה תלוי בזה. כפי ביטול האדם ["לא אנחנו"] מתקרב אליו יתברך [לו אנחנו]. ודברי פי חכם חן. כי יש שתי בחינות בעבודת הבורא יתברך. לבטל הגוף והגשמיות, הוא בחינת שוטרים, לכוף את הגוף לשנות את טעמו, בחינת "סור מרע (תהלים ל"ד:ט"ו)." והשניה בחינת התקרבות אל הבורא יתברך, בחינת "עשה טוב (שם שם)." וזה "שופטים"—שהוא בהשגת הדעת. (5:72)

ב

בכל מקום אומרים שהוא "עת רצון" כמו באלול ובסעודה שלישית בשבת, הגם כי לשם יתברך לא שייך זמן. על כרחך הפירוש שהוא עת רצון באדם שיוכל לקרב עצמו ולדבק בקדוש ברוך הוא ברצון אמת בפנימיות הלב. כי הקדוש ברוך הוא מלא רצון. ורק מי שזוכה יוכל להתקרב אליו. כי "כמים הפנים לפנים, כן לב האדם לאדם (משלי כ"ז:י"ט)." וכפי התעוררות רחמים בלב על עצמו, איך שיש בו נקודה קדושה מהקדוש ברוך הוא ונטבע בחומר וגשמיות, כפי התעוררות לבו מתעוררים עליו רחמים רבים בשמים גם כן. (5:68)

(דברים י״ב:ב)״ לנקות ארץ ישראל מכל פסולת ואחר כך ״לשכנו תדרשו.״
כי הנה דיש בשבת במקדש כתוב ״מנוחה ונחלה (דברים י״ב:ט).״ דכמו דיש בשבת
מנוחה שהיא הקדושה המתגלה בזמן ומתעברין מיני (ועוברים ממנו) כל
חשכות הזמן—לכן נקראת ״מנוחה.״ כמו כן יש בעולם מקום, בית המקדש
דהוא מנוחה, שסטרא אחרא אין לו שליטה שם. וכמו כן בנפשות, רוח
הקודש נקראת מנוחה. כמו שכתוב גבי ברוך ״ומנוחה לא מצאתי (ירמיה
מ״ה:ג).״ עיין שם. והאדם צריך לדרוש לאותן המקומות והזמנים והנפשות
שהקדושה מתגלה בהם—וזה ״לשכנו תדרשו.״

ובאמת כל זו המצוה שייך בכל אדם שצריכין מקודם לעקור מנפשו כל
הסטרא אחרא, ואחר כך ״לשכנו תדרשו.״ מכל שכן בכלל ישראל לדרוש
ולבקש להתחנן להקדוש ברוך הוא שיחזיר לנו הנבואה ורוח הקודש שישרה
בינינו כימי קדם. (62:5)

ד

״כי ירחיב ה׳ אלהיך את גבולך כאשר דבר לך ואמרת אוכלה בשר כי תאוה
נפשך לאכול בשר, בכל אות נפשך תאכל בשר (דברים י״ב:כ).״

במדרש (דברים רבה ד:ח,ט) ״מתן אדם ירחיב לו, ולפני גדולים ינחנו
(משלי י״ח:ט״ז).״ ״עושה משפט לעשוקים נותן לחם לרעבים ה׳ מתיר
אסורים (תהלים קמ״ו:ז).״

פשוט: מי שנותן נדבת לבו להשם יתברך זה עצמו מרחיב לו. כי כל
המיצר נעשה רק מהסתרת החיצוניות—ורק לנסיון. וכשאדם גובר רצונו
ומניחו בעבור רצון השם יתברך, זה עצמו פותח הפנימיות ומבטל ההסתר.
וזה ״ירחיב לו.״

וכתיב ״בכל אות נפשך תאכל בשר״ וכבר כתיב ״ואמרת אוכלה בשר.״
אך המפרשים דקדקו שלא כתיב אות גופך רק נפשך. עיין בר׳ משה
אלשיך. ו״בכל אות נפשך״ הוא כמו שכתוב ״ואהבת את ה׳ אלהיך בכל
לבבך ובכל נפשך ובכל מאדך (דברים ו:ה).״ אם כן מאחר שכתוב ״בכל
אות נפשך,״ על כרחך הכוונה לשמים.

... כי אם לא יתבטל מפנימיות הדביקות להשם יתברך, אף ברצון זה,
אז יוכל לאכול. ולא שיבטל על ידי זה אהבה העיקרית. וזה שכתב ״בכל
אות נפשך״ ואז כשעיקר האהבה נדבקת בו להשם יתברך, זה מתיר
האיסור וכח סטרא אחרא שיש בכל דבר גשמיות. וזה שכתוב ״ה׳ מתיר
אסורים.״

כי הווית כל דבר ממנו, רק שהנקודה סתומה וצריכין להרחיבה. וזה
תלוי בנקודה שבאדם. כפי הרחבתה בנפשו, כן מתגלה אליו בכל מקום. וזה
שכתוב ״כי ירחיב ה׳ אלהיך את גבולך״—שתתפשט הנקודה ותתרחב בכל
נפש האדם. (54:5)

ה

במדרש ״שמעו והאזינו, אל תגבהו כי ה׳ דבר (ירמיה י״ג:ט״ו).״ אמר רבי
תנחומא ׳אמר הקדוש ברוך הוא׳: שמעו לדברי תורה ואל תדברו גבוהות כי
ה׳ דבר. (דברים רבה ד:ב)״ דכתיב ״ראה אנכי נותן לפניכם היום ברכה

כי בכל דבר יש נקודת חיות מחי החיים. רק שבעולם הזה נסתר הפנימיות. וזה המבוקש מאיש ישראל: לעורר ולגלות הפנימיות שיש בכל דבר על ידי המצוות. שבכל מעשה נמצא ממצוות השם יתברך, עשה או לא תעשה. ועל ידי המצוה מקרב כל המעשים אליו יתברך. וזה "נרי בידך" כי צריך כל אדם להאיר הנקודה הטמונה. וכאלו היא במאסר עד שיגבור האדם להאירה מחשיכה.

ונקודה זו היא "הברכה" בעצמה "אשר תשמעו." כשמדבק עצמו בנקודה שבכל דבר—אז רואה שזאת הברכה. וזה "ראה" על ידי הביטול לנקודה הנ"ל.

וכן בשבת כתוב "ויברך (בראשית ב:ג)." כי זאת היא בחינת שבת, להיבטל ולהיכלל לנקודה הנ"ל—ושם שורה ברכה. אמרו חז"ל "כלי מחזיק ברכה... שלום (עוקצים ג:י"ב)." והיא הנקודה מהשם יתברך שמהוה כל ונקרא "שלום"—שהיא שלימות כל הנבראים. והיא הברכה. (5:54)

ב

["ראה אנכי נותן לפניכם היום ברכה וקללה. את הברכה אשר תשמעו אל מצוות ה' אלהיכם אשר אנכי מצוה אתכם היום. והקללה אם לא תשמעו... (דברים י"א:כ"ו-כ"ח)."]

בברכה כתיב "אשר תשמעו" ולהיפוך כתיב "אם." כי הטוב בבני ישראל בעצם, והחטא במקרה. לכן בישראל מחשבה טובה מצרפין—ולא לרעה. כי בכלל בוודאי שמעו וקיבלו בני ישראל. לכן גם אם כי נפלו אחר כך מזה, יש להם בכל יום בחירה חדשה. כמו שכתוב "אנכי נותן לפניכם היום." "אנכי" מצד קבלת התורה נתחדש בני ישראל בכל יום אלה שני הדרכים. וכך צריך להיות קבלת מלכות שמים בקריאת שמע בכל יום היינו "אשר תשמעו." ולכן אף שנמצא איזה חטא—כי גם בצדיק כתיב "אין צדיק בארץ אשר יעשה טוב ולא יחטא (קהלת ז:כ)"—רק שהוא בדרך עראי. (5:61)

ג

בפסוק "כי אם אל המקום אשר יבחר ה' אלהיכם מכל שבטיכם לשום את שמו שם לשכנו תדרשו ובאת שמה (דברים י"ב:ה)."

אמרו חז"ל "דרוש על פי נביא. דרוש ותמצא, ואחר כך יאמר לך נביא. כמו שכתוב בדוד המלך ע"ה 'אם אבא באהל ביתי, אם אעלה על ערש יצועי, אם אתן שנת לעיני לעפעפי תנומה—עד אמצא מקום לה' משכנות לאביר יעקב (תהלים קל"ב:ג-ה).'" עיין שם בספרי (פרשת ראה י).

דהנה כתיב "אשר יבחר ה'" ולא גילה להם המקום מיד, רק שיהיה בכח דרישת בני ישראל. כי ארץ ישראל ובית המקדש תלוים בעבודת בני ישראל. וזה שאמרו חז"ל דבעי [צריך] דרישה.

וכמו שכתוב באברהם אבינו ע"ה "לך לך... אל הארץ אשר אראך (בראשית י"ב:א)" ולא גילה לו מיד. כמו כן פרטות מקום המקדש היו צריכין בני ישראל לדרוש.

ומקודם כתיב "אבד תאבדון את כל המקומות אשר עבדו שם הגוים

והוא בחינת אהבת חסד מה שזיכה אותנו הקדוש ברוך הוא במצוותיו.
כמו שאמרו "רצה הקדוש ברוך הוא לזכות את בני ישראל. לפיכך הרבה
להם תורה ומצוות (אבות ו:י"א)." שעל ידי זה מזדככין מעשיהם להתדמות
אל הבורא. ותרי"ג (613) מצוות מזככין רמ"ח ושס"ה [248 איברים 365
גידים] שבאדם. ובזה זוכין לאהבת ה'. (5:50-1)

ג

במצות ברכת המזון "ואכלת ושבעת וברכת (דברים ח:י)" דכתיב "ואכלת
ושבעת... השמרו לכם (שם י"ט:ט"ו-ט"ז)" ש"אין אדם מורד אלא מתוך
שביעה (ספרי עקב י"א)." אם כן נראה ד"וברכת" הוא תיקון שלא יבא
לידי מרידה. ואדרבה! יכול לקבל ברכה מתוך אכילה.

דהנה כתיב "כי לא על הלחם לבדו יחיה האדם כי על כל מוצא פי ה'
יחיה האדם (דברים ח:ג)." ופירש האר"י ז"ל שחיות המאמרו יתברך שיש
בתוך המאכל הוא חיות אל הנפש, והגשמיות אל הגוף. עיין שם. שעל ידי
ברכות זוכין למצוא פנימיות המזון שהוא מזון הנפש. כי בוודאי כשנעשה
השם יתברך המאכל להיות מזון אל האדם הוא מזון גם בפנימיות. ועל ידי
התורה זוכין למצוא זה המזון.

יש "זכור" ו"שמור" בכלל כל המצוות. "זכור" הוא בחינת מצוות עשה
לעורר הפנימיות וניצוצי קדושה שיש בכל דבר על ידי מצוות עשה. ו"שמור"
על ידי ה"לא תעשה" לשמור החיצוניות וקליפות שלא יתמשכו יותר מדאי.
ושני אלו הם בכל דבר שבעולם. לכן כתיב "ושבעת וברכת" הוא בחינת
"זכור" בפה. "השמרו לכם" בחינת "שמור" בלב.

לכן אמרו חז"ל שלחן שאמרו עליו דברי תורה כאילו אכלו משלחנו
של מקום ברוך הוא דכתיב "וידבר אלי זה השלחן אשר לפני ה' (יחזקאל
מ"א:כ"ב)." כיון שדיבר עליו דברי תורה הוא שולחנו של מקום,
והוא שעל ידי דברי תורה זוכין למצוא פנימיות המזון שבקדושה.

ועל זה רמזו חז"ל "אם אין קמח אין תורה (אבות ג:י"ז)" הוא פנימיות
הקמח שמזין אל הנפש. וגם כן "אם אין תורה אין קמח (שם)" שבלי כח
התורה אין פנימיות המזון מתגלה. ולכן אמרו בגמרא (ברכות מ"ט ע"א)
שצריכין להזכיר בברכת המזון ברית ותורה, שעל ידי בריתו שחתם בבשרנו
ועל ידי התורה יכולין אנו למצוא מזון הפנימיות—שהוא מצד הקדושה
ומחיה ומזין את הנפש. (5:46)

ראה

א

["ראה אנכי נותן לפניכם היום ברכה וקללה. את הברכה אשר תשמעו אל
מצות ה' אלהיכם. (דברים י"א:כ"ו-כ"ז)."]

ובמדרש "הנפש והתורה נמשלו בנר. הנפש דכתיב 'נר ה' נשמת אדם
(משלי כ:כ"ז)' והתורה דכתיב 'כי נר מצוה ותורה אור (שם ו:כ"ג).' אמר
הקדוש ברוך הוא... 'נרי בידך ונרך בידי. נרי בידך זו התורה, ונרך בידי זו
הנפש (דברים רבה ד:ד).'"

"ומדוע לא יראתם לדבר בעבדי במשה (שם)."

וזה שאמר משה רבינו ע"ה שעל ידי שלא עלו למדרגה זאת כמוהו ואמרו "קרב אתה" ו"לא ראיתם כל תמונה," אם כן אין נפשותם נבדלין מכל הגשמיות וצריכין מאוד שמירה. כי אם היו במדרגת משה רבינו ע"ה, הוא כולו טוב כידוע, ואינו צריך שמירה. (5:25)

עקב

א

בפרשת "והיה אם שמוע תשמעו אל מצותי... (דברים י"א:י"ג)." ברש"י מספרי (י"א:י"ג) "אזהרה ליחיד אזהרה לרבים." פירושו: בכל יום מתחדשת אזהרת התורה בנפשות בני ישראל בפרט ובכלל. אבל כפי עבודת האדם זוכה להרגיש בזה הקול "אשר אנכי מצוך היום"—והכל תלוי באדם.

וזה שכתוב "אם שמוע תשמעו." פירושו: להשמיע את הקול ולשמוע לקבל את הציווי. כמו שכתוב "עושי דברו (תהלים ק"ג:כ-כ"א)" והדר [וחוזר] "לשמוע בקול דברו (שם)."

"... מצוה אתכם היום": כי הכל נברא בכ"ב אותיות התורה, ויש לכל איש ישראל רשימות מאותיות השייכות אליו—ובכלל ישראל הכ"ב אתוון [אותיות]. ואלה האותיות מתחדשין בכל יום ויום בצירופים שונים. וזה "מצוה אתכם" בכ"ב אתוון שבכם.

ואם זוכין בני ישראל להתחדשות הזאת, מתברכת להם כל הבריאה כמו שכתוב "ונתתי עשב בשדך כו' (דברים י"א:ט"ו)." וזה "כימי השמים על הארץ (דברים י"א:כ"א)"—ימים הם הארות. שכפי מה שימי השמים מאירים על הארץ ויכולין להתגלות בעולם, כך זוכין בני ישראל לנחול את הארץ. (5:49)

ב

בפסוק "והיה אם שמוע תשמעו אל מצותי... לאהבה את ה' אלהיכם ולעבדו בכל לבבכם (דברים י"א:י"ג)." פירש רש"י "שלא תאמר 'הרי אני לומד בשביל שאהיה עשיר, בשביל שאקרא רב, בשביל שאקבל שכר,' אלא כל מה שתעשה—עשה מאהבה."

פירוש הפסוק כי תכלית המצוות הם כדי לבא לאהבת ה', כי איך אפשר לבשר ודם לבא לאהבת הבורא! וכן הקשו הפלוסופים כי איך שייך ציווי באהבה אם אין הנפש אוהב בעצם! ולא מחכמה שאלו זאת, רק מחסרון המצוות שלהם. אבל בני ישראל על ידי המצוות מתעוררת בהם האהבה.

ובספר הישר לרבינו תם איתא כי שורש אהבה התדמות האוהב אל הנאהב. עיין שם. ולכן כאשר "קדשנו" הקדוש ברוך הוא "במצוותיו" ומדותיו, ומתדמין במעשינו ומדותינו אל מידות הבורא יתברך שמו ולמעשיו—בזה יש לנו דביקות בו יתברך כמו שכתוב "הדבק במדותיו (על פי סוטה י"ד ע"א)." ולכן נקראת מצוה על שם החיבור ודביקות וכמו שכתוב "לוית חן הם לראשך (משלי א:ט)."

ב

קושיית המפרשים בשם הרמב"ם על מצות "ואהבת (דברים ו:ה)" וכדומה: איך שייך ציווי בדבר התלוי בטבע האדם? והאמת כי הקושיה היא עצמה התירוץ, שמזה נלמד שיש בטבע כל איש ישראל לאהוב להשם יתברך בכל לבו ונפשו. ורק שנטמן בעומק הלב, ועל ידי הרצון והתשוקה למצוא זאת האהבה—על זה נאמר "יגעתי ומצאתי (מגילה ו ע"ב)."

ובספרי (ואתחנן ח) "והיו הדברים האלה... על לבבך (דברים ו:ו)" למה נאמר? לפי שנאמר "ואהבת כו'" ואיני יודע כיצד—אלא מתוך שאתה נותן הדברים אל לבך, תכיר מי שאמר והיה העולם. פירוש שעל ידי שמשים האדם זה ללבו תמיד ומשתוקק לבוא לאהבת בוראו, נגלה לו רוח הקדושה אשר בקרבו. ועל זה נאמר "חיי עולם נטע בתוכנו."

והכלל שכל מצוות שבתורה הם כללים. והפרטים איך לבוא לקיום המצוה הוא בחינת תורה שבעל פה. לכן "חביבים דברי סופרים מדברי תורה (שיר השירים רבה א:י"ח)" שדברי חכמים הם הקדמות איך לבוא לקיים מצוות המפורשות בתורה. כי דברי התורה נאמרים לאדם השלם שיש בו השלימות שיכול להשיג מעצמו. והוא תורה שבעל פה.

ואף שקשה לצייר לקיים "בכל לבבך," מכל מקום צריך להיות הרצון והתשוקה לבוא לזה בכל עת. ועל ידי זה נפתחים השערים שבלב האדם. (5:20)

ג

בפסוק "היום הזה ראינו כי ידבר אלהים את האדם וחי. ועתה למה נמות כי תאכלנו האש הגדולה הזאת אם יוספים אנחנו לשמוע... קרב אתה ושמע את כל אשר יאמר ה' אלהינו ואת תדבר אלינו (דברים ה:כ"א-כ"ד)."..

בכל דיבור מעשרת הדברות ניתוספה חיות חדשה בבני ישראל. ויש ללמוד קל וחומר דכתיב "ויפח באפיו נשמת חיים ויהי האדם לנפש חיה (בראשית ב:ז)" ממשהו רוח אלהים. מכל שכן כשדיבר השם יתברך הדברות לבני ישראל בוודאי נעשו בריאה חדשה בכל דיבור ודיבור. לכן הגידו חז"ל "בכל דיבור יצאת נשמתן של ישראל (שבת פ"ח ע"ב)." כי כשנעשין בריאה חדשה מתבטלת מדרגה הקודמת, כמו שצריכין למות קודם תחית המתים שלעתיד.

וזה שכתוב "ידבר אלהים את האדם וחי," שנתוספה בהם חיות בכל דיבור יותר ויותר. ונתעלו הרבה מדרגות זו אחר זו שהיו מוכנים להיות ממש כמלאכי השרת, וכמדרגת משה רבינו ע"ה איש אלהים בביטול כל הגשמיות. ולא יכלו בני ישראל לקבל כל כך. לכן אמרו "קרב אתה" והלא היה עומד שם. רק שבכל עת היו צריכין לעלות מדרגה אחר מדרגה ולא היו יכולים כל כך לעלות.

ויש לאמר ממה שכתוב "ונשמרתם מאוד לנפשותיכם כי לא ראיתם כל תמונה (דברים ד:ט"ו)" כי במשה רבינו ע"ה נאמר "ותמונת ה' יביט (במדבר י"ב:ח)" על ידי שהיה נבדל לגמרי מכל הגשמיות. לכן זכה להביט. כי בוודאי אי אפשר להשיג תמונת ה' בעוד יש שייכות של תמונה גשמית. רק כשנתבטלה הגשמיות "ותמונת ה' יביט (שם)." לכן הוכיח השם יתברך את אהרן ומרים

בעולמו, לא ברא אלא לכבודו (אבות ו:י"א)." אין כבוד אלא תורה. שיש מכל בריאה איזה לימוד ודרך ללמוד ממנו כבודו ורצונו של הקדוש ברוך הוא. זהו בחינת השירה שיש בכל דבר.

ולעתיד שיהיה מתוקן הכל ו"יתרון לשון אלם," כי מכל הלשונות יהיה מבורר כבודו ורצונו של הקדוש ברוך הוא. אך עתה הלשון נאלם והגשמיות מכסה שלא יהא ניכר הפנימיות הגנוז בו. ובכח לשון הקודש שניתן לבני ישראל יהיה תיקון לכל הלשונות. וכמו שכתוב "באר את התורה (דברים א:ה)" בשבעים לשון.

וכן מה שכתוב "אלה הדברים אשר דיבר משה... במדבר בערבה מול סוף בין פארן ובין תפל... (דברים א:א)." כל אלה המקומות היו מרוחקים מן הקדושה, ומשה רבינו ע"ה פתח פתחים ושערי תורה גם בכל אלה המקומות—מעין מה שיהיה לעתיד. זה שכתוב "הואיל באר" התחיל—ומשיח בן דוד יהיה הגומר. (5:16-7)

ג

[בהפטרה] "ידע שור קונהו וחמור אבוס בעליו, ישראל לא ידע עמי לא התבונן (ישעיה א:ג)." חס וחלילה שאין בני ישראל מכירין השם יתברך כשור, הלא מברכין ומתפללין אליו יתברך.

אבל רצון השם יתברך שבני ישראל יברֶרו מלכותו יתברך בכל הנבראים. כי כן היה בזמן השלימות שבית המקדש היה קיים והקרבנו תמידין בכל יום. היה זה קירוב והתדבקות חיות כל הנבראים אליו יתברך. והיו גם האומות בהכנעה מהשם יתברך. וכן מה שכתוב [גבי ירושלים] "קריה נאמנה (ישעיה א:כ"א)" גם כן על כל העולם, שאז היו נמשכים כל הנבראים אחר השורש. וזה שכתוב "ישראל לא ידע" שצריכין להמשיך ידיעה וחיבור לכל הנבראים. (5:1)

ואתחנן

א

במדרש (דברים רבה ב:ל"ב) "ואהבת את ה' (דברים ו:ה)." "מי לי בשמים ועמך לא חפצתי בארץ (תהלים ע"ג:כ"ה)." פירושו שלא להיות נמצא שום רצון אחר—רק להשם יתברך. "נפשך'—בכל נפש ונפש שברא בך (דברים רבה ב:ל"ז)."

פירוש "בכל לבבך" אינו כמו "עם כל לבבך" כמו שמפרשין העולם. רק ממש בכל הרגשה שבאדם ידע שהוא רק חיותו מהשם יתברך. ש"אין אדם נוקף אצבעו מלמטה, אלא אם כן מכריזין עליו מלמעלה (חולין ז ע"ב)" והוא כגרזן ביד החוצב.

וזה "ה' אחד" פירושו: לבד שהוא אלהי אחד, רק שהוא אחד אין עוד—שלכל דבר הוה הוא הוא חיותו יתברך ממש, רק שנסתר. וכן רצונו יתברך. אם כן צריך להיות נמצא אהבתו יתברך בכל הרגש שבאדם—וזה "בכל לבבך." (5:18)

ספר דברים
דברים
א

"אלה הדברים אשר דבר משה (דברים א:א)." במדרש "מרפא לשון עץ חיים
(משלי ט"ו:ד) (דברים רבה א:א)." איתא בזוהר הקדוש (חי"ב ר"ב ע"א)
שנמשלת התורה לאילן שיש בו ענפים ופירות ועלין וקליפות, לבד מגוף
האילן שכולן אחוזין בו. כמו כן התורה נותנת שפע וחיות לכל הבריאה, וכל
אחד יש לו דביקות כפי ערך קדושתו. כי באורייתא ברא קודשא בריך הוא
עלמא [בתורה ברא הקדוש ברוך הוא את העולם]. וכל הדברים הם כמו
לבוש לנקודה הפנימית.

והלשונות שמתפרשים בהם דברי תורה הם גם כן רק לבוש, כי המאמר
הוא התורה עצמה ומתלבש בלשונות אחרים. ועל ידי זה "מרפא הלשון."
לכן התירו שיכתבו ספרים בכל לשון. וכתיב "הואיל משה באר את התורה
הזאת (דברים א:ה)." פירש רש"י "בשבעים לשון פירשה להם." וכתוב
"באר" שכפי התרחבות הארת התורה במלבושים החיצוניים, יותר שמתקרב
הכל לפנימיות. על ידי זה נפתח המעין הפנימי ביותר.

כתיב "שתה מים מבורך, ונוזלים מתוך בארך (משלי ה:ט"ו)." כי
הקדוש ברוך הוא נתן בטבע עצמו של כל בריאה נקודה קדושה, בפרט
באיש ישראל שיש לו נפש קדושה. ונקרא "בורך" שדבוק בגופו. וכפי מה
שמקבל הארת הנפש וממשיך כל מעשיו אחר זו ההארה, כן ניתוסף לו רוח
ונשמה יתירה ונפתח מעין מעין שאין לו סוף. וזהו "ונוזלים מתוך בארך."

ולכן גם כן אחר כל המסעות במדבר שהמשיכו בני ישראל הארה
קדושה לתוך כל המקומות הללו—אחר כך "הואיל משה באר." (5:2)

ב

במדרש "מרפא לשון עץ חיים (משלי ט"ו:ד)'... לשונה של תורה מתיר את
הלשון (דברים רבה א:א)'. ומדרש תנחומא מביא "אז ידלג כאיל פסח ותרון
לשון אלם (ישעיה ל"ה:ו)" עיין שם. דאיתא לפי שאמר משה רבינו ע"ה "לא
איש דברים אנכי (שמות ד:י)" זכה ל"אלה הדברים (דברים א:א)." דאיתא
"במדה שאדם מודד מודדין לו (מגילה י"ב ע"ב)." משה רבינו ע"ה השתוקק
להיות כולו תורה. זהו "לא איש דברים אנכי." "איש דברים" [שרצה משה]
להיות—כולו תורה. כי כן צריך להיות אדם שנקרא "מדבר," צריך לבטל כל
הכוחות וציור שבו לבחינת הדיבור וכח הנשמה ואלוהות שבו.

וזה שרמזו חז"ל (שמות רבה ג:ד) "מי אנכי כי אלך אל פרעה (שמות
ג:י"א)." הלא אמרת "ואנכי אעלך (בראשית מ"ו:ד)"? ובאמת נתקיים הדבר
במשה—שנעשה כולו תורה ושכינה מדברת מתוך גרונו.

וכתיב "כה דברי כאש נאום ה' (ירמיה כ"ג:כ"ט)." דרך האש, כל
המתקרב אצלו נהפך לאש. וכן נעשה משה רבינו ע"ה כולו תורה. ומעין זה
כל העוסק בתורה מתהפך להיות בעל תורה כפי רוב העסק בתורה.

ובאמת כל הבריאה בכח התורה, כמו שכתוב "בראשית ברא"—"הביט
בתורה וברא (בראשית רבה א"א)." וכמו כן "כל הנקרא בשמי לכבודי
בראתיו (ישעיה מ"ג:ז)" כמו שאמרו חז"ל "כל מה שברא הקדוש ברוך הוא

הכנת בני ישראל בכניסתם לשם אז ירד משמים בחינת ארץ ישראל לארץ
ישראל הגשמי. כמו שאמרו ז"ל (ירושלמי ברכות ד:ה) בית המקדש שלמטה
מכוון לבית המקדש למעלה—וכמו כן ארץ ישראל וירושלים. וזאת הארץ
הפנימית הראה הקדוש ברוך הוא למשה רבינו ע"ה.

כי בני ישראל הם גבולים שיוכל להתפשט הקדושה בתוכו. ולכן על ידי
כניסת הי"ב שבטים לגבולותיהם, אז תפול הארץ בנחלה. לכן צוה השם
יתברך שלא יניחו מהכנענים, כי הארץ העליונה לא תוכל לסבול אותם.

וכן נוהג בכל איש פרטי גם כן. כפי הכנת התורה בלב ונפש, אז השם
יתברך משרה בו הקדושה, כמו שאמרו חז"ל "קדוש שרוי בתוך מעיו
(תענית י"א ע"ב)." (4:194)

ג.

אמרו חז"ל "המענג את השבת נותנין לו נחלה בלי מצרים כמו שכתוב '...
נחלת יעקב אביך (ישעיה נ"ח:י"ד)' (שבת קי"ח ע"א-ב)."

כי מצד שפעו יתברך אין הפסק ומצר. רק על ידי שכל ההשפעה אל
האדם צריך לבוא על ידי עולם הזה, כי האדם בגופו נדבק בעולם הזה,
לכן מצד הקבלה יש מצרים. ובשבת קודש כל הנבראים יש להם עליה
למקומם. כמו שכתוב "אל יצא איש ממקומו (שמות ט"ז:כ"ט)." פירשו
בזוהר הקדוש (רעיא מהימנא פינחס ח"ג רמ"ב ע"א): "מקומו של עולם"
והוא השם יתברך, שבשבת קודש מתבטלין הכל אליו יתברך—ממילא
הוא נחלה בלי מצרים. והוא נשמה יתירה שיש לבני ישראל בשבת קודש.
כי השגת האדם היא במדה בכל הימים, אבל בשבת קודש הוא בלי מדה
ושיעור.

והוא על ידי האבות. שכשהאדם מבטל עצמו לשורשו באמת מסייעת
לו זכות האבות.

ונשמה יתירה בשבת קודש משארת רושם בגוף האדם גם כן. כמו
כשאמרו בספרים שמנשמת האדם נשאר "הבל דגרמי" גם אחר הסתלקותו.
כמו כן מנשמה יתירה נשאר רשימה על כל ימי השבוע. וזהו תלוי בהתדבקות
האדם בנשמה יתירה, ומשתוקק שלא להיות נפרד ממנה וקשה אליו פרידתה.
(4:194)

הדבר אשר צוה ה' (במדבר ל:ב)' (ספרי מטות ב')." ענין הפרש זה כמו החילוק בין עשרה מאמרות לעשרת הדיברות. כי "מאמר" הוא רק לחוץ להודיע הרצון [למשל] "יהי רקיע," "יהי מאורות." ו"דיבור" הוא פנימיות עצם הדיבור. כענין שם "מדבר" שנקרא האדם מדבר ולא "אומר." כי הדיבור הוא בעצם, לא במקרה כמו המאמר.

ואמת שזה עצמו ענין החילוק בין "יהי" ל"כה." כי יש כמה מדריגות בנבואה. ועצם הדיבור מתלבש ומתפשט אחר כך למדריגות אמירה ולכן באמירה כתיב "כה" ובדיבור "זה." לכן כתוב "וידבר ה' את כל הדברים האלה לאמר (שמות כ:א)" כי מהדיבור באה אחר כך אמירה. וכן היתה מעלת בני ישראל בקבלת התורה שנעלה פנימיות דבר ה' בדיברות יותר מעשרה מאמרות.

ומעין זה החילוק בין ימי המעשה [לשבת קודש. בכל יום מימי המעשה], שהוא כח עשרה מאמרות שבכל יום, היתה בריאה מיוחדת: "יהי אור," "יהי רקיע." ובשבת לא היתה בריאה וכתוב "ויברך אלהים את יום השביעי" אם כן הוא בחינת עצם הדיבור. ובכל הימים שכתוב "ברכה" "ויברך... לאמר..." וכתוב "ויברך... ויאמר להם... פרו ורבו (בראשית א:כ"ח)." ובשבת קודש כתיב "ויברך" סתם—והוא עצם הדיבור.

ולכן בשבת ניתנה תורה שהיא בחינת עשרת הדיברות. וזהו עצמו שאמרו בזוהר הקדוש "בשבת דלא אשתכח ביה מזוני מה ברכתא אשתכח כו' [שלא נמצא מזון המן, איזו ברכה יש בה? אבל ברכה נמצאת] (ח"ב פ"ח ע"א)" אלא שהיא שורש הברכה. עיין שם. (4:190)

מסעי

א

"אלה מסעי בני ישראל אשר יצאו מארץ מצרים... ויכתוב משה את מוצאיהם למסעיהם על פי ה'. ואלה מסעיהם למוצאיהם (במדבר ל"ג:א-ב)."

הלשונות בתחלת הפסוק וסוף הפסוק מהופכים. יש לאמר כי הכתוב תולה המסעות ביציאת מצרים. ונראה שאחר כל המסעות, נגמרה יציאת מצרים. כי בכל מסע נתרחקו יותר ממצרים עד שבאו לארץ ישראל.

וצריך להיות הרצון של האדם בפרישותו מגשמיות כדי להתדבק בהשם יתברך, שיוכל להיות בר לבב, אבל לא מצד שנבזית בעיניו הגשמיות. ולכך נתן השם יתברך חן לגשמיות כדי שיהיה מעשה האדם רק לשם שמים. וזהו "מוצאיהם למסעיהם" ואחר כך כפי מה שנוסע האדם ומתקרב להשם יתברך, נגמרה ההוצאה, שהפריש עצמו מגשמיות. וכל אחד מהם מסייע לשני. (4-193:4)

ב

בפסוק "זאת הארץ אשר תפול לכם בנחלה (במדבר ל"ד:ב)." ובמדרש (על פי במדבר רבה כ"ג:ה) שהראה הקדוש ברוך הוא למשה רבינו ע"ה [כל מה שהיה ועתיד להיות] דור ודורשיו.

כי בוודאי הכנענים לא ראו מעולם בחינת "ארץ ישראל." ואכן על ידי

והקבלה, רק שעל ידי הקבלה יכולין לדמות המעשה אל הקבלה. (186:4)

ב

במדרש (במדבר רבה כ״ב:א) ״ונשבעת חי ה׳ באמת, במשפט, ובצדקה (ירמיה ד:ב).״ כי הנה עיקר השבועה בשמו יתברך הוא לסייע לעובד ה׳. ״מגדל עוז שם ה׳ בו ירוץ צדיק ונשגב (משלי י״ח:י).״ וגם לאנשים פשוטים מישראל, התעסקות בדברי תורה ותפלה נותן להם קדושה ומסייע להם לטהר לבם. מכל שכן לגדולים שבישראל, כענין שיש בעליונים כדאיתא במדרשים (חגיגה י״ג ע״ב; פסיקתא רבתי כ׳, צ״ז ע״ב) שאין להם רשות לעלות כל כך, ומשביעין את הכתר ועולה לראשו של מלך. כמו כן בצדיקים האמיתיים השבועה בשמו יתברך עומדת להם בשעה הצריכה להם.

אבל ״לא כל מי שרוצה ליטול את השם יטול (ברכות ט״ז ע״ב).״ רק כדמפרש במדרש ״ה׳ אלהיך תירא אותו תעבוד ובו תדבק (דברים י:כ)״ אחר כך ״ובשמו תשבע (שם).״

ולכן מסר כח השבועה לראשי המטות. עם כל זה גם לקטנים שבישראל הקבלה שמקבלין בפה עול מלכות שמים בכל יום הוא גם כן שבועה. כמו שכתוב ״שבע ביום הללתיך (תהלים קי״ט:קס״ד)״ על קריאת שמע וברכותיה בכל יום. וקבלה זו מסייעת להם שניתן להם כמו כן סיוע מלמעלה. כענין שאמרו (נידה ל ע״ב) שמשביעין את האדם קודם שבא לעולם ״תהי צדיק ולא רשע,״ כן הקדוש ברוך הוא מחדש בכל יום מעשה בראשית ומשביעין לאדם בכל יום על זה. וזה שכתוב ״אשר אנכי מצוך היום (דברים ו:ו).״ אך זה תלוי בהתעוררות התחתונים כדכתיב ״את ה׳ האמרת... וה׳ האמירך (דברים כ״ו:י״ז-ח).״ (187:4)

ג

והנה איתא (סנהדרין ע״ד ע״א) שלוש עבירות שצריכין למסור נפש עליהם: עבודה זרה, גלוי עריות, ושפיכת דמים. ולשון הרע שקול נגד כולם כדאיתא במדרשים (על פי ערכין ט״ו ע״א). וכמו כן זה לעומת זה שלוש המדרגות: ״תירא... תעבוד... תדבוק (דברים י:כ).״ ״ובשמו תשבע (שם)״ הוא כח הפה ולשון צדיק שעושה רושם בשמים ובארץ. והארבע בחינות אלו הם בחינת שלושה אבות ודוד המלך ע״ה.

ומענין זה נמצא בכל אדם. שמקודם צריכין לייגע עצמנו בתורה ומצוות הערוכים לפנינו, ואחר כך זוכה האדם להוסיף מדעתו. ועל זה אמרו ״אם יאמר לך אדם... יגעתי ומצאתי—תאמין (מגילה ו ע״ב).״ דאיתא ״חיי עולם נטע בתוכינו״ שהקדוש ברוך הוא גנז בפיהן של ישראל סודות התורה. כדכתיב ״ואשים דברי בפיך (ישעיה נ״א:ט״ז).״ ועל ידי היגיעה בתורה אז חוזר וניער בחינת תורה שבעל פה—שהוא בלבן ופיהן של בני ישראל. (189:4)

ד

אמרו חז״ל ״כל הנביאים נתנבאו ב׳כה אמר ה׳.׳ מוסיף עליהם משה ב׳זה

ג

בפסוק "צו את בני ישראל ואמרת אליהם את קרבני לחמי לאשי... להקריב
לי (במדבר כ"ח:ב)." ברש"י ומדרש (ספרי כ"ד) משל לבת מלך שהיתה
נפטרת מן העולם והיתה מפקדת בעלה על בניה [והוא משיב לה] "עד
שאתה מצוני על בני [לשמרם], צוה בני עלי [שלא למרוד בי]."

הענין הוא שיש לחם מן השמים ומן הארץ והן בחינות תורה שבכתב
ושבעל פה. ומשה רבינו ע"ה הוריד התורה מן השמים לארץ דכתיב
"הנני ממטיר... לחם מן השמים (שמות ט"ז:ד)." ורצה משה רבינו ע"ה
להשאיר זאת גם אחריו. אבל באמת התחיל עתה בחינת לחם מן הארץ,
היינו התקרבות מצד התחתונים לשמים, היינו "צוה את בני עלי." והיא
בחינת הקרבנות וכן תפלה שבמקום תמידין איתקן והוא עבודה שבלב.
פירוש על ידי השתוקקות בלב להתדבק בשורש עליון.

אם כי עתה נפלנו אחורנית יכולין לחזור למקומנו הראשון, וזה שכתוב
"עולת תמיד העשויה בהר סיני (במדבר כ"ח:ו)." שעל ידי שכבר היינו
במדריגה עליונה בהר סיני דכתיב "וירד ה' על הר סיני (שמות י"ט:כ),"
יכולין שוב עתה להעלות עצמינו לשמים.

ולכן התפלל משה רבינו ע"ה כדכתיב "ואתחנן אל ה' בעת ההוא
לאמר (דברים ג:כ"ג)" ולמדו חז"ל (ברכות ל"ב ע"א) דיני תפלה מתפלתו
של משה רבינו ע"ה, שהיה זה הכנה שהכין משה רבינו ע"ה בחינת תפלה.
שמקודם היה בחינת תורה אספקלריא המאירה, והיה הכל בגלוי. ועתה
התחיל הדרך למצוא הכל על ידי יגיעה כמו שאמרו "מעשיך יקרבוך
(עדיות ה:ז)."

וזהו ענין הקרבנות והתפלות. והבן כל זה. (4:170)

מטות

א

במדרש (במדבר רבה כ"ב:א) "ונשבעת חי ה' באמת, במשפט, ובצדקה (ירמיה
ד:ב)." כבר כתבתי כי אלו השלוש הן בחינות: "בכל לבבך, ובכל נפשך, ובכל
מאודך (דברים ו:ה)." כי "באמת" בחינת "נפשך" שהיא חיות הפנימיות.
"במשפט" בחינת "לבבך" שיש שני לבבות וצריך בירור ומשפט. "בצדקה"
בחינת "מאודך." אחר כך "והיו הדברים האלה אשר אנכי מצוך היום על
לבבך (שם שם ו)." שאחר תיקון הגוף והנפש יכולין לקבל דבורי התורה.

כי באמת כל התורה שמותיו של הקדוש ברוך הוא, ואלה הדיבורים
של התורה הקדושה מדבקין לבות בני ישראל אליו יתברך. ולכן "והגית בו
יומם ולילה (יהושע א:ח)." וכן מצות קריאת שמע ותפלה—"ודברת בם
(דברים ו:ז)," שמוסיפין חיות אל. ועל ידי קבלת מלכות שמים בכל יום
בפה מלא, מסייעין אלה הדיבורים להיות נמשך המעשה כפי הקבלה. כמו
שכתוב "נשבעתי ואקימה (תהלים קי"ט:ק"ו)" ונודרין לקיים את המצוות.
והנדר מסייע כמו שכתוב "ככל היוצא מפיו יעשה (במדבר ל:ג)."

והוא הבטחה גם כן כי יוכל האדם לקיים אחר כך במעשה כפי הקבלה
בפה. ולכן כתיב "ככל" ולא "כל." כי באמת המעשה רחוק מאוד מהרצון

פינחס

א

ענין היוד שניתוסף לפינחס, שהוא אות שלום. כי באות יוד אין חלל והפסק
כמו בכל האותיות, וכמו כן באות ואו. והם שתי שלמויות כמו שכתוב
"שלום שלום לרחוק ולקרוב (ישעיה נ"ז:י"ט)." ואיתא בזוהר הקדוש (ח"א
ו ע"א-ב) לרחוק זה יעקב ולקרוב זה יוסף. והם שתי שלמויות. יעקב עושה
שלום בין אברהם ויצחק. והוא שכתוב "וישבתי בשלום אל בית אבי (בראשית
כ"ח:כ"א)" למתק דיני יצחק. וכמו כן יוסף עושה שלום בין השבטים.

ואיתא (רעיא מהימנא פינחס ח"ג רל"ז ע"א) כי פינחס גמטריא ר"ח
כמו יצחק—והיה בחינת מדת הדין. והכהונה היא בחינת החסד וניתן לו
[לפינחס] במתנה הכהונה. והוא כמו שאמרו "כשישראל זוכין אף השמאל
נעשה ימין (תנחומא בשלח ט"ז)." וכן יש מזה בזוהר הקדוש (ח"ג רי"ד
ע"א) כי לכך הוצרך להנתן לו הכהונה דמאן דקטיל נפשא [מי שהרג אדם]
פסול הוא לכהונתא. והרמז כמו שאמרתי שהיה בחינת מדת הדין.

וכתוב "עושה שלום במרומיו (איוב כ"ה:ב)" הקדוש ברוך הוא עושה
שלום בין מלאכי החסד והגבורה. וכמו כן יש יש מלאך אחד שיש בו שתי
המדות. וכמו כן פינחס בעולם הזה ניתנה לו ברית שלום להיות כהן, אף על
פי שהיה בו בחינת הדין. (4:182)

ב

בפסוק "לאלה תחלק הארץ (במדבר כ"ו:נ:ג)" ואיתא (ירושלמי סנהדרין כ"ז
ע"ב) שהיה על פי גורל וברוח הקודש.

והענין הוא דכתיב "חבלים נפלו לי בנעימים אף נחלת שפרה עלי
(תהלים ט"ז:ו)." כי מתנת ארץ ישראל העיקר בשורש העליון, שיש לכל בני
ישראל חלק בשורש ארץ ישראל למעלה ולמטה. ולכן המנין שהיה קודם
כניסתם לארץ ישראל, להעמיד כל אחד על שורשו כמו שהיה המנין מקודם
—והיינו תורה שבכתב ושבעל פה. ובשתי אלו יש לכל בני ישראל חלק, כמו
שאומרים "יהי רצון מלפניך שיבנה בית המקדש ותן חלקנו בתורתך."

ואיתא "כל ישראל יש להם חלק לעולם הבא דכתיב יעמך כלם
צדיקים לעולם יירשו ארץ (ישעיה ס:כ"א)' (משנה סנהדרין י:א)." והגם
דפירוש "ארץ" כפשוטו בארץ ישראל, מכל מקום זה הוא הסימן שיש להם
חלק לעולם הבא במה שזוכין בעולם הזה להתדבק בארץ ישראל, שהוא
השורש של נפשות בני ישראל.

וכתוב "ששם עלו שבטים שבטי יה עדות לישראל להודות לשם ה'
(תהלים קכ"ב:ד)." שבעלייתן נגד בית המקדש היה עדות שיש להם דביקות
בשורשם. וזהו ה"ישם" שמעיד עליהם ועל יחוסם—על ידי זה שיכולין
לעלות לבית המקדש.

וזה היה השיר שהלויים מזמרים בבית המקדש על ט"ו (15) מעלות.
והמה הט"ו מעלות מיציאת מצרים עד "ובנה לנו בית הבחירה (בפזמון
'דיינו' בהגדה של פסח)." והמה ט"ו בחינות ודרכים להתקשר עד השורש.
(4:174)

הוא בכלל פיהן של ישראל. וכמו בפרט כל איש על ידי הפה מוציא הכח הפנימי... כמו כן בכלל הנביא הוא פיהן של בני ישראל. לכן תלוי כח הנביא בעבודת כלל בני ישראל כדכתיב "נביא מקרבך... יקים לך (דברים י״ח:ט״ו)." ויותר ממה שבני ישראל צריכין אל הנביא, צריך הנביא להם. והוא "כלל הצריך לפרט ופרט הצריך לכלל" (בכורות י״ט ע״א)." ולכן הנביאים הם עדות על הכלל.

והאומות אינם מוכנים אל הנבואה. לכן נתן להם הקדוש ברוך הוא בלעם, שהיה כלי לנבואה. אך בעבור כי אינם מוכנים לזה, לא עלתה הנבואות בידו לטוב. וכמו כן נוכל לומר מה שניטלה מאתנו הנבואה, הגם כי בעוונותינו הוא, אבל הוא גם כן עדות על בני ישראל, שלא יאמרו אומות העולם: על ידי שקרבנו והעמיד לנו נביאים נמשכנו אחריו. לכן נלקח מאתנו הנבואה, ואף על פי כן בני ישראל מתחזקים באמונתו יתברך ועוסקין במצוותיו להודיע כי הפנימיות נמצא בבני ישראל הגם שאין לנו נביאים להוציא הפעולה מן הכח אל הפועל. כמו שכתוב "אותותינו לא ראינו, אין עוד נביא, ולא אתנו יודע עד מה (תהלים ע״ד:ט)."... (4:158)

ג

בפסוק "מה טבו אהליך יעקב, משכנותיך ישראל (במדבר כ״ד:ה)": הקדושה נמשכת אחר בני ישראל בכל מקום שהם, כמו שכתוב "בכל המקום אשר אזכיר את שמי אבוא אליך וברכתיך (שמות כ:כ״ד)." והנה ארץ ישראל ובית המקדש מיוחד בקביעות בני ישראל. וזה "משכנותיך ישראל." אבל אפילו בכל מקום שבני ישראל שרוין, אפילו בדרך עראי, שם מגלה להם הקדושה. כמו שכתוב "כנחלים נטיו (שם שם כ״ה)" כי מעין התורה נמשך בכל מקומות מושבותיהם. וזה בחינת יעקב שהלך לחוץ לארץ, וכמו כן במדבר שעדיין לא נכנסו לארץ ישראל. (4:163-4)

ד

... איתא "שברי לוחות מונחים בארון (במדבר רבה ד:כ, בבא בתרא י״ד ע״ב)." והיינו כי בוודאי המתנה שנתן לנו הקדוש ברוך הוא לא היה למגן. ואם כי לא היינו ראוים לקבל ונגנז בארון.

ונשברו הלוחות בי״ז בתמוז. וצריכין לתקן כל אלה השברים. וזה הוא באמת כמו פיזור וגלות בני ישראל בכל הארצות, כדי ללקוט אותן השברים. וכשיתוקן הכל, נוכל לקבל הלוחות הראשונים.

ולכן איתא בשם האר״י ז״ל [אמר אהרן במעשה עגל הזהב] "חג לה' מחר (שמות ל״ב:ה)" שלעתיד יהיה י״ז בתמוז יום טוב. כי מצד נתינת הלוחות, בוודאי היה יום טוב גדול. ורק מצד שאיננו יכולים לקבל, נהפך לנו לאבל מחולנו. וכשיתוקן הכל, יהפך לנו שבעה עשר בתמוז לששון ושמחה. וכמו שכתוב "צום הרביעי... יהיה... לששון (זכריה ז:ח)." (4:157-8)

רחבה—מתלמידיו של בלעם הרשע [על פי אבות ה:י״ט].״ גילו לנו חז״ל כי אותו הרשע היה היפוך מצדקת אבינו אברהם ע״ה.

והענין הוא על פי מה שאמרו חז״ל (ברכות ז ע״א) בפסוק ״מה אקב לא קבה אל ומה אזעם לא זעם ה׳ (במדבר כ״ג:ח)?״ כי הרשע היה מכוין רגע זעמו של הקדוש ברוך הוא דכתיב ״ואל זועם בכל יום (תהלים ז:י״ב)״ וכמה זעמו?—רגע, וכתוב ״חסד אל כל היום (שם נ״ב:ג)...״. והרשע כל מגמתו למצוא אותו [רגע] הזעם.

אבל הצדיקים מכוונים למצוא עת רצון בשמים כמו שכתוב ״ואני תפלתי... עת רצון (שם ס״ט:י״ד).״ ולא עוד אלא שזוכין למצוא החוט של חסד בעולם הזה. שבעולם הזה אדרבא על דינא מתקיים עלמא [על הדין מתקיים העולם]—רק שנמצא בכל יום חוט של חסד. והצדיקים—מגמתם למצוא אותה נקודה של חסד ועת הרצון.

ובאמת כל רגע הזעם למעלה היא על ידי הרשעים. כדאיתא (ברכות ז ע״א) כשעובדין לחמה הקדוש ברוך הוא כועס כו׳. וכמו כן החוט של חסד שנמצא בעולם הזה, הוא על ידי הצדיקים. ואברהם אבינו ע״ה זכה להוציא מכח אל הפועל החוט של חסד להיות נמצא בעולם. כמו שכתוב על ידי שאמר ״אם מחוט ועד שרוך נעל ואם אקח (בראשית י״ד:כ״ג).״

וזה שאמר התנא שעל ידי אותן השלוש מדות טובות מתלמידיו של אברהם אבינו ע״ה זוכין למצוא החסד בכל יום בעולם הזה ״למיחלים לחסדו (על פי תהלים ל״ג:י״ח).״ והרשע, על ידי מדות הרעות הוציא מכח אל הפועל זעמו של הקדוש ברוך הוא למעלה. ומכל מקום מצינו כי מדה טובה מרובה, והצדיקים שזוכין למצוא חסד ה׳ בעולם—אין כל הרשעים יכולין לבטל מהם, כמו שכתוב ״מים רבים לא יוכלו לכבות את האהבה, ונהרות לא ישטפוה. אם יתן איש את כל הון ביתו באהבה, בוז יבוזו לו (שיר השירים ח:ז).״

וכן העיד אותו הרשע [בלעם] ״אם יתן לי בלק מלא ביתו כסף וזהב לא אוכל לעבור את פי ה׳ אלהי (במדבר כ״ב:י״ח).״ אבל הזעם רגע בשמים, כשהרשעים רוצים להתגבר בו, מונע הקדוש ברוך הוא הזעם. כדאיתא (ברכות ז ע״א) שלא היה כועס כל אותן הימים כדכתוב ״למען דעת צדקות ה׳ (מיכה ו:ה).״

והנה מלחמה זו היא בכל יום. וגם בפרט כל נפש מישראל שצריכין לעורר מדת החסד בכל יום, וכמו כן הרשעים ויצר הרע מתגברים בכל יום לעורר הדינין. וזה שאמרו חז״ל (ברכות י״ב ע״ב) שרצו לקבוע פרשת בלק בקריאת שמע. (156:4)

ב

במדרש (על פי במדבר רבה כ:א) ״הצור תמים פעלו כי כל דרכיו משפט (דברים ל״ב:ד).״ שלא הניח [הקדוש ברוך הוא] פתחון פה לאומות העולם [לעתיד לבוא לומר שאתה רחקתנו. מה עשה הקדוש ברוך הוא?] העמיד להם נביאים.

הענין היא כי הנבואה היא להוציא הכח אל הפועל בדיבור. כי הנביא

במעיו להיות נשבע מהמאכל.

ורמז לדבר דאיתא במדרש שיר השירים "מ"ח (48) פעמים נזכר באר בתורה, נגד מ"ח דברים שהתורה נקנית בהם (על פי שיר השירים רבה ד:ל"א)." עיין שם. ופירוש זה כי התורה שבכתב מתנה מן השמים לכל מי שירצה. אבל להיות נקנית התורה, להיות לאדם חלק בתורה, להיות נקרא "בן תורה," להיות דברי תורה נבלעים בדמיו—הוא בכח מ"ח דברים.

ולכן שירה הראשונה היתה קודם התורה אז "ישיר משה ובני ישראל" שהרגישו בנפשותם שנעשו עבדי ה' להיות מוכנים לשמוע דבר ה'. ושירה זו האחרונה היתה שהרגישו שנבלעו דברי תורה בדמיהן כי זה היה סוף מ' שנה. וכענין שאמרו חז"ל (תנחומא בובר כי תשא י"ב) כשלמד משה רבינו ע"ה מ' ימים בהר שכח, עד שלבסוף נתן לו הקדוש ברוך הוא התורה במתנה. כן היתה עבודת בני ישראל מ' שנה במדבר, שיגעו בתורה עד שלבסוף ניתנה להם במתנה. ולכן לא נזכר משה רבינו ע"ה בשירה זו שהיא למעלה מזו המדריגה, והוא מוריד התורה מן השמים. (4:145)

ד

במדרש "'וישלח ישראל מלאכים אל סיחון (במדבר כ"א:כ"א).' 'בטח בה' ועשה טוב שכן ארץ ורעה אמונה (תהלים ל"ז:ג).' 'סור מרע ועשה טוב בקש שלום ורדפהו (שם ל"ד:ט"ו).' ...אם באו לידך את מצוה עליהם ולא לרדוף אחריהם. אבל השלום 'בקש שלום ורדפהו' במקום אחר (במדבר רבה י"ט:כ"ז)."

כי מצינו רדיפה בשני דברים: באמת ושלום. "צדק צדק תרדוף (דברים ט"ז:כ)" ו"בקש שלום ורדפהו." כי שני דברים אלו הם היפוך מעולם הזה. כמו שאמרו "אמת ושלום אמרו 'אל יברא [האדם] דכולא [שכולו] שקרים, דכולא קטטה (בראשית רבה ח:ה).'" ואין דברים אלו בנמצא בעלמא דשקרא [עולם השקר]. לכן צריכין רדיפה להשיג סייעתא דשמיא [עזרה מן השמים], כמו שזכו בני ישראל אל תורת אמת מן השמים. כמו שכתוב "ה' עוז לעמו יתן ה' יברך את עמו בשלום (תהלים כ"ט:י"א)."

ומשה רבינו ע"ה היה בחינת אמת: "בכל ביתי נאמן הוא (במדבר י"ב:ז)" והוריד תורה מן השמים. ואהרן בחינת שלום. ואל השלום זכו בני ישראל בזכות המדבר, שהוא חוץ מן הישוב. זהו "'רדפהו' חוץ ממקומך." ולפי שבטחו בה' ונמשכו אחריו במדבר, זכו אל בחינת השלום. ולכן נקראו (בשיר השירים) בני ישראל ה"שולמית."

וכתוב "אני שלום (תהלים ק"כ:ז)," ולפי שיש לבני ישראל בחינת השלום, היה בכחם לקרב כל האומות אל השם יתברך. (4:147)

בלק

א

במשנה "כל שיש בו שלושה דברים הללו מתלמידיו של אברהם אבינו ע"ה, ושלושה דברים אחרים מתלמידיו של בלעם הרשע. עין טובה, ורוח נמוכה, ונפש שפלה—מתלמידיו של אברהם אבינו. עין רעה, ורוח גבוהה, ונפש

ב

בענין פי הבאר שנברא בערב שבת:

דכתיב "שתה מים מבורך ונוזלים מתוך בארך (משלי ה:טייו)." דאיתא "האומר [בברכת המזון] 'מטובו חיינו' הרי זה בור. [האומר] 'בטובו חיינו' הוא תלמיד חכם (על פי ברכות נ עייא)." ופרשנו כי "מטובו" הוא חלק מן הטוב ונפרד ממנו. "בטובו" הוא דביקות בגוף הטוב.

דהנה הכל נמשך מן התורה שנקראת "טוב" כדאיתא "בראשית ברא" בשביל התורה שנקראת "ראשית" (תהלים קיייא:י)." אם כן שורש הכל מן התורה. וכדאיתא בזוהר הקדוש (תקונא שתין ותשע קייח עייב) דאורייתא אית בה פירות שרשין עלין וקליפין. ובני ישראל ותלמידי חכמים דביקין בגופא דאילנא. וזה החילוק בין בור לבאר: כי בור הוא מים מכונסין, ולכן הם גם כן במדה וצמצום כפי הכלי. אבל באר הוא דבוק בשורש המעין—שהוא נובע תמיד.

וכן הוא בפנימיות שיש בכל נפש הארה וחכמה. כמו שכתוב "כולם בחכמה עשית (תהלים קיייד:כייד)" והוא בחינת בור.

ובאמת הוא ענין ימי המעשה, שכתוב בהם "יהיה סגור (יחזקאל מייו:א)," שאין נפתח שער הפנימי, אבל בשבת קודש נפתח המעיין נובע. לכן הוא "נחלה בלי מצרים (שבת קייח עייא)." וזה נקרא "פי הבאר" שנפתח שער הפנימי.

ויש שני פתחים, כדכתיב "וביום שבת יפתח וביום החודש יפתח (יחזקאל מייו:א)." והם שתי יודין על הנאו [שמהם נעשה האות אלף] ונעשה מייבור"—"באר." כי יוד היא שער. ועל זה איתא בספרים בפסוק "פותח את ידיך (תהלים קמייה:טייז)"—יוד-יך. כי מקודם כתיב "אכלם בעתו (שם שם טייו)" והיא עת ומדה מיוחדת בפרט כל מקבל. ו"פותח את ידיך" היא השורש "ומשביע לכל חי רצון" הוא הצנור ודביקות בשורש. (5-144:4)

ג

בענין שירת הבאר (במדבר כייא:יייז כו') שלא נזכר משה רבינו עייה. ובשירה הראשונה "ישיר משה ובני ישראל (שמות טייו:א)."

דהנה באר הוא התורה שבעל פה. כמו שאמרו זייל "אין מים אלא תורה," ויש תורה שבכתב הוא בחינת "לחם מן השמים (שמות טייז:ד)." זהו בחינת משה רבינו עייה שהוריד התורה מן השמים, וזהו מן "בזכות משה" שהוא לחם. ובאר הוא בחינת מים—תורה שבעל פה.

ושמעתי ממורי זקני זייל מה שהתורה יש ברכה לפניה ולאחריה, הוא כמו בסעודה שיש ברכה לפניה על מה שהזמין השם יתברך לנו האוכל ולאחריה על השביעה, מה שמקבל האדם מזון וחיות מן המאכל. ולכן שיעור זמן ברכת המזון עובר אחר זמן עיכול המזון. כן יש בתורה ברכה לאחריה על מה שזוכין למשוך חיות מדברי תורה להיות נבלע בנפש האדם. עד כאן דבריו זייל. וזה ענין תורה שבעל פה, שנעשה האדם "בן תורה" להיות לו דביקות בתורה; זהו שכתוב "וחיי עולם נטע בתוכנו." וזה ענין הבאר מים כמו שאמרו חזייל "ואכלת (דברים ח:י)' זו אכילה, ושבעת (שם)' זו שתיה (ברכות מייט עייב ועוד)." כי השתיה גורם שיתעכל המזון

השיג בחינה זו.

ויש לומר עוד על פי מה שאמרו במדרש (שמות רבה נ״ב:ה) שלוש בחינות קרא לה: בת, אחות, אם. וקרח אמר ״העדה כולם קדושים (במדבר ט״ז:ג)״ ושמעו ״אנכי ה׳ אלהיך (שמות כ:ב).״ היה סבור שאין מעלה עליונה בישראל מקבלת התורה. ולפי שהלוים לא היו בחטא העגל, נתגאה על אהרן. אבל באמת אהרן זכה וזיכה את הרבים. ונעלו אחר החטא למעלה ממדריגה שהיתה להם בקבלת התורה. וזה רמז המדרש (במדבר רבה י״ח:א) ״אח נפשע מקרית עוז (משלי י״ח:י״ט).״

ואלה שלוש הבחינות: בת, אחות, אם—הן עצמן בחינות שלושה רגלים. וכמו שהיה בדור המדבר, כך הוא לעולם, שצריך איש ישראל לתקן אלה שלוש הבחינות: להגאל מיצר הרע וסטרא אחרא—בחינת יציאת מצרים וחירות. ואחר כך לזכות לתורה—בחינת רוח. ואחר כך צריך לחדש איזה תיקון בעולם שעל זה נשתלח האדם. ויש לכל איש ישראל חלק בזה. על ידי תפלה ותשובה יוכל אפילו איש פשוט לעורר איזהו תיקון בבחינה המיוחדת אליו, כל חד לפום שיעורא דיהב ליה ידיה [כל אחד לפי השיעור שלו].

והנה כתיב ״ויקח קרח״ ואתפליג [בתרגום כתוב ״ויחלוק״]. כי משה רבינו ע״ה היה בחיר שבנביאים וביטל עצמו לכלל ישראל, כמו שכתוב ״מורשה קהלת יעקב״ שהכניס עצמו לפי מצב כל ישראל. וכשירדו בני ישראל על ידי החטא ממדריגתם, הכניס משה רבינו עצמו בתוך הכלל. וקרח, ברוב חכמה שהיה בו, החזיק בו ולא רצה לבטל עצמו אל הכלל—ולכן לא בחר בו ה׳. (4:130)

חקת

א

״זאת חקת התורה (במדבר י״ט:ב).״ תלה הכתוב הטהרה בתורה, שהיא עץ החיים—ומזה באה הטהרה, היפוך מעץ הדעת, שעל ידו באה מיתה, שהוא אבי אבות הטומאה. ועל ידי התורה יכולין בני ישראל להטהר מן הטומאה. והיא בחינת ״הנשמה שנתת בי טהורה היא.״ פירוש ״טהורה״ שאינה מקבלת טומאה דכתיב ״ויפח כו׳ נשמת חיים (בראשית ב:ז).״

והנשמה של איש ישראל היא בחינת תורה—דבר ה׳. ויש לכל נשמה חלק בתורה, או באות או בנקודה. והיא בחינת נשמת החיים שבו ואינה מקבלת טומאה. כמו שאמרו חז״ל ״וכה דברי כאש (ירמיה כ״ג:כ״ט).״ מה אש אינו מקבל טומאה, אף דברי תורה אינן מקבלין טומאה (ברכות כ״ב ע״א).״

וזה שכתוב ״מי יתן טהור מטמא (איוב י״ד:ד)״ דרשו חז״ל (נידה ט ע״א) על טיפת שכבת זרע שהיא טמאה ואדם נוצר ממנה והוא טהור. שעל ידי שהנשמה באה אל הטיפה מקבלת חיות ויוצאת מטומאה לטהרה. כן הוא לעולם העוסק בתורה זוכה לנשמה ולטהרה. ואמרו חז״ל ״אין לך אות בתורה שאין בה תחיית המתים אלא שאין אנו יודעין לדרוש (ספרי האזינו פיסקא א).״ (4:149)

דהנה קרח היה אדם גדול, כמו שאמרו חז״ל (במדבר רבה י״ח:ג) שהיה
מנושאי הארון. אכן ידוע שיש בחינת עובדא ומילולא [מעשים ומלים] כמו
שכתוב בזוהר תרומה ״אורייתא מאן דבעי זכה אבל מלה דקיימא בעובדא
צריך סייעתא דשמיא [תורה—מי שרוצה—זכה. אבל לקיים מעשה, צריך
עזרה מן השמים] (על פי ח״ב קכ״ח ע״א).״ וזה היה בחינת הכהן עובד ה׳,
וכל העולם נתחדש בכל יום בעבודתו בבית המקדש. זה שכתוב ״אשר
יבחר״ לשון עתיד דכתיב ״מי זה האיש ירא ה׳ יורנו בדרך יבחר (תהלים
כ״ה:י״ב).״

כי בכל יום יש דרך חדש. כדאיתא במדרשות (ב״ר מ״ט:ב) בכל יום
הקדוש ברוך הוא מחדש הלכה ״הגה מפיו יצא (איוב ל״ז:ב).״ והירא ה׳
לאמיתו מראין לו הדרכים המתחדשים בכל יום. וגם מי שאינו במדריגה
זו, כמו אנחנו בגלות, עם כל זה על ידי יראה זוכין לכוון כפי מה
שמתחדש בשמים.

אכן בזמן המקדש היה [זה] בהתגלות, בפרט [אצל] משה ואהרן שכל
העולם נשען עליהם. ועל זה כתיב ״חסדך ואמיתך תמיד יצרוני (תהלים
מ:י״ב).״ זה בחינת משה ואהרן, שעל ידי הכהן הגדול נמשך חוט של חסד
בכל יום לעולם. וזו היתה העדות על אהרן בכל יום ויום, שהמשיך אור
חדש לעולם.

וזה שאמר משה רבינו ע״ה ״בוקר ויודע ה׳ כו׳.״ איך יכולין לערר על
הכהן הגדול! הרי כל יום ויום מעיד עליו... (117:4)

ג

איתא ״תכלת דומה לים, וים דומה לרקיע, ורקיע דומה לכסא הכבוד
(במדבר רבה ד:י״ג).״ נראה דהני שלוש מדריגות הם לזכור כל אלה השלשה.
יציאת מצרים כמו שכתוב ״אני ה׳ אלהיכם אשר הוצאתי אתכם (במדבר
ט״ו:מ״א)״ וסוף הגאולה היה על הים כמו שכתוב ״ויושע ה׳ ביום ההוא
את ישראל (שמות י״ד:ל).״ ו״רקיע״ רומז לקבלת התורה מן השמים. ו״כסא
הכבוד״ רומז להשראת השכינה במשכן וענני הכבוד.

ואלה שלוש מתנות שהיו לישראל גם כן. באר [בזכות מרים]—בחינת
ים. ורקיע—לחם מן השמים, מן בזכות משה. וענני הכבוד—בזכות אהרן.
והם בחינת שלושה רגלים גם כן. ועיקר הדבר רומז לבחינת נפש, רוח,
נשמה. שביציאת מצרים היתה הגאולה בנפש. ובקבלת התורה קבלו בחינת
רוח, ואחר כך הנשמה.

והגם כי מדריגת משה רבינו ע״ה גדולה, אבל אהרן בכח שהחזיר בני
ישראל בתשובה, זכה למעלה עליונה וניתנה לו עבודת יום הכפורים לפני
ולפנים בחינת התשובה—והוא בחינת נשמה. ועל זה אמרו ״במקום שבעלי
תשובה עומדין, אין צדיקים גמורים יכולין לעמוד (ברכות ל״ד ע״ב).״
ו״גדולה תשובה שמגעת עד כסא הכבוד (יומא פ״ו ע״א).״ לכן ענני הכבוד
בזכות אהרן.

ובזה יובן מחלוקת קרח שעשה טלית שכולה תכלת. ומשה רבינו ע״ה
אמר שצריכין דוקא חוט של תכלת, שמבחינת תכלת העליונה אינו יכול
להמשיך רק הארה מועטת—וכולי האי ואולי [וגם זה לא בטוח]. וקרח לא

"יראה." שהם בזכות שלושה אבות שהנבואה ניתנה להם כדכתיב "וארא
אל אברהם, אל יצחק, ואל יעקב (שמות ו:ג)." מרוב אהבת אברהם אבינו
ע"ה אל הבורא יתברך נגלה אליו. ויצחק מרוב היראה. יראה לשון ראיה.
ויעקב מתוך האמת. והקדוש ברוך הוא נתן לבני ישראל המצוה שיוכלו
לבוא למדריגת האבות. וגם זה אמת שעל ידי מצוה זו חל השגחת הקדוש
ברוך הוא על איש ישראל כמו שאמר "מציץ מן החרכים."

וכמו כן בראיה ברגל בא לראות ולהיראות כמו שכתוב "יִרְאֶה יֵרָאֶה
(חגיגה ב ע"א ועוד)." והנה כתיב "אתה הראת לדעת (דברים ד:ל"ה)" שיש
לבני ישראל בחינת ידיעה וראיה... לפי שהם עדות. וכתיב "או ראה או ידע
(ויקרא ה:א)." ובזוהר הקדוש "וארא כי בחינת ידיעה למעלה מראיה דרגא
דמשה רבינו ע"ה (תקוני הזהר ה ע"ב)." ואפשר שלכך ניתן להם עתה מצות
ציצית. כשנפלו ממדריגתם, ולא נמשכו לגמרי אחרי הנהגת משה רבינו ע"ה,
הן צרכו לבחינת ראיה—שהיא למטה מידיעה. (106:4)

קרח

א

"ויקח קרח (במדבר ט"ז:א)" ואתפליג [בתרגום כתוב "ויחלוק"]. במשנה:
"מחלוקת שהיא לשם שמים, סופה להתקים ושאינה לשם שמים, אין סופה
להתקים. איזו היא מחלוקת שהיא לשם שנים? זו מחלוקת הלל ושמאי.
ושאינה לשם שמים—זו מחלוקת קרח וכל עדתו (אבות ה:י"ז)."

כי באמת העולם הזה נקרא "עלמא דפרודא [עולם הפירוד]," שכל
הנבראים יש לכל אחד בחינת לעצמו. ולכן "כולא קטנה (בראשית רבה
ח:ה)." אבל בני ישראל זוכין אל השלום בכח התורה. וכל עובד ה' לשמו
יתברך כדי להיות נגמר רצונו יתברך בעולם, אם מתכוון באמת לשם
שמים, אין בו שום קנאה על חבירו. כי מה האדם שיהיו מעשיו מתקבלים
בשמים? רק מכלל ישראל נגמר רצונו יתברך בעולם. ולכן צריך כל אחד
למסור חלקו יפה יפה לצבור. וממילא אין הפרש אצלו בינו לבין חבירו.

וזו היתה מדת אהרן "אוהב שלום ורודף שלום (אבות א:י"ב)," לכן
בחר בו הקדוש ברוך הוא לכהן. ולכן כתיב "ואהרן מה הוא כי תלינו עליו
(במדבר ט"ז:י"א)" כי לא היה נפרד כלל לעצמו, וכל מעשיו מסר לצבור.
אבל בקרח כתיב "ויקח" לעצמו. ואפילו יהיה גדול שבגדולים, כשהוא
לעצמו—מה הוא?

וכתיב "ואהבת לרעך כמוך אני ה' (ויקרא י"ט:י"ח)" ואמרו "זה כלל
גדול בתורה (ב"ר כ"ד:ז)." רש"י פירש "רעך" זה הקדוש ברוך הוא. והיינו
כשעובד ה' לשמו יתברך, ממילא אוהב את חבירו העובד ה' כמוהו. וזה כלל
גדול בתורה. רעך הקדוש ברוך הוא ורעך ממש—הכל אחד... (127:4)

ב

בפסוק "בקר וידע ה' את אשר לו ואת הקדוש... ואת אשר יבחר בו...
(במדבר ט"ז:ה)" דרשו חז"ל "כשם שהבדיל בין בוקר לערב אור לחושך, כן
הבדיל את אהרן לקדשו (תנחומא בובר קרח פרק י)."

התועים ולחסות בצל הקודש. כי באמת כפי מה שנבדלין בני ישראל מעולם הזה, כך יכולין לכנוס בצלו יתברך. וכתיב "בצלו חמדתי וישבתי (שיר השירים ב:ג)." (4:97-8)

ד

חז"ל דרשו "וראיתם אותו (במדבר ט"ו:ל"ט)" על השכינה. "שמי שמקיים מצות ציצית זוכה לראות פני השכינה כו' (על פי מנחות מ"ג ע"ב)."

והסתכלות זו היא כבוד מלכותו יתברך שיש בכל דבר כדכתיב "מלא כל הארץ כבודו (ישעיה ו:ג)"—רק שהוא נסתר. והאמת כי על ידי הביטול להשם יתברך בכל לב [רואים את כבודו]. שכן ענין עטיפה בציצית "וראיתם" כפשוטו הוא להיות כל החפץ והסתכלות האדם רק לראות ולהכיר כבוד שמו. על ידי זה יוכל לראות זיו יקרי'. וכן איתא:

נחזי ביקרי' [נראה כבודו]

ויחזי לן סתרי' [ויראה לנו סתרו]

דאתאמר בלחישא.

פירוש שיש הארה גנוזה בכל דבר רק שנסתר. ועל ידי הביטול שנקרא "לחישא" שמבטל כל ההרגשות להשם יתברך—חרש. על ידי זה מתגלה לו, וזה פירוש "דאתאמר בלחישא."

וזה שכתוב "וראיתם אותו" הוא האות שיש בכל דבר שהוא עדות על השם יתברך. כמו שאמרו ז"ל "צבאות אות הוא בצבא שלו (מכילתא פרשת השירה פרשה א)." וכל צבא שמים וארץ נקראו "צבאיו" שהם אות על מלכותו רק שנסתר בעולם הזה.

"וזכרתם את כל מצות ה' ועשיתם אותם ולא תתורו אחרי לבבכם ואחרי עיניכם למען תזכרו ועשיתם את כל מצותי והייתם קדושים לאלהיכם (במדבר ט"ו:ל"ט-מ)." שגם קיום המצות צריך להיות על כוונה זו כדי להתדבק בהשם יתברך ולזכור תמיד שנברא רק לקיום רצונו. שזכרון הוא דביקות... גם פירוש "ולא תתורו" יהיה זה כדי לזכור להתדבק.

כי יוכל בר שכל למאוס בעולם הזה מעצמו. ואמרו ז"ל אל יאמר אדם "אי אפשי בבשר חזיר," רק "אבי שבשמים גזר עלי (ספרא קדושים פרק ט)." וזה שכתוב "ולא תתורו... למען תזכרו... והייתם קדושים" שהפרישה מגשמיות תהיה לאלהיכם, כדי להתדבק בו. כי באמת מה שבכח איש ישראל למאוס בגשמיות הוא על ידי שהוציאנו ממצרים וזה שאמר "אני ה' אלהיכם אשר הוצאתי אתכם מארץ מצרים אני ה' אלהיכם (במדבר ט"ו:מ"א)." (4:88)

ה

בפרשת ציצית. במדרש (במדבר רבה י"ז:ה) "אור זרוע לצדיק (תהלים צ"ז:י"א)." כי ציצית, פירש רש"י, מלשון "מציץ מן החרכים (שיר השירים ב:ט)." שזו המצוה לפתוח עיני איש ישראל, כמו שאמרו בגמרא "הזהיר במצות ציצית זוכה להקביל פני השכינה (על פי מנחות מ"ג ע"ב)" דכתיב "וראיתם אותו."

והנה כתיב [מצות הציצית] שלוש פעמים, מעין שלוש פעמים בשנה

דכתיב "לכל זמן ועת לכל חפץ תחת השמים (קהלת ג:א)." ולא היו מוכנים לכנוס עד אחר מ' שנה. אך תחת כל השמים כתיב. אבל דור המדבר דורו של משה רבינו ע"ה היו כל תהליכות שלהם למעלה מן השמים. וזהו שרמזו חז"ל "עלה נעלה (במדבר י"ג:ל)": "אפילו יאמר 'עשו סולמות לעלות לשמים' לא נשמע לו (על פי סוטה ל"ה ע"א)." הם הדברים שדברנו, כי על פי הטבע לא היו מוכנים לעלות. וזהו "שלח לך" כי אם היו מצליחים בשליחותם והיו נכנסין באופן זה שלמעלה מן הזמן והטבע, היה גם משה רבינו ע"ה נכנס עמהם.

וכן כתיב בגאולה העתידה "בעתה אחישנה (ישעיה ס:כ"ב)"—[פירוש]: זכו—אחישנה כו'. והכל תלוי ברצון בני ישראל שעל ידי תשוקה באהבה רבה להשם יתברך מעוררין רצונו יתברך, ואז אין מניעה מצד הזמן והטבע. וזה שכתוב "אם חפץ בנו ה' והביא אותנו כו'."

ולכן יש לנו ללמוד מזו הפרשה שהגם שבאמת לא היה הזמן, מכל מקום אם היה הרצון בלבות בני ישראל להשם יתברך כראוי, היו באין. וכמו כן בגלות הזאת—אם היתה לנו תשוקה של אמת לשוב אליו יתברך, יחיש וימהר גאולתינו. אמן. (94:4‑5)

ג

בפרשת ציצית: "על כנפי בגדיהם (במדבר ט"ו:ל"ח)."

ענין עטיפת הטלית להתאחד בשורש האחדות. ובזוהר הקדוש (רעיא מהימנא ח"ג קע"ה ע"א) מביא הפסוק "מכנף הארץ זמירות שמענו (ישעיה כ"ד:ט"ז)" עיין שם. ואיתא בתוספות סנהדרין ל"ז ע"ב דכתיב שש כנפים בחיות הקודש ובכל יום אומרים שירה בכנף אחד. ובשבת אומרים "אין לנו עוד כנף" ואומר הקדוש ברוך הוא "יש לי כנף אחד בארץ" עיין שם. ויראה שזה ענין "מזמור שיר ליום השבת טוב להודות לה' (תהלים צ"ב:א‑ב)" כי השיר הוא על ידי התאחדות. וזאת האחדות אינה בנמצא בעלמא דפרודא [בעולם הפרוד]. רק לבני ישראל ניתנה זו האחדות בנפש.

וכמו כן בימים. נמצא בשבת קודש התאחדות "ברזא דאחד" כדאיתא בזוהר הקדוש (ח"ב קל"ה ע"א). ובעולם הוא בארץ ישראל ובית המקדש. ותרגום יונתן "מכנף הארץ" מארעא דישראל, עיין שם. כי הוא מקום הכולל כל המקומות ונקראת "מכנף הארץ." ומכח זה היה השיר בבית המקדש. וכמו כן בשבת קודש, שמתאחדת כל הבריאה לכן "טוב להודות לה'."

ולבני ישראל ניתן זה הכח להתעטף ולקבץ כל הכנפות. ועל זה מבקשין "וקבצנו מארבע כנפות הארץ." כדפירש רש"י ארבע כנפות רומז ארבע לשונות של גאולה. פירוש דכתיב "כארבע רוחות השמים פרשתי אתכם (זכריה ב"י)" שבני ישראל נשתלחו בכל המקומות לאסוף ולקבץ על ידיהם כל הניצוצות להחזירם אל השורש. ועל ידי מצות הציצית יכול איש ישראל להכניס עצמו לכלל האחדות. ולכן כתיב בציצית "לדורותם (במדבר ט"ו:ל"ח)" כי בכל מקום שהם נדחים מכל מקום מצוה זו מסייעת שלא להיות נפרד מן השורש. וכשאדם מתעטף בטלית מציצית הוא כאלו נפרש ומובדל מזה העולם שהיא פריסת סוכת שלום. שהקדוש ברוך הוא נתן לנו להבדילנו מן

וידבר אליו (במדבר ז:פ"ט)" למעט את אהרן. שזה בחינת משה רבינו שיש לו דביקות בעצם התורה. ואחר כך פרשת הנרות שהוא להתדבק בתורה בכח תיקון המלבוש על ידי המצוות.

וכן כתיב סוף הפרשה הבדל בין נבואת משה רבינו [לנבואת אהרן ומרים]. "אם יהיה נביאכם... במראה אליו אתודע (במדבר י"ב:ו)." "במראה" גימטריא רמ"ח שהוא על ידי הרמ"ח מצוות [נודע]. ומשה רבינו "פה אל פה אדבר בו (שם שם ח)."

ואיתא כי בשבת קודש מחזיר משה רבינו לבני ישראל הכתרים מהקדמת "נעשה" ל"נשמע" [וכך אנו מתפללים "ישמח משה במתנת חלקו"]. כי בקבלת התורה היו כל בני ישראל דבקים בעצם התורה בחינת משה. ולכן בעשרת הדברות נכללו כל התרי"ג מצוות שהיא עצם התורה אור. "אנכי ה' אלהיך (שמות כ:ב)"—וזה כל התורה.

אך אחר שנפלנו ממדריגה זו, בא אור תורה באמצעות תרי"ג פקודין. וזה "למען צדקו יגדיל תורה." ולפי שבשבת יש נשמה יתירה, והיא הארה מעצם אור תורה למעלה מהתלבשות התרי"ג פקודין, לכן נקרא "יתירה"—שאינו מתלבש בגוף. כי הנשמה בימי המעשה היא בהתלבשות בחינת "נר מצוה." ובשבת קודש למעלה מזה—הארה מבחינת מתן תורה. ולכן ניתנה תורה בשבת, שהיה גלוי וידוע לפניו יתברך שמו כי בשבת ישארו בני ישראל לעולם במדריגה זו. (4:82-3)

שלח

א

במדרש "אין חביב לפני הקדוש ברוך הוא כשליח שנשתלח לעשות מצוה ונותן נפשו שיצליח בשליחותו (במדבר רבה ט"ז:א)." נודע דברי אדוני אבי זקני מורי ורבי ז"ל כי כולנו שלוחי מצוה שנשתלחנו מהשם יתברך בעולם הזה לקיים מצוותיו כו'. ובוודאי לא היתה אפשרות להמשיך קדושת השם יתברך בעולם הזה—רק על ידי בני ישראל בעבודתם. והיתה העצה שיוכלו להתקיים בעולם הזה בקדושה על ידי המצוות כדכתיב "שלח אורך ואמתך המה ינחוני (תהלים מ"ג:ג)."

דהנה בכל דבר יש קדושה כדכתיב "מלכותך מלכות כל עולמים (שם קמ"ה:י"ג)." נמצא כל הנעשה הוא רצון עליון בלבד, רק שנסתר בעולם הזה. והמצוות נקראין "נרות" שמאירין בכח התורה לכל המעשים. כי אין לך מעשה שאין בו מצוה. ורק קודם כל דבר צריך האדם ליתן נפשו בשליחותו, והיינו שיאסוף כל רצונות שלו לבטלם רק לקיים רצון עליון. ועל ידי זה מצליח בשליחותו ועושה המצוה כתיקונה. ואף במעשה גשמי, על ידי ישוב הדעת שמברר אצלו וחפץ באמת שיתקיים רצון עליון שיש בזה—יוכל להנצל... (4:87-8)

ב

בפסוק "אם חפץ בנו ה' והביא אותנו אל הארץ הזאת ונתנה לנו (במדבר י"ד:ח)." כי בוודאי הרגישו המרגלים כי אינם מוכנים לכנוס לארץ ישראל...

העליונות לא יתבייש. ויעשה את שלו. "ויעש כן אהרן אל מול פני המנורה"
שלא שינה. פירוש שלא נעשה שינוי והסתר—והוא שבח גדול.

הוא כמו שיהיה לעתיד שכתבו חז"ל (ילקוט שמעוני בחקותי, רש"י)
על פסוק "והתהלכתי בתוככם (ויקרא כ"ו:י"ב)" שלא תהיו מזדעזעין כו'.
פירוש: שלא יצטרך האדם להתרחק על ידי היראה. וכמו מלאכי השרת
שנאמר "ונתתי לך מהלכים בין העומדים האלה (זכריה ג:ז)." שיכולין
לעמוד לשרת בפני הקדוש ברוך הוא אף שהקדוש ברוך הוא גבוה ומרומם
על מלאכי השרת כמו על התחתונים. כי לפי רוממות הבורא, אין ניכר
ההפרש בין מלאכי השרת לתחתונים. רק שזה שלימות השרת שיכול
לעשות מה שנצטווה אף שרואה ומשיג התרוממות הבורא. והבן... (4:71)

ב

במדרש "'יקח את הלוים מתוך בני ישראל (במדבר ח:ו).' כמה נימין היו
בכנור שהיו הלוים מנגנים בו?... שבע... ולימות המשיח נעשית שמונה...
ולעתיד לבוא נעשית עשר: 'שיר חדש אשירה לך בנבל עשור (תהלים קמ"ד:ט)'
(במדבר רבה ט"ו:י"א)."

כי השירה תליא בזמן. ולכן בכל יום יש שיר אחר כי ההתחדשות שיש
בכל יום נותנת השירה כמו שאמרו ז"ל (תנחומא בובר אחרי מות י"ד) כי
השמש אומרת שירה וזורחת. עיין שם בפסוק "שמש בגבעון דום (יהושע
י:י"ב)." כי בכל יום יש הארה אחרת כדאיתא בשם האר"י ז"ל "אין כל
יום דומה לחבירו מבריאת עולם."

ונראה דהלוים מיוחדים לבחינת הזמן—דיש שלוש בחינות: עולם, שנה,
נפש. דצריך כל אדם בפרט, ומכל שכן כלל ישראל, לתקן המקום והזמן
שמיוחד לו בתיקון נפשו. ובני ישראל תקנו המקום בכח ארץ ישראל, ולכן
נתחלקה להם הארץ. ולשבט לוי לא היה חלק. והלוים מוכנים לתקן בחינת
שנה. לכן הלוים נפסלים בשנים ולא במומים. כמו שאמרו במשנה "כשר
בכהנים פסול בלוים (חולין א:ו)."

והכהן מיוחד לבחינת נפש. לכן צריך שלא יהיה בו מום, ואין נפסל
בשנים.

ולכן תליא השיר בבחינת הזמן. ולימות המשיח וכן לעתיד יהיה שינוי
בזמן וישתנה השיר. וכמו כן שבת מעין עולם הבא. לכן "מזמור שיר ליום
השבת (תהלים צ"ב:א)" כתיב בעשר: "עלי עשור (שם שם ג)." ושבת הוא
בחינת שיר השירים, שכולל כל השירים של ימי המעשה. (2-81:4)

ג

במדרש "ה' חפץ למען צדקו יגדיל תורה ויאדיר (ישעיה מ"ב:כ"א)" דכתיב
"נר מצוה ותורה אור (משלי ו:כ"ג)" כי אור התורה הוא למעלה מהשגת
האדם. ולכן אין יכולים להתדבק באור תורה רק על ידי המצוות, שהן
כלים לתקן הרמ"ח [248] איברים וגידים—להיות כלי מוכן לאחוז בהם
אור התורה.

והנה משה רבינו ע"ה הוא בחינת "תורה אור" ואהרן הוא "נר מצוה"
בעובדא [מעשה]. לכן כתיב סוף פרק נשא "וישמע את הקול מדבר אליו

נקודה קטנה כמו הרבה—והבן כל זה. (4:55)

ג

במדרש (במדבר רבה ו:י) "ולבני קהת לא נתן כי עבודת הקדש עליהם בכתף ישאו (במדבר ז:ט)" דורש על השירה כמו שכתוב "שאו זמרה ותנו תף כנור נעים עם נבל (תהלים פ״א:ג)." וקשה. מה "בכתף"?

ויתבאר העניין (בעבודה זרה כ״ד ע״ב) על פי מה שכתוב "וישרנה הפרות בדרך (שמואל א ו:י״ב)." שעל ידי שנשאו הארון ניתנה בהם דעת לשורר ולזמר, כמו שאמר בזוהר הקדוש בלק—"ארונא דעל גבייהו עביד להון לזמרא [הארון על גביהם נתן להם לשיר] (ח״א קכ״ג ע״א-ב)." כן הלוים, במה שנשאו על כתפיהם [את הארון], בכח זה הרימו קול זמרה. וכמו כן הוא בכל עובד ה' שמתמלא זיו ושמחה על ידי עבודת אמת.

ועל זה נאמר "עם זו יצרתי לי תהלתי יספרו (ישעיה מ״ג:כ״א)." כי עיקר העבודה בתורה ובמצוות—וממילא נתמלא פיו שירה וזמרה. וזה עצמו העדות, שהאמת עד לעצמו, שהעובד ה' מבין בנפשו שהוא דבוק בשורש האמת ולבו שמח. והוא עדות על הבורא יתברך.

וכמו כן יש בכל יום תפילות ושירות. ומקודם יש מצוות בעובדא, ואחר כך במילולא דפומא [אמירת הפה] כידוע. (4:57-8)

בהעלתך

א

"בהעלתך את הנרות אל מול פני המנורה יאירו שבעת הנרות. ויעש כן אהרן אל מול פני המנורה העלה נרותיה (במדבר ח:ב-ג)." להבין הפירוש "מול פני המנורה," וגם השבח מאהרן שלא שינה. גם קשה "שבעת הנרות." הלא רק ששה נרות יאירו אל מול האמצעי.

ויראה לפרש על פי המדרש (במדבר רבה ט״ו:ח) המשל שאמר המלך לאוהבו "הכן לי סעודה." ובא המלך עם כל כבודו והטמין האוהב אשר הכין. ושאל המלך "היכן" ואמר שנתבייש. וצוה המלך להטמין הכל ולהשתמש רק בהכנת האוהב.

והנראה מזה המשל כי באמת היתה הדרך הנכונה שיכין האוהב אשר לו—אף שראה כלים של המלך, אף על פי כן יעשה הוא את שלו. רק בעבור שנתבייש האוהב, צוה המלך להטמין כל כבודו.

אבל באמת למה יגרע מכבוד המלך? וזה יש לפרש מאמר הכתוב "מול פני המנורה" פירוש: מנורה העליונה—יאירו שבעת הנרות, שלא יצטרך הקדוש ברוך הוא להסתיר אור העליון. כי באמת כל מה שנסתר בעולם הזה כבודו יתברך וקדושתו, הוא לצורך עבודת האדם. כי אם היה נתגלה, היו מתבטלין כל העבודות מידי בשר ודם.

אך הצדיק בעבודת השם יתברך יכול לעשות את שלו אף שלו אף שרואה כבודו יתברך. ולכן מי שמוכן לזה מראין לו כל מה שבעולמות העליונים, כי כל ההסתר בעבור חסרון העבודה.

וזה מאמר הכתוב "אל מול פני המנורה" יאירו שאף שיראה כל ההארות

המדות הם מושרשים בנפשות בני ישראל. רק להוציאם מכח אל הפועל הוא על ידי עסק התורה. כמו שכתוב "ברחובות תתן קולה (משלי א:כ)" שעל ידי היגיעה מתפשט כח פנימיות של התורה לתוך המלבוש—מתחבר המלבוש להפנימיות. וזה נקרא לשמה... (4:6)

ג

בענין המנין "לגלגלתם (במדבר א:ב)." דכתיב "לתבונתו אין מספר (תהלים קמ"ז:ה)." פירוש דאיתא בזוהר הקדוש "נודע בשערים בעלה (משלי ל"א:כ"ג)' כל חד לפום שעורין דלבא [כל אחד לפי השיעור שבלב] (ח"א ק"ג ע"א)." ולכל איש ישראל נמצא ידיעה ובינה מיוחדת להיות נודע גדולתו של הקדוש ברוך הוא כפום דרגא דיהב ליה ידיה [כפי הדרגה שניתן לידו]—מה שאינו יכול להתוודע לאחר. וזה שאמרו במשנה: "להגיד גדולתו של יוצר בראשית, שכולם נטבעו בחותמו של אדם הראשון—ואין פרצופיהן דומין זה לזה (על פי סנהדרין ד:ה)." ובמדרש פינחס (במדבר רבה כ"א:ב): כשם שאין פרצופיהן דומין, כך אין דעתו של זה כדעתו של זה. וכל אחד מתפעל באיזה בחינה אחרת, וזה "לתבונתו אין מספר."

ובזה המנין ניתן לכל אחד דעת ומוחין השייכין אליו, וזה "לגלגלתם" לבית אבותם. כי האבות כוללין הדיעות של הבנים, רק שהיה בכלל. ואחר כך מתפשטין לפרטים. וזה שאמרו במדרש (מדבר רבה ב:ח) "אשא דעי למרחוק (איוב ל"ו:ג)." (4:14)

נשא

א

אדוני אבי זקני ז"ל אמר על מה שכתוב מצות תשובה "והתוודו את חטאתם (במדבר ה:ז)" בגזילה. כי כל עבירה בכלל גזל, שמי שמחזיר כל הדברים להשם יתברך שהוא המחיה הכל והוא בעלים [ולו בעלות] של כל הנבראים. ומי שיודע זה אינו חוטא בודאי. (4:54)

ב

במדרש (במדבר רבה י"א:א) "ישא ה' פניו אליך (במדבר ו:כ"ו)" וכתיב "אשר לא ישא פנים (דברים י:י"ז)." כאן כשעושין רצונו של מקום, [וכאן כשאין עושין רצונו של מקום. כשעושין—"ישא ה'" וכשאין עושין—"אשר לא ישא פנים"]... כשעושין רצונו של מקום, מה צורך לנשיאת פנים! רק שיקבל הקדוש ברוך הוא המעט עבודה כמו הרבה. והוא עצמו מה שאמרו במדרש "הן נושאין לי פנים, כך אני נושא להם פנים." פירוש: הכלל [הוא] כפי מה שאדם עצמו שמח במעשה הטוב וחביב בעיניו שזכה לעשות רצון המקום—הן רב הן מעט, כמו כן מקבל הבורא יתברך ממנו בסבר פנים יפות. והאמת כי הוא לאות על הפנימיות שבאדם שמשם באה השמחה.

וזה שכתוב "וישם לך שלום" כי בחינת השלימות היא נקודת האמיתיות, שבכל הארה מועטת נמצא הכל. [ולכן] נקרא הקדוש ברוך הוא "שלום" שהוא שלימות הכל. וכשיש לבני ישראל זאת השלימות, אם כן נחשבת

ספר במדבר
במדבר

א

רבי מאיר אומר "כל העוסק בתורה לשמה זוכה לדברים הרבה (אבות ו:א)." פירוש הפשוט: כדי לעשות. וזה שם "תורה" כדי להורות לאדם המעשה. כי בודאי עיקר הגיעה בתורה לבטל שכלו ודעתו כדי לידע ולהבין רצון השם יתברך ודעת התורה.

ובמדרש (נדרים נ"ה ע"א, במדבר רבה י"ג:כ"ו) נמשלה תורה במדבר, שצריך להיות הפקר כמדבר כמו שכתוב "וממדבר מתנה (במדבר כ"א:י"ח)." משל "לנשיא שנכנס למדינה וראו אותו בני המדינה וברחו. נכנס למדבר וקיבלוהו בכבוד אמר הנשיא זו העיר טובה היא מכל המדינות. כאן אני בונה כס נאה (על פי במדבר רבה א:ב)." פירוש "דבר" הוא מנהיג ומושל. ו"מדבר" הוא להיות נכנע תחת המנהיג. והיינו שאדם מבטל עצמו שאין לו שום כח ופעולה בלי חיות השם יתברך. וזה ההפרש בין בני המדינה שברחו, והיתה להם גם כן יראה ממנו, אך היה להם גם כח בפני עצמם [ובין בני המדבר]. וכעניין שכתוב שאומות קורין להשם יתברך "אלקי דאלקיא [אלהי האלהים]." אבל בני ישראל כמדבר, שאין להם שום כח והנהגה בפני עצמם כלל.

וזה שאמרו [על] ירא שמים: "בסתר ובגלוי (סידור)." פירוש "בגלוי" על ידי שיודע שהשם יתברך משגיח על כל דבר נופלת עליו יראה. ו"בסתר" הוא להיות נדבק יראתו יתברך בחיות האדם, שלא יהיה שום פעולה ותנועה שישכח שהוא בכח השם יתברך. ו[האדם] רק כגרזן ביד החוצב בו.

וכן עסק התורה, להיות בטל אל הנהגת התורה, לעשות כל מעשה רק להיות נעשה רצון השם יתברך ומבוקשו. כי באורייתא ברא קודשא בריך הוא עלמא, ונמצא כי יוכל להתדבק בהשם יתברך בכל מעשה —ממש על ידי כח התורה. ועל ידי שמכניע עצמו ומתבטל בכל מעשה אל חיות הפנימיות חיותו יתברך, על ידי אותיות התורה שיש בכל מעשה. וזה לשמה. כי הנבראים לכבודו ברא... והוא בחינת כבוד שמו יתברך והבן. (4:1-2)

ב

[באותה משנה] מאי "לשמה"? כי נודע שהתורה "לא ידע אנוש ערכה (איוב כ"ח:י"ג)."

אך התורה שלפנינו היא לבוש התורה, ועל ידי עסק האדם בתורה זו מתעורר כח הפנימיות. וזה עיקר הכח שניתן לבני ישראל שיכולין לעורר שורש התורה. כי נפש האדם היא גם כן כך, שהיא מלבוש לכח הנשמה שהיא חלק אלהי ממעל.

וזה שאמרו במדרש "והיה מספר בני ישראל כמספר הסופר כו' (על פי במדבר רבה ב:י"ג)." פירוש: כמו התורה שיש אותיות ותיבות במניין, אף על פי כן שורש התורה אין מכל זה, כמו כן נפשות בני ישראל אם כי בעולם הזה יש להם מספר, אבל שרשם למעלה ממספר. וכן כתוב בספרים הקדושים שס' ריבוא נפשות בני ישראל—ס' ריבוא אותיות שיש בתורה.

וזה השכר שלומד לשמה, זוכה לאלה המדות טובות בעבור שכל אלה

הבירור, זוכה אחר כך לקבל הארה אחרת—וכן לעולם. וזהו רמז הכתוב
"והשיג לכם דיש" שהוא הבירור. (3:205)

ה

"[אני ה' אלהיכם...] ואולך אתכם קוממיות (ויקרא כ"ו:י"ג)." פירש רש"י
מתורת כהנים: בקומה זקופה. אף על פי שאמרו חכמים שאסור לילך
בקומה זקופה, אך כאשר יהיה התיקון כראוי, כמו לעתיד, יוכל האדם
לקבל מורא שמים אף בקומה זקופה. כי הרי כך נברא; רק שבעולם הזה,
מחמת הבלי עולם, אי אפשר לקבל היראה רק על ידי כפיפות קומה
והכנעה רבה.

וזה עצמו ענין אמרם ז"ל בתורת כהנים (על פי ספרא בחוקותי פרק ג)
על "והתהלכתי בתוככם (שם שם י"ב)" לא תהיו מזדעזעים... יכול לא
תיראו?... אני ה' אלהכם. פירוש שיוכלו לקבל עול מלכות שמים כמו שהם
בלי השתנות ושפלות יתירה. והיא ההבטחה שיוכלו לילך בקומה זקופה.
(205-6:3)

והחקיקות שחקק הקדוש ברוך הוא בנפש האדם. כמו שאמרו במדרש
"חוקים שהם חקוקים על היצר הרע (ויקרא רבה ל"ה:ה)." פירוש: כמו
שיש המשכות בהרגשות הנפש לתאוות היצר, מכל שכן שנמצא ממש
מיוחד דרכים ושערים בנפש האדם מיוחדים להשם יתברך. והם רשימות
וחקיקות בנפש האדם. אך להוציא מכח אל הפועל הוא בעזר השם על ידי
הרצון של האדם והגיעה בתורה. כמו שאמרו "יגעתי ומצאתי–תאמין
(מגילה ו ע"ב)."

וזה שכתוב "חשבתי דרכי"–לשון רבים, שחישב תמיד למצוא הדרכים
המיוחדים אליו. ומרוב המחשבות שהרהר בהם תמיד היה לו סייעתא
דשמיא [עזרה מן השמים].

"ואשיבה רגלי" הוא תיקון הטבע והרגילות, להכניס בהם אור החכמה
והדעת. וכאשר חכמים הגידו "הרהורי עבירה קשין מעבירה (יומא כ"ט
ע"א)," יש לנו ללמוד כי הרהורי מצוה נוחין מהמצוה גופא. שתיקון הנפש
תלוי ברוב הרהור ותשוקה לעבודת הבורא יתברך. (3:208-9)

ג

[פירוש אחר על אותו מדרש:] דכתוב "כל פעל ה' למענהו (משלי ט"ז:ד)"
אמרו חז"ל (על פי ראש השנה כ"ב ע"ב) לעדותו, להעיד עליו. וזו העדות
מוטלת על איש ישראל כמו שכתוב "אתם עדי (ישעיה מ"ג:י)." לכן צריך
האדם למצוא בכל דבר ובכל מקום זו העדות.

וכן התפאר עצמו דוד המלך ע"ה כי כל המחשבות שעברו לפניו כל
היום ביקר מהם עדות ה'. ובגמרא סוף ברכות "איזוהי פרשה קטנה שכל
גופי תורה תלוין בה? 'בכל דרכיך דעהו (משלי ג:ו) (ס"ג ע"א)'"–למצוא זו
העדות בכל הדברים.

ועניין "לבתי כנסיות ובתי מדרשות" דאיתא (תפילת שחרית לשבת)
"גדלו וטובו מלא עולם." "גדלו" בחינת בריאת עולם בעשרה מאמרות.
"טובו" זו התורה–עשרת הדברות. והם "מלא עולם," שאין לך מקום ודבר
שאין בהם כח מעשרה מאמרות ומעשרת הדברות. ואיש ישראל צריך לברר
זאת ולמצוא הארת התורה בכל מקום.

וכל אותן הדברים והמחשבות העוברין על האדם, כולם לברר זו
העדות. והם בחינת דרישות וחקירות ובדיקות שבודקין העדים, והם
בירור העדות.

וכמו דשבת דסהדותא איקרי [נקראת עד], וכל הדברים שבששת ימי
המעשה מתברר מהם הטוב שיש להם עליה בשבת–וזו עדות השבת, כמו
כן בני ישראל נקראו עדים, שעל ידיהם מתברר טוב מרע ועל ידי האדם
מתברר ומתעלה למעלה הטוב מזה התערובת. לכן כתיב "אתם עדי."
(3:213)

ד

"והשיג לכם דיש את בציר, ובציר ישיג את זרע (ויקרא כ"ו:ה)." דכתיב
"אור זרוע לצדיק (תהלים צ"ז:י"א)." והוא הארת התורה שאדם מקבל
בלבו ועושה פירות, ואחר כך צריך לברר מעשיו להיות בלי פסולת. וכפי

כמו שכתוב "וספרת לך (ויקרא כ״ה:ח)" ומקדשין בית דין שנת השמיטה
והיובל.

וכל זה הכח נמסר לבני ישראל בקבלת התורה לכן נאמר "בהר סיני."
ביד לשון הוא רמז לבני ישראל שנמסר להם לשון הקודש, כדכתיב. מקודם
היתה שפה אחת לכולם, ובדור הפלגה נתבלבלו הלשונות ונמסר אחר כך
לבני ישראל בפרט בקבלת התורה. (3:200)

בחוקותי

א

"אם בחוקותי תלכו (ויקרא כ״ו:ג)" פירש רש״י מתורת כהנים להיות עמלים
בתורה. זהו נקרא עמל בתורה להלוך בחקיו יתברך. לכן אפילו אינו מבין,
מכל מקום מייגע עצמו בתורה שחביב בעיניו להגות במאמרו יתברך אפילו
שאינו זוכה להשיג הטעם. כי התורה "נעלמה מעיני כל חי (איוב כ״ח:כ״א)."
והאדם צריך לעסוק בתורה אחר הידיעה שאי אפשר להשיג אחד מני אלף
שבה. ואז יש לו חלק בשורש התורה.

לכן כתב המהר״ל שמברכין "לעסוק בדברי תורה." הגם שאינו יכול
להשיג, מכל מקום עוסק הוא בתורה. וכך הוא תמיד בזוהר הקדוש "לאשתדלא
באורייתא [להשתדל בתורה]." ובגמרא נדרים (פ״א ע״א) "ולא הלכו בה
(ירמיה ט׳:י״ב)" שלא ברכו בתורה תחילה. פירוש: פשיטא אחר שזוכין
לטעום טעמי תורה מי פתי לא יתמלא שמחה וחדוה לברכו יתברך. אך
העיקר בתחילה—קודם שמשיג—רק מתאווה להגות בדברי קודש, דברי
אלהים חיים.

ומסיים הפסוק "]אם בחוקותי תלכו ואת מצוותי תשמרו...[ונתתי
גשמיכם בעתם" כי הגם שאמרו חז״ל "שכר מצוה בהאי עלמא ליכא [אין
בעולם הזה]" (קידושין ל״ט ע״ב) היינו מצד השכל ועבודת האדם כך הוא.
אבל באמת השם יתברך נתן חוק להיות כל העולם הזה תלוי בתורה.
כדאיתא "באורייתא ברא קודשא בריך הוא עלמא (זוהר ח״א ה ע״א)."
וזאת ההתקשרות היא למעלה מן השכל. ומי שמבטל עצמו כענין "בחוקותי
תלכו," אז התורה נותנת לו מזון גם בעולם הזה. (3:210)

ב

במדרש "חשבתי דרכי, ואשיבה רגלי אל עדותיך (תהלים קי״ט:נ״ט).' אמר
דוד, רבונו של עולם, בכל יום ויום הייתי מחשב ואומר—למקום פלוני
ולבית דירה פלונית אני הולך. והיו רגלי מביאות אותי לבתי כנסיות ולבתי
מדרשות (ויקרא רבה ל״ה:א)" דכתיב "מה' מצעדי גבר כוננו ודרכו יחפץ
(תהלים ל״ז:כ״ג)."

פירוש שיש ששה דרכים מיוחדים לאיש ישראל, והעובד ה' אשר משתוקק
תמיד למצוא הדרכים המיוחדים אליו—ינחהו ה' בדרך האמת. כמו שאמרו
"ויהיו רגלי מביאות" על ידי זה שבכל יום היה מחשב ומשתוקק למצוא
דרך ה'.

וזה שכתוב "אם בחוקותי תלכו" שהוא בכח האדם לראות הדרכים

ובאמת אין נס גדול ונפלא כמו הטבע, שהוא הגדול שבנפלאות המושגים
לנו. ואז כשזו האמונה מתבררת לבני ישראל, אין עסק להיות ניזון על פי
נס. רק ״וכי תאמרו 'מה נאכל'״ אז ״וצויתי את הברכה.״

ונס הוא לשון הרמה, פירוש שהיא הנהגה מתרוממת מהנהגת
הטבע—ומיוחדת לבני ישראל. וכן כתב המהר״ל כי כמו שיש סדר להטבע,
כן יש סדר להנסים. וסדר זה מיוחד לבני ישראל.

ובאמת הדורות שנעשו להם הנסים היתה קבועה בהם האמונה, והיה
שווה להם הטבע והנסים. לכן נהג השם יתברך עמהם בנסים. (3:190-1)

ג

״כי תבאו אל הארץ אשר אני נותן לכם ושבתה הארץ שבת לה' (ויקרא
כ״ה:ב).״ כי השם יתברך נתן לנו ארץ ישראל להודיע כי לה' הארץ. כדאיתא
בתנחומא (בהר א) השם יתברך הקנה העולם לאברהם וחזר והקנה לו. וזה
מצוות השמיטה: שניתנה לבני ישראל הארץ מחדש, ובכל שמיטה מתחדשת
המתנה. כעניין שכתוב בפרשת תולדות ״ויתן לך האלהים (בראשית
כ״ז:כ״ח)״—יתן ויחזור ויתן. עיין שם. וזה שכתוב ״אשר אני נותן״ לשון
הווה.

ובני ישראל הם מוכנים לקבל זו המתנה. וזה שכתוב ״כי גרים ותושבים
אתם עמדי (ויקרא כ״ה:כ״ג)״ הוא שבחן של בני ישראל שיודעין שהם גרים
ומברירין כי ״לה' הארץ״ ודבקים תמיד בכח הנתינה. ובזה יתכן לפרש מה
דכתיב ״וכרות עמו הברית לתת את ארץ הכנעני החתי האמורי והפרזי
והיבוסי והגרגשי לתת לזרעו (נחמיה ט:ח).״ תרתי למה לי [למה כתוב
״לתת״ פעמיים]? רק שיהיה להם תמיד בחינת הנתינה—יתן ויחזור ויתן.
שבכל שמיטה ״ושבתה... הארץ לה.״

וכעין שכתוב באור החיים על כל שבת שניתנת חיות חדשה לבריאה.
עיין שם פסוק ״ויכולו השמים והארץ (בראשית ב:א).״ וכשם שנאמר בשבת
בראשית כן בשמיטה. (3:196)

ד

במדרש ״״מות וחיים ביד לשון (משלי י״ח:כ״א)' בר סירא אמר 'היתה
לפניו גחלת ונפח בה ובערה, רקק בה וכבתה (ויקרא רבה ל״ג:א).'״

זו הגחלת היא בכל מקום, והיא ניצוצין מן התורה שנקרא אש. כמו
שכתוב בספרים כי ״גחלתי״ גימטריא ״אמת.״ ואין אמת אלא תורה. והכל
נברא מהתורה ונמצא מזו הגחלת בכל מקום וכל דבר.

אך ביד איש ישראל להוציא מכח אל הפועל זה הניצוץ. ועל זה כתיב
״ויפח באפיו נשמת חיים ויהי האדם לנפש חיה (בראשית ב:ז)״ [ובתרגום
שם] ״לרוח ממללא.״ היינו שיש כח בפיו לעורר החיות בכל מקום. ועל זה
אמרו ״אם בחוקותי תלכו (ויקרא כ״ו:ג)״ להיות עמלים בתורה. פירוש
ליגיע עצמו למצוא דברי תורה בכל מקום—הרשימות וחקיקות מהתורה
שנמצאות בכל מקום. כמו שאמרו במדרש ״חוקים שבהם חקקתי את...
הירח (ויקרא רבה ל״ה:ד).״ ולכן הזמנים נמסרו ביד בני ישראל כמו שאמרו
(ברכות מ״ט ע״א) ישראל דקדשינהו לזמנים. וכן במנין שמיטין ויובלות

בהר

א

[״וידבר ה׳ אל משה בהר סיני לאמר (ויקרא ה׳׳ה:א).״] ענין שמיטין ויובלות
להר סיני:

על פי המדרש ״׳ברכו ה׳ מלאכיו, גיבורי כח עושי דברו (תהלים ק׳׳ג:כ).׳...
בשומרי שביעית הכתוב מדבר (ויקרא רבה א:א).״ וחז׳׳ל דרשו ״שהקדימו
בני ישראל ׳נעשה׳ ל׳נשמע׳ אמר הקדוש ברוך הוא ׳מי גילה לבני רז
שמלאכי השרת משתמשין (על פי שבת פ׳׳ח ע׳׳א).׳״

כי בני ישראל היו מוכנים בקבלת התורה להיות כמלאכי השרת. כי
באמת גם התחתונים שלוחיו של מקום הם, דהכל לכבודו ברא. רק ההפרש
הוא שהמלאך אין בו דבר אחר, רק זו השליחות. ונקרא כולו ״מלאך״ על
שם השליחות. ולפי שבטל במציאות אליו יתברך, לכן ניזון מזיו השכינה—כמו
שעתידין צדיקים להיות בעולם הבא.

ובני ישראל בקבלת התורה היו מוכנים גם כן לזה. לכן ניזונו ״מלחם
שמלאכי השרת אוכלין (יומא ע׳׳ה ע׳׳ב).״ כי באמת ״בזעת אפיך תאכל
לחם (בראשית ג:י׳׳ט)״ היא הקללה לאחר החטא, ומקודם היתה כל אכילת
אדם מגן עדן. וכמו כן היו בני ישראל מוכנים להיות בהר סיני. וכן כתוב
״אמרתי ׳אלהים אתם (תהלים פ׳׳ב:ו).׳״

אך גם אחר החטא נשארו לבני ישראל זמנים שמתעורר להם זה הכח
הראשון. וכמו בשבת קודש שמתבטלין מכל מלאכה ומוכנים רק לעבודת
השם יתברך. לכן המזון ביום שבת קודש הוא בקדושה. ובזמן שהיו שמיטין
ויובלות היתה כל השנה שנת שבתון, ולא היו עוסקין בזריעה וקצירה...

ובשמיטין ויובלות ושבתות יש לבני ישראל מדרך הראשון שקודם
החטא. ולכן היו שובתין בזמנים הללו, והיו חוזרין למדרגה הראשונה
שקבלו בהר סיני. וזה עיקר החירות ביובל דכתיב, ״ושבתם איש אל
אחוזתו (ויקרא כ׳׳ה:י)״ שהיתה להם דביקות בשורשם.

ולכן שומרי שביעית נקראו ״מלאכיו עושי דברו״ שאין להם רק זה
השליחות, ואין עוסקין בדרך ארץ כלל, רק כמלאכי השרת. ולכן היה המזון
שלהם על פי נס. ואיתא בספרים בפסוק ״וכי תאמרו ׳מה נאכל בשנה
השביעית (שם שם כ)?׳״ כי רצונו יתברך היה שלא יהרהרו כלל, ואז היו
נהנים ממעשה נסים ממש. ועל ידי השאלה הוצרך להיות המזון בדרך
ברכה. (6-195:3)

ב

בפסוק ״וכי תאמרו ׳מה נאכל בשנה השביעית (ויקרא כ׳׳ה:כ)?׳״ בספר נועם
אלימלך בשם אחיו ז׳׳ל כי על ידי השאלה יצטרך המקום לצוות את
הברכה. עיין שם.

ביאור הדברים: מה קושיא היא זו ״מה נאכל?״ מאן דיהיב חיי יהיב
מזונא [מי שנתן חיים יתן מזון]! אך כי אם כן יהיה קיום בני ישראל על פי
נס, ואין כל הדורות ראוין לנסים. לכן אמרו ״מה נאכל?״ והתירוץ שיהיה
בדרך ברכה, וברכה היא קצת בטבע.

אך באמת צריכין בני ישראל לידע כי הנסים והטבעים—הכל אחד.

ה

במדרש "'והבאתם את עומר ראשית קצירכם אל הכהן (ויקרא כ"ג:י) ' 'מה יתרון לאדם בכל עמלו שיעמל תחת השמש (קהלת א:ג)?'... אמר ר' שמואל בר נחמני 'ביקשו לגנוז ספר קהלת שמצאו בו דברים שהם נוטין לצד מינות.' אמרו 'כך היה שלמה צריך לומר—מה יתרון לאדם—יכול אף בעמלה של תורה במשמע?' חזרו ואמרו, 'אלו אמר, יגע עמל—תשתק, היינו אומרים אף בעמלה של תורה במשמע הוא, הא אינו אומר אלא 'בכל עמלו—בעמלו הוא, שאינו מועיל. אבל בעמלה של תורה מועיל (ויקרא רבה כ"ח:א). ".

ואין מובן הסלקא הדעתך [הדעה שמנגד]. דהלא עיקר דברי קהלת הם לההביל כל מעשי עולם הזה רק לעסוק בתורה ומצוות. אכן נראה דבאמת כל מה שברא הקדוש ברוך הוא לכבודו ברא, וי"י בחכמה יסד ארץ (משלי ג:י"ט). לכן יש יתרון בכל מעשה בראשית, לאפוקי [להוציא] מדעת המינים שאומרים "עזב ה' את הארץ (יחזקאל ח:י"ב). ".

אכן אין יכולים למצוא החכמה הגנוזה [ב]מעשה בראשית רק בכח התורה כדכתיב "בראשית ברא (בראשית א:א)" בשביל התורה שנקרא "ראשית." ובעמלה של תורה יכולים להעלות זה הראשית שנמצא בתוך הטבע. וזה נקרא "עמלה של תורה" לעמול למצוא דברי תורה בכל מקום. שצריך איש ישראל להאמין שהכל שהכל תורה, וכח העשרה מאמרות שהם בתוך הטבע גנוזים. וכדכתיב "אמרות ה' אמרות טהורות כסף צרוף (תהלים י"ב:ז). " פירוש: כמו שהכסף נמצא תוך העפר וצריכין לצרפו ולזקקו עד שנעשה כסף טהור, כן נמצא בכל הבריאה גנוזים דברי תורה. ועל זה כתיב "[אם תבקשנה ככסף] וכמטמונים תחפשנה (משלי ב:ד). ".

ובאמת זה בחינת גאולה וחירות, להוציא יקר מזולל. והנה בני ישראל הם כלים לזה. וכשיצאו ממצרים נעשה בירור זה על ידם בכלל העולם עד שנתבררו עשרה מאמרות מאמרות ונעשה מהם עשרת הדיברות.

ולא זה בלבד, רק בכל שנה ושנה ממחרת הפסח נתעלה חלק ראשית בכח גאולת מצרים. לכן "והבאתם את עומר ראשית קצירכם" וזה הראשית נתברר במ"ט [49] ימים עד שנעשה מזה תורה ממש, כמו שהיה אז ביציאת מצרים בכלל.

שעל זה נאמר "אנכי ה' אלהיך אשר הוצאתיך מארץ מצרים (שמות כ:ב)" ודייק וקרא. כן בכל שנה יש ענין פרטי עד לעתיד "מלאה הארץ דעה (ישעיה י"א:ט)" שיהיה הכל תורה ממש. והכל על ידי בני ישראל. לכן נקראו "עושי דברו (תהלים קג:כ)" וכדאיתא (אבות ה:א) שצדיקים מקיימים העולם שנברא בעשרה מאמרות. (5-184:3)

ג

במדרש (ויקרא רבה כ״ו:ו) ״יראת ה׳ טהורה, עומדת לעד (תהלים י״ט:י)״
מורא שנתירא אהרן זכה לדורות כו׳...

דהנה יראת ה׳ לחיים היא יראת הרוממות. וכהן עובד ה׳ במקדש חל
עליו מורא שמים כמלאך משרת. דאיתא ״אין מדותיו של הקדוש ברוך הוא
כבשר ודם מוראו [של הקדוש ברוך הוא] על הקרובים יותר כדכתיב
יוסביביו נשערה מאד (תהלים נ:ג)׳ (על פי מכילתא בשלח ח׳ לשמות
ט״ו:י״א).״

ועיקר היראה ממלכות שמים היה בבית המקדש. וגם בני ישראל
קיבלו יראה זו שלוש פעמים בשנה כדכתיב ״יראה כל זכורך (דברים
ט״ז:ט״ז).״ ועל זה אנו מבקשים ״ושם נעבדך ביראה.״ וכן כתוב על אהרן
״בריתי היתה אתו החיים והשלום, ואתנם לו מורא וייראני, ומפני שמי
נחת הוא (מלאכי ב:ה).״

והנה בזוהר הקדוש יתרו איתא כי עיקר השלימות הוא ליראי ה׳ כמו
שכתוב ״אין מחסור ליראיו (תהלים ל״ד:י).״ ממשמע דאין מחסור— שלום
איקרי [נקרא], עיין שם. ולכן זכה אהרן למדת השלום, אוהב ורודף שלום.
כי שלום שמו של הקדוש ברוך הוא. ולפי שחל עליו יראת ה׳ טהורה, לכן
זכה אל השלום.

ומהאי טעמא נקראת עיר הקודש ״ירושלים,״ על היראה והשלימות
שנמצאות בה.

וגם שבת קודש, שחל יראת ה׳ על בני ישראל, כדאיתא ״אפילו עם
הארץ—אימת שבת עליו (על פי תוספתא דמאי פרק ה),״ נקרא ״שלום.״
(3:181)

ד

בפסוק ״ונקדשתי בתוך בני ישראל, אני ה׳ מקדשכם, המוציא אתכם מארץ
מצרים להיות לכם לאלהים, אני ה׳ (ויקרא כ״ב:ל״ב-ל״ג).״ פירש רש״י
מתורת כהנים ״על מנת כן״ עיין שם.

פירוש: בכל עת שאיש ישראל מוסר נפשו בעבור קדושת שמו מתעוררת
יציאת מצרים. כי תכלית יציאת מצרים ״להיות לכם לאלהים.״ ובמסירת
נפש מקבל עליו אלהותו יתברך ומתעורר כח יציאת מצרים. ובזה הכח יכול
למסור נפשו בפועל.

והנה כתיב ״בתוך בני ישראל״ כי הקדושה גנוזה בכלל ישראל כמו
שכתוב ״חלק ה׳ עמו (דברים ל״ב:ט).״ ואמרו חז״ל ״כל בי עשרה שכינתא
שריא [בכל בית של עשרה השכינה שורה] (סנהדרין ל״ט ע״א).״ פירוש ״בי
עשרה״ כשנעשין באמת אחד בלב אחד. דכתיב ״תוך בני ישראל״ הוא הלב
כי הנפשות קרובים, רק החומר מעכב התאחדות. אבל כשנמסר נפשו ניטל
הגשמיות, אז בא לכלל ישראל באמת ואז ״ונקדשתי.״

ולכן תיקנו חז״ל יציאת מצרים בקריאת שמע, שעל ידי קבלת מלכותו
יתברך שמו במסירת נפש בפרשת ״שמע ישראל,״ באין אל האחדות. [לכן]
נזכר כח יציאת מצרים. (3:186)

יכניס אהבת ה׳ בלב חבירו.
לכן אמרו שהוא כלל גדול בתורה. (159:3)

ד

במדרש ״וכי תבאו אל הארץ ונטעתם כל עץ מאכל (ויקרא י״ט:כ״ג)׳... ׳עץ
חיים היא למחזיקים בה (משלי ג:י״ח)׳ (ויקרא רבה כ״ה:א).״

פירוש: כח הנטיעה ניתן לבני ישראל, שיכולין לנטוע ולדבק כל דבר
לשורשו בכח התורה—וזה שכתוב ״חיי עולם נטע בתוכינו.״ ״ונטעתם כל
עץ מאכל״ לראות לבטל כל דבר לשרשו. והיא עיקר בחינת ארץ ישראל,
ועל זה מבקשין ״ותטענו בגבולנו (תפילת מוסף לשבת)״ שמקודם צריכין
לנטוע נפשותינו בשורש כי ״האדם עץ השדה (דברים כ:י״ט).״ (156:3)

אמור

א

בפסוק ״וקדשתו כו׳ (ויקרא כ״א:ח)״ פירוש שקדושת הכהנים תלויה בקדושת
בני ישראל, שצריכין להתקדש אף מי שאינו יכול להיות קדוש ממש. אף על
פי כן מעט קדושה שלו מוסיף כח לזה האיש המיוחד לקדושה להתקדש
כראוי. וכן כתוב ״הכהן הגדול מאחיו.״ דרשו חז״ל ״גדלהו משל אחיו
(ספרא אמור פרשתא ב),״ והוא כדברינו הנ״ל והבן. (172:3)

ב

במדרש (ויקרא רבה כ״ו:א) ״אמרות ה׳ אמרות טהרות (תהלים י״ב:ז).״
כי התורה ניתנה לבני ישראל לתקן על ידה כל המעשים. לכן אין דברי
תורה מקבלין טומאה. וזה הרבותא [של] טהורות: בכל המקומות שמכניסין
שם דברי תורה—אין בהם מגע נכרי.

ולכן אין אדם זוכה לתורה רק כפי הטהרה שנמצא בו. לכן ניתקנו ימי
הספירה, להיות מטהרים ומוכנים לקבל דברי תורה. כי הגם שכל אחד
לומד, אבל להיות לו דביקות בפנימיות התורה שנקרא ״אמרות ה׳״ כמו
שכתוב ״ודבק לבנו בתורתך״ דייקא, זה תלוי בטהרה. וזה עצמו העדות
שאמרותיו טהורין על ידי שכל אחד כפי הטהרה שבו כך זוכה לתורה. כמו
שכתוב ״ככסף צרוף בעליל לארץ (שם)״ כי התורה אמת ועד לעצמה. כי כפי
הטהרה, כך נכנסת באדם. ואם לא, לא יועילו כל התחבולות.

אכן גם זה אמת: כי דברי תורה מטהרין להעוסק בהם כמו שאמרו
חז״ל ״מה מים מטהרין, כך דברי תורה מטהרין (סדר אליהו רבה פרק
י״ח).״ ומקודם כתיב ״יכרת ה׳ כל שפתי חלקות, לשון מדברת גדלות. אשר
אמרו ללשוננו נגביר, שפתינו אתנו. מי אדון לנו?׳ (שם שם ד-ה).״ וזאת
כוונת המדרש, שכמו שלשון הרע הוא מגונה עד מאד, כך לשון הקודש
מביא לידי טהרה. וכלפי שאמר ״יכרת ה׳ כו׳״ מסיים ״אמרות ה׳ אמרות
טהרות״ וקאי על העוסקים באמרות ה׳. לכן מסיים ״אתה ה׳ תשמרם (שם
שם ח) על התינוקות [העוסקים בתורה] כמו שאמרו במדרש. (4-173:3)

רק כשזוכין לקדושה.

ועניין קהילה זו שייך בכל פרט גם כן, לאסוף כל הרמ״ח [248] אברים וכל הרצונות לדבר אחד. כמו שכתבו חז״ל (זהר ח״ג ע״ה ע״ב) בפסוק ״כי ה׳ אלהיך מתהלך בקרב מחנך... והיה מחניך קדוש (דברים כ״ג:ט״ו)״ ברמ״ח אברים שבך. ולכן, על ידי המצוות זוכין לקדושה. כמו שאומרים ״קדשנו במצותיו״ ומבקשין ״קדשנו במצותיך״ כי על ידי המצוות מתחברין הרמ״ח אברים לזכות לבחינת האחדות. ואז יש קדושה.

אבל קדושת כלל ישראל היא גבוהה ביותר. ולכן כנסיה שהיא לשם שמים סופה להתקיים, שחל עליה שם שמים וקדושה שורה בהם. וכמו כן בפועל על ידי שהיתה אחדות בישראל, היו להם משכן ובית המקדש, והשכינה היתה שורה ביניהם. ועתה, על ידי שנאת חנם חרב, שאין קדושה רק באחדות. (3:158-9)

ב

״קדושים תהיו.״ פירש רש״י הוו זהירין מן העריות ועבירה. ורמב״ן ז״ל כתב לקדש במותר לו.

ולפי עניות דעתי יפה כיון רש״י ז״ל, כי בודאי מצוות ״קדושים תהיו״ הוא מדברים שאין להם שיעור. וכפי הפרישה, כך זוכין לקדושה—ואין לדבר סוף. לכן כתיב ״תהיו״ כי לעולם צריך האדם להתקדש, קדושה על קדושה. והרמז לדבר בפסוק ״וקדשתם היום ומחר (שמות י״ט:י).״ כלומר שאין סוף לומר ״כבר קדוש אני!״ והראיה כי הלא אותו הדור היו באמת כל העדה כולם קדושים, ונאמר להם ״קדושים תהיו.״

וזה שרמז המדרש ״יכול כמוני כו׳ (ויקרא רבה כ״ד:ט)״ היינו שכיון שהפסוק אומר שאין סוף להקדושה עד שנתן גבול: ״קדושתי למעלה מקדושתכם (שם).״ ממילא מובן איך אין סוף לקדושה זו, שיכולין בני ישראל להתקדש בעולם הזה יותר מהשרפים.

אכן ודאי אתחלת הקדושה היא להיות פרושין מעריות ועבירה. אז מתחילין לכנוס בגדר הקדושה, שזה החיוב של הקדושה לכל איש ישראל. ואז יש לו להרבות תוספות קדושה. כעניין תלמוד תורה וכדומה, שאין להם שיעור. (3:157)

ג

בפסוק ״לא תשנא את אחיך בלבבך, הוכח תוכיח את עמיתך ולא תשא עליו חטא (ויקרא י״ט:י״ז)״ כתבו המפרשים להיות המוכיח בכלל התוכחה. פירוש: לידע שיש לו חלק בהחטא. כמו שכתוב ״ולא תשא עליו חטא״ פירוש שלא להשליך כל החטא על החוטא, רק להתערב עצמו ולשוב על זה. וממילא ירגיש גם חבירו ויתעורר בתשובה.

״ואהבת לרעך כמוך (שם שם י״ח)״ פרשנו לשון פועל יוצא, וקאי [מתיחס] על אהבת ה׳. כי היכן מצינו שיאהב האדם את עצמו שאמר ״כמוך״? רק הפירוש להאהיב את השם לרעך כמו לך. כמו שכתבו חז״ל ״ואהבת את ה׳ אלהיך (דברים ו:ה)׳ להיות שם שמים מתאהב על ידך (יומא פ״ו ע״א).״ וכמו שהאדם מייגע עצמו להכניס אהבת ה׳ בלבו, כן

כוללת כל העולמות. ועל ידי מעשה בני ישראל בתורה, נותנת להם חיים בעולם הזה גם כן. ועל זה מסר לנו הקדוש ברוך הוא התורה שעל ידינו תתפשט הארת התורה גם בעולם הזה. (147:3)

ג

בפסוק ״אשר יעשה אותם האדם וחי בהם (ויקרא י״ח:ה).״ פירשו חז״ל לעולם הבא, שבעולם הזה סופו מת. כי המצוות הם מתקנים צלם האדם הפנימי רמ״ח [248 אברים—מצוות עשה] ושס״ה [365 גידים—מצוות לא תעשה]. וכשזוכה אדם לזה המלבוש, אין מיתה שולטת בו, כמו שהיה לאדם הראשון קודם החטא. אך אחר החטא נתלבש בגוף שיש בו מיתה. ועל ידי המצוות זוכין למלבוש הראשון.

וגם פירוש זה נכלל ב״אשר יעשה אותם וחי בהם.״ פירשו באמצעיותם נעשה ציור האדם. וגם כפשוטו, שעל ידי המצוות נעשה כלי לקבל חיות שאין בו מיתה כדכתיב ״ויפח באפיו נשמת חיים (בראשית ב:ז).״ אם כן, לא שייך מיתה. רק שעל ידי החטא נאבד מאתנו כלי הראשון, ובעולם הבא נזכה לזה בהכנת המצוות.

וכתיב כאן ״יעשה״ וכתיב התם ״עין לא ראתה אלהים זולתך יעשה למחכה לו (ישעיה ס״ד:ג).״ הרמז כי עין הוא ציור ודמות, ועתידין בני ישראל להתלבש בציור רוחניי שאין מושג לשום בריאה כמו שכתוב ״זולתך.״ וכמו שכתבו ז״ל שעתידין בני ישראל לומר לפניהם ״קדוש.״ והכל באמצעיות המצוות בעולם הזה.

והנה שבת אמרו חז״ל שהוא מעין עולם הבא. ולכן נתגלה בו מעין ציור וצלם. לכן אמרו ״אין דומה מאור פניו של אדם [בחול למראה פניו בשבת] (על פי ב״ר י״א:ב).״ (149:3)

קדושים

א

״דבר אל כל עדת בני ישראל ואמרת אלהם קדושים תהיו כי קדוש אני ה' אלהיכם (ויקרא י״ט:ב).״ ״פרשה זו נאמרה בהקהל [על פי ספרא]״ שאיננו יכולים לזכות לקדושה רק על ידי הביטול לכלל ישראל. דכתיב ״כל העדה כולם קדושים (במדבר ט״ז:ג),״ פירושו כשהם באחדות אחת. לכן רוב דיני פרשה זו שבין אדם לחבירו. וגם כשבני ישראל הם אחד, אין יד האומות שולטת בהם ונבדלין מהם. ועל ידי זה שורה קדושה בישראל. כדכתב רש״י ״כל מקום שיש גדר ערוה יש קדושה״ לכן בשבת קודש ״דמתאחדין ברזא דאחד״ ו״סטרא אחרא מתעברין (זהר רזא דשבת)״ יש קדושה.

וכתוב ״כי קדוש אני ה' אלהיכם״ פירוש שגם הקדושה צריך להיות לשם ה', כדי לזכות להתדבק בו יתברך. וזה רמז המדרש ״יכול כמוני (ויקרא רבה כ״ד:ט)״ ולמדין מפרשת פרעה ״אני פרעה (בראשית מ״א:מ״ד).״ פירוש: כמו שפרעה לא העמיד את יוסף רק לטובת עצמו—שראה שהוא חכם העמידו לשמור את מלכותו של פרעה—כן לא תהיה הקדושה דבר נפרד, רק כדי להתדבק בו יתברך. ״כי קדוש אני״ ואיננו יכולים להדבק בו

"כל צפור טהורה תאכלו (דברים י"ד:י"א)' לרבות המשולחת (קידושין נ"ז
ע"א)" שרומז על הדיבור הטהור שזה עיקר האדם. "לנפש חיה (בראשית
ב:ז)" [תרגומו] רוח ממללא... (3:143)

אחרי מות

א

"כמעשה ארץ מצרים אשר ישבתם בה לא תעשו וכמעשה ארץ כנען אשר
אני מביא אתכם שמה לא תעשו ובחקותיהם לא תלכו. את משפטי תעשו
ואת חקותי תשמרו ללכת בהם... אשר יעשה אותם האדם וחי בהם...
(ויקרא י"ח:ג-ה)."

קשה: אי מכוון הפסוק על עריות המפורשין, למה תלה אותם הכתוב
במעשה מצרים וכנען? אבל נראה כי המכוון כי בכל המעשים לא נעשה אותם
כמו שעושין אותם בארץ מצרים וכנען. כי בכל המעשים יש בהם פנימיות
וחיצוניות, ובוודאי שורש כל המעשים הוא בקדושה—כי הכל לכבודו ברא.
ונקודה הפנימיות ניתן לבני ישראל וזה "כל מעשיך יהיו לשם שמים
(אבות ב:י"ב)."

לכן נקרא מעשה הגוים "חוקות" כמו שכתוב "ובחקתיהם לא תלכו."
כי אין להם שייכות לפנימיות הטעמים של כל המעשים, ודבקים רק
בחיצוניות.

ובאמת בני ישראל יכולים לעשות כל המעשים בקדושה על ידי המצוות.
וזה שכתוב "את משפטי תעשו." על ידי זה תוכלו לעשות כל המעשים שלא
כמעשה ארץ מצרים וכנען. וזה שכתוב "ללכת בהם... אשר יעשה האדם וחי
בהם." פרשנו גם כן שעל ידי המצוות ימשך החיות לכל הדברים. פשוט כמו
שכתבו ז"ל כל מצוות עשה נגד אבר מיוחד. וכפי מה שמבטל חיות כל
האבר אל המצווה, חוזר וממשיך חיות מהמצווה אל האבר. ועל ידי זה
יכול לעשות כל המעשים בקדושה כמו שאומרים "קדשנו במצוותיו."...
(3:144-5)

ב

ומפי אבי מורי זקני ז"ל שמעתי "אשר יעשה אותם האדם וחי בהם (ויקרא
י"ח:ה)" שניחת האדם עיקר החיות בתורה ומצוות, עד כאן דבריו.

ויש להוסיף על זה כי באמת על ידי זה "וחי בהם." כי התורה נותנת
חיים לעושיה בעולם הזה ובעולם הבא. וכמו שהרשעים, שעיקר רצונם
לחיות כדי ליהנות מעולם הזה, לכן כל חיותם על ידי אכילה ושתיה—אבל
הצדיקים, שעיקר רצונם לחיות כדי לקיים מצוות ה' ותורתו, לכן התורה
ומצוות הם החיים שלהם. כמו שכתוב "כי הם חיינו וארך ימינו." דייקא
שלנו נותנת התורה החיים.

ואמרו חז"ל "ללכת בהם' עשה עיקר ולא תעשה טפל (ספרא אחרי
מות פרק י"ג סימן י)." ובאמת זה תלוי בעבודת האדם. כפי מה שעושה
עיקר מתורה ומצוות, אז התורה נותנת לו חיים גם בעולם הזה. וזה שכתוב
"אשר יעשה אותם האדם" ואז "וחי בהם." כי התורה עיקרה למעלה והיא

והוא באמת מטמוניות—שבכל דבר הגשמי ביותר מוטמן בו ניצוצי
קדושה ביותר... (139-40:3)

ב

במדרש "ולרשע אמר אלהים: מה לך לספר חקי ותשא בריתי עלי פיך
(תהלים נ:ט"ז)"... שאין הקדוש ברוך הוא חפץ בקלוסו של אדם רשע
(ויקרא רבה ט"ז:ד)."

כי התורה נותנת עצה לבני ישראל לפי הזמן דכתיב "שלום שלום
לרחוק ולקרוב (ישעיה נ"ז:י"ט)." ובמדרש (ויקרא רבה ט"ז:ט) "רחוק" זה
מצורע, שהיה רחוק ונתקרב.

כי יש מי שמשיג השלימות על ידי הקירוב ויש על ידי התרחקות. וזה
"שלום שלום כו'" ולשון הכתוב "אמר מה לך לספר כו'" שזה גם כן דרך
התורה שנאמר לרשע שירחק עצמו. וזה הרפואה שלו על ידי שילוחו חוץ
למחנה. וכן הוא באדם כשפגם מעשיו ומתרחק מן הקדושה [הוא] צריך
לקבל זה הריחוק באהבה ולידע כי זה הריחוק הוא תקנתו. ובמדרש (שמות
רבה כ"ו:ב) אין מדתו של הקדוש ברוך הוא כבשר ודם—מכה באיזמל
ומרפא ברטיה. והקדוש ברוך הוא בדבר שמכה מרפא. פירוש שהמכה
עצמה היא הרפואה.

וזה שכתוב "זאת תהיה תורת המצורע" כי התורה שלו היא על ידי
הריחוק. וזה רומז האזוב שעל ידי השפלות יזכה להתקרב, וכל הנהגות של
התורה הם לטובה דכתיב "וכל נתיבותיה שלום (משלי ג:י"ז)." היינו אפילו
הדרכים שנותנין ריחוק לאדם הוא מביא לשלימות כמו שכתוב "שלום
לרחוק." וכתיב "האלהי מקרוב אני נאם ה' ולא אלהי מרחוק (ירמיה
כ"ג:כ"ג)." ובמדרש יתרו "וכי מקרב אני ולא מרחק (על פי תנחומא יתרו
פרק ו')." הרמז שאלוהותו יתברך שמו אינו על ידי קירוב בלבד, רק אפילו
הריחוק שאלהים עושה מביא לקירוב... (141:3)

ג

"וצוה הכהן ולקח למטהר שתי צפרים חיות טהרות ועץ ארז ושני תולעת
ואזוב (ויקרא י"ד:ד)." ברש"י לפי שהנגעים באים על לשון הרע וצפרים
מפטפטי קול. דאיתא בזוהר הקדוש פרשת תזריע (חי"ג מ"י ע"ב) דהנגעים
באין על מלה בישא [דיבור רע] ועל מלין טבין דאתי לידיה ולא מלל [ועל
דברים טובים שבאו לידו ולא דיבר] "החשיתי מטוב וכאבי נעכר (תהלים
ל"ט:ג)" עיין שם.

דכתיב "מות וחיים ביד לשון (משלי י"ח:כ"א)" ולפי שכח הלשון גדול
מאוד צריכין להזהר לבער מדברים בטלים והם מעכבין הפה ולשון להוציא בהם
דברי קדושה כמו שכתוב "ודברת בם (דברים ו:ז)." אמרו חז"ל "השח שיחה
בטלה עובר בעשה ':בם' ולא בדברים אחרים (על פי יומא י"ט: ע"ב)." שהוא
תנאי שכפי מה ששומר פיו מדברים בטלים כך יכול "לדבר בם."...

והצפרים באים לתקן שני החטאים: השחוטה לבער ולפרוש עצמו
מדברים בטלים ומכל שכן לשון הרע. והמשולחת להכין הפה ולשון להוציא
בהם דברי תורה. ולכן השחוטה אסורה ומשולחת מותרת כמו שכתבו חז"ל

(בראשית ב:ז)" [בשני יו"דין] –שני יצירות: בעולם הזה ובעולם הבא. וכמו
שכתוב במדרש "זכה... נוחל שני עולמות." (3:131)

ג

[וידבר ה' אל משה... לאמר: אדם כי יהיה בעור בשרו שאת או ספחת...
(ויקרא י"ג:א-ב)."]

... דהנה הפסוק תולה הנגעים בעור על פי מה שכתוב "ויעש ה'
אלוהים לאדם ולאשתו כתנות עור וילבשם (בראשית ג:כ"א)." ובמדרש
"כתנות עור כו'" כידוע שעל ידי החטא הוצרך להתלבש בלבוש הגס, משכא
דחויא [עור הנחש], שמשם יש כל הגשמיות. מקודם היה [האדם] רוחני
כמו שכתוב לעתיד, וכמו שהיו בני ישראל מוכנים להיות במתן תורה, ולכן
במשה רבינו ע"ה כתוב "קרן עור פניו" שתיקן כל זה העור עד שהאיר
באספקלריא המאירה.

ואנחנו לא נשארנו בזו המדרגה, לכן חזרו הנגעים כמו שכתוב במדרש
(על פי ויקרא רבה ט"ז:א) שעל ידי החטא חזרו למומים. עיין שם.

וידוע גם כן שיש בעור נקבים נקבים להודיע שיש ביכולת האור
להעביר קליפות הללו. רק על ידי החטאים מסתתמין אותן הנקבים ו"החושך
יכסה ארץ (ישעיה ס:ב)" וזה נגע צרעת "סגירו" [שסוגר את הנקבים].

ולכן ניתנה הטהרה לאהרן הכהן ובניו שהוא היה מתקן חטא העגל.
(3:130)

מצורע

א

"כי תבאו אל ארץ כנען אשר אני נותן לכם לאחוזה ונתתי נגע צרעת בבית
ארץ אחוזתכם (ויקרא י"ד:ל"ד)."

וקשה מה בשורה היא זו. ופירש רש"י "שהטמינו כנענים (אמוריים)
מטמוניות של זהב בקירות בתיהם כל ארבעים שנה שהיו ישראל במדבר,
ועל ידי הנגע נותץ הבית ומוצאן." וקשה. וכי היה צריך הבורא יתברך אלה
העלות! ולמה נתן לכנענים זאת המחשבה להטמין ושיצטרכו בני ישראל
להחריב הבתים!

אמנם ודאי גוף ענין נגעי הבתים הוא פלא גדול והוא אות ומופת על
קדושת בני ישראל שמביאין קדושה וטהרה גם במקומות מושבותיהם.
ויש ללמוד קל וחומר דכתיב "אבן מקיר תזעק וכפיס מעץ יעננה (חבקוק
ב:י"א)" על החטא, שקירות ביתו של אדם מעידין. מכל שכן מדה טובה
מרובה שהצדיק צריך להביא הרגשת קדושה בכל השייך אליו וגם בצומח
ודומם.

והנה בני ישראל כן עשו שהוציאו ארץ כנען מיד הטומאה והכניסוהו
בקדושה, ש[רק] שנקרא ארץ ישראל השרה הבורא יתברך שכינתו בבית
המקדש. וזה בכלל "ובכל מאודך (דברים ו:ה)" שצריכין להביא לכל הנכסים
הארת הקדושה. ומצד זה יכול להיות טומאת נגע צרעת גם בבתים. וזאת
הבשורה הטובה שיוכלו לתקן כל המקומות גם כן.

תזריע

א

במדרש ״׳אחור וקדם צרתני (תהלים קל״ט:ה)׳ אמר ר׳ יוחנן: אם זכה אדם נוחל שני עולמות—העולם הזה והעולם הבא... ואם לאו, בא ליתן דין וחשבון שנאמר ׳ותשת עלי כפכה (שם)׳ (ויקרא רבה י״ד:א).״

כי כל הבריאה צריכה תיקון, כמאמר ״...אשר ברא אלוהים לעשות (בראשית ב:ג).״ והאדם נברא אחרון למעשה וראשון לתיקון. כי על ידי האדם מתחברין הבריאה והתיקון. וזה שכתבו חז״ל (תוספתא סנהדרין פרק ח) שנברא באחרונה שיכנוס לשבת מיד, כי שבת הוא בחינת התיקון. ו״אחור״ הוא בחינת ימי המעשה שנקראו ימי עבודה לברר דברי עולם הזה אשר אינם מתוקנים. ועל ידי זה זוכין אחר כך לשבת בחינת ״קדם״ שהוא עולם המחשבה והתיקון.

האדם הוא מבריח ומחבר כל הבריאה. לכן יש בו גשמיות היותר מוגשם מכל, וגם רוחניות היותר עליון מכל. וכתוב ״בצלם אלהים עשה את האדם (בראשית ט:ו).״ אם כן כמו שידענו שהשם יתברך כולל כל ההויות כמאמר ״ואתה מחיה את כולם (נחמיה ט:ו),״ כמו כן ממש האדם כולל כל הנבראים אשר תחתיו. וכשהוא מתקן כל התלוים בו, אז זוכה למקומו המוכן לו למעלה מכולם. לכן ״אם זכה אדם, אומרים לו ׳אתה קדמת לכל מעשה בראשית׳ ואם לאו, אומרים לו ׳יתוש קדמך, שלשול קדמך (ויקרא רבה י״ד:א).׳״

רש״י: ״כשם שיצירתו של אדם אחר כל בהמה חיה ועוף במעשה בראשית, כך תורתו נתפרשה אחר תורת בהמה חיה ועוף [בספר ויקרא (רש״י על ויקרא י״ב:ב:א).״ פירוש שאין יכול להשיג דעת התורה המוכן לתהלוכת האדם באמת עד שמתקן מקודם תורת נפש הבהמיות שבאדם ומתקן הגשמיות. אחר כך בא ״תורת האדם.״ (128:3)

ב

... [על אותו מדרש] פירוש: האדם כולל כל צורת העולם הזה, ונקרא ״עולם קטן״—שכל העולם כלולין בו. לכן כל הדברים הם צורך האדם והם מזונות לו. אם כן, על כרחך נמצא בו שורש מהם. ולכן האדם כמו נשמה לכל הבריאה והם הגוף והחומר והוא הנשמה והצורה. לכן קדמה כל הבריאה קודם בריאת האדם, שהגוף קודם והבריאה קיבלה מקודם דברים הגופניים. אחר כך קיבלה הנשמה שהוא האדם. וזה שכתבו ״כדי שיכנס לשבת מיד (תוספתא סנהדרין פרק ח)״ שהוא יומא דנשמתין כדאיתא בזוהר הקדוש.

וכמו שיש אלה המדרגות במעשה בראשית, כן אחר כך בתורה, דאיתא ״האומר ועושה המדבר ומקיים.״ שבעשרה מאמרות נברא העולם, ובתורה ועשרת הדיברות מתקיים העולם. לכן נמצא בתורה חלק לכל פרטי הבריאה כמו שכתוב ״זאת תורת הבהמה ועוף כו׳ (ויקרא י״א:מ״ו)״ ואחר כך תורת האדם.

אכן פירוש ״אחור וקדם צרתני״ כי האדם כולל העליונים ותחתונים. וכמו שגוף האדם הוא צורת כל התחתונים, כן הנשמה יש בה צורת העליונים והיא בחינת ״קדם.״ ולכן דרשו חז״ל ״וייצר [ה׳... את האדם]

לעשות המצוה. וכמו כן אחר המצוה אם הוא בשלימות, חל עוד בושה על האדם. וזה עדות על שלימות המעשה.

נמצא שני הפירושים אמת: לפי שהיה ביישן זה ונבחר להיות כהן גדול, ועל ידי זה נקבע בו מדת הבושת. (3:123)

ד

במשנה "אל תהיו כעבדים המשמשים את הרב על מנת לקבל פרס, אלא הוו כעבדים המשמשין את הרב שלא על מנת לקבל פרס. ויהי מורא שמים עליכם (אבות א:ג)" הוצרך לו לומר—אל תשמשו על מנת לקבל פרס.

אך המכוון להיות כל מגמת האדם תמיד לעשות רצון בוראו. "ויהי מורא שמים עליכם" כי באמת יש בכל איש ישראל יראת ה'. אך שצריך עבודה לקרב הלב להאמת, ואל יתהלך בחשיכה. וכשיתעורר לב האדם תמיד בהפקת רצון ה', יפול עליו ממילא יראת ה'.

וכן נפרש הפסוק "זה הדבר אשר צוה ה' תעשו (ויקרא ט:ו)" כלומר להיות הרצון רק לעשות רצונו יתברך כאשר צוה. ועל ידי זה "וירא אליכם כבוד ה' (שם)" שיתגלה הישראת השכינה בלב האדם. (3:112)

ה

בפסוק "זאת החיה אשר תאכלו (ויקרא י"א:ב)" לפי שישראל דבוקים בחיים כמה שכתב רש"י.

ואיתא בגמרא על פסוק "[ולא תטמאו את נפשותיכם בכל השרץ הרומש על הארץ כי אני ה'] המעלה אתכם מארץ מצרים... (ויקרא י"א:מ"ד-ה)" "אלמלא לא העליתי את בני ישראל אלא לפי שאין מטמאין בשרצים די (בבא מציעא ס"א ע"ב)." דהנה המעלה אתכם הוא בחינה גדולה [יותר] מיציאת מצרים. והוא כמו שכתוב "הוצאתנו מארץ מצרים ופדיתנו מבית עבדים" כי יש גאולה מן המיצר, אבל יש בחינה יתירה שהוא למעלה מכל המקומות של צרה והוא בחינת "נחלה בלי מצרים." ולפי שהקדוש ברוך הוא הביא אותנו להיות בני חורין בעצם, לכן לא התיר לנו לאכול דברים שמשעבדין את הנפש אל הגוף. כי עיקר חירות הנפש שלא להתקשר בדברים גופניים... (3:121)

כי חיות התורה נמצא בכל מקום כמו שכתוב "כולם בחכמה עשית (תהלים ק"ד:כ"ד)." אבל יש דברים שאין יכולים להוציא החיות מחמת התערובות טוב ורע. וזה הסימן "מעלת גרה" ו"מפרסת פרסה." כי יש בכל דבר שני מפתחות: פנימית וחיצונית. וצריכין מקודם לפתוח הסגר הטבע והגשמיות שלא יהי מגושם ביותר. וזה הסימן "שוסעת שסע"—שלא נסגר לגמרי ויש סדק ושער לבטל הקליפה וההסתר. ואחר כך צריכין לפתוח נקודה הקדושה הפנימית. וזה הסימן [השני] "מעלה גרה"—שהרמז שיכולין להעלות הפנימיות.

ונמשכת אחר איש ישראל האוכל בקדושה. והמינים האסורים אין בכח להעלות הקדושה מהם. לכן הבדילנו הקדוש ברוך הוא מהם כנ"ל. (3:120)

בוודאי חביבין הם. אך אפילו נערים המה שלמטה, מכל מקום הסיוע שלמעלה שמאיר בהם מתקן אותם להיות הילדות טפל אל ההארה שמשפיע להן מלמעלה, כי סייעתא דשמיא הוא יותר מכל כח האדם שלמטה. ועיקר הידיעה בעולם כשנפתחים שערים שלמעלה... (119:3)

ב

איתא בתורת כהנים "ויהי ביום השמיני" שהיתה שמחה לפניו במרום כיום שנבראו שמים וארץ. כתיב התם "ויהי ערב ויהי בוקר יום אחד" ועל אותו היום נאמר "צאינה וראינה בנות ציון במלך שלמה בעטרה שעטרה לו אמו ביום חתונתו וביום שמחת לבו (שיר השירים ג:י"א)."

כי בני ישראל המשיכו עתה דרך חדשה בעולם על ידי התשובה שעשו. וזה היה הכנה לדורות כמו שכתבו חז"ל "לא היו בני ישראל ראוין לאותו מעשה [עבודת עגל הזהב] (עבודה זרה ד ע"ב)," כי אם להורות תשובה.

והאלוהים עשה האדם ישר, ומעשה בראשית הכל לכבודו ברא. והיה זה הדרך לצדיקים כמו שכתוב "ישרים דרכי ה' צדיקים ילכו בם [ופושעים יכשלו בם] (הושע י"ד:י)." אבל בני ישראל תקנו עתה דרך אפילו לנחשלים שנתעקמו יוכלו לחזור לדרך הישר על ידי תשובה. ודרך זו הוצרכו התחתונים להוציא מכח אל הפועל בעצמם כי "דרכי ה' [רק] ישרים" ולכן היתה שמחה לפניו כמו במעשה בראשית, כי זה תיקון העולם.

וזה שכתוב "שעטרה לו אמו" קָרָאָה אמו [קרא הכתוב לכנסת ישראל] שהמשיכו דרך חדש. ולכן כתוב "ביום השמיני" שהוא למעלה מדרך הטבע שהוא שבעה ימי בראשית.

וכמה גדולה התשובה כמו שכתבו ז"ל (על פי במדבר רבה י"א:ג) גדול החטא שמקודם [ראו] "מראה כבוד ה' (שמות כ"ד:י"ז)" ואחר החטא אפילו פני הסרסור [משה] יראו מגשת אליו. כמו כן אחר שעשו תשובה "וירא כבוד ה' אל כל העם (ויקרא ט:כ"ג)." (124:3)

ג

בפסוק "קרב אל המזבח (ויקרא ט:ז)" "שהיה אהרון בוש וירא לגשת. אמר לו משה 'למה אתה בוש, לכך נבחרת (רש"י שם).'" פירשו המפרשים בשביל הבושה שהיתה לו נבחר. ויתכן לומר גם כן שאדרבא, תכלית הבחירה לזכות לבוא לידי בושה כמו שכתוב במתן תורה "למען תהיה יראתו על פניכם לבלתי תחטאו (שמות כ:כ)." ואמרו חז"ל זו הבושת על שם ש"אין לו בושת בידוע שלא עמדו רגלי אבותיו על הר סיני (נדרים כ ע"א)." הרי תכלית קרבת בני ישראל להר סיני לזכות לבושת.

ולפי שהקדוש ברוך הוא כל מעשיו מדה במדה, ולפי שזה היה מדת אהרן, "אוהב את הבריות ומקרבן לתורה (אבות א:י"ב)," כמו שכתבו חז"ל (אבות דרבי נתן פרק י"ב) שהיה מקרב אפילו החוטאים כדי שיתבייישו מעצמם וישובו, כן מדד לו הבורא יתברך שמו שיקרבו להיות כהן גדול על כל ישראל, ונתביייש מאוד בעצמו—וזה תכלית השלימות.

ובאמת על ידי הבושה יכולין להתקרב לכל מצוה, כשמתבייש באמת בלבו. "איך יוכל גוש עפר לעשות רצון הבורא יתברך שמו?" בזה יכול

החטאים על ידי הקרבנות, לכן כתיב בכולן "תורת" לומר שבכח התורה יכולין בני ישראל לעולם לחזור ולהתקרב אליו יתברך שמו. וכתוב בשתי פעמים "והאש על המזבח תוקד בו לא תכבה (ויקרא ו:ה)" ואחר כך "אש תמיד תוקד על המזבח לא תכבה (שם שם ו)" לרמוז על שתי התורות, שבכתב ושבעל פה. ועליהם נאמר "סמכוני באשישות (שיר השירים ב:ה)" באש של מעלה ושל מטה. והיא תורה שבכתב ושבעל פה. כמו שכתבו "אף על פי שהאש יורדת מן השמים, מצוה להביא מן ההדיוט (עירובין ס"ג ע"א)."

ולעולם יש חלק לבני ישראל בשתי אשות הנ"ל. דכתוב "כה דברי כאש" בחינת תורה שבכתבה. וכתוב "בית יעקב אש (עבדיה א:י"ח)" בחינת "חיי עולם נטע בתוכנו" [תורה של בעל פה] דייקא. וזו היא (על פי שקלים ד ע"ב) מטבע של אש שהראה הקדוש ברוך הוא למשה רבינו ע"ה לומר שיש חלק לבני ישראל בצורה זו דאש—מחצית הצורה מלמעלה ומחצית מלמטה.

ובבית המקדש שהיה מוכן לאש מן השמים היתה המצוה לערוך גם כן אש תמיד שלמטה. וכן בזמן: בשבת שיורדת נשמה יתירה והיא מיוחדת לבני ישראל בחינת לחם משנה, מן השמים ומן הארץ. והם גם כן שתי אשות הנ"ל תורה שבכתב ושבעל פה.

ועיקר האהבה דכתיב "אהבתי אתכם אמר ה' (מלאכי א:ב)" הוא שקבלו בני ישראל במתן תורה "אנכי ה' אלהיך" שזה עיקר התורה שנחקק אלהותו יתברך בנפשות בני ישראל. וברשימה זו יכולין לחזור ולהתקרב אליו תמיד—וזה "עולת תמיד העשויה בהר סיני (במדבר כ"ח:ו)." (3:29)

שמיני

א

במדרש "ביום השמיני קרא משה לאהרן ולבניו ולזקני ישראל (ויקרא ט:א)' גדולה זקנה: אם זקנים הם—חביבין הם, אם נערים הם—נטפלה להן ילדות (ויקרא רבה י"א:ח)." ובתנחומא "[ה]' מקפיץ להם זקנה (שמיני י"א)" וצריך ביאור. והנה רבי עקיבא אומר "נמשלו ישראל לעוף, מה העוף הזה אינו יכול לעוף בלא כנפים, כך ישראל אין להם קיום רק על ידי הזקנים (על פי ויקרא רבה י"א:א:ח)." דהנה "קריאה" לשון חיבה ודביקות, לשון שמלאכי השרת משתמשין ["קרא זה אל זה ואמר...]" וזה התדבקות והתאחדות בשורש.

והנה כמו שיש למטה שבעים [זקנים ב]סנהדרין, כן למעלה. וזה הרמז במדרש "כחצי גורן עגולה (שם)." ורמזו עוד בפסוק "נודע בשערים בעלה, בשבתו עם זקני ארץ (משלי ל"א:כ"ג)." מה "ארץ"? רק שמדובר בשרים שלמעלה ויש שם שרים שממונים על שלמטה—לכן נקראו "זקני ארץ." ואותן שלמעלה לעולם מאירין למטה.

ובמדרש בהעלותך "אספה לי שבעים איש (במדבר י"א:ט"ז)'... בכל מקום שנאמר לי"י קיים לעולם (ספרי בהעלותך ל"ד)." עיין שם. היינו שנתקן על ידי שבעים איש שלמטה איש שלמעלה והם מאירין לעולם למטה. אכן כשהדור זכאי ונמצא למטה גם כן סנהדרין וזקנים שקנו חכמה

מ"ב:ט)" הוא "אש תמיד" "על מוקדה... כל הלילה."

וכן הוא הסדר בכל יום, כפי מה שאור התורה פועל באדם להיות שורף
ומבער מחשבות זרות. כי הכל הוא בתורה שנקרא אש. ויש אש מאיר–הוא
רמ"ח (248) מצוות עשה שבתורה מאהבה, ויש אש שורף–משס"ה (365)
[מצוות] לא תעשה מיראה.

ומצוות הרמת הדשן הוא לרמוז כי כפי מה ששורפין הפסולת, נעשה
מזה עליה בכל יום. ועל ידי זה יורד הארה חדשה אחר כך. ובכל יום ויום
נמצאים אלה התיקונים. ובעובד ה' כפשטו, כשמקבל בכל יום מלכות שמים
ב"קריאת שמע" "ואהבת" כו' וכתיב "והיו הדברים האלה אשר אנכי מצוך
היום..."–שהוא הארה המתחדשת בכל יום "על לבבך." "ודברת בם בשבתך
בביתך ובלכתך בדרך ובשכבך ובקומך" שצריכין לקבל זו ההארה עד השכיבה
והקימה–"כל הלילה עד הבוקר (ויקרא ו:ב). (3:24-5)."

ב

במדרש "על כל פשעים תכסה אהבה (משלי י:י"ב)" דכתיב "אש תמיד
תוקד... לא תכבה (ויקרא ו:ו)" וכתיב "מים רבים לא יוכלו לכבות את
האהבה (שיר השירים ח:ז)."

פירוש שיש בכל לב איש ישראל נקודה טמונה בהתלהבות לה' שלא יוכל
להיות נכבה. והגם כי "לא תכבה" הוא "לאו," אבל הוא הבטחה גם כן. וכמו
שכתבו חז"ל "אף על פי שאש יורד משמים מצוה להביא מן ההדיוט (יומא
כ"א ע"ב)," כמו כן בנפש האדם שצריך להיות תשוקת רשפי אש, בלב בוער
לעבודת הבורא יתברך ולחדש בכל יום זה ההתלהבות. כמו שכתוב "ובער
עליה הכהן (ויקרא ו:ה)" כל עובד ה' נקרא "כהן." והתעוררות אהבה הנ"ל
בלבות בני ישראל היא העבודה שבלב–זו תפלה שבמקום קרבן.

וכשיש זאת ההתלהבות, כל מחשבה זרה העולה על הלב נשרפת, כמו
שכתוב בזוהר הקדוש "מחשבה רעה העולה על מוקדה (ג:כ"ז ע"א)." כי
זאת היתה עיקר הכוונה בכל המחשבות העולות על הלב: שיהיו מתבטלים
בעלותן על לב עובד ה', ועל ידי זה מתעלין ומתבררין כל המחשבות זרות.

וזה שכתוב "כל הלילה עד הבוקר (ויקרא ו:ב). ולכאורה "עד הבוקר"
מיותר כיון דכתיב "כל הלילה." רק לרמוז שמזה התערובות והחושך של
מחשבות זרות המערבין לב העובד ה', מזה נעשה לבסוף בוקר, כי כן הסדר
"ויהי ערב ויהי בוקר" שמתברר התערובת טוב ורע. וכמו ימי המעשה הם
הכנה לשבת. וימי עולם הזה הכנה לימי עולם הבא. כן על ידי מלחמה הנ"ל
בלב עובד ה' "כל הלילה עד הבוקר." וכמו כן בימי הגלות שנקראים
"לילה" בוודאי יבוא מזה הבוקר... (3:23)

ג

במדרש "'זאת תורת העולה (ויקרא ו:ב)'... 'על כל פשעים תכסה אהבה
(משלי י:י"ב)' (ויקרא רבה ז:א)" דאיתא "עבירה מכבה מצוה ואינה מכבה
תורה (סוטה כ"א ע"א)." ועליו נאמר "אש תמיד תוקד (ויקרא ו:ו)"–התורה,
דכתיב "כה דברי כאש (ירמיה כ"ג:כ"ט)" "לא תכבה" כמו שכתוב בזוהר
הקדוש (רעיא מהמינא ח"ג כ"ח ע"ב). ולכן התורה מלמדת האיך לתקן כל

בחינת מחשבה, ולכן הם רברבין, כמו שבמחשבה יכולין לחשוב למעלה מהמציאות והטבע. והדיבור בחינת ממוצע בין המחשבה והמעשה, ולכן כתיב "ויקרא" באלף זעירא כי (על פי ברכות ל"ג ע"ב) הוא מלה זוטרתא [קטן] לגבי משה. ובמדרש (ויקרא רבה א:א) "עושי דברו לשמוע בקול דברו (תהלים ק"ג:כ)" כי צריכין לקשר המעשה בדיבור ודיבור במחשבה. ולכן ניתנה תורת הכהנים על ידי משה רבינו ע"ה שיקשר בחינת המעשה בדיבור כמו שכתוב במדרש (על פי ויקרא רבה א:ז) [משה משל לעבד שבנה למלך פלטין] על כל דבר ודבר שהיה בונה היה כותב עליו שמו של מלך, שכתב בכל דבר "כאשר צוה ה' את משה" עיין שם במדרש.

והענין הוא דכתיב "לעולם ה' דברך נצב בשמים (תהלים קי"ט:פ"ט)" כמו שכתוב "דבריו חיים וקיימים" שכל דיבור יתברך שמו קיים בשמים. ולכן המקיים המצוה לשמה, כמשה רבינו, מתקשר זה המעשה ממש בדבר ה' של זו המצוה. והוא חתימת שמו של מלך, ועל זה מבקשין "ויהי נועם ה' אלהינו עלינו כו' (שם צ:י"ז)" וזה פירוש "לשמה" כי כל התורה שמותיו של הקדוש ברוך הוא, נמצא יש שם מיוחד לכל מצוה שבתורה. וזהו "עושי דברו לשמוע בקול דברו."

ובימי המעשה זוכין אל התורה בכח העשיה. כמו שכתוב בזוהר הקדוש (ח"א קכ"ט ע"א): [מניחים] תפילין קודם התפלה [על שם] "ועשו לי מקדש ושכנתי בתוכם (שמות כ"ה:ח)." ובשבת אין צריכין תפילין שהם [ישראל] עצמם אות ומאיר אור התורה בעצם היום. וכמו כן נתמעט שבת ממלאכת המשכן בחינת "עושי דברו." (3:10)

צו

א

בפסוק "זאת תורת העולה (ויקרא א:ב)... אש תמיד תוקד על המזבח—לא תכבה (שם שם ו)."

והוא תכלית עבודת האדם. ובכל יום יורד הארה חדשה לעובד השם יתברך כמו שכתוב "ובער עליה הכהן עצים בבקר בבקר (ויקרא א:ה)." והוא שכתוב "מחדש בטובו בכל יום..." והוא בחינת אהבה שהיא במתנה בחסד עליון. אכן מזה האור צריך להיות נשאר רשימה בלב כל היום וכל הלילה "לא תכבה."

וממילא כל המחשבות וההרהורים העולים על הלב צריכין להיות נשרפין מהתלהבות רשימה זו. וזה שכתוב "היא העולה על מוקדה (שם א:ב)" כמו שכתוב בזוהר הקדוש [ח"ג כ"ז ע"א] מחשבה רעה לאוקדה לה בנורא [לבער אותה באש]. ופירוש "העולה על מוקדה" לומר כי אין מחשבה זרה רק כשיש מקודם מוכן כח ואש לשרוף אותה. כמו שכתב הרמב"ן ז"ל בכל נסיון שאין הקדוש ברוך הוא מביא לאדם רק כשיש בו כח לעמוד בו (ראה הרמב"ן לבראשית כ"ב:א).

ובאמת "אש תמיד"—הוא היראה, "ובער עליה הכהן עצים בבקר בבקר"—הוא האהבה. כמו שכתוב "בכל יום נמשך חוט של חסד (על פי עבודה זרה ג ע"ב)." "יומם יצוה ה' חסדו ובלילה שירה עמי (תהלים

ספר ויקרא
ויקרא

א

"ברכו ה׳ מלאכיו גיבורי כח עושי דברו לשמוע בקול דברו (תהלים ק״ג:כ)"
שהקדימו "נעשה" ל"נשמע." ביאור העניין על פי פשוטו, כמו שאמרו חכמים
"למה קדמה פרשת שמע ל'והיה אם שמוע'? שבתחלה יקבל עליו עול
מלכות שמים, אחר כך עול מצוות (על פי משנה ברכות ב:ב)." ו"כל אשר
דיבר ה׳ נעשה (שמות י״ט:ח)" הוא קבלת מלכותו עושי דברו בכלל. אחר
כך זוכין "לשמוע בקול דברו" הם המצוות, דכתיב "אם שמוע תשמעו אל
מצוותי (דברים י״א:י״ג)."

מכלל שיש קול דבר ה׳ בכל מצווה, כמו שכתבו חכמים (על פי רש״י
מכות כ״ג ע״ב) שכל אבר מבקש מאדם "קיים המצווה התלויה בי." וכל
קיום מצווה נקרא גם כן קבלת מלכותו. וזוכין אחר כך לשמוע יותר, וכך
צריך להיות: עושי דברו כדי לשמוע ביותר, ולא להיפטר בעצמו, רק לעשות
תמיד לשמוע יותר ולעשות יותר—בכל עת. (3:5)

ב

אדוני אבי זקני ז״ל הגיד בשם הרב [שמחה בונם] ז״ל מפרשיסחא על מה
שכתוב "אחד המרבה ואחד הממעיט ובלבד שיכוין לבו לשמים (ברכות ה
ע״ב)." והקשה בטורי זהב סימן א׳: אי גם המרבה ומכוון לשם שמים טפי
עדיף [רצוי יותר]? ותירץ הוא ז״ל למשל שני סוחרים שנסעו לדרך אחד,
והאחד בא מיד, והשני היו לו סיבות ומניעות עד שלזמן רב בא גם כן
ושאלוהו "מה זה שלא באת עד עתה?" והשיב "מאחר שבאתי גם כן, מה
שהיה היה!" עד כאן דברו ולא פירש יותר. ונראה פשוט שפירש "ובלבד
שיכוין לבו" שסוף ותכלית מעשיו יהיה שיהיה מכוון להשם יתברך כראוי,
בין שבא לו זה על ידי עבודה מעט או על ידי יגיעות הרבה—רק שיועילו
מעשיו לכוון לבו לשמים.

והדברים נכונים מאוד, שהרי גם כאן נאמר זה על הקרבן מנחה.
שמאחר שנתקרב קרבנו להשם יתברך, וזה תכלית המכוון וסוף דבר, אחר
כך אין נפקא מנה בין שהיה מרבה וממעיט—כי סוף הכל אחד שיתקרב
להשם יתברך. וזה עצמו פירוש "יכוון לבו" כעניין הקרבן להיות נמשך אחר
השורש והוא חיותו יתברך שניתן בכל דבר. (3:3)

ג

בעניין אלף זעירא [קטן] ד"ויקרא," דיש אתוון רברבין [אותיות גדולות]
ובינונים וזעירין. ובחינת אתוון זעירין נראה דהוא מלה דתליא בעובדא
[דבר שתלוי במעשה] שאור תורה מתפשט ומצמצם בתוך מעשה המצוות
בחינת "נר מצוה (משלי ו:כ״ג)." וזה עניין תורת כהנים שהוא בעובדא, דיש
בחינת מחשבה, דיבור ומעשה.

התורה היא בחינת הדיבור. וזה היה מיוחד למשה רבינו ע״ה כמו
שהיה במתן תורה דכתיב שם "ומשה עלה (שמות י״ט:ג)" מעצמו, שהיה
מיוחד למדריגה זו. ואתוון רברבין הם עוד למעלה בשורש התורה שבכתב

וכתיב ״ובצלאל... עשה את כל אשר צווה ה׳ את משה (שמות ל״ח:כ״ב).״ לפי שבעשיית המשכן נרמזין כל התרי״ג [613] מצוות דכמו שיש רמ״ח [248] מצוות עשה] ושס״ה [365] מצוות לא תעשה] לתקן כל ציור האדם להשרות בו הארת הקדושה. וזה תכלית המצוות: התקשרות האברים וגידין בשורשן. כמו כן במשכן נמצא זה הציור, ונקרא ״עבודת הלווים״ מלשון התחברות ודביקות אל השורש.

והכל ענין אחד. (239:2)

ב

"משכן העדות (שמות ל"ח:כ"א)" הוא לישראל שוויתר להם הקדוש ברוך הוא על מעשה העגל שהרי השרה שכינתו ביניהם.

ומה צריכין עדות! אך כי נשפלו מאוד בני ישראל על ידי החטא, ונתן להם הקדוש ברוך הוא עדות על ידי המשכן לחזק את לבם ולהראות שתיקנו כל החטא. ובאמת בני ישראל הם עדים על הקדוש ברוך הוא כדכתיב "אתם עדי (ישעיה מ"ג:י)." ובוודאי בני ישראל, שנבראו להעיד על אלהותו יתברך שמו שהוא אחד, איך יתכן שיהיו הם עובדי עבודה זרה חס וחלילה! ולכן נתרשלו בני ישראל בעדותן עד שהראה להם הקדוש ברוך הוא שלא היה זה החטא בעצם, רק במקרה—על ידי הערב רב. ושהם ראויין להעיד עליו יתברך שמו כבראשונה וכדאיתא "לא היו ראוין בני ישראל לאותו חטא, רק להורות תשובה (על פי עבודה זרה ד' ע"ב)." פירוש להודיע לכל בר תשובה שלא יהיה נופל ביותר בעיניו, וידע כי על ידי התשובה ניתקן כבראשונה.

וכמו כן אחר יום הכפורים שהוא יום סליחה ומחילה, ניתן מצות סוכה שהיא מעין השראת השכינה במקדש לחזק לכל בעלי תשובות. כי ראוים הם שתשרה שכינה עליהם. (239:2)

ג

"איש אמונות רב ברכות, ואץ להעשיר לא ינקה (משלי כ"ח:כ)."

במדרש "'איש אמונות רב ברכות'... זה משה... זה שהוא נאמן הקדוש ברוך הוא מביא ברכות על ידו. 'ואץ להעשיר' זה קרח (שמות רבה נ"א:א')." דאיתא "כלי מחזיק ברכה זה שלום (על פי משנה עוקצים ג:י"ב)." זה ענין איש אמונות להיות כל מעשיו דבוקים בשורשו כמו שכתוב "יתד במקום נאמן (ישעיה כ"ב:כ"ג)." אז נקרא שלום, כי החלק שלמטה אינו שלום רק בהתדבקות לחלק שלמעלה. וזה היה בחינת רבינו משה ע"ה "משה משה (שמות ג:ד)" בלי פסיק. ונקרא "איש האלהים (תהלים צ:א)' חציו איש וחציו אלהים (מדרש תהילים שם)." וכן היה "המשכן משכן (שמות ל"ח:כ"א)" כמו שכתוב "כעיר שחוברה לה יחדיו (תהלים קכ"ב:ג)."

וזה היה תכלית כל המשכן להיות כלי מחזיק ברכה לכל העולם. וכמו כן שבת בזמן, שכל מעשיה כפולים: לחם משנה, מזמור שיר, זכור ושמור... ונותנת ברכה לכל הזמן... כענין איש אמונות בנפש. ומשה רבינו ע"ה נתן ברכה לכל הנפשות כמו שכתוב "וזאת הברכה אשר ברך משה איש האלהים את בני ישראל (דברים ל"ג:א)" לפי שהוא איש אמונות. ובקרח כתיב "ויקח קרח (במדבר ט"ז:א)" ואתפליג בעל מחלוקת, היפוך בחינת השלום...

והנה כתיב "משכן העדות" כי זה עיקר העדות של בני ישראל להמשיך שפע קודש בעולם דכתיב "אתם עדי נאום ה' (ישעיה מ"ג:י"ב)" פירוש: כשנענים מן השמים. ולכן יש עדות במקום ובזמן כמו שזכו בני ישראל במעשיהם לעשות המשכן ולשכן השכינה בתוכם. וכמו כן בשבתות וזמנים שהקדושה יורדת בזכותן של בני ישראל. וכמו כן בנפשות כשזוכין להמשיך הקדושה מלמעלה בנפש.

ונהרות לא ישטפוה (שיר השירים ח:ז)'... בני עשו לי מקדש של יריעות עזים
ושכנתי בתוכם (שמות רבה מ"ט:א).״

והענין הוא כי האהבה והדביקות אשר קיבלו בני ישראל בהר סיני הן
חיות וקיימות לעולם. אבל על ידי החטא אינן יכולות להוציא מכח אל
הפועל אהבה הגנוזה. ולכן אחר החטא הוצרכו לזו הנדבה, שבכח התרומה
הזו הוציאו הנדיבות והתשוקה והדביקות מכח אל הפועל עד שהמשיכו את
השכינה למטה. ולכן נקרא ״משכן העדות,״ שהוא עדות שהשכינה שורה
בישראל.

ובזמן המשכן והמקדש היתה באמת השראת השכינה. ומה זו עדות?
רק שהיא עדות גם לכל הדורות, שאף על פי שאין הקדושה בהתגלות, מכל
מקום בפנימיות לבות בני ישראל נשאר רושם הקדושה.

ובאמת בכל המצוות הוא כן, אשר הן עצות איך להוציא הנדיבות
והרצון מהכח אל הפועל כמו שכתוב כאן ״כל נדיב לבו.״ פירוש שתרומה זו
הוציאה כל הנדיבות והרצונות שהיו טמונים בלבותם, כן כל מצוות שנקראות
נר כמו שכתוב ״נר מצוה ותורה אור (משלי ו:כ:ג)״ וכתיב ״נר ה' נשמת
אדם חופש כל חדרי בטן (שם כ:כ"ז)״ ויכולין להעלות כל הרצונות לה' על
ידי המצוות.

ומלאכת המשכן היתה עדות על כל הדורות להודיע שאף על פי שהחטא
מבדיל, מכל מקום לא יוכל לכבות האהבה כנ"ל. (2:227)

ג

״ששת ימים תעשה מלאכה (שמות ל"ה:ב)״ כי כל הארבע רוחות ולמעלה
ולמטה הוא בחינת התאספות כל הכוחות והמדות להיות היכל לנקודת
הפנימיות שהיא השבת. והוא בנין המשכן ממש כמו שכתוב ״אי זה בית
אשר תבנו לי (ישעיה ס"ו:א).״ (2:221)

פקודי

א

בפסוק ״ותכל כל עבודת משכן אהל מועד, ויעשו בני ישראל ככל אשר צווה
ה' את משה, כן עשו (שמות ל"ט:ל"ב).״

המשכן היה תיקון העשיה. לכן כתבו חז"ל (שבת מ"ט ע"ב) כי כל מה
שהיה במשכן נקרא ״מלאכה.״ כי נתקנו בעבודת המשכן כל המעשים
הנמצאים בעולם. ונקרא ״משכן העדות״ שבירר בני ישראל במעשה זו כי
כל הבריאה של הקדוש ברוך הוא. וכמו במעשה בראשית היה מאמר על כל
דבר ״וירא אלהים כי טוב״ ואחר כך בכלל ״וירא אלהים את כל אשר עשה
והנה טוב מאד... ויכל... ויברך (בראשית א:ל"א—ב:ג)״ כמו כן במשכן בכל
פרט ״כאשר צווה ה' (שמות ל"ט:מ"ב)״ ואחר כך ״ותכל כל עבודת משכן
אהל מועד... (שם שם ל"ב) ״וירא משה את כל המלאכה והנה עשו אותה
כאשר צווה ה'... ויברך אותם משה (שם שם מ"ג).״

רק שהיה עתה תיקון הבריאה מצד מיוחד לבני ישראל בפרט. לכן
נעשה על ידי משה. (2:232)

שהוא המייחד אותם באופן זה הציווי שנאמר אליו—הוא להם—כי הוא
אחדות אחת עמהם. ונמצא זה פתחון פה על החטא: כי בוודאי קודם
החטא, נפלו מזאת האחדות. ונמצא שלא היה הציווי להם כל כך בזה המדריגה.
אך החטא הוא מה שבאו לידי כך ליפול מכללות האחדות, אבל אינו חמור
כמו גוף החטא. עד כאן דברו ז״ל. (2:200)

ד

לפי שיטת רש״י שהמשכן נצטוו לעשות אחר החטא. אם כן נראה שלוחות
ראשונות היו מוכנים להיות נמצא בתוך בני ישראל בלי ארון ומשכן, שהיו
מיוחדים בני ישראל להיות בלי גשמיות.

וחז״ל רמזו במשכן ״בכל מקום שתלך קיטון אחד עשה לי שאדור
ביניכם (שמות רבה ל״ג:א).״ כנראה כי קודם החטא לא היו נפרדים כלל
מהבורא יתברך, רק אחר כך שהיה קצת פירוד היתה העצה על ידי המשכן
וכליו. (2:204)

ויקהל

א

״״מרבים העם להביא׳... ויצו משה ויעבירו קול במחנה לאמר ׳איש ואשה
אל יעשו עוד מלאכה לתרומת הקודש.׳ ויכלא העם מהביא. ׳והמלאכה
היתה דים לכל המלאכה לעשות אותה והותר (שמות ל״ו:ה-ז).״

ביאור הענין על פי דברי מדרש תנחומא [על הפסוק] ״וירא משה את
כל המלאכה (שם ל״ט:מ״ג),״ ״מלאכת המשכן״ אין כתיב. רק ״כל
המלאכה״—הוא מעשה בראשית כו׳ עיין שם. וכלל הדברים שכל מלאכת
המשכן היתה לתקן כל הבריאה. וכמו דמצינו שם ״וירא אלהים את כל
אשר עשה והנה טוב מאד... ויכלו השמים והארץ... ויברך אלהים (בראשית
א:ל״א–ב:ג).״ כמו כן המשכן שהוא קיום העולם היה על ידי ״וירא משה...
(שמות ל״ט:מ״ג)״ והוטב בעיניו ״ויברך אותם משה (שם).״ כדאיתא בזוהר
הקדוש בכמה דוכתי שהקדוש ברוך הוא ברא העולם בכח התורה, והצדיקים
מקיימים העולם בכח התורה. עיין שם.

וזה שכתבו ״וירא משה״ שתיקנו כל המלאכה, היינו כל הנבראים וכל
העשיה ניתקנו...

וכמו דמצינו שנתרחבו שמים וארץ עד שאמר הקדוש ברוך הוא לעולמו
״די,״ כמו כן התנדבו בני ישראל עד שנאמר להם ״די.״ וזהו פירוש הכתוב
״והמלאכה היתה דים (שמות ל״ו:ז)״ ומקשין כיון ש״הותר״ אין זה לשון
״די״ והם תרתי דסתרי [סותרים זה את זה]. אמנם אינו קושיא כי כך היה
צריך להיות, שיתנדבו במותר עד שיאמר להם ״די.״ וזה עצמו גם כן בכלל
המלאכה שנצרכה להמשכן. (2:222)

ב

בפסוק ״קחו מאתכם תרומה לה׳ כל נדיב לבו יביאה את תרומת ה׳
(שמות ל״ה:ה),״ דאיתא במדרש ״״מים רבים לא יוכלו לכבות את האהבה,

(פסחים קי"ו ע"א)." הרמז הוא שבו נגלה סוד הפנימיות שזה פעולת היין. "ותירוש ינובב בתולות (זכריה ט:י"ז)" ואיתא "נכנס יין יצא סוד (עירובין ס"ה ע"א)."

ובספר תורת חיים כתב לבעבור כי שבת רומז לעולם הבא, לכן מקדשין על היין לרמוז על יין המשומר בענביו לעולם הבא. עיין שם בפרק חלק בסנהדרין ופרק שני דעירובין. ופנימיות הענין הוא שייין המשומר בענביו הוא עצמו כח הנשמה הנסתרת בגוף. ואין יכול לשלוט בה מגע נכרי כי היא סתומה. ועליו נאמר "עין לא ראתה אלהים זולתך (ישעיה ס"ד:ג)' זה יין המשומר." ולעתיד צדיקים יושבין ועטרותיהם בראשיהם הוא התגלות הנשמה בשלימות.

אך כי שבת הוא מעין עולם הבא לכן יש בו מעט התגלות הנשמה כמו שכתבו חז"ל (ביצה ט"ז ע"א) נשמה יתירה בשבת קודש. לכן מקדשין על היין לרמוז על התגלות הנשמה, ולכן יין צריך שמירה ממגע נכרי. (2:208-9)

ג

במדרש "וישלך מידו את הלוחות וישבר אותם (שמות ל"ב:י"ט)' כיון שראה משה רבינו ע"ה לישראל עמידה, חבר עצמו עמהם ושבר את הלוחות. ואמר להקדוש ברוך הוא, 'הם חטאו, ואני חטאתי ששברתי הלוחות. אם מוחל אתה להם, אף לי מחול, שנאמר יועתה אם תשא חטאתם (שם שם לב)' כן לחטאתי מחול. ואם אין' אתה מוחל להם, אל תמחול לי אלא 'מחני נא מספרך אשר כתבת (שם)' (שיר מ"ו:א)." ואינו מובן. וגם קשה הא איתא [שם] שראה אותיות פורחות באויר לכן שיבר אותם.

ונראה ביאור הענין כי בוודאי התורה תלויה בני ישראל שהם מקבלי התורה. וכתיב "חרות על הלוחות (שמות ל"ב:טז)." חֵרות מיצר הרע, ממלאך המות, ממיתה כו'. וקשה מה פירוש "חרות על הלוחות?" רק כפי מה שנחקקה ונחרתה הארת התורה בלבות בני ישראל, כך נחקקו האותיות בלוחות גם כן. שעיקר הכתיבה בלב, כמו שכתוב "כתבם על לוח לבך (משלי ג:ג)."

ולכן כשחטאו בני ישראל "אותיות פורחות כו'." אמנם משה רבינו ע"ה לא חטא באמת. והיה בכחו להחזיק התורה כמו שאמר לו הקדוש ברוך הוא "ואעשה אותך לגוי גדול (שמות ל"ב:י)." אך כי מסר נפשו בעבור בני ישראל ולא רצה לפרוד עצמו מהם על ידי זה חיבר עצמו עמהם ולא נפרש מהם, שהיה חביב אצלו כללות בני ישראל מהלוחות, שהיה יודע רצון הבורא שכנסת ישראל חביבין אליו מהכל. ועל ידי זה גופא היו האותיות פורחות ולכן שיבר אותן.

ובאמת על ידי זה שחיבר עצמו לכללות בני ישראל, על ידי זה תיקן אותם. כי כמו שהיה הוא עמהם באופן זה ההתכללות, לא חטאו כי בשעת החטא לא היה עמהם.

וכעין זה שמעתי מפה קדוש אדוני אבי זקני מורי ורבי זצ"ל שפירש מה שאמרו חז"ל (על פי שיר מ"ג:ה) "אנכי ה' אלהיך (שמות כ:ב)' בלשון יחידה ליתן פתחון פה למשה "לי אמרת ולא להם." ופירש שוודאי הציווי היה לכלל ישראל, אך כמו שהם אחדות אחת ודבוקים במשה רבינו ע"ה

אך זה כח התורה דכתיב בה "יקרה היא מפנינים" (משלי ג:ט"ו)" ממי
שנכנס לפני ולפנים, שהיא מעמדת ומקיימת כל העולם. ובזה ניחם הקדוש
ברוך הוא למשה כי אי אפשר לו להתפרש מכלל ישראל. ולפי שמסר משה
רבינו ע"ה נפשו על כלל ישראל, שילם לו הקדוש ברוך הוא להיות כחו
נשאר בכלל ישראל. וכמעט כל איש ישראל יש בו הארה וניצוץ ממשה
רבינו ע"ה.

ולכן לא ניתנה לו הכהונה, כי הכהן צריך להיות נבדל. וכן אמרו חז"ל
(על פי קהלת רבה ז:ב) כתר כהונה זכה אהרן ונטלו; כתר מלכות זכה דוד.
אבל כתר תורה מונח לכל איש ישראל. (163:2)

כי תשא

א

"את שבתותי תשמרו (שמות לי"א:י"ג)"—לשון רבים. כי יש בכל דבר חיות
משבת קודש והיא הנקודה המשלמת הכל כמו שכתב רש"י ז"ל "ויכל
אלהים ביום השביעי (בראשית ב:ב)" שבשבת נגמרה המלאכה.

הפירוש: ששבת משלים כל דבר, והוא הגמר והקיום של כל דבר שהוא
שורש החיות. ובשבת קודש מתעורר שורש זה בכל דבר. ולכך נקרא מנוחה,
שמחזיר כל דבר לשורשו.

וכתב רש"י ז"ל "וישבת שבתון (שמות לי"א:ט"ו)" מנוחת מרגוע ולא
מנוחת עראי." פירוש כי ודאי כל איש ישראל מניח מלאכתו ואינו עושה
בשבת. אבל צריך להיות שלא יהיה לעול מה שעוזב מעשיו ביום זה. רק
אדרבה, להיות מצפה כל ימות השבוע לבוא לשורשו ומקום מנוחתו—והוא
שבת קודש. שבעוזבו כל מעשיו, זה עיקר מקום חיותו. וזהו פירוש "שמירה"
שיושב ומצפה כל ימי השבוע מתי יבוא שבת קודש ויחזור למקומו.

"ואך את שבתותי תשמרו (שמות לי"א:י"ג)" פירוש שלא להיות רצון
ותשוקה לדבר אחר בעולם. רק להשם יתברך שהוא שורש חיות האדם
שמתדבק בו בשבת קודש.

גם מה שכתוב "לעשות את השבת (שם שם ט"ז)" אף כי המצוה שלא
לעשות. גם מה שמירה שייך לשבת? אדרבה, שבת שומר אותנו. אך הפירוש
להמשיך קדושת שבת לכל מעשה החול גם כן, ושם צריך שמירה בודאי...
(198:2)

ב

בפסוק "אך את שבתותי תשמרו כי אות הוא ביני וביניכם לדורותיכם
לדעת כי אני ה' מקדשכם (שמות לי"א:י"ג)" אמרו חז"ל (ביצה ט"ז ע"א)
שבת ניתנה בצינעא. הענין על פי מה שכתוב "שער החצר הפנימית הפונה
קדים יהיה סגור ששת ימי המעשה וביום השבת יפתח... (יחזקאל מ"ו:א)"
כי בשבת נגלית הפנימיות הנסתרת. וכמו שהוא מצדו יתברך שמו, כן
בנפשות בני ישראל נפתחת פנימיות הלב בשבת קודש. ובכל מקום הפנימיות
צריכה שמירה, לכן כתיב "תשמרו."

וחז"ל אמרו "זכור את יום השבת לקדשו (שמות כ:ח)"—זכרהו על היין

עשה עצמו. עיין שם בסנהדרין פרק חלק. ושני הפירושים הם אחד כי תיקון האדם הוא על ידי המצוות שצריך להיות מיוחד להשם יתברך, שהוא משלוח בעולם רק לעשות רצון בוראו, ונצמא הוא עצמו המצוה. וכן פירוש "אשר קדשנו במצוותיו וצוונו"—[עשה אותנו מצוות]. (2:154)

ב

במדרש (ב"ר ל"ו:א) "ואתה תצוה (שמות כ"ז:כ)"—"זית רענן יפה פרי תאר קרא ה' שמך (ירמיה י"א:ט:ז)."

ביאור הענין שיש בנפשות בני ישראל נקודה טמונה אשר על זה נאמר "אם תבקשנה ככסף וכמטמונים תחפשנה (משלי ב:ד)." ועל ידי רוב יגיעות נפש ויגיעות בשר לזכך החומר מתגלה הפנימיות. וזה הדמיון לזית רענן שצריך כמה יגיעות להוציא השמן.

והנה כתיב "נר מצוה ותורה אור ודרך חיים תוכחות מוסר (שם ו:כ"ג)." פירוש שנפשות בני ישראל הם הפתילות להמשיך השמן אחר האור. ומשה רבינו ע"ה שורש התורה הוא האור. ולכן נאמר "ויקחו אליך שמן זית (שמות כ"ז:כ)" להיות נמשך אחר הפתילה. והמצוות הם הכלים שבאמצעות המצוות מתחברין השמן והפתילה להאור.

וכמו כן באדם עצמו יש כל אלה העניינים הנצמאים בכלל ישראל כמו כן בכל פרט. ובמדרש "ממנו פנה ממנו יתד (זכריה י:ד)" שהקדוש ברוך הוא עשה האדם ישר שנמצא בו שלמות של כל הבראים מתהום ארעא עד רום רקיעא. והנה אהרן הכהן נבחר להיות עובד ה', והיה זה לטובת בני ישראל אחר החטא שהיה בהם תערובות טוב ורע. היה עצתו של הקדוש ברוך הוא להיות בוחר אדם מיוחד לדורותיו אחריו להיות טהור. ועל ידי זה ימשך מכחו טהרה לכלל ישראל.

וכמו כן יש ללמוד אשר טוב לאדם ליחד מדה מיוחדת ומצוה מיוחדת לעשותה תמיד בשמירה עצומה. ועל ידי זה יוכל למשוך הארה ותיקון לכל מידות. וזה שכתוב במדרש "ממנו יתד" שעל ידי בחירת אהרן היה יתד קבוע לבני ישראל. כי הקדוש ברוך הוא הרים אותו שיהיה נפרש מכל דבר רע. וממילא על ידי זה היו יכולין בני ישראל לחזור תמיד להתדבק בבורא יתברך. (2:155)

ג

במדרש "לולי תורתך שעשועי אז אבדתי בעניי (תהלים קי"ט:צ"ב)": כשאמר הקדוש ברוך הוא למשה יואתה הקרב אליך (שמות כ"ח:א),' הרע לו. אמר לו, 'תורה היתה לי ונתתיה לך, שאלולי היא הייתי מאבד עולמי (על פי שיר ל"ז:ד).'"

פירוש: הגם כי היה משה רבינו גדול מאהרן, מכל מקום הכהונה ניתנה לאהרן שהוא נבדל מן העם, כמו שכתוב "ויבדל אהרן (דברי הימים א כ"ג:י"ג)." אבל משה רבינו ע"ה, שהוא שר התורה, צריך להיות דבוק בכלל ישראל. ולכן לא הוריש משה רבינו ע"ה כתרו לבניו, רק "מורשה קהלת יעקב (דברים ל"ג:ד)." ואילו היה גם משה רבינו ע"ה נבדל לא היה, חס וחלילה, לנו תקומה.

ובתלמידי חכמים זה שונה סדר זרעים וזה סדר מועד. השנו זה לזה ביד כל
אחד שני סדרים.

העניין הוא כי יש לכל איש ישראל חלק מיוחד בתורה, והתורה מחברת
נפשות בני ישראל כמו שכתוב "תמימה משיבת נפש (תהלים י"ט:ח)."
ונעשין אחדות אחת בכח התורה כמו שכתוב "מורשה קהלת יעקב (דברים
ל"ג:ד)." ומקבלין זה מזה הדעת המיוחד לכל אחד.

וכתוב "ה' עוז לעמו יתן" ובזה "ה' יברך את עמו בשלום (תהלים
כ"ט:י"א)." שמו של הקדוש ברוך הוא "שלום," מלך שהשלום שלו, ועושה
שלום במרומיו. וכמו כן התורה שמותיו של הקדוש ברוך הוא. ולכן על ידי
התורה זוכין לשלום. וכן כתוב "לכולם בשם יקרא (ישעיה מ:כ"ו)" לפי
ששמו יתברך כולל כל צבא מעלה לכן מתחברין על ידי השם. כמו כן
נפשות בני ישראל מתחברין על ידי התורה.

וכמו כן בנדבת המשכן שהיה נעשה על ידי נדבת כל איש ונתחברו על
ידי המשכן להיות אחד. ואז זכו להשראת השכינה.

ובאמת צריך להיות האחדות במעשה, דיבור, ומחשבה. ובמשכן ובמקדש
נתאחדו במעשה, ובתורה בדיבור, ובהקדוש ברוך הוא במחשבה.

כמו שכתוב "שבעים נפש (שמות א:ה)" בלשון יחיד. לפי שעובדין לאל
אחד, זה בחינת הרצון ותשוקה שבלב שפונים כולם אליו יתברך שמו, ובזה
נעשין גוי אחד. (150:2)

תצוה
א

במדרש "נר ה' נשמת אדם (משלי כ:כ"ז)' אמר הקדוש ברוך הוא, 'יהא נרי
בידך ונרך בידי.' ואיזו נרו של הקדוש ברוך הוא? זו תורה, שנאמר 'כי נר
מצוה ותורה אור (שם ו:כ"ג).' מהו 'כי נר מצוה,' אלא כל מי שעושה מצוה
הוא כאלו מדליק נר לפני הקדוש ברוך הוא ומחיה נפשו שנקראת נר,
שנאמר 'נר ה' נשמת אדם (ב"ר ל"ו:ג).'"

פירוש "נר ה'" כי השגחתו יתברך בתחתונים הוא על ידי נשמות בני
ישראל. וכפי עבודת בני ישראל ממשיכין השגחת השם יתברך והארת פניו
בעולם.

ויש שני מיני חושך. אחד על ידי היצר הרע וסטרא אחרא שהוא חושך
ממש, ועל ידי המצוות מבטלות זה החושך. וזה שכתוב "כאילו מדליק נר
לפני הקדוש ברוך הוא" פירוש שמכין מקום לחול שם כבוד מלכותו יתברך.
ועל ידי זה "מחיה נפשו" שנקרא "נר."... גם אור העליון נקרא אצלינו חושך
כמו שכתוב בספרים שהוא גבוה מהשגתינו, לכן נקרא חושך. וכפי מה
שהאדם מאיר בחושך הגשמי על ידי נרות המצוות, כמו כן זוכה להמשיך
אור על נשמתו ונפשו מאור העליון.

ופירוש "ואתה תצוה (שמות כ"ז:כ)" שיכניס המצוה בנפשות בני ישראל
שיהיו הם עצמם המצוות. כי באמת רמ"ח (248) איברים מיוחדים להמצוות.
ובגמרא "ועשיתם אותם (במדבר ט"ו:ל"ט)" [יש] שני פירושים: אחד כי מי
שמקיים מצוה מעלה עליו הקדוש ברוך הוא כאלו עשאה. והשני—כאלו

ח:ו)"—אך על ידי התפילין מצא מין את מינו. ולכן בשבת קודש איתא [על פי
עירובין צ"ו ע"א] שהם [ישראל] בעצמם אות ואין צורך לתפילין.

בשבת קודש יש התגלות הארת קבלת התורה מעין מה שהיה לבני
ישראל קודם החטא, כדאיתא שמשה רבינו ע"ה מחזיר לבני ישראל בשבת
קודש הכתרים של "נעשה ונשמע (שמות כ"ד:ז)" עיין שם. לכן גם מלאכת
המשכן לא נעשתה בשבת כדכתיב ברש"י בפרשת כי תשא "אך את שבתותי
תשמרו (שם ל"א:י"ג)" למעט שבת ממלאכת המשכן. כי בשבת קודש יש
התגלות הקדושה כמו קודם החטא. ולא הוצרכו לצמצום המשכן. (2:144-5)

ב

במדרש [על פי שה"ש ל"ג:ג ושיר השירים רבה ה:ב] "אני ישנה ולבי ער קול
דודי דופק פתחי לי (שיר השירים ה:ב)" אני ישנה בגלות ולבי ער-ער
לגאלני. אני ישנה מן העגל, ודודי מרתיק עלי. "ויקחו לי תרומה (שמות
כ"ה:ב)"—עד מתי אהיה מתהלך בחוץ [בלא בית]? הענין הוא שיש לבני
ישראל חלק בתורה שהוא למעלה מהשמש, וזה השורש לעולם אינו נפסק.
כאשר אמר השם יתברך בסיני "אנכי ה' אלהיך" מאז יש בכל איש ישראל
כח אלהי, ומכל שכן תוך כלל ישראל. אכן על ידי החטא מתרחק הגוף
מהפנימיות שהוא בחינת הנשמה, אבל השורש בשמים מלמד זכות ומבקש
לחזור למקומו.

ואמת כי גם זה תלוי בהשתוקקות האדם למטה להתדבק בשורש.
[כמו שהאדם משתוקק מלמטה] כן משתוקק השורש אליו. וזו בחינת
"שחורה אני ונאוה (שיר השירים א:ה)" על שחרות המלבוש והגוף, ותפארת
הפנימיות-הנשמה והשורש. וזה שכתוב "ולבי ער" שהוא בחינת אלהות
שכביכול משתוקקת לחול על בני ישראל התחתונים. כמו שכתוב "עד מתי
אהיה מתהלך בלי בית (שי"ר ל"ג:ג)." וזה נמשך מהשתוקקות שיש בלבות
בני ישראל.

ובוודאי לא לחינם אמר השם יתברך "ויקחו לי תרומה." רק שהיו
משתוקקים מאוד לעלות למדרגה ראשונה שהיתה להם בקבלת התורה.
ולא היו יכולין להוציא מכח אל הפועל על ידי החטא, עד שרחם השם
יתברך עליהם ונתן להם עצה על ידי המשכן וכליו.

וכל זה כתוב בתורה להודיענו כי בכל עת נמצא זה הרצון בלבות בני
ישראל. ואם היו מבקשים מאוד, היו זוכים להשראת השכינה. ואדרבה
קל וחומר הוא עתה שכבר היה לנו המשכן ובתי מקדשות, בנקל יותר
להשיג מה שכבר זכינו לו. וזה עצמו הרמז "וכן תעשו (שמות כ"ה:ט)" כי
לעולם כפי הרצון והנדיבות שיהיה להם יוכלו לעשות לי מקדש. רק
שצריך להיות בכלות הנפש כמו שמצינו בדוד "אם אתן שנת לעיני לעפעפי
תנומה, עד אמצא מקום לה' משכנות לאביר יעקב (תהלים קל"ב:ד-ה)."
וזכה לזה. (2:141)

ג

במדרש תנחומא "לקח טוב נתתי לכם (משלי ד:ב)" שני סוחרים: לזה
מטכסא [לבוש משי] ולזה פלפלין. החליפו מה שביד זה אינו ביד זה.

וצריך האדם לתקן עצמו בדברים שבינו למקום לזכות לתורה שבכתב,
ולתקן שבינו לחבירו לזכות לתורה שבעל פה. ולא עוד אלא שזו מדריגה
יתירה דכתיב "מגיד דבריו ליעקב חקיו ומשפטיו לישראל (שם קמ"ז:י"ט)"
וידוע דשם ישראל למעלה משם יעקב. לומר שהוא זכות גדול כשזוכין
לתקן שבין אדם לחבירו והוא הישרות שנקרא "ישר אל." כי "האלהים
עשה את האדם ישר כו' (על פי קהלת ז:כ"ט). ואחר החטא שנעשו "חשבונות
רבים (שם)" צריכין לתקן ולישר העקמימות והקנאה והשנאה. וזוכין לזה
על ידי המשפטים.

ולכן כתיב "אלה המשפטים אשר תשים לפניהם (שמות כ"א:א)" מלשון
"ושמו את שמי על בני ישראל (במדבר ו:כ"ז)" כמו שתרגם "דתהסדר קדמיהון."
שזה המעין שיש בבני ישראל צריכין להוציאו מכח אל הפועל לברר האמת
מתוך השקר. ובבחינה זו כתיב "ישרים דרכי ה' וצדיקים ילכו בם (הושע
י"ד:י)." וזה "לפניהם." (117:2)

תרומה
א

במדרש (שי"ר כ"ח:א) "עלית למרום שָׁבִיתָ שֶׁבִי לקחת מתנות באדם, ואף
סוררים לשכון יה אלהים (תהלים ס"ח:י"ט)." פירוש כי בזכות התורה זכו
בני ישראל להשראת השכינה בתוכם. ואיתא בזוהר הקדוש בפרשת פנחס
כי היו מוכנים בני ישראל שיוריד להם הקדוש ברוך הוא המקדש שלמעלה
כמו שיהיה לעתיד. ועל ידי שירדו מזו המדריגה על ידי החטא הוצרך להיות
השראת השכינה בצמצום המשכן ובית המקדש שלמטה.

וזה שכתוב "לקחת מתנות באדם" דייקא, שהיו מוכנים להיות השראת
השכינה באדם בלי שום אמצעות. וזה שכתוב "מכון לשבתך פעלת ה'
(שמות ט"ו:י"ז)" שהרגישו בני ישראל על הים כי המה כלים שהם מוכנים
להיות השכינה שורה בתוכם, כמו שכתוב "זה אלי ואנוהו (שם שם ב)"
אבנה לו מקדש. פירוש: בני ישראל עצמם הם "מכון לשבתך." ואחר החטא
הוצרך להיות "ועשו לי מקדש" ועל ידי זה "ושכנתי בתוכם (שמות כ"ה:ח)."

ובאמת הוא ענין ימי המעשה שבהם התגלות הקדושה בעשית גשמיות,
ובשבת קודש ההארה מתגלה ברוחניות. וזה שכתוב במדרש המשל לבת
מלך "בא אחד מן המלכים ונטלה, בקש לילך לו לארצו ולטול לאשתו. אמר
לו [אבי הכלה] 'בתי שנתתי לך יחידית היא, לפרוש ממנה איני יכול ולומר
לך 'אל תטלה' איני יכול, לפי שהיא אשתך. אלא זו טובה עשה לי, שכל
מקום שאתה הולך, קיטון אחד עשה לי (שי"ר ל"ג:א)." והיינו שמקודם היו
בני ישראל דביקים בעצם. ואחר כך כשירדו ממדרגה זו כתוב "ועשו לי
מקדש" קיטון אחד, ואדור ביניכם.

ויתכן לפרש שהוא מצוות התפילין שהם בתים מיוחדים להיות שורה
הקדושה בתוכם. והשמות שבפרשות התפילין הם מושכין קדושה לאדם
כדאיתא בזוהר הקדוש (פרשת חיי שרה קכ"ט) "ועשו לי מקדש ושכנתי
בתוכם" הוא רזא [סוד] דתפילין עיין שם. ובאמת רשימות אלו הם נרשמים
בפנימיות נפשות בני ישראל כמו שכתוב "שימני כחותם על לבך (שיר השירים

שבכח איש ישראל למשוך בכל עת התחדשות, לחול עליו מלבוש הקדושה
על ידי תורה ומצוות. וכתוב "עלה אלי ההרה והיה שם כו' (שם כ״ד:י״ב)"
היינו שנתהפך משה רבינו ע״ה להיוה חדשה כמלאכי השרת כמו שכתבו
חז״ל "נכנס בענן נתלבש בענן כו' (על פי יומא ד ע״א)" לשומו כמלאכי
השרת. ולכן היו ארבעים יום, כיצירת הוולד בארבעים יום. כן קיבל
בשלימות אותו הציור. ובזוהר חדש (שיר השירים) איתא "ויהיה שם"
שנעשה שם הקדוש.

ויש לכל ישראל חלק בצורה זו. וקודם החטא [של העגל הזהב] כתוב
"אמרתי 'אלהים אתם (תהלים פ״ב:ו)'" ואיתא כי בשבת קודש מחזיר משה
רבינו ע״ה אותה ההארה לכל בני ישראל. וזו בחינת נשמה יתירה, שלכן
"אין דומה מאור פניו של אדם בשבת (על פי ב״ר י״א:ב)" לימי המעשה.
ולזה ציור הקדושה זוכין על ידי תרי״ג מצוות שהם נגד תרי״ג איברים וגידים.
ובעולם הזה נדמה כי העיקר הגוף, והוא רומז לתרי״ג מצוות. אבל באמת
"נהפוך הוא" כי עיקר ציור האדם הוא תרי״ג אברים רוחניים [שהם] שורש
התרי״ג מצוות. ואלה האברים שבגוף הם רמזים אל הפנימיות.

ובמשה רבינו ע״ה נתגלה פנימיות המלבוש. וכפי מה שמתרחקין מן
הגשמיות, זוכין לפנימיות. ובימי המעשה צריכין לייגע עצמינו להתרחק
מהגשמיות, ובשבת קודש צריכין לייגע לקבל הארה פנימיות ורוחניות. (שם)

ג

בשם הרב הקדוש ז״ל מקאצק על פסוק "ואנשי קודש תהיון לי (שמות
כ״ב:ל)" להיות שמירת הקדושה במעשה אנוש ותחבולותיו. פירוש שאין
מחסור להשם יתברך מלאכי עליון שרפים וחיות הקודש. רק שמתאוה
לקדושת אנשים ולכן המשיך נצוצי קדושה גם בעולם הזה במדה וצמצום.
לכן "בשר בשדה טרפה לא תאכלו (שם)" דרשו חז״ל (זבחים פ״ב ע״ב) כלל
על כל היוצא מחוץ למחיצתו נאסר. פירוש שיש בכל דבר התפשטות
קדושה במדה, וצריכין לשמור הגשמיות שלא לצאת מגבול הקדושה.

גם פירוש "תהיון לי" הוא הבטחה שיהיו בני ישראל בסוף קודש לה'.
לכן צריכין לשמור עצמינו עתה להיות מוכנים להינתן בראשו של מלך.
כדאיתא במדרש (ויקרא רבה ב:ה) המשל מה שאתה יכול לקבוע אבנים
טובות ומרגליות—קבע, שהיא עתידה להיות בראשו של מלך. (111:2)

ד

"ואלה המשפטים כו'" מוסיף על ענין ראשון. כי [עשרת] הדברות הם
דברים שבין אדם למקום. ומשפטים שבין אדם לחבירו. ונסמכו לומר כי
זוכין לתורה על ידי השלום שנעשין בני ישראל אחדות אחת. כמו שכתבו
רז״ל "ואהבת לרעך כמוך (ויקרא י״ט:י״ח)' זה כלל גדול בתורה (ב״ר
כ״ד:ז)'" דכתיב "ה' עוז לעמו יתן (תהלים כ״ט:י״א)"—והיא התורה. "ה'
יברך את עמו בשלום (שם)" הוא באר התורה שבעל פה שעליה מברכין
"וחיי עולם נטע בתוכינו." וזה הבאר נפתח על ידי השלום שנעשה על ידי
המשפטים האלה. כמו שכתוב במדרש (שי״ר ל:א) "אתה כוננת מישרים
(תהלים צ״ט:ד)" שעל ידי המשפטים נעשין אוהבין זה לזה.

תמיד—כי הם פנימיות עשרה מאמרות. ועל זה איתא במשנה "ליתן שכר טוב לצדיקים שמקיימין את העולם שנברא בעשרה מאמרות (אבות ה:א)." ואין שכר טוב אלא תורה.

וכתוב "ה' בחכמה יסד ארץ, כונן שמים בתבונה (משלי ג:י"ט)." "יסד" [בלשון עבר] מעשה בראשית [מאז], "כונן שמים בתבונה"—"כונן" [בלשון הוה] תמיד, כמו שכתוב בזוהר הקדוש. והיא התורה שהיא מתחדשת בכל עת, ולא עוד אלא שבכח התורה מתחדשין גם העשרה מאמרות. ועל זה נאמר "בטובו מחדש בכל יום מעשה בראשית." ועל ידי מצוות התורה יכולין למצוא התחדשות התורה בכל יום... (2:103)

משפטים

א

במדרש "ואלה המשפטים אשר תשים לפניהם (שמות כ"א:א).' 'ואלה' מוסיף על הראשונים [עיין שמות ט"ו:כ"ה וי"ח:כ"ב]... משל למטרונה שהיתה מהלכת, הזיין [החייל] מכאן והזיין מכאן והיא באמצע, כך [מתן] התורה, דיניה מלפניה ודיניין מאחריה והיא באמצע (שי"ר ל:ג)."

וברש"י "מה הראשונים מסיני [אף האחרונים מסיני]," כי באמת הכל מן התורה. והיא נותנת ברכה לפניה ולאחריה, וכמו שכל הבריאה נבראה בשביל התורה. והדור שקבלו התורה הוציאו מכח אל הפועל, ומכל מקום קיום דורות הקודמים היה להיות הכנה לתורה.

וכמו כן ממש בפרטות בבני ישראל שמקודם הוצרכו ליישר עצמם כענין "התקן עצמך ללמוד תורה (אבות ב:י"ב)," והוא המשפטים שקודם התורה. לכן כתיב שם [לפני מתן תורה] "ושפטו את העם בכל עת (שמות י"ח:כ"ב)" ולא היו ביחוד למשה רבינו ע"ה—כי הם המשפטים שקודמים לתורה. ואחר כך כתיב "ואלה המשפטים" המיוחדים, לאחר קבלת התורה.

ואלה המדריגות הם תמיד בכל עובד ה'. כפי מה שמיישר מעשיו—זוכה לתורה. ואחר כך בכח התורה מיישר מעשיו כראוי וכן לעולם. וזה שהקדימו בני ישראל "נעשה" ל"נשמע" (שמות כ"ד:ז) אינו לפי שעה, רק שכן הוא לעולם, שצריכין מקודם לתקן המעשים, ואחר כך זוכין לשמוע. ואחר השמיעה הוא הזמן שצריכין לתקן המעשים ביותר—על פי התורה. ואז זוכין לשמוע יותר פנימיות התורה.

אכן העיקר הוא שצריך להיות המכוון לשם שמים. והאדם העובד ליישר לבבו כדי להיות מוכן לתורה, ולעבודת השם יתברך, אז התורה מסייעת לו שיוכל לגמור המכוון. וכן כתיב "ואנשי קודש תהיון לי (שם כ"ב:ל)" שצריך האדם לבקש הקדושה כדי להיות מוכן לעבדו יתברך שמו, ולא להיות רוצה להיות קדוש. כי קודש הוא למעלה מהטבע. ואיזה דרך יהיה מציאות הקדושה בעולם הזה? רק בכח התורה והקדוש ברוך הוא שקדשנו במצוותיו. וזה שכתוב "תהיון לי."... (2:116-7)

ב

פירוש "ואנשי קודש תהיון לי (שמות כ"ב:ל)" "תהיון" הוא הויה חדשה,

ועל זה אומרין "פורס סוכת שלום עלינו." (2:102)

ג

במדרש (שי"ר כ"ז:ד) "ה' עוזי ומעוזי ומנוסי ביום צרה אליך גוים יבאו מאפסי ארץ (ירמיה ט"ז:י"ט)." כי השם יתברך בחר לו בני ישראל לחלקו. והיה עולה על הדעת כי על ידי זה נתרחקו האומות. אבל באמת אדרבא: זו עצה עמוקה של הבורא יתברך לקרב כל האומות אליו יתברך על ידי בני ישראל. ובני ישראל מבינים זאת והם חפצים לקרב הכל אליו יתברך, לולא הרשעים שמעכבין כמו שכתוב "ויבא עמלק וילחם עם ישראל (שמות י"ז:ח)." ויתרו שבא קרבו אותו בכל כחם. "ה' עוזי" תקפן של בני ישראל, ו"מעוזי" שמסר העוז לבני ישראל, שיהיה התוקף בידם בכח התורה שמסר להם, כמו שכתוב "ה' עוז לעמו יתן (תהלים כ"ט:י"א)," כיון שהם שלוחים לקרב כל הברואים אליו יתברך.

זה שכתוב "וידבר אלהים את כל הדברים האלה לאמר: אנכי ה' אלהיך (שמות כ:א-ב)" פירוש כי הבורא יתברך נתן להם התורה, כי אין ביכולת האומות לזה. וגם בני ישראל פרחה נשמתן ונזדככו כמלאכי השרת. לכן כתוב "יום אשר עמדת לפני ה' אלהיך בחרב (דברים ד:י)," כמלאכים שנקראו "עומדים." והמכוון שבני ישראל יאמרו וימשכו אותן הדברות מדרגה אחר מדרגה עד שיתקרבו כל הברואים. כי חיות הכל בתורה, ותיקון הכל בכח התורה. וזה שכתוב "לאמר (שמות כ:א)" שצריך כל אדם מישראל להעיד בכל יום על הבורא יתברך כמו שאומרים "שמע ישראל" פעמיים בכל יום. ודברים אלו מאירין לכל העולם ולכל הברואים.

וברש"י "לאמר" מלמד שהיו עונין על הן [מצוות עשה] והן ועל לאו [מצוות לא תעשה] לאו," והיינו שאין דיברות הבורא יתברך כדיברות בשר ודם—רק הדיברות היו חקוקים בלבם. והיינו דכתיב "רואים את הקולות (שם שם י"ח)" היינו בלבם ראו שנתקיים מיד, ונתקנו נפשותם שנמשכו אחר הדיברות. וזהו ענין תורה שבעל פה שכתוב "חיי עולם נטע בתוכינו" שנבללו דברי תורה בנפשותם. וזה שכתוב "ומעוזי" היינו שנעשו מעצמות בני ישראל תורה שנקראת "עוז." (2:91)

ד

מצוות זכירת מתן תורה [בכל יום], כמו שכתוב "יום אשר עמדת לפני ה' (דברים ד:י) וכתוב "אשר אנכי מצוך היום (שם ו:ו)" והוא "אנכי" דעשרת הדיברות. וכמו כן "אשר אנכי מצוה אתכם (דברים י"א:י"ג)" בפרשה שניה [של קריאת שמע] דהוא הציווי בפרט ובכלל [לשון יחיד בראשון ולשון רבים בשני].

ומתעוררת מצות התורה בכל יום, דעשרת הדיברות הם כלל כל התורה ומצוות. והם מכוונים מול עשרה מאמרות. וכמו דכל מעשה בראשית וכל מה שמתהווה בעולם בכלל ובפרט היו נכללים בעשרה מאמרות—כמו כן כל התורה ומצוות שנעשו מכל בני ישראל, בכלל ובפרט, הכל נכלל בעשרת הדיברות.

והחילוק הוא דמאמרות הם קבועים בטבע, והדיברות הם מתחדשים

אחר יציאת מצרים היו בני ישראל מוכנים לעץ החיים, כמו שכתוב "אני אמרתי אלהים אתם ובני עליון כלכם (תהלים פ"ב:ו)." וניתן להם "לחם שמלאכי השרת אוכלין."

ואמרו חז"ל "אילו שמרו בני ישראל שבת ראשונה לא שלטה בהם אומה, דכתיב 'ויהי ביום השביעי יצאו מן העם ללקוט (שמות ט"ז:כ"ז)' וכתיב בתריה 'ויבא עמלק וילחם עם ישראל (שם י"ז:ח)' (שבת קי"ח ע"ב)." פרשנו שבת ראשונה ממש, כמו שהיה אז בשבת בראשית "ויניחהו בגן עדן." והוא עיקר השביתה והרצון שעלה לפניו יתברך שמו.

ובאמת בכל שבת קודש יש הארה יש מזה. לכן יורדת נשמה יתירה מגן עדן—ונקראת מנוחה... (2:75)

ד

מפרשת המן איתא במדרש (ש"ר כ"ה:ה) שזכו בני ישראל אל המן בזכות שהאכיל אברהם אבינו ע"ה לחם אל מלאכי השרת. באלוש ניתנה להם (עיין במדבר ל"ג:י"ד) בזכות "לושי ועשי עוגות (בראשית י"ח:ו)." הרמז הוא כי זכו ונזדככו נפשות בני ישראל להיות ניזונין מלחם שמלאכי השרת ניזונים בו בזכות אברהם, שנזדכך כל כך שהכין לחם למלאכים, כמו שכתוב "והוא עומד עליהם תחת העץ ויאכלו (שם שם ח)." כל כך היו מעשי האבות בקדושה, והשכינה שורה במעשי ידיהם, לכן אכלו המלאכים הלחם שלו.

וכתוב "לכו לחמו בלחמי (משלי ט:ה)" שיש לחם מן הארץ הם התיקונים שצדיקים מתקנים בעולם הזה. ויש להם עליה למעלה. וכמו כן הלחם יורד להם מן השמים. ולכן בשבת לחם משנה רומז על שני [מיני] לחם [אלו]. כדאיתא בזוהר הקדוש "ביני ובין בני ישראל (שמות ל"א:י"ז)" שסעודת שבת מתענגים בו עליונים ותחתונים עיין שם פרשת ויקהל. (2:84)

יתרו
א

בפסוק "וכל העם רואים את הקולות (שמות כ:י"ח)" פירוש כמו שכתוב "אנכי ה' אלהיך (שם שם ב)" [בלשון יחיד]. שראו בני ישראל כל אחד את שורש חיותו וראו עין בעין חלק נשמת ה' ממעל שיש לכל אחד. ולא היו צריכין "להאמין" את הדיברות, רק ראו את הקולות—שכך הוא כאשר ה' דובר. (2:91)

ב

בעניין מעמד הר סיני דכתיב "יום אשר עמדת לפני ה' אלהיך בחורב (דברים ד:י)"? כי בהר סיני באו בני ישראל לתכלית השלימות והיו כמלאכים. דהאדם נקרא מהלך, ובכל עת צריך לילך ממדרגה למדרגה לבוא אל השלימות—ואז נקרא עומד. והארה מעין שלימות זו יש בכל שבת, לכן יש בו מנוחה שביתה. וכתוב "אם תשיב משבת רגלך (ישעיה נ"ח:י"ג)" וי"אל יצא איש ממקומו (שמות ט"ז:כ"ט)."

להעיד על הבורא יתברך, כמו שכתוב "עם זו יצרתי לי, תהלתי יספרו (ישעיה מ"ג:כ"א)." ועל ידי הגלות במצרים נזדככו בכור הברזל להיות כלים לשיר ולזמר לפניו יתברך. לכן כשנגמרה הגאולה, נפתח פיהם ואמרו שירה. ולכן האמינו.

כשיצאו ממצרים לא הבינו מה יתרון נעשה על ידי הגלות. ואחר כך הבינו שנעשו כלים, כמו שכתוב במדרש (שי"ר כ"א:ה) "יונתי בחגוי הסלע בסתר המדרגה הראיני את מראיך, השמיעיני את קולך (שיר השירים ב:י"ד)" שכל מה שהיה בחגוי ובסתר המדרגה, הכל להוציא מכח אל הפועל להשמיע קולם.

ומעין זה יש בכל יום, שצריך אדם לתקן מדי יום ביומו כל מה שיצרו מתגבר עליו בכל יום לקיים "יונתי בחגוי הסלע כו'." ואחר כך, כשזוכה לטהר לבו, יכול לקרות קריאת שמע ולהתפלל. (2:78)

ב

"אז ישיר משה ובני ישראל (שמות ט"ו:א)" פירוש אחר יציאת מצרים נעשו בני ישראל כלים להעיד על הבורא, כמו שכתוב "עם זו יצרתי לי, תהלתי יספרו (ישעיה מ"ג:כ"א)." ובמדרש (שי"ר כ"ג:י"ב) "ויעלני מבור שאון... ויתן בפי שיר חדש, תהילה לאלהינו (תהלים מ:ג-ד)."

פירוש "חדש" שהוא לעולם בכח התחדשות, ואינו יכול להיות נשכח מנפשות בני ישראל. לא לחנם קבעו לומר השירה בכל יום. וזו האמונה שהאמינו בני ישראל כי הישועה היא לדורות, כמו שכתוב "ויהי לי לישועה (שמות ט"ו:ב)." אמרו חז"ל "היה לי לשעבר ויהיה לי לעתיד (מכילתא פרשת השירה פרשה ג)."

וזו השירה והדביקות היו נטועים בנפשות בני ישראל מעולם. אך קודם יציאת מצרים, לא היו יכולין להוציאן מכח אל הפועל. ואחר יציאת מצרים נתגלתה זו התשוקה. ועל זה כתוב "נפשנו כצפור נמלטה מפח יוקשים (תהלים קכ"ד:ז)." שהיה הרצון נאסר במצרים כענין שכתוב "הוציאה ממסגר נפשי להודות את שמך (שם קמ"ב:ח)."

וכן בכל שבת קודש יש גאולה וחירות לזה הנפש והרצון. לכן הוא "זכר ליציאת מצרים." ולכן "טוב להודות לה' (שם צ"ב:ב)" בשיר ליום השבת. (2:83)

ג

לפרשת המן—"לחם מן השמים (שמות ט"ז:ד)." במדרש (שי"ר כ"ה:ז) "לכו לחמו בלחמי ושתו ביין מסכתי (משלי ט:ה)" עיין שם. פירוש שדור המדבר היה הלחם שלהם מבחינת התורה ממש. ונקרא "לחם מן השמים."

והיה מעין הכנה ראשונה, דכתיב "ויניחהו בגן עדן (בראשית ב:ט"ו)" אחר כך כתוב "פן ישלח ידו ולקח גם מעץ החיים (שם ג:כ"ב)... ויגרש את האדם... ואת להט החרב המתהפכת לשמור את דרך עץ החיים (שם שם כ"ד)."

והיינו דמאן דנצח לחויא יסב לברתא דמלכא... [מי שנצח את הנחש, ינשא את בת המלך] (על פי תקוני הזהר תקונא תליסר דף כ"ט ע"ב)." לכן

ישראל נתקיים באמת הנהגת הבורא בעולם. כמו שכתוב ״ואתם עדי... ואני אל (ישעיה מ״ג:י״ב).״ ודוד המלך ע״ה אמר ״גם אני אודך בכלי נבל אמתך אלהי (תהלים ע״א:כ״ב).״ והוא דבר פלא כי האמת תלויה בעבודת האדם בעלמא דשיקרא [בעולם השקר]. ועל זה כתוב ״אמת מארץ תצמח (שם פ״ה:י״ב)״ ראשי תיבות ״אמת.״

אם כן האמת נסתר בעולם הזה, ״החושך יכסה ארץ (ישעיה ס:ב).״ ולמעלה נגלה ומבורר האמת, ״וי׳ אלהים אמת.״ אך גם פעולתו אמת, והוא בחינת כח הפועל בנפעל—וזה נקודת אלהות שבאדם. על זה אמר ״אמתך אלהי.״ כי הרשעים מהפכים, ובחייהם נקראים מתים. ונסתלק מהם כח אלהות ומתהפך להם האמת לשקר. והצדיקים מברירים האמת. וזה הענין עצמו מתברר לכל עובד ה׳ כפי היגיעה בעבודת ה׳, כמו שכתוב ״ישרים דרכי ה׳, וצדיקים ילכו בם ופושעים יכשלו בם (הושע י״ד:י).״ ובאמת על הכל על ידי כח התורה שנקראת ״תורת אמת.״.. (2:63)

ג

במדרש (על פי ש״ר י״ז:ג) על פסוק ״ולקחתם אגדת אזוב וטבלתם בדם אשר בסף והגעתם אל המשקוף ואל שתי המזוזות... (שמות י״ב:כ״ב)״ פירוש שאף על פי שהם שפלים... מכל מקום על ידי שיתאספו להיות אגודת אזוב, מתוך השפלות יבא להם עזר מקודש.

כי ביציאת מצרים היתה רק התחלה שיצאו לחירות מתחת יד פרעה, להיות מוכן אחר כך לכנוס בכלל עבדי ה׳ בקבלת התורה. וזה הרמז בהזאה על המשקוף ומזוזות—לידע כי עדיין הוא רק התחלה, כמו שכתוב ״פתחי לי [אחותי רעיתי] (שיר השירים ה:ב)״ דרשו חז״ל ״כחודה של מחט, ואפתח לכם כפתחו של היכל (על פי שיר השירים רבה ה:ג).״ וזה נתקיים אז, כי ביציאת מצרים היתה רק פתיחת הפתח. והשם יתברך הגין על נקודה מעוטת זו כמו שכתוב ״ופסח ה׳ על הפתח (שמות י״ב:כ״ג).״

והגם שיצאו ביד רמה, רצה השם יתברך שיהיו בני ישראל בעיניהם אגודת אזוב. ולידע כי הם עדיין אצל הפתח לקוות לכנוס לפני ולפנים, כמו שכתוב ״הביאני המלך חדריו (שיר השירים א:ד)״ במתן תורה. (2:49)

בשלח

א

במדרש ״הקורא את שמע צריך להזכיר קריעת ים סוף... ב׳אמת ויציב.׳ ואם לא הזכיר, אין מחזירין אותו, אבל אם לא הזכיר יציאת מצרים, מחזירין אותו... (ש״ר כ״ב:ג).״ ולמה צריך להזכיר קריעת ים סוף ב״אמת ויציב?״ לפי שכיון שקרע להם את הים האמינו בו, שנאמר ״ויאמינו בה׳ ובמשה עבדו (שמות י״ד:ל״א).״ ובזכות האמונה שהאמינו זכו לומר שירה, ושרתה עליהם שכינה... וכשם שהן טהרו לבם ואמרו שירה... כך צריך אדם לטהר לבו קודם שיתפלל.

הענין הוא דכתיב ״אז ישיר משה ובני ישראל (שמות ט״ו:א)״ משמע ש״אז״ נגמר עיקר המכוון של הגאולה. כי העיקר היה שנבראו בני ישראל

ולכן מקדימין יציאת מצרים לקריאת שמע, שעל ידי גאולת מצרים יכולים להיפנות ממחשבה זרה להיות מוכנים לשמוע דבר ה׳. (2:40)

בא

א

בפסוק ״[כי אני הכבדתי את לבו ואת לב עבדיו] למען שתי אותתי אלה בקרבו (שמות י:א)״ פירש רש״י ש[צריך היה לומר] ״אשית״ לשון עתיד. ויש לפרש נמי בלשון עבר, כי כל אלה המעשים שנעשו במצרים היו בעבור כי כבר שם ה׳ במצרים מטמוניות שהוצרכו בני ישראל להוציאם משם. ״ואותתי״ אלה הם אותיות שנבראו בהם שמים וארץ. ובני ישראל, שהיו מוכנים לקבל התורה, הוצרכו מקודם להוציא הדיבורים ואותיות שכבר היו נמצאים תוך העולם.

כתוב במדרשות כי מקודם היו רק שבע מצוות. אחר כך, כשבאו בני ישראל, זכו לכל התורה. לכן הוצרכו מקודם לברר הארת התורה שהיתה נמצאת גם בטבע. וזה ענין ״דרך ארץ״ שקדמה לתורה. הוא הארה שנטבעת בטבע. וכן לעולם צריכין מקודם לתקן הגוף והטבע, אחר כך זוכין להשגות חדשות.

ואמר הטעם כי למה עשה הקדוש ברוך הוא כן להיות שם ״אותתיו בקרבו״. הוא שעל ידי זה כשמוציאין ההארות משם, הם מבוררין יותר והם חיים וקיימים לדורות. וזה שכתוב ״ולמען תספר באזני בנך ובן בנך (שם שם ב)״ שעל ידי זה היה דבר של קיימא יותר. (2:48)

ב

״כי אני הכבדתי את לבו ואת לב עבדיו למען שתי אותתי אלה בקרבו (שמות י:א)״ ובמדרש (שי״ר יי״ג:א) ״כבד אבן ונטל החול וכעס אויל כבד משניהם (משלי כ״ז:ג).״

והנה בני ישראל שהם עדים על הבורא יתברך כמו שכתוב ״אתם עדי נאום ה׳ (ישעיה מ״ג:י)״ כמו שצריכין להעיד ולברר כי הקדוש ברוך הוא ברא העולם, כמו כן צריכין להעיד כי כל הבחירה ומעשי אדם ותחבולותיו—הכל ברצון הבורא יתברך שמו, לבטל ״כעס אויל״ שאומר ״בכח ידי עשיתי.״

וזה נתגלה לבני ישראל במצרים. וכתוב ״אתה הראת לדעת (דברים ד:ל״ה)״ פירש רש״י שפתח להם שבעה רקיעים. וכשם שפתח העליונים, כן פתח התחתונים [וראו שהוא יחידי] עיין שם.

ובאמת זה הוא ענין סתירת הידיעה והבחירה שדיברו בה ראשונים ואחרונים. והאמת כי כל זה עבודת איש ישראל: והוא יכול לברר ידיעת הבורא יתברך, [ואז] לבטל הבחירה—הן בנפשו, הן בכלל העולם. כמו שראינו שעשה הקדוש ברוך הוא נסים ונפלאות בעבורינו ״וידעו מצרים״ וניטל מהם הבחירה—הן במה שחיזק לבו בעל כרחו , ובמה ששלח אותנו בעל כרחו.

וכתוב ״על פי שני עדים... יקום הדבר (שם יי״ט:ט״ו)״ שעל פי עדות בני

ב

"וארא אל אברהם אל יצחק ואל יעקב באל שדי, ושמי ה' לא נודעתי להם
(שמות ו:ג)." וכן כתיב אחר כל ארבע לשונות של גאולה "וידעתם כי אני ה'
(שם שם ז)" שזה תכלית כל הגאולה, ושעל זה הוצרכו להיות ארבע מאות
שנה במצרים—לזכות לבחינת הדעת, והוא התורה. וכתוב "ה' יתן חכמה
מפיו דעת ותבונה (משלי ב:ו)." ואיתא במדרש (על פי מדרש תנחומא כי
תשא פרק י) גדולה החכמה, ודעת גדולה ממנה... למי שהוא אוהב, נותן לו
פרוסה מתוך פיו עיין שם. כי "ראיה" היא בחכמה, ויכולין לראות גם
מרחוק כדכתיב "מרחוק ה' נראה לי (ירמיה לא:ג)." אבל הדעת היא
דביקות וידיעה בעצם הנפש.

ובני ישראל הם עדים על השם יתברך כדכתיב "אתם עדי נאם ה'
(ישעיה מ"ג:י)." וכתוב בעד "או ראה או ידע (ויקרא ה:א)" שיש עדות
בראיה ובידיעה. ובאמת "כל פעל ה' למענהו (משלי טז:ד)" —לעדותו, כמו
שכתוב במדרשות. אם כן כל העולם ומלואו עדים על הקדוש ברוך הוא.
ואפילו חכמי האומות בעל כרחם מעידין על הבורא, שהחכם בטבעיות גם
כן רואה נפלאות הבורא יתברך שמו.

אבל לבני ישראל כתוב "אתה הראת לדעת (דברים ד:לייה)" שהם עדים
בראיה ובידיעה. וזכו לזה ביציאת מצרים וקבלת התורה, כמו שכתוב על
זה "ישקני מנשיקות פיהו (שיר השירים א:ב)."... (2:40)

ג

בפסוק "הן בני ישראל לא שמעו אלי, ואיך ישמעני פרעה ואני ערל שפתים
(שמות ו:יייב)." פרשנו כבר כי על ידי שבני ישראל לא שמעו, לכן הוא ערל
שפתים. כי הנביא מתנבא בכח שמיעת בני ישראל כדכתיב "נביא מקרבך...
אליו תשמעון (דברים י"ח:טייו)" והנה כתוב "שמעה עמי ואדברה (תהלים
נ:ז)" ואמרו חז"ל "אין מעידין אלא בשומע (רות רבה פתיחתא סימן א')."
וזה היה עיכוב עשרת הדיברות. והיה הדיבור בגלות כל זמן שלא הוכנו
המקבלים לשמוע דבר ה'. ובמדרש "ולא שמעו אל משה (שמות ו:ט)" שהיה
קשה להם לפרוש מעבודה זרה. כמו שכתוב "איש את שקוצי עיניהם לא
השליכו (יחזקאל כ:ח)." ואין הפירוש דוקא עבודה זרה ממש, רק עבודה
שהיא זרה להם.

כי השמיעה צריכה להיות פנויה מכל דבר. כמו שכתוב "שמעי בת וראי
והטי אזנך, ושכחי עמך ובית אביך (תהלים מ"ד:י"א)." וזה עיקר הגלות גם
עתה, מה שאיננו יכולים להתפנות ולשכוח הבלי עולם להיות הלב פנוי
לשמוע דבר ה' בלי מחשבה זרה. כמו שכתוב "ולא תתורו אחרי לבבכם
ואחרי עיניכם (במדבר ט"ו ל"ט)," וזה שכתוב "איש את שקוצי עיניהם לא
השליכו," ולכן בגלולי מצרים הלכו. כי אם היו מוכנים לשמוע דבר ה', היו
נגאלים מיד.

והנה עתה שכבר ניתנה התורה לבני ישראל וכתוב "קול גדול ולא יסף
(דברים ה:יייט)"—לא פסק. ואומרים בכל יום "שמע ישראל ה' אלהינו ה'
אחד (דברים ו:ד)" והוא המאמר "אנכי ה' אלוהיך (שמות כ:א)," אשר לא
פסק. אבל צריך להכין עצמו לשמוע פרשת קריאת שמע בלי מחשבה זרה.

הוציאו עדיין בני ישראל מכח אל הפועל—מכל מקום "קול דודי דופק פתחי לי"" שיוציאו מכח אל הפועל על ידי הפתח "כחודו של מחט (שיר השירים רבה ה:ג)."

כמו שכתבו חז"ל כי אין הקדושה יכולה להתגלות בעולם הזה רק על ידי פתח שבני ישראל פותחין. ולכן גם מה שהקדמנו "נעשה" ל"נשמע" (ראה שמות כ"ד:ז) הכל מכח אור התורה, שהיה דבוק בהם בעצם, בתוך תוכם. ומכל שכן עתה, שכבר קבלנו התורה בסיני, בוודאי קול התורה דופק בלבות בני ישראל. הגם שהוא נסתר בגלות, רק שצריכים להשתוקק לזה ההתגלות, כמו שהיה בגלות מצרים "עד שנגלה עליהם מלך מלכי המלכים הקדוש ברוך הוא וגאלם (הגדה)."

וכתוב "כימי צאתך מארץ מצרים, אראנו נפלאות (מיכה ז:ט"ו)." 2:19

וארא

א

"וארא אל אברהם אל יצחק ואל יעקב באל שדי, ושמי ה' לא נודעתי להם (שמות ו:ג)."

כל עבודתם היתה עבור בני ישראל, לכן נקראו אבות. והלכו בכל המקומות הנסתרים תוך הטבע. ויגעו עד שמצאו גם שם הארה הקדושה. ובחינה זו היא ההנהגה בשם "אל שדי." כמו שכתבו ז"ל שיש די באלהותו לכל בריאה. פירוש זה שהשם יתברך נתן בכל דבר דבר נקודת חיות אלהות, שיהיה כח למשוך כל הסביבות לנקודה זו.

כי בעולם הזה שנקרא "עלמא דשקרא [עולם השקר]" יש הרבה שקר לכל נקודה של אמת, כמו שכתוב "סביב רשעים יתהלכון (תהלים י"ב:ט)" ועל זה נאמר "הצילה נפשי משפת שקר (שם ק"כ:ב)." כי לכל נקודה של אמת, השקר סובב בכל צד. ועם כל זה, על ידי יגיעה—נוכל למצוא נקודה של אמת בכל מקום.

וזו היתה עבודת האבות. לכן נאמר "ארץ מגוריהם אשר גרו (שמות ו:ד)" מלשון גר. כמו שכתוב "אברהם גייר גיורים [ושרה גיירה גיורות] (ב"ר פ"ד:ד)." פירוש לשון המשכה, שהמשיכו כל הדברים לשורשן. ובגלות מצרים, וכן בכל הגלות, יש בחינה זו. ועומדת לזה זכות האבות.

ואיתא "משה ראה באספקלריא דנהרא [מאירה] ושאר נביאים באספקלריא דלא נהרא (על פי ויקרא רבה א:י"ד)." ולמה נקרא אספקלריא, כיון דלא נהרא? רק הפירוש שיש הסתר לנקודה, שמתגלה בתוך הסתר. ומשה רבינו ע"ה זכה כמו שיהיה לעתיד—ה' ושמו אחד—שלא יהיה שום דבר רק חיות אלהית. ובעולם הזה, נתלבש הכל בטבע. וכפי התקדשות האדם בעניני עולם הזה, זוכה להשיג דבר מה. ובחינה זו נקראת אספקלריא דלא נהרא, שעל ידי ההסתר, זוכה להתגלות. וזו היא עבודה קשה. וכדמיון זה הוא עבודת ימות החול. ושבת קדש אספקלריא דנהרא. שבשבת יש התגלות יותר לכל נפש מישראל... (2:25)

כדאיתא במדרש שגלות מצרים היתה הקדמת יסורין קודם התורה. וכל
הגליות שאחרי כן עד עתה הן הכנות יסורין קודם עולם הבא. ולכן כמו
שאז היה "כאשר יענו... כן ירבה (שמות א:י"ב)" כן בכל הגלויות. וכיון
שהשכר של ימות המשיח ועולם הבא הוא בלי קצבה, לכן גם הקדמת
היסורין הם בלי זמן קץ.

ונחזור לדברינו. הראה לו [למשה] הקדוש ברוך הוא האור הצפון
ומיוחד להיות נולד מזה הצער. וזה שכתוב "יודיע דרכיו למשה כו'." מה
שבני ישראל ראו אחרי כן, כשנגמר בפועל, וזה שכתוב "עלילותיו." ולמשה
הראה דרכיו בעוד שלא יצא לפועל וזה שכתוב "בלבת אש מתוך הסנה
(שם ג:ב)." כמו כן הצדיקים שמשתתפין תמיד בצער גלות—השכינה ובני
ישראל—זוכין להרגיש הארות מגאולה העתידה. (2:11)

ג

במדרש (שי"ר ג:א) "ומשה היה רועה כו' (שמות ג:א)" מוכן לגאולה עיין שם
ובתנחומא. זה שכתוב "משגב לעתות בצרה (תהלים ט:י)." "משגב" גימטריא
"משה." והוא שר התורה שנקרא עוז. וכל החירות תלויה בתורה כמו
שכתבו חז"ל "אין לך בן חורין אלא העוסק בתורה (אבות ו:ב)." ומאחר
שהעוסק בתורה הוא בן חורין, ממילא משה רבינו ע"ה שהוריד התורה מן
השמים, הוא בעל החירות.

ובאמת עיקר החירות שבא בכח התורה להיות הנפש בן חורין ממאסר
הגוף. ובאמת כל זה נעשה בכח התורה כדאיתא "בראשית ברא (בראשית
א:א)" בשביל התורה שנקראת "ראשית" ונתייעץ הקדוש ברוך הוא בתורה
וברא העולם. שזאת היתה דרך התורה—לברוא העולם ולהעלים בו כח
מעשיו. ושעל ידי התורה יוציאו בני ישראל מכח אל הפועל האור הגנוז
במעשה בראשית.

ולכן כתוב "ואלה שמות (שמות א:א)" מוסיף על הראשונות על ספר
בראשית (שי"ר א:ב)—שכמו שנברא העולם בתורה, כמו כן כל גלות וגאולת
מצרים היו בכח התורה. וזה גמר הבריאה. "הפה שאסר הוא הפה שהתיר
(כתובות ב:א)." ובכח התורה נסתר הכל בטבע, ובכח התורה לפתוח המאסר
"לאמר לאסירים, יצאו (ישעיה מ"ט:ט)."" (2:17-18)

ד

ובמדרש "בלבת אש מתוך הסנה (שמות ג:ב)" להודיעך "שאין מקום פנוי
בלי שכינה—אפילו סנה (שי"ר ב:ה)." פירוש שזה מכוון הגלות, שיבררו בני
ישראל מלכותו יתברך שמו, שהוא בכל מקום. שורש שם "גלות" על שם
"התגלות," שיתגלה כבוד מלכותו יתברך שמו בכל מקום. וזה נגמר על ידי
נשמות בני ישראל בעולם הזה. כמו שכתוב במדרש (שי"ר ב:ה) "אני ישנה
ולבי ער, קול דודי דופק 'פתחי לי (שיר השירים ה:ב).'"

כי הקדוש ברוך הוא בחר בנו ונתן לנו התורה, והתורה למעלה מן
הזמן. והקדוש ברוך הוא וברוך שמו שלפניו עבר ועתיד הכל אחד. אם כן,
הבחירה שבחר בבני ישראל ונתדבקו בו במתן תורה, היה גלוי לפניו גם
מקודם. וזה כח הדביקות של התורה—הגם שהיתה נסתרת עוד כי לא

ספר שמות

שמות

א

בפסוק "ויהי בימים הרבים ההם וימת מלך מצרים ויאנחו בני ישראל מן
העבודה ויזעקו ותעל שועתם אל האלהים מן העבודה (שמות ב:כ"ג)","
פירש מורי זקני ז"ל כי קודם שמת היו שרוים כל כך בגלות כי לא הרגישו
שהם בגלות. ועתה התחיל קצת גאולה שהבינו הגלות והתאנחו. וכן פירוש
מה שכתוב "והוצאתי אתכם מתחת סבלות מצרים (שם ו:ו)" שלא יוכלו
לסבול דרך מצרים.

ובודאי יש בכל גלות הרבה מדריגות. ואיתא "מוציא אסירים," פודה
ענוים," "עוזר דלים." והם שלוש בחינות [של גלות].

הבינונים הם במאסר בגלות, ואינם יכולים להרחיב נקודת חיות אלקות
שבהם. ועל זה נאמר "מוציא אסירים." ו"פודה ענוים" הם הצדיקים
שבעצמם אינם בגלות, רק בעבור הכלל, כמו שהיה במשה רבינו ע"ה. ומשה
היה "רועה" מוכן לגאולה—פירוש כי לא היה בעצם בגלות—רק [בתור]
הכנה לגאול את ישראל. וכמו כן הארת השבעים נפש שבאו למצרים,
להיות הכנה לגאולה. ועליהם נאמר "פודה ענוים." ו"עוזר דלים" הם
השפלים שאינם מרגישין כל הגלות, ואלה צריכין ישועה גדולה. והיא
ראשית הגאולה כמו שכתוב "והוצאתי אתכם מתחת סבלות מצרים."

ולכן יש ארבע לשונות של גאולה [בתורה, והרביעית היא] "ולקחתי
אתכם לי לעם (שם שם ז)"—זו תכלית הגאולה העליונה, שבעבור זה היה
כל הגלות.

ומעין זה נמצא בכל גלות. וגדולה מזו נראה שגם בכל פרט ופרט
נמצאים כל אלה המדריגות. שיש בכל איש ישראל איזה בחינה שהוא בן
חורין בפרט. אחר יציאת מצרים יש חלק חירות בכל איש ישראל. וזה החלק
מסייע לאדם, והוא הכנה לגאולה, דכמו שהוא בכלל כמו כן בפרט. (2:18)

ב

במדרש (שי"ר ב:א) "יודיע דרכיו למשה, לבני ישראל עלילותיו (תהלים
ק"ג:ז)" דאיתא "המשתתף בצערן של ציבור, זוכה ורואה בנחמת ציבור (על
פי תענית י"א ע"א)." וכמו כן באבילות החורבן "שישו אתה משוש כל
המתאבלים עליה (ישעיה ס"ו:י)." וצריך הבנה: אם הפירוש שיראה בבנין
ירושלים אם יהיה בימיו, מדוע לא יזכה כמו כל הדור? ואם הפירוש שיחיה
עד הבנין, והלא כמה צדיקים שנסתלקו מקודם?

רק הפירוש שזוכה לראות בנחמת ציבור גם תוך הצער, כי הגלות הוא
רק הסתר. אבל מי שזוכה להסיר ממנו ההסתר, כפי בירור וזכות לבו, כך
יוכל לראות בנחמת ציבור. וכמו שכתוב "שישו אתה... עליה" כמו בחינת
כנסת ישראל בעצמה אם כי היא בגלות, עם כל זאת השמחה גנוזה בה, כי
יודעת שעתידה להיות עטרה בראשו של מלך. כן מי שמשתתף עמה בצערה,
זוכה לראות גם בשמחתה.

וזה נתקיים במשה שכתיב "וירא משה בסבלותם (שמות ב:י"א)" לכן הראה
לו הקדוש ברוך הוא הגאולה ומתן תורה, שזה היה כל תכלית הגלות.

אבינו ע״ה להעלים מעשיו מהשם יתברך! אך הפירוש כי ביקש להראותם עומק הרע. ושיתגלה להם מלכותו יתברך בכל המקומות עד דרגא תתאה [דרגה תחתונה]. כמו שכתוב ״באחרית הימים (בראשית מ״ט:א).״ וזה הוא בעת הסתרת פנים.

והקדוש ברוך הוא לא רצה בזה, כדי שיהיה הגלות, שכך רצונו ברוך הוא. לכן נגלה עליו [ליעקב] השכינה. ועל ידי שהייתה התגלות, לא היה יכול ״לגלות הקץ.״ שזה רק בעת ההסתר.

וכן הייתה דרכו של יעקב אבינו ע״ה: תמיד להכניס עצמו במקומות אשר המה מסוכנים. כי היה מפתח לבנים. ורמז לדבר ״המלאך הגואל אותי מכל רע ״יברך את הנערים] (בראשית מ״ח:ט״ז)״ מכלל שירד לכל מקומות הרעים וניצל מהם. ודרך הזו רצה ללמד לבניו—ונסתם ממנו.   (1:267-8)

ג

בפסוק ״ויקרא יעקב אל בניו, ויאמר ׳האספו ואגידה לכם את אשר יקרא אתכם באחרית הימים (בראשית מ״ט:א).׳״ ובמדרש (ב״ר צ״ח:ג): מהיכן זכו ישראל לקריאת שמע?—מיעקב, דכתיב ״וזאת אשר דבר להם אביהם (בראשית מ״ט:כ״ח),״ שמסר להם כח הדיבור.

בזה הכח מעידין בני ישראל על הבורא וכתיב ״שפת אמת תכון לעד (משלי י״ב:י״ט).״ יעקב הוא האמת כדכתיב ״תתן אמת ליעקב (מיכה ז:כ).״ והשבטים הם ״שפת אמת״ כי הדיבור נשלם על ידי השפתים. ומקודם הייתה שפה אחת. ובדור הפלגה, על ידי שלא היו דבוקים באמת, ניטל מהם כח הדיבור ונשאר רק לבני ישראל. וכתוב ״אתם עדי נאום ה׳ (ישעיה מ״ג:י).״ פירוש בכח כ״ב [22] אותיות [בתיבת ״אתם״ א–ת] ולשון הקודש שנמסרו לבני ישראל—לשון שמלאכי השרת משתמשין בו. והוא אחד מהדברים שדומה האדם לעליונים, שמדבר בלשון הקודש.

וזה החילוק בין ״שפה״ ל״שפת״: כי השפתים הם להשלים הדיבור, וגם לסתום ולהעציר מה שאין צריך לדבר ולגלות. שפה—״ה״ פתוחה. ושפת ב״תיו״—סתומה עד לעתיד. דכתיב ״אז אהפוך אל עמים שפה ברורה לקרא כלם בשם ה׳ (צפניה ג:ט).״

ובאמת על ידי שפת אמת של בני ישראל יהיה כל התיקון לעתיד. וזה ״תכון לעד״ פועל יוצא: שעל ידי שפת אמת יתתקנו כל הלשונות. וזה כח לשון הקודש הנחיל יעקב לבניו. ועל זה כתיב ״זכור ימות עולם, בינו שנות דור ודור. שאל אביך ויגדך זקניך ויאמרו לך (דברים ל״ב:ז).״ ״ויגדך״ כמו שכתוב ״ואגידה לכם (בראשית מ״ט:א).״ ובני ישראל צריכין בכל יום לבקש האמת, ומתגלה להם. כדכתיב ״תתן אמת ליעקב״—לשון הווה, בכל יום בכח קריאת שמע...   (1:281)

שנקרא גר שמגייר עצמו גם כן על שם זה, שמוציא נקודה קדושה שהיה
נטבע באומות. וכן ענין גלות מצרים שכתוב "גר יהיה זרעך כו' (בראשית
ט"ו:א"ג)" גם כן הפירוש להוציא ניצוצות קדושים שנטבעו במצרים. וזה
שכתוב "ואחרי כן יצאו ברכוש גדול (שם י"ד)."

וזה שכתב רש"י ז"ל "[יעקב] ביקש לגלות הקץ ונסתם ממנו (בראשית
מ"ז:כ"ח)." פירוש שרצה לברר זה שהגלות רק הסתר, והכח הפנימי הוא רק
מהשם יתברך. רק אם היה נגלה זה, לא היה גלות כלל, ו[לכן] נסתם. ומכל
מקום כתוב בזוהר הקדוש שגילה מה שרצה לגלות, רק בדרך הסתר.
והפירוש על ידי אמונה יכולין למצוא האמת, להתברר שהוא רק הסתר.

ולכך "ויחי יעקב" סתום [הפרשה מתחילה באמצע העמוד]. שזה מקור
החיות להיות נמצא גם בארץ מצרים זה נקרא [ולכך נקרא שהתחיל
השעבוד]. וכמדומה לי שאדוני אבי זקני ז"ל הגיד בשם הרב מפרשיסחא
ז"ל שהקשה: למה רצה לגלות הקץ? ותירץ: שכשנודע הקץ הגלות בנקל. עד
כאן אני זוכר. ונראה כנזכר לעיל שפירשתי גילוי הקץ לידע שיש קץ לגלות,
והוא על ידי שהוא רק הסתר, ואינו כח בפני עצמו חס וחלילה. כי הפנימיות
שהיא אמת–אין לו קץ; וההסתר–יש לו קץ. ורצה שיהיה זה נגלה, ולא
היה גלות כלל, ונשאר סתום. ומכל מקום על ידי אמונה שמאמינים זה בני
ישראל שאין שום כח בלתי השם יתברך, רק כל זה, רק הסתר, אף שאין
רואין זה בעין, מכל מקום על ידי אמונה גם כן יכולין לראות האמת. רק
יעקב אבינו ע"ה רצה שלא נוכל לטעות כלל, שיהיה זה נגלה. ונשאר סתום,
שצריכין יגיעה למצוא זה.

וזה בחינת דוד המלך ע"ה, "דלית ליה מגרמיה [שאין לו מעצמו] (זוהר
ח"א קכ"ה ע"א)." ומשיג האמת רק על ידי הביטול. וזה ההפרש שבין אמת
לאמונה. וכמו כן [אמר] אדוני אבי זקני מורי זצ"ל על "יעקב אבינו לא
מת... מקרא אני דורש כו' (תענית ה ע"ב)." שכשאדם דורש ומייגע עצמו,
שזה בחינת תורה שבעל פה, יכול למצוא הארה מחיות יעקב אבינו גם
בתוך ההסתר... (264:1)

ב

במדרש (ב"ר צ"ו:א) למה פרשה זו סתומה כו'? פירוש כי הכתוב משבח
מעשה יעקב אבינו ע"ה, אשר חי במצרים י"ז (17) שנים כי היה דבוק
בחיים. ולא היתה כל טומאת מצרים עומדת לנגד קדושתו. והיו י"ז שנים
אלו הכנה לכל הגלות.

אך כי פרשה זו סתומה לנו. פירוש שאין אנו משיגין איך המשיך חיות
הקדושה במצרים. כי אם היו משיגין זאת לא היה הגלות כלל. ובוודאי יש
בכח איש ישראל לעורר החיות בכל מקום. ועל זה נאמר, "השם נפשנו
בחיים (תהלים ס"ו:ט)," דכתיב, "ויפח באפיו נשמת חיים ויהי האדם לנפש
חיה (בראשית ב:ז)." פירוש "נפשי"–הרצון. שהאדם יכול לעורר החיות
ברצונו, ובני ישראל דבוקים בחיים.

ומה שכתבו חז"ל (ב"ר צ"ח:ב) [יעקב] ביקש לגלות הקץ ונסתם . משל
[לאחד] שרצה לגלות מסטורין [סודות] של המלך. ראה שהמלך עומד [שם]
והשיח [דבריו] לדברים אחרים. והוא תימה, כי חס וחלילה שירצה יעקב

(יחזקאל ל"ו:כ:ה)," והוא בחינת תורה שבכתב. ו"מים עמוקים בלב" הוא
תורה שבעל פה– "חיי עולם נטע בתוכינו."

ויש מטמוניות גנוזות בלב איש. ועל זה נאמר "אם תבקשנה ככסף
וכמטמונים תחפשנה (משלי ב:ד)." והרב הקדוש מפרשיסחא [ר' שמחה
בונם] ז"ל אמר פירוש הכתוב "תבקשנה ככסף תחפשנה כמטמונים" כי
בקשה הוא כאדם המבקש למצוא מציאות. וחיפוש הוא דבר הנאבד ממנו
וחופש אחריו. והחילוק הוא כי מי שנאבד לו דבר מצטער ביותר לחפש
אחריו. אבל כשמצאו אין השמחה גדולה כל כך כי כבר היה לו דבר זה
מעולם. ומי שמבקש מציאות הוא להיפוך. אין הצער גדול, והשמחה גדולה.
ולכן אמר הכתוב כי בעבודת השם יתברך צריך להיות שניהם, להיות הצער
גדול לייגע עצמו למצוא כדבר הנאבד ממנו. ואחר כך, כשזוכה למצוא,
צריך להיות השמחה גדולה כמוצא שלל רב. עד כאן דבריו ז"ל דברי פי
חכם חן ושפתים יושק.

ונראה לי כי שניהם אמת, שיש שתי אלו העבודות בכל איש. שצריך
למצוא השלימות להוציא מכח אל הפועל מה שמוכן לו, והוא מטמון בנפשו
ונאבד ממנו, וצריך לחזור אחר אבידתו. והוא בחינת ימי המעשה. ויש גם
כן לבקש עזר מקודש (ראה תהלים כ:ג) למצוא התחדשות מן השמים, והוא
השבת שנקרא "מתנה טובה." לכן בשבת השמחה והעונג. ובימי המעשה
העיקר היגיעה והעבודה. (257:1-8)

ויחי

א

אדוני אבי זקני מורי ורבי זצ"ל הגיד, "ויחי יעקב בארץ מצרים (בראשית
מ"ז:כ"ח)' כי על ידי בחינת אמת יכולין לחיות גם בארץ מצרים. וכתוב
'תתן אמת ליעקב (מיכה ז:כ).'" דהנה לא היה לו לומר רק "ויהי יעקב
בארץ מצרים." ומשמע דעיקר הרבותא מה שהיה בחינת חיים, גם בארץ
מצרים. ופירוש "חיים" הוא דביקות בשורש ומקור שמשם נמשך תמיד
חיות. וכן כתוב בזוהר הקדוש [בפרשת] ויגש על פסוק "ותחי רוח יעקב
(בראשית מ"ה:כ"ז)."

ונראה לי שהוא מלשון "מים חיים." שעל ידי שמחת הנפש מעורר
מקור החיים, וניתוסף חיות. {ונראה לי שזה שכתוב "ויהי האדם לנפש חיה
(בראשית ב:ז)." פירוש "נפש"–הרצון; על ידי פנימיות הנפש נמשך חיות
תמיד.}

והגם שהיה בארץ מצרים, ידע שכל ה"מצרים" הם רק "קליפה" והסתר,
אבל הפנימיות היא חיות השם יתברך. ולכך, אמרו חז"ל, כי ה"רשעים
בחייהם נקראים מתים (ברכות יי"ח ע"ב)" שנפרשים ממקור החיות כנזכר
לעיל.

וכתוב במדרש (ב"ר צ"ו:ב) "גרים אנחנו לפניך (דברי הימים א כ"ט:ט"ו)"
כי כל בריאת אדם בעולם הזה לא היה כדי להידבק, חס וחלילה, בעולם
הזה. רק להיפוך: שעל ידי דביקות האדם בעיקר החיות, מתמשך גם ענייני
עולם הזה להשם יתברך. ו"גר" לשון המשכה, כמו מעלה גֵרָה שגם מה

ב

בפסוק "ולא יכול יוסף להתאפק" דכתיב "ויגש אליו יהודה (בראשית
מ"ד:י"ח)" פירוש "אליו" ליוסף, גם אל עצמותו, פירוש לעצמו, וגם פירוש
"אליו" להקדוש ברוך הוא. וביאור הענין כי הנה יהודה לא חידש דבר
באלה הדברים, וגם לא היתה לו טענה במה לבוא ליוסף. אף על פי כן
לאשר בירר אמיתות הענין, באה לו הישועה. כענין "אמת מארץ תצמח (
תהלים פ"ה:י"ב)."

והאמת כי כל כל פרשה זו מיוסף ואחיו הוא משל לעבודת בני ישראל
להקדוש ברוך הוא... ופירוש הנמשל כי השם יתברך מלא כל הארץ כבודו.
וגם במקום החושך שם נסתר כבוד מלכותו יתברך. כמאמר "גם חושך לא
יחשיך ממך (שם קל"ט:י"ב)." לזאת בכל עת צרה כשאדם מבטל עצמו אל
האמת ובמסירת נשמתו, כמו יהודה שאמר "איך אעלה אל אבי" ומסר
עצמו להיות עבד במצרים כדי שלא יהיה חוטא לפני אביו, על ידי זה
נתגלה לו האמת וראה כי הכל טוב ולא היה לו כלל ממה לירא כי "אני
יוסף." (249:1)

"ויגש אליו יהודה" שהאדם ערב על הנשמה בת מלך להחזירה לאביו
שבשמים. ואף שנתלכלך כל כך בחטא, עם כל זה על ידי תשובה מעומקא
דלבא [מעומק הלב כמו] "איך אעלה אל אבי" נהפכו עונות לזכיות—ונאמר
"אני יוסף כו'." ואף שאין יודעין להבין היטב איך נתהפך החטא לזכות, רק
כח הפועל בנפעל. וכמו שמהפך אדם לבו לשוב בתשובה, כן נהפכין כל
הפעולות שפעל בחטאיו.

ובאמת בני ישראל שהם חלק ה' ונחלתו, ו"אף על פי שחטא, ישראל
הוא (סנהדרין מ"ד ע"א)," לכן יכול להתחזק לגשת לכח אלהי אשר נסתר
בקרבו. ועל זה נאמר "ויגש אליו" לעצמותו. ונאמר "בי אדוני" וכבר כתבנו
מזה. (248:1)

ממילא "ולא יכול יוסף להתאפק" הוא הנקודה הפנימיות שבכל דבר
שנקרא יוסף. רק שעל ידי הקלקול נסתר זה. והקליפה מחשיך ומסתיר
כאלו, חס וחלילה, דבר נפרד מהשם יתברך. ועל ידי הכנעה וביטול אמת
מתגלה הפנימיות ונתודע שהוא "אחיהם."

וזהו "בי אדוני" שהאמין שמכל מקום יש בפנימיותו חיות השם יתברך,
אף שנסתר לו ואינו יודע היאך. כל זה גרם החטא. אבל באמת "בי אדוני"
כן יש בכל הסתר... (246:1)

ג

במדרש (ב"ר צ"ג:ד) "מים עמוקים עצה בלב איש, ואיש תבונה ידלנה
(משלי כ:ה)" זאת היתה עבודת יהודה והשבטים—לדלות מים מבורות
עמוקים כדכתיב "שתה מים מבורך ונוזלים מתוך בארך (שם ה:ט"ו)."
והוא שיש בכל איש ישראל בפרט בעולם הזה, וגם בעולם הזה בכלל,
הארות גנוזות. כמו שכתוב "ה' בחכמה יסד ארץ (שם ג:י"ט)" והוא עבודת
ימי המעשה—לברר אוכל מתוך פסולת.

ובחינת יוסף הוא להמשיך אור חדש מן השורש בשמים. וזהו "ונוזלים
מתוך בארך," מעין נובע תמיד. וכענין שנאמר "וזרקתי עליכם מים טהורים

ובברית הלשון [מתן תורה] תליא בברית המעור [מילה]. ושתי בריתות אלו הם בחינת יהודה ויוסף. והגם כי עיקר העדות בפה, וזה כחו של יהודה, לכן החזיקו השבטים ביהודה, אבל שורש פתיחות הפה והעדות תליא ביוסף לכן "עדות ביהוסף שמו" כי העדות תלויה בו.

בגמרא (סוטה ל"ו ע"ב) איתא יוסף שקידש שם שמים בסתר, ניתן לו אות "ה" משמו של הקדוש ברוך הוא. יהודה, שקידש שם שמים בגלוי, נקרא כולו על שמו של הקדוש ברוך הוא. והוא כנזכר לעיל כי עיקר הדיבור בהתגלות ליהודה, אבל שורש הדיבור באתכסיא [בסתר] הוא ליוסף. (196:1)

ויגש

א

בזמר האר"י ז"ל "אזמר בשבחין למיעל גו פתחין דבחקל תפוחין [אזמר בשבחים להכנס תוך פתחי שדה התפוחים]" וקשה. מאי "גו פתחין דבחקל תפוחין." היה צריך לומר "למיעל בחקל תפוחין."

אבל האמת כי חקל תפוחין הוא בכל מקום כמו שכתוב "מלא כל הארץ כבודו (ישעיה ו:ג)." וכדאיתא "ראה ריח בני כריח שדה (בראשית כז:כז)."

רק שעיקר העבודה לפתוח נקודה זאת. ובשבת נפתח זה השער כמו שכתוב "שער החצר הפנימית... יהיה סגור ששת ימי המעשה וביום השבת יפתח... (יחזקאל מ"ו:א)." וכמו שראינו קדושת שבת בין הימים - אף שהוא תוך הזמן - אף על פי כן הוא מעין עולם הבא. וההפרש בין ימות החול לשבת שנפתחת בה הפנימיות, ו"אין דומה מאור פניו של אדם בשבת כבחול (ב"ר י"א:ב)," שבנקל להרגיש הקדושה בשבת.

וכמו כן יכולין להבין כי כבוד מלכותו יתברך הוא בכל מקום, אף שאינו נגלה, וזה האמונה של כל איש ישראל: ה' אחד. פירוש "אחד" שאין דבר רק השם יתברך בעצמו, הוא הכל. ואף שאין יכולין להשיג את זה כראוי, צריכין להאמין בזה. ועל ידי אמונה באים אל האמת.

וכמו שכתוב במקום אחר כי אמת ואמונה הן שתי מדרגות, והוא ענין יוסף ויהודה דכתיב במדרש "אחד באחד יגשו (איוב מ"א:ח וב"ר צ"ג:ב)." כענין שנאמר "ביום ההוא יהיה ה' אחד ושמו אחד (זכריה י"ד:ט)." ולעתיד יתברר זה האחדות שיש בתוך הבריאה. וזה נקרא "רזא [סוד] דאחד (זוהר ח"ב קל"ט ע"ב)" כי הוא עתה בסוד נסתר. וה' אחד הוא למעלה מהשגת הנבראים, כמו שכתוב "כל הנקרא בשמי ולכבודי בראתיו יצרתיו אף עשיתיו (ישעיה מ"ג:ז)," כי העולם הזה נברא בשמו יתברך.

וזה שכתוב "בי אדוני (בראשית מ"ד:י"ח)" ופירש האר"י ז"ל "ה' בי" באותיות יהודה. והפירוש שעל ידי זה יכול כל אדם לתקן עצמו, אף בעת ההסתר, על ידי האמונה שהשם יתברך משגיח בכל. ויאמין כי יש בו נשמת אל חי כמו שאומר כל אחד מישראל "נשמה שנתת בי טהורה היא."

ועל ידי שמבטל עצמו לנקודת חיות מהשם יתברך, ורוצה להכיר את האמת, מתגלה לו. כמו שמצינו ביהודה [אחר שהוא אמר "בי אדוני"] "ולא יכול יוסף להתאפק (שם מ"ה:א)." (247:1)

מקץ

א

ענין החלום שכתוב בתורה משבע שני שובע ורעב. הרמז שגם כח הסטרא
אחרא רק על ידי גלות השפע בתוך ההסתר. אבל אין להם כח חס וחלילה
מבלעדי חיות השם יתברך. וזה שכתוב "ותבלענה השבלים הדקות את שבע
השבלים הבריאות" (בראשית מ"א:ז)," "ותאכלנה הפרות הדקות... ולא
נודע כי בא אל קרבנה (שם שם כ–כ"א)." ונדמה כאלו יש להם כח חס
וחלילה בעצמותם. ואינו כן.

והיה זה להראות לפרעה קודם הגלות, שידע שאף שבני ישראל יהיו
כבושין תחת ידו, מכל מקום אין לו כח נגד השם יתברך. ובאמת כתוב
"אשר לא ידע את יוסף (שמות א:ח)" ששכח גם כן בחינה זו.

ומה שיש ללמוד מפרשה זו, להכין לעצמו בימים הטובים שנתגלה
הקדושה בהם ולקבוע ההארות בלב היטב כדי להיות על ימי הרע כשהקדושה
נסתרת... (1:182)

ב

"עדות ביהוסף שמו [באות "יה" בשמו של יוסף] בצאתו על ארץ מצרים
שפת לא ידעתי אשמע (תהלים פ"א:ו)." במדרש (סוטה ל"ו ע"ב) כי בא
גבריאל ולימד אותו שבעים לשון, לא הוי גמיר [היה למד]. הוסיף לו
[האות] "יה" בשמו וגמיר. ותמוה: חדא, כי מה תורה היא זו לידע שבעים
לשון? ופרעה ידע, ויוסף לא היה יכול לידע? וגם מה תועלת אות "יה" בזה?

אכן יובן על פי המדרש (ב"ר מ"ט:ב), "הואיל משה באר את התורה
הזאת (דברים א:ה)" בשבעים לשון פירשה להם. כי כל השבעים לשון
מתפשטין מלשון הקודש. כי התורה נותנת חיים לכל הלשונות, והם רק
כמו לבושים כי המכוון כי המכון אחד הוא. רק הלשונות משונים בתנועותיהם, אבל
הן הדברים שנאמרו בתורה מתלבשין בכל אלו הלשונות.

ויוסף הצדיק, שבא למלוך במצרים בכח התורה, היה צריך לידע ולקשר
כל הלשונות בלשון הקודש. והיה זה הכנה קודם גלות מצרים, שהיא גלות
ראשונה שבישראל, היה צריך יוסף לשלוט אל כל אלה הלשונות. ולכן
נתוסף לו אות "יה" "שביה' נברא העולם הזה, כמו שכתוב 'ב-ה-בראם
(בראשית ב:ד)' (ב"ר י"ב:י)," ולכן בכח האות הזו להמשיך כל הלשונות
אחרי חיות הפנימיות, שהוא לשון הקודש כנזכר לעיל. (1:185)

ג

"עדות ביהוסף שמו בצאתו על ארץ מצרים שפת לא ידעתי אשמע (תהלים
פ"א:ו)." כי ירידת יוסף למצרים היתה הכנה אל גלות מצרים. ותכלית גלות
מצרים היתה הכנה לקבלת התורה, לתקן הדיבור. ולכן כתיב "אנכי ה'
אלוהיך המעלך מארץ מצרים הרחב פיך ואמלאהו (שם י"א)."

וכן כשיצא יוסף מבית האסורים זכה לשבעים לשון, הכל הכנה לכלל
ישראל שנבראו להעיד על הבורא. ולכן צריכין לברר העדות בכל הלשונות
כמו שכתוב "שמע ישראל (דברים ו:ד),"—"שמע: בכל לשון שאתה שומע
(מגילה י"ז ע"א)."

אצל אביהם. אבל מקודם שהיה מעלה דבתם רעה היה מוכרח לירד
למצרים.

ומה שנתכנה החטא אל השבטים [שמכרו את יוסף למצרים], כי אם היו
כולם מתוקנים כראוי, ולא היה חשש במה שיעלה כל מעשיהם לאביו, לא
היה נצרך לירד למצרים. נמצא שהם היו סיבה לירידתו למצרים. (165:1)

ב

ויש שני מיני נסיונות: אחד שיכול האדם לגבור בכחו, ויש נסיון עצום מזה
שאין באפשרי לגבור כלל. רק על ידי רצון ולב אמת וצדק, שיש להצדיק,
זוכה שיקחו ממנו הבחירה—שיצא מהנסיון. ופירוש שיסייענו משמים.

וזה שכתוב [על יוסף בנסיונו] "וימאן ויאמר אל אשת אדוניו הן אדני
לא ידע אתי מה בבית וכל אשר יש לו נתן בידי (בראשית ל"ט:ח)." וכתבתי
במקום אחר פירוש זה, שנתן הקדוש ברוך הוא הבחירה לאדם בכל מעשה
אשר ירצה לעשות. רק אחת מבקש השם יתברך מאדם: אשר יזכור בעול
מלכותו יתברך, וישדע שהכל מאתו. וצריך על כל פנים האדם לשמור זאת.

והנה אלה הדברים בדברי יוסף הצדיק "ולא חשך ממני מאומה כי אם
אותך באשר את אשתו (שם ט)." ודי למבין.

ועל ידי זה זכה יוסף הצדיק לצאת מהבחירה על ידי שזכר שגם
הבחירה נתן הקדוש ברוך הוא, ושאין זה יושר לעבור על רצונו יתברך. לכן
אף כי לא היה יכול לגבור בכחו, על ידי המרירות שהיתה לו, על זה הוציאו
הקדוש ברוך הוא מהנסיון.

וזה היה הכנה לכל הגליות. כי גלות מצרים הוא כלל כל הגליות. ועיקר
הגלות הוא תוספת הבחירה כי אם לא היה הבחירה כלל לאדם, היה ממש
בן חורין. ולכן כשזוכין לצאת מהבחירה הוא גאולה שלימה. והבן. (164:1)

ג

בפסוק "ויעזוב בגדו בידה וינס ויצא החוצה (בראשית ל"ט:י"ב)" פירוש
חוץ ממלבוש הגוף כמו [שעשה ה' לאברהם] "ויוצא אותו החוצה (שם
ט"ו:ה)," כמו שכתבתי במקום אחר.

והנה כתיב "הרכבת אנוש לראשינו באנו באש ובמים, ותוציאנו לרויה
(תהלים ס"ו:י"ב)." פירוש שעל ידי חטא הראשון נעשה כתנות עור ממשכא
דחויא [נחש הקדמון], ונתלבש באנושיות וגשמיות. "באנו באש ובמים,
ותוציאנו לרויה." [פירוש] שעתה צריכין מקודם לתקן הגוף על ידי יראה
ואהבה—שמדות אלו הם בהרגשות הגוף. אחר כך זוכין לפנימיות.

ובכלל האבות תקנו חטא אדם הראשון. "אש ומים" בחינת אברהם
ויצחק. "ותוציאנו לרויה" בחינת יעקב, "תתן אמת ליעקב (מיכה ז:כ)."
"אמת" הוא כמו שהיה קודם החטא, כי הנחש הביא השקר בעולם.

ויוסף נמשך אחר בחינת יעקב כמו שכתוב "אלה תולדות יעקב יוסף
(בראשית ל"ז:ב)." "ויעשה לו כתונת פסים (שם שם ג)" הוא "כתנות אור
[שהיו בגן עדן] (ב"ר כ:י"ב)," לכן "וינס החוצה"—התפשטות הגשמיות.
(180:1)

יש בו נקודת חיות מהשם יתברך, ובנקודה זו כלול הכל. כמו שכתוב במדרש, "הכל בחזקת סומא (ב"ר נ"ג:כ"ז)" גבי הגר שמצאה הבאר. עיין שם.

והפירוש שבכל מקום יש הכל ממש, על ידי שיש בו חיות מהשם יתברך. וזה שנקרא ה׳ שלום: שכל נקודה מכח השם יתברך—נמצא שם הכל. ועל ידי זה מי שמדבק כל דבר בשרשו, יש לו הכל. ואין חילוק אם יש לו רב או משהו.

וזהו בחינת שבת: ש"כל חפציך עשוים," ואין חסר כלל—כי הוא שלימות הכל. אבל עשו אמר "רב," והוא הרבוי שבא מכח האדם. כי מה שבא בכח ה׳ הוא אחדות, ושם נמצא הכל. וזה שכתבו ז"ל "יפה שעה אחת בתשובה ומעשים טובים מכל חיי עולם הבא (אבות ד:י"ז)" ומכל שכן חיי עולם הזה. ופירוש "שעה אחת" הוא כנזכר לעיל, להיות הכל באחדות, דבוק בשורש עליון. ולכך אמר יעקב "יש לי כל." והבן. (1:140-1)

ד

בפסוק "ויחן את פני העיר (בראשית ל"ג:י"ח)" איתא "חן מקום על יושביו (על פי ב"ר ל"ד:ט"ז)," כי ארץ ישראל מיוחד לבני ישראל ולאבותינו הקדושים. ומצא מין את מינו דכתיב "בחר ה׳ בציון (תהלים קל"ב:י"ג)" וכתיב "יעקב בחר לו יה (תהלים קל"ה:ד)." ולכן כתיב "לא יטוש את עמו, ולא יעזוב את נחלתו (שם צ"ד:י"ד)," כי זה בזה תלוי.

ובכח האבות נעשה ארץ הקדושה מקום קדוש, להיות בו משכן כבודו יתברך שמו. וזהו שכתוב "אשרי יושבי ביתך (שם פ"ד:ה)." כמו שדרשו חז"ל (שבת פ"ה ע"א) ב"שעיר החורי יושבי הארץ (בראשית ל"ו:כ)" שהיו טועמין את הארץ, שהם היו מבינים בגשמיות הארץ לעשותו ישוב. ובני ישראל עושין ישוב הפנימי, ולכן נקראין [רק ישראל] "יושבי ביתך," שיודעין ומבינים המקום המוכן לקדושה. וכתוב "אוה למושב לו (תהלים קל"ב:י"ג)." וזה נגמר על ידי האבות ודוד המלך ע"ה, כמו שכתוב "אם אבא באהל ביתי, אם אעלה על ערש יצועי, אם אתן שנת לעיני, לעפעפי תנומה, עד אמצא מקום לה׳ משכנות לאביר יעקב (שם ג-ד)." (1:154-5)

וישב

א

"ויראו אחיו כי אותו אהב אביהם מכל אחיו, וישנאו אתו, ולא יכלו דברו לשלום (בראשית ל"ז:ד)." בפסוק לא נזכר ששנאת האחים היה בעבור הדיבה. וקרוב הדבר כי יעקב לא הגיד להם שיוסף הביא דיבתם רעה. אמנם נראה כי טעם "ויבא יוסף את דבתם רעה אל אביהם (שם:ב)" היא סיבה שלכך נצרך יוסף להיות נמכר למצרים. כי היו, חס וחלילה, נדחין השבטים אם היה יוסף אצל אביהם והיה מעלה דבתם רעה.

וביאור הענין כי הצדיק מעלה לפני הבורא יתברך מעשים טובים של בני ישראל. אבל עדיין יוסף לא היה בשלימות עד אחר הנסיון. ואז נקרא יוסף הצדיק ומעלה רק מעשיהם הטובים. ולכן אחר כך היו כולם ביחד

וישלח

א

בפסוק "ויאבק איש עמו עד עלות השחר (בראשית ל"ב:כ"ה)" אמרו חז"ל
(חולין צ"א ע"א) שהעלו אבק עד כסא הכבוד.

הרמז הוא כי מאחר שצורתו של יעקב חקוקה בכסא הכבוד, כן כח
מלחמת הסטרא אחרא [מגיע] עד שם, כמו שכתוב "כי יד על כס יה (שמות
י"ז:ט"ז)" שאין הכסא שלם עד שימחה שם עמלק.

וכי שייך פגם, חס וחלילה, בכסא כבודו יתברך שמו? רק הפירוש
שאינו יכול להיות גילוי כבודו יתברך בעולם כל זמן שעמלק נמצא. וכמו כן
התפשטות כחו של יעקב וגילוי צורתו אינו יכול להיות בשלימות. "על כן
לא יאכלו בני ישראל את גיד הנשה אשר על כף הירך עד היום הזה, כי נגע
בכף ירך יעקב בגיד הנשה (שם ל"ג)." ובו עצמו כתיב "ויזרח לו השמש (שם
ל"ב)."

זה שכתוב במדרש (ב"ר ע"ז:א) "ויותר יעקב לבדו (שם כ"ה)" כמו
"ונשגב ה' לבדו ביום ההוא (ישעיה ב:י"א)" שאינם יכולים להתגלות עד
לעתיד. (156:1)

ב

"לא יעקב יאמר עוד שמך כי אם ישראל, כי שרית עם אלהים ועם אנשים
ותוכל (בראשית ל"ב:כ"ט)." ושני שמות אלו זכו בהם בני ישראל, והם
בחינת הגוף והנשמה. כי צריך כל אדם לתקן הגוף עד שיחול עליו כח
נשמתו, ואז נקרא ישראל.

ועניין מלחמת יעקב עם המלאך: כי נשמת אדם גדלה מעלתה מהמלאך
כידוע. רק שזה בבחינת הנשמה בלבד. אבל גוף המלאך גדלה מעלתו על גוף
האדם, כי גוף האדם בעולם העשיה.

אך יעקב אבינו ע"ה תיקן גופו עד שזכה להיות מרכבה להשם יתברך.
נמצא גם גופו כמו נשמה. ולכן גם בחומר גופו היה יכול להלחם עם
המלאך. וזה שכתוב "לא יקרא שמך עוד יעקב," פירוש שגם הגוף שמכונה
בשם יעקב איננו אצלו בבחינת גוף, ונהפך לרוחניות כמו הנשמה. וזה
שכתוב "ויבוא יעקב שלם (שם ל"ג:י"ח)," השתוות הגוף לנשמה נקרא
שלום.

כי בכל איש ישראל יש מחלוקת זו בין הגוף והנשמה. וכפי תיקון הגוף,
כך השלימות שבו. ולכן גם שבת נקרא שלום, כי יש בו תיקון הגוף שהוא
מעין עולם הבא. ולעתיד לבוא יהיו הגופות מתוקנים ממש כמו נשמות.
ובשבת קדש יש מעין זה... (143:1)

ג

באור החיים "כי חנני אלהים וכי יש לי כל (בראשית ל"ג:י"א)" כתב כי על
ידי המתנה לא יחסר—עיין שם פירוש "מכל כל."

והפירוש כי לכאורה "כל" יותר מ"רב (שם ח)" שאמר עשו. אך איך
יוכל אדם לומר "כל?" והרי כמה דברים היו שלא היו לו.

אך מי שדבוק בשורש עליון, מה שיש לו—הוא בחינת כל. כי כל דבר

ג

אדוני אבי זקני ז״ל הגיד בשם אדוננו רבי יצחק [לוריא] ז״ל כי שבת נקרא
שדה כדכתיב ״[לכה דודי] נצא השדה (שיר השירים ז:י״ב).״ כי עולם הזה
הוא מדבר, שאין ניכר בו השגחת השם יתברך. ובשבת נקראת ״שדה״
הראוי לזריעה, שנתעורר כח הפנימיות—נקודת חיות—מהשם יתברך. ועל
ידי זה [השדה/השבת] מקבלת זריעה כנזכר לעיל.

ועל פי זה נפרש הפסוק ״והנה באר בשדה כו׳ שלשה עדרי צאן כו׳
והאבן גדולה על פי הבאר ונאספו כו׳ (בראשית כ״ט:ב-ג).״ פירוש שבשבת
נפתח מקור מים חיים וזהו ״באר בשדה.״ ו״שלשה עדרי צאן״ הם מה שבני
ישראל מתבטלין בשבת להשם יתברך בכל לבבך ונפשך ומאדך. ונקראות
[שלש דרגות של הנשמה שהן] נפש, רוח, ונשמה, שצריך האדם לבטל הכל
להשם יתברך. (124:1)

ד

בפסוק ״והאבן גדולה על פי הבאר (בראשית כ״ט:ב)״ היה לו לומר ״ואבן
גדולה.״ ויתכן לרמוז כי האבן מכשול שהוא היצר הרע. הוא נמצא בכל
מקום, אבל על פי הבאר הוא גדול ביותר. והוא שאינו מניח לפתוח הפה
בתפלה שהיא עבודה שבלב, שהיא בחינת הבאר, תורה שבעל פה שהיא
תפילה. ועל זה מבקשין ״אדני שפתי תפתח.״ וכל מגמת היצר הרע לעכב
התפלה כידוע לכל עובד ה׳, וכדאיתא ״מאן דנצח לחוייא לנסוב ברתא
דמלכא [מי שמנצח את הנחש, נושא את בת המלך] (תקוני זוהר י״ג דף
כ״ט ע״ב).״

והאמת כי אין עצה לתפלה. רק כפי עבודת האדם בכל מעשיו, כך הוא
יכול לפתוח פה בתפלה. לכן קראוה ״עבודה שבלב,״ שתלויה בהשתוקקות
הלב בכל היום, בכל מעשיו. וזה הרמז ״ונאספו שמה כל העדרים,״ שזאת
תכלית הנולדת מכל העבודות.

וביעקב כתיב ״ויגל (בראשית כ״ט:י)״ דרשו ״כמעביר הפקק מעל פי
החביות (רש״י על פי קהלת רבה ט:י״ג).״ הרמז כי הצדיק יודע ומבין כי
זאת האבן טובה היא לשמירה מעולה, כמו שהחביות צריכות פקק לשמור
מהפסולת. והעומד בחוץ נדמה לו כאלו חס וחלילה משמים מעכבין אותו,
ומשימין אבן על לבו. אבל הוא רק לטובה.

וכתיב ״ויגש יעקב (בראשית כ״ט:י)״ יתכן לרמוז כמו שכתוב במדרש
(ב״ר מ״ט:ח) ״ויגש אברהם (בראשית י״ח:כ״ג)״ לשלושה דברים: פיוס,
מלחמה, ותפילה, כמו שכתוב ״בוא וקרב.״ עיין שם. והרמז לשלוש התפלות
בכל יום שמסתמא הם שלוש מיני תפלות... ובכל אלה השלושה עדרי צאן
יכולין לגלול האבן. (130:1)

ויצא

א

בפסוק "הארץ אשר אתה שוכב עליה לך אתננה ולזרעך (בראשית כ"ח:י"ג)."
דרשו חז"ל (חולין צ"א ע"ב) קיפל הקדוש ברוך הוא כל ארץ ישראל תחתיו.
כמו שאבינו יעקב היה כולל כל נפשות [ישראל]—שהוא האדם שברא
הקדוש ברוך הוא בעולמו ודמותו חקוקה תחת כסא הכבוד (על פי ב"ר
פ"ב:ב)—ממילא [המקום הזה] שייך לו, זה המקום שכולל כל המקומות.

ובגמרא "המענג את השבת, נותנין לו נחלה בלי מצרים, 'אז תתענג על
ה' והרכבתיך על במותי ארץ, והאכלתיך נחלת יעקב אביך (ישעיה נ"ח:י"ד).'
לא כאברהם שכתוב בו 'קום התהלך בארץ לארכה ולרחבה (בראשית
י"ג:י"ז),' כיעקב שנאמר בו 'ופרצת ימה וקדמה וצפונה ונגבה (שם כ"ח:י"ד)'
(שבת קי"ח ע"א-ב)." הענין הוא כי השבת הוא להיות עליית כל דבר
לשרשו כדכתיב "אל יצא איש ממקומו ביום השביעי (שמות ט"ז:כ"ט)."
וזהו/תכלית מעשה האדם למצוא המקום השייך אליו וממילא שורה בו
ברכה "ופרצת כו'." זהו שכתוב "הארץ אשר אתה שוכב עליה לך אתננה"
שהוא המקום השייך אליו. ויעקב אבינו ע"ה הוא כולל כל השש קצוות.
וזהו רמז ה"סולם מצב ארצה וראשו מגיע השמימה (בראשית כ"ח:י"ב)"
והוא מעלה ומטה. אחר כך "ופרצת ימה כו'" הוא ארבע רוחות... (1:131)

ב

"וירא והנה באר בשדה והנה שם שלשה עדרי צאן רובצים עליה כי מן
הבאר ההוא ישקו העדרים, והאבן גדולה על פי הבאר. ונאספו שמה כל
העדרים וגללו את האבן מעל פי הבאר והשקו את הצאן, והשיבו את האבן
על פי הבאר למקומה (בראשית כ"ט:ב-ג)."
בחינה זו נמצאת בכל דבר ובכל איש ישראל, שיש בכל דבר נקודה
הנותנת חיים ומחיה הדבר ההוא. וזהו באר בשדה. אף מה שנראה ונדמה
להפקר, כשדה, אך נגנז בו נקודה הנ"ל. ושכל האדם יוכל להרגיש ולידע
זאת תמיד. וזהו "שלשה עדרי צאן"—חכמה, בינה, דעת. שבחכמה ושכל
מבין האדם זאת הפנימיות, שבכל דבר יש כח הפועל בנפעל.
אך "והאבן גדולה על פי הבאר." היינו כשמתפשט בגשמיות יש הסתר,
שאין השכל דבוק במעשה תמיד. והעצה "ונאספו" הוא לאסוף כל הרצונות
וכל רמ"ח (248) אברים וגידים למסור נפשו להשם יתברך קודם כל מעשה.
ועל ידי זה "וגללו את האבן מעל פי הבאר והשקו את הצאן."
גם יש לומר "ונאספו" להכניס עצמו בכלל ישראל. כי כשכל הבריאה
מתאחדת אליו יתברך, נתבטל ההסתר. וזה יהיה לעתיד במהרה בימינו.
ועתה בני ישראל שמאספין הכל אליו יתברך. ואף איש אחד בפרט, כשמבטל
עצמו לכלל ישראל, ועושה בעבור כולם, נקרא בשם כל ישראל, ויוכל
לגלול ולהסיר ההסתר.
וזה שכתוב ביעקב אבינו ע"ה "ויגל את האבן מעל פי הבאר (שם שם
י')" מעצמו, ש[הוא] היה כלל ישראל. וגם היה צדיק יסוד עולם, שכל
העולם נתקיים בזכותו. "ויגל" מעצמו. (1:124)

יצחק ביאר איך לבוא ליראת ה׳ מכל הבריאה. וכל זה היה קודם התורה. "באר חפרוה שרים (במדבר כ"א:י"ח)" ואחר כך "וממדבר מתנה (שם)"—שניתנה התורה, שהיא מבארת טעם האמת של כל הבריאה, וזה אינו יכול להשיג רק במתנה.

ויעקב, שכתוב בו "תתן אמת ליעקב (מיכה ז:כ)," נזדמנה הבאר אליו מעצמה. כמו שכתוב "וירא והנה באר (בראשית כ"ט:ב)." (1:122)

ג

"ויאהב יצחק את עשו כי ציד בפיו (בראשית כ"ה:כ"ח)." הכתוב נותן טעם כי לא היתה אהבה אמיתית—רק [כי היתה] תלויה בדבר. לכן בטלה דבר, בטלה אהבה (אבות ה:ט"ז). ולכן כשהקדימו יעקב בצידה, אבדה האהבה.

אבל "רבקה אוהבת את יעקב (בראשית כ"ה:כ"ח)" בלי טעם, ונתקיימה האהבה לעד. וכן כוונת המדרש במה שכתוב "כל שהיתה שומעת קולו, היתה מוספת אהבה (ב"ר ס"ג:י)." פירוש ש[אהבתה] לא היתה תלויה בדבר.

וכן אהבת המקום ברוך הוא לבני ישראל גם כן אינה תלויה בדבר, אף לא במעשיהם. רק בחר לו: "כי חלק ה׳ עמו (דברים ל"ב:ט)." כמו שכתבו עליו—עשיר ישמח בחלקו (אבות ד:א). וזה שכתוב "׳אהבתי אתכם׳ אמר ה׳ ואמרתם ׳במה אהבתנו?׳ ׳הלוא אח עשו ליעקב... ואהב את יעקב (מלאכי א:ב)." פירוש שאין טעם במה לתלות האהבה, רק שבני ישראל מדובקין אליו יתברך בשורשם. (1:107)

ד

"ויתן לך האלוהים מטל השמים ומשמני הארץ (בראשית כ"ז:כ"ח)." במדרש "יתן לך אלוהותו כו׳ (ב"ר ס"ו:ג)." הגם כי הפסוק מסיים "מטל השמים ומשמני הארץ."

אך הכוונה שצריך איש ישראל לקבל אלוהותו יתברך שמו מכל נמצא שבעולם. והיינו דכתיב "ואהבת את ה׳ אלוהיך בכל לבבך ובכל נפשך ובכל מאודך (דברים ו:ה)" לקבל אלוהות מכל הדברים. כי חיות הכל מהקדוש ברוך הוא, ואפס זולתו. והיא הברכה שיתן לך האלוהים "מטל השמים ומשמני הארץ" בכל זה תמצא אלוהותו יתברך שמו.

ובאמת דורש המדרש אחר זה "מטל השמים ומשמני הארץ" על מנחות ונסכים וקרבנות. והכל ענין אחד להראות כי בבית המקדש על ידי הקרבנות נתקרבו כל הדברים האלה אל השורש. וכל זה עדות כי בכל מקום "מלא כל הארץ כבודו (ישעיה ו:ג)."

וממשמע שנאמר "משמני הארץ," שנמצא דברי חפץ בעולם הזה אפילו בארציות ממש, אך שצריכין להוציאו מכח אל הפועל. והכל בחכמה עשה. ולכן צריכה הארץ כמה עבודות: חרישה, זריעה, קצירה כו׳ עד שנעשה מאכל—להראות כי בכח עבודת האדם יכול להוציא מאכל וניצוצי קדושה הגנוזים בעולם הזה... (1:120)

מה שעובר עליו. ויש נסיון לעני ויש לעשיר.

ושרה בתחלת ימיה עברו עליה כמה זמנים קשים ברעבון ובלקיחתה לפרעה ואבימלך. ובסוף ימיהם היה להם כל טוב ולא נעשה בה שום שינוי בכל השינוים האלה.

וזה מאמר המשנה (אבות ה:ד): עשרה נסיונות נתנסה אברהם אבינו ע״ה. פירוש: ברוב אהבתו להקדוש ברוך הוא, כל הרוחות שבעולם אין מזיזין אותו ממקומו, ועמד בתמימותו. ולא הרגיש כלל בכל מה שעבר עליו, לא כדרך אדם שיש לו כמה שינוים בכל יום. והם [שרה ואברהם], כל שנותיהם לא נעשה בהם שינוי. ועליהם נאמר ״גמלתהו טוב ולא רע כל ימי חייה (משלי ל״א:י״ב).״ כולל כל מיני שינוים ונסיונות בעוני ובעושר. ואמר ״כשם שהם תמימים, כך שנותיהם.״...

ועיקר התמימות הוא להיות דבוק בשורש העליון כמו שכתוב ״תמים תהיה עם ה׳ אלהיך (דברים י״ח:י״ג)״ כי כל דבר שלמטה יש לו שורש למעלה. וכשהחלק שלמטה דבוק בשרשו, הוא דבר תם ושלם. וזה תכלית עבודת האדם: לידבק עצמו בשורש העליון... (1:98-99)

תולדות

א

אמר מורי זקני ז״ל על ענין הבארות שחפרו האבות: שיש בכל מקום נקודה גנוזה מהשם יתברך. רק שצריכין להסיר החיצוניות לגלות נקודת הפנימיות שנקראת ״באר מים חיים (בראשית כ״ו:י״ט, שיר השירים ד:ט״ו).״ ובימות החול נקרא ״עשק,״ ו״שטנה״ ובשבת ״רחובות״ (ראה בראשית כ״ו:כ-כ״א). ודברי פי חכם חן.

וכתוב ״חכמות בחוץ תרונה ברחבות תתן קולה (משלי א:כ)״ כי קול התורה מעורר תמיד לבות בני ישראל, רק שצריך האדם להטות אזניו, כמו שכתוב בזוהר הקדוש ״לית מאן דירכין אודני [אין מי שיטה אוזנו].״ וכתוב ״שמוע תשמעו בקולי (שמות י״ט:ה)״ וכתוב ״עקב שמע אברהם בקולי (בראשית כ״ו:ה)״ מכלל שיש תמיד קול מהשם יתברך. והוא מעשרה מאמרות [שבהם נברא העולם] ועשרת הדברות שנתן השם יתברך כח דבריו לכלל הבריאה.

ובשבת שבני ישראל מעידין כי להשם יתברך הארץ ומלואה, מתעורר קול השם יתברך, ובנקל לאדם לשמוע בשבת קודש. וזה שכתוב ״ברחובות תתן קולה.״ (1:105)

ב

בענין הבארות שחפרו האבות: ״באר״ הוא כמו ״הואיל משה באר את התורה (דברים א:ה).״ כמו כן קודם קבלת התורה היו האבות מבארים חכמת הבריאה, שהכל בתורה נברא. ״ולכבודי בראתיו (ישעיה מ״ג:ז).״ וצריך האדם להתבונן בכל הבריאה להבין כוונת הבורא יתברך שמו.

ואברהם אבינו ע״ה ביאר איך לבוא מכל הבריאה לאהבת הבורא, ולהסתכל בחסדים וטובות הבורא, שכבודו וגדלו וטובו מלא עולם. וכמו כן

חיי שרה

א

"ויהיו חיי שרה מאה שנה ועשרים שנה ושבע שנים שני חיי שרה (בראשית
כ״ג:א)." ברש״י "שני חיי שרה' [למה לא נכתב 'מאה עשרים ושבע שנה׳?]
שכולן שוין לטובה." יש לומר כי דרך האדם הפשוט, על ידי שנזקן נתוסף
בו דיעה ומיישב אורחותיו. ונמצא כי כל מה שנזקן יותר, מניח מדות
ומעשים רעים שהיה עושה. ואם כן, אינו נקרא "ימי חייו" רק רגע האחרון
שהוא בשלימות הראויה—אם זוכה לכך.

אבל בשרה הצדקת היו כל ימיה בטוב ובלי קלקול. אף כי וודאי
נתעלתה בימי הזקנה. אבל לא על ידי דחיית מעשים הקודמין בימי הנעורים,
רק שנתעלתה כפי מה שנבראת. שכל ימיו של אדם קצובין לתקן בכל יום
דבר מיוחד, ולהתעלות מדריגה אחר מדריגה. אבל לא היה לה פגם וקלקול
לחזור להתנהג בכשרות. וזה שכתוב "כולן שוין לטובה," והבן. (82:1)

ב

"ויהיו חיי שרה מאה שנה ועשרים שנה ושבע שנים שני חיי שרה (בראשית
כ״ג:א)." במדרש "'יודע ה' ימי תמימים, ונחלתם לעולם תהיה (תהלים
ל״ז:י״ח).' כשם שהם תמימים, כך שנותיהם תמימים (ב״ר נ״ח:א)."...

פירוש "תמים" מתפרש שאין בו מום והוא בשלימות. ולזה שייך גם
הזמן. כי האדם נברא להוציא שלימותו מכח אל הפועל. וכיון שנברא
בעולם הזה, ויש לכל אחד זמן קצוב, על כרחך שיש שייכות הזמן לשלימותו.

ופשוטו: על ידי שמתחדש לו ידיעות בכל יום, וכמו שאמר זקני מורי ז״ל,
כי יום נקרא על שם ההארה כמו שכתוב, "ויקרא אלהים לאור יום (בראשית
א:ד)," עד כאן דבריו. והיינו שבכל יום הקדוש ברוך הוא "מחדש בטובו
מעשה בראשית." נמצא שנותן הקדוש ברוך הוא בכל יום נקודת התעוררות
בכל איש ישראל להתדבק בו. וזה שכתוב ".... אשר אנכי מצוך היום (דברים
ו:ו)," "בכל יום כחדשים (שולחן ערוך אורח חיים סימן ס״א סעיף ב'.")

ומי שמקבל כל אלו ההארות, על זה נאמר "יודע ה' ימי תמימים" שעל
ידי הימים נגמר שלימותו. וכן כתוב בזוהר הקדוש שעל ידי הימים נעשה
"לבוש" אל האדם. והיינו שיש בעולם העליון גם כן הסתרות מסטרא
אחרא, שלא יוכל כל אחד לגשת להקודש. ועל ידי הכנעת עולם הזה
והתהפכות הטבע נעשה לבוש שמתחבר הטבע, שמכונה בשם זמן, טפל אל
הקדושה. וזהו שכתוב "שנותיהם תמימים," שהצדיק מדבק כל יום בשורשו.
ועל ידי שמקבל ידיעות והשגות בהמשך הזמן, על ידי זה מראה תועלת
בהזמן ומתעלה גם כן.

"ויודע ה' ימי תמימים"—פשוט שימי הצדיקים הם רק בידיעת ה'
שנתוסף לו תמיד ידיעות חדשות. (84:1)

ג

במדרש "'יודע ה' ימי תמימים' כשם שהם תמימים כך שנותיהם תמימים."
ורש״י פירש "שני חיי שרה' כולן שוין לטובה." והוא מדת השתוות שכתב
בספר חובת הלבבות. והוא מעלה גדולה להיות אדם עומד בתמימותו בכל

(שמות ל"א:י"ז)" "וי, אבדה נפש" שבימי המעשה נאבדה אותה התשוקה
והרצון. כמו מילה בנפש, כן שבת בזמן. (1:81)

ג

במדרש (ב"ר מ"ח:ב): "מבשרי אחזה אלוה" (איוב (י"ט:כ"ו).". "אלולי שעשיתי
כן, מהיכן היה הקדוש ברוך הוא נגלה אלי?!" פירוש דכתיב אחר המילה
"וירא אליו (בראשית י"ח:א).".
וזה בחינת המצוות, שהם תיקון הרמ"ח (248) איברים להיות חל
עליהם נועם ה'. והיא חיבה יתירה שיתגלה צלם אלוהים בנפש האדם בכח
המצוות. ומילה היא מצווה ראשונה מתרי"ג (613) מצוות המיוחדים לבני
ישראל. והוא שורש אברהם אבינו ע"ה, בחינת מצוות עשה כמו שכתוב
"אשר יצוה את בניו (שם ט).". דאיתא (בסידור התפלה) "באור פניך נתת
לנו תורת חיים ואהבת חסד." "אהבת חסד" בחינת המצוות, שהוא "אהבה
רבה" להתדבק בכל אברי הגוף אל הבורא יתברך בכח המצוות.
אברהם אבינו בחינת רמ"ח [248] מצוות עשה, ויצחק בחינת שס"ה
(365) מצוות לא תעשה, ויעקב [שהוא כולל שניהם] "תורת חיים." ומרוב
אהבת אברהם אבינו זכה להמשיך כח המצוות "אהבת חסד" כנזכר לעיל.
וזה "וירא אליו" ו"מבשרי אחזה אלוה"—זה בריתו של אברהם אבינו.
שעל ידי עשיית מצווה שלמטה, יתדבק בשורש העליון. ויהי נועם ה' עליו
בכח הברית שכרת חסם יתברך לאברהם. ועל ידי מצוות מילה נכנסין לזה
הברית. ועל זה מברכין [בברית מילה] "להכניסו בבריתו של אברהם
אבינו.(9-1:78)

ד

בפסוק "עתה ידעתי כי ירא אלהים אתה (בראשית כ"ב:י"ב).". ומקשין:
הלא עבודתו של אברהם היתה בחינת אהבת ה', שהיא למעלה מעובד
מיראה! ולמה ייחס לו הכתוב יראת אלוהים?
אבל התירוץ הוא כי זה עצמו היה הנסיון. כי ודאי אברהם אבינו ע"ה,
שעזב ארצו ומולדתו והשליך עצמו לכבשן האש בעבור הבורא יתברך, מה
נסיון הוא [לגבי אדם כזה] לשחוט את בנו! אבל התירוץ הוא כי בוודאי
העובד מאהבה, כמו אברהם, נמשך לבו ומעיו לעשות רצון קונו עד שכל
איבריו נמשכין בטבעם לעשות רצון קונם. וכל רמ"ח (248) איברים שבו,
כל חיותם, המצוות של השם יתברך.
אכן באמת לא היה רצונו של הקדוש ברוך הוא לשחוט את יצחק. ולבו
של אברהם לא הרגיש דביקות ואהבה בזו העובדא [מעשה], על ידי שבאמת
לא היה כן רצונו של השם יתברך, ולכן היה נסיון. לכך נאמר "וירא את
המקום מרחוק (שם ד).". ולכן היתה עבודתו עתה רק בבחינת "ירא אלוהים"
שלא הרהר אחריו יתברך כלום.
ולכן ביקש [אברהם] שלא ינסה אותו עוד (ב"ר נ"ו:י"א). פירוש שלא
יהיה לו רחקות עוד, שדרכו של אברהם אבינו ע"ה בחינת אהבה כנזכר
לעיל. (1:67)

למצות מילה, והוא תיקון עולם העשיה, שיזכה האדם להסיר הערלה במעשה ידיו.

לכן כל עובד ה׳ אין לו להרהר על אלה ההסתרות שנמצאים לכל עובד ה׳, כי "לפום צערא אגרא [לפי הצער השכר] (אבות ה:ב:כ"ג)." וזה בחר לו אבינו אברהם. מאהבתו את השם יתברך הכניס עצמו במקומות מסוכנים לתקן אליו כל הבריאה. לכן נקרא על שמו "בהבראם׳ [אותיות] באברהם (ב"ר י"ב:ט)."

וכן הוא לדורות. "בראשית" בשביל "ישראל שנקראו ראשית׳ (רש"י בראשית א:א)." על ידי שמקריבין כל הבריאה אליו יתברך ומעוררים כח הראשית בעולם.

ואיתא אברהם תיקן תפלת שחרית דכתיב "וישכם אל המקום אשר עמד שם את פני ה׳ (בראשית י"ט:כ"ז)." פירוש הפשוט: שמיד בהקיצו משנתו בא לו אל המקום אשר עמד בו אתמול בשכבו.

וזה סדר עובד ה׳ הנקרא מהלך, כמאמר "ודברת בם בשבתך בביתך ובלכתך בדרך ובשכבך ובקומך (דברים ו:ז)." כי כל ימי האדם הם הילוך אחד. ועליו נאמר "בא בימים (בראשית כ"ד:א)." וכמו שאומרים בתפלה "ונשכים ונמצא ייחול לבבנו כו׳." שזה סימן לאהבת הבורא יתברך שמיד בהשכמה קודם כל עובדא [מעשה]... לכן אברהם, שהוא עמוד האהבה כמו שכתוב "אברהם אוהבי (ישעיה מ"א:ח)" העיד עליו הכתוב "וישכם אברהם אל המקום אשר עמד שם (בראשית י"ט:כ"ז)." ועל זה אמרו שתיקן תפלת שחרית, שהניח זה הכח לכל איש ישראל שיוכל להיות מעורר את השחר בכל יום. (1:67)

ב

ברש"י מן המדרש והגמרא "וירא אליו ה׳ (בראשית י"ח:א)׳ לבקר את החולה."

כתוב "חולת אהבה אני (שיר השירים ב:ה)" שכנסת ישראל יש להם אהבה והשתוקקות להתדבק בהקדוש ברוך הוא. כמו שכתוב "׳צדיק כתמר יפרח (תהלים צ"ב:י"ג)׳ מה תמר יש לה תאווה, כך צדיקים תאוותן להקדוש ברוך הוא."

כי הנפש והרוח מתאווין אל השורש, רק שהם אסורין בגוף, ועל ידי המילה והסרת הערלה, גוברת תאוות הנפש והרוח. ובאמת ציור הגוף כציור הנפש. כמו שכתבו חז"ל "אין צור כאלוהינו (שמואל א ב:ב)׳ - אין צייר כאלוהינו (ברכות י ע"א)." וכמו בגוף, התאווה והתשוקה בזה האבר, כן הוא בפנימיות.

ולכן "צדיק כתמר יפרח" כי הנר"ן [נפש-רוח-נשמה] באמת חפצים לעלות, ככל עלול המשתוקק אל עילתו. רק כשהערלה מכסה, הגוף גובר. ואין הרשעים יודעין כלל שהם במאסר הגוף. ואחר המילה נעשה האדם בריה חדשה. ומרגיש שהוא תוך המאסר, ונעשה חולת אהבה.

וכן הוא בשבת קודש דמתעברת [שעוברת] סטרא אחרא ומתגלה הארת הנר"ן. וזהו בחינת "נפש יתירה" שהרצון והשתוקקות הנפש מתגלים בשבת קודש. כמו שכתוב "ויכֻלו (בראשית ב:א)" לשון חמדה והשתוקקות. "ויִנפש

ד

והאדם שנשתלח בעולם הזה לילך ולתקן כל המקומות, ולהוציא מהם
הניצוצות הקדושים. וזה היה כל תהלוכות אברהם אבינו ע״ה ממקום
למקום, ואחר כך למצרים. כמו שאמרו ז״ל (ב״ר מ:ו) שהיתה [ירידת
מצרים] הכנה לבני ישראל וכתיב [על אברהם כשהוא חזר ממצרים], "כבד
מאד במקנה בכסף וזהב (בראשית י״ג:א)." שהעלה הרבה ניצוצות קדושים
משם. "כסף" ו"זהב" רומז לאהבה ויראה, שהיתה עליתו משם בדחילו
ורחימו [יראה ואהבה] לשם שמים, לכן ניתקן הכל.

ובלוט לא כתיב כסף וזהב, רק "וגם ללוט... היה צאן ובקר ואהלים
(שם ה)." ולכן בא לוט אחר הנסיעה ממצרים לידי חטא, שלא היה בדחילו
ורחימו כראוי. ורמז וגם ללוט כמו שכתוב במצרים "וגם ערב רב כי' (שמות
י״ב:ל״ח)" ובבני ישראל כתיב "ויוציאם בכסף וזהב (תהלים ק״ה:ל״ז)"
כנזכר לעיל. לכן "אין בשבטיו [של ישראל] כושל (שם)," שאלה הניצוצות
הקדושים שבאו ממקומות הסטרא אחרא צריכין שמירה רבה, שלא להביא
מכשולות אחר כך על ידיהם. (1:54)

ה

במדרש תנחומא על פסוק "התהלך לפני והיה תמים (בראשית י״ז:א)" תמה
אברהם, "עד עתה אני חסר, וכשאמול עצמי אהיה שלם? כו'."

פירוש: שזה באמת השלימות, מה שאדם מחסר את עצמו כדי להיבטל
להשם יתברך, ולהראות כי אין שלימות לנברא רק בהשפעת הבורא. זה
עצמו הוא הנותן לו השלימות; וביטולו של דבר זה קיומו.

ולכן ניתנה מצווה זו באבר הזה אשר בו כח ההשפעה והתולדות של
האדם. שזה עיקר כח ומעלת האדם. וצריך להיות שם אות ורמז כי הוא
חסר מעצמו, וצריך להשלמת הבורא יתברך...

ולכך נקרא ברית, שהוא התקשרות המקבל אל המשפיע, והיא השלימות.
ונראה שלכך ניתן זה לאדם. והקשו הערלים: "אם חביבה המילה, למה לא
נברא מהולו?" כמו שכתוב במדרש; עיין שם (ב״ר י״א:ו). והתירוץ: שבאמת
במילה הוא מחסר הגוף, רק מצד שהאדם הוא העושה זאת בעבור הבורא,
הוא השלימות. אבל לא שייך שיהיה נברא כך. (1:45)

וירא

א

איתא "אברהם בירר לו את הגלות (על פי שמות רבה נ״א:ז)." כי אמרו
"לא גלו ישראל רק שיתוספו עליהם גרים (פסחים פ״ז ע״ב)." היינו המשכת
כל הברואים לתורה. שזה היה בחירתו של אברהם שהכניס עצמו בכל
המקומות לתקנם ולהעלותם. לכן איתא כי "נח היה צריך סעד לתומכו
(רש״י בראשית ו:ט)" ואברהם היה מתחזק בצדקו מאליו כי "בדרך שאדם
רוצה לילך מוליכין אותו (מכות י ע״ב)." והוא בחר לו זו הדרך, שמעצמו
ימצא לו דרך האמת

ולכן הצדיקים שהיו מקודם היו נולדים מהול. והוא בעבודתו זכה

עיקר תיקון האדם כפי מה ששוכח הבלי עולם, כמו שכתוב ״שכחי
עמך״ ולזכור כי נשתלח בעולם הזה לעשות שליחותו. וזה בחינת ״זכור״
ו״שמור״ [״את יום השבת״—בשתי גירסות של עשרת הדברות] מצוות עשה
ומצוות לא תעשה.

הוא בחינת זכירה ושכחה ששניהם צריכין לאדם. לשכוח הבלי עולם
ואז יכול לזכור ולהתדבק בעולם העליון. וזה שרמזו ״מי שישנו בשמירה
ישנו בזכירה (ברכות כ ע״ב).״

ובאמת בשבת, שכל ישראל שובתין ממלאכה, והוא בחינת שכחה מעולם
הזה. לכן זוכין לנשמה יתירה; זכירה ודביקות בעולם הבא בשבת קודש,
שהוא ״מעין עולם הבא.״ וזה ״זכור״ ו״שמור״ בשבת.

אבל באמת השבת ללמד על הכלל כולו יצא. שאיש ישראל צריך לעולם
לשמור שתי בחינות הנזכרות לעיל: ״שמעי בתי״ [זכור] ו״שכחי.״ ואברהם
היה הראשון שהשליך הבלי עולם וזכה למשוך אור בעולם. ועליו נאמר ״מי
העיר ממזרח כו׳ (ישעיה מ״א:ב).״

וזה העניין של בירה דולקת. כי כל עולם הזה נברא רק כדי לשכוח
ולבטל הבלי עולם; וזה קיום העולם, שהוא הפרוזדור כדי לכנוס לטרקלין
(אבות ד:טז). וכן רצון בעל הבירה שתהיה הבירה דולקת ומתבטלת. וזה
בחינת הנר: אשא חוורא [אש לבן] על אשא אוכמא [אש שחור] שהוא אש אש
שורף. וכפי מה ששורף כך, יאור עליו אשא אשא חוורא (זוהר ח״א נ״א ע״א) והם
בחינת ״זכור״ ו״שמור״ כנזכר לעיל. וזה רמז אור הנר בשבת. (1:58)

ג

[על אותו פסוק ומשל]. שהאדם נקרא מהלך, שצריך תמיד לילך ממדריגה
למדריגה. כי ההרגל נעשה טבע, והטבע משכח ומסתיר פנימיות החיות.
ואפילו בתורה ומצוות: אם נעשין הרגל, נעשה טבע, ושוכח הפנימיות. לכן
צריך בכל עת לחפש דרך ועצה חדשה.

ולכן הקדוש ברוך הוא ״מחדש בטובו בכל יום מעשה בראשית״ שלא
להיות גובר הטבע. וזה הבירה שדולקת, עולם הזה הטבעי, כל מה שנכנס
בה, אף על פי שכל הטבע על ידי נקודה חיות מלמעלה, אבל היא נטבע
בטבע, והטבע מכלה הכל, כעניין שכתוב ״ולא נודע כי באו אל קרבנה
(בראשית מ״ו:כ״א).״ ולכן הקדוש ברוך הוא ״בטובו מחדש בכל יום מעשה
בראשית.״ והאדם צריך לחפש למצוא זאת ההתחדשות, כמו שכתוב ״לשקוד
על דלתותי יום יום (משלי ח:ל״ד).״

ולכן כתוב ״שמעי בת כו׳,״ ואחר כך שנית ״הטי אזנך״ לומר שתמיד
צריך להיות מוכן לשמוע, וזה שכתוב ״לך לך״; לעולם צריך להיות מהלך.
״אל אשר אראך״ תמיד השגה חדשה. לכן נקרא האדם מהלך. שכל
העומד בלי התחדשות, מיד הטבע שולט בו. ולכן מלאכים למעלה, שאינם
תוך הטבע, נקראים ״עומדים (ישעיה ו:ב).״ ובעולם הזה נקרא האדם
מהלך. (1:60)

וכן היה האדם קודם הירידה. ואחר-כך נגרש מגן עדן "לעבוד את האדמה" ומכל מקום היה עוד לשון אחד [לשון הקדוש] ועל ידי התחברות כ"ב אתוון שלמטה היה לו עוד אחיזה בכ"ב אתוון דלעילא [שלמעלה]. וכמו שכתוב בזוהר הקדוש "דמתאחדים לתתא ברזא דאחד [שמתאחדים למטה בסוד של אחד] כגוונא דלעילא [כמו למעלה] (ח"ב קל"ה)." דיש כמה מדריגות באותיות, אתוון רברבין, וזעירין, ובינונים.

אבל כח האחדות שלמטה צריך להיות רק הכנה לשרש האחדות שלמעלה כמו שכתוב "הבונה בשמים מעלותיו ואגודתו על ארץ יסדה (עמוס ט:ו)." ולפי שדור הפלגה לא היה כנסיה לשם שמים, שעזבו את העיקר והפרידו בין אחדות שלמעלה לאחדות שלמטה, לכן נפלו גם מאחדות שלמטה. ונתפלגו לשבעים לשונות.

אך לשון הקודש נשאר לבני ישראל ונקראו "גוי אחד בארץ" שהם "כנסיה לשם שמים וסופה להתקיים (אבות ד:י"א)." (1:39)

לך לך

א

"לך לך מארצך ממולדתך ומבית אביך (בראשית י"ב:א)." במדרש: "שמעי בת וראי והטי אזנך ושכחי עמך ובית אביך (תהלים מ"ה:י"א)." כי אברהם אבינו ע"ה היה חכם גדול גם מקודם, כדאיתא בזוהר הקדוש (ח"ב קנ"ז ע"ב), "והקדוש ברוך הוא יהיב [נותן] חכמה לחכימין (דניאל ב:כ"א)."

ובודאי האדם נברא על דבר מיוחד שיוכל לתקנו ולהשיגו. ואז נקרא צדיק, שמיישר אורחותיו על פי המשפט. אבל אברהם אבינו ע"ה היה חסיד הנכנס לפנים משורת הדין. והיינו שהעובד ה' מאהבה יכול להפיק רצון מהשם יתברך להשפיע לו ממקור נשמתו, מה שאין איש [יכול] להשיג בשכל אנושי כענין שנאמר בפסוק, "עֹשֵׂי דברו לשמע בקול דברו (תהלים ק"ג:כ)." שעל ידי תיקון המעשים כראוי, זוכין לשמוע יותר ויותר. וכן לעולם. כי החסיד עובד ה' כדי לזכות להתדבק בשורש המצווה, ומבקש לשמוע בכל עת חדשות.

וזה שכתוב אחר "שמעי בת" שהוא מה שיכולין להשיג, אחר כך "הטי אזנך" שהוא לבטל כל ההאזנה והשמיעה אליו יתברך. ועל ידי הביטול לגמרי כענין "לך לך מארצך וממולדתך ומבית אביך," על ידי זה זוכין להארה חדשה שלמעלה מהטבע, כאשר השיג אברהם אבינו ע"ה.

"אשר אראך" אחר כך. הוא מה שאינו יכול להשיג ולראות מעצמו. וכן בני ישראל, אחר שנמשכו אחריו למדבר, בארץ לא זרועה, זכו לתורה אש דת... (1:48)

ב

במדרש "'שמעי בת וראי, והטי אזנך ושכחי עמך ובית אביך' משל לאחד שהיה עובר ממקום למקום וראה בירה אחת דולקת, אמר 'תאמר שבירה זו בלא מנהיג?' הציץ עליו בעל הבירה, אמר לו, 'אני הוא בעל הבירה' (ב"ר ל"ט:א)."

נקודה קדושה בכל הבריאה. והנבראים, בפרט בני אדם, צריכין להרחיב נקודה זאת שתתפשט כחה בכל הארץ. אך כי אלו התולדות הם רק על ידי הביטול, שאדם מבטל עצמו להבורא יתברך, ויודע ומבין כי אין בכחו מעצמו לעשות תולדות, ואינו מוצא לו מעצמו מקום, רק בכח הבורא יתברך. וכפי מה שיודע זאת, כך עושה תולדות.

וזהו שכתב הפסוק "אלה תולדות נח": בחינת מנוחה וישוב הדעת, לחזור כל אחד לשרשו ולהבין כי אין לו חיות מעצמו כלל. ועל ידי זה עושה תולדות. אף כי בחינה זו היפוך התולדות וההתפשטות, עם כל זה עיקר התולדות תלויין בזה.

ובזהר הקדוש (ח"ב פ"ח ע"ב) על "ויברך אלוהים את יום השביעי ויקדש אותו (בראשית ב:ג)" [אמרו] במן. והקשה, כיון דלא אשתכח ביה מנא, מה ברכתא אשתכח ביה [כיון שלא נמצא בו מן, איזו ברכה נמצאת בו]? אלא כולא בשביעאה תליא [הכל תלוי בשביעי] וכו'. פירושו: מה שאין בו התפשטות, רק הביטול אליו יתברך, מזה עצמו באין כל התולדות. ושבת נותן ברכה לכל ימות החול על ידי שבשבת כל הברואים מתבטלים לשרשן. וזה כבודו יתברך!... (1:23)

ב

ברש"י: עיקר תולדותיהם של צדיקים מצוות ומעשים טובים. ולא כתוב עיקר תולדות מצוות ומעשים טובים. וממילא נדע כי הצדיק עושה מצוות. אבל לא כל מצוה עושה תולדה להאדם, רק הצדיק שכל החיות שלו דבוק במצוות, "ומבשרי אחזה אלוה (איוב י"ט:כ"ו)." כמו זיווג גשמי, על ידי שכל החיות נמשך בו, נוצר מזה תולדה, כן כשאדם עושה מצוה בכל כחו וחיותו, נעשה תולדה.

ואמת כי מכל מצוה נעשה תולדה. כי כן יסד השם יתברך להיות תלוי מעשה עליון בתחתון. אבל להיות נקרא תולדותיו של אדם להיות לו דביקות ושייכות להתולדה, זה תלוי ברצון ועשיית המצוה כנזכר לעיל.

והפסוק כפשוטו: על ידי שהיה צדיק, ממילא תולדותיו היו כראוי, על ידי שגם בזיווג היה העיקר למצוות ומעשים טובים, ונמשך התולדה אחר העיקר. (1:21)

ג

בענין דור הפלגה בפסוק "הן עם אחד ושפה אחת לכולם (בראשית י"א:ו)" התורה מלמדת אותנו איך נפלו התחתונים משורש האחדות. מקודם כתוב "הן האדם היה כאחד ממנו (בראשית ג:כ"ב)" שהיה דבוק ממש באחדות. דרשו חז"ל "כאחד ממלאכי השרת דכתיב יקרא זה אל זה' (ישעיה ו:ג)" דמתחברין להיות אחד כמו שאומרים "ומשמיעין יחד בקול דברי אלקים חיים" (ב"ר כ"א:ה).

כי הקדוש ברוך הוא ברא הכל בכ"ב (22) אותיות וכל כתות המלאכים מתעלין אל שורש האותיות המיוחד להם. ומתחברין כל כ"ב אתוון [אותיות] הבאין מכל מיני צרופים של הכ"ב אתוון שאין להם סוף וחקר, ונעשין אחד.

(יהושע י״ד:א)׳ שהיה אברהם אבינו ע״ה גדול מאדם הראשון... (ב״ר
י״ד:ו) (1:18).״

ה

במדרש (ב״ר ה:א) בפסוק ״יקוו המים מתחת השמים אל מקום אחד,
ותראה היבשה (בראשית א:ט).״ משל למלך שהושיב אילמים והיו שואלים
שלומו של מלך ברמיזה. אמר אם יהיו פקחים על אחת כמה וכמה. והושיב
פקחין והחזיקו בפלטין כו׳.

דכל מה שברא הקדוש ברוך הוא לכבודו ברא, להעיד עליו. וכתוב
״השמים מספרים כבוד אל, ומעשה ידיו מגיד הרקיע (תהלים י״ט:ב).״ ״אין
אומר ואין דברים בלי נשמע קולם (שם שם ד).״ שכל הברואים מרמזין
ומעידין על הבורא. אך האדם, שהוא בר דעת ודיבור, הוא מוציא כל
העדות מכח אל הפועל. ועל זה נתן הקדוש ברוך הוא חכמה ודעת לאדם,
לידע להעיד עליו. והדעת תלויה בעדות זו. וכפי מה שאדם נותן דעתו
וחכמתו רק כדי לידע את ה׳ ולהעיד עליו, כך ניתוספות לו דעת וחכמה.
כמו שכתוב, ״עדות ה׳ נאמנה מחכימת פתי (שם שם ח).״ כי על ידי העדות
זוכה יותר להשיג ולהעיד עליו.

וכן אמרו ״ארון נשא את נושאיו (סוטה ל״ה ע״ב).״ וכן הוא בכל
הדברים הנעשין לשמו יתברך. המעשים מוסיפין לו כח להבין איך לעשות.

אך עצת הנחש הקדמוני, ימח שמו, היה ״והייתם כאלהים (בראשית
ג:ה)״—זה תערובות רע בטוב, שיחפוץ בדעת להיות בפני עצמו מושל על
השפלים ממנו. והדעת לא ניתנה רק לידע את הבורא יתברך שמו ולהעיד
עליו . לכן נברא אדם סמוך לשבת, כי שבת סהדותא [עדות] שזה תכלית
הבריאה, האדם שמעיד בדעת על הבורא יתברך שמו.

ועל ידי החטא בדעת נתמעטו הדעת והחכמה שלו. ולזה הדעת זכו בני
ישראל במתן תורה כמו שכתוב, ״אתה הראת לדעת כי ה׳ הוא האלהים,
אין עוד מלבדו (דברים ד:ל״ה)״ דכתיב ״עם זו יצרתי לי תהלתי יספרו
(ישעיה מ״ג:כ״א),״ ״ואשים דברי בפיך ובצל ידי כסיתיך לנטוע שמים
וליסד ארץ ולאמר לציון, ׳עמי אתה׳ (שם נ״א:ט״ז).״ ואיתא בזוהר הקדוש
״עמי בשותפות (על פי הקדמת ספר הזוהר חי״א ה ע״א).״

כיון שתכלית בריאת שמים וארץ כדי להעיד עליו, לכן נתחדשה הבריאה
כפי העדות שנמצאת בישראל, ומכל שכן בשבת קודש שהוא מיוחד לעדות
בזמן, כמו שבני ישראל מיוחדין לעדות בנפשות. ולכן האומר ״ויכולו השמים
והארץ (בראשית ב:א)״ נעשה שותף להקדוש ברוך הוא במעשה בראשית,
כיון שזה תכלית הבריאה. (1:19)

נח
א

״אלה תולדות נח, נח איש צדיק (בראשית ה:ט).״ בזוהר הקדוש כתוב ״נח
הוא בחינת שבת והוא עושה תולדות (ח״א נ״ט ע״ב)״ עיין שם. ברש״י:
״עיקר תולדותיהם של צדיקים מצוות ומעשים טובים.״

כל הנבראים צריכים לעשות תולדות, פירושו כי השם יתברך נתן

מהזמן והטבע. ובריאה המפורשת בתורה הוא רק במדה וקצבה.

לכן איתא במדרש (ב"ר י"א:ז), יעקב שכתוב בו שמירת שבת ירש העולם שלא במדה על ידי השלימות שנעשה בשבת קודש, והוא כלי המחזיק ברכה. ושורה בו כח השורש שאין לו הפסק ומדה. (1:9)

ג

במדרש "ויכלו השמים והארץ (בראשית ב:א)', יׁלכל תכלה ראיתי קץ, רחבה מצותך מאד (תהלים קי"ט:צ"ו)' לכל יש סיקוסים [שיעור], ולתורה אין כו' (ב"ר י:א)."

כי התורה נותנת חיים לכל הבריאה, ובמדה לכל בריאה. ואותה נקודה חיות שמתלבשת באיזה מקום להחיותו—זו הנקודה אין לה שיעור, כי היא למעלה מן הזמן והטבע. ועל נקודה זו נאמר, "הוא מקומו של עולם ואין עולמו מקומו (ב"ר ס"ח:ו)."

וכתוב, "רחבה מצותך מאד" ו"מאוד" הוא יותר ממקום התלבשות. וכמו שכתבו חכמינו ז"ל על "וארץ ישראל צבי היא לכל הארצות (יחזקאל כ:ו)' שאין עורו מחזיק בשרו: בזמן שישראל עליה מתרחבת כו' (גיטין נ"ז ע"א)." כן בכל דבר נקודה פנימיות, אין לה מדה וגבול.

וכן הוא בנשמת אדם שאין לה שיעור. וכמו שכתוב, "יוצר רוח האדם בקרבו (זכריה י"ב:א)." וכפי התפשטות הגוף, כך תוכל לקבל מהנשמה. והיא אין לה שיעור. וכמו כן נשמה שבכלל העולם, כי אדם עולם קטן הוא.

ושבת היא התגלות הפנימיות. ונקרא "יומא דנשמתא ולאו דגופא [יום הנשמה ולא יום הגוף] (זוהר חיב ר"ה ע"א)." ובמקום אחר פירשנו "ויכל אלוהים ביום השביעי מלאכתו אשר עשה (בראשית ב:ב)" כי השבת היא המודדת חיות לכל הדברים, כי "ויכל" הוא מדה... והשבת עצמה, אין לה מדה וגבול, כי היא מתוספות שלמעלה מהטבע. (1:9)

ד

"וישלחהו ה' אלוהים מגן עדן (בראשית ג:כ"ג)." הוא לשון שליחות, כי גם בגן עדן כתיב, "לעבדה ולשמרה (בראשית ב:ט"ו)' במצוות עשה ולא תעשה (ספרי דברים מ"א)." אבל [אדם הראשון] היה בבחינת בן לחפשא בגנזין דמלכא [לחפש באוצרותיו של המלך], פנימיות התורה והמצוות, דכתיב "ויקח את האדם (בראשית:ט"ו)" הוא לשון דביקות וחיבור כעין שדרשו חז"ל, "ויגרש את האדם (שם ג:כ"ד)' שנתן לו גירושין כאשה (סדר אליהו רבה א')." אם כן "ויקח את האדם" כמו, "כי יקח איש אשה (דברים כ"ד:א)."

ואחר החטא נשתלח לעבוד את האדמה בבחינת עבד. ואחר כך זכו בני ישראל לחזור ולכנוס בבחינת בנים. כשקבלו התורה בזכות האבות ומשה רבינו ע"ה, שתיקנו חטא אדם הראשון ונכנסו מתוך העבדות לבחינת בנים.

ועל זה נאמר, "עבד משכיל ימשול בבן מביש (תהלים י"ז:ב)" שאדם הראשון ביֵיש את כל העולם שהביא מיתה לעולם. ואברהם אבינו ע"ה שכתיב בו, "בעבור אברהם עבדי (בראשית כ"ו:כ"ד)" נתעלה מבחינת עבד לבן ונתעלה יותר מאדם הראשון כמו שכתבו חז"ל, "והאדם הגדול בענקים

ספר בראשית
בראשית

א

ברש״י ״אמר רבי יצחק: לא היה צריך להתחיל את התורה אלא מ״החודש
הזה לכם ראש חדשים (שמות י״ב:ב)׳ שהיא מצוה ראשונה שנצטוו בה
ישראל. ומה טעם פתח ב׳בראשית׳? משום ׳כח מעשיו הגיד לעמו (תהלים
קי״א:ו).׳״

ויש להבין מה התירוץ [הזה] על כל הפרשיות מ״בראשית״ עד ״החודש
הזה.״ אך פירוש הדבר כי אף שעיקר התורה למצותיה נאמר, זה תורה
שבכתב. אבל השם יתברך רצה לברר כי גם העולם הזה וכל הבריאה גם כן
על ידי כח התורה, כמו שכתוב ״בראשית׳: הביט בתורה וברא העולם (על
פי ב״ר א:א).״ וזהו ענין תורה שבעל פה, שתלויה במעשה האדם.

וזה כל הפרשיות ממעשי אבות, להראות כי נעשה ממעשיהם תורה. וזה
נקרא ״כח מעשיו״–הכח שנתן השם יתברך בתוך המעשה. ועל שם זה
נקרא ״מעשה בראשית״ להגיד כי בעשרה מאמרות נברא העולם, שגם חיות
העולם על ידי התורה. ועבודת האדם לברר זה שכל מעשה על ידי חיות
השם יתברך. וכשהאדם עושה מעשיו על פי כח התורה להשלים רצון
הבורא, אז מחדש האור שנגנז בטבע.

ועל זה נאמר ״ואשים דברי בפיך... לנטוע שמים וליסד ארץ ולאמר
לציון, ׳עמי אתה.׳״ ודרשו חז״ל בזוהר הקדוש (ח״א ה ע״א), אל תקרא
״עמי״ אלא ״עמי,״ שהוא שותף במעשה בראשית.

פירוש ״ציון/[ציון]״ הוא הנקודה, שיש בכל דבר רשימה ואות לזכור
שהוא מהשם יתברך. והוא החיות שמחיה כל דבר. והאדם הדבוק בנקודה
זו, וכל חיותו נמשך אחר זאת הנקודה, נעשה שותף במעשה בראשית... (1:5)

ב

בפסוק ״ויכֻלו השמים והארץ וכל צבאם (בראשית ב:א)״ במדרש (ב״ר י:ב)
נעשו כלים [ויכֻלו-כלים]. עוד שם ״לכל תכלה ראיתי קץ (תהלים קי״ט:צ״ו).״

הענין הוא על פי מה שאומרים בשבת קודש, ״פורס סוכת שלום.״
דלכל דבר יש שורש בשמים כדאיתא ״אין לך עשב מלמטה שאין לו מזל ברקיע
שמכה אותו ואומר לו, ׳גדל!׳ (ב״ר י:ו)״ דכתיב, ״ויבדל בין המים אשר
מתחת לרקיע ובין המים אשר מעל הרקיע (בראשית א:ז).״ ועל זה איתא
מים תחתונים בוכים, ״אנו בעינן למהוי קדם מלכא [אנחנו רוצים להיות
לפני המלך].״ ומה שנעשה ממים שמעל לרקיע לא נכתב בתורה. ובריאת
המלאכים [גם לא נכתב בתורה], מטעם כי הם בעצמם החלק השני השייך
לאותן הברואים שלמטה. והתחתונים הם חצי דבר. לכן בכל נברא נולד גם
למעלה בחלק העליון השייך לאותו בריאה.

ולכן בשבת קודש יורד אותו כח השורש ומתחברין שני החלקים. וזה
פריסת סוכת שלום, שיורד החלק שלמעלה, לכן אומרים שלום למלאכי
השרת בשבת קודש.

ולאותו חלק [העליון של כל דבר] באמת אין לו קץ שהוא למעלה

תוכן